Sir Robert Rhodes James was educated at Worcester College, Oxford. After time spent as Clerk of the House of Commons, Director of the Institute for the Study of International Organisations at the University of Sussex and Principal Officer in the Office of the Secretary-General of the United Nations, he was from 1976–92 the Conservative Member of Parliament for Cambridge. During his years in Parliament he held the posts of Chairman of the House of Commons and Parliamentary Secretary to the Foreign Office.

He is a fellow of the Royal Society of Literature, Fellow of the Royal Historical Society, Fellow of All Souls College, Oxford and Wolfson College, Cambridge. He holds an honorary D.Litt. from Westminster College, Missouri, and is an Honorary Professor at the University of Sussex. His publications include biographies of Lord Randolph Churchill, Anthony Eden (which won the Book of the Year Award) and Bob Boothby. His *Introduction to the House of Commons* was awarded the John Llewellyn Rhys Memorial Prize. He is also the editor of the complete speeches of Winston Churchill and the diaries of Sir Henry 'Chips' Channon.

ROSEBERY

Robert Rhodes James

PHŒNIX

For Angela

A PHOENIX PAPERBACK

First published in Great Britain
by Weidenfeld and Nicolson in 1963

This paperback edition published in 1995
by Phoenix, a division of Orion Books Ltd,
Orion House, 5 Upper St Martin's Lane,
London WC2H 9EA

A CIP catalogue record for this book is available
from the British Library.

ISBN: 1 85799 219 9

Printed and bound in Great Britain by
Butler & Tanner Ltd, Frome and London.

CONTENTS

LIST OF ILLUSTRATIONS

Preface

THE PERSONALITY AND CAREER of Archibald Philip Primrose, fifth Earl of Rosebery, have exerted a strange fascination over historians which is greater than his achievements would appear to warrant. As Mr Algernon Cecil has commented, 'It is one of the extraordinary things about him that he made so much display and left behind so much reputation with so little actually to his credit in the way of accomplishment.' A contemporary biographer, E. T. Raymond, aptly sub-titled his study of Rosebery 'The Man of Promise', and Sir Winston Churchill has related of Rosebery's numerous adherents and admirers, 'At first they said "He will come." Then for years "If only he would come." And finally, long after he had renounced politics for ever, "If only he would come back." ' Although it is over thirty years since Rosebery died, and nearly seventy since he relinquished office for the last time at the age of forty-eight, interest in his perplexing personality and strange political career has not declined to the extent that it has in the case of most of his contemporaries. 'In short', Raymond has remarked, 'the man was a puzzle, and puzzles are always interesting.'

In my researches for my biography of Lord Randolph Churchill I was struck by the considerable amount of new material in public archives relating to Rosebery's career—particularly in the papers of Sir Edward Hamilton at the British Museum, available to historians since 1956—and, as I had been long intrigued by the subject, I approached the Earl of Rosebery early in 1959 to enquire if a new biography of his father would have his support. Lord Rosebery doubted if a biography would command much public interest, but after further consideration he informed me in the summer of the same year that his family archives were at my disposal should I wish to make use of them. This most generous offer I at once accepted.

I confess that I first contemplated the Rosebery Papers— which had been conveyed to Barnbougle Castle on the Dalmeny

Estate—with mingled emotions of enchantment and alarm. Nearly a hundred box-files had been filled with letters, over a dozen tin trunks of formidable dimensions were crammed with papers, while in addition there were innumerable diaries, journals, assorted memoranda, and 'betting books' (in which Rosebery recorded interesting events and conversations); three more tin trunks—one filled with a lifetime's collection of cheque-book stubs—were subsequently discovered at Mentmore, and more papers were being discovered as late as the February of 1962. It would be hazardous to state with any confidence that the Barn-bougle collection of Rosebery's papers is complete, in spite of the meticulous and skilful compilation of the papers which was undertaken by Lady Rosebery, and which has eased my task considerably.

It cannot be contended that Lord Crewe's official biography of Rosebery—not unjustly described by Mr Cecil as 'a work of piety, weightily authenticated and warily discharged'—threw much light upon the subject's strange character, but the difficulties under which he worked were considerable. The Rosebery Papers, as he commented in a private note, were in a very 'higgledy-piggledy' condition, and he added that 'I cannot say that I may not have overlooked some matter of prime importance'. He was exceptionally unfortunate in this respect, since a considerable quantity of Rosebery's papers has been discovered in the last twenty years, including his important account of the events leading up to his accession to the Premiership and the complete Gladstone correspondence. Although there are occasions when Lord Crewe's selection of the documents at his disposal and his judgement of the relative significance of events—particularly the 1879–80 Midlothian campaigns and the 1892–3 Uganda Crisis—may be open to criticism, the difficulties of his task and the extent of his achievement should not be underrated. I am very grateful to the Marchioness of Crewe for the opportunity of using her husband's notes and papers, which have been of the greatest interest and value.

The problem of references is not easy to resolve. The serious student is understandably irritated by unverified statements, whereas the majority of readers, normally prepared to believe that the author has good reason for saying what he does, tend to be distracted by footnotes. Some authors have tried to compromise

by relegating all references to the end of the book, but, having
been maddened by this practice on several occasions, I decline to
incorporate it into any book of mine. Many footnotes can be
obviated by incorporating information in the text, and I have done
this wherever possible. Although I have endeavoured to reduce
the number of footnotes to the absolute minimum, I have borne
in mind the legitimate requirements of the historian.

The list of people to whom I am indebted for material and other
assistance is very long. I wish particularly to thank Sir Winston
Churchill, Lord Stanhope, Miss Cicely Stanhope, Lord Harcourt,
Lord Beaverbrook, Mr J. A. Waley-Cohen, Mr David Holland,
and Mr Nevile Masterman, each of whom has placed unpublished
papers at my disposal. The late Bishop Skelton sent me his
correspondence with Rosebery and a vivid memoir of his period
as Vicar of Mentmore and Rosebery's chaplain, and it was a
matter of deep regret to me that he died suddenly before I was
able to express my gratitude to him personally. I am very grateful
to my friend Mr Peter Stansky, of Harvard University,
Massachusetts, for lending me his detailed notes of the Harcourt,
Spencer, and Bryce Papers, and for allowing me to read the
typescript of his deeply informed forthcoming study of the Liberal
leadership from 1894 to 1899. The staffs of the British Museum,
the Libraries of the House of Commons and House of Lords, and
Mr Robert Mackworth-Young and Miss Price-Hill in matters
relating to the Royal Archives at Windsor, have been unfailingly
helpful and courteous, and I am deeply grateful.

Many friends, and some distinguished historians whom I pre-
sumptuously approached, have read the typescript and the proofs,
and have made many valuable suggestions and opened up new
lines of enquiry, for which I am indebted. But, as Sir Robert
Ensor once wrote on a similar occasion, 'believing that they will
be content with the private expressions of my sincere gratitude, I
do not propose to display their names here like a row of scalps'.

I find it impossible to express my gratitude to Lord and Lady
Rosebery with sufficient adequacy. As well as entertaining my wife
and myself on many occasions at Mentmore and Dalmeny, Lord
Rosebery gave me the use of Barnbougle Castle for my researches,
a privilege and a kindness which I deeply appreciated. As I am
able to give only a limited part of my time to historical research,

Lady Rosebery's preparatory work on the Rosebery Papers greatly shortened the length of time spent on assembling the material. Although it must be emphasised that this is in no sense an official biography, no biographer can have worked in more agreeable surroundings, under such pleasant circumstances, or have been showered with so many kindnesses.

I hope that my unfortunate wife has at last resigned herself to the melancholy fact that she has been unwittingly married to Mr Gladstone, Lord Randolph Churchill, the fifth Earl of Rosebery, and other worthies of the late nineteenth-century political scene. Even those who know her can only dimly realise what this book owes to her.

Priory Close,   ROBERT RHODES JAMES
Cartmel,
Lancashire.

CHAPTER ONE

'THE WISEST BOY THAT EVER LIVED'

... All the world looked kind
(As it will look sometimes with the first stare,
Which youth will not act ill to bear in mind.)
           BYRON: *Don Juan*

'LONDON IS EMPTYING FAST,' Lady Wilhelmina Stanhope, only daughter of the fourth Earl Stanhope, noted in her diary on July 16th, 1843, '& in a week or two we shall be migrating to Chevening, & thence to Walmer. I hope all the neighbours there are not so much wearied of me as I am of them. I think they must be *rather* sick of seeing me return, year after year, the same Lady Wilhelmina that I went, & I agree with them, that some new name might form an agreeable variety.' Lady Wilhelmina, twenty-four years old, was thoroughly bored by the dying 1843 Season. '*Another* ball!' her diary groaned on June 20th, and a week later after a ball at Buckingham Palace, she gave full rein to her irritation. 'The Queen is grown large, & very like George III,' she noted tartly. 'King Leopold [of the Belgians] came up & spoke to me for a long time: I was happily unconscious who he was, &, treating him only as a civil spoken old gentleman who seemed to know a good deal about England, never dreamt of rising from my seat, at which Mahon[1] was much overpowered. Came home heartily sick of Royalty & Royal attendants! One of the Belgian gentlemen, by the bye, introduced himself to me on the slight plea that he had once seen my *back* when walking on the Boulevards!'

Out of the throng of admirers who surrounded Lady Wilhelmina there had emerged the handsome thirty-four-year-old Lord Dalmeny, heir of the fourth Earl of Rosebery, 'the cleverest & most agreeable of all my partners,' she noted. His methods of courtship, however, appear to have been somewhat involved.

---

[1] Her brother, Lord Mahon, later fifth Earl Stanhope (1805-75).

Sunday, August 4th, 1843.—To Mrs Damer's *thé*—I, who fondly imagined the season over, & hoped to uncurl my hair, & retire into private life! It was very small. Lord Dalmeny never left me, as usual: but while people fancy he is proposing to me, he is in reality engaged in rating & finding fault with me in different ways, so that the theory of our flirtation, as impressed upon the lookers-on, is more agreeable than the reality.

But on the next day Dalmeny 'formally recanted all the disagreeable things he ever said to me, & assured me he had been finding fault with me for 2 months only to try my temper—which is very like a Scotchman!' On August 8th he at last proposed, and was accepted.

The wedding preparations were clouded by the serious illness of Lady Stanhope, and when it was realised that she was dying of cancer, the date of the wedding was brought forward to September 20th. On the night before, Lady Wilhelmina was sent to bed early, but 'being resolved to thwart them all, & sit up', she wrote up her Journal.

It seems as if the belief that I am going to be married is dawning upon me for the first time, & I can hardly think it *is* so: yet . . . I am strangely excited, & journalizing is a sedative. My morning was long, & dreary & lonely—I was quite left to myself—& my heart yearned for my mother's society—my mother's voice—my mother's smile: at length I went to sit with her, much to her maid's disapprobation, but she was drowsy with morphine, & sat in silence till she sent me away. . . . At one came Dalmeny, soon after two Mr Bouverie Primrose[1] whom I am *really* delighted with, & then I was fetched down to Papa's room to sign, & 'deliver as my act and deed'. Lord Rosebery, Mahon, Dalmeny, his brother, five lawyers & a clerk present: I am told I behaved with great self possession, but it is not one of the ordeals that alarms me, & the only two circumstances that impressed themselves on my mind were, that justice was not done to my handwriting by the crabbed corner of parchment allotted to it, & that the clerk who presented the blotting paper was excessively good looking. . . . I am now seriously going to bed—let me hope to sleep. I wish to look my best tomorrow, that Dalmeny may be proud of his bride—& Lady Wilhelmina Stanhope may 'appear for the last time', with credit.

Dalmeny had secured a rich prize. His bride was regarded not only as the most beautiful, but also the most intelligent, young lady of her generation. She had been one of Queen Victoria's

---

[1] Lord Dalmeny's younger brother (1813-98).

trainbearers at her Coronation—there had been no rehearsals, and she recorded in her diary that 'we carried the Queen's train very jerkily & badly, never keeping step properly'—and had been one of her bridesmaids at her wedding at the Chapel Royal in 1840. One contemporary described her when a girl as 'a very fine creature, and also a very agreeable converser'. Lockhart, Sir Walter Scott's son-in-law and biographer, met her at a ball in Kent before her marriage, and was 'seduced into dancing till three o'clock in the morning'. She had read widely, talked excellently, and was a gifted artist. 'She has the quickest, and the finest, perception of humor that I know, with an extraordinary power of expression, and the Stanhope wit,' Disraeli once noted; 'her conversation unceasing, but never long or wearying; a wondrous flow of drollery, information, social tattle, taste, eloquence; such a ceaseless flow of contemporary anecdote I never heard. And yet she never repeats.' Through her unpublished autobiography[1] it is possible to see what kind of things amused her. Social *gaffes* were her favourites, and none was better than that concerning old short-sighted Lord Portarlington who once said to Queen Victoria, 'I know your face quite well, but dammit I cannot put a name to it!' Lady Wilhelmina was always at her best in private conversation or at a small dinner-party. 'She spoke with an exquisite precision, both of utterance and of diction,' G. W. E. Russell has written. 'She hardly uttered a sentence without giving it a turn which one remembered: and her inclination to sarcasm was not unduly restrained. She was born in a learned home, and had lived all her life with clever and educated people. Her information was wide and varied, and she took keen interest in all the intellectual movements of her time. Her manner, like her figure, was exceedingly graceful, and her dignity of movement remarkable.'[2]

In spite of these attributes, a little of Lady Wilhelmina went a long way. Her brilliant headlong conversation was marked by a malicious streak, and, for all her acute observation of the world, she could lack penetration. As a young girl she had met Wordsworth, and dismissed him as 'amiable, simple-minded, kindly, & incapable of a joke . . . particularly plain, he wears a large pair of

[1] This amusing book was dictated by her in 1900, just before her death, but only covers the years 1819–51. It is in three bound volumes—in manuscript—at Dalmeny.
[2] G. W. E. Russell: *Portraits of the 'Seventies*, 454–5.

spectacles, & has a tedious, prosy manner'. She could also be cruel, and she possessed the Stanhope failing of self-absorption.

Lord Dalmeny was of a very different type. Tall, genial, and very good looking, he had been Liberal Member for Stirling Burghs since 1833, and for a short period had held junior office under Melbourne as a Lord of the Admiralty. He was a fervent believer in physical fitness—a subject which vaguely repelled the Stanhopes—and his sole literary production, a pamphlet unhappily entitled *An Address to the Middle Classes upon the Subject of Gymnastic Exercises*, was devoted to this fetish. He argued with great vehemence that although the upper and lower classes kept themselves in excellent condition—'Poverty compels the one, pleasure prompts the other, to adopt the habits and enjoy the benefits of physical exertion. The daily labour for daily bread maintains the vigour of the labourer. The chase, the gun, the foil, preserve the health of the gentleman'—the middle classes (by which Dalmeny meant shop-keepers) were deplorable in this respect. After a day of toil, the shop-keeper thought of relaxation. 'What is the nature of the relaxation or amusement ?' the pamphleteer indignantly enquired. 'Does he brace his nerves, re-animate his spirits or circulate his blood by gymnastic exercises, any invigorating game ?' He did nothing of the kind; he read *The Times*, repaired to a tavern, 'or sought the domestic hearth'. Dalmeny enthusiastically advocated the benefits of fencing. 'I have brought down the heathcock in Braemar, I have stalked the deer on Ben Macdhui, I have trod the Alpine solitudes of Switzerland, but never have I felt greater exhilaration of spirits or a more genial glow of health, more buoyancy of mind or greater vigour of body, than after an animated set-to with the foils at Messers Angelo's or Hamon's. . . . The pallid hue is replaced by the bloom of health, the narrow hollow chest expands, the flaccid, shrunk and withered muscles grow large and firm, the languid eye becomes bright, the nerves braced, the step elastic, the spirits brisk.'

Dalmeny's interest in health was apparently inexhaustible. He was one of the earliest amateur students to be convinced of the immense possibilities of anaesthetics, and in a letter to his father-in-law (January 2nd, 1847) he described recent experiments in ether. 'This discovery may be pregnant with consequences of incalculable importance. If its success be ascertained it ought to be hailed with enthusiasm and gratitude by all who desire to alleviate the sufferings of human nature.' Shortly afterwards he attended one of the first operations in which ether was used, and was greatly impressed by the statement of the patient that he had suffered no pain and had dreamed that he was in a public house in Suffolk. But in general Dalmeny disapproved of doctors and operations. 'I cherish a great antipathy to all medicine,' he informed Lord Stanhope on May 22nd, 1847, 'particularly to that of a mercurial description. Nature with me is the most skilful physician.' When a serious influenza epidemic was raging in the winter of 1847–8 the Dalmeny household was obliged to drink a glass of ice-cold water before breakfast, which he regarded as an elixir against the disease. When Lord Stanhope was suffering from a bladder complaint Dalmeny was appalled to discover that he was taking rhubarb juice to alleviate the condition, and earnestly advised him to cease the treatment, which, he was certain, only inflamed the ducts.

It is difficult to avoid the suspicion that Dalmeny was something of a hypochondriac, and in his voluminous correspondence with Lord Stanhope and his Stanhope in-laws there is hardly a letter which does not describe with pitiless detail the condition of his own health and the novel curative methods that he had devised. This is not to say that the letters were dull or dominated by self-pity, and indeed, Dalmeny enjoyed first-class health. Although political matters interested him only slightly, his comments on that subject were dominated by a basic common sense and a certain irony. 'It is a consolation to know', he wrote to Lord Stanhope on December 27th, 1845, on the subject of Macaulay, 'that if we lose a Whig Government we shall gain a Whig historian.'

Although the family history of the Roseberys could hardly compare with the brilliance of the Stanhopes, and could claim no connections with the genius of a Pitt or the eccentricity of a Lady Hester Stanhope, it was longer and almost as intriguing. The Primrose fortunes had been established in the seventeenth century by James Primrose, and were dramatically consolidated and enlarged by his son, Archibald (1616–79), who held high office and great influence in Scotland by means of a series of delicate and ingenious manoeuvres on the political tight-rope. Taken prisoner by the Parliament forces in 1646 at Philiphaugh, he was sentenced

to death but reprieved through the intercession of the Duke of
Argyll, and fame and fortune returned with the Restoration;
eventually he fell sheer after a career of extraordinary alternations
of great power and impotence, but not before he had skilfully
extracted the castle of Barnbougle on the Firth of Forth some
eight miles to the west of Edinburgh, the surrounding estates
of Dalmeny, and other properties in the Lothians from the
wreckage. Bishop Burnet in his *History of His Own Time* has
painted an admirable word-portrait of this shifty yet not unattractive man.

He was a dexterous man of business; he always had expedients
ready at any difficulty. He had an art of speaking to all men according
to their sense of things: and so drew out their secrets, while he concealed his own: for words went for nothing with him. He said everything that was necessary to persuade those he spoke to, that he was of
their mind: and did it in so genuine a way, that he seemed to speak his
heart. He was always for soft counsels and slow methods; and thought
that the chief thing that a great man ought to do was to raise his family
and his kindred, who naturally stick to him; for he had seen so much
of the world, that he did not depend much on friends, and so took no
care in making any.

The Primroses who followed the redoubtable Sir Archibald
flitted vaguely across the stage of history with little embellishment
to the family fortunes, although none of them was wholly without
personality. Sir Archibald's eldest son by his first marriage, Sir
William Primrose, was a sad failure; in the admirably laconic
account of Lord Crewe, he was 'jobbed into a high legal office
in his seventeenth year, neglected his duties, was dismissed,
became paralysed, and died young'.[1] The eldest son by Sir
Archibald's second marriage was created Viscount Rosebery in
1700 and was advanced to a Scottish earldom in 1703, becoming
Earl of Rosebery, Viscount of Rosebery, Viscount of Inver-
keithing, Lord Dalmeny and Primrose: his son, James, second
Earl of Rosebery (1691–1755), succeeded to the Dalmeny
estates and baronetcy in 1741 when the grandson of the first Sir
Archibald died.

The only outstanding features of these Primroses and Roseberys
were their matrimonial misdemeanours and misfortunes. James,

[1] The Marquess of Crewe, K.G.: *Lord Rosebery* (John Murray, 1931), 5. All
future references to this biography will be Crewe: *Rosebery*. I am most grateful to
the Marchioness of Crewe for allowing me to make these quotations.

first Lord Primrose (the son of the regrettable Sir William), was discovered by his wife's brother in Holland in the act of getting himself married to an innocent and very wealthy Dutch girl: Neil, second Lord Primrose, was described by Fanny Burney as 'the fattest, ugliest, and most disagreeable man in London'. Lord Dalmeny, the elder son of the second Earl of Rosebery, and who died before he succeeded to the title, secretly married a Catherine Canham in London and the couple retired to Italy as 'Mr and Mrs Williams'. After four years, 'Mrs Williams' died, and confessed on her death-bed that she was the wife of the Vicar of Thorpe-le-Soken in Essex, where she was buried in the presence of both her mourning husbands.

The family fortunes established by Sir Archibald Primrose had suffered serious depredations by the end of the eighteenth century, but were partially restored by the financial shrewdness of Neil, third Earl of Rosebery, who died in 1814. The restoration of the family's position was signified in 1819 by their moving from the ancient and spray-swept Barnbougle Castle on the Forth to a new Gothic-revival mansion—Dalmeny House—built nearby, but in a more sheltered position. The somewhat dilapidated condition of Barnbougle had been causing discomfort for some years, and the incident when Neil, third Earl, was 'knocked down by a wave' when walking to his dressing-room, was probably decisive. On another occasion a dinner-party was swamped when the sea burst through the windows. It was clearly time to be gone, and Barnbougle was left to moulder picturesquely for sixty years.

The first marriage of the fourth Earl of Rosebery ended in scandal and divorce, the wife being discovered by her mother-in-law in a compromising situation with Sir Harry Mildmay, with whom she later lived and from whom Lord Rosebery obtained subsequently £15,000 damages. But his second marriage, which took place in 1819, was extremely successful. Lord Rosebery held a distinguished position in English and Scottish public life, being MP for Helston and Cashel before he succeeded his father in 1814, and a Scottish Representative Peer in 1818, 1820, and 1826; he was an ardent supporter of Lord Grey's Reform Bill, for which he was made a Privy Councillor in 1831. In 1828, on the recommendation of Lord Goderich, he received an English barony. Lord Rosebery was a representative of the type of landed aristocrat more common in England than in Scotland; benevolent, generous, thoughtful, public-spirited, he enjoyed considerable local popularity in Edinburgh and the Lothians. His personal charm was considerable, and the atmosphere of Dalmeny was gentle and kindly. The future Mrs Gladstone and her brother Henry visited Dalmeny in the September of 1837, and the latter wrote that 'Music instrumental and vocal enlivens our evenings. Lady Rosebery on the harp, her son, Bouverie, on the cello, and the eldest daughter at the pianoforte. . . . A most lovely view of Arthur's Seat and Edinburgh Castle from the grounds; the scenery is enchanting. . . . Lord and Lady Rosebery are perfectly charming—it is the most delightful house I ever was in.'[1] Lord Rosebery was so highly esteemed that the 1845 *New Statistical Account of Scotland* remarked that if his example as a landowner was generally followed throughout Scotland it 'would greatly enhance the comforts and elevate the character of the deserving poor'. On one side of the union between the Primroses and the Stanhopes was a long line of Scottish *noblesse de robe*, and on the other over a century of brilliance, eccentricity and public eminence.

Lady Wilhelmina has left a long account of her wedding-day in her Journal, part of which may be related.

. . . we were quite a gay party going to St George's [Hanover Square], with some jokes about my veils being so thick I could see nothing thro' it, & must trust to Papa for not being married to the wrong person! I had always a strong feeling as to the good omens of fine weather for a bride—& never was there such a flood of sunshine as poured down upon me—summer seemed to have delayed its departure to give me joy! I talked to everyone in the vestry, & was not the least nervous during the ceremony; Dalmeny had repeatedly begged me not to cry & I was calm, tho' the words that bound me to him for life—'for better, for worse, for richer, for poorer, in sickness as in health'—had an awful sound to my ears. He led me out of the Church, (which was as full as it could possibly be)—& Ly Rosebery advanced first to embrace me, with the kindest affection: she was in tears, & called me 'Her own child now'. Everyone present was most cordial in their congratulations. . . .

There were large crowds in the streets, to which Lady Dalmeny bowed and waved. 'Papa was delighted—he & Dalmeny con-

Mary Drew: *Catherine Gladstone*, 16–17.

gratulating me upon behaving so well: I reached home crimson with excitement, & rushed upstairs to introduce Lady Dalmeny to Mama.' There followed a honeymoon on the Continent, entrancingly described in the Journal. They crossed from Portsmouth on the Le Havre packet and suffered bad weather; after a grim night Lady Dalmeny went up on deck to find her husband, who had been interned in a separate cabin with two men 'in the last stages of sea-sickness', gulping in the dawn air. He assured his wife that he had stuffed his ears with cottonwool and had managed to spend 'an excellent night'. But then there occurs a lapse of nearly six years in her diaries. On March 17th, 1849, they re-commence:

I have been amusing myself lately with reading over a Diary I kept in my young Lady days, & am tempted to try keeping one now, when five years & four children have sobered my mind & reduced my appearance to that of a thin, wizened, elderly woman.

Lady Dalmeny had endured an unnerving experience at the birth of her first child (Mary) in 1844. The Dalmenys had borrowed Bouverie Primrose's pleasant house at Wardie, on the outskirts of Edinburgh, which Lady Dalmeny—whose standards were not low—acidly described as 'a small jerry-built villa, well compared to a bathing machine': the walls were so thin, she averred, that she could hear every sound in the house, which was in any event positioned between a new railway line and the city meadows, which stank of 'rotten fish & other horrors'. She was very ill for some time after the birth of her daughter, and she took care that her other babies were born in the comfort of her father's London house, 20, Charles Street. A second daughter (Constance) was born in 1846, and, at ten minutes to three in the morning of May 7th, 1847, she gave birth to her first son, later christened Archibald Philip, and the subject of this biography. 'You will rejoice to learn', Dalmeny wrote to Lord Stanhope, 'that this morning at 10 minutes before 3, Wilhelmina was brought to bed of a son. She is wonderfully well.' According to her own account, Lady Dalmeny was ill for several weeks after the birth. Archibald was baptised at St George's on June 17th, when the god-parents were Lord Rosebery, Lord Stanhope, Lord Mahon, and the Countess of Effingham. When her second son and last child (Everard) was born in 1848 Lady Dalmeny—encouraged by her husband's enthusiastic accounts—used chloroform, to the horror of the rest of the family. 'My feelings towards babies', she later wrote in her Journal, 'were rapidly becoming modified. . . . I kept no diary during these four dull & dreary years, & few indeed are the events worth recording.'

Archibald was an exceptionally attractive child. On a wet Sunday afternoon at Chevening in the April of 1850, his mother amused herself by writing separate descriptions of her children, and on her elder son she wrote that 'He is a great darling, more affectionate than any child I ever knew: very tall, thin, & rather pale, with very fine large blue eyes, & the prettiest smile in the world. He has a very well formed high forehead, but I have his hair cut square, in the old fashion, & left long at the sides & behind. He has quantities of hair, as fine as floss-silk, which last year was quite flaxen, but I am happy to say is darkening fast. He is, I was going to say, never naughty: that is perhaps going too far: I can only say I have never seen him so: & tho' high-spirited & courageous, he is so sensitive that a harsh word throws him into a flood of tears: nor is he, like his sisters, one instant crying, the next laughing—he is some time recovering from a burst of sorrow. He has another great quality these mercurial young ladies are in great want of—he is not fidgetty, & so thoroughly gentle-manlike in his ways, that I think, even in a rage, he would look an aristocratic child. Everard is very different. . . . He is much cleverer, we think.'

Lady Dalmeny always regarded Everard with greater affection than she demonstrated towards her other children—possibly due to the emollient effects of the chloroform—and in most compari-sons Archibald fared badly. But her comment that her elder son 'is some time recovering from a burst of sorrow' is interesting, because it is not a common facet in a child, and remained a charac-teristic throughout his life. 'I cannot conceal from myself', his mother noted of him in her Journal for July 3rd, 1850, 'that he is a terribly dull little boy—Conny is a genius in comparison: but, tho' totally without an idea, he is, as Dalmeny emphatically calls him, an "*Excellent* little boy!".'

Archibald was not yet four when the first great disaster of his life occurred. In the autumn of 1850 his father fell seriously ill with pleurisy—occasioned, family legend has it, by walking into Edinburgh from Dalmeny House on a bitterly cold day, taking a

Turkish Bath, and then walking home again—and made a slow recovery. By the middle of the following January he was declared to be fully recovered, and on the evening of January 22nd, having received the good news from his doctors that day, he played exuberantly with his children in the nursery. His wife noticed particularly that he played most with Archie, his favourite, who clung delightedly to his knees. On the morning of the 23rd Dalmeny dressed for his first long walk since the previous October, and then had a sudden heart attack on the landing. It was subsequently discovered that he had an aneurism 'the size of a walnut' on the aorta, adhering closely to the air passage and rendering one lung almost useless. This condition was inoperable in those days, and death could have occurred at any moment. Lady Dalmeny was summoned by a terrified servant but was not in time to see him alive. After she had recovered from the terrible shock, her children were allowed to see her. Mary, Constance, and Everard, with the cruel resilience of childhood, recovered remarkably quickly, but Archie was ill for several weeks, causing considerable alarm to the family, and afterwards he was even more reserved and sensitive than before.

In spite of his quietness, he was a remarkably observant child, and on one occasion was almost hypnotised by the spectacle of the famous Duke of Cambridge calling upon his mother. Nor was this surprising, since he was one of the great eccentrics of his day, noted for remarking in a thunderous voice 'By all means!' in church when the prelate intoned 'Let us pray'. His contemporary fame also rested upon the remark that he was 'grattered and flatified' by a courteous civic reception. All interesting strangers fascinated Archie, and he was known to sit at the luncheon table without touching his food and never taking his eyes off the object of his interest. 'Once, when I was a child, I was taken to see Hatfield,' he related in 1898. 'In the library we saw a tall thin figure carrying a huge volume. The housekeeper paused with awe, saying, "That is Lord Robert Cecil".'[1] This was his first sight of the man who, as Robert, third Marquess of Salisbury, was to become his most formidable political opponent.

His mother did not remain a widow for long. In the August of 1854 she married Lord Harry Vane—later the fourth and last Duke of Cleveland—at Chevening Church. 'As Lord H. Vane

[1] Address to the Edinburgh Philosophical Institution, November 25th, 1898.

enjoys very good health the difference of age does not appear to
me very objectionable,' Lord Stanhope wrote to his daughter,
'for it has been well observed that the affection & anxiety to
please which is felt by men at his time of life is greater & more
constant than that which is usual in their younger days. His
personal appearance is not considered by me to be worthy of your
beauty, but if that is not an objection to yourself it cannot be so
to others.' The four children followed them to the church, the
two boys in Stewart tartan kilts. Although he was only seven,
the memory of that walk was indelibly printed on Archibald's
mind, and thirty-seven years later, when his step-father lay dying,
he recounted the details of the day to Mr Gladstone. It is difficult
to assess the impact that his mother's re-marriage had upon him,
and he never alluded to the subject in later life. But the event did
nothing to reduce the emotional shock of his father's death, and
his reserve was perceptibly increased.

But his mother's second marriage opened new horizons. The
family spent the winter of 1854 travelling in Europe, and the
seven-year-old Lord Dalmeny visited Naples for the first time,
which was later to fascinate him so profoundly. On their return
he was sent to Bayford House, a private school near Hertford.
The vast Cleveland possessions[1] had removed any financial
difficulties which might have limited the education of the Primrose children, and until he succeeded his brother as Duke of
Cleveland, Lord Harry rented a series of majestic houses, one
of which was the Palmerstons' home, Brocket. Lord Harry was
an affable and kindly person, but of little intellectual power. His
brother, whom he succeeded in 1864, famed himself for his contempt for literature and politics no less than for his almost morbid
consciousness of rank as the superior of ability. His widow survived him for many years, a redoubtable old lady who journeyed in
London in a magnificent yellow chariot with two powdered footmen hanging on behind, and who was noted for her asperity and
snobisme no less than for the determination with which she maintained her past grandeur. 'To see her descend at her house in
Piccadilly was as remarkable in its queer pomposity as a gener-

[1] When Lord Harry Vane inherited the Dukedom in 1864, the Cleveland estates
consisted of 104,194 acres (of which 55,837 were in County Durham) whose annual
income was assessed at £97,398 in 1878. (John Bateman: *The Great Landowners of
Great Britain*, 1878 edition.)

ation earlier it had been to see the Duke of Queensberry—"Old Q"—under his parasol, ogling the passing girls from his balcony a few doors away,' Lord Esher has written.[1]

Lady Wilhelmina's second marriage was extremely successful, although, to their dismay, they had no children, which occasioned the cruel entry in the Visitor's Book at Raby Castle, 'A pity at Raby there is no baby'. Lord Harry was very impressive in his appearance. 'He makes a good very Duke,' Disraeli once noted of him, 'tall and dignified, but very naturally, and, although not exactly good-looking, a good presence and a good expression of countenance, kind eyes.' When William Johnson first met him he recorded that 'I had, and valued, the gravity and plain lengthy statements of my host, who walked with me twice, and seemed to me . . . a truly honest and public spirited man.' Lady St Helier described him as 'a fine specimen of an English aristocrat and as he got older I think his picturesqueness increased. In the evening, when he wore his Ribbon of the Garter, standing up with his tall, erect figure, piercing eyes, and snow-white hair, he was always a very striking personage.'[2]

No doubt this was true enough, but Lord Harry was also shy, inarticulate, and slow-thinking, and was no match for the impetuous, brilliant and masterful woman he had married. His four step-children liked and respected him, but at a distance; he determined not to interfere with their lives in any way beyond providing handsomely for them, with the result that his remoteness from their day-to-day existence was accentuated. His wealth was enormous, and his possessions vast. On one occasion he had an argument with his brother-in-law—the fifth Earl Stanhope— about the outcome of a pending by-election. Stanhope had remarked on the Liberal prospects with favour, and was somewhat loftily contradicted by Lord Harry (by then the Duke of Cleveland). The discussion, which began to be rather warm, since none of the Stanhopes relished contradiction, was ended by the Duke's remark that he ought to know 'as the constituency is possessed by me'. Shortly before his death in 1890 he told Rosebery that when he was first elected Member for South Durham in 1841 his election expenses were £16,000, and each of the other candidates was charged the same price.

[1] Esher: *Cloud-capp'd Towers*, 9.
[2] Lady St Helier: *Memories of Fifty Years*, 94.

Their mother's re-marriage ended all financial worries. In her brief widowhood she had been generously assisted by her father, brother, and the Roseberys, and had an income in excess of £2,000. After her second marriage she continued to receive the £1,500 a year which was her marriage settlement from Dalmeny, £800 a year 'pin money'—this was the actual phrase used in the settlement—from Lord Harry, who also charged £40,000 on his estates for his wife's children. Lord Harry bought Battle Abbey in Sussex as their permanent home, which his wife enthusiastically redecorated at great expense but with little taste. One of her less amiable eccentricities was a Visitors' Book in which parting guests were obliged to write some remark about their stay. On one occasion a silent and somewhat despised young man stayed at the house; when he had gone the party made a rush to the Visitors' Book to see what banality he had written. The Duchess read out to the expectant throng, 'From Battle, murder, and sudden death, Good Lord deliver us!'

This was rather the opinion of Archie. Until Battle had been purchased, the family stayed often at Chevening, and it was this house, rather than any other, which he loved most. It is not easy to paint Chevening's portrait with justice. The estate, which lies a few miles to the north-west of Sevenoaks in Kent, was purchased in the reign of Henry VIII by the Lennard family, and the house was begun early in the seventeenth century by the thirteenth Lord Dacre. It was bought by the first Lord Stanhope in 1717, who entered upon a drastic rebuilding and remodelling of the house and estate, which was carried on by his widow after his sudden death in 1721. It was then a charming red-bricked mansion, simple but perfectly proportioned. 'Citizen' Stanhope, the great canal-builder and reformer, 'improved' the house over a long period between 1786 and 1816, with sad results. The red-brick on the house was covered with tiles of a grey-white texture, and another storey was built, which destroyed irretrievably the perfect proportions of the original building.

The fact that it has been in the same family for over two hundred years and loved by each generation has probably given the old house its gentle charm, and Archie adored it with an all-enfolding love. It was a perfectly self-contained community, with the servants and gamekeepers on the most friendly terms with the family. An old gardener brewed the uniquely delicious Chevening beer in a small hut on the estate, disappearing into it for weeks at a time and emerging gloriously cheerful, refusing to disclose to anyone the magic recipe, which eventually died with him. A barrel was reverently kept for the end of the 1914–18 war, but when it was ceremoniously opened on Armistice Day it was discovered to be undrinkable, to the bitter mortification not only of the family but the expectant tenants. Absolutely secluded, totally self-reliant, peaceful and gay, Chevening was always called 'Paradise' by Archie. As a child he spent long hours in the marvellous Library or shooting in the park. Once, when out with his cousins, he accidentally discharged his gun and nearly killed one of them while crossing a stile; for this terrible negligence he was promptly thrashed by the head gamekeeper, who achieved a certain amount of local fame for this exploit in later years.

In 1911, Rosebery dined at Knole, and invited himself to Chevening for the night. The family were away, and there was only Rayner, the old butler, in the house. Rosebery and Rayner visited every corner of the house, including the nursery floor, with oil lamps, as there was no electricity installed. He then wrote to Lady Stanhope (widow of the sixth Earl, and mother of the present Lord Stanhope) the following letter.

Paradise
July 31, 1911.

My dear Evelyn,

Your not being here knocked the bottom out of my day dream, but that apart, I have spent a very happy night here under the charge of the assiduous & sympathetic Rayner. This place is looking divine, and at all times has a greater charm for me than any other place. I can never be alone here—it is all peopled by ghosts, all of them pleasant and kindly. . . .

. . . Again a thousand thanks

Yr affec.
AR.

The only thing here that is short of perfection is the pens!

Archie was a quiet and, indeed, a solitary child, and the Stanhopes noticed how he used to detach himself from his sisters and cousins and wander off on his own into the park or up to the Library. In a rather unhappy childhood, the serene and happy atmosphere of Chevening stood out in sharp relief.

He appears to have been reasonably happy at Bayford, although Everard hated every minute at the place. His earliest letters to his mother were of a nature which will not be unfamiliar to parents of small boys at their first boarding-school:

> Bayford House, Herts.
> 1855 23rd of September.
>
> My dear Mama,
> I hope you are well. Do you know that Oliver Montagu had today a monitors licking the Monitors have daily to ask Mr Renaud if they may then they can have a stick of any thickness or thinness as they think proper and then generally he his [sic] then brought into the field where one of the Monitors hold him and the others lick him but today he was licked in the coach-house, I believe, and the three Monitors held him while the vice monitor and fourth monitor licked him give my love to mademoiselle & to everybody. Good bye
>
> Yours
> Archie.

His mother was not a very conscientious letter-writer, and towards the end of October Lady Rosebery received an earnest communication.

> Oct 27th Bayford House Hertford 1855
>
> My dear Grandmamma,
> I thank you for your kind letter. But I want to know where Mama is now for do you know I feel quite uneasy about her because I've not had a letter for a long time because she must have gone somewhere and I can't concieve [sic] where she is because I believe you would forward if she was not at Dalmeny.
> I hope you are well & Grandpapa also Good bye
>
> Yours
> Dalmeny.

Soon afterwards his mother received a direct reproof. 'I suppose you think I don't write often enough,' her elder son wrote sternly, 'but I think you ought to have written one line in answer to the long letter I wrote to you.' But his letters home were normally cheerful. 'W. Beresford & his brother', he wrote, unwittingly describing a future holder of the Victoria Cross, 'are the greatest bluberers in the school.' His most vivid memory of Bayford in later years was an attack of measles. 'Ten or twelve other patients in the room snoring or talking in their sleep, I feverish wakeful and utterly miserable. Parched also with thirst which could only be quenched with a thick beverage miscalled barley water which turned to a thick slime in one's mouth.' At the age of eleven he suffered severe concussion when he ran into a gate while playing a game of blind man's buff; the scar on his forehead was noticeable for the rest of his life, and for several weeks after the accident he was in a darkened room, refusing all conversation.

It is unlikely that this accident—as Lord Crewe has implied in his biography—had any permanent effects, although conceivably it may have contributed to the insomnia which first began to trouble him in his later twenties and which was to plague him more seriously from the age of forty until his death. Probably of greater importance was what the family called 'the Chevening tragedy' at the Christmas of 1858. One of the regular features of the Chevening Christmas was a huge snapdragon, heavily treated with brandy. The family were admiring it in the big kitchen when a fool of a manservant thrust a red-hot poker into it and it burst into flames, showering blazing pieces everywhere. Miss Sikes, the young daughter of the Rector of Chevening, was wearing a muslin dress which caught fire; the ten-year-old Archie, who was standing next to her, leaped to her assistance, and was most cruelly burned in his successful attempt to save her. His hands and arms heavily bandaged, he was given Macaulay's *Essays* to read by his mother while he was recovering. Rosebery always remembered the incident with mingled horror and pleasure, for although he bore the scars of his burns throughout his life, Macaulay made an immediate and dramatic impression upon him. 'There was much, of course, that I could not understand,' he wrote many years later to a friend. 'But I delighted in the eloquence, the grasp and the command of knowledge, the irresistible current of the style. And to that book I owe whatever ambitions or aspirations I have ever indulged in. No man can intellectually owe another more.' His mother then gave him Macaulay's *History of England*, and by the March of 1859 he had not only read this but had battled through Thiers' *History of the Consulate and the Empire*, and was already enslaved by Sir Walter

Scott. These early influences should not be underrated, for the glory of Scotland's history and the glitter of the eighteenth century bit deep into his imagination.

His precocious love of reading increased his aloofness from the rest of his family, and it surprised nobody when he passed into Eton at the age of thirteen at the top of the new boys, entering Lower Remove, which was the highest form he could enter as a new boy.

'I AM AN ETONIAN—there is something great in the name alone,' he wrote cheerfully to a friend in the autumn of 1860. He then went on to discuss American politics, berating Buchanan and speaking with enthusiasm of 'clever Mr Lincoln'. At Eton he boarded in the house of Mr Vidal and this accident brought him into contact with one of the most remarkable of all Eton masters, for Vidal's wife was the sister of William Johnson, then thirty-seven years of age, who made the house his headquarters.

Tall, very short sighted, with a high-pitched voice—'as if shouting in a high wind', as one of his pupils described it—stooping, sarcastic, energetic, caustic, and tenderly sensitive, William Johnson was the prince of schoolmasters. In some respects he was too brilliant for his charges, since much of his deep erudition and withering jibes were lost upon them. He taught contempt for cant and despised the commonplace; anything sloppy or conventional withered at his touch; his manner was brusque, and his sharp tongue made many enemies. Devoid of vanity, utterly intolerant of the second-rate, excellently versed in the vocabulary of contempt, he brought to Eton the undefinable air of the eccentric and fascinating University don. Palmerston, indeed, recommended him for the Professorship of Modern History at Cambridge University in 1860, but was overruled by the Prince Consort, who favoured Kingsley. His reports on his pupils were not noted for their sycophancy, and their disconcerting penetration was not always well received. The young Dalmeny had an early example of his *brusquerie*. Writing of Lord Stanhope's much-admired biography of his great-uncle Pitt, Johnson dismissed it as 'more like a shambling and scanty history of England, with an occasional insertion of something about Pitt, than a political biography'.

Dalmeny, in company with the thirteen-year-old Edward

Hamilton[1]—beside whom he had sat quaking on his first day—found Johnson an exhilarating if startling tutor. He would fall into great rages, or simulate them, stamping about his pupil-room with wild and extravagant gesticulations, vapouring his anger at the stupidity of his charges. Then he might sit, his legs crossed, in a curled-up posture, with a book held within an inch of his nose, interrupting the lesson with a rambling but riveting discourse upon any subject which crossed his extra-ordinarily active mind. 'His genius', his most recent biographer has justly written, 'was to make the smallest thing significant to those that had ears to hear and minds to respond. It might be a lesson in which he seemed to teach twenty things at once, and yet there was no confusion, but a blithe leaping from stone to stone in the rippling stream.'[2] 'Nothing that he taught could ever for a moment, while he taught it, be dull,' Herbert Paul, the historian, has written. 'He never seemed as if he tried to be interesting, but as if he could not be anything else. That he was teaching "dead languages" never occurred either to him or his pupils. It was the living voice that came to us.'

This wonderful facility was never shown to better advantage than in his translation of *Heraclitus* 'written for the boys doing Farnaby' (a school book of easy Greek pieces) in 1845.

> *They told me, Heraclitus, they told me you were dead,*
> *They brought me bitter news to hear and bitter tears to shed.*
> *I wept, as I remembered, how often you and I*
> *Had tired the sun with talking and sent him down the sky.*
>
> *And now that thou art lying, my dear old Carian guest,*
> *A handful of grey ashes, long, long ago at rest,*
> *Still are thy pleasant voices, thy Nightingales, awake;*
> *For Death, he taketh all away, but these he cannot take.*

Johnson had many enemies at Eton. It was whispered that he had too many favourites, and neglected those boys who were

---

[1] 1847–1908. Eldest son of Walter Kerr Hamilton, Bishop of Salisbury. Entered the Treasury in 1870, having been educated at Eton and Christ Church, Oxford. Private Secretary to Robert Lowe, Chancellor of the Exchequer, 1872–3; Mr Gladstone, 1873–4, and again, 1880–5. Principal Clerk of the Finance Division of the Treasury, 1885–92; assistant financial secretary, 1892–4; assistant secretary, 1894–1902, and permanent Financial Secretary and Joint Permanent Secretary (with Sir George Murray), 1902. C.B., 1885; K.C.B., 1894; G.C.B., 1906; P.C., 1908. Died at Brighton on September 3rd, 1908, after many years of cruel ill-health.

[2] Faith Compton Mackenzie: *William Cory*, 54–5.

neither beautiful nor brilliant. His teaching methods were so unorthodox that they inspired strong distrust and jealousy on the part of many of his colleagues. In spite of his veneration of scholarship, he frequently declared that it was a far greater thing for a man to get into the House of Commons than to get a First at Oxford. Then, like so many physically handicapped intellectuals, he had a singular thirst for military glory and prowess. In his hands the military history of England leaped into life. T. Earle Welby—not an Etonian—wrote of Johnson that 'He carried the military history of England in his head as men carry epics, and discerned the Homeric in the contemporary. . . . He touched dead and desiccated imagery, and it was restored to its original energy and significance.'

From ill-requited toil he turned
To ride with Picton and with Pack,
Among his grammars inly burned
To storm the Afghan mountain-track.

When midnight chimed, before Quebec
He watched with Wolfe till the morning star;
At noon he saw from Victory's *deck*
The sweep and splendour of England's war.

Beyond the book his teaching sped,
He left on whom he taught the trace
Of kinship with the deathless dead,
And faith in all the Island Race. . . .[1]

His critics were not wholly without justice; Johnson was a highly unorthodox teacher, and he was prone to favouritism. It was in the course of long voyages down the Thames in rowing boats on summer evenings no less than in the seclusion of the pupil room that he stamped his personality upon the favoured, pampered, brilliant few. He wrote poems for them, and to them; he sent them conspiratorial little notes; he hovered over all their Eton doings; he gave them childish nicknames like 'Mouse' (Frederick Wood, later Frederick Meynell, the fourth son of Lord Halifax) and 'Joab' (this was Dalmeny). It is in Johnson's poetry that the charm of Dalmeny's Eton days has been eternally preserved. After a rowing party in the June of 1864 from Eton

[1] *Ionicus*, by Sir Henry Newbolt.

to Henley and back 'by sunset and moonlight', of which Dalmeny
was a member, Johnson wrote:

> This sun, whose javelins strike and gild the wheat,
> Who gives the nectarine half an orb of bloom,
> Burns on my life no less, and beat by beat
> Shapes that grave hour when boyhood hears her doom.
>
> .   .   .   .   .   .
>
> Oh, Thames! My memories bloom with all thy flowers,
> Thy kindness sighs to me from every tree:
> Farewell! I thank thee for the frolic hours,
> I bid thee, whilst thou flowest, think of me.

Emotionally Johnson was an eighteenth-century Whig, and
was not without *snobisme*. Of the eighteenth century he wrote to
Dalmeny (August 29th, 1862) that it was 'the first age since the
time of Pliny when men were at leisure to worship virtue'. In a
letter to another pupil, Reginald Brett (later Lord Esher), in 1875
he expressed his philosophy, and incidentally foreshadowed
Rosebery's political life with remarkable accuracy.

> . . . I think, as a general rule, a young man commits himself incon-
> veniently if he proclaims that he is a Conservative; at least in England:
> he allows himself thereby to be claimed by selfish, lazy prudish folk.
> Laziness and scruples are sure to grow up fast enough anyhow. They
> can take care of themselves. An ardent reformer is pretty sure to be-
> come Conservative when he marries into a worldly family, when he
> has encumbrances, when he becomes post-prandial. He will be happier
> at 40 or 60 if his mind can fly back to a year of generous impulse and
> aspiration when he admired a Canning, a Peel, a Manin, a Cavour, a
> Hampden.

Johnson's influence over most of his pupils was considerable,
but for reasons which are not entirely clear, Dalmeny never fell
entirely under it. When his elder son went to Eton thirty years
later he spoke of the great Eton figures of his time—particularly
Hawtrey and Warre—who had influenced him, but he did not
mention Johnson. To some extent he was affected by Johnson's
view of life, and his admiration for a vanished age, his vague
thrillings at the emotional drum-beat, his intellectual arrogance
and cruelty of expression on occasion, were all accentuated by
Johnson's influence. But Johnson was no fool, and his reports

of Dalmeny's conduct and abilities, although tinged with real affection and admiration, were shrewd and revealing. Dalmeny had a mind of his own, and the fact that he did not slip easily into the Johnson mould gave the master's reports a detachment which they did not always reveal in the cases of more beautiful, more brilliant, and less obstinate boys.

Johnson was not particularly enthusiastic about Dalmeny before his arrival at Eton, as he held the view that all Brighton schools were below his standard; curiously enough, Dalmeny's Brighton headmaster advised Lady Harry not to send her brilliant son to Eton, of which institution he held a very low opinion. Under the headmastership of the great Hawtrey, Eton was emerging from a very bad period, but her reputation was slow in recovering from the effects of a series of inept appointments. Robert, third Marquess of Salisbury, described his Eton life as 'an existence among devils', and when Dr Hodgson became Provost his first statement was 'Now, please God, I will do something for these poor boys'. When Dalmeny entered Eton, Hawtrey had been Provost since 1858 and Dr Goodford was Headmaster, and the reforming zeal was still in full swing. As well as Johnson, other remarkably able masters were Oscar Browning, Stone, and Vidal. All were immediately struck by the grave, even solemn, demeanour of the thirteen-year-old Lord Dalmeny. 'When he arrived at Eton as a "new boy",' Lord Esher has recorded, 'he used to lie low while others talked, and wait for a chance of saying at his ease something unexpected and *sec* . . . he possessed, even then, that capacity for the true adjustment of two dissimilar things which make a spark, and is called wit.'[1] At the end of Dalmeny's first 'half' Lady Harry received the following report.

Eton College,
December 13th, 1860.

Dear Madam,

I have the pleasure of making my first report to you of your son's performance at Eton in terms decidedly favourable, warranted by a tolerably long and close observation.

I have several times heard him spoken of by Mr Stone, the teacher with whom he has done most of his work, including a good deal which does not come under my criticism, such as geography.

[1] Esher: *Cloud-capp'd Towers*, 21.

Mr Stone thought him singularly well-informed, but after some weeks he noticed his want of accurate grammatical knowledge: latterly I have heard only of his good doings in history: throughout he has been prudent and orderly in school and I hope to find, when the printed report comes, that he has taken a fair place in the terminal Examinations, which I must ask you to recognize hereafter under the name of 'Collections'.

I was less surprised than Mr Stone was with the boy's knowledge of history, which I have known surpassed by other boys on first coming to Eton: but it is very considerable.

I thought him at first rather over-educated and almost unnaturally intellectual, and his failures in writing Latin I thought would be wholesome in their humbling effect. On better acquaintance I find him endowed with heart as well as mind, very sociable, friendly, and gay.

I find he likes nearly everyone in his house, and is liked, apparently by all, certainly by those whom I know and like best.

He has been very patient in doing what is clearly against the grain, verses: he will not, I think, be distinguished in scholarship, but if he were to take constant pains for a year or two he would become accurate and idiomatic enough to do justice, in Latin, to his originality. But it is too early to express a confidential opinion as to his classics. I can only assure you that the attempt to become a good classical scholar would do him a great deal of good, even if he failed. . . .

Believe me to be, dear Madam,
Yours faithfully,
Wm. Johnson.

But the next report was not so flattering.

King's College,
Cambridge.
March 26, 1861.

Dear Madam,

I have not much to add to the last account I had the pleasure of writing to you of your Son's doings at Eton, because he has spent but little time in the active discharge of school duties since the Christmas holidays.

Mr Stone tells me that he has not been very efficient, and that he never construes a lesson thoroughly well, seeming sometimes not to have attended enough in the preparatory 'construing'.

I never observe that he is absent, or distracted; but I dare say he is not much interested in the lessons.

He does very short and unsatisfactory exercises.

I am ready however to hope that he may be drawn into the imitation

of two or three good students who are in the same house, and about
his own standing: it is not so unfashionable, as people seem to think,
for our boys to work for honour; and I believe by the time your Son
gets to Christ Church, for which he tells me he is destined, it will be
easier than it has been lately for a young man of good prospects to read
for honour even there. . . .

. . . I proceed to mention what hardly comes within the range of my
proper duties as a reporter, his marked and I think increasing kindness
of heart . . . he must have a high capacity for friendship, a quality of
which I seldom see the germs so early in a school career.

Again, I have hardly ever seen anyone show so much good feeling
towards Mr Vidal, who does not see the best side of boy-nature so
often as a tutor.

Alliances with schoolfellows of good habits are of course far more
important than friendly intercourse with grown-up people.

I think your Son likely in a singular way to combine both.

> I remain, dear Madam,
> Yours very truly,
> Wm. Johnson.

At the end of Dalmeny's first summer half his tutor was writing
(August 4th, 1861) to Lady Harry 'in rather more hopeful terms
as regards his head work and with increased respect for his
character'. Both Warre-Cornish and Stone spoke highly of him,
but from the mathematical tutor, Mr Ottley, came the report that
Dalmeny was 'irregular and indolent'. 'I am sure that he might be
a good scholar if he took pains,' Johnson wrote, but he had
excellent reports of Dalmeny's activities on the cricket field—
'playing with much zeal and gaiety'—and on the river, where 'the
new pleasures of boating . . . seem to bring with them at first a
special enlargement of mind and consciousness of promotion'.
Johnson also remarked on Dalmeny's habit of 'choosing companions almost fastidiously, but showing unusually strong regard
for the few with whom he associates', a feature of his character
which remained throughout life. Johnson was also struck by
Dalmeny's 'singular fineness of perception . . . so that it seems to
me sometimes as if I were talking to an experienced married *lady*:
at other times he reminds me in a mocking tone that merely veils
the serious thought and makes it more acceptable to one's taste,
of the ablest and most free-minded Cambridge men. Mr Cornish
was surprised by his talking (as he said to me) "quite wisely"
about Italian affairs, when five other boys were quite thrown out.

I have never had so young a pupil that drew me out so much. I certainly never had any, that in the course of a year's acquaintance became so intimate or gave me so much friendly sympathy. But I beg that you will not imagine that he is too old for his natural playmates: so far from that, he is, as he ought to be, primarily concerned with them, and only in a secondary degree with his elders.'

A contemporary subsequently wrote of Lord Dalmeny that

he had a slight figure and a fresh, prim, young-ladyish appearance. His family name of Primrose suited him to a nicety. He was not remarkable for scholarship, but he possessed plenty of cool assurance. He was always on the smile. If he was called up to construe, and did not know where to go on, nor much about the lesson, he would have the same luck as the legendary Titus Smalls of Boniface, who was not well prepared for his 'greats',

> But native cheek where facts were weak
> In triumph brought him through.

Under Dalmeny's dainty appearance there was some Scotch hard-headedness. He kept out of all scrapes. Walking very erect, with a tripping gait and a demure look, he was the pink of neatness, and seemed wrapt up in himself until you caught a glance of his shrewd eyes, which showed that he thought of weightier things than his personal appearance. Such eyes are like lighted windows, which reveal that house is not empty. Dalmeny steered the *St George* in 1862 . . . but he was not an energetic wet-bob or dry-bob. He read a good deal by himself—books of history and memoirs, newspapers, and the Parliamentary reports. . . . His patrician *hauteur* was unmistakable. Not an offensive *hauteur*, but that calm pride by which a man seems to ascend in a balloon out of earshot every time he is addressed by one not socially his equal.[1]

'We were very normal young scapegraces,' Esher has recorded, 'outwardly cynical, enjoying every hour of boyhood, whether strenuous or idle. We gossiped at street corners, we swung down the High Street in line, we lay eating cherries under the elms in Upper Club, we jumped off Acropolis into the river, we rowed races that we hated as though we loved them, we played House Matches in the field with rancorous delight, and spent long lazy

---

[1] James Brinsley-Richards: *Seven Years at Eton* (1883). Rosebery read his book in 1883 and was puzzled, as he could remember no Etonian of that name. In 1887 he met the author, whose real name was Grenville Murray.

evenings in "My Dame's" library playing them over and over again.'[1]

In the November of 1861 Dalmeny fell ill, and Johnson lamented to Lady Harry (November 12th) that he 'was just beginning to show some interest in Latin. . . . Besides this he has *twice* made a speech in our debating society with singular fluency, spirit and wit: I have hardly ever seen so promising a speaker. . . . But the loss of his company is much more to the point. He gives not only me, but many of the boys, the greatest pleasure we have: his influence, although unconsciously exerted, has quite reformed one boy, and done a great deal of good to some others; and I really think no one could be more missed than he would if he were to go away again for illness. He gives me more happiness than I can trust myself to speak of in writing. . . .' 'Good and dear friend,' he wrote to Dalmeny on November 28th, 'come back soon, as well as possible; for I miss you.'

This is not the normal type of letter written by a schoolmaster to a fourteen-year-old pupil, and another that Johnson wrote to Dalmeny in the March of the following year is even more strange.

Midnight. Sunday March 23 1862.

My dear Dalmeny,

What is the matter?

Wood says you say you are not coming here any more, because I cut you.

I don't agree to that.

You cut me for *four* days.

You came here on Thursday night and I was very polite, only Mr. Day's presence prevented any ordinary conversation.

On Friday night I made reasonable overtures, stomaching my pride, which is not less than yours: only reason convinces me that it must be subdued, or else I shall lose more than I can afford to lose in this dearth of sympathy.

Why could you not be civil enough to come in on Saturday, or to-day: I have been in, the whole of both days.

Some day you will lose a friend worth much more than me if you do not come to an understanding sooner after something has gone wrong.

Come and have it out, if you have any grievance.

I have been unhappy for a week without you, though too proud

---

[1] *Cloud-capp'd Towers*, 20–1.

to say so, till the gentle influence of Sunday and the peace-making Mouse prevailed.

On Wednesday night I had no companion but the dog Rabe and I was sorely tempted to remonstrate.

If I did not show sufficient joy at your appearance on Thursday night, it was out of pride, which you ought to make allowances for: I was really very glad when you came in and began to romp.

WJ

It is very much open to doubt whether any schoolmaster, however brilliant, can be regarded as a satisfactory influence if he regards his pupils with the emotions that Johnson did. His departure from Eton in 1872 is shrouded with considerable mystery, and Eton is still reticent on the subject. A popular—and possible—explanation is that the father of one of Johnson's favourites intercepted a letter to his son, was shocked by its tone, and reported it. Johnson did not have many allies on the staff, and even his name was removed from his text-books which were used at Eton for a further eighty years. The deep and mysterious silence which promptly descended, and which has never been penetrated, would appear to have been designed and perpetuated not to preserve Johnson's reputation but those who secured the resignation of the most brilliant of all Eton masters.

But even if the innuendoes concerning Johnson which have always been current are discounted, it is undeniable that his hero-worshipping of many boys did little good to their characters. But Dalmeny, as has been remarked, appeared to keep out of the charmed circle, and Johnson's irritation with his idleness and intellectual arrogance resulted in some very candid reports to Lady Harry.

King's Coll. Cambridge.
April 14, 1862.

Dear Madam,

The note which I enclose seems to me to give a correct estimate of Archie's general character at Eton as a student, and I have to report the entire failure of our attempts to get more work out of him. In all my experience it is the saddest case of the waste of faculties. We often have boys as clever as he is, whose cleverness takes another line and cannot be brought into the classical track, but he is a born Latinist, and might write the very best Latin prose and verse if he would but study the rules and increase his stock of words. Such a boy fifty years

ago would have done like Lords Grenville and Wellesley. Nowadays
it seems out of the question to get scholarship where there is an
assured prospect of social distinction without it.

Mr Wayte, who has always been heartily interested in your son, shares
my disappointment and speaks of his performances in Collections with
something more than regret.

It is possible that the next master he is with may have more influence
over him and may elicit some good composition.

I have no doubt that about four years hence he will himself see what
a mistake it is not to use these years of apprenticeship.

Meanwhile he seems to me to be falling off a little even in the power
of discussing rational topics: he was literary and thoughtful if not
studious, he is gradually becoming frivolous.

His position as steerer of a boat is valuable only so far as it enables
him eventually to become a member of the debating society in which
he can hardly fail to be a very conspicuous person, and, I am afraid,
when he is tired of the debates he will have nothing left at Eton to
care about.

I shall not cease however to put before him all that can attract him,
hereafter if not now, to high literature, believing that some day he will
take to it kindly.

                                        I am, dear Madam,
                                          Yours very truly,
                                            Wm. Johnson.

Johnson's annoyance at Dalmeny's lack of application was
increased by his awareness of the boy's remarkable abilities. In a
letter to a friend, Henry Bradshaw, in the spring of 1862, he
described how he and Dalmeny had gone 'Primrose hunting', and
that he had 'the natural eagerness of the budding bibliomaniac.
. . . He has the finest combination of qualities I have ever seen. . . .
I am doing all I can to make him a scholar; anyhow he will be an
orator, and, if not a poet, such a man as poets delight in.' In the
spring of 1862 he suggested to Dalmeny that he should begin to
collect material for his memoirs, which the boy commenced with
enthusiasm. Comments on contemporaries predominated. 'Of
Philip Stanhope,' he wrote on his cousin, 'who has great talents,
I think that if he could overcome an inordinate vanity, a passionate temper, and some trifling faults of petty deceit, etc., he may
grow up to be a great man.' He met Delane, the greatly feared
editor of *The Times*, at Chevening in the September of 1863 and
wrote him down as 'an insufferable snob, toadied by everyone for

the immense power he wields'. The arrival of the future Princess of Wales (later Queen Alexandra) for her wedding was described thus:

... The Provost was there in full fig with a couple of loyal addresses, the Rifle Corps were there in bedabbled uniforms. Suddenly a mounted policeman capered into the town, was nearly thrown from his horse & —capered on again. It was now perfectly dark. Then at last a carriage came—the corps having presented arms huddled after it like a flock of sheep, & it turned out to be the Royal Ladies' maids or something of that kind. Meanwhile the real Princess was galloping through. She rattled past the gaping Provost who however had the presence of mind to set off at a run & toss the Address into the carriage.

Eton matters were not often touched upon, but when they were recounted, the polished cynicism of this curious fourteen-year-old boy was given full rein. 'The Commissioners for Public Schools are down here now,' he recorded gleefully in the June of 1862, 'and wild is the terror which they inspire.' The visit of his mother and sisters to the Fourth of June celebrations in 1864 appears to have been a particularly dismal occasion. 'Suffice it to say that my mother paid 3£ for the most miserable vehicle I ever saw, which I confess I could not muster courage to enter, that the fireworks were bad, that my best clothes were all drenched, and that it was a scene of general misery.'

But he was usually concerned with more grand matters. Old Lord Rosebery, to whom he was devoted, was a wonderful fund of information, and carefully described Queen Victoria's first Council—which he had attended—to his fascinated grandson.

... Her behaviour, though a great red spot on either cheek showed her mental agitation, was perfectly composed & dignified. The scene was a plain dining room. The Queen entered supported on either side by a Royal Duke, the Dukes of Cumberland and Sussex. She then took possession of a dining room chair at the top of the room as Sovereign and read out a written speech. She then performed the first act of her [reign] as of every other Sovereign's reign since the Union, i.e. a declaration that she would support the Presbyterian Religion in Scotland. Ld. Melbourne then wrote on a slip of paper hurriedly, 'I appoint Henry, Marquis of Lansdowne, President of my Council,' which she read aloud. She then declared her Uncle's Privy Council to be her Privy Council; Lord Lansdowne then performed a great deal of reading as to the places where she should be proclaimed, etc. Several Councillors were affected to tears, none more so than Lord Melbourne. . . .

It was probably from the same source that he learned of the true circumstances of the death of the Duke of Hamilton, which occurred in a Paris brothel, and the full story was carefully recorded in the *Memoirs*. Dalmeny's first visit to the House of Commons occurred in the Easter holidays of 1864, when he heard Mr Gladstone introduce his Budget, and described his speech as 'grand & rolling, but very whimsical'. It was his first sight of the great man, then Chancellor of the Exchequer, but in 1865 he was invited to a dance at Hawarden and first made the acquaintance of that unique family which was to have so great an effect upon his life.

Johnson's report on the 1862 summer half to Lady Harry contained the usual praise of her son's exceptional ability and infuriating indolence.

. . . He has in himself wonderful delicacy of mind, penetration, sympathy, flexibility, capacity for friendship—all but the tenacious resolution of one that is to be great. The particular duty before him is to face week by week the difficulties of composing in a dead language. He has a rare literary faculty; one of my most learned & wise colleagues is forcibly struck by the fact that he urged me to set a particular bit of Homer for translation into verse . . . so rare is it for a boy to perceive any poetical beauty in one lesson more than another. Most boys that get credit for good taste are merely reflecting and reproducing what they get from their seniors; but Archie is infinitely above admiring what I admire, e.g. Sophocles. He is original all day long; too original to be very popular. He has more affection than tact, and quite as much antipathy as sympathy; so that he is not floating with the stream of popularity. All would come right if he were seriously engaged in a course of study, overcoming difficulties and competing with the many worthy rivals whom a great school contains . . .

Johnson's acuteness of judgement on Dalmeny is quite remarkable, for his comments could have been made with justice at any time in Rosebery's lifetime. There is a conspicuous absence of 'the tenacious resolution of one that is to be great'; he is 'original all day long' but 'too original to be very popular'; he has 'more affection than tact, and quite as much antipathy as sympathy'. The main features of a personality which was to bewilder and fascinate (or repel) Rosebery's contemporaries throughout his life were well marked in the schoolboy. On August 18th Johnson gave the boy a warning which he might well have taken more to heart.

> . . . I want you to be one that will not only understand, but *do justice to*, what passes in other minds—one that will not merely pick out and appropriate what pleases, but unconsciously attract and imperceptibly check and indirectly stir and elevate the minds of equals no less than of inferiors. If you face all reasonable difficulties in the way of headwork, you will become less fastidious and therefore far more influential in dealing with those in whom the head and heart go together, that is, the great bulk of active people. . . .

To Warre-Cornish, Johnson also wrote, at this time, 'I would give you a piece of plate if you would get that lad to work; *he is one of those who like the palm without the dust*'. As a description of Dalmeny this was accurate enough, but that single phrase—it was published by Cornish in his edition of Johnson's *Letters and Journals* in 1897—haunted Rosebery's reputation up to, and beyond, the grave. It has been seized upon by countless persons as the solution to his complex personality and the secret of his life, and there is hardly a book or an article on Rosebery which omits the phrase. It was written, it should be remembered, by a man whose standards were extremely high, of a boy of fifteen years of age, who was already outstripping most of his contemporaries, and who had just published (privately) a volume of poetry. Although Johnson's reports on Dalmeny were very frank and perceptive—which is why they occupy so much space in this chapter—he made the mistake of ascribing to indolence the Stanhope characteristic of only doing congenial work. The Stanhopes worked in fits and starts; there would be intermittent periods of feverish activity followed by apparent relapses. Dalmeny inherited these characteristics; he was constitutionally unfitted for the long haul, and although his powers of work were to become considerable, his memory quite exceptional, and his reading, even as a schoolboy, remarkably wide and deep, he could not, and would not, be forced into activity when he did not feel like it.

He was also greatly enjoying Eton life. His letters home were usually confined to amusing accounts of these activities, and one on the aftermath of the 1862 June 4th, in which he had steered the *Defiance*, having never been on the river before—an act which he subsequently described as the bravest action of his life, not excluding the acceptance of the Premiership—should not be omitted.

. . . At Surley, Poppy kept behind me faithfully. After two or three glasses of champagne, I looked round and saw that he wanted something; on which he pointed to his mouth, and began to eat jam tart largely. I believe also that Rickards, the captain of our boat, kept going in that direction with a glass of champagne, saying, 'Drink it, somebody!' on which Poppy immediately seized it. The result was, I believe, considerable excitement on the part of Poppy when he got home . . . the great beauty of the whole thing was that no one got drunk. One reason being, that there was no time to get drunk; and the next was, that the rain very considerably adulterated the champagne. . . .

He was becoming an excellent shot, but the quality of the game at Battle was not very good, and in the January of 1863 he wrote a mournful account of his endeavours to his cousin, Henry Stanhope. 'Lord Harry', he observed, 'seems to be keeping all the shooting on the estate for some day, but privately I don't believe that day will ever come. Meanwhile I wander about hedgerows disconsolately with a rusty old keeper and a rustier old dog and never get a shot. . . . I go back [to Eton] on Thursday which is, to say the least of it, no end of a bore.'

The concern of Lady Harry at her son's lack of progress at Eton was increased by Johnson's next report (March 24th, 1863).

. . . I could not give him a good character for industry; for I think he might have done a great deal more ever since he has been here, and, though he says he is improving, I cannot perceive it. One of his trial papers it was my duty to look over, and this was far below the average, and contained foolish mistakes. Even in the modern history, which one would suppose would have suited him, he showed no interest. He has done everything with me slowly, listlessly, and even clumsily. . .

. . . I have nothing to show for the nine weeks of instruction. It is one of the very many cases of waste and stagnation which men of my profession have to watch with patience but which they do not always report with frankness. . . .

But Dalmeny, heedless of the warnings of Johnson and the reproaches of his mother, continued to enjoy himself thoroughly. In the October of 1864 he was elected to the Eton Society—'Pop'

—and figured prominently in the monthly debates. His flippancy and studied use of irony were not disapproved of, and his own accounts of his speeches in the reports of the debates make interesting reading. He spoke in support of Pitt, and recorded that 'his polysyllabic arguments occupied 5¼ minutes (for a bet)': at the close of a debate on Dundee he said, 'I think Dundee was a very brave man. His life and death were equally romantic. I therefore give my vote in favour of Dundee.' In another speech, made in a debate on the subject of Mary, Queen of Scots, he recorded that 'Lord Dalmeny then addressed the House in his usual eloquent manner: he pointed out that there is a great difference between regarding a person with admiration and hatred, with many other wise remarks'. On another occasion he successfully led a revolt against the memory of Walpole, and his report reveals that 'Dalmeny spoke in his usual vein of sarcastic and cutting wit, making several of the members look very small'.

Johnson's reports continued to praise Dalmeny's character and potential ability, but to lament his lack of application. One master reported that he was 'not quick' to grasp a new subject, and that his Greek was 'very poor'; Johnson reported that in his classes he was 'weak' and 'not attentive', although 'he is not so easily bored as he was, and I look upon him as a favourable—or at least charitable—listener'. 'I believe', his letter of August 1st, 1863, continued, 'that he acts upon principle, and has high motives and aspiration. Now that he has got rid of a certain fastidiousness and peevishness he seems to me singularly enlightened, and high minded, with strong affections well regulated. To me personally he is almost a good genius; he makes me behave better to other people, and I am ashamed of dogmatising roughly in his presence. I cannot imagine a boy having more sympathy with a middle-aged man, than he has with me. He could not know so much of me if he had not, besides other gifts, the rare and precious gift of imagination. I hope he will grow up as an orator and a man of wide influence; if he goes on as he does now, it cannot be otherwise; and I think he has passed the crisis of public school life.'

In the December of 1863 Johnson visited Battle. He had dreaded the occasion, as its previous owners had been 'some awful old people . . . colder than the Sussex hills', but he consoled himself with the thought that he would find 'a friend there for whom

I would face a battery of beaux and belles'. Somewhat surprisingly, he was delighted with the house, and particularly with the 'sublime Library, in which books are sumptuously buried like Cheops in a Pyramid . . . radiant with blue velvet, and soporifically warm'. He enjoyed the grave company of Lord Harry no less than 'the merry frivolities of the lads'. Dalmeny showed him his treasures: a miniature of his father, his best books, Charles James Fox's copy of Virgil (given to him by Lady Holland), Chatham's letters to Camelford, which had been given to him by his uncle, Lord Stanhope, and his collection of autograph letters which included a letter from Lord Dalhousie declining an invitation because he was 'hardly presentable, for besides other tribulations he had become quite deaf'. The magpie collector who was to fill Barnbougle Castle and The Durdans with such an astonishing mixture of treasures was to be discerned also in the schoolboy.

The rift between Dalmeny and his mother was steadily increasing during these years. The reserve which Dalmeny had shown throughout his childhood irritated his mother, who found in the adoring and adored Everard a more worthwhile outlet for her affections. 'I have only one wish in the world for you', she wrote to her elder son in 1864, '—that you should learn to hold up your head, & not go about in your present slovenly, slouching way.' 'I must thank you for your letter, or rather for your good intention in writing,' she wrote again to him at this time, 'as dry & brief as they are, your letters seem to give you so much trouble, from the inability of finding anything to say. As regards myself, any, the smallest trifle, about you or Evy, would interest *me*, but for others, in this dearth of material, I would advise you to study the flowing & amplifying style of your uncle Stanhope or Grandmama. Each can write a very graceful, well composed & readable letter, upon *nothing at all*, & I think it a desirable talent in this way, that it can never lead their correspondents to think they are "getting over" an unwelcome task.'

The unfortunate Lord Harry, who had determined to remain aloof from all family squabbles, found himself being drawn into them, and felt obliged to take the mother's side. It is not possible, at this length of time, to catalogue the incidents which increased the mutual antipathy between son and mother, but from time to time a letter, or a recorded comment, illuminates the relationship with sad clarity. Lady Harry had almost every quality which one could desire; brilliance in conversation, an arresting personality, genuine charm and warm-heartedness, and exceptional talent as an artist, all these attributes were rightly ascribed to her by her many admirers. But, like so many masterful women, she was a demanding person, and resented the shyness and aloofness of her elder son. Everard and Mary (her elder daughter) were her favourites; and the inevitable consequence of this favouritism was that Archie and Constance were thrown together and became inseparable. 'No shadow of annoyance has ever come across me in connection with you that I can remember in the whole course of my life,' he once wrote to her in later years, in one of the many gentle letters which passed between them almost every month.

Thus, at an early stage the family quietly resolved itself into two camps, and although there were no scenes or instances of division, each part went its own way. When Everard—whose gentle nature was probably inherited from his father—died on active service in 1885 his mother wrote a biography of him which was privately printed, in which her excessive adoration of him shone in every page. Apart from the fact that he was a talented artist, very little about his personality has come down to us. Family legend hopefully credited him with a somewhat Bohemian private life about which his mother was blissfully unaware, but if this uncorroborated theory were true, it would be one of the few signs that he was not the placid slave of his mother that his correspondence and actions might imply.

Dalmeny's natural reserve was inevitably increased by his none-too-happy home life. At Eton, although happy, he was not popular, mainly on account of his aloofness, which was put down to patrician *hauteur* or conceit by his contemporaries. Johnson took him to Rome in 1864, and described him to a correspondent as 'the wisest boy that ever lived—and full of fun, too'. His mother, on the other hand, saw a morose, fastidious, undeniably talented but indolent boy, and her irritation with him increased proportionately.

Curiously enough, Johnson provided the excuse for her to make her last attempt to impose her will upon her incomprehensible and obstinate son. The reports continued to speak well of Dalmeny's character but with despair of his work, and she informed Johnson that her son was to leave Eton at the Easter of

1865 at the latest. The master was distressed, and wrote to her on
May 7th, 1864, pointing out the illogicality of her decision.

. . . Archie is quite old enough to care for himself at Oxford *now*;
and if he entered it in October this year he would save a *year*. He would
be able to get through the ordinary examinations of the University
without delay, and he might get his degree by the time he comes of age.
But if he enters Oxford next Easter he loses fourteen weeks of Eton
schooling (of course I cannot presume to hint that this is of the least
use); he gains in lieu of it only a few weeks of Oxford, with an immense
long vacation: in July he would be languishing in Hyde Park and
wishing he were with the schoolfellows of whom he is so singularly
fond.
It is quite in his power, I do not say that it is in his wishes, so to employ the fifty weeks of Eton schooling which he would get by August 1,
1865, as to fit himself for taking some form of *honours* at Oxford. . . .

Dalmeny was appalled by the prospect of losing his last summer
half at Eton, and the battle of wills began, with the unhappy step-
father trying to retain his doctrine of non-interference with some
difficulty. Dalmeny bitterly resented his mother's attitude, and
thirty years later he told his elder son that he had never forgiven
her for attempting to curtail his Eton life. The correspondence—
assuming that there was any—between Dalmeny and his mother
on this matter has disappeared, and it is from the letters of the
Duke of Cleveland (by which title Lord Harry Vane will hence-
forth be recognised) to his brother-in-law, Lord Stanhope,
that the progress of the family crisis can most easily be traced.
Dalmeny's obstinacy matched that of his mother, but by the
January of 1865 it was clear that he was going to win the day.
The Duke wrote to Stanhope:

. . . I have generally abstained from giving advice on the subject,
but I did say that at Archie's time of life & in his peculiar position of
independence it was a matter for consideration whether she would not
lose her authority over him. . . . Wilhelmina has not answered Archie's
letter,[1] but said altho' she was herself agst. giving way that she wd.
write to Mr Warburton[2] to ask him whether he could take Archie as he[3]
proposes on the 1st August. . . . If he does not accept, Wilhelmina is
against giving way & says that she would wash her hands of him

[1] Missing from the Duchess' papers.
[2] The tutor engaged for Dalmeny's coaching before going up to Oxford.
[3] i.e. Dalmeny.

altogether (to use her own expression) if it was decided to give way to him. Archie's case is peculiar, [for] if it had been my own son I should have taken him away, as it is clear to me that the passion for remaining at Eton arises from it not being a place of study as it ought to be, but of freedom, enjoyment, & independence. . . .

The principal support for Dalmeny came from Johnson and the Roseberys, and when Mr Warburton said that he could take Dalmeny on August 1st rather than at Easter, the Duchess capitulated, and 'washed her hands of him altogether'. 'I trust', she wrote coldly to her son on May 8th, 'you will not let this last half at Eton be an idle one, with Mr Johnson or without him, & not let the golden days slip unimproved through your fingers.' Before this decision was reached, Johnson had written to Dalmeny a famous letter of condolence.[1]

. . . I quite conceive and almost feel myself what you must feel at leaving your friends at Easter, and giving up the delightful summer at Eton; the last summer, which is often so full of interest as to blot out the memory of all earlier years. It is a loss which ladies cannot be expected to understand, and not many men of fifty can estimate aright —perhaps no one who has not been at Eton. I never spent such a summer myself, but I have watched many boys in their enjoyment of it, and caught the glow and lustre by reflection. Nor would I preach to the effect that similar and greater enjoyment and companionship will be found at Oxford, or elsewhere. Even if it were so, human life is not so long or well arranged as to spare one such summer. It is the pearl in the crown of years. I can half weep to think that I shall never again see a Pelham or a Holland stepping through those weeks of kindness and brotherly sympathy. May there be many generations of such happy cricketers, though I be out of earshot. . . .

Eton is not a mere place of residence for people working avowedly for an examination; a place where one is to leave as soon as one ceases to acquire fresh knowledge. It is a place which contains its own remedies for idleness, if people will only apply them: a place in which there is charity as well as selfish prudence, that goes on hoping, and looks to a distant point.

No tutor single-handed, and particularly in the upper part of the school, where tutors and pupils do so little together, can contend against idleness. He can speak plainly if he is beaten in the endeavour to get something done, and then he can try again. . . .

<hr/>

[1] *The Letters and Journals of William Cory*, edited by F. Warre-Cornish (1897), 157-8.

Although Johnson supported Dalmeny in his controversy with the Duchess, he did not relax his criticisms of his work, and he lamented the decision to send him to Christ Church, an institution he despised; he urged Balliol upon the Duchess, but without effect. At the end of the 1864 summer half (*July 30th, 1864*) he tried again.

. . . I feel tolerably sure that in the course of the next few years he will wish for instruction, and that he will not find at the wretched place of his future residence any one half so ready or able to instruct him as I am: for though they are far more learned at Christchurch they are above their business. Having a fine mind before me I try to cultivate its reasoning powers, and I am baffled by a fixed indisposition. He will listen to any amount of talk about persons but to nothing else.

I have stated this, not as a complaint, but as an explanation. . . . Your son is letting year after year drift away without learning what in theory he should be learning, the art of expressing himself, *like a reasoner*. . . .

. . . On the other hand he has been gaining bodily strength, animal spirits, experience, friendship, tact, and almost everything that will eventually make him a happy and influential member of society. I have watched with the purest pleasure his enjoyment of companionship with the excellent and delightful people who make Eton the best possible place of residence. His affection for his school-fellows is worth all that anyone can extract from all possible libraries on systems of philosophy: and if the critics and our employers were content with the education of the *heart*, I should be quite at my ease: only they unluckily cry aloud for knowledge, and in order to meet that demand I am obliged to scold and worry those who set themselves against having knowledge thrust upon them.

I should not in this particular case deeply lament the loss of time and of opportunities, if I did not know that at Christchurch there will be no chance of making up the arrears.

If he were going to live at the age of nineteen and twenty-two with zealous intellectual men, he might well afford to trifle now. But with nothing else to look forward to but a set of fashionable triflers, gamblers, loungers, and cricketers, *wholly left to themselves* except as far as the University frightens them into spasmodic cramming for six weeks a year, I have a dismal foreboding of this rare, fine, intellect being wasted, either on 'society' or the turf.

I have written this in anticipation of what will be said by Archie's family friends about five or six years hence. . . . But to tell him that he is to go to Christchurch is tantamount to giving him leave to be a mere man of pleasure.

He is assuming at Eton the attitude assumed before him by the scores of young men whom I have seen disqualifying themselves for public usefulness, but there is far more in him to spoil than in his fellow victims. . . .

There were many signs of Dalmeny's growing fondness for 'society' and the Turf, and in the Eton Society he moved 'That Baily's Turf Magazine be taken, but on the disapproval of the House, the motion was withdrawn'. It was with reason that Johnson viewed Christ Church as the Nemesis of all his hopes, and he never relaxed his endeavours to push Rosebery into other less glittering but more rewarding channels. ' "Society" ', he wrote to him on November 25th, 1866, 'is not enough. Society has made a thorough mess of English politics these last few years, though kept it straight to some extent by the doctrinaires whom it smiles at. The kind of people you see at Battle or Raby are clever but not wise.'

Even at the age of eighteen, Lord Dalmeny was something of an enigma. That he was remarkably able was undeniable, but any good impression which this might have made was often weakened by an irritating pose of casual flippancy; his literary and oratorical styles, although highly burnished, were distinguished principally for their irony and sarcasm. His epigrams were regarded—particularly by himself—as of singular brilliance and penetration, but were perhaps best described by Johnson's tart adjective, 'Clever'. He was a moody, unpredictable boy, self-enfolded and solitary, yet in his letters to his Primrose aunts and Rosebery grandparents one discerns the warmth and charm which could make him such an enchanting and fascinating companion. He was remarkably mature and accomplished, and his correspondence, conversation and manner belied his surprisingly youthful appearance, which he retained until his forties. Few young men of his generation could emulate his accomplishments or his wonderful prospects, and the great country houses of England and Scotland welcomed him enthusiastically as a brilliant new recruit, while the worlds of society and the Turf were already beginning to court him.

Beneath the glittering surface, his character had been perceptibly altered by his years at Eton. The natural reserve which had been increased by his father's death and his alienation from his mother had already become part of his personality, so that what had begun as a pose which served to protect himself from unpleasant realities had been woven into the fabric of his character. The knowledge that he would shortly be entirely independent undoubtedly affected his attitude to hard work, although he had so much of the Stanhope in him that without interest there could be little application. His conspicuous aloofness had caused, as one of its side-effects, a certain fastidiousness which, although it repelled many people, undeniably made him more interesting, and gave him an air of maturity even as a schoolboy. Within the chosen circle of friends he was the most delightful of companions, wonderfully gay, a cruel mimic, sardonic, generous, and irreverent. But the outward appearance of a somewhat priggish youth concealed an acutely sensitive nature. Something of a dreamer and romantic, he had the opportunity of shutting out the unpleasant aspects of life. Unquestionably he was affected by the adulation of his elders and contemporaries, and it was already noticeable that he surrounded himself only with those friends and relatives who most admired him. The devotion of his sister, Constance (now Lady Leconfield), was always present to counterbalance his alienation from his mother. Success at Eton had come rather too easily, and Johnson's warnings were unheeded. That he possessed a 'rare, fine intellect' was not doubted by the few who knew him well; the great question was whether he possessed the character to make use of it.

He left Eton in a haze of glory, undimmed by a final fling on his last evening, when he and other Eton swells went to a local theatre, clambered into the boxes from the pit, and barracked the unfortunate actors and pelted them with rubbish until the leading man cried in anguish that 'I can bear your ridicule, but I would rather not be made a target of'. The rioters relented only in this aspect, and the curtain fell amid a perfect tumult of disapprobation. Dalmeny, like all Etonians, was deeply moved by his last Chapel. 'God grant I may never have such a wrench again,' he recorded in his diary for August 4th, 1865. 'I cannot take in that I am no longer an Etonian. It must have taken place at some time. Why not now?' Eton was always one of his great loves. 'There is one consolation in getting older as an Etonian', he declared in 1898, '—that you keep the pride that has always been in you since you went to Eton, the pride of the prowess of your school. I never knew but one Etonian who said he did not like Eton, and he very soon went to the devil.'[1]

Rosebery did not have many contacts with Johnson in later life. In 1872 Johnson resigned his Eton appointments, subsequently changed his name to Cory, and had twenty years more of a strange, melancholy life, enduring some hardship of body and much of mind. After his death in 1892 Rosebery wrote to Warre-Cornish that 'he was always burning his idols, though the shrine was never empty. Music was perhaps the only one that lasted him his life.' His pupils, almost without exception, rose to the most exalted levels in every sphere of life, and all honoured Johnson's reverence for freedom of spirit, depth of character, and sentiment. This was his greatest contribution to their personalities, for he had helped to inculcate in them a fierce contempt for anything second-rate, petty, or narrow-minded, while at the same time fostering admiration for physical courage, a liberal spirit, and the grand gesture. Johnson was, in the last analysis, a great romantic, admiring the man of imagination and idealism. He has written his own epitaph in the last stanzas of his moving *Academus* (1858).

> *I'll borrow life, and not grow old;*
> *And nightingales and trees*
> *Shall keep me, though the veins be cold,*
> *As young as Sophocles.*
> *And when I may no longer live,*
> *They'll say, who know the truth,*
> *He gave whate'er he had to give*
> *To freedom and to youth.*

[1] This speech was given at a dinner in honour of Lord Curzon, Lord Minto, and Bishop Welldon in 1898, and his concluding words brought a shout of laughter which disconcerted Rosebery, who had not been aware of the fact that Lord Salisbury (then Prime Minister) had refused an invitation because of his ineradicable hatred of Eton!

CHAPTER TWO

POLITICS, AND OTHER DIVERSIONS

Riches are a good handmaid, but the worst mistress.
BACON: *De Dignitate*

IN THE AUGUST OF 1865 Mr and Mrs Disraeli paid a visit to
Raby Castle in County Durham, the seat of the Duke and Duchess
of Cleveland. 'On a red October evening, with the stags roaring
through the rising mist, it was a stately picture of feudal grandeur,'
Lord Crewe has written of this imposing establishment, whose
entrance hall was so enormous that carriages actually drove into
it to deposit their startled loads. 'The general effect feudal and
Plantagenet,' Disraeli remarked with truth, for Raby, grandiose,
bleak, and freezing cold in winter, was administered on feudal
lines, with its own chaplain and armies of servants. The eighteen-
year-old Lord Dalmeny was already desperately bored when the
interesting visitors arrived as part of a large party which included Montagu Corry, who had never met Disraeli before and
who was to become his confidant and private secretary. But
Corry was not the only young man who attracted the great man's
attention; 'Dalmeny seemed to me very intelligent and formed
for his time of life (not yet of age),' Disraeli noted, 'and not a
prig, which might be feared.'[1]

Dalmeny was entranced by the strange couple, and recorded
their visit with the greatest care. Disraeli entered his profession
in the visitors' book as 'patriotism'—Gladstone later wrote
'apprentice' in the same column—and quickly established himself
with his hostess, as Dalmeny's account records.

Mama came in from riding when they were all in the library; so she
said, 'I was so sorry to be so rude as not to be here to receive you, but
the fact is that I had such a bad headache that I was obliged to go and
take a ride.' To which Dizzy replied with an air, 'The pleasure of seeing

---

[1] Monypenny & Buckle: *Disraeli*, II, 153 (two-volume edition).

Your Grace in your riding habit makes up for the loss of your society'
—the sort of compliment in fact that one sees in *Coningsby*.

I sat next Mrs Disraeli at dinner. May I have memory and strength
to write down some of our conversation. She began by asking me where
I was going to. I replied 'Oxford'; so she exclaimed, 'Oh, yes, I love
Oxford, they are all so fond of Mr Dizzy there, they all applaud him
so.' So I said, 'Yes, I suppose Mr Disraeli took an Honorary Degree
there ?' 'Yes,' said she, 'he was made a D.T.C.L., or something of the
sort.' She then asked me if I were fond of reading, and after a little
talk, she said that the only novels she liked were those that improved
and instructed her. 'I think *Coningsby* is that,' I hinted. 'Of course,'
she said, 'written by a clever man like him.' . . .

. . . 'Do you care for politics, Mrs Disraeli ?' 'No, I have no time,
I have so many books and pamphlets to read and see if his name is in
any of them! and I have everything to manage, and write his stupid
letters. I am sorry when he is in office, because then I lose him altogether, and though I have many people who call themselves my
friends, yet I have no friend like him. I have not been separated from
him since we have been in the country, except when I have been in the
woods, and I cannot lose him' (here her voice trembled touchingly). . . .

. . . I think this half-crazy, warm-hearted woman's talk is worth
setting down, for she is an uncommon specimen. Parts are very
touching. . . .

September 1st. Mrs Disraeli greeted me at breakfast with 'We have
been talking about you.' 'I am indeed honoured, Mrs Disraeli.' 'Oh,
but I did not say it was very good.' 'But to be talked about by you is
enough honour.' I cannot help quizzing her by talking in this way,
though I really like her. She praised me in her own and her husband's
name very warmly this evening.

September 2nd. After breakfast Dizzy came up and asked me how much
we had shot. I said that partridges were scarce and that we intended,
therefore, to kill nothing but time today. 'Then you have a certain bag.'

During the visit Disraeli took Dalmeny for a long walk in the
park and they discussed politics. In spite of all that has been
written about him, the secret of Disraeli's extraordinary fascination still eludes us. But part of the admiration he evoked in
young people was due to his interest in their doings, the apparent
seriousness with which he considered their sayings, and his complete lack of condescension. Although most people laughed
at his extravagant language and studied courtesy, they were
secretly flattered, and young people in particular were very
receptive to his kindly interest in their affairs. Dalmeny returned

from his walk excited and impressed; Disraeli gave him a copy of *Lord George Bentinck* with the inscription, 'For Dalmeny, in remembrance of a walk at Raby, 1865, from B. Disraeli', and Rosebery later told his sons that his political aspirations really began as a result of this conversation. But they did not move in a Tory direction. Mrs Disraeli told him that her husband was 'so delighted with his walk, and so pleased with you. He is so sorry there is no chance of your being in the House of Commons. He would so like to have some young men like you to follow him. But then you are a Whig.' 'Who told you?' Dalmeny asked. 'He did.'

After an autumn spent with a tutor at Revesby, Dalmeny matriculated at Christ Church on January 19th, 1866, as 'Hon^lis Archibaldus Philippus Primrose, Baro de Dalmeny'. From the beginning he took up an independent attitude by failing to attend morning chapel, which was obligatory in those days. 'Sent for by Dean,' he noted laconically in his diary on one occasion; 'Told him the morning was too cold. Very amiable.' Dalmeny found at Christ Church a somewhat indolent, charming, and privileged circle of Eton friends, strengthened by the addition of Lord Lansdowne at Balliol and the irrepressible and slightly outrageous Randolph Churchill at Merton. Through 'the unifying influence' of the Bullingdon Club they formed a coterie which, as Rosebery later admitted, 'saw regrettably little of the rest of the University'. Having an ample allowance from his step-father and grandfather, Dalmeny lived in some state, and greatly enjoyed the varied pleasures of his Oxford existence. On one not uncharacteristic day he played racquets in the morning, worked in the afternoon, wined with friends at six o'clock, went to a concert, supped at the Mitre off oysters and Chablis, drank more wine in a friend's room afterwards, and concluded an enjoyable day by piling furniture against the 'oak' of another friend's rooms so that he had to be rescued by his scout in the morning. On February 6th, (1867) he attended the opening of Parliament and lunched at the House of Lords. In May he attended his first Derby and, betting discreetly, made a net profit of £10 in the week. Dinners at the Mitre followed in regular succession, and not infrequently there was 'considerable intoxication' as Dalmeny recorded in his diary. His family noted these doings with some alarm. 'In our class of life', his mother wrote meaningly to him, 'self indulgence is what we have most to guard against; it seems to extinguish the more generous feelings, & deadens the heart to the sense of sin.' Dalmeny's first year of Oxford did not contain much hard work and was mainly taken up with much visiting of country houses, dinners at the Mitre, wine in rooms, and chaff and chatter.

He was a frequent traveller. In the March of 1867 he went to Italy and renewed his adoration of Naples. He went to the races at the Campo di Marte where, as a boy of seven, he had seen Ferdinand II review his troops. 'It is something', he noted in a copious and meticulously kept Journal of his travels, 'to have lived out a dynasty at twenty!' He used to visit Lady Holland regularly when staying in Naples, dining with her at the Palazzo Roccella, and making numerous local expeditions with her and her adopted daughter Mary.[1] Mary was very beautiful and Dalmeny was undoubtedly smitten, but it is difficult to determine to what extent. Their relationship ended under somewhat mysterious circumstances. According to Fox family legend, Dalmeny proposed and was refused; some plausibility is given to this story by the fact that he gained possession of his letters to Mary Fox in 1910 and destroyed them in spite of an assurance to the contrary which he had given to Lord Ilchester. But Rosebery's version was different, and after re-reading the letters he noted that

I cannot understand these letters, and my memory does not supply the clue.

I certainly never proposed to Mary Fox, but this seems to me the base of Lady Holland's letter to me and that Mary refused me on account of religion. After racking my brain I seem to remember that Miss Fox took me aside into a room at St Anne's & declared spontaneously that she could not change her religion on marriage. I was very fond of her with a boy and girl affection (I was only 20 in 1868 & Mary Fox only 16) but I cannot think that I contemplated marriage, which Mary and Lady Holland certainly must have done. My recollection is that I was terribly embarrassed by Mary's declaration, which I saw would put an end to our friendship and to my delightful life under Lady Holland's roof.

Mary Fox's letters to Rosebery have survived, and give no hint of any romantic attachment, at least on her side. Lady Holland, on

[1] After Lady Holland's death Rosebery was sent the papers relating to Mary's parentage: she was an illegitimate child of a French serving-maid, and when Lord Bute was informed of these facts he had broken off his engagement to Mary. She died in 1878.

the other hand, was clearly very anxious for an engagement, and when Mary married Prince Aloysius Lichtenstein in 1872, she wrote to Rosebery with some bitterness that 'the wound is very deep—very painful—but it is healing. She is not worth the tears I have shed—what a bitter disappointment. Where is her head? Even *that* might have remained where the heart was wanting—but no—she makes herself ridiculous and disliked! You would have guided her better than that fool—but I am happier as it is, thinking that you are free, and that no evil influence has robbed (me) of your friendship. God bless you, dearest. . . .'

Much of Dalmeny's intellectual promise was being fulfilled at Oxford. His own diaries are filled with accounts of gay evenings and expensive racing weeks, but he must have been working fairly hard, as he did exceptionally well in 'Moderations' in the November of 1867, and his tutor confidently predicted a First in Greats. 'I should say that whilst he was universally liked he was not one who at that time had many bosom friends, possibly because he was intellectually so immeasurably superior to all his contemporaries,' Henry Tollemache has written.[1] '. . . I was always in bitter conflict with the authorities, whereas his influence was always on the side of Law and Order. It was in the lighter side of University life that I saw most of him.' His life was a curious mixture. In September he stayed at Hughenden as the guest of the Disraelis, and although Disraeli had a bad cold and was less communicative than usual, they had a long walk together in the park and earnestly discussed contemporary politics. On November 11th Dalmeny dined with the Vice-Chancellor and on his return to Christ Church was jostled by a large and angry Oxford crowd which had been rioting almost continuously since November 9th; Dalmeny leapt on to a mounting-block and harangued the mob; his speech must have been of a strong Radical nature, as he was cheered enthusiastically and allowed to pass unmolested on his way back to college.

In October, possibly as a result of a hint from Hughenden, Dalmeny was approached by the Conservatives of Darlington with an invitation to stand as candidate in the next election, expected to be in 1869. Dalmeny declined the offer partly on financial grounds and partly on political. To the surprise of his

[1] Henry Tollemache to Lord Crewe, August 27th, 1929 (*Crewe Papers*). Part of this letter was quoted on pages 44–5 of volume I of Crewe's *Rosebery*.

mother he gave hints of more radical tendencies. 'The Conservative party has practically ceased to exist,' he wrote somewhat loftily to her on October 27th, 'and I think we shall see an entire transmutation of parties before 1869. Anyhow, it is not the time for a young man to commit himself in any way on either side.' The Duchess replied that she agreed with him about the transitional state of parties 'though I think the old names will go on, no one can say what they may not represent in 1869. . . . I am sorry to think you should not be in the House of Commons, even for a short time; it is such a good, inspiriting, though rather hard, school: whereas the House of Lords is a chilling, formal, debating society'. This was destined to be one of the few subjects on which mother and son were in complete agreement.

As it happened, Dalmeny could never have taken his seat in the Commons. On March 3rd, 1868, he was summoned from Oxford to London, where he found old Lord Rosebery unconscious and dangerously ill. He sat by the bedside all night until his grandfather died at 10.15 on the morning of the 4th. Lord Dalmeny was hailed as Archibald Philip, fifth Earl of Rosebery.

After his grandfather's funeral at Dalmeny, Rosebery could contemplate the results of his succession. Financially, it made an immense difference to his life. His annual income from his Scottish property—which he had not visited for six years— (15,568 acres in Midlothian, 5,680 in Linlithgow) and shale mines was over £20,000, and another property in Norfolk of over two thousand acres yielded a further £3,500 a year. Including other assets inherited from his grandfather, Rosebery's gross income was probably in excess of £30,000, and with the pound worth at least five times what it is today and with no income tax worth mentioning, it was a considerable fortune. A proportion was put back into the estates, and Rosebery gave his grandmother £1,000 a year as well as maintaining her, but there were no other major calls upon his purse. After his marriage he was one of the wealthiest men in Britain, but even before it he was extremely rich. He was never particularly expert at managing his financial affairs, but he had a great deal of Scots shrewdness, was never wasteful with his money, and for the rest of his life was supremely ignorant of the worries and compromises which dominate the lives of most men. Although he could talk with great feeling about poverty, was intellectually enraged by social injustice, and almost excessively generous—another Scottish characteristic, although not often comprehended—he simply did not know what it was to be worried about money. If he wished to go to Naples for a month's holiday, or buy a picture, or bet heavily on a horse, he could do so without any qualms. His hospitality at Dalmeny, and later at The Durdans and Mentmore, was always princely. He enjoyed his wealth, and he used it wisely, but inevitably took it for granted.

Financial independence can be the most invaluable asset for a public man, and Aristotle's philosophy that statesmen should not have to bother about bread-and-butter matters so that they can devote all their energies to affairs of state is often quoted as a counsel of perfection. But the hazards of wealth for a public man are not inconsiderable, and the greatest of these is that he may become divorced from the factors which influence and impel the thoughts and actions of the vast majority of mankind. For, unless (as in the conspicuous case of Gladstone) there are counterbalancing forces of ambition and principle, there is a tendency to drift into a comfortable but unreal independence. The other temptations of wealth, particularly indolence or the cultivation of diverse interests which sap personal ambition for, and even interest in, public life, do not require emphasis. The young Rosebery, being ambitious, high-principled and earnest, used his independence wisely and profitably, but in later years it was to provide opportunities for withdrawal from situations which were not congenial to him, and increasingly removed him from the great social and political movements of late nineteenth-century England. Rosebery was not indolent, although he has often been accused of being so, but the absence of any serious intellectual opposition in his formative years and the independence which his wealth gave him combined to make him increasingly averse from doing things he did not want to do, or in which he saw no immediate purpose. Thus although capable of taking a long view on important matters, and demonstrating remarkable prescience on occasion, he became too easily impatient with the petty vexations and compromises of the hour. It was not Pride—as he came to believe in the last years of his life—which proved his undoing, but the streak of Stanhope irresponsibility in his personality and the absence of any element of struggle in his earlier years. He became too used to getting his own way, and tended to surround himself with people who were not up to his intellectual level, so that when the inevitable period of clash and strain occurred, he was poorly equipped to meet it. And to this unfortunate state of affairs his private wealth was an important—although by no means the only—contributory factor.

His family and friends were seriously concerned by his apparently aimless doings at this time. In the spring of 1868 he visited Italy again, noted severely that Florence was 'swamped with Cook's Tourists', and in May he took his seat in the Lords. He betted rather more heavily at Epsom, losing £165 on the Oaks, and entered the racing world as an owner, registering his colours as primrose and rose hoops, rose cap. Throughout his life Rosebery's knowledge of racing was never equal to his enthusiasm. He had an unfortunate habit of taking the advice of his jockey rather than that of his trainer, and he was not a good judge of a horse. The fact that he himself was a very poor horseman contributed to this defect. In 1868 he was very green, and he set his heart upon winning the Derby while still an undergraduate. He bought a horse called *Ladas*, by *Lambton* out of *Zenobia*, which had enjoyed a good season and which he entrusted to James Dover of Ilsley for training. His friends were unenthusiastic about his purchase. Reginald Brett, Randolph Churchill, Tollemache, and Edward Marjoribanks with a few other bloods travelled to Ilsley to see *Ladas* gallop and were greatly unimpressed. 'A brute of a beggar', Randolph declared with characteristic bluntness, but Rosebery, intoxicated by the prospect of leading in *Ladas* amid the tumult of the Epsom crowd, was heedless of all criticism.

'The Turf' was regarded with justifiable aversion by the aristocracy at the close of the 1860's. The Marquis of Hastings had just run through a considerable fortune in an impressively short time and had died at the age of 26 heavily in debt to an obnoxious money-lender named Padwick who made a handsome living out of foolish rich young men. The Duke of Newcastle and the Earl of Westmorland—both members of the Jockey Club—also ruined themselves, and Padwick narrowly escaped lynching when he had the impudence to present himself at the sale of Newcastle's estates. The Christ Church authorities were as disturbed as his family by Rosebery's registration as a racehorse owner, but for different reasons.

By now Rosebery was something of an Oxford figure. In the autumn of 1868 he travelled to Russia with Lord Bute, and

Everard remarked in a letter to his mother that it was becoming impossible to track his brother's movements, 'staying a few minutes in Russia, five in London, and some seconds in Durham'. Something of a dandy in his dress, journeying about Oxford in a dog-cart, frequently dining in state at the Mitre, he was a conspicuous personality. 'As his surviving bills show,' Sir Keith Feiling has remarked, 'his breakfast parties were numerous and expensive.'[1] He regarded the Union with contempt as a place where children played at being politicians, a view shared by Randolph Churchill, the remainder of his friends, and the majority of adult undergraduates down the years. There is a good photograph of him at this time, standing outside his Christ Church rooms with Lord Lansdowne, cigar in one hand, the other thrust into a jacket pocket, self-assured and merry.[2]

1869 opened propitiously. Disraeli had been swept from his briefly-held Premiership in the previous year, and Mr Gladstone's Liberal Administration, supported by huge majorities in the House of Commons, had entered upon a period of unprecedented reforming zeal. Ancient fortifications of prejudice, ignorance, and incompetence crumbled at the onslaught, and a new exhilaration swept through political life as probably the most talented and balanced of nineteenth-century Governments, headed by a leader of outstanding capacity and vision at the height of his powers, drove through Parliament a series of reforming measures whose impetus and comprehension captivated its adherents and appalled its opponents. Lord Granville,[3] always on the look-out for new recruits to this invigorating Liberal crusade, invited Rosebery to second the Address in the House of Lords 'if you feel sufficient confidence in Gladstone's Government', and Rosebery replied as follows.

Christ Church,
Oxford.
January 31st, 1869

Dear Lord Granville,

Many thanks for your kind note. But it has puzzled me a good deal. I cannot be insensible of the flattering nature of your offer, however

---

[1] Sir Keith Feiling: *In Christ Church Hall*, 188.

[2] Reproduced facing page 51.

[3] George, second Earl Granville (1815–91). MP, 1836–46; Foreign Secretary, 1851; President of the Council, 1853; Leader of the House of Lords, 1855; Colonial Secretary, 1868–70; Foreign Secretary, 1870–4, and 1880–5; Colonial Secretary, 1886.

incapable I feel of seconding the Address in a way either satisfactory
to myself or anybody else. But you probably do not know that I am
only a resident undergraduate of Oxford working for a pass degree;
and it might damage the Government if, with no counter-balancing
quality, the Peer who seconded the Address was a lad *in statu pupillari*.

I have never yet professed any political principles of any kind; for
I think that when special profession is necessary, it is much better for
a young man to reserve it, but my private sympathies and my reason
have been wholly enlisted in the Liberal cause for some years; and as
in June I must take one side or the other, I see no use in postponing
that choice for a few months, when I have so thoroughly made up my
mind, and so excellent an opportunity occurs of making that mind
known to you.

I can never hope to be of the slightest use to the party, though I
should be proud of any opportunity of showing my attachment to its
principles.

Still I sincerely feel that the fact I mentioned at the beginning of my
letter might be a disadvantage to the Government; so that I feel I must
decline your kind offer.

I only got your letter today. I wish I could have spared you so long
a rigmarole as this, plastered with the personal pronoun.

> Believe me,
>
> Most gratefully and respectfully yours,
> Rosebery.

'Pussy' Granville, that apparently most indolent yet shrewd
of men, must have been highly satisfied with this insufferably
pompous letter; Rosebery had committed himself. Young noble-
men of wealth and promise (and not a few with neither) were
eagerly courted by political parties in those days, and it was
already apparent that Rosebery would be a rich prize for any
party.

But for the moment politics were of secondary interest. The
Duchess had frequently complained about her elder son's
frivolous activities, and on his coming of age (May 7th, 1868)
she had written austerely that 'I hold there is no perfect character
without a grain of ambition, and I cannot but regret its absence in
you'. For the moment, there was only one ambition, and at this
juncture the Christ Church authorities stepped in. They were no
doubt unaware of the fact that Rosebery had just lost over £1,000
at the Northampton meeting—most of which was recouped by a
successful Epsom week—but they ruled that the actual possession

of a racehorse was the ground on which they would impeach him. Rosebery was startled and indignant: he was told, in effect, that either his horse went or he did; Rosebery unhesitatingly chose the latter course, and at Easter 1869 he left Christ Church without a degree, to the astonishment of his tutor, the admiration of the Bullingdon set, and the horror of his family. 'Dear Mother,' he wrote to the Duchess, 'I have left Oxford. I have secured a house in Berkeley Square; and I have bought a horse to win the Derby. Your affectionate Archie.' It was an impulsive and stupid action which he soon deeply regretted. In public he adopted a studied air of perfect indifference, and circulated a forecast of the Derby result to the Loder's Club of Christ Church, admirably described by Sir Keith Feiling as 'a small co-opted society in which for over a century sons of the country houses sacrificed at their ancestral altars of fox-hunting, Church, and King'.[1]

It is the Derby Wednesday, carrier pigeons come in flights,
There is terror in St James's street, and agony in White's.
From Hayling Isle to Newmarket they have begun to toast
The foremost horse that stayed the course and foremost passed the post.

From Dan and from Beersheba, from Joppa and Gilgal,
The Israelites are flocking, resolved to stand or fall:
From the Baron[2] to the broker each one is like a lion, he
Having staked his bottom shekel on the son of bay Hermione.

The Christ Church tutors put a tax on those who came in late,
And they were puzzled how to spend the tribute of the Gate.
So they put it on the Derby, and pitched upon a horse
Who took his rise from Lambton's *thighs, and cannot stay the course.*

There was wailing in the Common Room, the Censors tore their hair,
Some scraped themselves with potsherds, and some began to swear,
They d — d the race of Lambton, *and cursed* Zenobia's *womb,*
And wished the race of racehorses a universal tomb.

[An alternative verse ran as follows:

---

[1] *In Christ Church Hall*, 188. It is characteristic of Lord Crewe's excessive tact that he declined to publish these verses in his *Life of Rosebery* as being 'unfit for publication in an official biography'. They are published here, I believe, for the first time.

[2] Baron Meyer de Rothschild.

There was wailing in the Common Room, the Censors tore their hair,
They turned away from port and punch, and some began to swear,
They cursed the race of Lambton, *and wished* Zenobia *sterile,*
And wept that for so poor a colt their souls they should imperil.]

'They're off!' They stream along the hill at a pace to try the bellows,
Which tomorrow will want mending in the ' Drums and Masaniellos.
Bright as a scattered rainbow, swift as the dawn of day,
No living horse can stay the course in that breakneck sort of way.

They come along a cracker, now the ruck begins to shirk,
Padwick is flogging Ethus, *and the Baron is at work;*
And from the hill arises a wail of souls in pain,
Where Gad and where Jeshurua bewail their vanished gain.

And now from out the beaten crowd a flogging four there come,
Pero Gomez *and* Pretender, Ladas *and* Belladrum.
They have passed the Judge's tribune—Good heavens, what a pot!
And all shout 'What the devil's won?' and Echo answers 'What?'

'Pretender's Derby' was a lamentable fiasco so far as Rosebery
and *Ladas* were concerned. Backed heavily by Christ Church at
66 to 1, he trailed in an ignominious last. Rosebery was bitterly
disappointed, but he rallied himself to send out a postscript to his
verses to his unfortunate backers.

Now thank your prophet, Gentlemen, ye who plunged upon the Drummer,
Who lumped it upon Rupert *or on* Ladas *went a bummer.*
For he told the first two horses who the Judge's tribune passed
Then he wrote a warning comma—and the names of the two last.

Rosebery had been the guest of the affable Henry Chaplin—
who had sensationally won the Derby with *Hermit* in 1867—for
the Epsom week, and there met Colonel Forester, nicknamed 'The
Lad' and an eminent racing man of his day, for the first time. On
the morning of the Derby Rosebery found a dead hedgehog in
the garden, and 'The Lad' said that this was an evil omen. Twenty-
five years later on another Derby morning in which the second
Ladas was running Rosebery saw a hedgehog running in the
garden of The Durdans; 'The Lad' declared that this was an
excellent augury, and so it proved to be.

Racing now began to occupy a quite disproportionate amount
of Rosebery's time and money. At Doncaster in September he

lost £1,698 in a day ('A fair day's racing,' he remarked in his diary), won nearly £6,000 on the St Leger, and promptly lost £725 and £460 respectively on the following two days. He argued with literal truth that he had made a good net profit on his week but his family was thoroughly alarmed by the reports of his heavy betting. On the other hand, his attendance at the House of Lords was surprisingly good, and his sister, Connie, who had married Lord Leconfield in 1867, reported to the Duchess in July that 'Archie seems to have taken a very strong Radical turn, which I am very sorry for. Henry [Lord Leconfield] has seen a great deal of him in the House of Lords, & tells me that he seems very cold indeed about racing.' This was before Doncaster, when Rosebery's coldness did not appear very noticeable. But shortly afterwards he announced that he had done with racing and put up his few horses for sale at Tattersalls in the November sales. This announcement caused considerable dismay and perplexity in racing circles. What had happened was that he had entered *Mavela* for a selling plate at Stockton and had backed very lightly. The locals, however, feeling that Rosebery would not have entered his horse unless he felt it was going to win, backed it heavily, and were extremely angry when it performed poorly and was later sold for £17 at a public auction. A sporting newspaper printed an angry letter from one of *Mavela*'s chagrined supporters which hinted that the whole affair was distinctly suspicious.

This was virtually the first occasion that anyone had expressed public criticism of Rosebery, and he reacted violently. Announcing angrily that if he could not lose a paltry selling race without rendering himself liable to unworthy suspicions racing was not worth following as a pastime, he put his horses up for sale. The paper which had published the offending letter printed an abject apology, and *Baily's Monthly Magazine of Sports and Pastimes* assured Rosebery that 'he may rest assured that his first retirement from the Turf, far from diminishing him in the estimation of the Racing World, has only served to increase the loss they feel they have sustained by the premature withdrawal of his horses'. Mollified, Rosebery returned to the Turf, and in the November of 1870 he was elected to the Jockey Club. Shortly afterwards the tide began to turn in his favour, for he bought *Paraffin* as a brood mare and started a stud at The Durdans, a large house and estate hard by Epsom Downs, which he purchased in 1872. Epsom in

those days was a charming small Surrey county town, well leafed
and peaceful, and The Durdans—always called simply 'Durdans'
by Rosebery—with its encrusted ivy, spacious grounds, large
stables, and sweeping lawns, became Rosebery's real home. 'When
I first came to live at Epsom a quarter of a century ago', he wrote
in 1901, 'it was a little sleepy town, surrounded by long stretches
of down and common. Its perennial slumber was broken twice a
year by race meetings, when the followers and camp followers of
the Turf stormed the neighbourhood during a few agitated days,
then struck their tents and left the town, sodden and exhausted.
Thereafter the calm recommenced, and the inhabitants could
saunter over miles of open turf to breathe the purest air in England. But the memory of those six days of carnival kept off the
speculative builder and his serious clients. Thus the town remained rural and old-fashioned. Now all that is changed.'[1]
Dalmeny, which he had seldom visited at this time, never really
won his affection to the extent that Chevening or The Durdans
did. One might suspect that the warmth of the south and the less
magnificent surroundings fitted in more appropriately with his
personality than the bleakness of the Forth. But the fact that The
Durdans was his own purchase, where he could do what he liked,
was probably more important.

In 1873 he had his first major success when *Padaroshna* won the
Gimcrack Stakes, and in 1874 he won the City and Suburban with
Aldrich. He delighted in 'matches', and these often took place
in the early morning of summer days on the Downs, after which
his opposing owner would come to breakfast at The Durdans. He
greatly enjoyed his racing, not because he was particularly know-
ledgeable about horses but because he loved the thrill of possession
and of meeting the extraordinary variety of personalities who follow the sport. A contemporary has described Newmarket as it
was when Rosebery first knew it.

How delightful it was then compared to what it is now! There was
only a small stand at the Rowley Mile post, containing one large
room for luncheon with a balcony outside, and a small room downstairs to afford shelter from the rain. The only possible way of doing
Newmarket in any comfort or satisfaction was to ride all day long. I
well recollect how delightful it was on a fine bracing day to gallop
up to the Birdcage, to hastily alight, and throw one's reins to one of

[1] Preface to *Epsom: Its History and Its Surroundings*, by Gordon Home.

the many men on the look-out for a shilling; take stock of the horses, remark the number of runners, and settle what to back; then came the hurried stampede of the riders to their horses, the mad race down the Ring, the forcing one's way in to get at the chief bookmakers, the booking of the bets, and the rush to see the race.[1]

Rosebery drew around him in his racing weeks a curious collection of racing characters who would have greatly shocked the Duchess of Cleveland had she ever come across them. His losses, although comparatively small in relation to his income, were not inconsiderable. In Doncaster week in 1872, for example, he made a net loss of over £1,000, and a few days later lost over £60 at 'that d—d écarté' after dinner. Apart from 'The Lad' and Chaplin, a great racing friend was Ouseley Higgins, a wealthy soldier who ate, slept, and drank gambling, and in whom Rosebery delighted. 'Circumstances (pecuniary) over which I need not dwell', he wrote mournfully to Higgins in October 1871, 'did not allow of my going to Newmarket at my own expense. Thank Heavens the Turf knows me no more till it covers me. I have had a bad year racing this year, & if it had not been for some ill-smelling Paraffin I must have left the country. Pray burn Paraffin & nothing else.' 'You are welcome', he wrote banteringly in September 1872, 'to take the Brompton lady and have an ozone bath with her at Ramsgate. She cost me last year as much as Marshal Bazaine, and so I have advised her to go into a convent, where she can practise her profession in ease and safety.'

Rosebery was in fact going through a somewhat undergraduate phase which usually comes rather earlier in life. His racing correspondence and his passion for rather silly little clubs and societies were manifestations of this period. From all sides came admonitions about his way of life, and his uncle, Bouverie Primrose, was particularly severe in his strictures. It is difficult to believe that Rosebery was quite as irresponsible as some of these rebukes would suggest. 'Even a Scottish peer cannot be ruined by four racehorses, especially when they win!' he replied to one of his mentors. Deliberately giving the appearance of a wealthy young man about town, comfortably installed in his pleasant London home, 2, Berkeley Square—described in later years by a contemporary as 'a little band-box of a place facing Lansdowne House'—or presiding at gay dinner-parties at The Durdans, in

[1] Sir George Chetwynd: *Racing Reminiscences and Experiences of the Turf.*

fact he was casting an acute gaze at the society in which he dwelt. His frivolous correspondence with men like Higgins ('How you do win!' he writes in November 1872; 'the putting on of your Sandringham pants will be an evil moment for the Princely cheque-book') and awesome expenditure on the Turf were more than counterbalanced by his deep reading and growing interest in the manifestations of the new popular movements.

The contrasts of Rosebery's double life may be illustrated by an incident which occurred in 1873. Francis Knollys, the Prince of Wales' Private Secretary, asked him if he would be willing to make his London house a rendezvous for the Prince of Wales and the Duke of Edinburgh to meet their 'actress friends'. Rosebery, although no prude, evidently felt that this was the limit, and replied that his house was too small and that he trusted that the matter would not be raised again. Through Knollys he was kept well informed of the many escapades of the Prince of Wales' *entourage*—Knollys himself in his younger days being by no means the most innocent member of it—but although he always liked and even admired the Prince, he detested his younger brother, the Duke of Edinburgh. But although he was normally a distant and mocking observer of the princes' pleasure-seeking existence, he was present at an extraordinary debauch held at 2, Brook Street, the home of Frank Lawley of the *Daily Telegraph*, in the April of 1873. The Prince and the Duke, in company with their euphemistically named 'actress friends', were the principal guests, and there was much drinking, organised cockfighting, and other amusements provided throughout the night. Rosebery left at an early hour, and was up early the next morning to go to hear Spurgeon, the mighty hot-gospeller of the day, deliver one of his renowned sermons at the City Tabernacle. 'The audience is entirely middle-class,' Rosebery observed, 'without, so far as I can see, a single exception. Neither the upper nor the lower classes are represented. Spurgeon is the apostle of the grocers.'

I went away thinking of this vast power wielded by one man. He has raised a sort of spiritual city in the midst of London. . . . And all this influence has been achieved by a man like a butler out of place, with a face resembling an ape covered perpetually by nature with a silly grin.

Influence over whom? There is the second matter for thought. Not a soul in the church had I ever seen. Here is a great multitude, powerful, wealthy, devoted, with a perfect organization and independence, with a leader of genius, as completely unknown to the world in which I live as if it did not exist. Its aims are not our aims, its language is not our language, its aspirations and ideas are wholly alien to our aspirations and ideas. Would it not be well for 'society' to ponder this ? Which would win in battle, 'society' flabby flippant and enervated with no even ostensible strength except that wealth which is in reality its greatest weakness,—or this serious band of ironsides and roundheads, nerved by conviction and animated by genius ? The battle has been fought before, and we know the certain result.

It was shortly after this episode that Rosebery made tentative suggestions to friends that he might be allowed to assist in working-class organisations, and was warmly encouraged by the gay William Rogers, Rector of Bishopsgate and Prebendary of St Paul's, who had already become a close friend. Rogers was an Eton and Oxford man—where he had gained a rowing Blue— and was notorious for his alleged dismissal of doctrine by the phrase 'Hang Theology', which clung to him like a burr for the rest of his life. Crippled by rheumatism, he remained a merry, sardonic, and outspoken advocate for his wretchedly poor East London parish, where he was adored. It was from Rogers that Rosebery gained his first-hand knowledge of conditions in East London and acquired many of the ideas of civic reform that he was to carry into effect when he became the first Chairman of the London County Council in 1889. At the invitation of Henry Solly, Rosebery made an appearance at a meeting of the Artisans' Institute on the north side of the Strand. Peers with these curious interests were regarded with considerable suspicion. The pride of the artisans was already surmounting any feelings of awe which the aristocracy may have inspired in the past. A Republican saddler on this occasion made a considerable point of referring to the distinguished visitor with some contempt as 'Mr Rosebery', and ignored the shocked remonstrances of Solly, who was in the Chair. After the meeting Rosebery walked up to the offender, and said, 'Come, let us shake hands. I'm not such a bad fellow after all.' This story spread, and was often quoted as an example of the contrast between the boorish stupidity of the Republican and the civilised courtesy of the Peer. But at this length of time it is difficult not to feel some sympathy with the saddler and his distrust of aristocrats intent on 'good works'; Rosebery himself had the sense to see this, and to realise that much more was needed than good intentions to secure the confidence of the people.

His interest in the Working Men's Club and Institute Union, then in its infancy, was considerable, and in a speech to the Union on July 17th, 1875, he startled his audience by a pungent exposition of what the aims and methods of the Union ought to be. 'Each Club should be altogether free from all vexatious infantile restrictions on the consumption of intoxicating drinks and all similar matters,' he declared, 'restrictions which tend to make these Institutions moral nurseries rather than Clubs intended for the use of the citizens of a great Empire.... From time to time one reads in the papers of persons discoursing to the members of these Clubs, and drawing pictures of enlightened miners returning from their underground toil to the consumption of aesthetic tea or the discussion of the subtleties of *Hamlet* or the mysticism of Greek literature.... I believe that the labour of those who would ameliorate the conditions of the working classes is slower and more imperceptible than that of the insect which raises the coral reef from the bed of the ocean.'

As might be expected, a young man with Rosebery's accomplishments had the *entrée* to virtually every great house in England. The Queen, who met him in May 1870, noted in her Journal that he was 'pleasing & gentleman-like, & wonderfully young looking'.[1] He was an acute and fascinated observer of every facet of human behaviour. He was always particularly interested in the Gladstones and Disraelis, often visiting both men in the same day. Although now definitely in the Liberal camp, Rosebery found the Disraelis a never-ending source of interest, and he began a novel which never got beyond two draft chapters, but which has certain Disraelian characteristics. It opened with the death of a great Duke, residing in a mansion which bears suspicious resemblances to Raby.

... What wonder if Corker the butler should require a glass or two of the ducal sherry to support him under the sudden removal of his master, or that the Reverend Howlett, rector of the parish and chaplain to his late Grace, should at once retire to his closet and elaborate a sermon in which the great deceased should be compared to Jonathan, Lorenzo de Medici and Henry, Prince of Wales, which should be

[1] *Royal Archives.*

delivered to a sympathetic audience on the Sunday following his patron's funeral, and should ultimately be printed on luxurious paper edged with black for private circulation ? . . .

His Commonplace Books and Journals abound with amusing comments and more serious opinions.

I love a circus, I don't know why: I think it is because there is no talking on the stage, except occasionally the clown's jokes which I know as well as my own name and which have a soothing effect on the digestion. However it was a capital circus: I have been there before, won't I go back ? About twenty little boys who turned summersaults and were pelted with oranges, like bouquets, when their performance was over. Then there was a great equestrian who jumped through a hoop the size of a virgin's waist. Then there were two brothers who made our teeth chatter and our hearts stop beating with terror and admiration. And there was a man who had upon my honour no single bone or joint in his body but spent his time in—as far as I could make out—looking at the back of his own head underneath his left arm. Awed and delighted, I walked home. (*Paris, April 8th, 1873*)

When pondering on autobiography, he writes:

Why, then, do we neglect our own history ? Is it that to look back on the year is to look back on a Golgotha, that our shrines are empty, that our memorials are shadows: is it that we fear to look back upon our lives just as we dread to look beyond them, that the end of the year does not resemble the happy close of a well spent day but rather the uneasy waking from a disturbed slumber ? Let us ask ourselves. (*1872*)

On biography he reflects that 'After all is said and done, there is no writing or reading so charming as biography. In the writing of it there is the secret delight of identifying yourself more and more with the man you describe till at last you seem to be able to give a sequence, a character and a reason for every action of his life. Such a revelation is more like that of some fairy tale where the mountain that shews only its barren rock to the ordinary traveller opens to the favoured enquirer her mystic side within which he shall find treasures such as it is not in the mind of man to imagine.'

A few weeks later he returned to this theme.

History becomes more real, more familiar, more—so to speak—human, when viewed through the medium of biography. . . . The reign of George III for instance in its earlier part seems to us nothing but a record of favouritism and cabal. We read Boswell's *Life of Johnson* and the dormant figures start into life. Lord North awakes from his good humoured slumber, Burke comes to sit at the foot of the philosopher and receive the rare tribute of his admiration. Burke brings Wyndham; nay, the beefy King himself shows some curiosity to see the Great Bear, and cunningly contrives to find him by chance in the Royal Library. It was not all then wars and subsidies and ribands and sinecures and Hessian hirelings; there was something more real than the grim fantastic stageplay of Chatham and the cringing impotence of Newcastle.

. . . The figures move upon the murky canvas when the lantern of biography is thrown upon it. . . . We are not remote descendants gazing idly on a long unmeaning dumbshow; we are sitting in the Mitre talking with the best and greatest minds of the country on contemporary men and events.

In a more frivolous mood he traced the terrible decline and fall of a Country Squire, Booby, who inherits great estates and revels in the army of servants and gamekeepers, the slaughter of birds, and the possession of Booby Hall, 'a Wyattville Gothic house with a Venetian campanile,' where 'the only way to the drawing room is through the kitchen, and to the kitchen through the Chapel'. Booby pays one disastrous unrepeated visit to London, and meets two Oxford friends, Mal and Pal.

. . . 'Glad to see you,' says Mal. 'Dear old fellow,' says Pal. 'What regiment are you in—I never can remember,' says Mal. 'Indian Civil Service I thought,' says Pal. 'I am living on my property in Grandshire,' says Booby with dignity. 'I hope you will come and look me up some day.' 'Charmed,' says Mal. 'Delighted,' says Pal, 'and we will have a good crack about old times.' They move on. 'Good heavens, *Grandshire*, just fancy!' ejaculates Mal. 'Stop! The bare idea,' interposes Pal. . . .

Booby marries a plain artless local girl, daughter of a neighbouring Squire, and together they descend contentfully into rustic oblivion. It is probable that in his portrait of Booby Hall, Rosebery was thinking of Dalmeny, which he rarely visited at this time, and of whose ugliness he was always talking. 'My grandfather, whom I loved very tenderly, built the house I live in,' he wrote in 1904 to a correspondent who had protested at Rosebery's criticisms of Epsom Church which had been designed by his grandfather, 'and I am compelled very frequently to indicate my opinion of its consummate ugliness.'

His notebooks and diaries are filled with records of conversations with great or interesting men. He met Henry James, the novelist, at this time, who told him that 'I mean to write a great novel before I die, but I do not mean to be in a hurry', and that he had decided never to marry. Disraeliana were innumerable.

Disraeli . . . once said to him (John Bright) of, and, I think, in, the House of Commons, 'This is *the* place, because it is where one acquires power. I might have occupied a literary throne, but I preferred to come & contend here.' (*1875*)

Lady Cowper (Ann) met Disraeli after the passing of the Reform Bill in 1867. She said, 'Oh, Mr Disraeli, I have not seen you since you ruined the country.' He replied with a low bow, 'I assure you that if that is so it is your fault.' She said, 'Why ? I had nothing to do with it.' 'No,' said Disraeli, 'but I called several times in St James's Square to take your Ladyship's advice on political affairs, and it is to me never having found you in that I attribute any defect there may be in the Bill!' (*December, 1870*)

Disraeli told me an amusing anecdote of the present and the late Sir Robert Peel. When Mr Peel (as he then was) had been misconducting himself in various ways, and was completely out of favour with Sir Robert, Sir Henry Bulwer wrote to Disraeli from Madrid where Mr Peel then was to ask him to assist in a plan for recommending the Son to the Father. Sir Harry was to write a long private letter to Disraeli about Spanish politics which Disraeli was to show to Sir Robert as being interesting, and it was to end with a postscript giving a laudatory account of Mr Peel's goings on. Disraeli agreed & the letter came. He watched his opportunity for weeks. At last, sitting on the Opposition bench behind Sir Robert he found an occasion for talking about Spanish affairs and saying 'There is a letter from Bulwer about these matters; towards the end there is some private matter, but it may interest you too'. Sir Robert took the letter and read it with evident interest: at last he came to the postscript, but then his face lengthened ominously, and, folding up the letter, he grimly handed it back to Disraeli. As Disraeli said—the plot was blown at once, he smoked the whole thing in a minute. (*December, 1870*)

Had a chat with Mr Disraeli at his house, but, as Lady Beaconsfield was present, it was not so uninterrupted as I could have wished.

'Lytton', he said when I shewed him a passage in Cooper's autobiography about Lord Lytton, 'is here described to the life.' (Cooper says that Lytton 'received me, smoking with a thousand smiles &c.') 'He is an excellent friend—in adversity. But he cannot forgive me for having succeeded in pursuits better than him to which he attached perhaps too much importance. It is only by long experience that I have learned the power of envy. It is not in me—I do not claim it as a merit, for everyone should have it slightly—but I do not know it.' (*May 5th, 1872*)

A pretty party at the Foreign Office. Disraeli dressed as an Admiral, having dined as an Elder Brother at the Trinity House. Lady Beaconsfield in wonderful spirits, though I am afraid she is very ill. I took her through the rooms, and she insisted on introducing me to the Burmese Ambassador as her son! (*June 19th, 1872*)

I was once witness of a curious scene at Marlborough House. It was on the occasion of some party or ball. I saw Mr Disraeli and Mr Gladstone, the latter with his daughter, Mary, making their way towards the front hall for their departure. They were coming from different directions, and did not observe each other, and I hurried on, thinking there must be a curious encounter.

Mr Disraeli (I forget if he was then Lord Beaconsfield or not) stood with his back to the fireplace, and, I think, on the fender, as he seemed taller than usual: while Mr Gladstone stood in front, and they exchanged hollow greetings. Mr Gladstone, to ease over an irksome meeting, began to tell the story, which had recently appeared in Lord Shelburne's Autobiography, of Sir James Lowther sitting in that very hall and being mistaken for a beggar.

Mr Disraeli assumed an expression of supercilious boredom, and, indeed, Mr Gladstone, telling his anecdote under such circumstances, did not have the advantage. No man, indeed, could assume so quickly an expression of utter scorn and ennui as did Disraeli.

Then Mr Gladstone's carriage was called, and I was left alone with Disraeli. He said 'Why didn't he offer me a lift ? He might just as well, and I would have taken it, as my carriage has not come. Had the girl been alone I should have asked her without hesitation.'

The scene is fixed in my mind even now.[1]

Disraeli's letters to Rosebery were in marked contrast with those from Gladstone: whereas the latter's were marked by ancient courtesy and paternal kindness, Disraeli's breathed a wonderful air of comradeship.

'Dear Lord Rosebery,' Mr Gladstone wrote to him in 1872, 'If I am not taking too great a liberty, I would ask you to call on me in the forenoon of any day which may be convenient to you. Faithfully yours, W. E. Gladstone.' 'Your graceful & affectionate

---

[1] This recollection was dictated by Rosebery early in the 1920's. There is another account in Lucy Masterman, *Mary Gladstone*, 468.

present had only one deficiency,' Disraeli wrote to him in March 1876, 'You should have inscribed your name in it—the name of one I greatly regard. My dear, I want you to dine with me on Wednesday the 22nd. I hope you are disengaged.' Disraeli wrote to Lady Chesterfield of the Prince of Wales' Ball at Marlborough House in the July of 1874 that 'It was a great success; gorgeous, brilliant, fantastic. The male dresses much more successful than the ladies'. The most striking and the most perfect and finished was Lord Rosebery as Barbe Bleu.'[1] It was not surprising that Rosebery was bewitched by this strange, enchanting man. Throughout his life he continued to collect information about Disraeli, and it is sad that he refused the invitation to write Disraeli's official biography which was eventually entrusted to the more stolid Mr Monypenny.[2]

J. Greenwood told me of the last time he saw Dizzy in 1879. Colonel Home, who D admired & liked very much, had just died.

D—'So Home is gone—I had destined him for high command.' Then silence: D patting his knee gently, & G, watching, saw tears stealing down his cheeks. After a pause, he complained of his difficulties in the Cabinet—all agst him—*only one* minister with him. But G did not discover the name. (*April 7th, 1890*)

The Queen. She talked abt Dizzy.

'He had a way when we differed about some matter (of course nothing of importance) of saying "Dear Madam" so persuasively' & she either put her head on one side or said that he did so—I forget which.

'On my birthday he once sent me without any inscription a little box: on one side was a heart transfixed by an arrow, and on the other the word "Fideliter". Was it not touching ?' (*October, 1893*)

In her last days Ly B[eaconsfield] told R[owton] that they induced her to send for a clergyman. 'He told me to turn my thoughts to Jesus Christ, but I couldn't. You know Dizzy is my J.C.'

She was mad the last week—the cancer had gone to her brain—& denounced Dizzy to M.C. [Corry]—D shedding tears outside the door. (*May 14th, 1899*)

---

[1] Lord Zetland (Editor): *Letters of Disraeli to Lady Bradford and Lady Chesterfield*, I, 117.

[2] The select tribe of biographers may reflect with awe and discontentment that Rosebery was offered £20,000 by the Disraeli Trustees; when invited to write Gladstone's official biography—again refused—an even higher sum was tentatively mentioned.

W. H. Russell's story of Delane leaving dinner at Stafford House to go to his office, & Granville then asking Dizzy what he thought of him. Dizzy, carefully putting up his eyeglass, looked round & said 'I observe that Mr Delane has left the room, but I am under the impression that he is still alive & still editor of *The Times*, & so I would rather not answer'. (*June 23rd, 1899*)

In September 1870 Rosebery was invited to Balmoral for the first time, and kept a careful account of life in the Royal household.

. . . I arrived here about in time for dinner at 8.40 with Her Majesty. One goes into a drawing room where one finds the other guests. The page suddenly enters and announces the Queen's approach. The ladies rush out to the foot of the stairs, the gentlemen cower in a doorway. Down comes the Queen, shakes hands as she passes with any strange lady, and passes into the dining room followed by Princess Louise and Prince Arthur. . . . The conversation during dinner was sustained and almost gay. If one talks to one's neighbours the Queen, who has a very sharp ear, joins in the conversation. The dinner is served very rapidly, & coffee after it. When coffee is finished, the Queen rises, we also rise and stand behind our chairs, and the Queen comes slowly round the circle, talking for five minutes or so with each. When this circuit is finished she retires with Princess Louise, and the rest with Prince Arthur adjourn to the billiard room & play at billiard bowls. We retire about 11.30.

Saturday, September 3. Today Pickard[1] & I went out grouse shooting, Colonel Ponsonby[2] driving with us to the rendezvous. As we were in the waggonette at the door a telegram was put into Colonel Ponsonby's hand. It was the telegram announcing the capitulation of Macmahon's army at Sedan, & the surrender of the Emperor. What a thunderbolt! We, like true Englishmen, drove off at once & slaughtered a few brace of grouse, but I think we were moved. What an ending to so much brilliancy & fortune & to such a name. Six short weeks ago the Empire was a powerful, stable & splendid institution, at the head of it was a magnificent Sovereign who had held the destinies of Europe, at its base a great army rich with the memory of great traditions & their emulation in the future. All this is now gone, and its epitaph is written in a somewhat canting telegram of the King of Prussia's. We killed 13½ brace of grouse: the birds were very wild. I dined with the Household this evening. . . .

[1] Equerry to Prince Arthur.
[2] Later Sir Henry Ponsonby, Private Secretary to the Queen.

... After dinner we went off to the dreary & uninhabited drawing room where we found the Queen & the Royal dinner party. The Queen, who seemed very shy, spoke a few words to some of us & retired. ...

The excitement of being at Balmoral just now is intense: for telegrams arrive at every hour of the day. ...

Sunday, September 4th. After breakfast, which all the Household take together, Mr Sahl the Librarian & I went over the library & other rooms together. The ornaments are strictly Scotch, and the curtains and the covers are of 'dress Stuart' tartan. But the effect is not very pretty. We afterwards went to Crathie Church which is near the Castle over the Dee bridge. There was a crowd of tourists standing up inside and outside of the Church who had arrived there at some fabulously early hour. The Royal Family waited outside for the Queen. ...

The luncheon, which is always taken by the Household in common, has two distinguishing features on Sunday. The first is that it begins with mutton broth; and the second is the introduction of an odious drink called birch wine. On tasting it I remarked that I thought the bottle was corked, an observation which was received with enthusiasm, as that taste is the purest natural flavour of the wine!

There is, I am informed, only one quality of every wine drunk in the Castle & that is the best. So that if you ask for a glass of claret to put in your water at luncheon you are supplied with Chateau Lafite. It is not an economical arrangement. ...

Monday, September 5th. The day was so rough & stormy that I was not sent out shooting, but remained to walk with Prince Arthur & Pickard to the village of Crathie, where there is a 'merchant' or general shopkeeper called Symon, who is a great character & the gossip & pet of the households of Abergeldie & Balmoral. Today Prince Arthur took him his photograph, and we drew Mr Symon out on the subject of his visit to London, where he went to the Opera, & to avoid a difference with the doorkeeper on the subject of costume, he pinned back the tails of his morning black coat. He seemed, however, to have been chiefly struck by the Alhambra. We were weighed, which is a solemn ceremony. First two rustic swings are let down from the ceiling into one of which is placed the person to be weighed. A large screw and a piece of broken gaspipe are then placed in his hands to equalise the different weight of the two seats. Into the other seat meanwhile bags of shot & weights & a general collection of old metal is placed till the balance is found. Then arrives the prodigious moment of calculation; and the rapture of the merchant when the weights are approximately right is charming to witness. I paid for my introduction to this worthy by the purchase of some trophies in Balmoral granite. ...

After luncheon there was to have been a ride, but it rained too heavily for that, so Pickard & I went out and clambered among the hills and enjoyed the glorious effect of light & mist along the hills, making the distant valley look like the mountain guarded cauldron of hell, sending up a lurid vapour.

I dined with the Queen. . . . The atmosphere was somewhat stiffer than usual, an effect produced perhaps by the proclamation of the French Republic of which we received the tidings today. However, for a wonder, Princess Louise was allowed to remain after the Queen & to go to the billiard room, where as usual we played bowls.

Tuesday, September 6th. At last, a lovely morning, so I strolled out before breakfast & watched Ross, the head piper (who also acts as butler at the Queen's dinner) performing his daily morning duty. At half past nine he starts at the Tower & walks along the front of the Castle to the Queen's side, where he pipes during breakfast. The Queen at this time of year generally breakfasts in a tent in the open air, I believe. She lunches in the library, where she dines. . . .

Rosebery attended the annual cricket match between the Households of Balmoral and Abergeldie, watched by the Queen and all the Royal Family, Prince Arthur captaining the Balmoral team, which was narrowly defeated. Rosebery was introduced to the future King George V and his elder brother—the ill-fated Duke of Clarence—whom he described as 'very amusing riotous children'. There was an enormous tea under the trees ('Life here is one perpetual and astounding meal,' Rosebery remarked) and Rosebery thought that Princess Beatrice was 'a pale young lady who seems to require more of the open air than she gets'.

There was a last dinner with the Queen, who presented him with her Balmoral accolade in the form of *Our Life in the Highlands*. There was a contretemps at dinner with the formidable Ross, who asked Rosebery if he would like sherry or claret. Rosebery asked for claret, and Ross poured out sherry: Rosebery pointed out that he had asked for claret, and Ross, remarking loudly and censoriously 'You *said* sherry', dourly changed his glass.

'The Queen in her own house is far from a Constitutional Sovereign,' Rosebery wrote after he had reached Dalmeny. 'She allows her family (at least, and I think the whole household) no fires at this time of year, and finding one in Prince Arthur's room the other day, made him put a jug of water over it. He professes to suffer much from cold.'

'What I have written here seems very flunkeyish to me,' he wrote carefully on this record. 'But that is what I wanted. Flunkeyism in this sense is the minute description of what Royalty & great people generally do with themselves. I wanted to reproduce for myself an exact account of the monotonous country life of the Court here, and if I am as flunkeyish as I fancy, these notes have more than answered my most sanguine expectations. But they are meaned for no eyes but mine,' he concluded rather mysteriously, 'and even for them they are only intended as landmarks which will recall other things.'

Not content with living a very full and interesting life in England, Rosebery was a constant traveller. In 1870 he spent three months in Italy with three friends—one of whom was Edward ('Blackie') Hope—and kept a copious Journal of their doings. In his old age, Rosebery re-discovered this volume, and wrote on it, 'Terrible trash, but it was great fun'. In 1873 he went to America, armed with several introductions provided by Frank Lawley, warned by another friend to 'Beware those d—d heartless mothers', and was welcomed rapturously. 'It is evident that "the Hearl" is enjoying himself,' Lawley wrote to Ouseley Higgins on January 2nd, 1874, enclosing a bundle of press-cuttings, 'but Heaven grant that the affection with which he is regarded by the American girls may not be reciprocated by him, for most of them are the most heartless & worldly b—s that can be imagined.' Higgins had already received an account of their friend's travels, sent from a hotel near Niagara Falls on October 21st.

. . . I left New York this day fortnight and have only been four nights in bed during all that time: and one of those nights was spent in the bed of a Mormon Bishop who had several wives. Need I say that my moral feelings did not allow me to sleep ? The curses of travelling here are the stove-heat of the carriages and the babies. Every carriage reeks with children of all ages varying from two days to three years. The first receive natural nourishment in a disagreeably public way, the second will seek food in any part of the carriage under your legs or in your hat. Moreover, they howl abominably, which I suppose is why they all grow into practised public speakers. . . .

It was during his visit to New York that he met an enchanting friend of Lawley's, Samuel Ward, who had already got through two fortunes with charming facility. When Rosebery asked him what he would do if Providence gave him a third he replied that he would appoint three trustees and have himself declared a lunatic, 'otherwise it would all be got out of me in a week'. He shared Rosebery's delight in rather jejeune clubs and together they founded the 'Mendacious Club', of which 'Uncle Sam' Ward was the President and Rosebery 'The Sycophant'. 'In New York his name is still remembered as a synonym for all that is gracious and accomplished,' T. H. S. Escott wrote somewhat unctuously in 1898,[1] but as well as amusing himself Rosebery found time for more serious matters. He visited Salt Lake City, conversed with President Grant, lunched with Longfellow, and witnessed a huge torchlight procession winding its way to the Democrat Convention in New York. He returned home deeply impressed. 'When one returns to England', he noted, 'one finds oneself in a neatly constructed dilemma. If you say you dislike America, the answer is "Ah, I knew you would be shocked when you saw your principles carried into practice: you see what Liberalism would bring us to." If, as I did, you say that you are greatly pleased with America: "Ah, I thought you would be delighted at their toadying to you: they always do make so much of a lord." '

The October of 1874 found Rosebery on the steamship *Algeria* on his way to America for another journey of discovery. His vessel's dilatory progress resulted in an exasperated poem.

She is a beauteous object, for although she toileth not,
She spinneth daily onwards, proud of an hourly knot,
With naked spars and crowded decks and stormy winds abreast,
She's like the Flying Dutchman—taking a little rest.

The other day a landbird came and perched upon our bark,
This moved us all to bitter tears—he thought it was the Ark,—
But, not recognising Noah, he set off again to rove,
As the waters did not lessen and the vessel did not move.

Sweet is our pleasant cabin, except to him who thinks
That, having been at Cologne, he knows the worst of stinks,
Oil, cooking and corruption blend until the dinner bell,
Then aggravate and culminate in one stupendous SMELL.

[1] T. H. S. Escott: *Personal Forces of the Period.*

Then bless thee, gentle Ship, if e'er a Catholic I be,
I'll spend my forty days of Lent in crossing out with Thee;
For you make (remember proudly if your passengers repine)
Double the longest passage of any ship upon the line.

On this visit he concentrated more upon the South; Savannah was 'the most heavenly place except Naples which I have ever seen', which was praise indeed. Cuba, where he went in December, he loathed. 'If anyone would know how low and degrading vice may be made, let him go to Havana. . . . I never was so sickened in my life at any sight.' Trinidad, he later recorded, was nearly as bad. But at Memphis he had an interview with the aged Jefferson Davies.

. . . tall and slight with a small keen head and sharp features, one eye apparently blind, very feeble. All the evening he sat hardly speaking, languidly fondling his youngest daughter, Winny, who sat on his lap.

He said that the United States Government was the basest and simplest tyranny now existing. (*January 15th, 1875*)

When he made a third visit a year later, the gossip-writers were in ecstasies. Randolph Churchill had just married Jennie Jerome, and another American marriage into a great British family was eagerly expected. But Rosebery, although greatly lionised by hostesses with beautiful daughters, kept carefully out of all entanglements and continued to roam up and down the country, making detailed notes of his impressions. When he returned he met Lord Beaconsfield—Disraeli having accepted a peerage in 1876 after two years of his Premiership—at a dinner given by Ferdinand Rothschild, and the Premier wrote to Lady Bradford that 'Rosebery came up to me, and talked very well—just come from America—his third visit, and full as an egg of fun and quaint observations'.

Rosebery was indeed a remarkably equipped young man. His travelling through Europe and America had been almost continuous since he had left Oxford, and in every country he had not contented himself with pleasure but with serious conversations with local politicians, backed by considerable study. In the spring of 1873, for example, he spent several weeks in Paris, enjoying himself at circuses, which were always a passion with him, and studying the political make-up of the insecure new

Republic. His reactions were unfavourable, and his life-long mistrust of France's political reliability was born at this time. In his Journal he recorded:

Anything less like a Republic than Paris at this moment it is impossible to conceive . . . so bastard and ridiculous a Republic was never seen. It is like the Gothic castles of Wimbledon or Nice. . . . What would Cato think of Paris ? Would Brutus find himself at home at Versailles ? They would either be arrested as communists, or would be compelled to have cards printed with 'Msr. le duc d'Utica' and 'Le chevalier Cassius, député'. These republicans are reeds shaken by the wind, they are clothed in soft raiment, behold, Solomon in all his glory was not arrayed like one of these. They dance and they sing. They give greater prices for pictures and knicknacks than ever were given. It takes a Debrett or a Burke to understand and announce their titles.

In the lives of most public men there comes a point at which they step from obscurity and first interest and impress their contemporaries with some exceptional speech or action. Randolph Churchill was to make his sensational *début* in 1877 with a speech on Irish politics at Woodstock which attacked not only the Government of which he was a nominal supporter, but English rule for the past century; Gladstone had made a prodigious undergraduate reputation with a speech on the Reform Bill in the Oxford Union; Disraeli had emerged with decisive force with a series of wickedly brilliant attacks upon Sir Robert Peel in the early months of 1846; Arthur Balfour gave the first hint of promise in a speech on the 'Kilmainham Treaty' in 1882 in the House of Commons, which he described as 'standing alone in its infamy'. Rosebery's *entrée* was less spectacular than any of these, but its impact was considerable.

By 1870 he was decisively committed to the Liberal cause. Heredity, upbringing, intellectual indignation had all played their parts in this process. He had all the aristocratic Whig contempt for Tories, and an almost Disraelian concept of the function of the radical aristocrat championing the rights of the oppressed. 'The Tories', he wrote to 'Uncle Sam', 'profess anything but liberalism, they would call themselves Communists to get seats, but when they have got them they are as illiberal as ever.' From the glittering circle in which he moved with such ease and charm he saw the other side of the nation with great clarity. In Scotland the division of classes was even more conspicuous, and since 1871 Rosebery had made much more use of Dalmeny.

Politically, he started quietly. He made his maiden speech in the Lords in February 1871, when he seconded the Address, attired in the uniform of a Royal Scottish Archer, and fulfilled the difficult task with competence, even the vinegary *Standard* conceding that although the matter was unremarkable, 'the manner was, after a fashion, very good'. Early in 1872 he was invited to join the Government as a junior Minister representing the Board of Rating (formerly the Poor Law Board) in the Lords, but declined. In 1873 he accepted the Lord Lieutenancy of Linlithgow after first refusing the offer. This incident was a foretaste of future characteristics. In his letter of refusal, Rosebery explained that he did not know much about the county, and did not relish 'other obligations of society and residence by which at present I should be very unwilling to bind myself'. Bouverie Primrose descended in fury upon his haughty nephew, and pointed out that the late Lord Rosebery had been honoured to hold the position, and that if he persisted in his refusal, no one would understand his reasons and dismiss him as a conceited or lazy young fool. He delivered an admonition which Rosebery might have taken more to heart.

. . . Such incomprehensibility is not to the advantage of a man's public or private character, and is liable to give rise to a number of false surmises which may not only influence the public and private estimation in which he is held, but be made to recoil upon himself in ways he least expects, at moments not the least looked for and in modes most disagreeable and permanently annoying. . . .

Rosebery bowed reluctantly to this pressure, and on May 25th informed Gladstone that 'though I cannot bring my mind into accordance with the views you expressed, I can bring my will into subjection. This I am quite ready to do.'

There had already been public signs of Rosebery's radical outlook. In the November of 1871 he had startled and impressed the Edinburgh Philosophical Society with a brilliant exposition of the Union. If proof were needed of the immense work which he must have been doing quietly since his departure from Oxford, this speech would provide it. He was only 24, yet his oratorical style was astonishingly mature. His speech abounded in happy phrases and penetrating epigrams. James I had 'turned the Privy Council

Chamber of Scotland into a dissecting room'; the career of Hamilton 'is one which may well be spared from history to be framed in fiction, for it derives but little lustre from facts'; on Belhaven's speeches, 'that they were absurdly pedantic, that they were painfully prepared to the very least monosyllable, that the delivery no less than the style was intolerably affected, are hindrances perhaps to our pleasure in reading them, but formed no obstacle to their popularity in Scotland'. 'Our ancestors', he concluded, 'put their hands to a mighty work, and it prospered. They welded two great nations into one great Empire, and moulded local jealousies into a common patriotism. On such an achievement we must gaze with awe and astonishment, the means were so adverse and the result so surprising, but we should look on it also with emulous eyes. Great as the Union was, a greater still remains.' One passage in particular riveted the audience in Edinburgh and eventually a larger one outside.

It is not monarchs, or even statesmen, that give to a country prosperity and power. France in 1789 had a virtuous monarch and able statesmen. But the different classes of the community had then become completely estranged, and the upper crust of society was shivered to dust by the volcano beneath. In this country, the artificial barriers which separate class from class are high enough, but, thank God, they are not insuperable. Let us one and all prevent their coming so.

The Duchess added her severe condemnation to the storm which these mild phrases evoked. It must be remembered that the Scottish aristocracy was even more divorced from other classes than were the English, and were proportionately loathed by the mass of the people. It was startling to discover one member of this hated clique speaking with conspicuous disrespect of class barriers and uttering warnings about 'the volcano beneath'. The comparison with the French Revolution was particularly alarming. The Duchess wrote grimly to say that 'Men are not better esteemed in other classes for depreciating their own', and Rosebery replied simply that 'your argument strikes at the very root of political morality. I hope it will be long in England before people act or speak merely to please a class or classes.' Rosebery followed up his good start by taking a keen interest in educational matters in Scotland, and he championed the not very popular cause of the Irish Catholics.

I do not believe in the charity which meets two ragged children in the street, which asks them what their religion is, and when one answers, 'I am a Protestant,' says, 'Come home little Protestant, and take your porridge; but as for you, little Catholic, you may die or starve or emigrate, it is no matter to me. I do not agree with any of the articles of your dogma, and therefore you may be left to your own ways and your own doing.' That, as I have said, is a very narrow spirit of charity.

In the House of Lords he intervened rarely in debate, but when he did he always spoke with wit and incisiveness, and as early as May 1871 he succeeded in 'drawing' Lord Salisbury after a vigorous onslaught on the principle of lay patronage, a subject very near to Salisbury's heart. In the debate on the consequences of the *Alabama* claims of the United States in the June of 1872 Rosebery strongly attacked Lord Russell, who had descended with all the panoply of an ex-Premier to urge rejection of the arbitration unless all indirect claims of the American government were abandoned, and declared that he preferred his own insignificance to the eminence—'the mischievous eminence'—of the noble lord.

But it was his speech to the Social Science Congress at Glasgow in 1874 which really made Scotland sit up. 'The most vital and perpetual question before this Congress', he declared, 'is the well-being of the working classes; a vital question, because on the apt solution of it depends the commercial supremacy, the political solidarity, nay, the very existence of our empire. . . . Our civilisation is but little removed from barbarism.' He illustrated his argument by citing the ghastly conditions of children working in the brickfields near Glasgow, whose ages ranged from 3½ to 17 years, commenting that 'It would not be difficult, and it would be painfully instructive, to draw out a dismal catalogue of facts to prove how little the splendour of our civilisation differs from the worst horrors of barbarism.' He rebutted the canard—as common in 1962 as in 1874—that the working classes did not know how to spend their money properly, by the simple argument that it was not surprising that a man who had been near starvation most of his life used an increase in his wages unwisely. Compulsory education he regarded as the first vital step, 'the true leverage of Empire'. He then delivered a prolonged, acid, and riotously applauded onslaught upon the House of Lords. E. T. Raymond was exaggerating when he wrote that 'In the House of Lords, Rosebery adopted rather the tone of a very consciously sane chaplain addressing the inmates of a home for imbeciles',[1] but Rosebery's life-long contempt for that venerable institution had already become perfectly apparent to their Lordships, and explains his slender hold upon their affections. In some characteristically weak but unambiguous doggerel verses he described in one of his Journals the eventual decline of the House of Lords into a national museum.

> *The plastic Tussaud our hall will hire—*
> *Dispute our useless ermine with the moth,*
> *Our benches she will fill with waxen peers*
> *Or with her choicest murderers, or both.*

When invited in America to enumerate the powers of the Lords, he simply replied 'That of adjourning themselves'. 'We have no hereditary surgeons, or priests, or soldiers, or lawyers,' he declared at Glasgow. 'We have, however, a large body of men who are hereditary legislators during good behaviour, for they, and their fathers before them, have sat in Parliament so long as they were solvent and respectable. But for these, technical education is not provided nor even contemplated. We agree that an artisan cannot do his work properly without special instruction; but for those to whom we entrust our fates, our fortunes, and our honour, no such training is requisite. It is expected and assumed that a peer shall take to politics as a duck takes to swimming.'

From all sides came stern rebukes, and Francis Knollys was instructed to convey the severe displeasure of the Royal Family for such outrageous sentiments. In Scotland, however, there was great joy.

Behold him, then, in his late twenties, 'an Eton boy grown heavy,' of middle height, sturdily built, with remarkably clear blue eyes which could either be utterly blank or glittering with life. He gave an impression of elegant and highly polished maturity, which could enchant but which could also create misgivings about the character behind the mask. Already he was noted as one of the best shots in Britain, a collector of rare discrimination and enthusiasm, a dapper figure at the racecourses, and one of the best-read young men of his generation. His becoming modesty and courtesy made him a welcome guest and a

[1] *The Man of Promise: Lord Rosebery*, 34.

perfect host, 'the Prince Charming of the age,' as Mr John Raymond has felicitously remarked, 'courted by his elders and envied by his contemporaries in much the same fashion as Zuleika's worshippers envied the Duke of Dorset.'[1] His voice was already remarked upon, being astonishingly flexible and clear, with a deep rich intonation which was ideally suited for public speaking and which was comparable only to those of the remarkable Spurgeon and Mr Gladstone himself.

He had given an appearance of maturity since he had left Eton, and his friends found it difficult to imagine that he had ever really been young. 'I have seldom met one so young who had so well digested his reading or who gave more earnest of a wise & firm manhood,' Frank Lawley wrote to Higgins in 1872. His erudition, wit, sarcasm, and the blazing temper which could erupt with startling suddenness were characteristics of the Rosebery of twenty-five. Shrewder friends had noted his moodiness, his deliberate cultivation of an air of mystery, his calculated perverseness on occasion, and his excessive inclination towards cynical *bon mots* which convulsed select dinner parties, but gave an appearance of flippancy which made many write him down as a brilliant but shallow *politico-littéraire* with undefined and insincere radical tendencies. There was something vaguely Foxite about his pose as the aristocratic champion of the people while at the same time he spent enormous sums on racing and his several large and imposing mansions. These suspicions were never relaxed throughout Rosebery's life by his detractors, and have survived down to the present day.

What most contemporaries did not see was the apprehension and the indecision which lay at the root of his character. The accidents of his estrangement from his mother and his early independence had caused a façade of cynical self-confidence which either impressed or annoyed contemporaries, but which was entirely a defensive pose. The admiring audiences of his public speeches had no notion of the immense trouble and the mental anguish which had preceded these triumphs, nor of the acute nervousness—almost amounting to terror—with which he inwardly confronted a large gathering. Giving the appearance of remorseless progress, confident of his way, he was consumed with doubts. In his most intimate papers these doubts were occasion-

[1] *The Doge of Dover*, 15.

ally committed to paper. On his birthday in 1875 he wrote at length of these tangled emotions.

> *Born on this day. Now silent years have rolled*
> *And merged their motion in the swell of time:*
> *Childhood and youth have cast their crowns of gold*
> *Before the throne of Mystery Sublime.*
>
> *Born on this day. The sheen of sunrise gone,*
> *The dawn's cool rapture and unreasoning life:*
> *Pass we in reverence to the mellower moon*
> *Where zeal is rivalry and work is strife.*
>
> *The cup of pleasure has not lost its savour,*
> *Shall we not quaff where we have quaffed?*
> *Winking and smiling with its palled sweet flavour,*
> *Shall we not laugh where often we have laughed?*
>
> *Leave it awhile and gaze upon thy years,*
> *The years to come that break upon thy dream:*
> *How cold they glitter, like a grove of spears;*
> *How sharp their points, how sinister their gleam.*

. . . . . .

> *The dreams of boyhood and the hopes of pride*
> *The high ambitions that have torn thy soul;*
> *Live on and rush with them—or, creep aside*
> *And die, unpitied, wounded in a hole.*

CHAPTER THREE

MARRIAGE AND MIDLOTHIAN

'I AM SORRY ROSEBERY is still addicted to *badinage*,' William Johnson (who had changed his name to Cory) wrote to Reginald Brett at this time, 'let him fall in love.' Rosebery had no lack of feminine admirers, both in England and America, but apart from the mysterious Mary Fox episode, very little is known of his early affairs, if, indeed, there were any. Although amused by the wild doings of the Prince of Wales' set, about which he was admirably informed by Francis Knollys as well as by his personal observation, he remained very much on the fringe, slightly shocked as well as amused. The social columnists often spoke hopefully of possible wives, and at one time there was talk of a Royal romance; Rosebery's papers and the Royal Archives are silent on this matter, but one or two mysterious references in letters from Francis Knollys reveal that at least the Prince and Princess of Wales took the possibility of an engagement seriously at one stage.

Rosebery's attitude to women, to judge from his letters to close friends, was marked with the superficial cynicism which he liked to simulate at this time. We hear much of the personal fortunes of his women-friends, their extravagance and general unsuitability. In 1874 he was involved in a hilarious misadventure undertaken on behalf of 'Blackie' Hope, who had fallen headlong in love with Miss Grey, the daughter of Lord and Lady Grey, but who trembled to approach her personally to declare his love. In a series of heartbroken letters he implored Rosebery to tell Miss Grey of his feelings, which he reluctantly agreed to do. In the event Rosebery bungled the business hopelessly, choosing a Marlborough House party as the occasion. Miss Grey at first thought that Rosebery was proposing, and when this had been sorted out, and the true situation discovered, the Greys descended upon Hope with a cold fury. Albert Grey was obliged to deliver a savage letter from his mother, ordering the miserable Blackie

never to speak to her daughter again, and although Hope forgave Rosebery, he determined never more to interfere in such
grave matters.

But while the gossip-columnists[1] speculated about the future
Lady Rosebery at great length, and even his closest friends were
wondering what he was going to do, the matter had already been
privately arranged. On January 4th, 1878, Gladstone received a
letter whose contents surprised and delighted him.

My dear Mr Gladstone,
    I want to write to you & explain in one line why you have heard
no more from me as to my visit to Hawarden. I am engaged to be
married to Miss Hannah Rothschild, and your good wishes on this,
the most momentous event of my life, would make me very proud and
very happy.

I am,
Yours very respectfully,
Rosebery.

Rosebery had been introduced to Hannah de Rothschild by Mrs
Disraeli at Newmarket in 1868. She was then seventeen years old,
the only child of Baron and Baroness Meyer de Rothschild, who
died in 1874 and 1877 respectively, leaving Hannah with a considerable fortune and Mentmore, a majestic mansion set in magnificent parkland near Leighton Buzzard in Bedfordshire. Baron
Meyer—of whom Rosebery had written so irreverently in *Pretender's Derby*—was the youngest of the four sons of Nathan
Meyer de Rothschild who had arrived in England in 1789 to
found the London branch of the family banking house. Within
twenty years the foundations of the Rothschild fortune had been
established, and three of Nathan's sons—the fourth settled in
Paris—virtually took possession of the Vale of Aylesbury and in
the course of time either built or restored imposing mansions.[2]

----

[1] It is a popular misconception that these personages are a modern phenomenon.
In fact no modern columnist would dare to print half the things that their predecessors did, and it is curious that although Rosebery was desperately sensitive
to newspaper criticism, he seldom minded very much about this aspect, and kept
many scurrilous comments about himself.

[2] Baron Meyer (1818–74) built Mentmore in 1852–5; his brothers, Sir Anthony
(1810–76) bought Aston Clinton in 1851, and Lionel (1808–79), who fought a
long and successful battle to enter the House of Commons between 1847 and
1858 and take the Jewish oath, who is portrayed as 'Sidonia' in *Coningsby*, and
who raced under the name of 'Mr Acton'—winning the 1879 Derby—built

On the recommendation of Metternich, Nathan Meyer was granted a patent of nobility by the Austrian Emperor in 1815, and in 1822 the title of Baron of the Austrian Empire was conferred on each of the brothers. Baron Meyer took little part in the affairs of the family firm or in the House of Commons, where he sat as Liberal Member for Hythe from 1859 until his death, but he was widely known as a sportsman and collector of art treasures. He established a stud-farm in the village of Crafton near Mentmore, and became a highly successful racehorse owner, winning the Thousand Guineas in 1854, 1864, and 1871, and the Goodwood Cup in 1869 and 1872. 1871 was known as 'the Baron's year', in which he won the Derby with *Favonius*, the One Thousand Guineas, the Oaks and the St Leger with *Hannah*, and the Cesarewitch with *Corisande*.

As a collector of pictures, furniture, and ornaments the Baron was half a century ahead of his time. One of his *dicta* was the sensible observation that it was cheaper to buy antique French furniture than to go to Maples', and in the course of his travels on the Continent he amassed a collection of treasures which included some of Marie Antoinette's furniture, the chimney-piece designed by Rubens which had been in his Antwerp house, some magnificent tapestries, a wealth of Limoges enamels and Sévres porcelain, some remarkable items from the Doges' Palace at Venice, and paintings by Rembrandt—thrown in by a seller to 'make up' a lot!—Murillo, and the young Turner among others, which testified to the Baron's exceptional taste and demanded a suitable magnificent setting. This was provided by the famous landscape gardener and architect Joseph Paxton on the Baron's Mentmore estate.

Mentmore—designed and built between 1850 and 1855—is in essence a copy of Wollaton, the home of the Willoughby family near Nottingham, but with subtle amendments and built in the warmer Ancaster stone. Although it is probable that Paxton was assisted by his son-in-law in his plans for the house,[1] it is clear that the magnificent siting of Mentmore was the vision of Paxton

Halton. Nathan Meyer (1840–1915), who was created Baron Rothschild of Tring in 1885, built Tring; Leopold bought and enlarged Ascott; and Baron Ferdinand (1838–98)—a cousin of Baron Meyer—built Waddesdon between 1875–80.

[1] See Pevsner: *The Buildings of England, Buckinghamshire* (1960), and G. F. Chadwick: *The Works of Joseph Paxton* (1961).

himself. As was to be expected from the architect of the Crystal Palace, skilful and indeed revolutionary use was made of plate glass, particularly in the immense central hall—fifty feet deep, forty feet wide, and forty feet tall—which is lit by a glass ceiling, has tall plate-glass doors, and overlooks a marvellous view of the Chilterns through lofty windows. Mentmore has always had its critics, and has been stigmatised as 'a tedious imitation', but although these criticisms may be justified when applied to the exterior plan and treatment, the spaciousness and light of the interior and the inspired siting which gives a breathtaking view from almost every one of the great windows, deserve higher commendation than that usually given to Paxton for his design. He was also limited to some extent by the necessity for building the mansion around Baron Meyer's enormous collections. The great hall, for example, had to accommodate the huge gilt lanterns from the Doges' barge and the Rubens chimney-piece.

Long before the Baron's death Rosebery was an intimate friend of the family and had frequently stayed at Mentmore and had joined racing-parties at Newmarket and Epsom. Baron Ferdinand was perhaps Rosebery's greatest Rothschild friend, and everything about that remarkable family appealed warmly to him. It was not long before Hannah fell deeply in love with him, but the courtship was prolonged. The religious difficulty was a very real one, since although the Rothschilds would not have vetoed a Gentile alliance, they anticipated—and their forebodings were fully justified in the event—that there would be intense opposition from the majority of the Jewish faith; furthermore, although she counted for very little in Rosebery's life, the Duchess of Cleveland had a violent Semitic antipathy on both religious and racial grounds (Disraeli seems to have been an exception). But as early as 1876 it was apparent that there could be only one end to their relationship, and when the Baroness—who warmly favoured the match—died suddenly in 1877 it was Rosebery who consoled 'Miss Hannah'. She was extremely shy and nervous, and Sir James Lacaita, an old friend of her father, undertook to play the part of 'the honest broker'.

Hannah, living alone in her great palace-museum, probably the greatest heiress of her age, was indeed much to be pitied. She had been outrageously spoilt as a child, and her education had been badly neglected. In a private note her cousin, Lady Battersea, once wrote in reminiscence, 'She never was allowed to enter a cottage, to go where sickness and sorrow dwelt, she was never brought face to face with want or sickness. "The poor" was merely a phraseology for her. She had but few redeeming qualities as a child.'[1] Rosebery, almost as shy and equally lonely, admired and liked by her uncles and cousins, quickly became the only real interest in Hannah's life, and when he proposed on January 3rd, 1878, he was at once accepted. To the person he had always loved most he wrote a short note.

My darling Connie,

I was engaged to Hannah yesterday. I love her so much that I can never be happy if you do not love her too.

Ever yr loving brother,
A.

His sister at once telegraphed her delighted congratulations, to which Rosebery replied:

My darling,

Your telegram has made me so very happy that I must send one line to say so before running off to shew it to Hannah.

Yr loving
A.

You must tell the chicks of their new aunt.
The Rothschilds appear pleased.

Lady Leconfield hastened to London to meet Hannah as soon as she could, and they took to each other at once. After she had left, Hannah, who was always rather shy, wrote to her from 107, Piccadilly, on January 16th.

My dearest Connie,

Please let me call you so, for you cannot imagine how delighted your visit made me, it felt so homelike! I am indeed thankful for my intense happiness.

You must tell me, dear, everything I should do; I look to you for advice. I want very ardently to make him happy. I could not thank you from my heart for your journey to see me, though I felt it in my heart and love you already.

Believe me Yrs affly,
Hannah de Rothschild.

[1] *Lady Battersea's Papers.* (British Museum Additional Manuscripts 47,956 (Diaries for November 19th and 25th, 1890).)

Hannah's shyness with her fiancé was very noticeable, and he did all he could to ease this by arranging that when she met his friends and relatives he was not hovering in the background. 'She gets on with people much better when I am not in the room, and though of course I should be in & out, yet you would know her more easily in that way,' he had written to Lady Leconfield when making arrangements for their meeting.

Very few of Rosebery's letters to his wife, or those from her to him, are in existence, as Rosebery destroyed most of them in his agony after her death. One breathless note from 2, Berkeley Square, on February 14th, 1878, has survived.

My darling,
I am on the point of being late for Uncle John's dinner so I am in a hurry. I have just come back from the House. Everything looks to me very warlike.[1] It did not rain much here today. I only just caught the train. I have had no invitation from the Stanhopes. I have had a lovely cigarette case in pure gold from H. Tyrwhitt. C. Sykes spent an hour here this morning & interrupted me in my letter but I like him so much I forgave him. He says Ferdy's ball was the most beautiful & perfect thing he ever saw. Goodbye, my own darling,

Yr loving
A

I am better with my tongue than my pen, I think.

Opposition to the marriage in the Jewish press had been growing since the previous autumn when the rumours of the engagement had begun to assume an authoritative nature. *The Jewish Chronicle* of October 5th, 1877, had spoken of 'the most poignant grief' at the news. 'The rabbinical query is on every lip. If the flame seized on the cedars, how will fare the hyssop on the wall: if the leviathan is brought up with a hook, how will the minnows escape? . . . The intelligence has thrilled through the communal frame. It quivers under the impact. And shall we suppress the cry of pain heaved forth from the soul?' The fact that Hannah Rothschild kept this particular article, and others in the Jewish press hostile to her marriage, reveals to some extent how this aspect of her engagement troubled her. There was never any question of her giving up her religion, and indeed Rosebery strongly opposed any such suggestion; had he not done so, for

[1] A reference to the critical situation in the Middle East.

all her adoration of him, there is very little doubt that she would not have married him.

The Duchess of Cleveland was deeply mortified by the news, and could not trust herself to write to her son for several days. 'I must surprise you, even as I was myself surprised yesterday,' Everard Primrose wrote to his cousin, Henry Stanhope. 'Archie is to marry Miss Hannah Rothschild and her millions! I really believe the young woman has annually some 80,000£ worth of hard cash!¹ I think that is enough to buy the consent of a whole tribe—were it even of Levi. . . . I cannot conceal from myself that this marriage will be a great blow to my mother—whose house hitherto has alone stood out against an infusion of Jewish society —and whose sentiments even on the report were expressed with force.' At length the Duchess penned what Rosebery described to Lady Leconfield as a 'not altogether ungracious' letter.

> Battle Abbey,
> Battle
> Tuesday [January 9th]

My dear Archie,

I would sooner have answered your letter, but I have been very much cut up, & not at all well: & both the Duke & I judged it best to wait till I could write with sufficient composure on a subject that touches me so deeply. You are right in believing that I should dislike this marriage on religious grounds: & to me the question is of grave importance. You can easily suppose how unhappy I must feel in finding

¹ This was something of an understatement. Lady Rosebery's will was proved at £724,892 gross in 1890 (£719,876 net), but this took account solely of her personal invested fortune, and did not include Mentmore (made over to Rosebery on his marriage) or other properties in Buckinghamshire and Hertfordshire which yielded an average annual income of approximately £8,000. Disraeli wrote to Lady Chesterfield in the July of 1875 that Baron Meyer had left £3,000,000 to his wife and daughter, as well as Mentmore which was worth £600,000. 'They say the poor Baroness cannot live but a very short time, bad dropsy rapidly developing itself— so Miss de R. will have Mentmore and three millions sterling besides *absolutely*; not a Trust created.' (Zetland: *Letters of Disraeli to Lady Bradford and Lady Chesterfield*, I, 256.) This was evidently rather an exaggeration; it is doubtful if Miss de Rothschild's fortune (including Mentmore) was more than £2 million. After his marriage, Rosebery's income from his estates (including mines) was approximately £40,000, and that from the trust fund of £700,000 set up in the marriage settlement over £100,000. His total gross income was therefore approximately £30,000 per annum before his marriage and £140,000 after it; in later years of his life it was depleted by taxation and the fall in the value of land, but his will was proved in 1929 at £1,554,339 gross, a sum which did not include Mentmore and other extensive properties, made over to his heir several years before.

that you have chosen as your wife, & the mother of your children, one who has not the faith & hope of Christ. . . . I myself do honestly, & from the bottom of my heart, disapprove of such marriages, & I could not say otherwise without acting against my conscientious convictions.

You would not wish me to do that, or to approach my own child, on the most important occasion of his life, with any words that were not the exact truth upon my lips. I can at least sincerely say that I am glad to hear of your great happiness; & in this feeling the Duke cordially joins. I will receive the future Lady Rosebery with all the kindness & consideration that are her due, & I do not think she will ever have occasion to complain of me. But for the present I would plead to be spared any agitating interviews on the score of my own health. I am not strong, & rapidly feeling myself growing old; with a feeble heart (like my poor brother's): & any strong emotion makes me physically ill. But if you are really anxious that I should come up to London to see her, I will of course do so.

Ever yr affte mother,
C. L. W. Cleveland.

Although Rosebery may have felt somewhat sceptical about his mother's complaints of poor health—she was as strong as an ox, and lived for another twenty years—he handled her with great gentleness, and she thawed slightly, although she said that the Duke and herself would not attend the wedding unless it were in a church, and wrote that 'I do not in the least suppose—owing to the difference in our religious opinions—that you can estimate the trial that it will be to me. . . . I am glad to find that you intend your wedding to be a very quiet one.'

If this was Rosebery's intention, it was certainly carried out in a curious manner. There were two ceremonies, the first a civil one at the Board-room of the Guardians in Mount Street and the second at Christ Church, Down Street, Piccadilly. The first ceremony took place at a quarter to ten on the morning of March 20th, and the dull room was almost suffocatingly decorated with £60-worth of flowers, the registrar's table being so swamped that it almost resembled an altar. Only about thirty close friends and representative Rothschild and Rosebery tenants were present, but the ceremony at Christ Church was considerably more elaborate. The Prime Minister—now the Earl of Beaconsfield—gave the bride away, and, Harry Tyrwhitt being ill, Lord Carrington was best man. The bride's veil alone, the press recorded with awe,

cost over £700, while the groom, apparently determined not to
be completely outshone, wore a blue frock-coat with a red rose
in his buttonhole. The ceremony was performed by the much-
beloved Canon Rogers, and the garrulous reporter of the *Morning
Post* informed his readers that 'Lord Rosebery said his say like a
man, with no *tremolo* or nonsense. His wife was, pardonably
enough, inaudible. The Premier acted the heavy father *à ravir*.'
Beaconsfield, the Prince of Wales, Lady Leconfield, the Duke of
Cleveland and Everard Primrose signed the register, and at the
wedding breakfast at 107, Piccadilly, the Prince proposed the
health of the couple. By two o'clock the couple had departed for
their honeymoon at Petworth, Lady Rosebery now in a greatly
admired sapphire blue velvet dress, trimmed with blue fox fur,
with her muff also in blue fox fur. All in all, it was a magnificent
affair, and one which left London Society humming for several
weeks. After a week or so Hannah wrote to Lady Leconfield:

. . . You will be surprised to hear Archie is not yet quite bored.
We two old bachelors agree & are becoming accustomed to married
life though I may own that he usually gets his own way; you see we
are both (as he said if you remember) spoilt children & I being the
laziest, am the more amenable. . . . My husband sends his love. . . .

In the following March Mary Gladstone dined alone with
Hannah Rosebery, and recorded that 'she is very serenely happy,
and going to have a baby'.

Rosebery's marriage was so important an event in his life that
it merits detailed examination. It is a subject over which more
misunderstandings have arisen than is usual in the marriages of
public men. A curious legend had grown up to the effect that
Rosebery had once said that he had three ambitions in life: to win
the Derby, marry an heiress, and become Prime Minister. The
source of this legend is untraceable, and although it is quite possible that he did once make such an observation, it is extremely
unlikely that it was meant seriously. As a young man he was very
much a *poseur*, which had irritated a number of people who had
met him casually, and he did sometimes say outrageous things
merely to observe their effect, and he could be witheringly sarcastic. Yet this particular phrase—which Rosebery always
vehemently denied ever saying—is so out of character that it at
once falls under suspicion. Throughout his life Rosebery was

always surrounded with peculiarly malicious gossip, and his riches fitted in excellently with the Derby-heiress-Prime Minister legend, and was regarded as the truth in many quarters. Rosebery's public irritation with his obviously adoring wife gave added credence to the picture, but his was a nature so highly-strung that quite trivial things could disconcert and infuriate him.

Lord Crewe has described their marriage as 'founded on admiration and warm affection on the one side, admiration and adoring devotion on the other'. Rosebery was not a man who wore his heart on his sleeve, and he was most reserved about those things which were most sacred to him. Hannah Rosebery possessed those qualities in which he was most deficient. She had great common sense and tact, although—as she herself admitted—her impetuous enthusiasm on her husband's behalf was not infrequently misinterpreted. Being very shy, she disliked entertaining on any scale and hated the official functions which the position of wife to the Foreign Secretary later entailed, but she was always inviting local people whom she believed her husband ought to meet to Mentmore, Dalmeny, and The Durdans, and she was probably the only person who made him do things which he did not want to do. Indeed, much of the popularity which Rosebery enjoyed in Edinburgh, Buckinghamshire, and Epsom was due to his wife.

Although a remarkably shrewd judge of character and full of gossip, she was also endearingly naïve. Her adoration of her husband was obvious enough to be almost embarrassing. 'I never saw a woman so wholly absorbed in a man,' Edward Hamilton wrote after her death. 'Everything she did was done with the object of serving him. If he was in the room, nothing could turn her thoughts or eyes from him. It was the most touching fidelity I ever saw.' Understandably, Rosebery was often impatient at this perhaps excessive devotion, and there are countless stories—many of them undoubtedly true—of his rudeness to her. He had a cruel gift of mimicry, and had the unattractive habit of scoring off a 'butt', and when, as occasionally happened, Hannah was the unwitting butt, chance acquaintances were naturally shocked. But it is important to note that the very few intimate friends of the Roseberys, notably Hamilton, Lady Battersea (who always disliked Hannah), and Ferdinand de Rothschild never even hint in their private papers that the marriage was anything but supremely happy and successful.

She gave to her husband all the affection and sympathy which he had lacked in his childhood, and for which he craved. Her adoration was undeniably tinged with awe, and Lady Leconfield —who was devoted to her—was frequently the recipient of her hopes and fears. On one occasion she had to fulfil an engagement in Edinburgh in her husband's place, and on her return to Dalmeny wrote a long account of the evening, anxiously enquiring at every point if she had done the correct thing. So eager was she not to let him down, and so conscious of the deficiencies in her education, that she asked Principal Donaldson to coach her in Scottish literature and history. One cannot avoid the impression of Hannah Rosebery following nervously in Rosebery's footsteps throughout their married life, utterly devoted but consumed with alarm lest she made some dreadful mistake. Although he often made fun of her—'I am leaving tonight; Hannah and the rest of the heavy baggage will follow later' was one of his alleged *mots*— Rosebery depended upon her sympathy and loyalty far more than he probably ever realised. Against this background of serene family happiness Rosebery's sensitive and febrile personality demonstrated the warmth and tenderness which he was normally so anxious to suppress. Her kindness, gaiety and charm were very difficult to resist; Rosebery used to laugh at her love of anniversaries of all kinds, but found after her death that he, like his children, had acquired this delight. In all Rosebery's papers, the detailed accounts of his birthdays and those of his children are among the most charming.

Watts' well-known portrait of Hannah Rosebery conveys something of her warmth, but a water-colour portrait by an unknown artist which Rosebery kept in his tiny, lonely bedroom at Barnbougle, captures her artless charm more exactly, standing in a simple white dress in the great hall at Mentmore, pretty, composed, and smiling shyly.

Politics, that insidious seductress, was remorselessly exerting her fascination over Rosebery. The somewhat impetuous dissolution of February 1874 had been the last official act of the exhausted Liberal Ministry which had secured so triumphant a victory in 1868, but which had forfeited much of its cohesion and popu-

larity after 1872, and the Tories achieved a majority of about fifty
over all other parties. 'The Tories are mad with joy,' Rosebery
wrote ruefully to 'Uncle Sam'. 'They condole with one, they
sympathise with one, they pat one on the back. I nearly died of
it.' Mr Gladstone tendered his resignation, Mr Disraeli accepted
the Queen's Commission, and within a year the Liberal leader had
resigned his pre-eminent position and had retired 'to a position
of greater freedom and less responsibility'. The Liberal leadership
was divided between Lord Hartington in the Commons and Lord
Granville in the Lords and suffered a consequential debilitation.
For a period the Disraeli administration carried all before it and
it was not until 1876 that the Liberals began to cause the Ministry
any great concern, when the supposedly retired Gladstone suddenly
emerged with a white-hot castigation of the Turkish atrocities in
Bulgaria in the September of 1876. The news that over twelve
thousand Bulgarian men, women, and children had been mas-
sacred by Turkish irregular troops was slow in filtering across
Europe, but when the fact was established there was a shattering
reaction in Britain. Beaconsfield's cynical flippancy further excited the already impassioned Gladstone, and on September 6th
his electrifying pamphlet, *The Bulgarian Horrors and the Question of
the East*, was published and sold over two hundred thousand
copies in three weeks. In a series of enormous meetings Gladstone
continued his ferocious denunciation of the Turk and the Ministry, and at no time was the relationship between himself and
Beaconsfield marked by such a degree of bitterness. Harcourt
wrote to Sir Charles Dilke on October 10th, 1876, that 'Gladstone
and Dizzy seem to cap one another in folly and imprudence, and I
don't know which has made the greatest ass of himself'. Gladstone's language caused a reciprocal bitterness which disfigured
British public life for the remainder of his life.

The Liberal Party at Westminster was sorely divided over the
Bulgarian Question, but Rosebery lost no time in coming down
with surprising vigour on Gladstone's side. His interventions in
debates in the House of Lords since 1874 had been skilful and
admired, but fitful and quickly forgotten. In the October of 1876
he made his first really arresting partisan speech in unmitigated
castigation of the Tory Ministry at Dumfries and savoured the
heady wine of the delighted cheering of a large audience. In the
House of Lords he became more active, concentrating increas-

ingly on foreign affairs. In the spring and early summer of 1877 he delivered a series of informed and impressive attacks on the Eastern policy of the Government, and when the Congress of Berlin was convened in the following year he spoke with a harshness which was quite unexpected, and in a speech at Aberdeen on October 10th, 1878, he denounced the 'Peace with Honour' claim of the Prime Minister for the Congress. 'They have partitioned Turkey, they have secured a doubtful fragment of the spoil for themselves. They have abandoned Greece, they have incurred responsibilities of a vast and unknown kind, which no British Government has a right to incur without consulting the British Parliament and the British people. . . . You will have observed, all through these negotiations, that we actually treated Turkey as a great Power. There never was so deliberate a mistake as that. Turkey is not a great power, *she is an impotence*.' He concluded his speech, which was punctuated throughout with wild applause, with a denunciation of the argument that the Congress had secured the preservation of the route to India. 'I believe it is no more necessary for the preservation of India than it is necessary that we should damage Spain in order to keep Gibraltar. But I do say this, that we may pay too great a price even for the preservation of India.'

The Congress of Berlin marked the highest point of the fortunes of the Beaconsfield Administration, and temporarily obliterated the effects of Gladstone's campaign against the Turk. But the opportune moment for an appeal to the country was allowed to pass. Ireland, quiescent for a decade, began to give hints of the terrible eruption of 1880–2; the amiable, peaceable, constitutional Irish Parliamentary Party leader, Mr Isaac Butt, was replaced by the cold, unamiable, implacably hostile Anglo-Irish aristocrat Charles Stewart Parnell, who raised Parliamentary obstruction to an art, paralysed the work of the House of Commons by contemptuous disregard for the customs and conventions of centuries, and provided the leadership for which the divergent elements of Irish Nationalism had craved since the death of O'Connell. The serious decline in British agriculture towards the end of the 1870's gave the cause of Irish Nationalism its most formidable allies, hunger and despair.

The autumn of 1878 saw two vitally significant events in the career of the newly-married Scottish peer. He was invited to stand as Liberal candidate for the Lord Rectorship of Aberdeen University, which invitation he at once accepted. Matters were complicated by the threatened intervention of Lord Aberdeen, a young peer exactly the same age as Rosebery, but who had not yet publicly declared his allegiance to the Liberal cause. Mr Gladstone was enthusiastic that Aberdeen should stand, but Rosebery demonstrated an unexpected degree of toughness which startled his friends. When asked to withdraw he wrote to Gladstone on October 2nd:

. . . It appears to me if I must speak with perfect frankness that as it is Lord Aberdeen who has got himself into this difficulty that it is he who should withdraw. Why I am to expiate his political aberrations is a point that I do not clearly understand. . . .

Aberdeen decided not to appear as a rival Liberal candidate, and Rosebery won the contest by three votes over the Conservative nominee, Sir Richard Cross. The victory marked the first substantial step towards the domination of Lowland Liberalism which Rosebery was never to forfeit. It also opened a few eyes so far as Rosebery was concerned, and there was some feeling that he had not treated Aberdeen fairly; in fact, Rosebery had offered to withdraw from the contest if he was the only political candidate, but on the advice of W. P. Adam, the Liberal Whip, decided to go forward with his candidature.

Of infinitely greater moment was the capture of Gladstone as Liberal candidate for Midlothian. In 1876 W. P. Adam, the architect of the reconstruction of the central Liberal Party machine since 1874, had established the East and North of Scotland Liberal Association and the West and South-West of Scotland Association, and had appointed Secretaries. John James Reid, the Secretary of the East and North of Scotland Association (situated in Edinburgh), was in effect the party agent for the whole of Scotland, and the two bodies were amalgamated in 1881. The importance with which Adam regarded Scotland may be gauged from the fact that he supplied Reid with considerable sums of money from central funds; in the November of 1880 Reid's secret reserve stood at £1,588 12s.[1] and presumably must have been considerably higher before the General Election of that year. Adam was extremely anxious to persuade Gladstone to stand for

[1] H. J. Hanham: *Elections and Party Management*, 159.

a Scottish constituency, but his first approaches in the autumn
of 1876 were unsuccessful. Gladstone would not even attend a
banquet in his honour in Edinburgh, since, as he wrote to Adam
(October 4th), 'I am a follower & not a leader in the Liberal
party, and nothing will induce me to do an act indicative of a
desire to change my position. Any such act would be a positive
breach of faith on my part towards those whom I importuned as
I may say to allow me to retire, and whom I left to undertake a
difficult and invidious office. True, I have been forced, by obligations growing out of the past, to take a prominent part on the
Eastern question: but I postponed it as long as I could, and have
done all in my power, perhaps too much, to keep it apart from
the general course of politics & of party connection.'[1] Nevertheless, Adam did not abandon his ambition. Gladstone, deeply
chagrined by his narrow victory at Greenwich in 1874, was
anxious to represent a great industrial constituency; Leeds
wanted to adopt him, but the Liberals were so firmly entrenched
in that enormous constituency that there would be little glory in
victory.

Midlothian, although a county constituency, was a highly
marginal seat, which had been recovered for the Conservatives by
Lord Dalkeith—son and heir of the fifth Duke of Buccleuch—in
1874, but the Midlothian Liberal Association was convinced that
this was a temporary reversal which did not reflect the true temper
of the constituency. When searching for an attractive candidate,
Sir David Wedderburn, a distinguished Edinburgh personality,
was favoured by the association, and Adam privately urged
Wedderburn to abandon Devonport—where he had also been
selected—and accept the offer of the Midlothian Liberals. Donald
Crawford[2] was deputed to approach Wedderburn, who expressed
himself willing to stand but could only promise £1,000 towards
the expenses of the campaign. This was regarded as wholly inadequate, and the Midlothian Association was still without a
candidate. Rosebery saw much of Adam and Crawford at this
time, and it is probable that it was he who proposed that Gladstone should be approached. Adam, who later felt that his share

[1] *Gladstone Papers*.
[2] 1837–1919. Fellow of Lincoln College, Oxford, 1861–81; advocate at Scottish
Bar, 1862; legal secretary to the Lord Advocate, 1880–5; MP(L) North-East
Lanarkshire, 1885–95. Married, 1st, Virginia Smith in 1880 (dissolved in 1886) and
2nd, Hon Lilian Moncreiff, daughter of third Baron Moncreiff (1876–1950).

in the events of 1878–80 had been inadequately recognised, sub-sequently wrote to H. W. Lucy that 'I have really had all the responsibility of Mr G.'s going there. He does nothing without my advice. I got Granville and Hartington to consent to his going to contest Midlothian, which he would not otherwise have done. . . . Rosebery and I were the original joint conspirators who set the whole thing in motion. He, very properly, has got plenty of kudos, but nobody thinks of the poor slave of the lamp who grubs underground.'[1]

Gladstone, when approached by Adam in the autumn of 1878, was some time coming to a decision. His friendship with the Duke of Buccleuch, the perils of the undertaking, and his uneasy position in the political world, all played their part in his hesita-tion. By the December of 1878 things had so far progressed that Adam was writing to Rosebery to say that 'W.E.G. will not *finally* decide and has asked us to call in Wolverton[2] to consult in the matter. I have seen Wolverton & asked him to see you. He is not so hot on Midlothian as you and I are. W.E.G. will be bound by what we three consider best. I am to see Wolverton on Tues-day at my office at 11 and go over some constituencies. He will probably see you before then but if you choose to come on that day I shall be very glad to have your support.' On December 11th Wolverton wrote to Rosebery to say that Gladstone was prepared to accept the proposal of the Midlothian Liberals under certain conditions.

. . . I went fully into the matter with Mr G & he is ready to stand if you can get him a strong requisition from the County—he said at first that he ought to have a majority of the electors but upon my urging the position this would place the tenant farmers in (who rely upon the ballot) he gave way saying you had urged the same point; but before he accepts he will require such a requisition as will give him a *reason* for presenting himself to the County in which he has no ties and which wd also justify him in disturbing the peace of the Duke [of Buccleuch]—I don't think he feels strongly upon the *latter* point!— but he is not disposed to move without a requisition strong enough to justify the step. I have no doubt you can take steps to secure this. . . .

[1] H. W. Lucy: *Sixty Years in the Wilderness*, 194.
[2] George Grenfell Glyn, second Baron Wolverton (1824–87). MP for Shaftesbury, 1857–73, when he succeeded his father. Joint Secretary to the Treasury, 1868–73; Paymaster-General, 1880–5; Postmaster-General, 1886.

Gladstone himself wrote to Adam on January 22nd, 1878, that

My first desire would be to find myself justified in closing my Parliamentary life at the next dissolution. If, as is possible, this could not properly be done, my next wish is to make what may remain of that life as quiet and unobtrusive—assuming that there are no more Eastern Questions—as possible. It is not likely that I could have my old seat at Newark but the most tranquil seat would be to me the most valuable & satisfactory. I should not in any case be able to undertake the charges of a County Election. But, subject to these qualifications, I should wish that my selection of a seat, or a candidature, should be governed by a regard to the interests of the Liberal party, on which, now that my official life is over, and, when I read them in the light of the present period of Tory Government, I set a higher value than ever.

From this, I think, you can measure exactly my position as to the idea you have broached of the Midlothian seat. And though I cannot even now dismiss all old recollections about the Duke of Buccleuch, I think that a pronouncement by a distinct majority of the constituency would get over that difficulty, which otherwise might remain.[1]

This important and illuminating letter followed one from Adam of January 15th, which stated that 'The whole expenses of the contest will be arranged by the Liberals in the county, and I am in a position distinctly to assure you (which I now do) that you will not be held responsible for any part of the expense either preliminary or during the contest'.[2]

The Midlothian Association had met on January 7th to approve the invitation to Gladstone to become the Liberal candidate, and Rosebery had travelled from Paris to attend this historic meeting at the urgent request of Reid, since 'there may be a tendency to walk on the art of some of those present which your lordship's presence would check'. The 'Requisition' to Gladstone was magnificently bound in leather, and the Conservatives of Midlothian—particularly the appalled Dalkeith—were confronted with the most serious challenge that could be conceived. Reid and Ralph Richardson—secretary of the Midlothian Association—had carried out a secret canvass at the urgent request of Adam and were able to report at the beginning of 1879 that a small Liberal majority existed. The triumvirate of Adam, Reid, and Richardson

[1] Adam forwarded this letter to Rosebery, and it is now in the *Rosebery Papers*. There is no copy in the *Gladstone Papers*.
[2] *Gladstone Papers*.

ordered another and more detailed canvass to provide a definite estimate.

Although there were less than three thousand registered electors in the constituency, the Liberals faced formidable difficulties and it was decided that Gladstone's candidature for Leeds should not be abandoned. Buccleuch possessed some 430,000 acres in the Lowlands, and although only 3,436 in Midlothian itself, this property was extremely valuable and comparatively heavily tenanted. This was the crucial matter from the beginning. Eviction for voting against the laird was so ingrained a feature of Scottish politics that the 1872 Ballot Act had had surprisingly little effect in these relatively remote areas. Furthermore, both Dalkeith and his father were popular in the constituency, and their wealth enormous. The creation of 'faggot votes'—a device by which voters were added to the Register by obtaining a property qualification, usually achieved by registering them as tenants or lessees of houses with the necessary value—was another ancient feature of Scottish electioneering and of the total 2,889 Scottish electors in 1820, some 1,200 were 'faggot voters'.[1] The Reform Acts of 1832 and 1867 had not seriously changed the situation, which was that the owners or tenants of a dwelling-house with a yearly value of £14 (£10 in England) were eligible to be registered. £14 was a high rent in Scottish county districts in the 1870's, so the creation of faggot votes by 'assisting' tenants, or by actually moving workmen or casual labourers into houses with a £14 yearly value, was a comparatively simple operation, and one into which both parties hurled themselves with enthusiasm. As early as January 17th, 1879, Adam was warning Gladstone that the Tories were taking energetic steps to improve the Register, 'but we can counteract them by some rows of new houses which have lately been built and are inhabited by Liberals almost entirely. Of course', he concluded virtuously but untruthfully, 'we never condescend to faggot making.' 'The Tories', he wrote to Rosebery on January 23rd, 'are making faggots like mad, but I doubt that they will be able to do anything seriously to shake the position.'

The process of vote-making and persuasion raged fiercely throughout 1879. The Liberal tactics were more discreet and better planned than those of their opponents, but they played the same

[1] Porritt: *The Unreformed House of Commons*, 157.

game. Cramond, adjacent to Dalmeny, disclosed an anti-Glad-
stone majority of 59 to 52, with 8 uncertain. 'As your lordship
may be able to influence some of the voters,' Richardson wrote
meaningly to Rosebery, 'I attach a list with politics marked.' The
Liberals estimated that the Tories had only created about a hundred 'faggots', and plastered the constituency with posters urging
electors not to sell any property to the Buccleuch agents. Other
more subtle stratagems were employed. On December 14th,
1879, Reid wrote to Rosebery that

. . . The building scheme of McLaren and Lang Todd looks as if it
were to be favoured by weather. It is a complete thaw at present.
Another scheme of the same kind is being devised at Penicuik but with
this *material* difference. The houses are there: the working men are
in them as tenants, & the only thing would be to enable them by a
slight temporary advance to get the title of owners. From any point
of view these are genuine voters whether by property, residence or
otherwise. They number nearly a 100 I hear, but a friend of mine is
going quietly out to see about it all tomorrow or next day. I hope it
will be arranged.
    Lang Todd has closed with his sellers as the Tory agent was pressing
for possession to get a hold of it for faggot-voters. . . .

And then, on the same subject, January 22nd, 1880:

. . . From what I can learn, the Tynecastle workmen's buildings are
rapidly approaching completion. The Tories seeing it could be done in
so short a time are said to have attempted a rival movement, though
not for working-men inhabitants. Their attempt failed as the hard
frost came on just after outside work & roofing was finished on the
original work. . . .

By the February of 1880 Reid calculated that 272 Liberal voters
had been added to the Register since the December of 1878 by
these methods, and to the present day 'Mr Gladstone's cottages'
are still pointed out by older inhabitants of Edinburgh to interested visitors. 'Midlothian is ours till 1 Nov. 1880,' Richardson
reported to Rosebery in the February of 1880, '& I hear the other
side now admit Mr Gladstone will win—they say by 100.' The
official Liberal calculation at this stage was Gladstone 1,781,
Dalkeith 1,144, Uncertain, 253, an estimate so wildly inaccurate
that it is evident that the Liberal canvassers had received many

false promises. Gladstone himself was uneasy. 'Adam was here yesterday', he wrote to Rosebery on October 30th, 'and reported the *same* favourable state of computations and expectations in Midlothian as at the outset. There is, however, something singular in the very confident statements on the other side.'

The Eatanswill atmosphere of the Midlothian preparations enchanted Rosebery, who entered into the work with zest. In the August of 1879 he invited Gladstone to make Dalmeny his headquarters and urged him 'to make use of us as much as possible'. At this point the second stage of the campaign, that of making the maximum effect of their candidate's personality, really began, and Rosebery's experience of the Democrat Convention in New York in 1873, when he had watched with awe a vast torchlight procession, was invaluable. Every aspect of Gladstone's visit was planned in the most meticulous detail, and the imaginative touches were all Rosebery's.

Gladstone and his wife travelled north on November 24th, and from Liverpool to Edinburgh crowds of Liberal enthusiasts thronged the platforms and even, at some points, lined the tracks. These gatherings were by no means spontaneous or accidental. Rosebery and Richardson between them decided that the Gladstones should travel by the Midland Railway to Edinburgh by way of Hawick, Galashiels, and Melrose, where the local Liberal Associations were instructed to lay on demonstrations. The Midland Railway was chosen because it had recently introduced new Pullman coaches from America which had a platform at the back from which the great man could conveniently address crowds of well-wishers. Gladstone spoke from this vantage point at Carlisle, Hawick, Galashiels, and Melrose, but these crowds were as nothing when compared with the vast multitude which awaited him at Waverley Station. Midlothian and Edinburgh had been suffering from election fever for months before his arrival, and Gladstone's visit came at the end of an intense period of acrimonious argument between the two parties. Rosebery met the Gladstones at the station, and a procession of carriages, led by a single horseman and flanked by flamboyantly-dressed out-riders, wended its way through packed streets out of the city to Dalmeny, 'the noise more than deafening, hundreds flying along by the side of the carriage, and the whole way to Dalmeny more or less lined with people and torches and fireworks and bonfires,' Mary

Gladstone excitedly wrote.[1] Bonfires blazed on the hills, and fire-works cascaded into the night sky. Excited Liberal crowds roamed the streets of Edinburgh amid scenes of belligerent enthusiasm, but all Tories seemed to have vanished. 'I have never', Gladstone wrote, 'gone through a more extraordinary day.'

On the next day (November 25th) Gladstone drove into Edin-burgh through packed streets with Rosebery to speak at the Music Hall in George Street; his speech to a vast and almost frenetic audience was a measured denunciation of the Ministry and all its works. On the 26th he was greeted as a god at Dalkeith, where he spoke at the Corn Exchange amid 'a perfect storm of applause', and then to the Foresters' Hall, where he attacked militarism, exhorting his wildly cheering audience to 'Remember the rights of the savage, as we call him. Remember that the happiness of his humble home, remember that the sanctity of life in the hill vil-lages of Afghanistan, among the winter snows, is as inviolable in the eye of Almighty God as can be your own.' 'Several times we went through horrors from the reckless crowding of the people,' Mary Gladstone wrote to a friend, 'pressing on to the carriage, hanging on to the wheels, such pinched, haggard, eager faces.'[2] The torchbearers in serried ranks lined the streets as the *entourage* returned to Dalmeny, where large crowds lined the long drive and stood in front of the house to catch a glimpse of the great man. The excitement of Midlothian was now almost frightening in its intensity, and the appalled Conservative agents sent mes-sages of panic to their central organisation.

On November 27th Gladstone visited West Calder through streets bestrode with triumphal arches to find the town itself brilliantly illuminated and decorated, and hurled himself into a furious attack upon the foreign policy of the Disraeli Ministry; by now he had captured Lowland Scotland, for crowds from hundreds of miles away poured into the constituency to hear this incredible man. On November 29th he held an audience of five thousand spellbound at the Corn Exchange, where Rosebery pre-sided and was thunderously applauded; they then went to the Waverley Market, where a crowd of over twenty thousand was crammed. Rosebery's own account of the scene should be re-corded.

[1] Lucy Masterman: *Mary Gladstone*, 178.   [2] *Ibid.*, 179.

. . . a strange sight. Gladstone calmly perorating about Bulgaria while the fainting people were lifted over pale & motionless into the reporters' enclosure. He felt it though he did not shew it & spoke for barely 20 minutes. A frightful business getting back to the carriage through the mob.

In Rosebery's speech at the Corn Exchange, which he privately described as 'an admirable financial statement', he described Gladstone's progress—with unintentional candour—as 'a series of well-ordered triumphs'.

. . . From his home in Wales to the Metropolis of Scotland there has been no village too small to afford a crowd to greet him—there has been no cottager so humble that could not find a light to put in his window as he passed. Mothers have brought their babes to lisp a 'hurrah', old men have crept forth from their homes to see him before they died. These have been no prepared ebullitions of sympathy; these have been no calculated demonstrations. The heart of the nation has been touched. . . .

December 5th was the outstanding day. In the morning Gladstone spoke at Glasgow as Lord Rector, pouring scorn on Disraeli's remark in the previous Address that 'Nothing succeeds like success'. In the afternoon he spoke to six thousand people in St Andrew's Hall for an hour and a half, returning to his favourite theme of the 'pestilential' nature of the Disraelian concept of national policy; the assumption by the Queen of the title of Empress of India was 'theatrical bombast and folly'; the Ministry was attempting to lead the British people along a road 'which plunges into suffering, discredit, and dishonour'. And then there was a dinner at the City Hall where the Grand Old Man, not a whit exhausted, continued his thrilling denunciation of the Government. At the close of his speech there were cries of 'Rosebery! Rosebery!' which mounted in volume until Rosebery made a brief speech which was greeted with tumultuous applause. It was apparent that it was not only in Edinburgh that Gladstone's young sponsor was regarded as the rising star of Scotland. 'As to the exhibition of Liberal feeling,' Gladstone wrote to Granville (December 21st), 'it would be hard to describe, impossible to exaggerate. . . . Rosebery has made a great impression, and is a hero not only in Edinburgh but in Glasgow.'

Mr Gladstone and his excited family returned to Hawarden on December 8th. The passions aroused by the first Midlothian campaign did not abate for a decade, and the immediate reactions were violent. 'Lies, invectives, misstatements, imputations of every kind, spring up thickly in every part of the country,' Gladstone wrote to Rosebery on his return to Hawarden, 'and what between answering and determining what to answer, and my huge correspondence rather aggravated, I am a veritable slave. But I hope the tempest will abate.' The tempest, however, grew more fierce as the months passed. The Roseberys—with their baby daughter, Sybil, who had been born in September—spent Christmas at Nice. Midlothian affairs still occupied much of his time, but by now the Liberal organisers were jubilant and were concerned solely with the consolidation of the triumph of November. For Rosebery things were never the same in Scotland again. Lord Crewe's statement that 'The Midlothian campaign of 1879–80 belongs to Gladstone's biography, not to his [Rosebery's]'[1] is a serious misinterpretation of the effects of the campaigns. The impact of the campaign upon the electorate as a whole is a matter of considerable historical controversy; its effects upon Gladstone's claims to the Liberal leadership and upon Rosebery's subsequent career, however, were incalculably great. 'The first time I ever saw Lord Rosebery was in Edinburgh when I was a student,' J. M. Barrie has written, 'and I flung a clod of earth at him. He was a peer; those were my politics. . . . During the first Midlothian campaign Mr Gladstone and Lord Rosebery were the father and son of the Scottish people. Lord Rosebery rode into fame on the top of that wave, and has kept his place in the hearts of the people, and in oleographs on their walls, ever since.'[2]

The first Midlothian campaign gave Rosebery a fabulous reputation in his own country, and not even Chamberlain in Birmingham ever commanded the admiration and veneration which surrounded Rosebery in Scotland. Although he was debarred as a peer from active participation in the campaign, this distinction was neatly drawn by the Liberal organisers. In the November of 1879, for example, Lord Dalkeith made a personal visit to St Cuthbert's Parish, greatly ingratiating himself with the villagers.

[1] Crewe: *Rosebery*, I, 127.
[2] *An Edinburgh Eleven* (1889).

A few days later, prodded urgently by Reid, the Roseberys happened to pass through the village and walked around it, speaking to the cottagers and generally making themselves pleasant. The effect of this fortuitous visit was reported by Reid as 'excellent', and that it had done 'much good in a rather neglected corner'. The Liberal organisers had a tremendous admiration for him, and an unfaltering faith in his power to swing voters. When a particularly nasty pamphlet was issued by the Tories, Richardson wrote with almost awesome deference to Rosebery on February 27th, 1880, that 'If your Ldship were well enough & in the humour, I daresay you could dispose of this clumsily & obscurely expressed attack on Gladstone in a few brilliant sentences'.

The Midlothian campaign affected Rosebery in other ways; for the first time he was genuinely excited by politics, and when in later years he referred to the campaign as 'a chivalrous adventure' he was not posing; the counting of heads, foiling of the Tory agents, and all the rest of the pre-campaign manoeuvres were wholly enjoyable, in the best eighteenth-century traditions, while the regal progress of the old leader touched a very real chord in Rosebery's romantic nature. He was to a considerable extent intoxicated by the glorious events of the first campaign, and, with his name ringing through the land, who can censure him for dreaming spectacular dreams?

It was freely alleged by the disgruntled Conservatives that the Midlothian campaigns cost Rosebery a fortune out of his own pocket, and some credence is given to this story by Edward Hamilton's diary for June 30th, 1882. 'Rosebery said he wanted to economise a little. He had determined to pay the last General Election expenses to which he had been put out of income, and these amounted to £50,000!'[1] This staggering sum of money in a constituency of under three thousand electors—the total Liberal Party central election fund in 1880 was only £33,000[2]—falls under suspicion when examined. Richardson wrote to Rosebery on December 17th, 1879, that 'All the Liberals' expenses (Registra-

---

[1] *Edward Hamilton's Diary* (Brit. Mus. Add. MSS. 48,632).

[2] H. J. Hanham ('British Party Finance, 1868–1880' [*Bulletin of the Institute of Historical Research*, XXVII (1954)]) has stated that 19 Liberal peers contributed approximately £6,000–£8,000 to the 1880 election fund. These calculations, of course, only relate to contributions to central funds.

tion & otherwise) connected with Midlothian are now paid (we
have spent only £168 of yr Ldship's kind donation) & we shall
begin 1880 without a shilling of debt, which is more than Her
Majesty's Ministers can say.' In the January of 1880 Reid reported
that there had been a net loss of £100 on the Corn Exchange
demonstration, and Rosebery, as he had previously promised,
made good this loss. These are the only financial matters mentioned in the considerable collection of papers on the Midlothian
campaigns in Rosebery's papers. It is possible that Rosebery in
his conversation with Hamilton included in his estimate of his
expenditure on the elections the purchase of property in Midlothian—of which the largest single element was the Malleny
estate—which took place at this time. The Liberal organisers
were eager that Rosebery should buy the property for the purpose
of creating faggot votes, but his lawyers, Tods, Murray, and
Jamieson, held a large mortgage on Malleny which they were
anxious to pay off, and Esson, the chief partner and a friend of
Rosebery's, regarded it as an excellent investment (which it
proved to be). Although it is possible that Rosebery would not
have bought Malleny had it not been for the Liberal agents' drawing his attention to the political possibilities of the property, the
final reason was a financial one, and it would not be reasonable
to include it as part of his expenses on the Midlothian elections.
In any event, the purchase of Malleny was not completed
until early in 1882, when Rosebery bought the estate for over
£100,000.

Therefore, the only recorded expenditure by Rosebery directly
related to the Midlothian election was an unknown but probably
small contribution early in the campaign (out of which the £168
mentioned by Richardson in his letter of December 17th, 1879,
was taken) and the £100 to cover the loss on the Corn Exchange
meeting.[1]

Immediately after his return from France in the February of
1880 Rosebery took a Turkish bath in London, a rash developed,
and he felt very unwell; scarlet fever—in those days a serious
malady—was diagnosed, and before he had any chance to make
anything like a full recovery it was apparent that the long-
awaited dissolution was imminent, and, swayed by two un-

[1] Unfortunately the Liberal records of contributions to the election were destroyed
in the last war.

expected by-election victories in February at Southwark[1] and
Liverpool, Beaconsfield announced the impending dissolution of
Parliament on March 8th and issued a manifesto declaring that
peace depended upon Britain's ascendancy in the Councils of
Europe, and that the agitation for Irish Home Rule was a menace
'scarcely less disastrous than pestilence and famine'.

The Midlothian Liberals were delighted, since their campaign
was now reaching its peak. 'On the assumption that a Dissolution
may take place at Easter,' Richardson had written to Rosebery on
February 25th, 'we are making every preparation in Midlothian
for our Election. . . . We expect to see Lord Dalkeith badly
beaten. . . . I have entered into written contracts with cab proprietors to supply us on the Election Day with 73 cabs.'

On March 16th Gladstone commenced the second Midlothian
campaign, with the unwell Rosebery again acting as his host at
Dalmeny. Gladstone was greeted at Edinburgh on the 16th with
a huge crowd, and commenced a whirlwind campaign, speaking
almost every day, and taking in almost all the constituency. On
the 17th Rosebery rented 120, George Street 'as a den of refuge'
and he only made two speeches, at the Glasgow University Gladstone Club (March 29th) and at the Inaugural Banquet of the
Scottish Liberal Club: he had been piqued by a remark of Sir
Stafford Northcote's about his motives for acting as Gladstone's
sponsor, but in the end confined himself to an acid observation at
the banquet on the 31st that 'Proscribed and hunted as our party
is, I never knew, till it fell from the lips of the Chancellor of the
Exchequer, that the very right of asylum is denied to the arch-
criminal of his country (*cheers and laughter*).'

April 5th was the day of decision. The Liberal tide was sweeping strongly in England, but in spite of a façade of confidence,
the Liberal organisers in Midlothian were desperately anxious. A
statement by Dalkeith's agents that the vote was not secret and
that the ballot papers could be examined after the election to see
how people had voted had caused perturbation in what Reid
called 'The Ducal tenantry', and a Liberal denial was not alto-

---

[1] On February 18th Gladstone received the following telegram: 'Southwark
distressing fear success in Midlothian problematical plausible excuse for withdrawal
deserves consideration. . . . Rosebery.' Gladstone, although puzzled, was not completely hoaxed: 'Forgery is within my experience of Tory tactics,' he wrote to
Rosebery. It was subsequently discovered that it had been sent by Lord Claud
Hamilton.

gether convincing. Eviction for voting the wrong way had been
a feature of Scottish politics for so long that the fear remained,
and there was no doubt in the minds of Richardson, Reid, and
Rosebery that many votes would be affected.

April 5th was cold and cheerless. After a nervous morning the
Gladstones drove into Edinburgh at three o'clock and the Roseberys followed two hours later. They all dined together at 120,
George Street at seven o'clock, and at 7.15 Reid was shown into the
dining-room. With some sense of occasion he went up to Gladstone and said, 'Mr Gladstone, I have the pleasure of announcing
to you that you have been elected for Midlothian by a majority of
211.' The figures were Gladstone 1,579, Dalkeith 1,368. Shortly
afterwards the Chief Constable sent a message to the effect that
there was an enormous crowd of over fifteen thousand people in
the street which refused to disperse until Gladstone spoke to
them. He went out on the drawing-room balcony, with his wife
and daughter on either side, holding candles. Rosebery 'sneaked
back to dinner but had a similar message',[1] and went out to find
the crowd swaying and roaring 'Rozbury! Rozbury!' in unison.
He spoke briefly, saying that the victory was one for oppressed
nationalities throughout the world, and that 'To use the words
of Mr Pitt, I will only say that Midlothian, having saved herself
by her exertions, will now save Great Britain by her example.'

Rosebery eventually escaped from the house by an underground
passage to a nearby hotel and 'Thence away by a side street to
Lord Young's. The rest of the party followed for a minute, and
then we drove out to Dalmeny.'

On the following evening the Gladstones were taken in a
brougham to the station with Rosebery on the box and safely
caught their train to Hawarden, 'only the people in or near the
station getting the scent'.

The results were now pouring in from all over the country, and
a large Liberal majority was evident long before over half the
returns were made. Had the franchise not been so limited—particularly in the county districts—the Conservative *débâcle* would
have been on the 1906 scale. Joseph Chamberlain—the forty-four-
year-old champion of truculent Midland radicalism—could
exultantly claim that much of the credit should go to his National

[1] Rosebery's diary for April 5th and 6th, 1880, from which this account is mainly
taken.

Liberal Federation, but in fact it was almost a single-handed victory. It is difficult at this space of time to recapture the astonishing dominance Gladstone exerted over his contemporaries in 1880, particularly when it is contrasted with his bitter unpopularity even a few years before; his shining integrity, his supreme courage, almost hypnotising oratory, all had their effect; but the secret would probably lie in less easily definable factors; how can one explain the devotion of the tens of thousands of unfranchised men and women who flocked to Midlothian save that to them Gladstone was little short of a god? One grows dizzy when compiling the numbers of the crowds which listened to his speeches and crammed the streets just to see his carriage pass by. Although much of what he said was far above their heads, he seemed to confer upon them the glory of equality by treating them with complete sincerity as his fellow-crusaders. 'I am sorry to say we cannot reckon upon the landed aristocracy!' he said to a huge gathering at West Calder on April 2nd. 'We cannot reckon upon the clergy of the Established Church either in England or in Scotland! . . . We cannot reckon upon the wealth of the county, nor upon the wealth of the country! . . . In the main these powers are against us. . . . We must set them down among our most determined foes! But, gentlemen, above all these, and behind all these, *there is the nation itself*. And this great trial is now proceeding before the nation. The nation is a power hard to rouse, but when roused harder still and more hopeless to resist.'

Arthur Godley—who later became Lord Kilbracken—has rescued from obscurity the essay of a young man who attended Gladstone's Marylebone meeting and who was 'Gladstonized'. 'The petty politics of the hour figured as first principles, and the opinions of the people became as the edicts of eternity. As it went on, we became persuaded that the Government . . . were the most incompetent set of reprobates that an angry heaven had ever sent to be the curse of a country. It grew upon us as a marvel why we had not seen this earlier. Why we had lived under such diabolical ineptitude astounded us with a sense of shame; and ever and again was rolled out our patent of nobility, "Fellow-electors of Marrilbone", until we became enlarged, quickened, glorified by our fraternity. . . . All through a speech of long tortuous sentences he endowed us with a faculty of apprehension we did not know we possessed. . . . When I stood in the free air outside once more, it seemed somewhat unreasoning, all this ecstasy; clearly I had been Gladstonized; and I voted for him at that election.'[1]

The one really fascinating fact which emerges from a close study of the Midlothian campaigns is that they seem to have had a surprisingly limited effect upon the few Midlothian electors; the calculations prepared by Reid and Richardson, apart from being very optimistic and inaccurate, show that the bulk of the Gladstonian vote had been secured before Gladstone ever came to the constituency. The suspicions about the Ballot Act, the creation of faggot votes by the Tories, the genuine respect enjoyed by Dalkeith, seem to have had their cumulative effect. Of the vast multitudes who flocked to hear Gladstone in Midlothian only a small minority can have had votes, and of these only a few can have been Midlothian voters. The train of Liberal victories in Scotland must be regarded as the one certain effect of the Midlothian campaigns; the impact upon the English constituencies of what Beaconsfield described as 'the pilgrimage of passion' is more problematical, but was undoubtedly considerable.

There was no doubt of the national revulsion against the last Beaconsfield Administration; the Liberals had won 347 seats, against 240 Conservatives and 65 Irish Nationalists. The Queen, aghast at this calamity, invited Hartington and Granville to form an Administration, but they realised what everyone knew and which the Queen for a time tried not to understand, that Midlothian had swept away their claims. By the evening of April 23rd Gladstone had accepted the Queen's reluctantly proffered commission and had commenced the task of forming his second Administration.

After the triumph Gladstone and Rosebery had exchanged letters of mutual congratulations and goodwill, and at no time was their relationship closer than at this moment. 'I should like to write about these marvellous events but how can I?' Gladstone wrote on April 10th from Hawarden. 'The romance of politics, which befall my old age in Scotland, has spread over the whole land. . . . I suppose the Conservative Scotch will fill a first class compartment, or nearly so, but no more. Wales, I beg you to observe, has not (as I think) been behind Scotland in her achievements. . . . As to Midlothian, the moral effect, before and after, has I think surpassed all our hopes.'

To superficial spectators there seemed very little in common

[1] Lord Kilbracken: *Reminiscences*, 109-12.

between the seventy-year-old statesman, grave, over-earnest, product of Liverpool and Oxford, and the thirty-two-year-old Scottish Peer, possessed of great wealth, a keen votary of the Turf, greatly popular at week-end parties in great houses, with a mordant wit and keen sense of the ridiculous. But Gladstone saw in the younger man a basic seriousness and application which struck a responsive chord; there was his entrancing conversation—of which, perhaps unconsciously, Gladstone was something of a connoisseur—and his fondness for books; above all there was the contempt for anything mean or treacherous and the concept of public life as being something considerably better than a squalid battle for place, which created a bond. Writing of Rosebery to Granville on March 26th, Gladstone declared that 'He is very decidedly a remarkable man, not a mere clever man: and is to be evidently the leader of the Liberal party in Scotland. . . . From the first time I ever saw him I liked him & thought highly of him: but he has opened out upon me marvellously.'

Lord Crewe has remarked that 'Gladstone liked the old ways; and if Hartington or Rosebery enjoyed breeding or running horses, as landowners and statesmen had done for generations in the past, he saw no reason to object to them, any more than to Spencer's hereditary pack of hounds.' But even at this early and most happy period of their relationship it is noticeable that Gladstone's 1880 letters still begin 'My dear Lord Rosebery', and that in his contributions there is little echo to the banter of Rosebery's letters.

On the morrow of Midlothian there was great speculation as to what office Rosebery would receive, but although he was undoubtedly eager to enter the Government, there were difficulties. It was apparent to Lady Rosebery and his doctors that the strain of the second Midlothian campaign had seriously postponed his recovery from the scarlet fever, and he was very seedy at this time. The Conservative charge—repeated on almost every platform in Scotland—that he had only sponsored Gladstone for his own ends stung Rosebery, always acutely sensitive to criticism, to a degree which surprised many of his more experienced political friends. Granville told the Queen on April 28th that 'Lord Rosebery would accept nothing, as he said it would look as if Mr Gladstone had paid him for what he had done.'[1]

[1] *Royal Archives.*

Rosebery was at The Durdans on April 23rd, and received several telegrams from Gladstone asking him to come to London. Perversely, he refused, but at last decided to catch the 5.45 from Epsom, and the events of that evening are best recounted in Rosebery's own words in his diary.

At Vauxhall Hannah met me & told me I could go back as Mr G had been sent for by the Queen. So I returned & telegraphed to Mrs G that I had gone back but wd come up if she telegraphed. Ferdy [Rothschild] at the Durdans just returning redhot to London. . . . In the middle of dinner comes a telegram from Mrs G asking me to come up. So I went up & drove to Harley St. Mr G had returned & was closeted with Granville & Hartington. . . . Presently the Trio came out, Mr G announcing that he had taken the Treasury & Exchequer, & Granville the FO. Hartington told me his office was not quite decided. Drove to the Turf.

On the next morning Rosebery went to The Durdans to collect some papers and on his return to London told his wife that he was off to Mentmore 'to get out of the way'. The diary continues:

. . . H went & told the Gs. Mr G at once said 'Going out of London, he can't go out of London, I want to see him.' H replied that I was very tired & had to start in half an hour. 'Then I will go to him—take me there in your brougham.' H said this was impossible & went to fetch me. When he & I were alone together he said that there were two departments of paramount importance & difficulty in the Govt—one was Foreign Office, the other India. Granville had taken one, Hartington the other. He asked me to represent India in House of Lds— pointing out the great advantage in the fearful odds against me etc. I in a troubled voice told him of my resolution taken a year ago to accept no office. He argued vehemently agst this, took my hand & said there were things between us which he could never forget etc. I much pressed begged for a reprieve. Then we went into the drawing room & he made tea for Mrs G & H & us. He spoke very kindly to H & urged her to use her influence etc.

On April 25th Rosebery decided definitely to refuse office in the Government for the moment, having 'lain awake nearly all night thinking it over, for of course to me it is the most critical moment of my life'.

. . . If I take this appointment, [he wrote to Gladstone] I lose the certainty that what I have done in the matter of the elections, however slight, has been disinterested. In losing that I lose more than political distinction could repay me: I should feel that where I only meant personal devotion & public spirit, others would see & perhaps with reason personal ambition & public office seeking. . . . No, with all gratitude to you, I must remain as I am. Yesterday is a day I can never forget, when I sat with you treated like a son & in possession of this high proof of your confidence and esteem. The memory of that no one can take away from me, whatever motives may be assigned for my answer. . . .

Lord Granville sent a personal appeal, begging Rosebery to reconsider his decision, but without success. 'And so ends my one chance of public life, & I subside to obscurity & turnips,' he recorded in his diary.

'. . . I cannot express to you my feelings of the last 20 hours,' Lady Rosebery wrote to Mrs Gladstone on April 25th. 'I should be more than insincere were I to pretend not to have conjectured about the office Mr Gladstone wd. make to Archie. Perhaps I overestimate my husband's powers, but you both have been invariably kind in your expressions. I felt sure the opportunity for distinction would be offered him. . . . I knew the scruples which would make Archie refuse. No post could be more congenial to him than that which Mr Gladstone has offered. This is a most trying moment for him. Few know, or can realize, the tremendous sacrifice he is making of what he holds most dear, to scruples which few will understand. But you & Mr Gladstone *will* understand, and I will take up no more of your time. . . .'

Health was an additional factor, for Rosebery had not recovered from his attack of scarlet fever, and both his doctors and his wife were insistent that he should take a complete rest. 'There is nothing "grand" in what I have done,' he wrote to Mary Gladstone: '. . . moreover, my real motives are so well known that it would be a waste of time in me to dilate on them. They are:

1. Annoyance at not being asked to join the Cabinet.
2. Dislike of hard work. 3. Passion for the Turf. . . .'[1]

[1] Mr Roy Jenkins, in his biography of Dilke, has stated that Rosebery at this time 'looked forward with some impatience to rapid political preferment. This impatience so impressed itself upon Dilke that, after a walk at Mentmore . . . one Sunday afternoon in May, 1880, he "came to the conclusion that Rosebery was the most ambitious man I had ever met".' (*Sir Charles Dilke: A Victorian Tragedy*, 145–6.) In fact, this comment was not written in 1880 but in 1890 when Dilke was preparing some autobiographical notes and after he had severed his connection with the Roseberys. The full extract from Dilke's Memoir runs, 'From Saturday the 22nd

It was not very long before Gladstone was again pressing him to enter his Administration. On May 9th he tried to persuade him to change his decision in the course of a conversation at Mentmore, and in July the post of Under-Secretary at the India Office (under Hartington) became vacant on the resignation of Lansdowne, and Gladstone invited Rosebery—convalescing at Salzburg—to fill the position. Edward Hamilton, who had just become one of Gladstone's private secretaries for the second time, noted in his diary on July 10th that 'I doubt him accepting the offer, in spite of the "reek" of the election (as Mr G put it to him) being over.' Rosebery's 'cure' was not progressing satisfactorily (on June 21st he recorded in his diary, 'Began my cure. . . . Result of cure, complete depression & exhaustion.') and he wrote gloomily to the Prime Minister on July 14th that 'I may say in strict secrecy that I no longer feel the confidence I did then that my position with regard to my immediate chief would be as mutually agreeable as I then fancied', but his health was the principal factor.

. . . I do not know what is the matter with me, medically speaking, but speaking as the patient, it is prostration physical and mental. I felt tired when I left London, but not the annihilation of the present moment. . . . I hope I am neither a fool nor a hypochondriac. Whether I ever become one or the other I know that I am like a sucked orange now, and that it would be criminal in me to undertake any public function. . . .

'Your father's note burnt a hole in my pocket for four days (and more emphatically four nights) before I sent my answer,' he

May to Monday the 24th [1880] I was at Mentmore with the Roseberys, meeting the Lansdownes and Lord Fife, and in the course of a short walk I discovered Rosebery's immediate ambition, which was to be Governor either of Victoria or New South Wales. . . . I came to the conclusion that Rosebery was about the most ambitious man that I had ever met.' (*Dilke Papers:* Brit. Mus. Add. MSS. 43,934, ff. 195-7.) Even if this opinion has any historical value, it is somewhat difficult to equate Rosebery's ambitions with regard to the 'Governorship of New South Wales' with Mr Jenkins' interpretation of the passage.

Mr Jenkins also states (*op. cit.*, p. 146) that 'Throughout the early years of the Parliament he [Rosebery] and his wife hovered over Dilke's life, as discontented half-friends, constantly inviting him to visit them at their various houses.' In fact, between the beginning of 1880 and the June of 1885 there were only eight such invitations, which seems hardly an excessive amount. Moreover, one of the invitations was at the request of Herbert Bismarck while he was staying with the Roseberys, and another was simply to ask Dilke to spend a night at Dalmeny in the November of 1882 when he was fulfilling a public engagement in Edinburgh. (*Dilke Papers:* Brit. Mus. Add. MSS. 43,876, ff. 104-68.)

wrote to Mary Gladstone on July 21st. 'I had no option. . . .' This is the first indirect reference to the insomnia from which Rosebery had begun to suffer in the late 1870's and which was to plague him at moments of stress and anxiety for the remainder of his life with increasing severity.

When Edward Hamilton wrote to Rosebery, expressing his regret at the decision, he replied from Gastein on July 19th that 'At any rate I could not undertake an office which, if I went home to enter upon, I might have to resign in a month: and which, if I had availed myself of Mr Gladstone's & Hartington's kind offer, I might not have been able to fill after all.' These reasons were accepted by the Prime Minister, who remarked that Rosebery seemed 'low about himself'. Hamilton noted on July 21st that 'His doctors say he must have further rest & not, for the present, take to an official life. But for this, he evidently would now be pleased to take office.'

Rosebery continued to be 'low about himself' for the rest of the summer and early autumn. On August 18th he announced that he would be humbugged by no more cures and was returning home: the Roseberys arrived at The Durdans on September 3rd, and the only entry in his diary for that day is 'Durdans—Repose'. He did not improve matters by taking a bad fall off a horse at Mentmore on September 16th. 'My bill for coats & trousers should be nothing this year,' he informed Gladstone on September 17th, 'but I anticipate ruin in dressing gowns & slippers!' In November he was still grumbling and 'rather in the dumps at being so easily tired'. 'Rosebery is greatly better,' Gladstone wrote to Granville from Mentmore, 'but he is *physically* rather too self-conscious, perhaps, for his health.'

There was some dismay in certain political quarters at Rosebery's absence from the Ministry. There had been acute disillusionment on the Radical wing when Gladstone had announced his Government, for of the eleven major positions, eight went to confirmed Whigs. Only Joseph Chamberlain, entering the Cabinet in the humble capacity of President of the Board of Trade, Sir William Harcourt (Home Secretary), and the aged John Bright (Chancellor of the Duchy of Lancaster) could be properly described as belonging to the radical element in the Liberal Party, while Sir Charles Dilke had to be content with the undersecretaryship of the Foreign Office. This serious imbalance was the basic defect of the Government, and Harcourt, Chamberlain, and Dilke were anxious that Rosebery should join in some capacity. Lady Rosebery was often approached by them to see if she could persuade her husband to change his mind, but she could only reply that his recovery must precede any possibility of political activity. There were several people who did not believe her, and when she tackled Gladstone after a dinner in the August of 1880 she found herself being misunderstood.

Mr and Mrs G dined with us. After dinner I seized a moment to talk about Archie, and said I wished he had some work to do, as I believed it was what his brain required and should do good to his physical health. He answered, alluding to official work, 'But then there is nothing now to give him'. I was horrified at seeming to hint at office, when I meant nothing of the sort, and endeavoured to explain I meant to work at a subject. Mr Gladstone may be a marvel of erudition, but he will never understand a man, still less a woman. . . .

It was the first of many similar misunderstandings which were caused by Lady Rosebery's all-absorbing interest in her husband and by Rosebery's own reserve and fastidiousness. His interest in politics was now fully aroused, and occupied much of his time and thoughts; he was undeniably ambitious, and his fear of appearing to 'push' himself did not obscure his desire to rise to high office and wield power which he felt he was qualified to do. These legitimate aspirations were bedevilled by his quite extraordinary position in Scotland.

On November 5th, still suffering from the after-effects of his illness, he gave his delayed Rectorial Address at Aberdeen. He was met at the station by a wildly excited crowd which insisted upon dragging his carriage to the hotel where he was staying. After the Principal of the University had been unable to make a single sentence audible above the clamour of 'miniature fog-horns, toy musical instruments, bells, and other contrivances', Rosebery's speech was listened to in a respectful silence and was tumultuously applauded for several minutes after he had sat down. He began with the modest observation that he must have been elected as Rector by the students 'from sympathy rather than respect, from a sense of kinship rather than a hope of guidance', and from that moment the audience was captured. 'The history of Scotland, which has been for centuries little less than a long martyrdom', he said, 'is not a cold register of dates and treaties; it stirs the blood like a trumpet.' His description of Scotland's position in the Union as 'like nothing so much as a poor man marrying an heiress' was sly in view of the canards about his marriage which still circulated and about which Rosebery was painfully aware. 'It is mortifying to pride at first; irksome perhaps occasionally; in the long run harmonious, because founded on interest; eventually it may be moulded into love by the beauty of its off-spring.'

On the day after the Aberdeen speech it was announced that he had been elected Lord Rector of Edinburgh University after a close contest with a very popular local Conservative. At the beginning of November he presided over a banquet in Edinburgh in honour of W. P. Adam, who had been appointed Governor of Madras; it was a vast affair, with much impassioned speechifying. 'When my health was proposed', Rosebery wrote to Gladstone on November 4th, 'the audience which had been 500 was about the ordinary quorum of the House of Lords.'

1881 opened with the birth of a second daughter[1] for the Rose-berys at The Durdans on January 1st. Her arrival was somewhat premature and Mrs Lionel Cohen, Lady Rosebery's aunt, super-intended the delivery. When all was over at two o'clock in the afternoon the doctors arrived. Shortly after this event Rosebery was the object of much condolence when he was blackballed for the Travellers' Club. His proposers were distraught, but Rosebery was unconcerned. 'One of the minor results of the Midlothian Election was to close to me any London Club of which I was not a member,' he wrote to Lord Houghton on February 4th. 'As I was already a member of eighteen this was of the less conse-quence.'

Throughout the winter of 1880-1 Rosebery immersed himself in the subject of Scottish administration. The situation was ripe for critical examination, since Scotland had no Secretary of State, and was administered, so far as the central government was concerned, by the Lord Advocate. For some time this ridiculous state of affairs had been the subject of Scottish protest but nothing whatever had been done. Early in December Harcourt paid a visit to Mentmore and was so struck by Rosebery's arguments that he urged Gladstone to appoint a Scottish Minister, but with-

[1] Lady Margaret Primrose. She married the Marquess of Crewe in 1899.

out effect. Rosebery summarised his objections to the existing arrangements in a memorandum sent to Harcourt a month later.

> . . . Now my object in writing is to point out that this is both bad & absurd. You choose your Scottish minister . . . from among one or two Scottish lawyers who may never have been in the House of Commons at all and have had little experience of the world outside the law courts of Edinburgh. . . . At present you have no Scottish lawyer in the House, for though one has been elected he has not taken his seat, while you have a dozen tried & experienced Scottish members who would represent Scotland admirably in the House but who are debarred from doing so by the fact that they are not lawyers. . . .
>
> It has often been proposed that there should be revived the secretaryship of state for Scotland. I think this is more than is required. The late Government, on the other hand, wished to establish an undersecretaryship for Scotland, which appears open to the opposite objection that it would be not quite enough. There would be a feeling of soreness in Scotland at being handed over to an under secretary, for the Scots as you know are touchy & sensitive in these matters. But that is a difficulty that would be easily got over. Take one of the old Scottish offices, & attach it to the Home Office. There is, for instance, the post of President of the Privy Council of Scotland which was suppressed at the time of the Union. . . .

In a further letter, Rosebery drew attention to another absurdity in the arrangement. 'When the ministry goes out, the Lord Advocate usually takes refuge on the bench. If a Scottish lawyer languishes in opposition he usually languishes in Edinburgh looking after his practice. . . . The fact is that hardly any Scottish lawyer can *afford* to lead a political life in Opposition. . . .'

Harcourt was so impressed by the desirability of getting Rosebery into the Government that when the talented but erratic Duke of Argyll severed his somewhat tenuous connection with the Ministry in the spring of 1881, he urged Gladstone to appoint Rosebery to the vacant post of Lord Privy Seal. Rosebery, Harcourt wrote, seemed to be irritated and disappointed by the fact that he had been left alone for so long, and the offer of the Privy Seal might help to soothe his ruffled feelings. Harcourt also believed that Rosebery was piqued at not being consulted as to Argyll's successor. 'I did my best to smooth him down, but only with partial success,' Harcourt wrote. 'One of the symptoms of provocation is that he wholly declines to be consulted on Scotch business, on which I was in the habit of taking his opinion, as he says "that he has now no relations of any kind with the Government. . . ." I am sure you will be able to administer an anodyne to his wounded spirit when you return to town—but it is wanted.' Gladstone was understandably startled by this information, and replied to Harcourt that 'The notion of a title to be consulted on succession to a Cabinet office is absurd . . . I believe Rosebery to have a very modest estimate of himself, and trust he has not fallen into so gross an error.'

Lady Rosebery had the first of several sharp exchanges with Mrs Gladstone, which subsequently caused her considerable alarm. On April 25th she asked for Dilke's advice. 'She has been silly,' Dilke wrote in his Diary, 'but Mrs Gladstone is so silly also that rows are inevitable.'[1]

Edward Hamilton was as surprised as the Premier and noted in his diary for April 22nd:

It appears that Rosebery positively was mortified at the idea of not having been consulted about the succession to the Privy Seal. Really, to set up such a claim is preposterous. I am very sorry for it, for I believed better things of him. Mr G is extremely concerned. What Rosebery evidently wants is to be lifted straight into the Cabinet without subordinate office; and if that is not feasible to be taken into consultation regarding the constitution of the Cabinet! on which Cabinet Ministers themselves are not consulted except such men as Ld G[ranville] & Ld Hartington.

This was probably unfair, as both Gladstone and Hamilton soon realised. 'I begin to believe the Rosebery rumours are a canard only,' Gladstone wrote to Granville on April 26th. 'If you talk to him confidentially on public matters, it will probably blow over.' 'But it is no canard,' Granville replied on the 27th. On the 29th he repeated that Gladstone should treat Rosebery more considerately. 'I very much doubt communications with the Countess,' he added. 'Women always are more unreasonable than their husbands about the claims of these, and this seems to be especially the case with Hannah. A little confidential talk with him on the state of Affairs would more likely soothe him than anything else.'

Harcourt's advocacy and reports of Rosebery's discontent had

[1] *Dilke Papers.*

gone rather further than even Lady Rosebery, whose attitude prompted his approach to the Prime Minister, had intended. It would appear, indeed, that Rosebery himself was ignorant of the whole affair from beginning to end. 'As to asking me for news,' he wrote to Mary Gladstone on April 22nd from The Durdans, 'you might as well ask a toad which has been imbedded in marble for a thousand years. My news is how much milk & eggs we produce daily or the direction of the wind & the prospects of rain.' All correspondence on the incident was between Harcourt and Lady Rosebery, who was mortified by the fact that her husband was still fretting in comparative idleness, and restless beyond measure. The letters which passed between Harcourt and Lady Rosebery have a faintly conspiratorial air, and it is noticeable that it was to the wife that Harcourt conveyed his regrets at the outcome of his intervention. On Good Friday he wrote to her as follows:

. . . But do not believe that I shall let this affair rest where it is. I believe you know the real admiration & respect I feel for Rosebery & how much I desire that he should achieve the position which his abilities—and what is more his industry (without which ability goes but little way) honestly deserves. But it is for this very reason that I preach to you above all things at the present moment *Patience Patience Patience*. 'Tout vient à qui sait attendre' and you will never regret the self control of today. Be satisfied he has good friends who will not allow his just claims to be forgotten or neglected & leave to us the best time and manner of advancing them. In these things a man's friends are better judges than he can be himself and—forgive me for saying it—than his *wife*.

Above all don't let a word be whispered to Scotland. Rosebery's position there is far too considerable and assured to allow of its being jeopardised—and it ought not to be compromised for a moment by a foolish step.

Rely upon it that all that ought to be said will be said in the quarters it ought to reach.

I have nothing more at heart than to repay the immense kindness I have received from R by establishing the right to be looked upon as a *true friend*. . . .

In view of Harcourt's probably unintentional disservice to Rosebery, some of the weighty sentiments in this tendentious letter might have appeared somewhat curious to Lady Rosebery, but, unaware of the true situation, she replied at once.

. . . Had I required any assurance of your friendship your kind letter, received yesterday, would have amply given it to me. I can only say I thoroughly believe and trust your feeling for Archie in which I hope I may consider to have a share. I am not impatient in the sense you describe; certainly not to the degree you imagine, but as I owned to you I feel pained at the manner of the last proceedings to an extent which I cannot find words to express and which shakes completely my belief in those whose friendliness hitherto I could scarcely doubt. . . .

In this incident and its sequel a pattern of events is seen which was to recur again and again in the complicated Rosebery-Gladstone relationship. Gladstone frequently misinterpreted the actions of the Roseberys as being motivated by personal ambition; this neither surprised nor particularly disturbed Gladstone, who was remarkably sturdy in his attitude to the political jungle, and surprisingly generous to ambitious juniors, particularly men like Dilke and Chamberlain, whose principles distressed him no less than their curious attitude to Cabinet secrecy.[1] It is difficult to believe that many modern Prime Ministers would be so lenient towards their junior colleagues, but Gladstone was less sensitive on these matters than many historians have imagined.

But Rosebery was one of his blind spots, and was always to remain so. He admired him intensely, and praised him with great enthusiasm to his closest colleagues, but he seemed to shy away from saying the same things to the man himself. This was destined to be the fundamental cause of the subsequent cleavage between the two men in the years 1892–5; at almost every stage of their complex and tragic relationship a word of sympathy, understanding, and encouragement from the older man to the younger would have averted countless misunderstandings. Rosebery was still unwell in the spring of 1881, and wrote to Gladstone on February 23rd that 'I am still a leper as regards putting pen to paper & a pariah as regards society.' His letters at this time were rather formal and even gloomy; when he invited the Gladstones to Dalmeny (March 16th) he ended his letter, 'Pray do not summarily dismiss the idea', and when Gladstone asked him to call upon him to discuss local government reform and Rosebery omitted to reply to the invitation, the Prime Minister was not

[1] Chamberlain, Dilke, and W. E. Forster (then Chief Secretary for Ireland) all communicated Cabinet secrets to the Press at this time.

unjustifiably irritated, and thus, at even this early period, the pattern of mutual incomprehension between the two men was established. But it was apparent that the time was rapidly approaching when Rosebery would again be urged to join the Ministry. 'As the months flew on', Lord Crewe has written, 'the absence from the Government of such a conspicuous figure ... became more and more noticeable.' 'I hope', a new acquaintance, John Morley (not yet in the House of Commons),[1] wrote to Rosebery, 'it is not an impertinence in me to say that I am getting rather impatient to see you among the Government magnates.'

[1] He had unsuccessfully contested Westminster in the 1880 election, and won Newcastle-on-Tyne in a by-election in February 1883.

CHAPTER FOUR

A MINISTERIAL INTERLUDE

THE ADMINISTRATION WHICH HAD ENTERED office in the spring of 1880 with such glowing expectations, supported by overwhelming majorities in the House of Commons, and fortified by the enthusiasm of the electorate, presented an unhappy spectacle within twelve months of its accession. The majority in the House of Commons had proved to be of an independent temper and had already inflicted a major humiliation upon the Ministry by expelling Mr Bradlaugh from the House against the advice of the Government after he had claimed his right to affirm rather than take the Oath of Allegiance. Other Government defeats on minor issues had illuminated the difficult nature of the Ministerial rank and file. These vexing disputations had not been confined to the back benches.

The problem of Ireland, which had seemed so comparatively trivial in the early summer of 1880, had assumed dark and sinister proportions by the autumn of the same year. Sheer hunger, bitter despair, the accumulated miseries of many years, all combined with grim coalition to render the condition of the peasants desperate. The well-intentioned but inopportune repeal of the Peace Preservation Act by the new Government had compromised its position when the appalling increase in evictions and the consequential agrarian outrages scarred the later months of 1880. The Viceroy (Lord Cowper) and the Chief Secretary, W. E. Forster, appealed to Whitehall for increased powers and reinforcements with which the Administration attempted to combat the rapidly deteriorating situation. The winter of 1880–1 was catastrophic for the Ministry. A prosecution for conspiracy was brought against Parnell and thirteen of his countrymen; the case ended in the disagreement of the jury, the dismissal of the charges, the elevation of Parnell's already considerable reputation in Ireland and the utter humiliation of the English Government.

The whole fabric of Irish society was shaken by the increasing number of outrages; cattle were maimed, houses fired, hay-ricks destroyed, and, after the shooting of Lord Mountmorres in County Galway, murder entered the armoury of the desperate peasants. 'Boycotting' was an effective novelty, almost impossible for the Government to combat; Parnell, bleak and chilling, did nothing to alleviate the deteriorating situation. The Ministry reluctantly and with indecision turned to coercion, and the struggle was transferred to the House of Commons, where the Irish Nationalist Members fought every provision with unexampled fierceness and resolution; 'obstruction' ceased to be a nuisance, and was developed into a highly organised and ruthless method of bringing the Commons to a standstill. The Speaker was obliged to bring a forty-hour sitting to an end on his own responsibility, and the ugly weapon of the Closure was conceived. Although the official Conservative Parliamentary Opposition was weak, a new and independent figure was emerging from below the gangway in the House of Commons on the Conservative side; Randolph Churchill, impudent, audacious, indefatigable, was embarking upon his astonishing rise to eminence.

As if all this was not enough, South Africa erupted when the Boers, impatient for the promised disannexation of the Transvaal, rose in the last month of 1880 and annihilated the wretchedly inadequate British force which advanced to crush the uprising. Majuba Hill marked the culmination of this humiliating episode, and the Ministry was forced to negotiate a peace which inflamed British public opinion and which lit the train for a later and more terrible conflagration. Beset on all sides with these grave issues, occupied with acrimonious Cabinets and doubting colleagues, it was not surprising that Gladstone had little time to devote to a single disgruntled follower.

In the train of coercive legislation for Ireland came remedial measures to ease the critical land question, and Scotland stirred at her continued neglect. Rosebery broached his scheme for a Minister for Scotland in a speech in the House of Lords which was widely reported in Scotland. 'The words Home Rule have begun to be distinctly and loudly mentioned in Scotland ... I believe that the late Lord Beaconsfield, on one occasion in Scotland, implored the people of Scotland to give up "mumbling the dry bones of political economy, and munching the remainder biscuit of effete Liberalism". I believe the people of Scotland, at the present moment, are mumbling the dry bones of political neglect, and munching the remainder biscuit of Irish legislation.' The Scottish Press, led by Charles Cooper in *The Scotsman*, took the cue, and the campaign steadily increased throughout the summer of 1881.

Various tentative proposals were made to Rosebery during the early summer of 1881. On May 9th, while staying at The Durdans, Granville invited Rosebery to take the Under-Secretaryship at the India Office, but the offer was refused. On May 14th Rosebery was invited to Downing Street and 'speaking with great plainness' told Gladstone that the office did not attract him as it would divorce him from Scotland. He added that he was concerned by Gladstone's attitude to ministerial promotion, where age and length of service were the paramount considerations, and that he did not wish 'to be buried in subordinate office till I was 60'. On the 18th Rosebery again saw Gladstone and repeated his objection. At the beginning of June Gladstone stayed at The Durdans, and was delighted by his visit, a delight which was not marred by Rosebery hitting a tennis ball through an open window behind which the Prime Minister was enjoying a peaceful Sunday.

At the end of July a vacancy occurred at the Home Office when Mr Leonard Courtney was promoted, and Harcourt wrote to Gladstone on the 27th to say 'I think you know how sincerely I am anxious that Rosebery should join the Government for all reasons, and particularly on the ground of my great personal regard for him.' Rosebery was accordingly offered the post with special responsibilities for Scottish business, and he accepted. 'You are always devising some friendly plan for me,' he wrote to the Prime Minister on August 1st, 'and I fear you must often have thought me crotchetty with regard to them.' 'I hope that among the many good works you may do at the Home Office', Eddie Hamilton wrote on August 5th, 'you will do your best to mollify the somewhat rough manners of your Secretary of State which too frequently give offence.'

The arrangement so far as Scottish business was clearly unsatisfactory, particularly as the control of the Lord Advocate appeared to be as complete as before, but Gladstone gave Rosebery a broad hint that it was purely temporary. 'I do not think that the arrangement would last very long in its present form,' he wrote to Rosebery. 'There *must* be within the next six months further manipulation of political affairs: and with this there is the likelihood of development uncertain as to time, but certain, and so more than a likelihood as to that element.' With this understanding, Rosebery entered the Government at the age of thirty-four, to the approbation of Scotland. His Ministerial career opened inauspiciously, as his diary for August 12th reveals.

Land Bill in House of Lords. I ordered a grouse punctually at 8 at Brooks', went to eat it, returned in about half an hour & found I had missed the divisions! A nice beginning for a subordinate of the Govt.

Not long after this sad episode, he narrowly escaped death on September 22nd when the horses of his coach stampeded while he and a friend were passing through Ayr on their return to Dalmeny from Ayr Races. The carriage rocketed down a very steep road, the postilion having been thrown off, and disaster was averted by the heroic intervention of a local farmer, Mr William Young, who grabbed one of the horses and eventually brought them under control. It was with some difficulty that the news of what was very nearly a fatal accident was kept from Lady Rosebery—who was expecting her third baby—but the secret was kept.

The arrangement under which Rosebery entered the Government was essentially a patchwork affair. Harcourt never lost an opportunity of assuring Rosebery that he earnestly desired a 'proper' Minister for Scotland, but that until Gladstone had resolved the Irish question there could be little hope of any positive action. It was not long before the impossible nature of the situation in which he found himself began to prey upon Rosebery's febrile and over-sensitive mind. 'Already I find the Department in confusion and despair at the loss of a House of Commons Under-Secretary,' Harcourt informed Gladstone within a week of Rosebery's appointment. When John Maclaren, the Lord Advocate, was removed from his position by Harcourt, Rosebery declared that he would resign if his name was associated with the incident. It was an unpleasant opening to their official relationship. Harcourt, as Sir Winston Churchill has written, 'was a genial, accomplished Parliamentarian, a party man, ambitious in a calculating style, a Falstaffian figure, with an eye fixed earnestly but by no means unerringly, upon the main chance'.[1] He had been

---

[1] *Great Contemporaries*, 23.

in public life for fifteen years before he entered the Cabinet, and had already acquired a reputation for rudeness and asperity; when he was proposed for Solicitor-General in 1873 Sir John (later Lord) Coleridge warned Gladstone that 'I think him not of a loyal temper & I am sure he would be found an impossible colleague', a forecast abundantly confirmed by events.[1] 'Wealth in the real sense being indifferent to him, small honours beneath his consideration, and overpowering enthusiasm for the greater ideals foreign to his nature,' E. T. Raymond has written, 'what remained as the motive power sufficing to propel the vast bulk of this political galleon through the cross currents of over thirty years of varied navigation? The answer would seem to be sheer love of the game of politics.'[2]

For a while after the Maclaren affair all went well. 'This letter', Rosebery wrote to Gladstone on August 30th from Dalmeny, 'is so trivial & rambling and generally futile that it may be well to mention that its object is to induce you to come here.' In October he was offered the vacant Order of the Thistle, which he politely declined, as he seemed to do to everything on principle at the first offer. Edward Hamilton stayed at Dalmeny for the first time in October and was delighted by his host and hostess. On November 28th he saw Rosebery at Woodcote, and found him 'perfectly charming and delightfully agreeable. He fascinates me greatly.' On December 29th he dined in the splendours of Lansdowne House, which the Roseberys had rented from Lansdowne at £3,000 a year.

It is certainly one of the most charming houses—if not *the* most charming house, in London. It has all the appearance of a country house deposited in the best part of Town. It just suits the Roseberys. They dislike and have outgrown their house in Piccadilly; & while they occupy Lansdowne House, Rosebery will have time to build on his new site at Knightsbridge.[3]

The friendship between the Roseberys and Hamilton grew very quickly. Hamilton, nicknamed 'the Cob' on account of his cheerfulness and jaunty little figure, was a hard-working, shrewd, and extremely affable person, and he shared Rosebery's love for

---

[1] See R. R. James, 'Mr. Gladstone and the Greenwich Seat'. (*History Today*, May, 1959.)

[2] *Portraits of the Nineties*, 151.

[3] This project came to nothing.

beautiful things and keen appreciation of good food and wine. He was one of the very few men who ever called Rosebery 'Archie'; in an age when christian names were rarely used, this betokened a very special relationship.[1] Although he was devoted to Rosebery, Hamilton was one of the few people who could argue with him on level terms, and Rosebery often took his advice, which was usually given extremely forcefully. He was an excellent *raconteur*, and Lady Rosebery became as fond of him as Rosebery was. The formal 'Dear Mr Hamilton' of her early letters became 'Dear Mr Eddie' or 'Dear Mr E' by 1881–2, eventually to become, like her husband's, 'My dear Eddie'. Her affection was warmly returned. After her death he wrote that 'Her judgement as a whole was singularly sound and calm: indeed, there was a sort of intuitive wisdom about the advice which she would tender, the course which she would recommend, or the consequences she would foretell. . . . Having the power of seeing through people quickly, she gauged the characters of her fellow-creatures with great perspicacity. . . . She was one of those born to direct; and with this birthright she had in a notable degree the faculty of getting other people to work and of quickening their energies.'

On April 18th, 1882, they went to see the notorious Lily Langtry in *She Stoops to Conquer*, which they both regarded as an appropriate title. To their surprise they found her 'very passable' on the stage. This visit was occasioned by the fact that Gladstone was endeavouring to 'rescue' Mrs Langrty, and had also recommenced his night-walking activities to recover prostitutes.[2] He had told Mrs Langtry that she could make use of the 'two envelope' arrangement when she wrote to him, so that her letters would not be opened by his secretaries. Her handwriting became rather too familiar for the peace of mind of the secretaries, and Hamilton and Rosebery agreed that Gladstone must be warned of the grave risk to his private and public reputation which he was running by these actions, which although of a most Christian nature, were open to some misconstruction. On February 9th, Rosebery and Hamilton tossed a coin to see who should under-

---

[1] It is always possible to date Rosebery's friendships. His Eton contemporaries called him 'Dalmeny' or just 'D', and Oxford friends 'Ladas'. Hamilton was one of the very few people outside the family circle who called him 'Archie'.

[2] See Magnus: *Gladstone*, 305–6.

take the delicate and disagreeable task of presenting these facts
to the Prime Minister. Rosebery lost, and, having made an
excuse for an interview, tactfully broached the subject on February 10th. 'Mr G took it in good grace,' Hamilton noted with
relief, '& was apparently impressed with Rosebery's words,
which will (I am in hopes) have a good effect.'

Rosebery's departmental duties were comparatively light and
mainly formal, while his Parliamentary responsibilities were
confined to a few answers and the occasional brief speech.
Harcourt, who wanted an Under-Secretary in the Commons, was
equally dissatisfied with the situation, but on the assumption that
the arrangement was only temporary they consented to carry on
with it for the time being. Rosebery's reputation in Scotland
continued to improve: he delivered a series of speeches in the
autumn of 1882 to very large crowds, dealing mainly with the
serious Irish situation, and in August he had been made a Privy
Councillor, the ceremony being performed at Holyrood. For
some reason—almost certainly the recollection of the Midlothian
campaigns—the Queen was extremely cold towards the Roseberys,[1]
and it was some time before the unfortunate impression which
she gave was removed. 1882 opened with the birth of a son, who
was christened Albert Edward Harry Meyer Archibald[2]—'names
enough in all conscience', the father remarked—whose godfathers
were the Prince of Wales and the Duke of Cleveland. The fact
that Rosebery had not yet shed his pose of world-weariness was
demonstrated by his reply to Mary Gladstone's congratulations.
'I cannot pretend to be much excited about an event which occurs
to almost every human being & which may cause me a good deal
of annoyance.' In March he wrote to invite the Gladstones to
The Durdans for Easter:

Forgive, GLADSTONIA, if I ask
In ardent phrase and halting rhyme,
What plans of pleasure thou has formed
For the recess at Eastertime?

---

[1] 'Council at 3. Queen black as thunder. I sworn in,' Rosebery recorded in his
diary for August 26th.
[2] The present Earl of Rosebery.

Thy mother shall adore the babes,
And all their budding charms admire:
Both Sybil pert and Margaret sweet,
And Albert Edward Harry Meyer. ....

In April there occurred a no less significant event in Rosebery's life. For many years Barnbougle Castle, which lies on a small promontory in the Firth of Forth barely half a mile from Dalmeny House, and which had been the headquarters of the Rosebery family until 1819, had been a gradually disintegrating ruin. Only the main tower was standing, and Rosebery's grandfather had thought of having it pulled down, but he was urged to preserve it by the local seamen who used it as a leading mark. Rosebery decided to rebuild the Castle around the tower. The new Barnbougle contained a large hall on the first and second floors with a minstrel's gallery, a large study for Rosebery, and a library, a bathroom—equipped with a gorgeous marble bath—and bedroom on the top floor. These rooms have a wonderful attraction. The bedroom, although very small, looks out over the sea on both sides, giving the impression of being a ship's cabin; a perfectly proportioned library, only a few yards from the bedroom, overlooks the Park, and, although small by Rosebery's standards, is peaceful and very comfortable. Rosebery planted a small wood between Barnbougle and Dalmeny House, which in a few years made the isolation of the Castle even more noticeable. In Barnbougle Rosebery gathered many of his books and collected and displayed his treasures, which even at this time were considerable. Barnbougle gradually became Rosebery's personal shrine, where he spent a great deal of his time, revelling in his isolation. Only a very few favoured persons were permitted to enter it; even his devoted sister, Lady Leconfield, never went into the Castle in her brother's lifetime. In later years, Barnbougle saw more of Rosebery than did Dalmeny itself, but even in the 1880's he spent much of his time there, and his children, looking out from the nursery, would see his stocky figure walking across the Park to lunch at the house, his cape fluttering around him. When the new Barnbougle was at last completed to his satisfaction, he wrote to his wife the first of innumerable letters from his new study.

Barnbougle Castle,
April 7 1882.
11.30 p.m.

My dear little woman—

I have just got here and write you the first line of tidings from the new-old house. I entered it with a bowl of salt resting on a bible according to the old Scottish custom I have somewhere read of. It is all beautiful & delightful. . . .

Your own
A

'It was a strange feeling re-inhabiting the disused home of one's predecessors,' he wrote in his diary. 'It was delightful sleeping in the room over the walnut room with the outlook entirely sea.'

Irish affairs caused a remorseless darkening of the political sky. Parnell and several of his leading supporters had been imprisoned in Kilmainham Jail in the autumn of 1881 after the announcement of his intention to hinder the working of the Land Act passed earlier in the year as Gladstone's first attempt to grapple with the injustices which lay behind the agrarian revolution. Rosebery's attitude to these events represented that of the vast majority of Liberal supporters: a real endeavour had been made to conciliate Irish feeling, and it had been contemptuously rejected; a situation which bordered on anarchy must be met with resolute measures, and it was not for the Conservatives to jeer at these actions. 'Have we advanced an inch, have we advanced a foot, have we advanced a yard, in the last century, towards making Ireland more reconciled and more prosperous under our rule?' he demanded in a great speech at Hull on December 7th, 1881. 'We can but sow the seed hoping that if we ourselves are not spared, others may reap the harvest.' He counselled patience in the face of extreme Irish provocation. 'We are dealing with an exceptional race, and an exceptional state of things; but even in dealing with these we need not tremble nor falter, if we are guided by the light of justice and truth.' (Greenock, November 4th, 1881.)

But Scotland's discontent at her treatment, fully shared by Rosebery, grew when she compared it with that accorded to Ireland. In the April of 1882 negotiations—in which Chamberlain took a leading part—were opened for Parnell's release, and in return for a promise to work for the improvement of the Irish Question from Parnell, the Government proposed an Arrears

Bill to indemnify those peasants not covered by the 1881 Land Act. On the public announcement of what was dubbed the 'Kilmainham Treaty', both Cowper and Forster resigned from the Government and the apparently defunct Conservative Opposition, finding an unexpected champion in the almost unknown young Arthur Balfour, assailed the Ministry in the Commons.

Rosebery was startled and dismayed by the situation. On May 3rd he had a long talk with Lord Frederick Cavendish, who had been appointed Chief Secretary in succession to Forster, and on May 4th he noted in his diary, 'Situation of affairs gloomy and desperate.' The Roseberys then went down to The Durdans, where Rosebery brooded unhappily over the crisis. 'I am clear that I disagree with the policy of Govt.,' he wrote in his diary for May 6th, 'but am almost clear that I ought not to resign.' He resolved to see Gladstone and to ask him about 'the exact position of a subordinate like myself with reference to Cabinet policy'.

He set down his views of the situation in a long personal memorandum which was destined never to be completed.[1]

My position is somewhat complicated at this moment. The Cabinet on its own responsibility has entered in an undertaking to be justified only by success. The men whom it releases are in no respect different to what they were when it imprisoned them. It is believed that if humoured they will range themselves on the side of order. The proof of this is but slender, and affects only one of them. But their predominance and success depend not upon order, but upon disorder; their influence will disappear if they act with the Government just as the influence of other Irish leaders disappeared under like circumstances. The head may come over, but will the tail follow?

Again, some measure of coercion or restraint must be introduced. There must be arrests and will be arrests, because there are irreconcilables in Ireland whom it is necessary to keep out of the way. How many arrests will this new alliance bear? How many will it be allowed to bear? If it bears any will it not be discredited? The first act of coercion will be the signal of a new departure not in the Government but in the Irish party, probably headed by Dillon. But, you will say, you could not leave them in for ever.—No, but why let them out

[1] On page 152 of volume I of Lord Crewe's *Rosebery*, it is stated that this document 'does not exist'. It was discovered, quite accidentally, together with the memorandum of the interview with Gladstone on August 1st, 1882, in the back of a loose-leaved notebook at Barnbougle at a late stage of my researches. This is an excellent example of the difficulty of presenting, at even this length of time, a complete catalogue of the Rosebery Papers.

before your new measures are promulgated? If they approve these measures they will wreck you. Would it not have been better to introduce all your measures and then, having shewn your hand both to the suspects and to Ireland, you would know the effect of them on Ireland and be able to sound the suspects and to judge if you could rely on the support of either or both. Now you are bound while they are free. The birds have flown; it is you who are in the cage.

What then is my personal relation to these events? This is not egotism, but honour. Nicety of honour can hardly be carried to too great a length.

This is emphatically a new departure. There was no question of alliance with, or reliance upon, Mr Parnell when I joined the Government. I suddenly find myself embarked on an enterprise which I cannot justify or defend. If I remain in the Government I am for life connected, however humbly, with this policy, just as every lord-in-waiting has to bear his share: and yet this policy I believe to be a fatal mistake.

What then am I to do? Should I not resign? This it would seem is my obvious course. But it is not so obvious. In the first place, my position in the Government is so humble and one that no one could believe that, if I remain in, I remain from regard to my place. It was no doubt higher than my merits deserved, but nevertheless to me personally the acceptance of it was a great sacrifice: nay, my retention of it is a sacrifice and irksome to a degree which many may not understand. So if I remain in office I cannot suspect my own motives whatever others may do.

In the second place there is my connection with Mr Gladstone. By that I mean my personal devotion to him, and my sense that he deserves all support at this moment. If I fail him in this hour of need, for such it is, it is a personal defection which he would feel much more than my position in the Government would indicate. I do not think that I could bring myself to join the Government now if I were outside it, but I am not sure that I should leave it, being inside it.

If I could find a pretext for leaving the Government without paining Mr Gladstone, I should go at once. If I were ill I should insist on going. If I were in the Cabinet it would have been necessary to go.

He then wrote to Gladstone, asking for an interview, and apologising for troubling him 'for I feel as if I were a fly perching on the incubus which already weighs down Atlas'.

The tortuous Memorandum was never completed and the letter to Gladstone never sent. On the morning of May 7th Rosebery went on 'a melancholy and perplexed ride' in the morning, and on his return to The Durdans at 1.15 he was told the shattering news of the assassination of Cavendish and the Permanent Secretary, Mr Burke, in Dublin's Phoenix Park on the very day of the Chief Secretary's arrival in Ireland. They had been cut down and hacked to death by a gang armed with long surgical knives, but which had been intent only on the murder of Burke. 'Of course this event cleared my course completely,' Rosebery wrote in his diary. 'All hands are wanted at the pumps.' The opportunity for the magnificent gesture which Rosebery always cherished had arrived. He hastened to London, and wrote to the Gladstones, 'I can only say "God sustain you all. It is past all words".' On the 9th he told Edward Hamilton that had he occupied a more responsible position in the Government he would have resigned with Forster and Cowper. For a while the fate of the Ministry tottered in the balance, and emerged from the crisis with its reputation seriously damaged.

Ten days after the Phoenix Park murders, with surprising insensitivity, Rosebery was back on his hobby-horse of the treatment of Scotland. A Junior Lordship of the Treasury was vacant, and on May 17th he urged the Prime Minister to appoint a Scotsman to the post.

. . . Though I do not pretend in any sense to represent Scotland or to assert that Scotland will be seriously outraged if you do not appoint a Scottish Lord of the Treasure, yet I would venture to remind you that 'many a little makes a mickle', that Scotland is the backbone of the Liberal party, and that, if I am rightly informed, there is some discontent as to her treatment. . . .

Gladstone replied that he was unable to accede to this advice, and Rosebery, feeling perhaps that his intervention had not been happily timed, hastened to apologise, but Gladstone replied through Hamilton that his 'interference was quite right & such as I desire & am grateful for'. Rosebery wrote to Hamilton.

My dear H,

I am glad Mr G is not angry.

But I confess I think Scotland is as usual treated abominably. Justice for Ireland means everything done for her even to the payment of the natives' debts.[1] Justice to Scotland means insulting neglect. I leave for Scotland next week with the view of blowing up a prison or shooting a policeman. . . .

Yrs ever
AR

[1] A reference to the Arrears Bill.

Rosebery was still preoccupied with accusations about 'pushing' himself. When it was suggested to him in June that he and his wife (who was expecting another baby) should do more Party entertaining, he refused. 'He told me', Hamilton noted on June 30th, 'he could not bear the thought of being considered to be pushing and going out of his way—of assuming as an Under Secretary the position of a Minister. He further said that in view of promotion in the future the one thing of all others he wished to avoid was a charge similar to that brought against Ld Carlingford[1] when he was married to Lady Waldegrave,—that he had "dined himself into the Cabinet".' He added that he was still engaged in recouping the money he had spent on the Midlothian campaigns.[2]

The Government's sagging fortunes were partially restored by the bombardment of Alexandria by the British Fleet in July, the landing of forces under General Wolseley, and the overwhelming defeat of the Egyptian forces under Arabi Pasha by the British armies at Tel-el-Kebir. The withdrawal of the French fleet at the eleventh hour and the spectacular nature of the British victory stunned Europe and gave a prestige to British arms which lasted until the Boer War. But the bombardment itself—however justified—resulted in John Bright's resignation and much heart-searching among many other Liberals. Bright told Rosebery in the incongruous surroundings of a Marlborough House garden party on July 13th that 'Dizzy had never done anything worse than, or so bad as, this bombardment'. Rosebery defended the Government, but Bright cut him off: 'Say no more about it, it's damnable!' On July 15th Rosebery again saw Bright, who spoke with Gladstone with some bitterness as having 'a flexible conscience: meaning that he was not unscrupulous but that his conscience followed the bent of his mind'. The Ministry was acutely embarrassed by its new acquisition, and a hopeless muddle seemed to overtake British foreign policy at this time. Granville was clearly failing, and Gladstone was reluctant to face the fact that evacuation was impossible until some stable administration was established. Thus, hesitantly and even feebly, did the British Government assume responsibility for this vast territory, its

---

[1] Chichester Fortescue, first Lord Carlingford. Chief Secretary for Ireland, 1868–70; President of Board of Trade, 1870–4; Lord Privy Seal, 1881–5.

[2] Hamilton mentions the sum of £50,000 in this connection, but I find it very difficult to accept this figure, as I mentioned on pages 101–2.

R.—10

sprawling multitudes, its debts, and its atrociously incompetent administration. In the Sudan a strange prophet who called himself the Mahdi proclaimed a holy war and plunged the British Government into further embarrassments and difficulties.

In spite of his support for their Egyptian policy, Rosebery continued to press for better treatment for Scotland, and on June 27th he urged the Prime Minister to give Government assistance to a Scottish Endowments Bill which was in peril through Government apathy for the third session running.

. . . What are indeed the facts as they appear to the most impartial eye ? The Prime Minister was returned by a Scottish constituency, backed by an overwhelming majority of Scottish members. From the day of the first meeting of the new Parliament until the present day of its third session, if I am correctly informed, not one minute of Government time has been allotted to Scotland or Scottish affairs. Can you be surprised that the people of Scotland complain ?

. . . You might well ask what business it is of mine: the Bill is not in the Home Office, and it is for Mundella to speak. But unfortunately the view is taken in Scotland that I have a considerable share in the responsibility; and certainly wherever the Scottish halfpence may go, I shall get the Scottish kicks.

That is an eventuality which I am not prepared to face, when I am of opinion that the aggressive boot contains a toe of justice. I literally do not know how Scotland is to be faced during the Recess if this Bill be not passed. . . .

Gladstone suggested in reply that the Bill might be sent to a Grand Committee of the House of Commons—in those days a very novel procedure—but this course did not commend itself to the Under-Secretary for the Home Department, who relapsed into a moody silence.

On August 1st, however, Rosebery dined with the Gladstones, nd after dinner they sat together on a sofa, and had a long conversation, in which Rosebery told the Prime Minister a few home truths. He bluntly criticised the delayed reconstruction of the Cabinet, which cast a slight upon Ministers outside the Cabinet, for the impression was given that none were capable of this promotion. 'I said that I had no personal feeling in the matter whatever he might think, and that to no human being in the world but him would I say this. He interrupted eagerly to assure me of his certainty of my having no personal feelings.' Rosebery considered

that Gladstone replied to his arguments 'very weakly'. '. . . I interrupted occasionally and we kept up a sort of running fire of small
arms with good and indeed affectionate manners on both sides
and perfect good temper. Gladstone said that "the position of the
Govt. was that of an army guarding five miles and a half of vale,
where half a mile was attacked and all the force had to be concentrated there." I replied that it was not a good policy to leave
the five miles entirely abandoned as Scotland had been. . . . We
then went into a general argument about Scottish legislation in
which he said that this session she would have got more than
England. "Yes," I said, "but this is all we have to show for three
sessions, and tomorrow we shall have our first minute of Government time since this Parliament met in 1880." '

The Roseberys had been invited to Windsor in July, when the
Queen dispelled the unfortunate impression of coldness which she
had given a year before at Holyrood. But August was a sad
month. Old Lady Rosebery, to whom Rosebery was devoted,
died after a pitifully long illness on August 19th. Rosebery recorded the event in his diary.

. . . I only hoped that the end might come soon.
It came at 6.15 as I rang the front door bell & I was just in time for
her very last sigh. She who had loved me longest, & whom I loved
tenderly, would no more be the centre & point of contact of so many
different persons whose only link was their affection for her. I could
not mourn at her death, having seen her long agony, but her disappearance I must always mourn.

Four days later a favourite groom was killed when his horse
bolted while he and Rosebery were riding to Leatherhead Downs.
The tragedy occurred within a few hundred yards of Cherkley
Court,[1] where he died without recovering consciousness. 'I had
left home at 10,' Rosebery noted in his Diary. 'It was 11.20 when
I returned, and what an abyss of horror between the two dates.'
This accident permanently affected Rosebery's attitude to riding,
which had never been noticeably enthusiastic. In fact he was
probably one of the worst horsemen of his generation, and the
despair of his grooms.

There was a brief visit to the beloved Naples in September
('At 12 we drove to the dear Villa Delahante which looked sub-

[1] Since 1911 the home of Lord Beaverbrook.

lime. I long for it & dread it. Without resolution it would be a
Capua. With a heavy heart we left Naples by the 3.47.') and most
of the autumn was spent in smouldering discontent at Dalmeny.

Rosebery's Scottish reputation rose further with his Rectorial
Address in Edinburgh on November 4th, of which one passage
deserves to be recorded.

There is no word so prostituted as patriotism. It is part of the base
coinage of controversy. Every government fails in it, and every
opposition glows with it. It dictates silence and speech, action and
inaction, interference and abstention, with unvarying force and facility.
It smiles impartially on the acceptance and the resignation of office;
it impels people to enter and to quit public life with equal reason and
equal precipitation. It urges to heroism, to self-sacrifice, to assassination, and to incendiarism. It re-built Jerusalem and burned Moscow;
it stabbed Marat, and put his bones in the Pantheon. It was the watchword of the Reign of Terror, and the motto of the guillotine. It raises
statues to the people whom it lodges in dungeons. It patronises almost
every crime and every virtue in history.

Cabinet changes were in the air, and on all sides—and particularly in Scotland—it was said that Rosebery's accession was
imminent. The Prime Minister, however, was in a position of
some embarrassment. He had to find places for Lord Derby and
Sir Charles Dilke in the face of the Queen's displeasure, and
decided that these were the only accessions he could contemplate
for the moment. On Monday, December 4th, Rosebery dined at
Lord Granville's, and afterwards he and the Gladstones went to
see the Gilbert and Sullivan opera *Iolanthe* at the Savoy. In the
interval the Prime Minister told Rosebery that only Derby and
Dilke were to enter the Cabinet in the proposed reconstruction.

This information, so casually given, profoundly irritated Rosebery, and on the next day he called on Gladstone to discuss the
matter. Gladstone told him that there was to be no change in
the management of Scottish affairs, that Rosebery was to remain
at the Home Office, and that, in view of 'prior claims', there was
no immediate prospect of promotion. Rosebery was surprised and
angered. His latent discontent with his ambiguous position at the
Home Office now erupted. Edward Hamilton, aware of the
difficult position in which his friend found himself, offered to
mediate, but this generous suggestion was refused by Rosebery.

My dear E,

I hope I am not such a repulsive idiot as to treat your most friendly suggestion as an 'impertinence'. My doubt arises from the fact that it does not seem quite right, considering my relations with Mr G, and might be displeasing to him, that I should appear to go whining to a third person instead of going directly & 'manfully' (as he would say) to him.

Of course I see the difficulty with regard to my amour propre in having written on such a subject but it does not seem to me that it would be less in having spoken to you & your having spoken to Mr G. I do not see daylight yet. But I am grateful for such a friend.

Y. ever
AR.

In his letter to Gladstone, written from the Home Office on December 6th, Rosebery fastened on to the sentence in the letter of August 1881 in which he had been offered the position and which referred to the temporary nature of the arrangement. The statement which Gladstone had made to him the day before 'places me in a position of extreme gravity, personally and officially'. He concluded by asking permission to consult his principal supporters in Scotland. He then left by the night train to Dalmeny, where his wife was awaiting the arrival of her baby with some impatience. Before he saw Gladstone, however, Edward Hamilton came to Lansdowne House, and Rosebery told him frankly of his disappointment. Hamilton has left a detailed record of this conversation.

He is greatly disconcerted & disappointed. He considers that the just expectations of Scotland to have their interests represented more effectually ought to be met; & he believed they would have been met. He had hoped that he might have been selected as the person to represent those interests in an improved manner. If length of service is to be the consideration entitling promotion, he will be the last to be promoted as he only joined the Govt. 16 months ago. From certain hints dropped by Mr G, and from the peculiar relations which Rosebery has held with Mr G, he had been led to expect that a step was in store for him. He is sure that his being kept in his present post under the present arrangements will be greatly misunderstood in Scotland. It will be thought that he has been tried & found wanting. He finds the present arrangements making him responsible for all Scotch affairs without any direct access to the Cabinet is unworkable. In short, he is grievously disappointed at not getting Cabinet office; and I must

say, taking everything into consideration, his disappointment is not
without reason. He asks to be relieved of his present place as Scotch
Minister; he will, so long as Mr G remains on, continue to serve the
Govt in a subordinate place; he will then give up politics. He is
evidently under the impression that Lord Granville does not like him
& has put a spoke in his political wheel. I hope I have not mis-
represented him.

If anybody else had taken the line he has, I should have said it
showed a want of patience, that it was unreasonable, and that it was
overrating himself too high. But considering the estimate which Mr G
has formed—and rightly formed—of Rosebery's abilities, and how
often Mr G has let Rosebery know what that estimate was, I am not
surprised at all at Rosebery's state of mind. The difficulty is this: if
Mr G were now to reconsider the point & give Rosebery (say) the
Chancellorship of the Duchy of Lancaster with a seat in the Cabinet &
a special commission to administer Scotch affairs, it would be almost
impossible for Rosebery to accept any such offer with proper regard to
his *amour propre*, now that he has made a representation to Mr G on
the subject of his own feelings.[1]

Having rejected Hamilton's offered mediation, Rosebery departed for Dalmeny, which was lapped in deep snow. On the 8th
he received Gladstone's reply to his letter, in which the Prime
Minister politely declined to agree that he had bound himself a
year before to keeping the arrangement temporary. 'I do not see
the signs of conflict between the two indications which present
themselves to your mind. . . . Perhaps if I understand your meaning more clearly I may be able to meet it better than in this imperfect note.' Rosebery, although disappointed, was not in an
unreasonable frame of mind at this stage of the crisis, and, if
carefully handled, his disappointment might have been eased, and
the whole affair speedily dealt with. To Hamilton he wrote on the
9th, 'Please forgive the bilious flood of egotism & patriotism that
I poured over you in one fell flood. But your friendship I shall not
easily forget.' In his letter to Gladstone, written on the 10th, he
explained his difficulty frankly. He specified his complaint about
Scottish business, and reminded Gladstone that he had already
pointed out to him how unworkable the arrangement was. 'The
experiment was always believed by me to be purely tentative,' the
letter continued, 'but in my humble opinion it was open to the
reproach of being both undefined and undignified. But I believed

---

[1] *Edward Hamilton's Diary*, Thursday, December 7th, 1882.

that it was intended to mark a new departure, to be a step in the right direction, and to contain the germ of a new office which would satisfy the country. I gathered, however, on Tuesday that it was your intention to enter upon the next session of Parliament with this system of administration unaltered. . . .' He then dealt with the difficult 'personal question'.

. . . If a somewhat Chinese principle of seniority is to prevail in my promotion, it will be many years before I cease, except by my own act or a party defeat, to be an Under-Secretary. I am almost, if not quite, the junior member of the Government. In merit I have no doubt that my inferiority would be equally undoubted. If I could ever hope to rise higher, it could only be by the favour and support of my fellow-countrymen. But if seniority is to be reckoned against me, that, and the probable succession of one, as well as the probable elevation of other ministers to the House of Lords, would keep me for ever in a subordinate position.

I do not value office at all. It is a sacrifice of much that renders life pleasant to me, leisure, and independence, and the life of the country. But, unattractive as it is, your remarks appeared to me to open a gloomier vista still: and if the result of all this should be my retirement into private life, I should have nothing personal to regret, while I should feel that I could be of more use both to Scotland and yourself as an independent member than in my present position.

Hamilton, with reason, considered that this letter was a great mistake, since Gladstone would regard it as an application for higher office in defiance of the principles in regard to Cabinet promotion which he held most tenaciously. Hamilton telegraphed on the 11th, asking Rosebery's permission to keep back the letter, which was given. Hamilton then wrote to him, begging him to withdraw or at least re-phrase the letter, but Rosebery refused, and on the evening of the 12th the letter was handed to the Prime Minister. 'I won't inflict myself further upon you,' Hamilton wrote coldly, 'I can only say that I regret your decision; & I can only hope that you know your own interests better than I do. . . . I have not had any talk with Mr G; but have now seen his reply to you. I can only hope it may induce you to let things stand for the moment.'

Rosebery replied to Hamilton on the 12th,

. . . But all that you say I have thoroughly weighed before. I know well what people will say south of the Tweed. North of the Tweed they will speak differently. . . .

When I became an official I did not lose the rights of an intelligent being. I accepted a certain office on what I believed to be a definite understanding. I find I was mistaken & I depart. I firmly believe that without such an understanding I should not have been serving the interests of my country but doing the reverse. I have no doubt that in remaining where I am I should be continuing an arrangement which would be distinctly injurious to my country. I have only consulted three intimate friends[1] as I do not wish the affair to be known before it is necessary, but they are all able and representative Scotsmen and they all agree with me in what I am saying.

Mr G, you say, might say that he would consider any suggestion as to a re-arrangement of Scottish business. To make uninvited suggestions would be an impertinence on my part. But even if it were not, it is no longer possible for me to make any suggestions. I view my retirement as inevitable, and indeed it can hardly be otherwise. I cannot now remain where I am, still less could I accept higher office under the circumstances without a self sacrifice which would be beyond my strength.

God knows all this is hard enough. But I cannot altogether blame myself. . . .

Gladstone's next letter, although tactful, had a sting in the tail. '. . . your prospects are brilliant as well as wide, but even you cannot dispense with much faith and patience.' 'Mr G's letter, kind as it is, does not touch the real question,' Rosebery wrote to Hamilton on the 13th, 'which I must repeat is a public & not a personal one.'

On the next day Lady Rosebery gave birth to her second son, who was christened Neil in the Hall at Barnbougle on January 21st. This event, together with the congratulatory letters which poured in, improved the relationship with the Gladstones for a short while. Mrs Gladstone sent Rosebery a typically charming and breathless letter on the subject of the ministerial crisis.

One little word unknown to my Husband, my dear friend.
1st Have you not considered him more as a Father?
2nd Have you not surely taken in his affection and deep interest?—
Why do you not trust him?
Leaving this, & trying to follow your own thoughts I give all the credit to you of high minded desire . . . forgive me therefore if I venture to point out that rash action would have the very contrary effect—damage Scotland—damage yourself. What? to wait even if it

[1] Lord Reay, Charles Cooper of *The Scotsman*, and the Lord Advocate, J. B. Balfour.

shall have seemed disadvantageous will assuredly compensate in the end. . . .

On the 15th Rosebery thanked her for 'your kind & affectionate letter, which was just like yourself, and I cannot praise it more'. He said that he could write no more about the 'absolutely nauseous' business, and that 'as regards politics & office I do not think I shall ever get the taste of it out of my mouth'.[1]

At this point, Rosebery was still in a conciliatory frame of mind, in spite of his feeling that Gladstone had—perhaps unintentionally—deceived him. With careful handling, it is possible that the storm might have blown over, but the Prime Minister, wrestling with the triple problems of Derby, Dilke, and the vacant Archbishopric of Canterbury, regarded Rosebery's somewhat tortuous soul-searching epistles as the final irritant. Whereas Gladstone's iron constitution could weather fierce controversies with astonishing resilience, it was incapable of sustaining just this kind of personal problem. In these circumstances he would be physically ill, with the result that the self-control and calm which he exhibited in the face of serious crises tended to disappear. On the 16th, after writing again to Gladstone, Rosebery wrote to Hamilton, saying that his kindness and that of the Gladstones 'are the only bright spots in this gloomy business'. After the 16th, however, the tone of the Prime Minister's letters changed sharply, and do not merit the comment of Lord Crewe (who, however, saw only a few of them) that they were 'affectionate but vague'.[2] They were not noticeably affectionate, and were very much to the point. Gladstone told his son, Herbert, at this time that he could see no analogy between a Secretary for Scotland and the Chief Secretary for Ireland; 'What would Peel have said to me if I had made a similar demand?' he asked. Herbert Gladstone wrote to his brother, Henry, that 'The people who bother him at this moment more than all England are the Queen and Lord Rosebery.'[3]

---

[1] This sentence has sometimes been quoted out of context to give the impression that Rosebery was now wholly captured by politics. In fact Rosebery wrote in the original letter, 'I do not think I shall ever get the taste *of this business* out of my mouth', which he altered for the sake of euphony, but which expressed his meaning better.

[2] Crewe: *Rosebery*, I, 160.

[3] Sir Charles Mallet: *Herbert Gladstone, A Memoir*, 97.

'He should confine himself to demanding improved arrangements for the conduct of Scotch business,' Hamilton noted on the 17th. 'I fear however he is inclined to be pig-headed.' On the next day the equally nettled Prime Minister brought a new note into his correspondence with the Under-Secretary for the Home Department.

. . . I am not however sure that you think I am working as hard as I can; indeed the inference from your letters wd seem to be the reverse. . . . I hardly think the time & circumstances thus viewed, to be appropriate for a complaint of what you seem to regard as a contumacious inattention. If you will lay before me your views of existing wants, & the proper mode of supplying them, so that they may be considered by me, & by the Cabinet, this shall not be neglected. At present I hardly know that I have any materials before me. . . .

This transformed the situation. On the 19th Rosebery wrote to Hamilton to say that a decision must be made at once; '. . . if Mr G still maintains the *non-possumus* attitude, there is no reason why matters should go on a day longer. It all depends on him.' To Gladstone he wrote in the same sense on the 20th: '. . . I hope you will allow me to say that I trust the matter may not then be protracted, but that I may at once be told either that a new arrangement will be made or that my resignation is accepted.' The Prime Minister was now very angry indeed. He told Hamilton on the 21st that he regarded the correspondence 'as astonishingly foolish—a tempest in a tea-kettle; & thought it marvellous how so clever a man as Rosebery could be so silly. He had however not lost his patience with Rosebery, & continued to treat R with kindness & much tact. . . . Whatever happens, R will I fear have damaged himself permanently in Mr G's estimation.'

This 'kindness and much tact' were not very evident in Gladstone's reply to Rosebery's ultimatum. 'I am sorry to say that Rosebery has inflicted on me a set of letters which appear to me astonishingly foolish', Gladstone wrote to Granville on December 19th, 'about the neglect of his country, the necessities of his position, and the like: a tempest in a tea-kettle. It is marvellous how a man of such character & such gifts can be so silly. Nor does it mend yet.'[1]

[1] See also Agatha Ramm (editor), *The Political Correspondence of Mr Gladstone and Lord Granville, 1876–1886*, I, 471–82.

Writing on the 21st, he asked Rosebery to submit his proposals to Harcourt, and continued:

... Am I to interpret your letter as really conveying to me that, you having never up to this time supplied any statement of the evils, or any plan or remedy, you now require to be told by me 'at once' either that the Government proposes a new arrangement (which it cannot do until it knows *what* the arrangement will be) or that your resignation is accepted? If this were so, I own I hardly should know, under the conditions of public affairs & my own limited powers, how to deal with you, or any man, upon such terms. ...

To Hamilton Gladstone confided that he was seriously contemplating cancelling a visit to Midlothian arranged for January 'if Rosebery continues in his present tempestuous state of mind'.

Rosebery's reply of the 22nd to Gladstone's letter of the 21st was the most formidable which he penned in the course of the protracted correspondence. He revealed that he had submitted several memoranda to Harcourt at Harcourt's request on Scottish business since the early summer of 1881, and imagined that the Government had considered the subject. He went on to speak of his 'sense of humiliation' at having to remove an impression that his actions were 'dictated by personal feeling & pique'.

... I am now running the risk of blighting my whole career in the official sense by leaving your Government, & of losing the intimacy with yourself which has been my happiness for three years & which made the drudgery of politics & office a grateful task. My personal devotion to you can never change: it began in darker days & has stood the test of stormy weather. But my personal relation to politics can never be the same again. I can only wish to leave them & forget them. Whereas formerly it would have been a pleasure to serve you in any higher offer you might have called me to, I never could willingly do so now. I entered upon office to secure attention to & a definite department for my country: I shall leave it because I have failed. Even if I should succeed, my satisfaction could only be of a very mingled & dreary kind. When therefore you see how desolate my position is, you will at least I hope give it the credit of disinterestedness. ...

On the 23rd the Prime Minister submitted the already sizeable correspondence on the subject to Lord Granville, and that shrewd observer, in a memorandum to Gladstone, brought the first draught of common sense into the controversy.

I do not see in your letters to him much trace of that warm affection or that remarkable appreciation of his character & abilities, just, but which would even be considered excessive by some, which you have so constantly and in so many different circumstances expressed to me.

On the other hand, the course which Rosebery seems inclined to take appears to me, a somewhat lymphatic observer, almost impossible. . . .

Rosebery has a brilliant career before him, & he once told me that it was the one thing he really cared about.[1] But brilliant as his career may be, there will be no brighter episode than his connection with you, and the work you achieved together. . . . I agree that you could hardly frame a scheme under the threat of a resignation of a friend.

If Rosebery insists upon resigning . . . it seems almost impossible that you should conduct the Midlothian campaign from his house. . . .

I cannot help thinking that, if you gave him some more definite assurance of considering the Scotch question while reserving perfect freedom of action & were to say only one tenth of what you have said to others as to the standard by which you judge him, this affair, so annoying to you, and so likely to be damaging to him, might be satisfactorily settled. . . .

This was a carefully prepared letter, designed to be shown to Rosebery. In a private note to Gladstone on December 23rd, Granville wrote: 'I doubt the use of my intervention. He is morbidly suspicious, which I do not attribute to politics, but to a point in his character, strengthened by Newmarket training. . . . You will observe the ingenuity with which I attack you—but my observations are not altogether without foundation.'[2]

Gladstone's letter of the 23rd (written before Rosebery's letter of the 22nd had been received) was almost paternal in tone. He related an incident in 1842 which 'helped to teach me what I have not even yet fully learned, the necessity for a political man of weighing the exterior as well as the interior bearings of my actions'. He had offered his resignation to Sir Robert Peel when the latter had made what Gladstone—then at the Board of Trade —regarded as 'an insufficient step' in relation to the Corn Laws.

[1] Rosebery, when told of this remark, strongly denied that he had ever said anything of this nature to Granville. It is clear from the tone of Granville's comments on Rosebery at this time and Rosebery's on Granville, that each regarded the other with a certain degree of suspicion.

[2] Granville had not seen Gladstone's sympathetic letter of December 12th, and when he had he wrote to Gladstone on December 28th that 'it cuts the ground from my criticism'. (Ramm, op. cit., I, 479.)

Peel was 'very sulky, and would hardly speak to me beyond saying "he should consider whether or not to break up the Government" '.

. . . I left him, rather dumb-founded—and I did not sleep that night as well as usual—but on the next forenoon I wrote to him, and told him I should continue where I was; not retracting what I had said of his measure but following what I thought the higher duty. Such is my tale. You can supply the ὁ μῦθος δηλοῖ. . . .

After he had written this, Rosebery's letter arrived, and Gladstone added a postscript to the effect that he had never considered personal ambition 'as the mainspring of your present movement'.

This warm glow faded quickly. In his letter of the 21st the Prime Minister had mentioned Harcourt 'who *is* the Minister for Scotland', and Rosebery, in his contribution on the 24th, took somewhat belated exception to this phrase. In a cold and rather portentous letter he reiterated all the old arguments about Scotland, his personal position, and the terms of his appointment. On Boxing Day there arrived from Hawarden 'a letter but little Christmas-like' in which the old ground was traversed anew, but in the meanwhile Rosebery had received Gladstone's kinder letter of the 23rd, and on the same Christmas Day that Gladstone was penning his bleak letter at his Hawarden desk, Rosebery was writing that 'I am disarmed. The mere hint of such a threat as you metaphorically convey, though of course I cannot believe in its full application, is a thrust I cannot parry. . . .' Mrs Gladstone sent another long incoherent appeal, which was touching in its artlessness.

My dear friend,
   I must write you this line though words cannot express how my heart bleeds for you in this miserable misunderstanding. I never knew anything so wretched; I can see so well now how it has all arisen & how nobody is to blame. His character is so extraordinarily simple I don't think he knows how to understand these ins and outs. But don't think he would ever for a moment dream of you as in any way a self seeker. To him in a way, political life is very simple; 'follow the man you trust & wait till that man sees the proper moment to rearrange.' Scotch business has never flourished before as it has done lately, & that for the moment has satisfied him. I see the huge sacrifice you make in now wishing to resign; there is one greater still to which you are called—& that is not to resign.

Have you quite faced what it wd mean ? Do not think me imperti-
nent—but how could the PM come to Dalmeny just then—it would
signify he thought a thing right which he actually thinks wrong. An
hotel has just been offered to him in Edinburgh. He has not yet
answered. Only think what it means if we have to go there instead of
to you. What I would implore is that for his sake, you would consider
all this wretched time as a dream. I think I know it is a tremendous
thing to ask. I think I understand *now* the whole position. And yet
even if it is you who has most to forgive & most to give in then to
you falls the higher part in forgiving. . . . You know he would forget
it all in a minute, & Dalmeny would be just what it was before, a
haven of delight & happiness. But if you resign & he cannot go there,
it would spoil it for ever.

But of course this would not count & ought not to count, if you
felt absolutely certain your only right course was resignation. But I
cannot *cannot* feel it could be right. Do you know, I think if you only
came here, all might be right in a few minutes.

Letters never are any good. . . .

By the end of December the situation had definitely improved.
'The atmosphere is unexpectedly clearer,' Rosebery remarked in
his diary on the 25th. Granville advised Gladstone to treat Rosebery more considerately, spoke of his claims to the next Cabinet
vacancy for a Peer, and urged Gladstone to give Rosebery a
pledge on these lines. On the 26th Rosebery telegraphed to Gladstone that 'the immediate subject of our recent correspondence is
disposed of'. 'The Rosebery *fracas* is smoothed over, thank
goodness, for the moment at any rate,' Hamilton noted in his
diary on the 29th. '. . . I am afraid however there is no denying
he has acted somewhat foolishly.' 'The Rosebery tumult is ap-
peased,' Gladstone wrote to Granville on December 30th.
'. . . I own however that for the present it leaves what you sometimes call "a bad taste in the mouth". I am by no means assured
that he has yet taken more than a superficial or newspaper article
view of the question.' 'Goodbye, thou damnable year,' Rosebery
wrote in his diary on December 31st at Dalmeny, after returning
from Edinburgh where he and Jack Tennant had gone to see the
Hogmanay celebrations.

Gladstone succumbed to the strain of these and other personal
tribulations and was ordered to bed at the beginning of 1883.
'My power of sleep,' he wrote to Rosebery on January 2nd,
which is my mainstay, has within the last few days given way in

a manner quite new to me.' Rosebery telegraphed his sympathy, and asked if he might visit Hawarden. 'I who know your kindness for your youthful colleagues am well aware you will have the robe and the ring and the fatted calf ready for him, and that the *mollia tempora fandi* will blot out the *litera scripta*,' Harcourt wrote to Gladstone on December 27th. 'Rosebery will be most welcome here,' Gladstone replied. 'It is a most singular case of strong self-delusion: a vein of foreign matter which runs straight across a clear and vigorous intellect and a high-toned character.'[1]

But the visit was not a success. The Gladstones received him somewhat coldly, and the Prime Minister never once alluded to the matter of the Scottish Office or to Rosebery's position. 'It is incredible', John Morley said to Hamilton in 1892, 'the want of *nous* which Mr Gladstone shows about Rosebery,' and this observation was as applicable to 1882–3. Rosebery left Hawarden on January 5th without 'a syllable having been said about the subject of our previous correspondence and the subject of my visit!'

On January 12th Mrs Gladstone and Lady Rosebery met in Edinburgh and had a sharp exchange. Mrs Gladstone related the many trials and tribulations besetting the Prime Minister, and strongly hinted that Hannah's husband was not the least of these. 'It is all right now,' she kept saying. 'He must not be in a hurry to mount the ladder, he is very young.' Lady Rosebery tried to explain that Scottish business was the bone of contention, not personal ambition, but this did not seem to be taken in. Mrs Gladstone concluded the conversation with an unpleasant allusion to the Turf which infuriated Lady Rosebery. Her account of this curious meeting concludes,

. . . She said, 'It will be all right.' I said, 'He knows best.' She said, 'He is so young.' I said, 'Not of head or heart, he knows what is right.' She went downstairs, and I had no need, thank God, to kiss and shake hands.

Charles Cooper was furious when he heard of this interview, and described Mrs Gladstone's tone in a letter to Lady Rosebery on January 19th as 'insolent'.

. . . It was the talk of a spiteful woman who could not resist saying what she thought were venomous things against those who had

[1] Gardiner: *Harcourt*, I, 466–7.

offended her. But having said this, I must add that I feel more convinced than ever that her conduct was proof that she knows they—
by which I mean Mr G & his family, who seem to me to know at least
enough of state affairs—have been convicted of conduct which could
not be called by any less name than ingratitude and might be not
unfairly described by other epithets, as shabby, selfish, etc. . . . .

This was going rather beyond what the Roseberys themselves
felt but it was not the reverse of their feelings. Both were angered
and irresolute; Charles Cooper urged resignation in the event of
the Government failing to satisfy legitimate Scottish demands.
'I am losing all belief in action being taken', he wrote to Lady
Rosebery on April 29th in one of many similar letters, 'and I am
gaining the certainty that the government will alienate many
people in Scotland. It is always to-morrow, and to-morrow, and
to-morrow. . . .' Rosebery gave up any attempt to conceal his true
feelings to his closest friends. He had little confidence in the
Government doing anything worthwhile for Scotland, and on the
personal aspect he was profoundly depressed by the poor prospects for advancement. On February 7th Harcourt telegraphed to
him about Scottish business details; Rosebery sent the information, but added that after his correspondence with Gladstone
he was under the impression that he had not 'any special connection' with Scottish affairs. Gladstone had no heart in the move
for Scottish reform. On March 18th he told Hamilton that in all
his administrative experience he could never remember a big
issue so 'irrationally handled' by a clever man. He suggested
that the subject should be delegated to a Parliamentary Committee, but Rosebery objected. 'How Rosebery is to be provided
for and retained', Hamilton recorded on March 18th, 'it is not
easy to say.' On March 20th Rosebery wrote a somewhat truculent letter to the Prime Minister which almost courted dismissal,
but Hamilton halted its progress and, with no small difficulty,
persuaded Rosebery to tear it up. On the 24th Rosebery wrote
in a more contrite frame of mind, and Gladstone was greatly
mollified, replying on the 27th that he fully understood his impatience and vexation and that 'I can assure you that I have
profoundly shared it'. 'Here is an excellent letter from Rosebery,'
Gladstone wrote to Granville on March 24th, 'which, though it
may leave behind the question what is to become of him for the
moment, seems to take the whole *virus* out of the affair, to my

great comfort.' Harcourt wrote soothingly to Rosebery to say
that the decision should be taken by Whitsun and that he (Harcourt) had strongly impressed the urgency of the matter upon the
Prime Minister.

But all proposals foundered on Gladstone's refusal to accept
a separate Scottish Ministry and Rosebery's determination not to
accept anything else. In these circumstances the numerous letters
and memoranda which sped to and fro, the meetings of senior
Ministers and the draft proposals which everyone was drawing up
were somewhat unreal. After a conversation with Rosebery on
April 4th, Hamilton realised that a crisis was imminent. His
friend was thoroughly bored with the Home Office, saw no chance
of promotion, had been misled by being assured that the 1881
arrangement was to be a temporary one, and so on. He frankly
wanted the vacant Privy Seal but no offer was made, although the
Press was saying on all sides that he was the inevitable choice.
Hamilton realised that nothing except complete victory could
avert Rosebery's resignation. Gladstone, Granville, Hamilton, and
the members of the Cabinet who knew about the crisis were
dimly beginning to realise that there was a deadly flaw in Rosebery's personality which has been admirably summarised by Sir
Winston Churchill:

In times of crisis and responsibility his active, fertile mind and
imagination preyed upon him. He was bereft of sleep.[1] He magnified
trifles. He failed to separate the awkward incidents of the hour from
the long swing of events, which he so clearly understood. Toughness
when nothing particular was happening was not the form of fortitude
in which he excelled. He was unduly attracted by the dramatic, and by
the pleasure of making a fine gesture.[2]

There were other symptoms of this failing. At the end of
March, Gladstone asked him to become a Trustee of the British
Museum. Characteristically, Rosebery asked for time in which to
consider the matter; on March 31st they met at Sandringham, and
Gladstone 'stormed my room & demanded an answer about the
Trusteeship'. Rosebery was unable to give a clear answer. 'I am
indifferent but anxious to refuse,' he wrote in his diary, 'but I did

---

[1] On December 12th, 1882, at the most critical point in the crisis, he recorded
'Slept at New Club—or rather, did not sleep.' On the 13th he noted, 'To Dalmeny.
. . . Dined alone.—Bad night.'
[2] Churchill: *Great Contemporaries*, 22.

not find on the spur of the moment an excuse.' On April 8th he wrote to decline the offer; Gladstone noted curtly on his letter, 'Too late'. When Hamilton conveyed to Rosebery the information that his name had already gone forward, he replied (April 9th) that 'The matter is as broad as it is long. For if I am appointed I resign at once.' He was persuaded not to take so ridiculous a step, but his utterly disproportionate annoyance over such a trivial matter increased the strong doubts about his reliability and common sense within the Liberal hierarchy.

Gladstone had bowed to the strong advice of Granville, and on April 7th he wrote to inform Rosebery that he was high on the list of Peers worthy of advancement to the Cabinet circle at the first vacancy. This might have had more effect had it been written several months earlier; at this late stage it merely irritated Rosebery, although he agreed on April 16th to postpone his resignation. He told Hamilton quite definitely that he had no hope that Childers[1] (who had been entrusted with the task of preparing a scheme) would produce anything satisfactory and that he would 'infallibly take himself off'.

On May 5th the Cabinet was presented with Childers' scheme to create a Local Government Board for Scotland with a Parliamentary President. Dilke, Chamberlain, and Harcourt supported the plan purely as a method of retaining Rosebery, and on these terms the Cabinet reluctantly consented to let the plan go forward. 'I regard the loss of R as a very serious matter not only from a personal point of view which you I know would feel as I do,' Harcourt wrote to Gladstone on May 4th, 'but I think in the present state of the Party it would have a most mischievous effect in the most loyal of all our battalions, the Scotch contingent. There is no doubt that he is much looked up to in Scotland, and the idea that he had suffered in their cause would produce the worst impression.' Gladstone's aloofness was most pronounced, and when he was appealed to for a statement of his views he merely remarked that he was prepared to submit to the decision of his colleagues. On the same evening Harcourt met Rosebery at the Royal Academy Dinner and told him, 'Well, you ought to be greatly flattered: the Cabinet agreed to-day to do a thing they do

[1] 1827–96. First Lord of the Admiralty, 1868–71; Chancellor of the Duchy of Lancaster, 1872–3; Secretary of State for War, 1880–2; Chancellor of the Exchequer, 1882–5; Home Secretary, 1886.

not care about doing, simply to please you.' 'On public grounds', Rosebery wrote somewhat bleakly to Gladstone on May 7th, 'I rejoice at the decision of the Cabinet.'

The decisive event which made Rosebery's resignation inevitable was the announcement in the *Morning Post* on May 9th that his elevation to the Cabinet was imminent; congratulations poured in, and Hamilton noted on May 10th that they did Rosebery 'incalculable harm'. Dilke met him at this time, and recorded that Rosebery 'broke out to me against Mr G. He swears he will resign, giving health as his reason. He is not a gentleman, for he reproaches Mr G with the benefits he has conferred upon him, but he has been ill-used.'[1] On May 29th and again on the next day Rosebery saw Hartington, and frankly stated his views. On May 31st came the occasion for resignation which Rosebery had been seeking for so long.

In a debate in the Commons on the Civil Service Estimates there were complaints about the absence of an under-secretary at the Home Office in the House, with which view Harcourt associated himself. Rosebery was about to leave for Edinburgh, but before he left he told Hamilton that he would now definitely resign.

It is a very unfortunate business; [*Hamilton wrote in his diary on June 2nd*] but Rosebery's personal position has got so much on his brain that a decisive step is almost a necessity. One cannot help making great allowances for him. He is so horribly over-sensitive; and this constant reappearance in the papers of his probable promotion goads him to desperation. He feels as if every one pointed their finger of scorn at him, and said that he had been tried and found wanting.

In Edinburgh Charles Cooper enthusiastically urged immediate resignation, arguing that such a wonderful opportunity might not present itself for some time. Rosebery entirely agreed with this view, as did his wife. Harcourt frantically implored mature consideration in the course of a series of urgent messages and letters, but on his return from Edinburgh early on the 4th Rosebery at once wrote to the Prime Minister to tender his resignation on the grounds of the criticisms levelled in the Commons. 'I am thus enabled to give effect to my own views on the subject, and at the same time afford a convenience to the Government without doing

[1] *Dilke Papers.*

any violence to my own feelings.' Hartington was deputed to arrange the details of the separation, and Lord Reay sent Lady Rosebery an accurate report of this meeting on June 4th.

Dear Lady Rosebery,

Lord H was commissioned to arrange matters and he said that the PM agreed to accept resignation on condition that the debate in the H of C was the reason to be given and that it should not interfere with acceptance of office hereafter if the Scotch department requires that Lord R should be its first head, though such a head should not be in the Cabinet. Lord R did not pledge himself to the latter course, but said of course that he was prepared for friendly intercourse with the PM on the subject when the time came.

He also told Lord H that he had had nothing to do with the Scotch Bill which was not good, but that bill is *not* to be mentioned. . . . Mr G spoke of a speedy re-arrangement of offices but of that Lord R said to Lord H he took no notice.

Yours truly,
R.[1]

There only remained a final interview between Rosebery and Gladstone, which was very cordial. 'It is a relief to both I think that a decision has at length been taken,' Hamilton truly remarked.

Rosebery's spirits were higher than they had been for over a year, and Lady Rosebery did not conceal her delight when Hamilton called on her on June 10th. The Scottish Press was not deceived by the published reasons for the resignation, and Cooper told Lady Rosebery on June 10th that the reception of the news in Scotland had had 'gratifying results. The PM is in the wrong and he knew it. . . . I should not wonder if Edinburgh offered the freedom of the city to Lord Rosebery.' There were a few final details to be settled. Harcourt was incensed by the implication, broadcast in several newspapers apart from *The Scotsman*, that he had been grossly disloyal to Rosebery; a contrived Question in the Commons had to be arranged as well as a public letter from Rosebery.

On June 6th Rosebery contentfully penned a valedictory letter to Eddie Hamilton.

[1] This version is confirmed by a considerably more detailed account in Rosebery's diary for June 4th.

. . . I hope we shall now see even more of each other than in the past. As to what has occurred I never was more happy in the consciousness of having done the right thing, & am restored to the position which I ought never to have quitted. On the other hand my official experience has been of great use to me, I don't doubt. . . .

I cannot tell you how sorry I am for all the trouble I have caused you, except for this, that it has tested in the furnace a friendship I did not & cannot deserve. How odd it would have seemed when we sat side by side, two shivering little scugs in Remove & in the library being examined for Remove, that *post varios casus et tot discrimine rerum* we should still be sitting side by side on the stage of the great theatre of politics. . . .

'Your departure, however temporary (as I earnestly hope it may be)', Hamilton wrote, 'is a sorrow to Mr Gladstone, a blow to the Government, a loss to the Country, and a great trouble to your friends.' 'I have known him intimately for twenty-three years,' Hamilton wrote to Sir Henry Ponsonby, '. . . and yet I have never really understood him. He is an extraordinary mixture. He has brilliant abilities and in many ways special aptitude for political life; but I fear his over-sensitive, thin-skinned nature will sadly stand in the way of a really successful political future. . . .'[1]

But the subject of this and many other comments was only concerned with his blissful liberty. The Season beckoned, and beyond that a project upon which he had been dwelling for some time. The Ministerial Interlude was over.

[1] Lord Ponsonby of Shulbrede: *Henry Ponsonby: His Life from His Letters*, 274–5

CHAPTER FIVE

LIBERAL IMPERIALISM

ROSEBERY'S POLITICAL FORTUNES had received a severe set-back. His resignation aroused perplexity in the political world and exasperation among his colleagues. It is too seldom realised that the existence of a junior Minister is not an enviable one, and is only tolerable if he is prepared, as a result of personal ambition or exceptional regard for the public interest, to put up with the countless vexations and frustrations of his position. He has no power: in the departmental hierarchy he is situated some way below the senior permanent officials; his relationship with the Minister is frequently distant; he is instructed to make a few carefully prepared statements, to answer the occasional Parliamentary question, to reply—again meticulously briefed—to debate. Even if the senior Minister is friendly, the life of his subordinate is a drudgery; if not, the junior Minister languishes in his office, fettered, and not undespised. Rosebery thought and lived on the grand scale; he was ambitious not for place, but for power and influence; he did not wish, nor was he able at this early stage of his career, to bring himself down from the lofty contemplation of the largest horizons to the examination of schemes of municipal rating and the laws relating to fire engines.[1]

Unquestionably he had been treated badly. He entered the Government with an assurance by the Prime Minister that the arrangements for Scottish business which he had criticised were to be amended: this assurance had not been carried out until too

[1] Mr Roy Jenkins states that a dispute with Dilke at the Local Government Board over the control of fire brigades 'was a contributory cause of his [Rosebery's] resignation in June and his departure from British politics for half a year's voyage around the world'. (*Dilke*, 166.) There is no evidence in Rosebery's or Gladstone's papers that this interdepartmental dispute had any relevance whatever. In his diary for April 12th, 1883, Dilke wrote that 'Rosebery is angry at my taking HO work, & refuses to do anything'. (Brit. Mus. Add. MSS. 43,925, f. 56.) This quite minor matter was symptomatic of Rosebery's discontent, but was in no sense 'a contributory factor'.

late, and by that time Rosebery's disenchantment with office was overpowering. But even after making every possible allowance in his favour, Rosebery's ministerial interlude had disclosed certain fundamental weaknesses in his capacity for public life which had surprised, disconcerted, and irritated even those Ministers and friends who sympathised with him. He had not demonstrated great ability in departmental work and had clearly not been a success in the Lords on the few occasions when he was permitted to speak. Moreover, he was dominated by a morbid conviction that Gladstone and Granville disliked and underrated him.

Gladstone made a last endeavour to retain Rosebery by offering him the position of the Scottish Ministership if the Local Government Board (Scotland) Bill were passed by the Lords, which seemed unlikely.[1] Granville was not enthusiastic about the offer, but Harcourt wrote to the Prime Minister to urge 'that the place ought to be offered to Rosebery *at once*'. Rosebery refused (July 30th) on the grounds that, as the most active supporter of the scheme, he would be open to accusations of self-interest, that the Minister should be in the Cabinet, and that he would never re-enter the Government except as a member of the Cabinet. 'I can quite understand', he wrote to Gladstone, 'that you will think this very presumptuous on my part. But the fact is that for office, *quâ office*, I do not greatly care. I am convinced that for me there is no middle term of usefulness between that of absolute inde-pendence and Cabinet office. As absolutely independent I hold a position in Scotland, of which I do not think so highly as some others may, but one which I greatly cherish. As a Cabinet Minister I should hold a position in Great Britain which it is an honour to covet. But by accepting office outside the Cabinet I lose both positions. On that point I have some experience to guide me. I hope I have made myself clear. . . .'

Gladstone's reaction was not unexpected. 'He does not like anyone to dictate their own political terms,' Hamilton noted (August 1st); 'and is certain that Rosebery requires further political training to fit him for the highest offices. I am sure it is a false step of Rosebery's.' In his reply, Gladstone thanked Rosebery for 'the thoroughly kind, frank, and cordial manner in which you have conveyed to me your intentions'. But on the 4th Rosebery told Hamilton that he was convinced that Gladstone wanted to

---

[1] It was in fact rejected by the Lords on August 21st by a majority of 15.

keep him out of the Cabinet: on the 10th they dined alone together, and Hamilton urged him to reconsider his decision, announced to Gladstone on July 30th, to go on a visit to Australasia with his wife. 'He was, however, immovable,' Hamilton recorded, '& when in such a mood he is not to be convinced. He can't get it out of his head that Mr G is thwarting him.' On the 15th Gladstone decided, without much enthusiasm, to ask Rosebery again to take the office, which he did after dinner at Lansdowne House. 'There is no concealing the fact, I fear, that Mr G is disappointed with R in two ways', Hamilton noted, '—disappointed with his official aptitude and his qualifications for a statesman's career, and disappointed with his conduct in first declining everything & disclaiming all selfish interests and now trying to dictate his own terms into the Cabinet.'

Rosebery saw Gladstone on August 20th, and definitely refused the offer; after the interview Mrs Gladstone told him that her husband had not pressed the office 'with heartiness' because he doubted if it could be carried on. 'She said the world wd call my refusal an act of want of courage, etc.—she was exceedingly angry.' 'I doubt', Hamilton wrote on July 6th, 'if the former close relations [between Rosebery and Gladstone] will ever be firmly re-established.' After a few farewell dinner parties to close friends at Lansdowne House the Roseberys left Liverpool for America on September 1st, arriving in Australia on November 17th.

Rosebery, always a romantic, was entranced and astounded by the continent which he had discovered. Throughout his early speeches it is not difficult to trace a growing awareness of the enormous potentialities of the British Empire, a subject almost entirely ignored by contemporary politicians and particularly by Liberals. Thus, in 1874, education is 'the true leverage of Empire', and 'if we have done our duty well, even though our history should pass away, and our country become

> *An island salt and bare,*
> *The haunt of seals, and orcs and sea-mew's clang,*

she may be remembered not ungratefully as the affluent mother of giant Commonwealths and peaceful Empires that shall perpetuate the best qualities of the race.' In 1882, in his Edinburgh Rectorial Address, the image was perhaps not altogether happy but the meaning plain, when he compared the British Empire to 'a sheet knit at the four corners, containing all manner of men, fitted for their separate climates and work and spheres of action, but honouring the common vessel which contains them'.

He kept a copious Journal of his Australian travels, recording that he preferred Sydney to Melbourne, although—or perhaps because—the latter 'is what we called a noble city', and that Tasmania was 'a pretty enclosed country, ridiculously like England, and with stations with names from Scotland', where the coaches were such 'venerable relics of antiquity' that Rosebery thought, 'not without emotion', of the House of Lords. His account of a long drive over the Old Man Plain in a dust storm should not be omitted.

An endless dust-coloured plain, occasionally a cinder coloured tree, the dust skimming swiftly after us like Furies, or any hostile pertinacious spirits. At the change, a lonely inn with a thirsty and exhausted host and hungry and animated flies, I sitting silent in the buggy for fear I should swallow dust, my companions exchanging an occasional murmur; this is a picture of that day, a fair shadow of Purgatory, if not worse; and yet—we were not unhappy.

'My present is all sightseeing, travelling, & listening to people', he wrote to Hamilton on December 13th from Government House, Melbourne, 'with the hideous interlude of a couple of speeches.' Two of these speeches revealed the remarkable—and crucial—effect of his visits and long conversations with British officials and Australian political leaders. He went to Australia with an idealistic concept of Empire; this was strengthened immensely by his experiences there, and found expression in his few public speeches. On December 10th, at a dinner held in his honour by the Speaker of the Legislative Assembly of the New South Wales Parliament, he declared that

People talk of the Roman colonies, of the Greek colonies, of the military colonies, and of the American colonies. They have interesting records, but they furnish no guidance now for the British Empire. We have outlived that time of minority and instruction. Britain's relations with her colonies are, it seems to me, of a complicated and intricate nature. . . . I would sum them up in a single sentence by saying that, in the strict sense of the word, she does not attempt to guide, she does not pretend to control, but she does regard her giant offspring with a pride which it would be the merest affectation to conceal.

At Melbourne (January 9th) Rosebery urged the Australians to preserve their system of local government—'our bitter experience in the old country should lead you to prize local government as the greatest of all gifts'—and spoke with enthusiasm of the future of the Empire.

There is an old tradition—I do not know if it remains good—that in the British Royal dockyards every rope that is manufactured, from the largest cable to the smallest twine, has a single red thread through it, which pervades the whole strand, and which, if unpacked, destroys the whole rope. That was the sign of the Royal production of those ropes. Though I distrust metaphors, I believe that that metaphor holds good to some extent of the British Empire. It is held together by the single red line, and that red line is the communion of races.

On January 18th, Rosebery delivered his last speech of his Australian tour at Adelaide in grilling heat. 'What with the hot wind my audience was languid,' he noted. 'What with the hot wind and the difficulty of coping with the Town Hall, I was languid. I had not had enough preparation, and there was an old drunkard who interrupted. The result was that though I spoke for an hour, it was uphill work.' Nearly forty years later Rosebery wrote to the Rev. H. A. (later Bishop) Skelton that 'I only stopped at Adelaide on my way back to England, and delivered an appalling speech of an hour in a hot wind; an experience I shall never forget, nor, I think, will my audience.'

In these depressing circumstances Rosebery delivered a speech which is to be numbered among the most noble and revealing of his utterances.

I say that these are no longer colonies in the ordinary sense of the term, but I claim that this is a nation—a nation not in aspiration or in the future, but in performance and fact. . . . Does this fact of your being a nation, and I think you feel yourselves to be a nation, imply separation from the Empire? God forbid! There is no need for any nation, however great, leaving the Empire, because the Empire is *a Commonwealth of Nations*. . . .

I think that each day that we live we shall be more and more unwilling to see this ancient Empire of ours—raised with so much toil, colonised with so much energy, cemented with the blood and sweat of so many generations—pass away like a camp struck noiselessly in the night, or split into isolated and sterile communities, jealous among themselves, disturbed by suburban disputes and parochial rivalries, dwindling possibly, like the Italian States of the Middle Ages, into political insignificance, or degenerating into idle and polite nonentity. And, Sir, let me remind this audience of the fact that Empires, and especially great Empires, when they crumble at all, are apt to crumble exceeding small.

The Roseberys returned to England by way of Ceylon ('It is impossible to conceive anything more perfect than gliding along this blue sea under the sunshine of this blue sky'), with which they were entranced. 'The outriggers, with naked bronze figures guiding them, the lonely, skinny fisher in his frail boat, the solemn Mohammedan merchant with his singularly inconvenient basket cap on the back of his head, the diver plunging for his sixpence, the washermen with their greasy certificates of worth by former passengers tendered to their successors, the hungry jewellers with their choicest gems tendered for a few shillings, every head turbaned, every form lean, every mouth blood-red with betel—all this one saw before one landed.' 'It is a golden dream to carry through life,' Rosebery recorded as their ship left Ceylon, 'a life which must always be brighter for this one little ray of the rare Eastern sunshine let in through a chink of time into the foggy chamber of a British existence.'

This idyll continued throughout the journey back to England. 'That we should have established ourselves, our coal, and fortifications to protect our coal, on a parched rock in Arabia, is full of suggestion,' he sagely noted at Aden. 'That we should have done so as an incident of our Indian Empire is a fact of tenacity. That we should there have received and revived the tanks of Solomon is a singular succession and a pregnant thought.'

The people of Dundee, when Rosebery received the freedom of that city on April 15th, were the first to learn of the startling effects of Rosebery's world tour. The image of Empire which that experience gave Rosebery was shortly to become distorted and extended in a manner which he loathed; yet there is nothing more noble in Rosebery's life than his Imperial concept, uncluttered as it was by the turgid emotionalism of Kipling, the ideological ruthlessness of Chamberlain, or the terrible misinterpretations of Milner, for each of whom he felt a strong antipathy. He was to live to see his prescient image of the Commonwealth of Nations accepted and magnified, but fortunately did not witness the fulfilment of his fears of 'isolated and sterile communities, jealous among themselves, disturbed by suburban disputes and parochial rivalries'. Although not blind to the many evils of the Empire, Rosebery was absolutely sincere when he described the Empire as 'the greatest secular agency for good that the world has seen'.

Rosebery returned from his world tour an Imperialist; he appreciated for the first time the vital importance of the chain of power to the East, depending upon the arsenals of Gibraltar and Aden, and the control of Egypt. This realisation was to have immense effects upon his subsequent career; his knowledge of Europe, based upon his friendships with the members of many leading families and officials in almost every European country, was already considerable; his interest in European affairs had been quickened by his friendship with Count Herbert Bismarck—son of the Chancellor—which had begun in 1882 and had developed rapidly; although his knowledge of the Empire was never so deep, it was greater than that of any of his political contemporaries and was to be increased by his travels in 1886-7.

'Imperialism, sane Imperialism, as distinguished from what I might call "wild cat" Imperialism, is nothing but this—a larger patriotism,' he declared in the autumn of 1885. '. . . If a Liberal Imperialist means that I am a Liberal who is passionately attached to the Empire—if it means, as I believe it does, that I am a Liberal who believes that the Empire is best maintained upon the basis of the widest democracy, and that the voice is most powerful when it represents the greatest number of persons and subjects—if these be accurate descriptions of what a Liberal Imperialist is, then I am a Liberal Imperialist, and I believe that you are Liberal Imperialists too.' The first rumblings of dissent to the concept of Liberal Imperialism came from old John Bright, who stigmatised the policy of Imperial Federation as 'childish and absurd', to which Rosebery replied in a speech at Epsom (February 9th, 1885) that 'It is with regret that I have appeared to differ in the remotest degree from one whom I admire and I owe so much as Mr Bright, but we cannot be snuffed out by epithets.' Thus, in an atmosphere of courteous disagreement over what appeared a trivial issue, was inaugurated the dispute which was to warp and destroy Rosebery's career and split the Liberal party irrevocably.

The Roseberys returned to England at the beginning of the March of 1884, and it was not long before another idiotic misunderstanding between Rosebery and the Prime Minister aroused doubts about the former's common sense. After attending the funeral of the Duke of Buccleuch, Rosebery returned to Dalmeny to find a letter from Gladstone offering him the Lord Lieutenancy of Midlothian which had been held by Buccleuch. Almost inevitably, Rosebery refused, and an absurd interchange of letters with Hamilton and Gladstone ensued before Rosebery acquiesced in characteristic manner. 'It must be understood', he wrote to Hamilton on May 6th, 'that I only do it as a final sacrifice to the party & to Mr G: and that I am not to be called upon till the resources of civilisation are exhausted. Perhaps you will understand how hateful this is to me. If you do not, so much the better. At any rate, I close my thirty-seventh year with an act of mortification which I trust may not have to be repeated in any other year.' Hamilton deduced, no doubt rightly, that 'Rosebery dislikes accepting favours and feels that a barren compliment has been paid him. . . . Even granting (which I cannot grant) that Mr G has done everything to thwart R and has treated him badly, such a frame of mind is suicidal to his political prospects and makes one despair of his future.'

Throughout the summer of 1884 tentative offers were made to Rosebery to induce him to return to the Government. Two difficulties stood in the way. In the first place, Rosebery was unhappy about the Egyptian policy—or rather, lack of policy—of the Government. The events of 1882 had placed the Liberal Government in an equivocal and potentially dangerous position in Egypt, which had been exacerbated by the annihilation of two British forces by the armies of the Mahdi at the end of 1883 which meant that—at least for the moment—the Sudan was effectively lost. The Government decided to withdraw the remaining Egyptian garrisons in the Sudan, and in a hapless moment entrusted the task to General Charles Gordon, who installed himself at Khartoum and proceeded to ignore his instructions. As the months passed, British public opinion became alarmed at his isolation, and pressure increased upon the undecided Government to send a relieving force.

In a speech at the Liverpool Reform Club in the autumn of 1884 Rosebery demanded a more powerful Navy and attacked the proposition that Egypt should be evacuated in the near future, insisting that a stable independent administration on which we could rely was essential before we left. This line, as Rosebery was well aware, was directly contrary to the view of the Prime Minister, who told him on June 17th that he would 'welcome political death in the cause of preserving England from the dangers of assuming responsibility for Egypt'. Not only did Rosebery regard the Government's irresolution on this vital matter with impatience, but there were unexpected difficulties in finding a vacancy for him in the Cabinet, as Lord Carlingford was proving remarkably difficult to remove from the Cabinet. 'Spencer made me nearly die of laughing by narrating his and Granville's abortive interview with Carlingford urging him to retire,' Rosebery recorded on October 13th. 'Granville as good as told him that there was no option but retirement or expulsion, which I thought too strong. S felt quite an emotion when G stood before the fire & said, "Now will you let me talk to you as I should to my brother Freddy in such a case." C said he had entered public life with great sorrow & reluctance, and could not . . . etc. etc.'

On September 24th the exasperated Hamilton noted that Carlingford's skin appeared to be made of buffalo hide, and on October 7th there was a conference between Gladstone, Harcourt, Spencer, Childers, and Hartington to consider how this embarrassing impediment might be removed. On October 10th Gladstone informed Rosebery of the situation, adding that 'the time, eminently suitable for your introduction [to the Cabinet], is not favourable to an ejectment'. Rosebery—'trussed like a fowl' after a serious riding accident at Dalmeny—replied that 'nothing would be more distasteful to me than to enter upon an office which had been compulsorily or even reluctantly vacated by another'.

Rosebery's star had unexpectedly risen since the ludicrous episode of the Midlothian Lord Lieutenancy. He declared his support for the Imperial Federation League at the end of June, and in September he made a thunderously applauded speech to the Trades Union Congress meeting at Aberdeen extolling the necessity for closer links with the Empire: 'The impulse for Imperial Federation must not come from Parliaments, but from the people.'

On June 20th he startled the House of Lords by moving for a Select Committee 'to consider the best means of promoting the efficiency of this House' and devoted considerable time to the history of the political complexion and public usefulness of the House, an investigation which was not greatly to that institution's advantage. He proposed that the Committee could examine proposals—for example the extension of the principle of life peerages—to increase the efficiency and usefulness of the House, but, to his anger, he was deserted by the Government front bench in the ensuing discussion and divisions; when the Question of referring the subject to the Committee was put, the members of the Government front bench walked out of the House.

Of far greater importance was his intervention over the Franchise Bill, proposed as part of the great measure of Parliamentary Reform. Rosebery for once captured the attention and the admiration of the Lords by a brilliant speech on second reading, but which failed to save the Bill. It was probably the first occasion that a member of their Lordships' House had laughed at them in their presence; the particular object of his derision was the Duke of Argyll—one of Rosebery's most consistent antipathies—who, he declared, had 'made a spirited defence of the country peers, and drew a picture of them studying politics in their rural retreats, and when the tocsin sounded, hurrying from these rustic retreats, redolent of the library and the hayfields, ready to confirm any decision which might be arrived at by the front bench opposite. . . . You are placing this House in a position for which it is most unsuited; I mean the risky position of trying to dam a torrent of popular feeling.' In the period of negotiation which followed, Rosebery strongly and successfully urged an agreed solution between the two parties.

At the end of August the Gladstones came to Dalmeny for a short Midlothian campaign. Eddie Hamilton was a member of the house party and was awed by the magnificence of the Roseberys' *grande tenue* and by the astounding enthusiasm with which Rosebery was received in Edinburgh. 'One realised for the first time', he wrote in his diary, 'the immensity of the position which he holds in Scotland. I doubt if there is any parallel for it.' Mary Gladstone was also immensely struck by Rosebery's popularity, noting that 'the passionate devotion to him was perhaps the most striking feature of the week'.[1] 'Mr Gladstone is the only other man who can make so many Scotsmen take politics as if it were the Highland Fling,' J. M. Barrie wrote in 1899.

[1] Lucy Masterman: *Mary Gladstone*, 328.

'Once when Lord Rosebery was firing an Edinburgh audience to the delirium point, an old man in the hall shouted out, "I dinna hear a word he says, but it's grand, it's grand!" '[1]

Although still distrustful of Gladstone, and upset because of imagined slights, Rosebery was evidently more cheerful about his political future, which at this time was centred upon the Colonial Office. When offered the Commissionership of Works in November, however, he declined on account of Egypt. 'As to your policy in Egypt,' he wrote on November 12th to the surprised Prime Minister, 'I do not think I have ever disguised from you that I regretted it.' In Gladstone's papers the words 'I have ever disguised from you' are underlined by the Prime Minister, and the comment 'Never mooted in any way between us I believe', added.[2] He replied simply that this was the first that he had ever heard of the difference.

The refusal was particularly annoying, since the leading members of the Government had decided to move Shaw-Lefevre to the Post Office and admit Rosebery as First Commissioner. Mrs Gladstone warned Lady Rosebery that her husband's refusal would seriously harm his career, and Granville urged her to use her influence; this she did, but without effect. Gladstone was extremely disappointed, and did not conceal this. 'He fears', Hamilton wrote (November 12th), 'that this sort of hesitancy of mind & angularity of disposition betray weakness of character and show an inability to pull with others and subordinate his individual views to those of the men with whom he is in general political harmony.' Matters were not improved when *The Scotsman* revealed that the offer had been made, but it was subsequently discovered that Dilke and not Rosebery had been responsible for this accidental disclosure. Rosebery was given to understand that the offer remained open.

It is not easy to define Rosebery's tangled emotions in this situation, since there were many factors which led him to over-

---

[1] *An Edinburgh Eleven.*

[2] Rosebery certainly believed that he had made his position clear. In his diary for April 9th, 1884, he recorded a long conversation with Gladstone on the Egyptian question at The Durdans. 'He asked me what I thought. I told him. He remained silent & after a minute said "You could probably not put that view of the case more forcibly", & retired into the house.' Rosebery recorded other conversations with Gladstone on the subject of Egypt on June 17th and November 9th, when he wrote that Gladstone 'behaved with great tact, delicacy and dignity'.

rule his wife's and his colleagues' arguments. His dissatisfaction
with the Government's foreign policy was very genuine. 'You
wish me (to put it concisely) to enter the government in order to
give the colonists confidence in a colonial administration in which
I feel no confidence at all,' he wrote to Hamilton (December
31st). 'Would not that be acting a lie?' He also enjoyed his independence—as he told Hamilton on January 25th in the course
of a long walk at Mentmore—and disliked the office proffered to
him. He also considered that the Government was rapidly declining into defeat, and was out of sympathy with the more
Radical element in the Cabinet—particularly Chamberlain—which
had deliberately brought the harsh voice of class warfare into the
struggle against the Lords over Parliamentary reform. In brief,
as he told Hamilton with complete candour, he declined to join
a ship whose crew he distrusted and which appeared to be on the
verge of catastrophic shipwreck. A conversation with Hartington
on January 28th did not lessen Rosebery's mistrust of the Cabinet.
'He, H, had a talk with W.E.G. last week as to the break-up
of the Liberal party, which seemed to him inevitable. W.E.G.
concurred, or rather thought there was too much reason to fear
it, but advised Hartington not to resign, if he must resign, on the
Egyptian question, a question no one cared a button about.'
When Rosebery himself saw Gladstone on January 3rd, he thought
'he seemed weary and unhinged'.

The offers were repeated, but refused. Mrs Gladstone (February
4th, 1885) again added her somewhat incoherent appeals to the
more dignified epistles of her husband.

The door is not shut: if upon reading my Husband's letter you *stop*
things—*surely surely*. Poor old Husband! that you wld be by his side.
. . . In all that affects you may God guide you to what is best. . . .

In the early hours of February 5th, news reached Downing
Street that a relieving force had reached Khartoum and found
Gordon already dead. Mr Gladstone, staying at Holker Hall,
near Cartmel, the Lancashire seat of Lord Hartington, returned
at once to London, receiving the Queen's notorious telegram of
vilification *en clair* from the embarrassed stationmaster of Carn-
forth Station. The Queen had not misjudged the mood of her
people. By the time that Gladstone reached Downing Street at

8 p.m., composed and inscrutable, the first fury of an almost unparalleled political storm was apparent.

Rosebery's reactions were characteristic. He at once wrote to Hamilton from Mentmore.

My dear E,

I am horrified & haunted by this news, but at any rate it must make us all determined to sink differences & stand by the Government although it seems hardly probable that it can survive.

But I do not wish to discuss politics any longer, but to put to you a simple question. You gave me to understand that you thought I could be of essential use to the Cabinet. Why I refused to join it you know. But what I meant to say is that though I do not share your view, yet if Mr Gladstone does I will swallow all my scruples and put my shoulder to the wheel if he has not already filled the office up.

But then doubts supervened, and the letter was not sent for three days, during which Rosebery anxiously re-examined the situation. On February 8th he decided to write to Gladstone 'in the sense of my original impulse'. To Hamilton he wrote: 'I am sure that I cannot be wrong in tendering myself, and the situation at this moment is hardly one to attract ambition or vanity.' To Gladstone he wrote that although he was still disturbed over the Egyptian policy of the Government, 'my only call of duty is plain and simple—to place myself at your disposal in the hour of difficulty and disaster'. To this characteristically romantic gesture Gladstone replied with what Rosebery described to Hamilton as 'icy dignity', accepting his offer and informing him that he would submit his name to the Queen.[1]

Hamilton was able to make matters smoother by suggesting to Granville that Rosebery should be offered the Privy Seal as well; Granville tactfully hinted at such an offer 'to sweeten the Works, as he is silly enough to care', and, in Hamilton's words, 'Mr G jumped at the idea at once without having any suspicions (he is certainly the most unsuspicious of mortals).'

It was obvious that the downfall of the Government could not be long delayed. The acute personal divergencies within the Cabinet, soon to be exacerbated further, were reflected in a deteriorating Parliamentary position. For the previous eighteen months the Government's handling of its legislative programme and its supporters had been palpably inept, and was reflected in

[1] The letter is quoted in full in Crewe: *Rosebery*, I, 217-18.

the bewilderment, independence, and apathy of the Ministerialist benches. Both Gladstone and Granville had lost their grip of Government business which had held together the 1868–74 Administration. As a modern commentator has remarked, 'In the end the art of government had eluded Gladstone, though the art of swaying opinion he never lost. He could not now manage the small teasing human difficulties, though he could still stir the mind and heart with the large ideas that often proved right in the end.'[1] Supported by the extraordinarily violent feeling of the country the once-defunct Opposition hurled itself furiously upon the Ministry, which survived a critical vote of censure in the Commons by only fourteen votes. Churchill, Salisbury, and Hicks-Beach, supported by a united Tory Party, harried the Government unmercifully. On the Afghan border a potentially grave situation between Russia and Britain was looming, the expiry of the Crimes Act in August meant a return to the controversies over coercive legislation for Ireland and an inevitable clash between the left and right wing members of the Cabinet, while the intractable Egyptian question provided fertile ground for dispute in an already divided Cabinet.

Rosebery attended his first Cabinet on February 16th, and was struck by the lack of harmony and the abruptness of manner in discussion. 'I wonder what you thought of us all?' Granville asked Rosebery in a note passed at the meeting. 'More numerous than the House of Lords', came the reply, 'and not quite so united.'

On February 28th—the morning after the Pyrrhic victory over the Sudan vote of censure—there was a confused discussion in the Cabinet over whether it should resign. Rosebery's long and detailed account reveals that there was a substantial majority in favour of resignation, and that the discussion was characterised by the petulance and childishness which was so conspicuous a feature of the second Gladstone Government. After Granville, Harcourt, Derby, and Chamberlain had spoken in favour of resigning, 'Hartington depreciated the majority by saying votes had been turned by his speech. Harcourt quoted persons who had been influenced by *his* speech. Hartington summed the matter up by saying [that] the two sections of the party can only be conciliated by uttering divergent opinions.' Chamberlain put

[1] Agatha Ramm, Introduction to *The Political Correspondence of Mr Gladstone and Lord Granville, 1876–1886*, xlviii.

forward a series of arguments against resignation, supported by
Dilke, but after Gladstone had spoken vehemently against this
course, Dilke changed his mind, as did Harcourt. 'Mr Gladstone
very pathetic as to the question,' Rosebery noted. ' "It is one for
those who in the future will have the responsibility. For me it is
evident that my retirement would mean something—definite"—
he paused before the last word.'

'We then branched off into discussions on the Suakin railway,
in the midst of which Childers soliloquised bitterly, "Kimberley
has spoken nineteen times & won't let me speak *once*". . . .
Hartington observed that all these differences only made him more
clear that the cabinet had better take this opportunity of resigning.' After four hours of this rambling and futile discussion the
matter was put to a vote, Rosebery abstaining. The numbers were
equal: Granville, Derby, Hartington, Selborne, Spencer, North-
brook, and Childers voting for resignation, with Kimberley,
Lefevre, Trevelyan, Harcourt, Dilke, Chamberlain, and Carlingford voting against. Gladstone gave his casting vote against
resignation, and so it was decided. 'Of course as a matter of fact
there was a large majority in favour of resignation,' Rosebery's
long account ends. 'Harcourt & Chamberlain were strong for it,
but voted against in deference to Mr Gladstone. Carlingford, as
he gave his vote, said "I suppose it is too late to change so I must
vote No".'

The drift and indecision of the doomed Government were
partially checked at the end of April, when the Russians suddenly
attacked Afghan troops at Penjdeh on the Afghan border while
negotiations on frontier delineations were in progress. The
Cabinet discussions on this vital matter were marked with a
childishness which exasperated Rosebery; at one meeting Harcourt threatened to resign merely because he had been interrupted
in the middle of a long discourse by Kimberley. Rosebery urged
strong action, and wrote a memorandum which attacked any
suggestion that the Russian aggression should be shrugged off.

All Europe is laughing at us, our nose has been pulled all over the
world. Throughout next week we shall be undergoing the same process
with France. Our Government smiles over it, and thinks it is not
humiliating. But it *is* humiliating. And they further say that we are so
strong we can afford it. But are we so strong ? Nations with armies of
two millions do not consider us strong.

In the event the Government pulled itself together, secured an emergency Vote of Credit of £11 million to demonstrate its earnestness, and the Russians quickly climbed down.

But it was not India, nor even the Sudan, but Ireland which provided the most fruitful source of division within the Cabinet. A major Irish crisis arose when Chamberlain brought forward an Irish plan of administrative devolution involving county boards and a national council. After hesitations and acrimonious discussions the 'Central Board Scheme' was taken to a vote on May 20th, all the commoners except Hartington supporting it and all the peers except Granville in opposition. Rosebery, with considerable reluctance, supported Lord Spencer, the Viceroy, in opposition to the proposals. At one meeting Rosebery passed a note to Chamberlain: 'Would you take a stroll to-morrow morning, or dine quietly to-morrow evening? I am a Scottish home-ruler as well as Irish.' After the adverse vote, Chamberlain and Dilke submitted their resignations, which were, however, held over temporarily.

Rosebery remained a junior and somewhat puzzled spectator of these curious manoeuvres. He wrote on the Ministry:

> *In fire lives the Salamander*
> *And in water lives the fish;*
> *On goose's sauce exists the gander,*
> *And the Whigs upon the Dish.*

> *Stranger far, upon devices*
> *Our Cabinet both lives and thrives;*
> *Devices to avoid the crisis*
> *Which forms the pleasure of our lives.*

He came to the conclusion that Childers and Shaw-Lefevre were the weakest members of the Cabinet, that Kimberley was more impressive than he had expected, and that Gladstone towered over all his colleagues in ability and personality. 'Rosebery says the key to the situation of the Cabinet is Mr G himself,' Hamilton wrote on May 16th. 'All Ministers individually want it to break up and yet none want to break away from the rest, disassociated from Mr G. They each want Mr G's aegis to be spread over them.' Gladstone was for his part increasingly impressed with Rosebery. 'It is impossible', he remarked to Hamilton at this time, 'to get anything out of Rosebery but a clever, and indeed brilliant, reply, no matter how uninteresting the subject.' In his letters and conversation with Rosebery, Gladstone did not conceal his mounting dislike for Chamberlain and Dilke. On the latter he remarked that he was 'curt and discourteous', and observed to Rosebery on May 21st that he was determined that Chamberlain and Dilke should not destroy the Government. Hamilton urged him to let them go, but Gladstone replied, 'I would, if they were ministerial nonentities; but they are great factors; and a quarrel with them is too big a job for me to face lightly.'

The closing weeks of the Ministry were disfigured with personal acrimonies, beset by grave international problems, and haunted by the mounting onslaught in the House of Commons. Childers' Budget produced farcical scenes in the Cabinet and frequent resignations by the Chancellor of the Exchequer. Rosebery's diary records these events.

April 20th: Cabinet at 2 on budget. Childers stated his case wretchedly ('bitched it' said WEG!) and got unmercifully handled. It was a Childers bait (as we should have said at Eton) for 2 hours.

Dilke threatens to resign (taking I suppose Chamberlain with him) if the beer duty of ½d. is persisted in, as it will alienate the new voters for ever. . . .

May 7th: At 2 Cabinet. It was agreed to resign if we were beaten on the question of the Registration payment. It was announced we shd certainly be beaten on the budget & if not shd break up on Ireland. I thought they were not enjoining Dick Grosvenor[1] (who was present) to whip zealously enough so I remarked 'We appear to contemplate a course of conduct which on the Turf wd bring us under the notice of the Jockey Club.'

May 10th: Cabinet at noon. A Childers worry. Childers wants to amend his budget. Says he must resign if we won't amend it.

If we can endure the odium of it surely the author can. He won't resign, nor would it matter if he did.

After his statement Harcourt simply remarked 'So far as I know the budget is as good a question to go out upon as any other & Tuesday as good a day.'

June 5th: Cabinet at 11. . . . Discussion on budget. Childers proposed an increased wine duty.—everybody against it. At last saying 'I am sorry to say I cannot agree' he stalked from the room. Harcourt the official pacificator hurried after him, followed shortly aftwds by

[1] Lord Richard Grosvenor, the Liberal Chief Whip.

Gladstone amid general mirth. They came back in 20 minutes saying he required an hour's thought. Then Granville & the Chancellor[1] were sent. (Shortly after the cabinet separated C withdrew his resignation.) Then general discussion on Ireland: Lefevre, Dilke & Chamberlain all agst 'coercion'. C[hamberlain] wrote on a piece of paper 'Can you not give us a lift in this matter? I fancy you are with us though I have not liked to ask you your opinions.' I replied that I was in favour of a strong local government measure, but cd not throw over anything wh Spencer declared to be the least possible legislation with wh Ireland cd be governed.

On June 8th Gladstone informed the Cabinet that there was 'some chance' of the Government being defeated on an amendment to the Budget on the proposed beer duties that evening. A heated argument on Ireland followed, principally between Spencer and Chamberlain, described by Rosebery in his diary as 'a long & confused & simultaneous discussion ending in nothing—adjourned till tomorrow'. That evening, to the inexpressible relief of most members of the Ministry, the Government were defeated by twelve votes in the House of Commons on the beer duties. Rosebery recorded the epitaph of the Ministry thus:

> *Here lies a Cabinet, I'll tell you why;*
> *It spelt its funeral bier without an i.*

The Cabinet met on the following morning in high spirits, except for the Prime Minister, who opened by saying that he would like to announce that they had agreed on the Irish Question, but the ensuing silence told him that that was impossible. Rosebery somewhat flippantly asked if the Cabinet could resign by telegraph, 'which horrified Mr G'.

The events of the next few days were confused. Lord Salisbury was summoned to Balmoral and accepted the Queen's Commission; under the terms of the Reform Act no dissolution was possible until the autumn, so unless assurances on business were given by the Liberals the Conservatives could not secure a majority in the Commons nor seek a dissolution. Salisbury was afflicted with an embarrassing personal decision, caused by Northcote trying to cling on to the fragments of his position as the nominal leader in the Commons and by Randolph Churchill insisting upon Northcote's removal to the Lords. On June 18th

[1] Lord Selborne.

the Cabinet met and refused to give any specific assurances to Salisbury; Rosebery had 'bustled up' from The Durdans with the Privy Seal for tendering to the Queen, only to discover that he was still in office. He travelled alone with Gladstone to Windsor in a special train in the afternoon.

. . . Mr G shewed me Salisbury's letters to the Queen & his replies. 'What do you think of the situation—of our going out?' 'Well, personally I am very glad.' He seemed nettled by the word 'personally', and said, 'not personally, but politically.' 'Well, the best result wd be that you should come back & form a new government.' 'Why?' 'Because we could not come back as we were, the cabinet shd. be reduced & some changes made.' 'What changes?' 'Well, for instance, Ld Carlingford is a very good man but he is not of much use.' 'I quite agree with you about him, as you know last autumn I tried everything with him except the *ultima ratio*.' 'I only give him as an instance.' 'Then what departments wd you change?' 'That is not my business, but if you want an example I should say that Ld Derby has not given satisfaction at the Colonial Office.' 'I doubt if there is any precedent for a minister in my position forming a fresh govt.' 'But you will have to, precedent or not. If you come back with what is falsely called Coercion, you lose Dilke, Chamberlain & Lefevre. If without, you lose Spencer & others who agree with him. You were face to face with this difficulty when we were beaten, but then you had not the means of meeting it: you had to find three H of C men for the Cabinet or get rid of some of your peers. By forming a fresh cabinet on whichever principle you adopt you get rid of the difficulty & have all offices at your disposal.' 'True,' & plunged in thought.

I asked him if he could tell me when we shd give up the seals. 'I really cannot say, the situation is so abnormal. Here is Salisbury practically forming a cabinet before entering into parliamentary negotiations.'

I had a brougham waiting for me at Windsor & drove to the races, where Hartington & Granville, thirsting for information.

Rosebery's disenchantment with his experience of Mr Gladstone's second Cabinet—short though it had been—had been profound. As he had told Gladstone, root and branch tactics were required to give it unity and efficiency. It was absurd, for example, that incompetent Ministers like Carlingford and Childers, regarded with derision by their colleagues, should continue in office year after year, or that the Ministry should confront the sombre Irish Question so desperately divided. On June 21st he told Hamilton that a major reconstruction was essential, with Carlingford to leave the Ministry, Granville to be removed from the Foreign Office and to be replaced by Dilke, Harcourt to become Lord Chancellor, Henry James to become Home Secretary, and Derby relegated (like Granville) to a nominal position. Rosebery said that his ambitions were for the Colonial Office. On the next day he set these thoughts down in a memorandum, which has only been recently discovered in his papers.

Reasons for not rejoining the cabinet if reinstated.

1. Because I consider, our resignation having been accepted, that a new state of things has arisen, and that every member of the government is at liberty to reconsider the position.

2. My experience of the present cabinet has convinced me that it cannot properly conduct the affairs of this country. It is too large and not homogenous enough. Under the circumstances in which I joined it I felt it my duty to remain in it whether I agreed with it or not. But now that stage of things has ended, and I am free to look to what is best for the country, and I have been long convinced that this government is not calculated to act efficiently.

Events did not make this step necessary. The required assurances as to essential business having been given, the Liberal Cabinet finally resigned on June 24th. Lord Salisbury headed what was derided by Chamberlain as 'the Ministry of Caretakers', with Lord Carnarvon as Viceroy of Ireland and Randolph Churchill at the India Office, clearly the second man in the Ministry. The unfortunate Sir Stafford Northcote—'offered up like the Greek virgin of antiquity to assist the success of the enterprise', as Rosebery observed in a speech at Paisley in the autumn—was bundled off to the House of Lords as the Earl of Iddesleigh with the honorific post of First Lord of the Treasury.

The events of the autumn and winter of 1885–6 mark a decisive point in modern British political history. While Gladstone pondered in isolation on the problems of the Irish Question and the possibilities of Home Rule, the Conservatives engaged in a dangerous flirtation with the Irish Nationalists which was destined to have a profound effect upon the history of the Liberal Party. The 1885 election campaign—which virtually began in July although voting did not begin until November—was characterised by a public display of Liberal disunity, seen most

conspicuously in the curt exchanges on Ireland between Hartington and Chamberlain, while Chamberlain himself embarked upon
an independent Radical campaign quickly labelled 'the Unauthorised Programme'. Gladstone, deaf to all entreaties from his
colleagues and supporters, maintained an Olympian detachment,
declining to enter into negotiations with Parnell, who, in an
evil moment for his cause, responded by issuing a manifesto on
the eve of the elections urging all Irishmen in England to support
the Conservatives.

Yet within three months, Chamberlain, who had harshly
denounced Salisbury in 1883 as 'the spokesman of a class who toil
not neither do they spin', found himself in political alliance with
the object of that onslaught; Hartington, compared by Randolph
Churchill to a boa constrictor in 1885, entered Churchill's camp;
the Liberal candidates of 1885 fighting against the Parnell *diktat*
were championing Irish Nationalism within the year. A more
unexpected or astounding political metamorphosis could hardly
be conceived. Home Rule became the sole banner, and Home
Rule the only test. On September 9th Gladstone set out his view
of the complex political position in a letter to Granville of which
Rosebery received a copy.

> . . . The problem for me is to make if possible a statement which
> will hold through the Election and not to go into conflict with either
> the right wing of the party for whom Hartington had spoken, or the
> left wing, for whom Chamberlain I suppose spoke last night. . . . I
> do not say they are to be treated as on a footing, but I must do no act
> disparaging to Chamberlain's wing. Dilke for the moment is under his
> mantle.[1]
> After the dissolution things will define themselves. . . . I shall write
> to Chamberlain. His socialism repels me. Some day mischief will come.
> The question is when. . .

Rosebery did not share Gladstone's confidence in Parnell. 'If
I had the power,' he declared in the course of a speech to the
Paisley Liberal Club, 'and if I were convinced that Ireland were
loyal to the connection with this country, there would be no
limits to the concessions that I would offer to Ireland. No de-

---

[1] Dilke had been cited as co-respondent in a divorce action brought by Rosebery's
friend, Donald Crawford, against his wife, which had been announced on August
5th. The case, and the question of Rosebery's implication in it, are discussed on
pages 181–189.

mands formulated by Mr Parnell should appal or deter me if I were sure of that one feature in the problem; no price should be too great to pay for a loyal and contented Ireland. But now, if we had to pay the price, what should we get? We can only surmise; but I am afraid the surmise of everyone in this hall would point in the same direction.'

'Parnell's declarations have filled me with pleasure,' he wrote to Gladstone on September 8th. 'It frees our hands to do what we think right without being misled by the will o' the wisp idea of satisfying the Irish party, while it renders impossible the unholy alliance with the other side.' Gladstone replied on the 10th that 'It would be a great relief indeed, if with you, I could feel pleasure at Parnell's recent declarations. I seem to be rather like the juror, who sat with eleven most obstinate men, that he could not convince of the truths he himself saw. . . . It is no pain to me to be relieved of the will o' the wisp idea of satisfying the Irish party, as I have never had that expectation or acted with such a view. What I do think of is the Irish nation, & the fame, duty & peace of my country. . . . Chamberlain says, what are 4 millions against 32? The answer depends wholly on the case. . . . I deeply regret our having lost the opportunity offered by the plan of a Central Board, which you favoured. . . . I am treading upon eggs at every step, & the shells are unusually brittle.'

By November, when the Gladstones came to Dalmeny for the Midlothian campaign, Gladstone's disgust with Chamberlain was predominant and he told Rosebery in a long walk in the park on November 10th that he distrusted him more than Parnell. Lady Rosebery had visited Hawarden just before this, and came away with the impression that the Gladstones were determined upon office. 'There is evident jealousy of Mr Chamberlain at Hawarden', she wrote to Hamilton, 'and an exaggerated belief in his power, which has been cultivated by Sir WH.' Gladstone was equally distrustful of Dilke, who in his speeches was taking a line almost as independent as that of Chamberlain. 'I said I had heard there was a chance of Dilke being beaten for Chelsea,' Rosebery recorded on November 20th; 'Mr G replied that worse things might happen.' On November 13th Gladstone prepared upon Dalmeny paper his view of the situation, which was that it would be disastrous for the Liberals to propose a Home Rule measure while in Opposition.

. . . I well know, from a thousand indications, past and present, that a mere project of mine, launched into the air, would have no momentum which would carry it to its aim. . . .

The *first* essential is a sufficient and independent Liberal majority; the second is to keep it together. If these two can be had, there is no fear of the House of Lords. It would not dare: and, if it did, would repent quickly, and probably in vain. . .

The results of the elections destroyed these expectations; the Conservatives, making spectacular inroads into the Liberal ascendancy in the boroughs, but losing heavily in the traditionally Conservative county constituencies, won 249 seats, the Liberals 335, and consequently Parnell's 86 Irish Nationalists held the balance of power. Gladstone held the Midlothian seat with an enormous majority (4,600) amid scenes of excitement which some observers thought were greater than in 1879–80. 'Just imagine doing a thing for the 4th time, and exactly the same, the same carriage and 4 horses, the same routes, the same people,' Mary Gladstone wrote on November 11th from Dalmeny. 'And yet as we drive to Edinburgh you would think it was the first time it ever happened, the 7 miles of road with its frantic little groups, the decorated cottages, the carriages, bicycles, traps of all description lining the way, the gradual increase of people as you get nearer Edinburgh, the crowds in the streets, the eager faces cramming every window high and low; it is all *exactly* the same as before.'[1] But the triumphal speeches at the Rosebery Club and Corn Exchange in Edinburgh were overshadowed by the inconclusiveness of the general election results. 'Somehow I felt the whole thing melancholy,' Rosebery noted; '. . . Mr G was older feebler less victorious by much than in 1880, if victorious at all, & somehow one felt as if one was witnessing the close of that long & brilliant career. Several of our party wept at the Rosebery Club meeting.' Eddie Hamilton was one of the Dalmeny party, and recorded that 'Mr G, whose voice was very husky, replied in a subdued, somewhat depressed, but stately tone. Rosebery followed with a most touching speech. . . . It was most pathetic—the delivery as touching as the matter. It drew many a tear. . . . There was a certain gloom which characterised the proceedings [at the Corn Exchange]. . . . The enthusiasm of the crowd outside the station for Rosebery knew no bounds. They mobbed

[1] Lucy Masterman: *Mary Gladstone*, 336.

him and shouted for him, "Rosbery, Rosbery" was the universal
cry, the crowd running with the carriage till we were fairly out of
the Town.'

On December 8th Rosebery was summoned to Hawarden to
confer with Gladstone and Spencer on the acute difficulties of
the situation. Gladstone said that if the Tories could come to an
agreement with Parnell he would support them; if not, they should
be at once opposed when Parliament reassembled, on a vote of
want of confidence on an issue unconnected with Ireland for
preference; if it were to be on Ireland, it should be moved by the
Liberal leaders and not by Parnell. 'Rosebery has returned from
Hawarden. Mr G's mind is bent,' Hamilton noted on December
12th. '. . . He has Ireland on the brain; & thinks himself bound
to make an effort, heedless of consequences, to effect a settlement.'
Rosebery, on Gladstone's instructions, saw Labouchere on December 12th to attempt to discover the views of Parnell and the
Tories; in his long account of this interview to Gladstone, Rosebery most strongly urged silence before Parliament reassembled.
'I agree most strongly that I must remain obstinately silent as to
my plans,' Gladstone replied on the 13th. '. . . If P and the Government cannot agree, that opens a new situation. . . . I do not mean
to be sat upon by D[ilke] or by D & C[hamberlain], if other
things call on me to act. . . . I think it may be best to ignore
Dilke.'

These careful plans were destroyed on December 16th by an
act of astonishing irresponsibility by Herbert Gladstone, who
deliberately briefed some journalists at the National Press Agency
that his father was contemplating a plan to provide 'for the
establishment of a Parliament in Dublin for dealing with purely
Irish affairs'. The 'Hawarden Kite' arose on the next morning in
The Standard and created an immense political sensation, which
was not allayed by a characteristically ambiguous denial from
Hawarden.

'I fully share your regrets as to H's indiscretions,' Rosebery
wrote to Hamilton on December 22nd. 'Proofs of them reach me
from all sides from newspaper editors & persons in railway
carriages. But I greatly fear that he has been encouraged to this
by an illustrious relative who is or has been most anxious that
his opinions on this subject should be known in various quarters.
That is why, I suspect, H has not heeded your remonstrances. I

am not at all sure that the country and the Liberal party will refuse to follow Mr G on this question. Disregard the London clubbites, who are sure to lead you wrong.' From the outset of the crisis Rosebery took his stand beside Gladstone. The romantic side of his nature was fired by the image of the aged statesman flinging down the gauntlet of Home Rule, facing the dismemberment of his party and savage attack for the sake of a great principle. He had, moreover, been taken into Gladstone's confidence at an early stage, and it would have been unthinkable to retreat at this point; Rosebery's attitude to Home Rule in 1886 was that it was the only practical alternative to coercion, and at least merited an experiment. He did not foresee the terrible penalty the Liberal Party was to pay for its actions, although even at this early stage he had a rooted distrust of Parnell. But he also appreciated the intense irritation of Gladstone's ex-colleagues—particularly Chamberlain and Harcourt—at being placed so unexpectedly in so dangerous a situation so soon after fighting a general election. 'Harcourt furious with Mr G, talking of "lying" etc., full of pique,' Rosebery noted on December 30th. 'I rather wish you could see your way to call a meeting of your late colleagues next week,' he wrote to Gladstone (January 2nd, 1886). 'It would nip in the bud jealousies and misunderstandings that might ripen into schism.' This suggestion was swept aside by the Liberal leader, and the situation continued to deteriorate. Eddie Hamilton agreed to write to Gladstone at Harcourt's instigation to inform him of his colleagues' reactions to the 'Hawarden Kite'; Gladstone noted in his diary that 'The contents of Hamilton's letter recd. today, I confess, made me indignant for a while.' Spencer, not easily aroused, wrote to Rosebery that he had never been so disgusted in his life as he had been by the Hawarden Kite, and added 'how odious (and maybe wicked) it is to think that Parnell and his crew are to govern Ireland'.

Rosebery, reluctantly convinced that Home Rule must be attempted as the only alternative to coercive rule, was opposed to the tactical suggestion that the Tories should be allowed to remain in office. He privately attacked this 'propping-up policy' as dishonourable and unrealistic. Harcourt came to Mentmore on January 9th to report that Chamberlain refused to accept either coercion or Home Rule. 'How then in Heaven's name', Rosebery retorted, 'is Ireland to be governed?' Hamilton told him that he was not personally bound to Gladstone's Irish policy and that his excessive loyalty might conflict with his personal interests, but 'there was nothing very unbending in his reply'. Throughout the crisis Rosebery demonstrated an unexpected tenacity and resolution; 'the two men on whom Mr G evidently leans most just now', Hamilton wrote on January 12th, 'are Ld Spencer & Rosebery.'

The Conservative Government was anxious to resign and force the public commitment of the Liberal leader to Home Rule, while Gladstone still clung to the belief that the Government would undertake a Home Rule measure, opening informal negotiations with Salisbury through Arthur Balfour on December 22nd. Chamberlain, whose initial reaction to the Hawarden Kite was to describe 'Mr G's Irish scheme' as 'Death and damnation',[1] was working increasingly closely with Randolph Churchill, whom he told on January 12th that the country was 'dead against' Home Rule. 'Joe did not conceal at all his hatred of Hartington and Goschen, and snarled awfully at both many times,' Churchill informed Salisbury on January 13th.[2] Although Gladstone's proposals were rejected by the Cabinet, there were serious differences among the Conservative leaders on the exact tactics to be adopted; Salisbury was resolved 'to get out of office, and at once', and a Coercion Bill was drafted, but Hicks-Beach and Churchill held out against this measure for several days. When Parliament reassembled on January 21st both political parties were suffering from divisions within the ranks of their leaders. On the 20th the Liberal ex-cabinet peers met Hartington and Harcourt, both of whom were bewildered by Gladstone's exact intentions. 'It reminded me of the Duke of Grafton's cabinet talking over the possible intentions of Ld Chatham,' Rosebery remarked in his diary. On the 21st the ex-cabinet met, but Gladstone declined, 'with great eloquence and vigour', to have his hand forced. 'I may resign my seat, but I will not part with my liberty,' he declared; the discussion then branched off into an argument between Gladstone and Hartington, and the meeting broke up after an hour and a half with little decided, some of its members—including Gladstone—embarrassed by the presence of Dilke, who sat 'morose in a corner', as Rosebery recorded. It

---

[1] Garvin: *Chamberlain*, II, 141.
[2] *Salisbury Papers*. (See R. R. James, *Lord Randolph Churchill*, 229.)

is impossible to condemn Gladstone's attitude to his colleagues too strongly. He should—as Rosebery urged him to do—have called them together, explained why he had been forced to conceal his conversion from them, and asked for their support. The fact that he had taken a few of them into his confidence and not the others made matters considerably worse, but a candid explanation might have cleared the air. On January 27th the Liberals struck at the Ministry on an agrarian amendment to the Address ('Three acres and a cow') moved by Jesse Collings, and in the critical division Hartington, Goschen, Henry James, and thirteen other Liberals voted in the Government lobby. That afternoon, however, the Conservatives had announced their intention to introduce a Coercion Bill, and it was Ireland and not allotments for owner-occupiers which occupied the thoughts of Members when the House divided. Salisbury resigned forthwith.

The dual problem facing Gladstone was to frame an Irish measure and to form a Ministry which would support it. Hartington, Goschen, and Henry James refused all offers, and Chamberlain entered very doubtfully as President of the Local Government Board. Lord Spencer, however, although it was his policy that had been overturned, took office as Lord President. The Queen had envisaged sending for Hartington to form a government, but Rosebery, when approached by Ponsonby for advice on January 24th, strongly urged the abandonment of this dangerous proposal.

The problem of the Foreign Secretaryship was particularly difficult to resolve. Granville's failing abilities had been only too painfully apparent to his colleagues in the late Ministry; Gladstone had been troubled by this question for some time, and had told Rosebery on December 9th that Granville's return to the Foreign Office would be 'inexpedient'; Dilke, as Gladstone somewhat curtly noted, was 'not available'. At a conference between Gladstone, Wolverton, and Rosebery on January 28th Rosebery said that it would be extremely difficult and embarrassing to remove a man 'who had been Foreign Minister for 33 years more or less and had absorbed all the experience of the party. Mr G said Kimberley would do.' The Queen made it known through Ponsonby on the 29th that she could not agree to Lord Kimberley, and proposed Rosebery. 'He did not object,' Ponsonby reported to the Queen, 'but thought he was rather

young.' The Prince of Wales, in a letter to Ponsonby on January
31st, urged the same proposal. Hamilton produced an enormous
memorandum on the subject of the new Cabinet—which he sent
to Lady Rosebery—and proposed to work for his friend's accession to the Foreign Office. 'I am not sure if you yet thoroughly
understand Archie,' she replied on January 29th. 'Anything right
and to prevent an incompetent person to hold a particular office
he will endeavour, but I doubt his even saying a syllable which
would even make an idea possible of his having entertained the
notion of taking a high post.' Granville, not surprisingly, was
deeply hurt when the suggestion was made to him that he should
relinquish the Foreign Office. When Rosebery saw Gladstone on
January 28th he learned that Kimberley was Gladstone's nominee;
this, of course, was before the Royal opposition to this proposal
was made known. On January 30th Spencer at last obtained
Granville's relinquishment of his claims to the Foreign Office
after an embarrassing and difficult interview. Granville—who, as
Spencer reported to Rosebery on February 1st, was 'very sore'—
insisted that he could only accept the Colonial Office, and this
appointment was subsequently agreed to. Rosebery's nomination
had the support of the principal members of the Cabinet. 'Harcourt, Spencer and D. Grosvenor[1] agree with me in choosing
Rosebery,' Granville wrote to Gladstone on February 2nd.
Rosebery was in London to attend the wedding of Mary Gladstone
to the Rev. Harry Drew at St Margaret's, and after the ceremony
Gladstone offered Rosebery the Foreign Office, adding that the
only alternative for him would be the Scottish Office. In spite of
his characteristic façade of indifference, Rosebery was thrilled by
the offer, as a man of thirty-eight might reasonably be at such
spectacular elevation to virtually the second place in the Government. When Hamilton had suggested in the September of 1885
that Rosebery should go to the Foreign Office he had laughed at
the notion, but, as Hamilton noted, 'I fancy I have given him the
place which in his heart of hearts he would prefer, though he
will not admit it.' But Rosebery was genuinely disturbed by the
circumstances of the offer, and in spite of the coldness which
Granville and he had regarded each other for the past five years,
he felt acutely the painful closure of the old man's career at the
Foreign Office. He asked for time to consider the offer,

[1] Lord Richard Grosvenor.

R.—13

but at 9 p.m.[1] on the same evening wrote to the Prime Minister.

Feb. 2. 1886.
Lansdowne House, Berkeley Square, W

My dear Mr Gladstone,

I have no right to leave your proposal unanswered any longer.

Though I have seen the suggestion mooted in the papers that I should go to the Foreign Office I have never seriously entertained it. I have absolutely no experience of the Foreign Office, which I have never entered except to attend a dinner. My French is I fear rusty. I have never had to face anything like what *you* would call hard work. I have no knowledge of diplomatic practice or forms, and little of diplomatic men. And I am sensible of many deficiencies of temper and manner. Moreover the Foreign Office is usually considered, and justly I think, to be the chief of all offices. I should gladly have climbed into it in ten or twenty years, had I been fit for it then. But I know very well that I am not fit for it now, and that you wish me to take it without that experience of other departments which seems to me as indispensable to a Foreign Secretary: without even that cabinet experience so essential to a minister of that rank.

Nevertheless, if you wish me to try my hand, and if you have that confidence in me which I have not in myself, I am willing to put my shoulder to the wheel and do my best; in spite of my gloomy and egotistical preface.

I need not say that the kindness you promised me on Lord Granville's behalf is a great element in the situation.

If, after receiving this, a new combination should occur to you that would enable you to dispense with me at the Foreign Office, you will of course consider your offer as not made.

I hope that if I am to be Foreign Minister, I may be consulted as to the Under Secretary in the House of Commons.

I write in some depression and much self-distrust, but with the most earnest anxiety to do my duty.

Believe me,
Yrs affy
Rosebery.

'Advisedly, upon the whole case, I am glad to accept your "Notwithstanding" (or "Nevertheless")', Gladstone replied at once, 'and I propose to submit your name to HM for the FO.' 'It is an awful scrape,' Rosebery confided to his diary. When he kissed hands at Osborne on the 6th the Queen noted that 'He

---

[1] Incorrectly stated as 3 p.m. in Crewe: *Rosebery*, I, 259.

seemed much impressed with the difficulties of his new Office of Foreign Sec?. & said it was "too much".' On the 8th he entered the Foreign Office for the first time as Foreign Secretary, and dictated his first official telegram. 'What a fly on a cartwheel!' he noted in his diary.

One of Rosebery's first acts upon entering the Foreign Office was to write to Sir Charles Dilke on February 4th.

My dear Dilke,
   You will know already what I have not been allowed to announce previously, that I have been appointed to the Foreign Office.
   One of my chief thoughts in this business has been of you.
   Had you not felt compelled to stand aside this office would have been yours by universal consent. You have all the knowledge & the ability I so sadly lack. You must feel this strongly, but you cannot feel it half so strongly as I do; and I venture to intrude upon you even at so trying a moment as this to assure you how constantly present it is to my own mind.
   I will not trouble you with more now, but will only sign myself
                                                  Yrs sincerely,
                                                       AR.

'I don't know how, with those terrible telegrams beginning to fly round you, you have time to write such letters,' Dilke replied. 'I could never have taken the Foreign Office without the heaviest misgivings, & I hope that whenever the Liberals are in, up to the close of my life, you may hold it.' On February 8th he wrote in similar terms, adding, 'If you are writing to Herbert Bismarck please remember me to him, & tell him from me that I have no FO ambitions.'

'Many thanks for your kind letter,' Rosebery replied on the next day. 'I never attributed any importance to the article except as shewing how many others feel like me what an excellent Foreign Secretary you would make. I have written your message verbatim to Herbert Bismarck. I called on you on Friday to consult you *de omnibus rebus et quibusdem aliis*. But you were out and I could not wait. Now that I am actually in harness I cannot leave the shaft for five minutes.'

The case of *Crawford v. Crawford and Dilke* came up on February 12th. The evidence against Dilke—the sole alleged co-respondent —was dismissed with costs, but Crawford was given his decree *nisi*, an apparently contradictory decision which naturally aroused some perplexity.[1] Dilke's counsel, Sir Charles Russell and Sir Henry James, had advised against him going into the witness-box and Russell had made matters even worse by referring in his statement to the Court to the fact that 'in the life of any man there may be found to have been some indiscretions'. Dilke soon discovered that although acquitted by the Court he had been found guilty by public opinion. The Prince of Wales told Hamilton on February 17th that it would be impossible for the Queen to receive Dilke as a Minister. Chamberlain told Rosebery on the 13th that if Dilke bided his time everything would be forgotten; Rosebery said that the failure to put Dilke into the witness-box had been unfortunate.

Dilke invoked the intervention of the Queen's Proctor,[2] but in the second case, held in July, Dilke was subjected to merciless cross-examination by Henry Mathews—who almost immediately afterwards became Home Secretary in Salisbury's second Ministry on the recommendation of Randolph Churchill—and was publicly branded as an adulterer and a perjurer, the jury taking only fifteen minutes to reach their decision. Dilke had recently lost his seat at Chelsea in the general election, and there was even a meeting of his ex-colleagues to consider whether his name should be struck off the list of Privy Councillors. Although he returned to the House of Commons in 1892 for the Forest of Dean and remained a Member until his death in 1911, he never held office nor exerted any political influence again.

The story of this shattering eclipse has recently been related by Mr Roy Jenkins.[3] 'He was', he writes of Dilke, 'the victim of a conspiracy, the main lines of which (and, indeed, the identity of the other participants in which) are shrouded in mystery and are likely always so to remain.'

Certain features of the Dilke case are extremely puzzling, and

[1] It is interesting to note that Selborne, the former Lord Chancellor, in a letter to Gladstone of February 14th, considered that Mrs Crawford's petition should have been dismissed and that the Judge's decision was incomprehensible. (*Gladstone Papers* (Brit. Mus. Add. MSS. 44,298, f. 205).)

[2] This official acts as a solicitor on the Crown's behalf in the Probate and Divorce Division of the High Court, and can intervene between the granting of a decree *nisi* and its being made absolute; if it can be proved that the decree was given 'contrary to the justice of the case by reason of material facts not brought to the knowledge of the Court', it can be quashed.

[3] *Sir Charles Dilke: A Victorian Tragedy* (1958)

remain so to this day. Henry Primrose, Rosebery's cousin, wrote to Lady Rosebery on December 12th, 1885, that he had dined with Crawford's solicitor, Stewart, and reported that 'he evidently is not confident of being able to establish any case agst. Dilke, but expects that some mud will stick and disfigure him for a time politically'. When it is appreciated that Stewart's sister, Mrs Rogerson, had written one of the anonymous letters which warned Crawford of his wife's alleged infidelity, the interest of this conversation becomes apparent. The Dilke Papers contain an alleged statement by C. A. Whitmore, the Conservative candidate for Chelsea, that Stewart offered to let him see the petitioner's case in advance 'so that he might "make capital" out of it during the contest'.[1] This, if true, was not out of character. It also appears from Rosebery's papers that Crawford was anxious to end his marriage as he wanted to marry Miss Valentine Munro Ferguson —who later jilted Haldane—and the fact that he was a Fellow of Lincoln College when Dilke's liaison with the Rector's wife was notorious may not be without significance. Mrs Crawford's mother—Mrs Eustace Smith—had been at one time Dilke's mistress, so that both the Crawfords were extremely well-informed about the details of Dilke's private life.

Dilke was a man with a 'reputation', and his conviction aroused little surprise in the small politico-social world. 'It does not surprise anyone who knows Dilke,' Hamilton wrote in the July of 1885 when the rumours of the impending action began to circulate. 'He is extraordinarily free & easy with ladies.' A man who is labelled is often libelled, but it was said that he attempted to seduce Lady Randolph Churchill, and went down on his knees in supplication; 'I never saw anything so ridiculous in my life,' she subsequently remarked. Dilke's relationship with the wife of Mark Pattison, the eminent Rector of Lincoln College, Oxford, in 1879–80 had been an Oxford scandal, and had contributed to Pattison's bitterness in his last years. Dilke married her in the October of 1885—the lady herself announcing the engagement[2]— and when Rosebery wrote to congratulate him he noted, some-what ungraciously, to his secretary, J. E. C. Bodley, 'Perhaps we

[1] Dilke Papers (Brit. Mus. Add. MSS. 49,454, f. 53.)
[2] Lady Battersea recorded in her Diary for February 3rd, 1885, that 'I spent two cheery days with Mrs Pattison, at Oxford. She is really engaged to Sir C. Dilke.' (Brit. Mus. Add. MSS. 47,955.)

ought to keep this of Rosebery's, for *she* is odd as you know.' To Rosebery he wrote, 'Mrs Pattison is my oldest friend, for our friendship dates from 1858, & seems to have strengthened under time & trial.'

In his book Mr Jenkins reveals the startling fact that the Dilkes at one time believed that the Roseberys—or, more particularly, Lady Rosebery—had given Mrs Crawford money to incriminate Dilke in order to further Rosebery's political career. Mr Jenkins quotes a note written by Dilke in the April of 1894, whose implications cast a very dark shadow over the characters of Rosebery and his wife.

John J. Louden of Killudunyan House, Westport (one of Parnell's solicitors), wrote naming Mrs Bridgmount, an Irish woman, as the author of the story of how Lord Rosebery found the bribe for Mrs Crawford to lie about me. Mrs Bridgmount lived with Rosebery both before and after his wife's time. I have never believed the story. Lady Rosebery found some money for Mrs Crawford as we know, but that was a different matter.[1]

Mr Jenkins, after quoting this document, continues:

Apart from the payment of money by Lady Rosebery to Mrs Crawford, there are two factors which give a certain superficial plausibility to the story. The first was that Dilke was a direct rival to the extremely ambitious Rosebery. . . . The second factor was Lady Rosebery's known capacity for trying to advance her husband's career by rather unfortunate methods. But there is a great difference between making scenes to Mr Gladstone and bribing Mrs Crawford to concoct a conspiracy. It is true that she was sometimes hysterically anxious for her husband's success and that Dilke stood directly in his way. But these truths do not begin to prove that she attempted to remove the obstacle. The theory of a conspiracy instigated by the Roseberys might be dramatically satisfying, but it cannot be held to have much hard evidence in its support.[2]

As an acquittal, this is perhaps less than warm, and Mr Jenkins' 'truths' merit closer examination. In the first place, there is no evidence, in Dilke's papers or in Rosebery's, that any money was ever given to either of the Crawfords by either of the Roseberys, although of course it is not impossible. The statement that 'Dilke

---

[1] *Dilke Papers*. (Brit. Mus. Add. MSS. 49,454, f. 22.)
[2] Jenkins: *Dilke*, 353.

was a direct rival to the extremely ambitious Rosebery' is not correct in the context of 1885–6; whatever Rosebery's ambitions for office were, they were centred on the Colonial rather than the Foreign Office. The adjective 'hysterical' when applied to Hannah Rosebery is capable of refinement; two quarrels with Mrs Gladstone might be regarded as unsatisfactory evidence for a 'known capacity for trying to advance her husband's career by rather unfortunate methods'. The two premisses upon which the theory of a Rosebery conspiracy might be based—Rosebery's personal ambitions and Dilke standing in their way—are not valid. In view of the characters of Rosebery and his wife the story is inherently improbable—indeed, absurdly so—and an examination of the evidence in support of this canard confirms this beyond question.

The Dilke Papers are open to serious objections as reliable historical material. They were most carefully collected and edited by Dilke and his wife, and subsequently by Lady Dilke's niece, the excessively devoted Miss Gertrude Tuckwell. The method employed was laceration, a mania of Dilke's which did him some harm at the two divorce cases, and which must compromise his papers.[1] Attached to the note which Dilke wrote in the April of 1894 is the original letter from Louden upon which it was based, and which was not quoted by Mr Jenkins. As a historical document it has disadvantages, being lacerated so severely that only a few sentences remain, as follows:

. . . Sir Charles. She got a very large sum of money from Lady Rosebery. I asked—why . . . [then occurs a break which covers almost all the letter] . . . on, with a Irishwoman—a Mrs *Bridgmount*. This person tells extraordinary stories about him.

Faithfully yours,
John J. Louden.[2]

It will be noted that there is no evidence that the 'she' at the beginning of the letter was Mrs Crawford, or that the 'him' at the end is Rosebery. It is unlikely—to put the matter at its most

---

[1] Even Sir Shane Leslie, a fervent believer in Dilke's innocence, has written that 'Miss Tuckwell was determined that nothing should survive which was not in favour of Dilke as a Galahad' (article in the *Daily Telegraph*, December 8th, 1960), to which might be added the comment that every scrap of innuendo concerning other people was most meticulously preserved and not infrequently 'edited'.

[2] *Dilke Papers*. (Brit. Mus. Add. MSS. 49,454, ff. 20–1.

mild—that such interesting facts would have been so meticulously cut out of Louden's letter, since the Dilkes and Miss Tuckwell most jealously preserved any information relating to Mrs Crawford. If Louden had actually referred to Mrs Crawford in the letter, the results of the subsequent enquiries were sadly disappointing, for even the mysterious Mrs Bridgmount is never heard of again. Dilke's statement that Mrs Bridgmount—of whom nothing is known—'lived with Rosebery both before and after his wife's time' has no evidence to support it.

The Crawford case had put Rosebery and his wife in a position of considerable embarrassment. Crawford was an old friend, who had frequently stayed at Dalmeny and Mentmore; Dilke, although he had occasionally visited the Roseberys, was a much more distant acquaintance. In his diaries at the time Rosebery always referred to 'this tragedy of Crawford and Dilke' or 'this sad story'. 'This CD business is all over the place,' he wrote to Hamilton from Homburg on August 1st. 'I only know that he emphatically contradicts it.' Naturally, his sympathies were with Crawford,[1] who was contesting North-East Lanarkshire for the first time as a Liberal candidate in the autumn of 1885. After his narrow victory he stayed at Dalmeny, and this innocent visit prompted a surprising letter from Dilke.

Secret.   76, Sloane Street. S.W.
                                                                    12th Decr [1885]

My dear Rosebery,
    Some time ago friends of mine who are also friends of Mr Crawford & of yourself expressed surprise that he was staying with you. I replied that I thought it not unnatural, there being nothing I know of against him. Today I have, however, a statement so incredible that I hesitate to repeat it to you even in a secret letter. It is that Mr Crawford states that Lady Rosebery has promised him *help* in his case. Now, no doubt he believes the wicked & monstrous lies that have been told him, but no one else who has any acquaintance with the matter believed them, & I make no doubt but that the nature & authorship of the plot against me will be fully exposed. Still, it is not pleasant to have a colleague's name used in this way, & I think it best to write

[1] In the August of 1936 J. L. Hammond wrote to Lord Crewe to inform him of the passage in Dilke's papers implying intervention by the Roseberys. 'As a matter of fact', Lord Crewe replied, 'the Roseberys' sympathies were entirely with Donald Crawford, whom I remember meeting at their house not long after the divorce.' (*Crewe Papers.*)

to you rather than to write to relations of Lady Rosebery's or to colleagues of ours or common friends.

Yrs sincerely,

Charles W. Dilke

Rosebery replied at once on December 13th from Dalmeny.

My dear Dilke,

I should have thought that even in this age of lies no human being could have invented so silly a lie as that you mention. But, if you wish me to contradict it, I will only say that there is not a vestige of truth or even possibility about it. Under no circumstances could I, much less my wife, connect myself with anything of the sort.

But I am very glad you have written for another reason, as I wished to explain to you my position in regard to this matter. Crawford is a very intimate friend of mine. He has repeatedly stayed with me, here and elsewhere. When I first heard with the rest of the public about this case,[1] I felt that as a friend of yours, and a friend of his, I was placed in a position of some embarrassment, and came to the conclusion that my only possible course was to keep clear of the case, not taking one side or the other, and behaving to both friends as if nothing had happened. Nothing has occurred to make me alter that resolution, and my earnest wish is to be with my friends as if this painful business had never been.

Yours sincerely,

AR.

Dilke replied on the 14th.

My dear Rosebery,

Your letter is all I could expect or wish. He thinks he has received the greatest of injuries at my hands. I have received none at his because I have never for an instant doubted his belief in what he was told.

Yours sincerely,

Chas W. D.

[1] This was not strictly true. In his diary for July 20th Rosebery recorded that 'it is rumoured that Dilke has been found out in an intrigue with Mrs Crawford'. On the 24th he saw the Lord Advocate—J. B. Balfour—and discussed the case 'for a long time'; on the 28th Rosebery saw Crawford at the House of Lords 'and had a long talk with him in a committee room about his tragedy'. The public announcement of the impending action was made on August 5th. It may be noted, however, that Randolph Churchill told Salisbury on July 25th that 'There is likely to be a great scandal against Sir C. Dilke, who has, it is said, played the deuce with the peace of a home in the most cold-blooded and debauched manner' (*Salisbury Papers*), and Hamilton, as has been stated, heard of the rumours on July 23rd. As Mrs Crawford had made her confession to her husband on the night of July 17th, the speed with which the news spread through London society was remarkable.

The events of 1886 ended the friendship—never particularly
warm—between Rosebery and Dilke, although until the second
case in July they corresponded occasionally. On July 8th Rosebery
sent his condolences upon Dilke's defeat at Chelsea, and received
a friendly letter of acknowledgement. The revelations in the
second case, however, convinced Rosebery—and almost everyone
else—that Dilke had perjured himself abominably and had
treated Crawford outrageously.[1] In his diary for July 23rd Rosebery recorded:

Dilke case decided. I told Mr G who at once began on the passage
in Corinthians I abt 'such sin as is not named'. Then he spoke abt the
Privy Council. Then abt Canning & his reported pedastry. I told him
I did not believe it. It rests on Granville's recollection of a tradition of
Stapleton's. Mr G agreed, but said he had been much struck by Canning's devotion to his brother Robertson then a handsome boy of 16
in Sir John's house at Liverpool.

So far as Rosebery was concerned, the wretched affair was
forgotten, and when Dilke returned to the Commons he at once
allied himself with Labouchere as a trenchant and persistent critic
of Rosebery. But the Dilkes appear to have persisted in relating
the story of the alleged Rosebery intrigue, and the sequel is
related in the following documents.

> 12 Nov, 1898.
> Pyrford, by Maybury
> Nr. Woking.

My dear Sir Wemyss Reid,
     McKenna saw me yesterday and told me of a conversation he had
had with you. He seems to have accepted a supposed story of Frederic's[2]
(that Lady Dilke had informed him of a certain story) as possible. I
think Frederic must have been misunderstood, as it was he who sent
her (not 'three years ago,' but at least 6) *The Country Gentleman* with
the paragraph marked. He informed her that the author of the story

---

[1] After the second case in the July of 1886 Dilke drew up a list of his friends,
subsequently heavily lacerated, which does not include Rosebery (Brit. Mus. Add.
MSS. 49,454, f. 55). This does not prove that the split came immediately after
the case, as the excisions could have been made in later years. Rosebery's son recalls
his father once saying about the case that Dilke had perjured himself in the witness-
box for two days. Unquestionably, in my view—supported by the abrupt end of
their correspondence in July 1886—Rosebery cut himself off from Dilke at this
point.
[2] Frederic Harrison.

was one 'Jope-Slade'. As this person afterwards died in a mad house, no importance need be attached to his unhappy revival of what was in fact a story of 1886, or Frederic's equally unhappy repetition of it.

The original story was, I think, the subject of direct communication by me to Lord Rosebery early in 1886, and of direct reply by him. At all events I saw, and I think I have, his reply. I accepted his contradiction. I do not think I had believed the story at the time, and I certainly never believed it since. Neither does Lady Dilke believe the story, and I sincerely regret any statement connecting Lady Dilke's with the absurd charges of Mr Jope-Slade.

> Believe me, my dear Sir Wemyss Reid,
> > Very truly yours,
> > > Charles W. Dilke.

Thirty-two years after Rosebery's death his elder son found the following paper at Dalmeny.

> > Oct. 27, 1909.
> > Durdans, Epsom.

I think it necessary to leave on record for the information of my children, in case Sir Charles Dilke should leave any records of his life speaking ill of me, that I was compelled to cut him dead, for having declared that my wife (then dead) had inspired Mrs Crawford to make a false accusation against him in order to get him out of the way of my career.

> > AR.

There is another reference to Mrs Crawford in the Rosebery Papers. At the 1889 World Fair held in Paris, a section on 'Morals in Society' had as its earnest and devoted secretary, a Mlle Eustace. Under this pseudonym was recognised the physically unmistakable, but spiritually reformed, Mrs Crawford.

CHAPTER SIX

'THE MAN OF THE FUTURE'

High hopes he conceived, and he smothered great fears,
In a life parti-coloured, half pleasure, half care.

THE CABINET FORMED BY MR GLADSTONE in the February of 1886 revealed a remarkable transformation in personnel when compared with the Administration which had resigned seven months previously. Hartington and Henry James were in the enemy ranks, Lord Herschell had replaced Selborne as Lord Chancellor, Harcourt went to the Treasury, Dilke was 'unavailable', Granville and Childers were in the shadows, Carlingford had been dropped; two newcomers were Henry Campbell-Bannerman, a shrewd, wealthy, commonsense businessman, who went to the War Office, and John Morley, a nervous, taut, and sensitive intellectual, who became Chief Secretary for Ireland. Chamberlain —who told Rosebery on February 13th that he coveted the Exchequer—returned to the Local Government Board, and was at once locked in an absurdly acrid controversy with Gladstone over the salary of his under-secretary, Jesse Collings, which salted the wound inflicted to his *amour propre* by Gladstone's failure to consult him over Home Rule. Chamberlain had been in secret contact with the Conservative leaders for several weeks before, and after what Rosebery described in his diary as 'a most painful and disagreeable scene' in the Cabinet, he and Trevelyan resigned on March 26th.

The story of the third Gladstone Ministry can be briefly related. Gladstone introduced the Home Rule Bill in a packed House of Commons on April 8th, and the Bill was rejected on second reading in the early hours of June 8th by 343 votes to 313, 93 Liberals voting in the majority. Parliament was dissolved at once, and, fighting on the single issue of Home Rule, its opponents won 394 seats (316 Conservatives and 78 Liberal Unionists), and its supporters only 276. The great Liberal Party, confident that it would hold power for a generation, was reduced to a shaken and disheartened minority. They had lost the election, the leadership of the great Whig families, and the inspiration of the new Chamberlainite radicalism, which had promised to provide a decisive and constructive Liberal programme for the next decade. Gladstone was obsessed by Home Rule, and told Rosebery with passion on April 9th that the issue would 'control and put aside all other political questions in England till it is settled'; in a sense he was right, but at the expense of the party which he had done more to create and inspire than any other man.

The Home Rule crisis had decisive effects upon Rosebery's career. He never believed that Home Rule of itself would cure Ireland's ills, but considered that it was the only alternative to separation, and must therefore be attempted. In company with Harcourt and many other Liberals, his enthusiasm for the cause faded when he appreciated the terrible price which the party was having to pay for it. The Liberal schism opened the way to his succession as leader of the party by eliminating virtually all his rivals, but ensured that that leadership would be a precarious and compromised position. All this was but dimly perceived in 1886. The immediate effect of Rosebery's unqualified support of Gladstone was to enhance his popularity enormously within a party stunned by the mass defection of its leaders. 'The spectacle of this eloquent, magnificent personage separating himself from the bulk of his class, "biding by the Buff and the Blue," excited the hostility of the Unionist party, and filled the Liberals in the shade with a sense of hope and expectancy for the future,' as Churchill has written.[1]

His brief tenure of the Foreign Office from February to July was mainly uneventful. He inherited Salisbury's policy completely, which was fundamentally one of careful isolation from Europe, using the main British weapon, sea-power, to maintain the *status quo*, but at the same time restoring good relations with Germany and Italy. Rosebery was even more of a Germanophile than Salisbury, and had a genuine admiration for Bismarck which was developed through his friendship with Herbert Bismarck, who seems to have realised at an early stage that Rosebery was the coming man. In the May of the previous year he had visited Berlin

[1] *Great Contemporaries*, 20.

to meet the great Chancellor—of whom he subsequently remarked that only he and Queen Victoria had ever thoroughly frightened him—and had recounted his experiences to the Foreign Office in a memorandum which began with the strange phrase, 'There is indeed something intensely repugnant to me in being a man's guest and writing down his careless utterances like an interviewer. ... I cannot forget that the Chancellor spoke to me in his own phrase "as one gentleman to another", and I feel certain that you will not allow any other human being to see my notes.' On January 17th, 1886, he told the German Ambassador, Hatzfeldt, at Mentmore that 'a *successful* foreign policy would not be overturned. The condition of continuity is success.'

The enunciation of the doctrine of the 'continuity of British Foreign Policy', which Rosebery emphasised again and again in his public and private declarations, had excellent short-term results. Criticism of Liberal foreign policy, which had been continuous and at times harsh in the previous five years, almost disappeared; the authority of the Ministry in foreign affairs was maintained, in spite of the fact that it was clinging on to office by its eyelids; to a Ministry working under intense Opposition pressure on almost every other issue it was a relief to contemplate the unflurried and warmly praised conduct of Foreign Affairs. Rosebery's great knowledge of Europe, his almost intuitive appreciation of the effects of apparently insignificant events, and his refusal to be ruffled by the unexpected, created a remarkable impression of competence and authority which evoked the respect of the foreign ambassadors no less than that of his colleagues. In a sense, he did nothing in particular, and did it very well.

He was fortunate in having the enthusiastic support of the Queen and Gladstone; the former described his as 'The only really *good* appointment', and as early as March 22nd Rosebery recorded that while he was talking to Gladstone on Foreign Office matters 'he suddenly burst out with an astounding & unprecedented eulogy, stating that if this Govt had existed for no other reason it wd have made him happy because of admin^n of FO, etc, etc. I never was so astounded'. His relations with the Queen were excellent, and indeed he was the only senior Minister of whom she approved. Her knowledge of foreign affairs and her common sense greatly impressed him; when he urged her to open the Indian and Colonial Exhibition 'with all pomp' she replied,

'With all the pomp you like—as long as I don't have to wear a low dress.'

Rosebery's main difficulties were in the confused and bloody Balkans, where Prince Alexander[1] of Bulgaria occupied an uneasy throne between Russian and Turkish ambitions. The Greek Government had taken up a belligerent attitude towards the Turks, and had been warned by Salisbury that the British Government would not support them; this was confirmed, by Rosebery who was, however, anxious to avert a joint French British, and, German blockade. He told the British Ambassador at Berlin, Malet, on February 24th that Admiral Lord John Hay, commanding the Mediterranean Fleet, 'has replied to our enquiry as to the facility of a blockade by a raw head and bloody bones telegram saying that it would involve the destruction of batteries, the occupation of islands, and the sinking of ships: operations compared to which Navarino would be amicable and Alexandria a flea-bite. None of us who are represented in the allied fleet would contemplate such measures.' But the Greeks declined to disarm, and in May the British, French, and German Governments presented a formal joint ultimatum to the Greek Government.

The crisis passed over. Alexander, protesting unreasonably that he had not received the indefinite assurance of his rule (he was granted a five-year period), retained his throne, but only until August, when he was deported to Russia, returned to Sofia, and obliged to abdicate. But this was after Rosebery had left the Foreign Office, and his careful handling of a potentially very serious situation won golden tributes from all sides, Gladstone writing with enthusiasm at one point, 'I do not remember an instance of such an achievement carried through in the *first quarter* of a Foreign Secretaryship. And it is one to which your personal action has beyond doubt largely contributed. It is a great act, and a good omen.'

In July Rosebery found himself the only European Minister prepared to defend the Treaty of Berlin when the Russians suddenly announced their intention of unilaterally tearing up that part of the Treaty which made Batoum a free port. Rosebery took a strong line, warmly supported by the Queen, who described

[1] The brother of Prince Louis of Battenberg, who served in the Royal Navy and later became First Sea Lord.

the Russian conduct as 'insolent and dishonest'. His formal protest (July 13th) was described by the Russian Chancellor, de Giers, as 'the most wounding communication that one Power could address to another', but neither the German nor the Austro-Hungarian Governments was particularly disturbed, and Rosebery could not prevail. It is, indeed, open to question whether his interpretation of the Russian action as a violation of the Treaty of Berlin was correct, but the Penjdeh Incident was barely a year in the past, and mistrust of Russian ambitions was deeply rooted in the Foreign Office. Rosebery had difficulties in getting his views brought before the Russian Government owing to the independence and indolence of the British Ambassador at St Petersburg, Sir Robert Morier, who was described by Granville in 1881 as having 'a temper, self-conceit, and huffiness beyond belief'.[1] On February 19th he was ordered to urge the Russian Government to drop their remaining objections to an agreement between Prince Alexander and Turkey and declined to do so. He was startled to be instructed with considerable acerbity to carry out his orders forthwith, since he had been under the illusory impression that his gushing reports had been well received. The contrary was the case. 'It is no consolation to Lord Rosebery to read in *The Times* this morning that Sir R. Morier has given one of the most successful balls of the season,' Rosebery wrote to the Queen on March 4th, 'or to hear from Sir R. Morier that the Czar is greatly pleased with Lord Rosebery's method of conducting business, of which indeed, owing to Sir R. Morier's proceedings, the Czar can know nothing.'

When Parliament was dissolved in June, and the clamour of the elections had become deafening, Gladstone, speaking at Manchester on June 25th before a huge audience, singled out Rosebery for special commendation; 'of whom I will say to the Liberal party of this country, and I say it not without reflection—for if I said it lightly I should be doing injustice no less to him than to them—in whom I say to the Liberal party that they see the man of the future'.

On October 28th, the elections disastrously over, Rosebery and his wife, accompanied by a new friend, Ronald Munro Ferguson

[1] Agatha Ramm: *The Political Correspondence of Mr Gladstone and Lord Granville, 1876–1886*, I, 260.

of Novar, who had been Rosebery's private secretary at the Foreign
Office, set out on a visit to India. Rosebery kept a copious journal
of this journey. As usual, they travelled in great style, and were
accorded an appropriately awed reverence. At Agra he worshipped
the Taj Mahal, and accorded it one of his more regrettable poems
which ended

> *So let us gaze a moment free from care.*
> *The Christian prays, the Moslem built a prayer.*

His enthusiasm for railway travelling found suitable opportunity. Bombay, Jaipur, Agra, Delhi, Lahore, Peshawar, the
Khyber Pass, Kohat, Quetta, and Lucknow were all inspected in
the course of two months. At Sibi he and Munro Ferguson were
greeted with banners which read 'Welcome Lord Rosebery' and
'Income tax hard'; another light moment occurred when a post
office official courteously but resolutely refused to transmit the
words 'God bless you' in a telegram which Rosebery wanted to
send to Gladstone on his birthday!

On their way back to England the Roseberys stayed for three
weeks in Egypt, where Rosebery met all the leading British and
Egyptian personalities, notably Sir Evelyn Baring, the British
Agent, already well established as the virtual ruler of the country.
In Rome they met Randolph Churchill on holiday with Harry
Tyrwhitt, a mutual friend, nicknamed 'the smiler'. Much had
happened since Rosebery had left England. Randolph Churchill,
Chancellor of the Exchequer and Leader of the House of Commons, prophet of 'Tory Democracy', darling of the Conservative
constituencies and leading exponent of the Unionist alliance—a
phrase which he himself had coined—had found himself challenged
by an older, infinitely more calculating and realistic statesman in
Lord Salisbury; pushed on by past successes, impatient of criticism, puzzled and restless through his isolation in the Cabinet,
and already affected by the cruel disease which was to kill him
'by inches in public', as Rosebery later wrote, Randolph had been
decisively outmanoeuvred and defeated by the Prime Minister.
His resignation just before Christmas had rocked the Government, but it had recovered, Goschen had taken Churchill's place,
and the *preux chevalier* of the Tory Party was hurled into the
political wilderness from which, after a poignant struggle against
denigration and disease, he was destined never to emerge.

R.—14

This extraordinary episode had removed Chamberlain's one ally in the Cabinet, but the Liberal 'round table' conference which followed had failed to reconcile the two sides, and from this moment any hope of repairing the havoc of 1886 gradually receded. The personal animosity between Gladstone and Chamberlain—exacerbated by the fact that Chamberlain still sat on the Opposition front bench among his former colleagues—was crucial. 'One does not like to formulate these things even to oneself', Gladstone said to Rosebery in the July of 1887, 'but it seems to me that Chamberlain is the greatest blackguard I have ever come across.' On August 4th, 1887, Rosebery noted after a long walk with Gladstone at Waddesdon, 'The defects of his strength grow on him. All black is very bla.k, all white very white.' This sad decline became more evident in these years. In the January of 1890 Rosebery stayed at Hawarden and wrote in his diary, 'Mr G changed: still wonderful, but changed—walks like an old man, sits down after climbing a slope, had lost also I think his quick snap of apprehension.'

There was much talk of Rosebery as 'the future leader' as a result of Gladstone's Manchester eulogy. 'As for the "leadership going a-begging", let it beg,' he wrote to Munro Ferguson on April 5th, 1887, 'you know that I would not entertain any idea of that sort.' 'No power that I wot of', he wrote on another occasion, 'will compel me to bound from the jungle into the arena.' On October 17th, 1887, he wrote to Munro Ferguson that

I have made one d—d dull speech at Ipswich (I was determined not to make a joke). I should have thought it the dullest of the year had I not since delivered one at Keighley on technical education which takes the cake. I speak worse & worse, and as I begin to be found out as a bore I may hope that invitations to speak may cease. I address Castle Douglas on Thursday which will probably make the Unionism of South West Scotland permanent.

Early in 1888 Rosebery returned to the subject of Lords reform, and on March 11th he brought forward a motion for a Committee to enquire into the constitution of the House. He proposed that a delegation from the whole peerage should represent the hereditary element, that there should be an elected element chosen by the new County Councils about to be called into existence by the County Councils Act, by the larger municipalities, or by the House of Commons, or by all three, and that in addition there should be representatives from the self-governing colonies. Apart from the imaginative concept of the colonial peers, the really significant feature of the proposals was that peers who were not selected for the new House could stand for the House of Commons without renouncing their titles. But the motion was defeated by 97 votes to 50, and when the Government, which had undertaken to introduce a measure of life peerages, produced their Bill it authorised the creation of only three life peerages a year, whose recipients were to be drawn from carefully-defined categories in the armed, civil, or diplomatic services. Rosebery, in one of his most attractively irreverent speeches, denounced the Bill as a proposal to turn the Lords 'into a sort of legislative Bath or Cheltenham, or, perhaps, if it is not disrespectful to say so, into a sort of legislative hydropathic establishment, where these noble persons will take more care of their own constitutions than of the constitution of this House'. The feeble measure disappeared, unmourned.

But Rosebery was genuinely depressed by the further shelving of a problem which was constantly exercising his mind. The Home Rule controversy had completed the process of turning the Lords into a Conservative assembly, always prepared at the suitable moment to paralyse the work of a Liberal Ministry. He believed that a major clash between the two Houses was inevitable, and that when it happened the Lords would either be abolished or have its powers emasculated to an extent whereby there would be virtually single-chamber government. For a time he seriously considered standing for the House of Commons and precipitating some kind of enquiry by the Government, but Herschell privately ruled that he would certainly lose his seat on petition, and the party managers were consequently unenthusiastic, so the proposal died.

By this time (1890) Rosebery had experienced the delights and difficulties of serving in an elective assembly. His interest in local government had always been considerable, and in his Australian speeches in particular he had spoken with regret of its decline in Britain. The newly-created London County Council offered an opportunity for service in this field, and, earnestly encouraged by Canon Rogers, he was elected as one of the four members for the

City of London early in 1889. 'It seemed to me', he later remarked, 'that the public was not aware of the magnitude of this experiment, and that the men of thought, leisure, and business capacity—with whom London abounds to an extent disproportionate even to its vast population—should come forward to give their best energies to so noble a work, and make it a success. I felt, however, that I could not expect others to do what I shrank from myself, and so, very reluctantly, and with a strong sense of unfitness, I became a candidate.'

The Progressive Party, which had won a decisive majority in the first L.C.C. elections, arrived at the first meeting of the Council at the Guildhall—loaned by the City Council—in a belligerent mood, and at once announced their intention of appropriating all nineteen aldermanic seats. Rosebery—who was an Independent member—rose on a point of order to urge tolerance and generosity by the majority. 'This quiet maiden speech,' John Benn, a fellow-councillor and friend of Rosebery, later wrote, 'in such striking contrast to the restless spirit of the majority, revealed a man of judicial mien, clear judgment, and rare oratorical gifts. From that moment he was designated by many of those present as the best possible first chairman of the greatest municipal body in the world.'[1] He was proposed for the Chair, but some of the more extreme Progressives were hostile, and after a debate of over two hours he was elected by 104 votes to 17. 'My thanks are due to the majority on the division,' he said in his first speech from the Chair, 'but [a pause] my sympathies are entirely with the minority.'

Within a few months of assuming the Chairmanship Rosebery had effectively captured the admiration of the new Council. His unruffled good sense and humour, his interest in every aspect of the Council's work, his aloofness from partisan argument, and, above all, his detailed application to the work of the Council and its numerous committees, quickly silenced the misgivings of the Progressives. He had a real feeling for London, delighting in prowling around forgotten decayed squares, searching out long-forgotten places of interest, and walking long hours in the less-frequented parts of the city. On July 1st, 1888, for example, he and John Morley walked to the City. 'We walked to Houndsditch and all about any nooks we could find. Stood on London Bridge,

[1] Quoted in A. G. Gardiner: *John Benn and the Progressive Movement*, 99.

and went in reverence to see the house in Bolt Court, where Johnson lived and died. A happy reverent morning.' On another occasion, 'To bed at 2.30 but not sleeping—rose at 4 & walked to Covent Garden Market & back by the silent parks. No one about but all the birds in the cages singing like mad.'

Rosebery's work as Chairman of the L.C.C. was in many respects the most important single factor in his advance to the Premiership. There was a new generation of Liberals entering the House of Commons, men who had discarded the old shibboleths and prejudices, and who believed in an enlightened social radicalism which would sweep away slums, build schools, and generally 'get things done'. Rosebery's appeal to Londoners to 'do something for the people', his determination to make London 'not a unit, but a unity', and his progressive social attitude reflected their own ambitions far more accurately than the doctrinaire approach of Gladstone, Harcourt, or even John Morley. His greatest contribution to the work of the L.C.C. was to weld it into a cohesive non-partisan body, and to rebut the sneer that it consisted solely of 'Rads, Cads, and Fads', while his radical approach—'I would make those great slum-landlords skip'— excited those new Liberal MPs like Asquith and Edward Grey, who looked at the L.C.C. with a certain degree of admiring envy from Westminster, where all debates led to Ireland. Rosebery was re-elected unanimously to the Chair in the November of 1889, and when he resigned from the position in the July of 1890 the tributes paid on all sides went far beyond the formalities customary on these occasions.

While Rosebery was establishing a reputation as a social reformer of the widest sympathies and imagination, and was immersing himself in the humdrum day-to-day business of the Council, the prospects of the Liberal Party were improving quite dramatically. The Unionists, proclaiming 'twenty years of resolute rule' in Ireland, were getting into serious difficulties at home, and the Chief Secretaryship of 'Bloody Balfour' aroused mounting criticism from the Opposition. But the decisive event was the public humiliation of Ministers when they unwisely applauded a series of sulphurous articles in *The Times* entitled 'Parnellism and Crime', which accused Parnell of direct implication in the outrages which had profoundly shocked the British people. The series included a facsimile of a letter from Parnell

condoning the Phoenix Park murders, and *The Times* dared Parnell
to sue for libel. Parnell ignored the challenge, but one of his
Irish Nationalist colleagues did sue *The Times*, and eventually the
Government set up a commission to investigate not only the
allegations of *The Times* but the whole question of Irish agitation.
It was a political commission, and for months it dragged along
with dwindling public interest until, at its fiftieth meeting, the
nation first heard the name of Pigott. Under merciless cross-
examination by Sir Charles Russell, whose junior was H. H.
Asquith, it was proved that Pigott had forged the letter published
in *The Times*, and when Pigott fled to Madrid and shot himself
the public repugnance against the Unionists was intense, and
from their own benches Randolph Churchill delivered one of the
most savage denunciations of a Ministry ever heard in the House
of Commons.

For a brief period the Liberals basked in the political sunshine.
There was an Eighty Club dinner to which Parnell was invited
and spoke; he then publicly shook hands with Rosebery and
Spencer amid emotional applause. Rosebery's speeches on Ireland
at this point were among the most serious and partisan of his
career, and on one occasion, at Bristol on November 13th, he
held an enormous audience of seven thousand on tiptoe for nearly
an hour with a harsh denunciation of the Union, and of 'that
part of the Constitution that was sown in corruption and raised
in dishonour'. But the period of Liberal triumph was short-lived.
Captain O'Shea filed an action for divorce against his wife, who
had been Parnell's mistress for over eight years, and the Home
Rule cause received its mortal blow 'in the stench of the divorce
court', the Irish Nationalist Party split into two bitter factions,
and when Parnell died at the end of 1891, exhausted by the strain
of the savage controversy which had raged for the previous
year, the cause for which he had devoted his life was fatally
compromised. The Liberals were learning the grim truth of
Morley's private dictum: 'Ireland would not be a difficult country
to govern—were it not that all the people are intractable and all
the problems insoluble.'

Other strains were becoming apparent within the Liberal
ranks. Imperialism had become a burning question of the day, its
less agreeable characteristics aroused by the patriotic fervour over
the Queen's Silver Jubilee in 1887 and the raucous voice of

Kipling. To men like Gladstone, Harcourt, and John Morley this was merely an appalling extension of the cheap jingoism against which they had struggled for their political lives. Rosebery, the first leading Liberal to identify himself with this new creed, found himself virtually isolated in the Liberal hierarchy. His speeches to the Imperial Federation League in these years were not redolent of the Liberalism of Bright and Mill, of the great principles 'for which Hampden died in the field and Sidney on the scaffold'; nor were they marked by the aggressiveness and tawdry patriotism of the Imperialism of the Tories, and thus he held a somewhat undefined position between both sides. Thus, in 1892 Rosebery declared to the City Liberal Club that 'Our great Empire has pulled us, so to speak, by the coat tails out of the European system, and ... we must recognise that our foreign policy has become a Colonial policy, and it is in reality dictated much more from the extremities of the Empire than from London itself.' But on another occasion he declared that the purpose of Empire must be 'that unswerving determination to develop and maintain', without which 'planting a flag here or there or demarcating regions with a red line are vain diversions'. To some extent, Rosebery was an Imperialist among Liberals and a Liberal among Imperialists.

Harcourt's increasing arrogance and his domineering insolence towards both his colleagues and his leader were causing some bitterness among the Liberal leaders. At a meeting of the ex-cabinet in the February of 1890 he jeered at Gladstone's draft Home Rule suggestions and violently opposed any proposal that the Irish Parliament should have equal status with the House of Commons; 'it should be in the position of a County Council,' he concluded, glancing imperiously in Rosebery's direction. This unhappy meeting was a taste of things to come. 'Mr G somewhat feeble & deaf & not very clear,' Rosebery recorded. 'Harcourt more contentious & weathercocking than ever.' A strong difference of opinion between Rosebery and his colleagues occurred in the June of 1890 over the Anglo-German Agreement whereby Britain received concessions in Africa in return for Heligoland, and it was Harcourt who inserted into the controversy a degree of venom which quickly brought matters to a crisis. Bryce was Rosebery's only supporter in opposition to the Agreement, and the events of June 19th are related in Rosebery's diary.

Discreditable business in H of C. Bryce wanted to ask a question as to whether govt. had consulted naval experts with regard to Heligoland. On Harcourt seeing it, scene of almost physical violence on front bench. Bryce came to ask me to suppress my question to preserve peace. Declined. Violent letter from H & strong letter from J M demanding meeting of ex-cabinet. H saying that whole of H of C front bench & unanimity of party hostile to me! on this subject (I having expressed no opinion): saying this more than Irish question, etc, etc, etc.

Harcourt, supported by Morley, demanded that Rosebery's attitude should be considered by the ex-cabinet, and some sharp letters passed.

> June 22, 1890
> Durdans

Dear J. M.

For the first and only time in my life I was not altogether sorry that you did not come down today, as it seems to me better now that we should not meet until after the High Commission which Harcourt & you have summoned to sit on the vile corpus of

> Y ever
> AR

> 95, Elm Park Gardens,
> S.W.
> June 22, '90

Dear Rosebery,

For the first and only time in my life—to use your phrase—I am altogether sorry to have your letter. Of course, it must be as you please.

> Ever yours,
> John Morley

But the cloud passed, so far as these contestants were concerned.

> 95, Elm Park Gardens,
> S.W.
> Midsummer Day, '90

Not only five minutes, my dear Rosebery, but five hours, five days, or five weeks—rather than one minute of misunderstanding.

> Ever yours,
> J. Morley

Although the crisis blew over, Rosebery was exercised by the revelation of Harcourt's vicious and unreasoning attitude, and had a council of war with Spencer and Morley in his new London home, 38, Berkeley Square,[1] on July 4th. 'All was most harmonious & satisfactory,' Rosebery recorded. 'I had by Mr Gladstone's leave shewn John Morley & now shewed Spencer, Harcourt's letter of June 19. It was agreed that by preserving a thorough understanding & communication on essential points we could give the next government that solidity & consistency wh. it was otherwise likely to want: that otherwise Harcourt would lead the cabinet such a dance as would discredit us: and that Mr G wd have to be sustained in face of the petulance of Harcourt & the hostility of the Queen.' Rosebery proposed that Harcourt, Parnell, and Campbell-Bannerman should come to Dalmeny in November when Gladstone was visiting his constituents; Gladstone himself was delighted, declaring that 'Parnell is the best man with whom I have ever had to do political business, so alive to the bearing of things.'

But already the shadow of the divorce court was falling over the fortunes of the Liberal Party, and when November came, there was no conference at Dalmeny.

By 1890 Rosebery was marked out as the glittering hope of the Liberal Party. His physical appearance belied his forty-three years, and at least part of his fascination lay in his surprising youthfulness, the light blue eyes which could blaze with anger, warm with merriment, or freeze with a chilling contempt. The indecision of his early years seemed to have gone, and he gave to casual acquaintances the strong impression of a determined and ambitious man. Lady Monkswell met him for the first time in 1889 and wrote that 'He looks to me like a man who fears neither God nor man, as clever as you please, knowing his own mind, perfectly determined to get on, hard, clear-headed and unremorseful. Nobody could be better fitted out than he for the nerve-destroying, heart-breaking work of political life.'[2] As an estimate of Rosebery's character this was something less than exact, but it is typical of contemporary comment at this time. 'At London dinner-parties half a century ago it was rare for Rosebery to be mentioned without some allusion being made to his three declared ambitions—to marry an heiress, to own a Derby winner,

[1] They had relinquished Lansdowne House in 1888.
[2] Hon. E. Collier: *A Victorian Diarist*, 168.

to be Prime Minister of England,' Algernon Cecil has written;
'... apocryphal or not, it gives if not Rosebery's measure as a
man, yet certainly the measure of him by the men of his time.'[1]
Jowett of Balliol wrote to Margot Tennant in the March of 1890
that he thought Rosebery 'very able, shy, sensitive, ambitious,
the last two qualities rather at war with each other—very likely a
future Prime Minister'.[2]

The series of personal triumphs since 1885 which Rosebery
had enjoyed had undoubtedly altered his attitude to public life.
He always resented criticism, and did not dismiss praise with the
elegant negligence which he liked to affect. In Scotland his
position was quite extraordinary. 'Whenever there was a crowd
in the streets or at the station, in either Glasgow or Edinburgh,'
Margot Asquith has related, 'and I enquired what it was all about
I always received the same reply: "Rozbury!"'[3] Never a party
'hack' speaker, he was nonetheless in great demand on Liberal
platforms, and he had acquired the reputation of being the most
witty and trenchant of contemporary speakers. He never spoke
to any but the greatest audiences, and Augustine Birrell has written
that 'His melodious voice ... his underlying strain of humour,
his choice of words, never either staled by vulgar usage or
tainted with foreign idiom, and above all his "out of the way"
personality, and a certain nervousness of manner that suggested
at times the possibility of a breakdown, kept his audience in a
flutter of enjoyment and excitement. He was certainly the most
"interesting" speaker I have ever heard.'[4]

But the façade of self-confidence only concealed the shyness,
reserve, and fastidiousness of his personality. He was only really
at ease in the company of a few close friends in congenial surroundings, when he would expand remarkably. 'It is difficult to
convey the pleasure I derived from his conversation', Winston
Churchill has written, 'as it ranged easily and spontaneously
upon all kinds of topics "from grave to gay, from lively to severe".
Its peculiar quality was the unexpected depths or suggestive
turns which revealed the size of the subject and his own background of knowledge and reflection. At the same time he was

---

[1] *Queen Victoria and Her Prime Ministers* 283.
[2] Margot Asquith: *Autobiography*, 122.
[3] *Ibid.*, 161.
[4] Birrell: *Things Past Redress*, 256.

full of fun. He made many things not only arresting, but merry. He seemed as much a master of trifles and gossip as of weighty matters. He was keenly conscious about every aspect of life. Sportsman, epicure, bookworm, literary critic, magpie collector of historical relics, appreciative owner of veritable museums of art treasures, he never needed to tear a theme to tatters. In lighter vein he flitted jauntily from flower to flower like a glittering insect, by no means unprovided with a sting. And then, in contrast, out would come his wise, matured judgments upon the great men and events of the past. But these treats were not always given.'[1] He was usually at his best at small dinner-parties, where gaiety was unrestrained. It is not possible to re-create these occasions. Birrell has written, 'How we passed the time, and what we talked about, have all gone from me. If I am asked "What good came of it all at last?" I have nothing to say except that *whilst* it lasted, it was great, and in the Tam O'Shanter sense of the word, "glorious fun". . . . Curiously enough, Lord Rosebery as an occasional "Lord of Misrule" was unrivalled.'[2] Rosebery's wit took many forms. There is the famous—and possibly apocryphal—story of how he rose one evening at Mentmore when he felt that his Rothschild relations had kept him up late enough, stretched, and cried 'To your tents, O Israel!' When Henry Ponsonby once remarked at Mentmore in 1887 that the Turkish Ambassador, another guest, appeared 'low', Rosebery remarked in his most solemn tones, 'So would you if you had just received a despatch saying that your Government intended to cease paying your salary.' He disliked puns, but when one sensitive guest said that she disliked the 'scent' from the Dalmeny shale mines, he quietly replied, 'I only like the per cent.' He was an excellent raconteur, and one of his best stories related how he made a speech in his younger days and referred to two leading members of his audience as 'the village Hampden' and 'the village Pym'; the latter gentleman, slightly befuddled by the effects of his dinner, left the room in considerable fury, believing that Rosebery had called him 'the village pimp'! His annotations in his books— particularly in some of the Beckford volumes—are very funny and quite unprintable, as are some of the essays which he occasionally prepared and circulated to a few friends. One of these,

[1] Churchill: *Great Contemporaries*, 16.
[2] Birrell: *Things Past Redress*, 147, 258.

an account of a lecture by Ferdinand de Rothschild and the Prince of Wales at the Imperial Institute on the subject of 'Copulation—Ancient and Modern', may be regarded as something of a collector's piece.

But throughout his life, and even in this happy period of it, he was a difficult man to live with. When in the mood, he was the most entrancing of companions, but when he was out of humour, as Churchill has related, 'he could cast a chill over all, and did not hesitate to freeze and snub. On these occasions his face became expressionless, almost a slab, and his eyes lost their light and fire. One saw an altogether different person. But after a bit one knew the real man was there all the time, hiding perversely behind a curtain.'[1] 'His moods were apt to vary,' John Buchan has written. 'He could be caustic and destructive, a master in the art of denigration; he could be punctiliously judicial; in certain matters he refused to be other than freakish, making brilliant fun out of bogus solemnities; he had also his deep and sober loves. To hear him talk of certain friends, certain books and figures of the past like Johnson and Sir Walter Scott, was to listen to a boyish enthusiasm. In all he said there was the antiseptic of humour and sound judgment. He took nothing at second hand, and his admirations were as individual as his antipathies. I have heard his talk called cynical, but the word is a misnomer. In all he said there was gusto, which is the opposite of cynicism, and where he condemned it was with a kind of frosty geniality. But the marvel of his conversation was its form. He spoke finished prose as compared with the slovenly patois of most of us, and his thoughts clothed themselves naturally with witty and memorable words.'[2] Buchan and Churchill were very much younger than Rosebery, but their comments on Rosebery's charm and unpredictability of conversation have been echoed by his contemporaries, particularly Hamilton, who once noted after dinner at The Durdans that 'there is so much sympathy and tenderness under his stolid and placid exterior which adds so greatly to his charm'.

Even in an age when considerable wealth was held in comparatively few hands, the splendour of Rosebery's existence startled and awed his contemporaries. His great mansions were run on

---

[1] Churchill: *Great Contemporaries*, 16.
[2] Memoir in the *Glasgow Herald*, May 22nd, 1929.

luxury lines, with what appeared to be armies of servants flitting endlessly and silently down the carpeted corridors, and his large estates were meticulously maintained and supervised. The smooth efficiency of his arrangements—particularly when he travelled—was the subject of amused admiration by his friends, and Edward Grey has described how Rosebery's valet would put the whole of Waterloo Station on the alert, so that when the great man arrived the stationmaster was ready to greet him and conduct him to his compartment amid the respectful salutings of the staff.[1] He frequently travelled by special train, and when this was not possible, expresses were known to stop at Cheddington or Dalmeny for his convenience. The calm efficiency of the Rosebery *entourage* was one of its most intimidating features; a horse once dropped dead in the traces near Dalmeny while the Gladstones were being brought from Edinburgh, and when Gladstone expressed his regret the postilion loftily replied, 'We have two of the same colour at Mentmore.' Edward Grey was one person who found this grandeur rather depressing. 'There are many glass doors,' he once remarked of Mentmore, 'but some are locked, and others open with difficulty—and egress and regress are more or less formal; you may go out or in but not slip out or in.'

His moods were always varied and frequently disconcerting throughout his life, and became increasingly perplexing as he grew older. He was known to ignore guests almost entirely, and his secretary vividly recalls one week-end party at Dalmeny which only saw their host once—when he had to go into the library to get a paper-knife. Conversation stopped at once, and the male guests rose from their chairs; Rosebery walked to his desk, got his paper-knife, and withdrew. Some visitors to his houses noticed that in spite of the splendour, in each room there was only one chair which could be called comfortable, and which was exclusively reserved for Rosebery. When staying at Dalmeny, he would often disappear into Barnbougle for days on end, going through his books, arranging his treasures, reading in the library, going for long solitary walks along the shore to Hound Point, or sitting in his tiny, bleak, bedroom, gazing at the changing texture and colour of the waters of the Forth.

An easily impatient man, quickly disconcerted by trifles, over-sensitive to atmosphere, and extraordinarily touchy when out of

[1] G. M. Trevelyan: *Grey of Fallodon*, 73.

humour, he was not an easy master to serve. Eddie Hamilton once noted at Mentmore (August 1900) that 'he is imperious, and everything must be done with the greatest smartness; otherwise they are spoken to very sharply, so much so that I have at times felt quite hot. All the same I think they like him and take a pride in serving him.' Henry Skelton, when Vicar of Mentmore, was struck by the same fact.

He used to go for a drive every night after dinner—this he said helped him to sleep. He always drove postilion, which, of course, is the ideal way to be driven as, instead of having nothing but the backs of coachmen and footmen to look at, one can look straight ahead instead of looking out sideways.

One lovely summer night, as we were nearing the end of our drive, he said to me 'I cannot think why more people don't do this—it really is lovely'. I said I could give him two very good reasons why they didn't. 1. Because very few people could afford it. 2. Because fewer still could get their servants to do it!

I pointed out to him that the same men had been on duty since 6 a.m. when they had started exercising the horses, that he had driven in the afternoon as well, that the carriage had to be cleaned and that it would be nearly midnight before they had got the horses cooled off and bedded them. He said 'They don't seem to mind—I think they rather like it.' And that was the wonderful thing—they did. All the people who worked for him seemed to worship the ground he trod on and would do simply anything for him.

His generosity towards his servants and tenants was largely responsible for this affection, but his touch—and that of his wife—was so sure that there was remarkably little of the condescending philanthropy which is such a depressing characteristic of the late-Victorian upper class. His generosity was so notorious that his secretaries were constantly urging him to curtail his benefactions, and achieved a great victory when he agreed never to open letters which were unstamped—the infallible hall-mark of the begging-letter writer. This decision caused more than one embarrassment—Lord Kimberley, who had forgotten to stamp an important official letter, was one of Rosebery's friends who were mystified by getting their letter back with the peremptory 'Not known—return to sender' written on the envelope—but the saving in time and money was not inconsiderable. When Randolph Churchill referred to Rosebery's 'enormous and unlimited wealth' in an 1886 election speech the victim mournfully replied,

. . . I do not complain of your speaking of my 'enormous and un-limited wealth' though as a matter of fact it is not enormous, and I have never had any difficulty in finding its limits. But what is mon-strous is this, that in consequence of what you said thousands of mendicant pens are being sharpened. The parson's widow, the bed-ridden Scot born at Dalmeny, the author who has long watched my career, the industrious grocer who has been ruined by backing my horses, the poet who has composed a sonnet to the GOM, the family that wishes to emigrate—all these, and a myriad others, are preparing for action. Not to speak of the hospital that wants a wing, the roofless church, the club of hearty Liberals in an impoverished district, the football club that wants a patron, the village band that wants instru-ments, all of which are preparing for the warpath. May heaven forgive you, for I cannot . . .

His benefactions were usually well concealed, and his corre-spondence is full of his consideration in such small matters as the doctor's bills for one of his tenants, the education of promising children and assistance in their careers. Among innumerable acts of generosity, the cost of a large social centre in the East End of London, which included a swimming bath (then a wonder), the gift of the Villa Delahante at Posilipo to the British Government for use as a summer residence of the Ambassador, and a contri-bution of over £2,000 to pay off Lord Granville's debts, may be particularly mentioned.

The Roseberys were not particularly extravagant, nor were they ostentatious, and as they both detested large gatherings, they entertained on a small scale and were generally regarded by London Society as being aloof and inaccessible. But, with an annual income equivalent to nearly £500,000 net in 1962 values, they could afford to live in a style which it is impossible to visua-lise today. As a young man Rosebery had gambled and betted heavily, and on one evening in Newmarket week in 1882 he won over £1,500 off Leopold Rothschild and the Sassoons at baccarat. But this phase passed, and in later years his principal extravagances were books, pictures, old silver, and young horses.

He had been an enthusiastic collector since he was a schoolboy, and as the years passed his purchases strained even the formidable capacities of his great mansions. He was fortunate in that he had money, some taste, and the love of acquisition at a time when Tiepolos were sold at the Cheyney Sale in 1883 for twenty-five guineas each, and when Horace Walpole's annotated copy of the superb *Stowe House and Gardens* (1777) cost £2 12s. at the Beckford Sale of 1882. The five superb Goya tapestries which now hang at Dalmeny cost under £100 each, most of his marvellous collection of Beckford books—over nine hundred in all—cost less than £2 each (many cost only a few shillings), while nineteen volumes of the Strawberry Hill Press imprints cost him £54 in 1875.

Books were Rosebery's greatest love, and in his lifetime he created libraries at The Durdans and Barnbougle which entranced even the most sophisticated bibliophiles. Barnbougle[1] was mainly devoted to his unique collection of rare Scottish books, broadsheets and pamphlets, of which over three thousand were presented to the National Library of Scotland in 1927. But the Castle also housed the fabulous Beckford collection—whose very existence was not suspected, even by the army of earnest Beckford scholars in America, until recently—numerous Burns letters, a perfect Kilmarnock (1786) edition of Burns in its original wrappers, and King Charles I's copy of *The Booke of Common Prayer* of 1637. This last volume is perhaps the greatest of the Barnbougle possessions, since it is annotated by the King and proves conclusively that the alterations made in the 1637 folio edition, usually termed Laud's Scotch Liturgy, emanated from Charles himself. The note by the King on the Order for Morning Prayer reads:

Charles R. I gave the Archb[p] of Canterbury command to make the alteracions expressed in this Book and to fit a Liturgy for the Church of Scotland and wheresoever they shall differ from another Booke signed by us at Hampt. Court Septemb[r] 28 1634 our pleasure is to have these followed rather than the former; unless the Archb[p] of St Andrews and his Brethren who are upon the place shall see apparent reason to the contrary. At Whitehall, April 19, 1636.

'This book', Rosebery used to say, 'cost the King his head.' Barnbougle also contained Gilbert Stuart's magnificent full-length portrait of George Washington, which Rosebery bought from Lord Lansdowne, and a letter signed by both the artist and the sitter which proves that it is the only full-length portrait of Washington painted from life. David's portrait of Napoleon—now in Washington—and Napoleon's superb travelling library

[1] See an article by the Countess of Rosebery in the spring 1962 issue of *The Book Collector* on the Barnbougle books.

were also at Barnbougle, as well as countless unusual treasures which include the original 'round-robin' signed by the Nore mutineers and Wellington's travelling chair, which he used on all his campaigns.

Although Rosebery was an avid reader of almost everything except military history, metaphysics, and some poetry—'perhaps I do not really taste it as I ought', he once wrote to Lord Crewe, 'for it always seems to me to express either too little or too much. . . . To appreciate poetry one must be in the heights rather than in the depths'—as a collector he delighted particularly in books with interesting connections. He had Bothwell's copy of Estienne La Roche's *Larismetique et geometrie* (1538), Mary Queen of Scots' Bible and copy of Paradin's *Chronique de Savoie* (1552), a copy of *The Statutes of the Order of the Thistle* which has the signatures of James II and Queen Anne, the 242 copies of Marat's broadsheet *L'Ami du Peuple* (originally *Le Publiciste Parisien*), and a book which had belonged to Marat and about which Rosebery remarked 'It seems strange to see a book of Marat's in so aristocratic a cover'. The Durdans library, of which John Buchan has written that it was 'so full of rarities that the casual visitor could scarcely believe them genuine', contained the first draft of Johnson's *Irene*, the original manuscript of Johnson's last prayer, the manuscript of Disraeli's *Vivian Grey*,[1] the papers of Bub Dodington (Baron Melcombe), including the complete Diaries from 1749 to 1761, and the household accounts of Frederick, Prince of Wales, and his wife (the parents of King George III). But apart from his interesting 'connection' books, which included a remarkable number of author's first edition presentation copies (one of which was Keats' copy of *Endymion* given to Leigh Hunt), Rosebery had some very rare volumes, of which the outstanding were a perfect first edition of the Authorised Version (1611), Kempis' *De Imitatione Christi* (1437), a 1549 Book of Common Prayer, and a Shakespeare First Folio which, when sold by Lady Sybil Grant at a rather unhappy but sensational sale of The Durdans library in 1933 at Sotheby's, brought the world record price of over £14,000.

His interest in books was surprisingly diverse, and gave his conversation much of its interest and charm. 'The Past stood ever at his elbow and was the counsellor upon whom he most relied,'

[1] That of *Alroy* is in Barnbougle.

Churchill has written. 'He seemed to be attended by Learning and History, and to carry into current events an air of ancient majesty. His voice was melodious and deep, and often, when listening, one felt in living contact with the centuries which are gone, and perceived the long continuity of our island tale.'[1] After a dinner-table argument on contemporary fiction at The Durdans in 1886 Eddie Hamilton remarked on Rosebery's contributions that 'one might think that he had never studied any other subject.' He had his prejudices; towards the end of his life his daughter-in-law (the present Countess of Rosebery) suggested that he should read Drinkwater's *Fox*, but he replied with some sharpness, 'I loathe Fox and abominate Drinkwater.' Although a lifelong member of the Roxburghe Club—and eventually its President—he once wrote to John Murray that 'I am, between ourselves, ardently of the opinion, which you hint at, that the great mass of the Roxburghe publications are twaddle—mere bibliomaniac reprints of dry superannuated husks, of no savour to man or beast.'

His own literary output, although limited in quantity, was notable. In 1889 and 1890 he became absorbed in a brief biography of the younger Pitt for Macmillan's 'Twelve English Statesmen' series, whose editor was John Morley. It was published in 1891 after some sharp correspondence between author and editor, and was greatly praised. Morley, who never took Rosebery very seriously as an author, commented that 'Nothing can be more agreeable to read, or more brightly written, in spite of a certain heaviness, due partly to excess of substantives, and partly to too great a desire to impress not only the author's meaning, but his opinion.' In conversation with Lord Crewe Morley described Rosebery's *Pitt* as 'a brilliant prize essay', and his criticisms are justified. The book was something of a best-seller,[2] and reached much the same type of reader that Duff Cooper was to charm with his *Talleyrand* some forty years later. There are, indeed, many points of similarity between the two books. Both are vividly written, the portraits glowing, the style perhaps self-consciously burnished, but wonderfully attractive. Thus, Rosebery describes Pitt's first Cabinet as 'a procession of ornamental phantoms', and writes of Shelburne that 'his good

[1] *Great Contemporaries*, 17.
[2] Up to the beginning of 1962, *Pitt* has had 27 printings and has sold 76,000 copies.

faith was always exemplary, but always in need of explanation'.
On George III he writes that

The character of George III is one which it is not easy to understand,
if we take the common and erroneous view that human nature is
consistent and coherent. The fact is, that congruity is the exception,
and that time and circumstance and opportunity paint with heedless
hands and garish colours on the canvas of a man's life; so that the
result is less frequently a finished picture than a palette of squeezed tints.

An admirable example of Rosebery's sardonic and compressed
style at its best is his account in *Pitt* of the rejection of Fox's
ill-fated East India Bill by the Lords.

When the Bill arrived at the House of Lords, the undertakers were
ready. The King had seen Temple, and empowered him to communicate
to all whom it might concern his august disapprobation. The uneasy
whisper circulated, and the joints of the lords became as water. The
peers, who yearned for lieutenancies or regiments, for stars or strawberry leaves; the prelates, who sought a larger sphere of usefulness;
the minions of the bedchamber and the janisseries of the closet; all,
temporal or spiritual, whose convictions were unequal to their appetite,
rallied to the royal nod.

Rosebery had given a foretaste of his facility to arrest the
attention of readers and listeners when unveiling a statue of
Burns on the Thames Embankment in the July of 1884.

It was not much for him to die so young; he died in noble company,
for he died at the age which took away Raphael and Byron, the age
which Lord Beaconsfield has called the fatal age of 37. After all, in life
there is but a very limited stock of life's breath; some draw it in deep
sighs and make an end; some draw it in quick draughts and have done
with it; and some draw it placidly through four-score quiet years; but
genius as a rule makes quick work with it. It crowds a lifetime into a
few brief years, and then passes away, as if glad to be delivered of its
message to the world, and glad to be delivered from an uncongenial
sphere. Byron and Burns together hardly more than exceeded those
three-score years and ten which are said to fulfil the life of man; but
none will deny that they had lived their full life—that they had done
the full work which was appointed them to do, and we have no right
to repine in view of so much achievement if to the mere mortal eye
they do not seem to live their full tale of years. They had exhausted
human frame and human happiness, and it was time for them to be
gone.

His outstanding quality as essayist and biographer was his compression of complicated events into a succinct and vivacious narrative. After an eloquent account of the wars of the eighteenth century he writes, 'Among all these stately figures and famous slaughters we see the central fact of the period, the shameless and naked cynicism of the eighteenth century, which, turning its back for ever on the wars of faith and conviction, looked only to contests of prey.' His characters are vividly portrayed. Cromwell 'comes tramping down to us through the ages in his great wide boots, a countenance swollen and reddish, a voice harsh, sharp and untunable, with a country-made suit, a hat with no band, doubtful linen with a speck of blood on it'. Napoleon arrives in Paris before the 18 Brumaire and 'appears before the Directory as it were *incognito*, dressed in the costume of a civilian, in a dark green great-coat with a Turkish scimitar. In this grotesque attire he seems sunburnt, emaciated, dried up: only in his eyes is there fire.' On the hatred of George II for his son he remarks, 'Frederick was a poor creature, no doubt, a vain and fatuous coxcomb. But human beings are constantly the parents of coxcombs without regarding them as vermin.' His humour is restrained, and principally owes its strength to irony; Gorgaud's proposal that Napoleon should set himself to translate the *Annual Register* is drily described as 'a remedy or a sedative unique perhaps among moral and intellectual prescriptions', while Lord Bathurst is dismissed as 'one of those strange children of our political system who fill the most dazzling offices with the most complete obscurity'. (*Napoleon: The Last Phase.*)

Although Rosebery as an author was perhaps too attracted by the picturesque and the dramatic, on occasion he could demonstrate a common sense and reality which illuminates a difficult subject. A good example is his memorable analysis of Chatham's oratory, which he concludes by remarking that the one vitally important feature was 'the character breathing through the sentences', and another is his characterisation of Sir Stafford Northcote's failure as a party leader.

He went through protracted campaigns in the provinces, delivering lengthy speeches accurately reported, from which the listener and the reader, however edified, carried away no phrase or passage that struck a spark. It was all excellent and irreproachable, but destitute of the art phrase which bequeaths a memory, still more of the fang that leaves a wound. When Northcote warmed there was, or seemed to be, a note of apology in his voice; there was also what is known as the academic twang, an inflection which cannot be defined, but which is not agreeable to the House of Commons. . . . Around him there gathered abundantly affection, loyalty, and gratitude, all just and deserved. But they availed him nothing. (*Lord Randolph Churchill.*)

Rosebery only wrote four books—*Pitt* (1891), *Napoleon: The Last Phase* (1900), *Lord Randolph Churchill* (1906), and *Chatham: His Early Life and Connections* (1910)—but many essays and appreciations, most of which were gathered together in 1921 by John Buchan in two volumes of 'Miscellanies'. Some critics have said that as what little he wrote was so good, it was tragic that he did not write more. It is true that he shrank from the labour of planning and executing a great work, and refused offers to write the biographies of Gladstone, Disraeli, and Kitchener, but there is a real place for the literary Hilliard, and it is absurd to criticise Rosebery on the score that his canvas was never large enough. His principal defect as a historian was an excessive preoccupation with the interesting and vivid, and with the polish of the final portrait rather than the meticulous accuracy of that portrait.

All of Rosebery's books—with the possible exception of *Chatham: His Early Life and Connections*, which is nevertheless considered by some to be his best book—are still read today, and unquestionably the one which most deserves to survive is his monograph on Lord Randolph Churchill. When Winston Churchill undertook his father's biography in 1903—with Rosebery's warm support and encouragement—Rosebery prepared a memoir of his ill-starred friend and proposed that it should be incorporated in the book. Churchill, not unnaturally, was touched and embarrassed by this proposal; moreover, he took exception to the harmless Eton adjective 'scug' which Rosebery had employed about his first sight of Randolph, and, after an unhappy correspondence, Rosebery declared that his contribution was withdrawn, and it was published separately. There was no ill-feeling over the matter, and Rosebery's friendship with Churchill was unimpaired, but his elder son—a Cabinet Minister himself nearly forty years later—was considerably startled when Churchill growled at him, '*Your* father called *my* father a scug!'

Rosebery's memoir of Randolph is a fraction of the size of

Churchill's lengthy official biography, but it tells us far more about Randolph's personality. In private, Rosebery took the view that Churchill's book, although brilliantly written and presented, was an unsatisfactory biography; indeed, he used to cite it as a classic example of his rule that close relatives should never write political biographies, remarking, 'If Winston couldn't do it, no one could.'

Rosebery's portrait of Randolph, although understandably tinged with affection and discretion, is so perfect that it is dangerous to select passages for quotation, save for the purpose of demonstrating its felicity.

Randolph's personality was one full of charm, both in public and in private life. His demeanour, his unexpectedness, his fits of caressing humility, his impulsiveness, his tinge of violent eccentricity, his apparent daredevilry, made him a fascinating companion: while his wit, his sarcasm, his piercing personalities, his elaborate irony, and his effective delivery, gave astonishing popularity to his speeches. Nor were his physical attributes without their attraction. His slim and boyish figure, his moustache which had an emotion of its own, his round protruding eye, gave a compound interest to his speeches and his conversation. His laugh, which has been described as 'jaylike', was indeed not melodious, but in its very weirdness and discordance it was merriment itself. . . .

He will be pathetically memorable, too, for the dark cloud which gradually enveloped him, and in which he passed away. He was the chief mourner at his own protracted funeral, a public pageant of gloomy years. It is a black moment when the heralds proclaim the passing of the dead, and the great officers break their staves. But it is sadder still when it is the victim's own voice that announces his decadence, when it is the victim's own hands that break the staff in public.

Rosebery's books and lectures, although vivid and in some cases memorable, rarely achieved the compression and interest of his jottings in his diaries, journals, or 'betting books'. Many have been quoted elsewhere in this book or in Lord Crewe's biography, but more deserve to be recorded. He was a lifelong 'collector' of interesting events or impressions. After dinner at White's on February 7th, 1882, for example,

I drove with H. Tyrwhitt to 50, Bryanston St. where Lonsdale[1] is dying. He is dying in this house he took to give actresses supper in,

[1] The third Earl of Lonsdale.

his wife does not leave Monte Carlo till tomorrow night, his brother & heir in the next room cheerfully smoking cigarettes till the end comes, passing away incognito as it were from a world which had appeared to reserve every blessing to continue for him & where he never spent a happy hour.

On meeting General Booth in 1908 he wrote,

He looks like an old prophet, drops his hs, but is strangely attractive; really earnest, but withal a man of the world in astuteness & common sense. Apart from his faith, he is sustained by his vanity. But a well-founded vanity, such as his, is not & should not be distasteful. I doubt if he will live long, and whether his organisation will long survive him.

His account of his first meeting with Cardinal Newman in 1880 at Norfolk House records that

He is much younger looking than his photographs, less wrinkled, has a deliciously soft voice and manner. Was dressed in a purple cassock with a red sash & biretta. We talked about insignificant matters. He said he was very gratified to me for my anxiety to see him, & was astonished at the kindness felt to him. I told him I had always had the *Apologia* in my room, at which he used even stronger expressions of courtly but apparently genuine surprise.

Rosebery's last portrait of Newman in 1890 jotted down in his diary, is hauntingly memorable.

The Cardinal just like a saint's remains over a high altar, waxy, distant, emaciated, in a mitre, rich gloves whereon the ring (which I kissed), rich slippers. With the hat at the foot.

And this was the end of the young Calvinist, the Oxford don, the austere vicar of St Mary's. It seemed as if a whole cycle of human thought and life were concentrated in that august repose. That was my overwhelming thought. Kindly light had led a guided Newman to this strange, brilliant, incomparable end.

Seeing him on his right side in outline one saw only an enormous nose and chin almost meeting—a St Dominic face. The left side was inconceivably sweet and soft, with that gentle corner of the mouth so greatly missed in the other view. The body, so frail and slight that it had ceased to be a body terrestrial.

Rosebery's strong religious convictions came as a surprise to the very few people who discovered them, but they lay very nearly at the root of his character. To say that he read the Bible daily and read prayers to his children—and often one of Newman's sermons —on Sundays and was a regular communicant is merely to brush against the reality and sincerity of his religion. John Buchan has rightly drawn attention to the essentially gloomy nature of Rosebery's religious outlook, which had become marked in his later years when Buchan knew him. 'Behind all his exterior urbanity and humour lay this haunting sense of transience, and, while to the world he seemed like some polished eighteenth century grandee, at heart he was the Calvinist of seventeenth century Scotland.' His obsession with death more than once gave the appearance of morbidity, and his habit of rushing off to see the remains of his friends before they were buried frequently aroused surprise, and Eddie Hamilton expressed considerable uneasiness when Rosebery hurriedly left Mentmore in 1899 for Waddesdon to see the body of Ferdinand Rothschild. Some of the most remarkable—and undeniably chilling—passages in Rosevery's diaries describe these strange visitations, but they were not out of character. In his bleak little bedroom at Barnbougle a crucifix faced the bed so that he saw it last thing at night and first in the morning, while his notes on services and sermons are copious and detailed. 'How I love this simple church and service,' he once noted at Gastein, 'bare as our Kirks—no meretricious madonna—only the picture of Christ—the devout congregation of mountaineers. Read prayers all day at home.' After a service at Cologne Cathedral he noted, 'The Cathedral more beautiful than I could have imagined. I sat through part of the afternoon service: the moaning of the priests almost drowned by the hammers of the builders; it was as if the old faith were feebly appealing for respite while its coffin was being hammered down.'

It would be wrong to deduce that Rosebery's religion was without solace to him, nor that it was invariably marked by pessimism. He always relished religious controversy, and in 1895 he had the courage of his convictions to appoint Dr Percival to Hereford in spite of the Queen's strongly-expressed hostility. He once had a notable encounter with his friend Canon Hunter of Christ Church, Epsom, who bravely rebuked him for walking out of the service before the sermon, a practice which tended to disconcert the clergyman ascending to the pulpit. 'We are delivering, however unworthily, what we believe to be God's message', Hunter wrote, '& I cannot think it wd be for the good of the people if they were generally to absent themselves whilst that message is being delivered. I think that possibly it may not have occurred to you how readily people are influenced by what you do; & sufficient as your reasons undoubtedly are, your example might be followed by others for very insufficient reasons.' This interpretation was challenged by Rosebery, who declared that the good done by the service was too often undone by the sermon, and that although many people return home criticising the sermon he had never heard of anyone criticising the prayers. The view that sermons were 'God's message' was summarily dismissed.

Rosebery himself wrote a sermon, which was delivered by Canon Rogers at St Paul's on Ash Wednesday, 1892, on the text 'Can these dry bones live?' Rosebery attended the sermon and recorded, 'It was not very successful, I think! I had no time to give it.' A year later he laid the foundation stone of the Bishopsgate Institute, Rogers' lifelong dream, and in his speech slyly referred to 'the admirable and interesting' sermon recently delivered at St Paul's by the writhing Rogers on the text of 'Can these dry bones live?'

Rosebery's addiction to the Turf was a feature of his life which often puzzled his more serious friends, and the fact that he was a notoriously poor judge of a horse increased this perplexity. Many people regarded it as part of a kind of Whig-grandee pose, and there was probably some truth in this. His pleasure in racing was centred on the peripheral delights, the friendship and *camaraderie* of the Turf, the excitements and frustrations of owning and breeding racehorses, the early morning matches on Epsom Downs followed by breakfast at The Durdans, the gay dinner-parties after the day's racing, the poring over *Ruff's Guide*, and the clatter, colour, and excitement of the meetings themselves. 'The noise, stench and villainy of the town of Doncaster are essentially part of the entertainment,' he once wrote to Lord Crewe when declining an invitation to Fryston. His Turf library was extensive, and some of Stubbs' most noble pictures—including that of *Eclipse*—graced the walls of The Durdans. 'Let not ambition mock these homely joys,' as Rosebery himself has remarked.

'If I am asked to give advice to those who are inclined to spend their time and their money on the Turf,' he genially remarked at the Gimcrack Dinner of 1897, 'I should give them the advice that

Punch gave to those about to marry—"Don't". That, I admit, is a discouraging remark for an assembly of sportsmen, and I perceive that it is received in the deadest silence. I will give you my reasons for that remark. In the first place, the apprenticeship is exceedingly expensive; in the next place, the pursuit is too engrossing for anyone who has anything else to do in this life; and, in the third place, the rewards, as compared with the disappointments, stand in the relation of, at the most, one per cent.'

Rosebery's proportion of successes was rather higher than this, and between 1875 and 1928 he won every great race with the exception of the Ascot Gold Cup. His colours came second in the 1874 Derby and *Camelford* was the unsuccessful favourite for that of 1928, and for over fifty years he was a consistently successful and popular personality of the British Turf. It must be admitted that these successes owed more to the amount of money he spent than to his judgement. His trainers did not find life very easy; after one of his horses had run second in the first race of the opening day of the Flat season he wrote caustically to his trainer, 'I see that we have struck our usual vein of "also rans".' He did not like losing. When once congratulated on the performance of a horse which ran fourth, he merely replied with some coldness, 'I am not aware that Messrs Wetherby pay for also-rans'; introducing his last trainer, Jack Jarvis, to his grandson at The Durdans, he said genially, 'This is Mr Jarvis, who trains winners for me', and then, casting a dark look at the gratified Jarvis, '—but not recently.' He was almost morbidly suspicious, and once sent his two boys home in the middle of Doncaster week as he was convinced that they were bringing him bad luck. As a stud owner, his brood mares, notably *Paraffin* and *Illuminata*, were extremely successful, but his sires were disappointing, and even a magnificent horse like *Velasquez*, who won five major races and came second in the 1897 Derby, never succeeded as a sire of winners. These vicissitudes are familiar to all who have embarked upon this extremely expensive and hazardous enterprise, but the reputation of the Mentmore Stud—more than maintained by Rosebery's son, himself the owner of two Derby winners—was always very high.

Rosebery's interests were so diverse that it is not surprising that his contemporaries were baffled. Much of the suspicion with which he was regarded stemmed from the doubt that a man who is interested in so much can be relied upon to be sufficiently qualified in any single field. Undoubtedly, he had very grand conceptions. In 1889 he planned an enormous new mansion to replace Dalmeny, but, fortunately for his descendants, the project lapsed, and the plans of his vast, hideous, fortalice now slumber at Dalmeny. His plans for the enlargement of Rosebery—his pleasant shooting-lodge in the Moorfoot Hills—were more happily conceived, but were also abandoned, not before he had built a chapel in the grounds which, to his fury, was never consecrated, since he had built it without episcopal permission. He also fell foul of Bishop Gore of Oxford when he proceeded to 'restore' the little Mentmore church without consulting the Bishop.

He had a tendency to be a law unto himself, resentful of outside interference, and easily angered by opposition or criticism. His temperament was notoriously uneven; he could be the most enchanting of companions, or he could be moody, severe, and autocratic. When in this latter mood, so strong was his personality that he could shrivel conversation with a glance, and chance acquaintances meeting him in this frame of mind were often very frightened of him. Even when he was old, the young and irrepressible Max Aitken left his presence chastened but admiring. His humour often had a sharp edge to it, as is seen in the following letter to the Queen of February 2nd, 1893.

Lord Rosebery had hoped that in the torpid and somnolent atmosphere of The Hague Sir Horace Rumbold's proverbial irritability would have lost something of its keen edge. To learn therefore from Your Majesty that he has managed to tax the endurance of the phlegmatic and impassive Dutch is almost more than Lord Rosebery can bear.

For it is impossible to move him. It would be wrong on the one hand to foster by his promotion the race of impracticable diplomatists of which he is the ideal, while on the other hand it is clear that the Court does not exist which would not, after the briefest experience, pant for his removal. A post as Queen's Messenger of an exalted and special description, which would keep him in constant flight through the principal capitals of Europe, would alone meet the case of this bird of sinister passage; but this, unfortunately, does not exist.

In a different vein, among his letters to Sir Henry Ponsonby there is a delightfully whimsical account of a Sunday journey from Windsor to Epsom.

... Thrice have I dined at Windsor on Saturday: thrice have I been turned out into a cold hard world like a new born lamb on Sunday morning. Twice have I escaped by special train. The third time, which was yesterday, I determined to try the road. I have now sufficiently recovered from these last experiences to narrate them.

I left Windsor at 8.45 by a tardy and chilly train for Staines. At Staines I met my carriage galloping up after a sixteen miles journey from Epsom. In it I pursued a cold and devious way through the counties of Middlesex and Surrey, of both of which I am now qualified to write a statistical account. They are level and monotonous in appearance, their roads are muddy, their population saturnine. The only variety was that one horse lost a shoe.

That detained me for half an hour's meditation at a forge on a lonely common, to which I proceeded at a foot's pace for four miles after the loss of the shoe being discovered. The solitary soliloquy gave me courage to meet the freezing looks of the church-goers along the road, who eyed me as if I were the Scarlet Lady of Babylon herself, instead of a guest returning from a visit to his Sovereign.

At the end of four hours' painful & incessant travel I reached my own door. But exposure to the winds & scorn of two counties has left its mark on my iron constitution, and long, long, will it be, I fear, before I can again face the rigours of a Royal Saturday. ...

A. G. Gardiner, in a remarkably acute contemporary vignette of Rosebery—which is probably the best essay on Rosebery ever written—has commented that

He has the temperament of the artist, not of the politician. The artist lives by the intensity of his emotions and his impressions. The world of things is coloured and transmuted in the realm of his mind. He is subjective, personal, a harp responsive to every breeze that blows. The breath of the May morning touches him to ecstasy; the east wind chills him to the bone. He passes quickly through the whole gamut of emotion, tasting a joy unknown to coarser minds, plunging to depths unplumbed by coarser minds. He is a creature of moods and moments, and spiritually he often dies young.[1]

The truth of this judgement can be tested again and again in Rosebery's life. One very good example can be seen in his relationship with Everard Primrose, who died in the April of 1885 in the Sudan from enteric fever. On the last occasion on which Rosebery saw Everard, his younger brother had come to ask for money; Rosebery's account of their conversation is curt, and merely

[1] Gardiner: *Prophets, Priests and Kings.*

records that Everard came for money, got £500, and departed at once. But when he received the news of Everard's death he wrote in his diary:

And so I strike the word brother from my dictionary. How hard it is to have been so hopelessly separated from him in this long illness, to have realised him sinking slowly, homelessly in the hard, hot glare of the desert sun, caring so much for all the people and all the things from which he was cut off. . . . What love, what faith, what sorrow moved him, or was he too feeble for thought? Farewell, Brother—word and fact—on this side time. Would that I could fill up the irreparable blank by calling my suffering fellow-men by that name, in action as well as speech, or rather by action instead of speech. The brotherhood of man is so noble and difficult in action, so silly and easy in mere speech.

Politics was never a central feature in Rosebery's life, but nor was anything else. He made almost a cult of dabbling in everything, with the result that his talents were dispersed, and through the accident of his peerage he never had that undefinable but strong tie to public life which is so remarkable a feature of the House of Commons. Detesting the House of Lords, he lacked a congenial political platform, and as partisan politics bored him, the temptation to return to his beloved books, his wide estates, and the company of his family and friends was sometimes irresistible. Sir Winston Churchill has written that

As the franchise broadened and the elegant, glittering, imposing trappings faded from British Parliamentary and public life, Lord Rosebery was conscious of an ever-widening gap between himself and the Radical electorate. The great principles 'for which Hampden died in the field and Sidney on the scaffold', the economics and philosophy of Mill, the venerable inspiration of Gladstonian memories, were no longer enough. One had to face the caucus, the wire-puller and the soap-box; one had to stand on platforms built of planks of all descriptions. He did not like it. He could not do it. He would not try. He knew what was wise and fair and true. He would not go through the laborious, vexatious and at times humiliating processes necessary under modern conditions to bring about these great ends. He would not stoop; he did not conquer.[1]

This is to over-simplify Rosebery's dilemma, although there is some truth in what Churchill says. The fact was that Rosebery never really knew what he wanted out of life. He relished power,

[1] *Great Contemporaries*, 19.

but shrank from the struggle; he was proud, sensitive, introspective—three qualities which are not appropriate in a leader of a modern political party. Being contemptuous of anything which savoured of cant, he was not misled by party cries, and too often made this abundantly plain in public. He reserved the right to make up his own mind on any subject as it arose, but he did not have the boldness or self-righteousness of a Gladstone, nor the unscrupulous flamboyancy of a Randolph Churchill or a Chamberlain. The 'great game of politics' never greatly amused or interested him, and, when bored, he could always retreat to his libraries. This fundamental boredom with politics as opposed to public life—for that never ceased to entrance him—was often manifested by a flippancy which amused but did not impress. 'The British people,' as Disraeli has remarked, 'being subject to fogs, and possessing a powerful Middle Class, require grave statesmen.' Rosebery himself was fully aware of this factor, but his irrepressible levity kept breaking through, as at the Royal Academy Banquet in the April of 1893, when he replied to the toast of 'Her Majesty's Ministers':

I have only to open a red box to be possessed of that magic carpet which took its possessor wherever he would go. Perhaps sometimes it carries me a little farther than that. I open it, and find myself at once in those regions where a travelled monarch and an intellectual Minister are endeavouring to reconcile the realms of Xerxes and Darius with the needs of nineteenth century civilisation. I smell the scent of the roses, and hear the song of the bulbul. I open another box, which enables me to share the sports of the fur-seal—his island loves, his boundless swims in the Pacific; I can even follow him to Paris and see him—the *corpus delicti*—laid on the table of the Court of Arbitration. . . . I follow every Court. Not a monarch leaves his capital on a journey, but I am on the platform in the spirit if not in the body. I am in spirit in the gallery of every Parliament. I am ready and anxious—but not always successful—to be present at the signing of every treaty. I think I have laid a sufficient claim before you to insist that, in future, when you consider Her Majesty's Ministers you may not consider them merely as political creatures, but as persons who have also their imaginative side, as official Ariels roaming through time and space, not on broomsticks, but on boxes.

From his young manhood Rosebery had surrounded himself with admirers, a perhaps unconscious manifestation of that craving for sympathy which, as Lord Welby once observed,

Rosebery always demonstrated. Hannah Rosebery's adoration may have irritated and embarrassed him on occasions, but his affection for her was very profound. His children remember how he would honour her religion, and how, at the end of the Day of Atonement, he would take up to her bedroom the tray of food with which she ended her fast, and how they would sit together, quietly talking, far into the night. Few of their letters have survived, but those that remain demonstrate the warmth and tenderness of their relationship. In 1884, to take one small example, Hannah commissioned a pictorial catalogue of the Mentmore treasures, and sent a copy to her husband with a gentle note explaining that she had undertaken the work in honour of her father. 'And now, in thus handing it over to your care, I feel yours are the only hands which are fitted to hold what he, whom I consider as perfect as any mortal may be, cared for. I could not speak this. Excuse a letter. Your loving Hannah.'

At the beginning of the October of 1890 it was evident that Lady Rosebery was seriously ill, and on October 9th her doctors pronounced that she was suffering from typhoid fever. From October 20th her condition deteriorated rapidly, and five days later Rosebery was told that her death was imminent. She was still conscious, and they had what both believed was to be their last conversation together. 'How short everything in life seems,' she said at one point. 'It seems only yesterday that you came to Mentmore and gave me a sapphire locket.' 'On that day', Rosebery later wrote, 'I felt all the bitterness of death.'

But the crisis passed, and on November 4th Lady Leconfield— who had come to Dalmeny at her brother's urgent request to nurse his wife—reported to the Duchess of Cleveland that 'I do not think that Archie will send any more telegraphic bulletins now, as Hannah seems really progressing, though very slowly'. For a short period Rosebery—who did not know, as the doctors did, that his wife was suffering from Bright's Disease, and could not hope to survive the typhoid for long—believed that she was recovering, and plans were made for a recuperative holiday in Corfu with the children. Herbert Bismarck called on November 9th, but Lady Leconfield noted that this visit, although well intentioned, 'is not quite chiming in with Archie's thirst for solitude'.

The length of the illness, the fluctuating hopes and fears, and the distressing periods of delirium, all exerted an almost unbearable strain on Rosebery and his sister. On November 17th, after days of acute anxiety, the doctors again prepared Rosebery for his wife's death. After the crisis of October 25th he could not bring himself to believe it, and in the afternoon he took the children—the boys were staying in Barnbougle and the girls with Principal Donaldson in Edinburgh—to Cramond Church. But a ghastly night of desperate endeavours to revive the patient and a dreadful vigil by the bed followed. Once she regained consciousness, smiled at him, and said quite clearly, 'Archie, Archie, I am going home', before relapsing into a final coma. At ten minutes to six, on the morning of November 18th, the terrible groaning breathing which had racked the listeners subsided into 'a gentle sigh of rest' which, Rosebery later wrote in his poignant account of this night, 'was almost pleasant to hear'.

Rosebery went down into the dark, silent hall, and walked out into the night. He crossed the park in the bitter-black hour which precedes the dawn, past the house with its few cheerless lights, through the little wood which he had planted, to Barnbougle. He climbed to his tiny bedroom, and 'watched a beautiful dawn of melting grey, until it was time to see the children'.

CHAPTER SEVEN

THE RELUCTANT MINISTER

But men must know, that in this theatre of man's life
it is reserved only for God and angels to be lookers-on.
BACON: *Advancement of Learning*

IT IS IMPOSSIBLE to exaggerate the shattering effect which his wife's death had on Rosebery. At the funeral at Willesden on November 25th Hamilton thought that his friend was in control of himself, but Ponsonby, in the course of a detailed account for the Queen, wrote that 'Lord Rosebery never spoke but remained close to the coffin till it was lowered into the grave. Lord Rothschild led him back to the Chapel but he looked down the whole time. He wishes to show in public that he is able to put aside his sorrow—but in private he breaks down.'[1] 'But alas!' he wrote to Ferdinand de Rothschild, 'if I write, what can I say? Our happy home is a wreck, her children are motherless, and I have lost the best wife ever man had. I do not see the elements of consolation, except in the memory of her beautiful unselfish life, and in the feeling of her still encompassing love.' To Hannah's old nurse, Doretta Morck, he wrote, 'We must go to Mentmore at once, or I shall never go there again; for every inch of it will be painful; so the plunge must be taken without delay.' 'There is, however, one incident of this tragedy only less painful than the actual loss,' he wrote to the Queen; 'which is that at the moment of death the difference of creed makes itself felt, and another religion steps in to claim the corpse. It was inevitable, and I do not complain: and my wife's family have been more than kind. But none the less it is exquisitely painful ... love, such as my wife's, cannot perish; it is with me as much as my skin or the air I breathe; and so it must be to the end.' To Scott Holland, an Eton friend now Canon of St Paul's, he wrote:

[1] *Royal Archives.*

R.—16

... How strange it seems to look back on our pupilroom days when our anxieties lay in our lame elegiacs and the probable eccentricities of our tutor, days that seem to be so near—and now you should be holding forth your hand to me as I pass through the valley of the shadow of death. And in that valley are all the stations of the cross by which one cannot but pause and meditate, whether one will or no: the great problems of life and eternity suddenly gape open on each side and will not be denied: they have each to be contemplated or considered. And so one is led to believe that Death, besides what it means for the one taken, is for the one or for those surviving the supreme warning of God, the call of the trumpet second only to the last; the summons to face once for all the awe and import of the visible and invisible world. And so one is led by the grim angel through a pilgrimage like that in the cartoons of Faust, where all that is actual or possible or past is lit up by the flashes of his lantern, and the blessed dead wrapped in real rest—a distant star of comfort...

His few intimate friends were surprised and even shocked by the dark depression into which Rosebery was plunged and from which he was slow to recover. His children were dressed in the most sombre black, and for the rest of his life Rosebery used notepaper disfigured with black borders. His wife's bedroom was kept exactly as it had been and was never occupied again during his lifetime,[1] while the anniversary of her death was observed in solitude at Barnbougle. He even added books to her library for the rest of his life. Hannah Rosebery's death drastically accentuated the gloomy—indeed, almost morbid—side of Rosebery's nature. 'The procession passes swiftly on from the seen to the unseen,' he wrote to the Queen at Christmas 1890; 'and while we are still straining to catch the last glimpse of one we loved, another has gone: and we begin to think that our hearts and our interests are not here, but in the great silence.' In the November of 1896 the Ripons came to Dalmeny, and Rosebery wrote that 'On the 19th you will not see me. It is the anniversary that is sacred to me, and a day which I spend alone. But I shall be in my castle, and my children will do their best to make the house pleasant.' It was five years before Rosebery realised that it was unreasonable to expect his children to feel as deeply as he did. 'I fasted at the Castle,' he wrote in his diary for November 19th, 1896. 'I did not

---

[1] The present Countess of Rosebery was installed in this room by error on the occasion of her first visit to Dalmeny, but after her future father-in-law was told, she found that her belongings had been transferred to another room.

see the girls, as I wished them to discontinue observing the anniversary. Why add a cloud to the beginning of their lives? Their
mother's memory should be associated with happiness and not
mourning.' In the May of 1894 he wrote to Lady Stanhope, 'I
have not dined out for nearly four years, and scarcely think I
shall ever dine out again.'

His wife's death was the greatest personal tragedy of his
life, and in a sense he never recovered from it; he had come to
rely far more on his wife's devotion and sympathy than he had
probably ever realised, and her loss revived his love of solitude
and his impatience with adversity and criticism. Her pride and
happiness in his success had been an important element in his
political career, particularly since 1886, and their removal, together with that of her common sense and ambition, effectively
destroyed what ambitions he had ever possessed. His insomnia,
which had hitherto only affected him at moments of crisis, plagued
him throughout 1891 and 1892. He took no part whatever in
public life in 1891, and most of his friends left him alone, thinking
that he would soon recover from the shock of his wife's death and
return to politics.

'I spent a couple of days with Rosebery last week,' Morley
wrote to Gladstone on August 18th: 'He is now himself again,
and though he uses language implying that his return to political
activity is quite conditional (I know not on what), I feel that he
will be at his post again by the end of the summer.' The only
event of note in the year was the publication of *Pitt* in November.

In December there was a Liberal conclave at Althorp described wonderfully by Morley.

After dinner, we went into what I do think was the most fascinating
room I ever saw in a house—great or small—one of the libraries, lined
with well-bound books on which enamelled shelves, with a few, but not
too many, nick-nacks lying about, and all illuminated with the soft
radiance of many clusters of wax candles. A picture to remember:
Spencer with his noble carriage and fine red beard; Mr G seated on a
low stool, discoursing as usual, playful, keen, versatile; Rosebery,
saying little, but now and then launching a pleasant *mot*; Harcourt
cheery, expansive, witty. Like a scene from one of Dizzy's novels, and
all the actors, men with parts to play.[1]

[1] Morley: *Recollections* I, 293-4.

On the following day (December 8th) Rosebery said that he must leave immediately after lunch for Mentmore, but Gladstone persuaded him to remain for an important discussion on Liberal policy. 'Rosebery took up a book and turned it sedulously over,' Morley has recorded, 'only interjecting a dry word now and then. Harcourt not diffuse.'[1] In his record of the 'long palaver', Rosebery remarked that 'We discussed every imaginable subject from a list brought down by Mr G; Egypt, as to which I said that the government which *simultaneously* gave HR to Ireland & evacuated Egypt wd be a bold one, finance, probably dissolution, Goschen's one pound notes, the navy, Harcourt copious on each, and at length Ireland. There was only time for a short discussion between Harcourt & Mr G as to the reduction of the Irish members, & as to an Irish second order & then I had to catch my train back to Mentmore.' Gladstone followed him to stay at Mentmore, and took the occasion to express the hope that Rosebery would soon be returning to public life. 'On this we talked with some fullness,' Rosebery noted. 'He was emphatic on the point that when one had attained to a certain point in politics it was not possible to retire.'

The close of 1891 marked the fifth anniversary of the Unionist domination. Although their 1886 Parliamentary majority of 116 had declined to 68, and was to be further reduced before the end of the Parliament, the Unionist leaders could with reason congratulate themselves upon their tactical position. The Tory leadership was unquestioned for the first time since the death of Beaconsfield; the fortunes of their opponents had received a terrible injury; the possibility of reunion between the Gladstonian Liberals and the Liberal Unionists had vanished; the Ministry which had appeared doomed to disintegration and collapse in its early period of office now held the reins of power with firmness and unity.

The Gladstonian Liberals, on the other hand, were experiencing the chagrin of a political confederation mocked by false dawns. The 'Newcastle Programme', announced by Gladstone himself at Newcastle on October 2nd, 1891, bore all the signs of cynical political expediency and merited the scalding invective of Chamberlain that 'It is a programme which begins by offering everything to everybody, and it will end by giving nothing to

[1] Morley: *Recollections*, I, 294.

nobody'. Church disestablishment in England and Wales, triennial Parliaments, 'one man, one vote', local vetoes on the sale of intoxicating liquor, employers' liability measures, compulsory land acquisition, and the provision of improved district and parish councils, were all promised, together with indefinite hints about the limitation of hours of work—a subject on which the Liberal leaders were acutely divided—the payment of Members of Parliament and vague threats against the House of Lords. The 'Newcastle Programme' was hastily concocted, was destined to cause sharp divisions within the Liberal Party, and probably had little electoral impact. The by-election swing against the Government was clearly losing its impetus, and a Liberal victory at Rossendale early in 1892—the election having been caused by Hartington's elevation to the Lords as the eighth Duke of Devonshire upon his father's death—could not be regarded as symptomatic of the national temper.

In the course of an audience with the Queen on January 30th Arthur Balfour admitted that the chances of a Unionist victory were not very great, but it was apparent to the organisers of both parties that it would be a desperately close-run affair. A speech by Lord Salisbury at Exeter on February 2nd heralded the beginning of the prolonged election campaign which occupied the energies of the political world for the remainder of the spring and early summer. The party orators followed each other up and down the country answering their opponents with wearying fidelity; the Unionists hinted darkly at the dismemberment of the Empire in the event of a Liberal victory; the Gladstonians attacked coercive rule in Ireland and aired the indefinite pledges of the Newcastle Programme; the Irish Nationalists continued their internecine controversy with unamended ferocity, while the Ulstermen thundered threateningly from across the Border.

In these circumstances the party struggle in the House of Commons became increasingly unreal. Balfour introduced an Irish Local Government Bill in February, and this hapless measure, praised mildly by its author, derided by the Liberals, and harshly denounced by the Irish, came to a peaceful and unlamented end later in the Session. With this exception, such Government business as there was proceeded silkily. There were no more by-election disturbances; North Hackney returned a Unionist candidate in May with a majority only slightly less than that of 1886.

The Liberal leaders approached the elections with mounting apprehension. It was evident that Gladstone's hitherto unquenchable fires were dying, and the magic of his name was waning in the country. He had his good days, and on these he was still incomparable, but they were becoming noticeably less frequent. He was eighty-two, and although still marvellously active for his years, several incidents demonstrated the fact that prolonged exertion quite exhausted him. His resolution to lead the Liberal Party into the elections never wavered, but among many of his most devoted supporters there was increasing concern lest his glorious career should end in pathetic anti-climax.

The position of Rosebery was another cause of perplexity in the inner councils of the party. Morley had visited him at The Durdans in the August of 1891 and recorded that 'He seemed to have recovered his usual spirits. . . . He is still restless . . . but he is again alert, ready, and *suivi*.'[1] Until the June of 1892 it appeared that he had thrown off the malaise which had afflicted him after his wife's death. He had agreed to stand for the East Finsbury Division in the London County Council elections in March, and then consented to resume the Chairmanship for a brief period, which he resigned in June. His conduct of Council business was as competent as ever and showed no diminution of the deftness of his touch, while a series of speeches delivered in May in Birmingham and Edinburgh were regarded as more trenchant than any he had previously made on partisan platforms. It is not surprising that neither Harcourt nor Morley had taken Rosebery's mysterious hints of withdrawal from public life very seriously. 'After all,' Harcourt wrote to Morley on January 28th, 'it is pretty Fanny's way, and we have survived a good deal of it for many years.'[2]

In fact Rosebery was passing through a period of acute personal unhappiness and indecision. January and February were spent in Italy and April in Spain, where he admired the Alhambra, discovered that he liked bullfighting, and bought for an absurdly low price five magnificent Goya tapestries which he brought back to Dalmeny. But in March he suffered an unpleasant private and financial shock when an American friend Van Zandt, who had been a regular and welcome visitor to Dalmeny, Mentmore, and The Durdans for several years, shot himself; he had been

[1] Morley: *Recollections*, I, 311.   [2] Gardiner: *Harcourt*, II, 167.

entrusted with a considerable amount of Rosebery's foreign investments, and it was discovered that Van Zandt's speculations had been disastrous and that nearly £20,000 of Rosebery's money had been lost. A week later, while addressing his L.C.C. constituents in Finsbury, the ruby in the engagement ring that his wife had given him in 1878 flew out of the clasp and was shattered on the stone floor. 'Verily,' he noted wearily in his diary, 'misfortunes never come single.' On his return from Edinburgh on May 13th after a triumphant speech at St Andrew's Hall he fell asleep and dreamed that he was dying and was trying to warn his wife; 'A tender, not a painful, dream' he noted in the bleak solitude of Barnbougle. It was one of several dreams about his dead wife which he had at this time, which naturally increased his melancholy. Insomnia was plaguing him constantly, and when he rose to speak in London at the St James's Hall in March on the eve of the Council elections, one observer noted 'the pathetic hint of sleeplessness in the eyes', the drooping of the once sprightly figure, touches of grey in the hair, and the low and broken voice in which he began his speech. It was soon apparent that his speaking was as vigorous as ever, and he appealed that 'London's work should be done, not in the spirit of vestrymen, but in the spirit of statesmen'. Lady Monkswell was among the audience on this occasion.

Altho' he is not handsome now, he looks so sad and ill, his very size and squareness and massive head impress one at once. Then directly he opens his mouth his deep rich voice, which for a good part of his speech he hardly raised, and his beautiful, refined, clear pronunciation, is delightful to listen to. He is an orator, without any effort he makes one's blood run faster, and he has a delightful power of humour. He has a hundred tones in his voice, and his face, whether truly or not, expresses deep earnestness. I can hardly believe, unless he gets a great deal better, that he is anything like well enough for public life. Two days ago he told Bob[1] that after making a speech he always has a sleepless night, and that he should probably never make another speech again. The one I listened to lasted ¾ hour. He was very pale when he began and very red when he finished.[2]

Rosebery's speeches in May and June, as well as delighting the Liberal rank and file, aroused the indignation of the Queen, who

[1] Robert, second Lord Monkswell (1845–1909).
[2] Hon. E. F. Collier: *A Victorian Diarist*, 205.

described his Birmingham speech to Ponsonby as 'radical to a degree to be almost communistic. Hitherto he always said he had nothing whatever to do with Home Rule, and only with Foreign Affairs, and *now* he is as violent as any one. Poor Lady Rosebery is not there to keep him back. Sir Henry must try and get at him through some one, so that he may know how grieved and shocked The Queen is at what he said. In case of the Govt's defeat The Queen meant to send for him first, but after this violent attack on Lord Salisbury, this attempt to stir up Ireland, it will be *impossible* and the GOM at 82 is a *very alarming lookout*.'

Very few people were aware of Rosebery's determination to leave public life after the elections. He had put himself in a quite impossible position, since neither the Liberal leaders nor the public realised that he intended to withdraw; only a handful of intimate friends like Hamilton knew the true situation. On May 11th Brett warned him of the obvious reactions to his return to the platform.

I agree with you that there is no necessity to take the public into your confidence. I was not arguing in favour of an open declaration. Hitherto you have kept comparatively silent upon the great political issues, and you have not taken a very prominent part in the struggle for power.

So long as you maintain this attitude, the private warnings to colleagues that you propose not to accept office are all that is necessary. Perhaps more than is necessary. If men vote for Liberal candidates, assuming that you will be a minister, it is their own miscalculation they will have to blame. But if you enter just now into the political fray, in my view you give hostages to the Party. You are not a 'plain and simple citizen', but a great deal more.

In private Rosebery persistently argued to his own satisfaction that he was bound in loyalty to Gladstone and the party to assist in the election campaign and that after this obligation was fulfilled he would be at liberty to retire. 'I do not wish it to be said that I am silent for tactical reasons or from indifference,' he had written to Arnold Morley[1] on April 5th. 'I am therefore ready to speak in May & June at Edinburgh (first), Birmingham and Glasgow, if I can do so on the distinct understanding that I am not to be committed thereby to continuance in office or to be considered as a possible candidate for office. If this cannot be I

[1] 1849–1016. MP for Nottingham 1880–1895; Liberal Chief Whip, 1886–1892; Postmaster-General, 1892–5.

should prefer to retire at once.' But in his speech in London on June 23rd he said that in the event of a Liberal victory 'we intend to try the experiment of having a continuous Foreign Policy. . . . I cannot doubt that Mr Gladstone's Government and Mr Gladstone's Foreign Secretary, whoever he may be—I am told in the newspapers this morning that that point has a peculiar and morbid interest for myself [*laughter and cheers*]—will continue Lord Salisbury's Foreign Policy.'

This ambivalence between private statements and public demeanour—for on no occasion did he even give the impression that he was about to leave public life—was not merely wrongheaded but essentially selfish. Rosebery's great failing as a politician was his self-enfoldment, which constantly rendered him liable to misinterpretation and which bewildered and exasperated his colleagues, and this defect was never demonstrated more clearly than in the summer of 1892. Here was a great public personality of the widest popularity, regarded by many as Mr Gladstone's inevitable successor, taking an active part in the pre-election campaign and then declining to enter the Government in the event of a Liberal victory. This aloofness would lay the Liberals open to the damning indictment that one of its most brilliant ornaments felt so little confidence in its policies and prospects that he would have nothing to do with it.

Hamilton visited Rosebery at The Durdans on May 29th and found him very pessimistic. He and Morley had visited the Gladstones on the previous day and had been depressed by the low quality of the great man's *entourage*, and he told Hamilton that he was already dreading the visit of the Gladstones to Dalmeny for the last Midlothian campaign. Morley went down to The Durdans on June 6th. 'The weather delicious,' he noted. 'We sauntered about the garden, talking books, politics, and persons. He was uncommonly keen about it all—for a man who comforts himself in vagrant moments with the thought that he has "done with public life". . . . After dinner we walked for an hour in the woods, the silver moon gleaming through the branches. R a charming companion.' Rosebery said that Morley was more 'sympathetic' to Liberals, who rarely came to see him but were always consulting Morley. 'This comparison paid me an undeserved compliment,' Morley wrote, 'for nobody surpassed him in that inner humanity which is the root of good manners and good feeling and other things lying at the core of character.'[1] Morley departed from The Durdans obviously convinced of the unreality of Rosebery's divorce from politics. In later years he portrayed Rosebery at this critical moment in his career.

He took with him to his roosting-place at Barnbougle all the elements of the widest popularity, and men were well justified in looking to him as leader in a popular party. . . . His known fondness for books and proficiency in book-knowledge, as well as the grace and finish of form alike in writing and speaking, had cultivated lively interest in the reading class. His diction was at once pure and full, periods were spaciously rounded, and fine imaginary flights did not impair the steadiness of the plain sense which is the essence of sound politics. . . . Keeping himself particularly well informed as to all the world's affairs, and to those who had a voice in them, he was the best and most brilliant of conversers, unless he chose to be silent. None of us could be sure . . . of the right English for *esprit*. Everybody felt that Rosebery had more of that enchanting gift than any Englishman of his day. Wit, humour, good humour, are rare and useful aids to public business, and in his case they deserve Clarendon's words of Charles II, 'that his was a pleasant, affable, recommending sort of wit'. He knew how to manage with easy and unaffected melody the rich voice that nature had given him, and his gesture and accent have always been equally attractive to audiences of every type. Let me add that the glories of the famous Midlothian campaign, in which he had so active a share, now shone upon him with a reflected glow that naturally lighted up new hopes for his party. He was at the stage that comes in an important career, when influence on public opinion finds itself transformed and is fixed into responsible power. The boldest may well be the most intent on survey and re-survey of the ground.[2]

Parliament was informed at the end of May that it was to be dissolved in July, and Members fled to their constituencies. Rosebery, having fulfilled what he regarded as his obligations to the party, was at The Durdans on June 13th when Hamilton descended upon him, resolved, if necessary, to jeopardise his long friendship. 'E. Hamilton came down & dined', Rosebery commented in his diary, '—in a high & mighty friendly fury.' 'He is still bent on standing aside from public affairs as soon as the fight is over,' Hamilton noted; '. . . on this occasion I determined not to mince matters.'

Hamilton employed every possible argument that he could lay

---

[1] Morley: *Recollections*, I, 314.   [2] *Ibid.*, I, 318–19.

hands on. For Rosebery to carry out his intention of retiring would be to desert Gladstone at the close of his career; it would be a triumph for the Unionists, since his defection would irreparably damage any Liberal Ministry; his wife would never have heard of it; he would be branded for ever as unreliable and treacherous, and so on. 'R was very stubborn,' Hamilton recorded, 'though he gave me a patient hearing.' In reply to his friend's tirade, Rosebery said that he had complete liberty of action provided that he stood by Gladstone until the elections; he was not enslaved to public life; he had his children and his private affairs to look after; he had never been wedded to Home Rule, which 'though he recognised that some form of it must come he did not believe it would be the panacea of Irish ills'; Kimberley would make an excellent Foreign Secretary, and John Morley had assured him that he would take that office if it went to a commoner! Hamilton returned to London fully aware that he had made no impression whatever upon his friend, and on the next day (June 15th) he tackled Gladstone on the subject.

He found the old man in a gloomy frame of mind. He was depressed about his eyesight and hearing, and viewed with unenthusiasm the 'unavoidable' victory at the polls. He warmed when he referred to the Unionist tactics and speeches, particularly in Ulster, but was untroubled by the possibility of Rosebery's retirement. 'Mr G pooh-poohed the idea of his withdrawal from public life being within the range of practical politics: the question was not arguable.' Ten days later, on the eve of the Gladstones' departure for Dalmeny, Hamilton was again unsuccessful when he broached the subject. Gladstone replied that Rosebery was too deeply committed to retire, 'though it must not be thought that there is no one else competent to take the Foreign Office. I don't see why John Morley should not be Foreign Secretary.' When Hamilton said that he could not think of anyone less suited to the post Gladstone simply retorted that in any case the problem would not arise.

The last Midlothian campaign was, in the main, a melancholy charade. Only once, in a speech at the Theatre Royal, Glasgow, on July 2nd, did Gladstone recapture the fervent enthusiasm and inspiration of the previous campaigns. The Gladstones were depressed, while Rosebery, suffering from a heavy cold and insomnia, wore his most black and uninviting façade. The cold

weather, the evident failure of the election campaign, Mrs
Gladstone's tactlessness and possessive adoration of her husband,
created an unbearable tension. Until driven to Dalmeny House
by his cold, Rosebery slept at Barnbougle, and refused to discuss
politics. Morley arrived for a hurried visit, was locked in discussion with Gladstone, and invaded Rosebery's room at eleven
in the evening to discuss offices but Rosebery, his cold 'overpowering', refused to be drawn. In his discussion with Morley,
Gladstone had said that Spencer had stronger claims than Rosebery. 'It is extraordinary', Morley reported to Hamilton on July
21st, 'the want of *nous* which Mr Gladstone showed about Rosebery.'

Into this strange atmosphere Sir Algernon West[1] arrived shortly
after Morley had left, and found 'an indescribable cloud over the
whole thing, which I cannot account for'. On July 4th the first
election results began to come in, and Rosebery seemed to take a
malicious pleasure in referring to '*your* victory' or '*your* defeat';
before he left Dalmeny, West was taken by Rosebery to Barnbougle—a rare privilege—and told of his determination to leave
public life.

The early results showed that the tide was flowing only weakly
in the Liberals' favour. Rosebery wrote to Hamilton on July 8th:

Mr G is in good spirits this morning, but on Wednesday morning
he felt the wreck of his high hopes severely. Yesterday he revived a
good deal, and he has borne his cruel disappointment heroically. I say
'cruel disappointment', because he would not hear of anything below
80 or 100 majority and insisted on forming governments etc—much
to my discomposure.

Two days later he wrote again:

My dear E,
Your views of the situation and Mr G's do not at all coincide. His
present view points to his taking office with the smallest of majorities.
Alas! Alas!
I cannot tell you what a week I have had since last Sunday, and I
have three days more of it.

[1] 1832–1921. Commissioner of Board of Inland Revenue, 1873–7; Deputy
Chairman, 1877–81; Chairman, 1881–92. Unofficial head of Gladstone's secre-
tariat, 1892–4. C.B. 1880, K.C.B. 1886, Privy Councillor 1894, G.C.B. 1902.

I hope to leave this place on Wednesday night and bid it a very long farewell. I am going to potter about the Western Highlands in a small yacht I have hired. Keep this to yourself.

Y ever,

AR.

Hamilton was naturally alarmed by the tone of these letters; and West, on his return to London, confirmed that the Gladstones were behaving inconsiderately and that Mrs Gladstone was making matters worse by her notorious tactlessness, but that Rosebery was not improving matters by his moroseness and refusal to discuss politics. Whenever Gladstone broached the subjects of policies and offices, his host deliberately evaded any discussion on these topics. On July 6th Gladstone drove down to Barnbougle; on the 7th he caught Rosebery in the library, but when he began to talk of prospective arrangements Rosebery said that this was very unlucky and averted the discussion; on the 8th they drove round the park in Rosebery's carriage, and Gladstone asked him if he had any comforting consideration to offer him, and Rosebery replied simply that he had not; on the evening of the 9th Gladstone handed Rosebery a list of measures to be introduced 'in case of a small majority'; on the 11th, while Rosebery was reading *Waverley* to his boys, Gladstone came in and at once started talking of the leadership of the Lords, urging Rosebery to take it; Rosebery replied that Kimberley or Spencer would be better qualified. 'Rosebery had a sort of presumptive title to the Foreign Office from a former tenure of it, although a very brief one, in 1886,' Gladstone later wrote in a record of the errors he had committed in his public career. 'But instead of founding a claim upon this tenure, he did everything in his power to avoid the resumption of it. Again and again he resisted my overtures.' Lady Fanny Marjoribanks—wife of Edward Marjoribanks and Randolph Churchill's sister—came to Dalmeny at this time, and saw that Rosebery was so wretchedly unhappy that she urged him to go away for a holiday at once, but he decided to stick it out.

The failure of the Midlothian meetings, the dreary weather, and the impenetrable wall of misunderstanding between the Gladstones and their unhappy host were not improved by the nature of the election results which were now pouring in. The English boroughs had given 34 victories to the Liberals, which was not nearly as many as had been hoped for, and still left the Unionists in a majority of 153 to 136. John Morley and Herbert Gladstone had nearly been defeated, and Midlothian nearly witnessed the supreme catastrophe. In his last contest in 1885 Gladstone had secured a majority of 4,631, which was extremely large for those days. The 1892 Conservative candidate, although a valiant soldier and a colourful personality, was somewhat inexperienced, but he came very close to toppling the Grand Old Man off his pedestal; the result—described by the Queen to Ponsonby as 'very cheering' —was Gladstone, 5,845, Colonel A. G. Wauchope, 5,155. Fortunately the Midlothian result was one of the last to be declared, or the effect upon the Liberal fortunes might have been calamitous.

Morley, stunned by his Pyrrhic victory at Newcastle, came to Dalmeny to see the Gladstones off. He and Rosebery drove back together from Dalmeny Station. 'It was a lovely evening,' Morley has written, 'the waters of the Forth lay glassy smooth in the sunlight. The stupendous structure of the Bridge, though only iron and mechanical, rose into the sky with a touch of the sublime. We dined alone, and had good political talk.' While discussing Ireland Rosebery said that Spencer must be Lord Lieutenant to give confidence to England; 'I did not explode or rail, but went cheerfully to my bed, while he sallied forth to Barnbougle.'[1] 'I had a still final wrestle at Dalmeny—feeling rather ashamed all the time that any wrestling should be needed, where the path both of personal and of public duty was so clear,' Morley reported to Gladstone on July 19th. 'I rather thought that his frame of mind was much more promising.' On July 16th Rosebery disappeared with his children in his yacht off the West Coast of Scotland, leaving the political world to contemplate the situation which the elections had caused.

The final result was a majority of 40 for Home Rule—355 to 315—leaving the Liberal Party completely dependent upon the Irish for its Parliamentary majority. Gladstone was in the library at Dalmeny when he heard of the size of the Liberal majority. One of the assembly tentatively remarked that it was sufficient. 'Too small, too small,' the great man sadly remarked, and silence fell upon the gathering.

[1] Morley: *Recollections*, I, 317. Rosebery recorded in his diary that 'J. Morley & I walked alone. He will not hear of being Chief Secretary with Spencer as Ld Lieut.'

Few Administrations have entered upon office under circumstances so uniformly inauspicious. Salisbury's decision not to resign at once but to confront Parliament—the last occasion but one on which that course was followed—gave the Liberals a priceless month in which to group their forces. There were early difficulties within the party hierarchy. Concern was expressed on Gladstone's health, and Morley became irritated and suspicious by a series of secret confabulations at Harcourt's house in Brook Street. The so-called 'Brook Street Conspiracy' resulted in a serious weakening of the alliance formed in the years of opposition between Morley and Harcourt's son, Lewis—invariably called 'Loulou'—at Malwood, Harcourt's house in the New Forest, to the effect that Morley would support Harcourt for the party leadership when Gladstone retired.[1] The 'Malwood Compact' was at best an uneasy alliance. Asquith has written of the incongruity of the two men:

They belonged not only to different generations, but in all essentials, except that of actual chronology, to different centuries. Both of them were men of high and rare cultivation; on the intellectual side, Morley was what Harcourt most loathed, an *ideologue*, and Harcourt was what jarred most upon Morley, a Philistine. Harcourt, with a supposed infusion (however diluted) of Plantagenet blood; the grandson of a Georgian Archbishop; brought up with the tastes and habits of the caste in which he was born; but a natural mutineer, with a really powerful intelligence, a mordant wit, and a masculine and challenging personality, soon shook off his hereditary fetters, and seemed at one time to be in training for the post of the great Condottiere of the political world. Morley, sprung from the Lancashire middle-class, dipped but not dyed in the waters of Oxford, a youthful acolyte of Mill, had hovered for a time around the threshold of the Comtean conventicle. . . . Political exigencies make strange stable companions, but rarely two, to all appearance, less well assorted than these. They had hardly even a prejudice in common. . . . Had they a common political faith? It is hard to say—except that, from different points of

[1] It has always been accepted that the 'Malwood Compact' was between Morley and Harcourt, but the unpublished Journals of Lewis Harcourt make it clear that the arrangement was between himself and Morley, and it is probable that the father was unaware of the compact. Unfortunately Loulou Harcourt's Journals do not start until 1892, so it is not possible to specify the date of the agreement. It seems probable, from the references in the Journals, that it was made in 1889 or 1890, and almost certainly before the row of January 1891 (see also, pages 242, 301–2).

view, they were equally ardent disciples of what used then to be called the Anti-Imperialist and 'Little England' school.[1]

Harcourt's *brusquerie* and Morley's touchiness had already led to some acute personal crises before 1892. In the January of 1891, for example, a letter from Harcourt on Irish matters so upset Morley that he refused to speak to Harcourt for several weeks except on official subjects, and then only in the presence of a third party. Harcourt apologised, and sent Loulou to smooth Morley down, but it was some time before the rift was healed. The reports of the mysterious conclaves in Brook Street were seen by Morley in the light of some strange letters from Harcourt to his colleagues. To Gladstone Harcourt wrote on July 16th demanding a strong Radical programme to carry out the promises of Newcastle, and Morley wrote warningly to him that 'I cruise under the green flag, come what will; if we founder, at least let us go down with honour'. Morley had a tendency to see intriguers all around him, and Rosebery once described him as 'a petulant spinster' when in this mood of suspicious moodiness; the events of August 1892 inflicted an initial strain on the 'Malwood Compact' which led to its complete and decisive disruption eighteen months later.

While the seekers after office jostled each other unceremoniously in London, Rosebery was pottering about the West Coast in his yacht. Although the Queen had abandoned her idea of sending for him on Salisbury's resignation, she was anxious to see him, and Ponsonby was instructed on July 13th to consult his personal friends and political colleagues.

The Queen, as Sir Henry will easily believe, is much distressed at the prospect of all the trouble & gt. anxiety for the *safety* of the *country* & Empire wh. these most unfortunate Elections have brought abt. . . .

Tho' she supposes she will have that dangerous old fanatic thrust down her throat—she thinks she wd. like to see Ld. Rosebery when the time comes, as she must have security for FA & she thinks Sir H. who knows all these people well cd. in an indirect manner let him & others know that the Queen will *resist any* attempt to change the foreign policy, any attempts to abandon our obligations towards Egypt & any truckling to France or Russia or giving in to any attempt of those 2 Powers to frighten or bully us. . . .[2]

[1] Asquith: *Fifty Years of Parliament*, I, 246–7.
[2] Ponsonby, 216.

Ponsonby saw Hamilton on the 19th; Hamilton said that it would be most unwise for the Queen to send for Rosebery, but suggested that she might write privately to him, urging him to take the Foreign Office. 'Lord Rosebery's friends are very much perplexed at his attitude,' Ponsonby wrote to the Queen on the 20th. 'He made two extreme speeches some time ago. One of his supporters at Kelso said he was full of eagerness. But now he seems to have grown quite indifferent. . . . Mr E. Hamilton cannot at present understand his movements.'[1] On the next day (July 21st) Ponsonby advised the Queen not to write to Rosebery, and made it clear that he thought Rosebery was merely attempting to improve his position. On the 26th Hamilton again put his sugges- tion before Ponsonby, and added that he thought the Queen could communicate with Rosebery simultaneously with Glad- stone, but Ponsonby was unimpressed. He told Hamilton frankly that he thought Rosebery was trying to dictate his own terms of admission, but Hamilton, in his note on these conversations, expressed the view that Ponsonby's hostility to Home Rule dominated his advice to the Queen.

At this stage irritation with Rosebery rather than concern was the predominant emotion among the Liberal leaders. Hamilton, who was the only person who was in a position to appreciate the seriousness of the situation, saw both Morley and Harcourt on July 21st, but could convince neither of them of the reality of Rosebery's withdrawal. Morley was particularly indignant; he told Hamilton that to desert Gladstone at this moment would be 'the meanest of acts', and that his statements about devoting his attention to his children and private affairs were worthless and selfish. 'What does it all mean, then? There must be two Rose- berys—one the fine noble minded Britisher; the other the cold calculating Scotsman. It is the second Rosebery that at times, and now is one of those times, predominates over the first Rosebery. If he deserts Mr Gladstone in his hour of need, he will never be forgiven by the party.' When he called at 1, Carlton Gardens— lent to the Gladstones by Lord Rendel—on July 29th, Hamilton found Mrs Gladstone in an equally militant frame of mind; and Gladstone told him on August 3rd that he had never been treated so badly by any colleague before as he had been by Rosebery. Both West and Hamilton tried on several occasions to put

[1] *Royal Archives.*

Rosebery's point of view to the Gladstones, but without success.

On July 31st Rosebery formally wrote to Gladstone that his views on retirement, expressed to him personally at Mentmore in the December of 1891 and in his letter to Arnold Morley, were unchanged, and that 'I could now retire without inconvenience'. He returned to Dalmeny on August 1st to be confronted with mounds of letters from colleagues and friends imploring him to state his intention of joining the Government. Rumours had been circulating in London about the possibility of his withdrawal for the past week, and had even been repeated in the newspapers, while the Ambassadors expressed their bewilderment in their secret reports. The tone of the volumes of letters which began to reach Dalmeny at the end of July was therefore one of considerable alarm. 'Spencer, John Morley and I are determined to make every effort to induce you to come to help us by your counsel and support in such a crisis,' Harcourt wrote, to which Rosebery replied, 'The eighteen months that I have spent in seclusion have convinced me that I was not intended or fitted for a political life; all my interest is now divorced from it; should I be forced back into it again, future extrication would be difficult if not impossible.' 'It may be impossible for me to hold my ground,' Rosebery confided to his diary on August 3rd, 'but I will make the best fight I can.'

By August 4th most of the Liberal leaders realised that the situation was becoming increasingly difficult, and West persuaded Gladstone to write a tactful letter of appeal to Rosebery. Gladstone said that it should be delivered personally by Lord Spencer, so West set out at once for Spencer House, only to discover that Spencer was out. He and Lady Spencer then drove to Brook Street and collected Harcourt before hastening to the House of Commons to see Morley. It was agreed that Morley should take the letter to Dalmeny that night, and Gladstone's assent was secured. The council then moved to the United Services Club, where Hamilton joined it, and, after further discussion, it was decided to try Spencer once more. Harcourt, Morley, Arnold Morley, Hamilton, and West went to Spencer House, but Spencer declared that John Morley would be a better emissary, and, as time was getting short, it was thus agreed; Morley wrote a hurried telegram to Rosebery, warning him of his imminent arrival, and departed in a cab for the Scottish Express.

In the discussion which ensued after Morley had left, Spencer said that Gladstone had recently remarked to him 'From nobody in public life had I received such warm affection, such unbounded kindness, such great generosity, as from Rosebery, and for no one have I warmer feeling. But in public life he is a perfect Bismarck—so unapproachable is he and so inexplicable in his conduct.'

Morley arrived at Dalmeny early the next morning, where he found Rosebery 'haggard-looking and distressed',[1] and delivered the letter from Gladstone. Rosebery had just received a characteristically incoherent appeal from Mrs Gladstone. 'I who know your love for my Husband, I must seek your sympathy. I remember well your talk at Mentmore & I was in the belief that my Husband had the happy feeling that his words then impressed you . . . though I cannot say enough for his friends' kindness & desire to help, without flattering you I know that *you* are the one who would do him *most good.*' Morley repeated his previous appeals, adding that Gladstone was sickened by Harcourt's rudeness and machinations and was prepared to offer Rosebery the *jus successionis* to the leadership. Rosebery only undertook to return to London, but Morley regarded this as an important concession, and informed his anxious colleagues that 'he had brought his bird with him, and that he, Rosebery, would now in all probability join'.[2] Morley wrote to Gladstone on his return that 'I am glad to be able to tell you that I have every ground for believing that your anxieties in that quarter are now pretty nearly at an end . . . he came up in the train with me, and has gone straight on to Paris, where he hopes to "clear the cobwebs out of his brain"—as he expressed it. He will be back on Monday night. I have no doubt now that he has made up his mind to join, and I expect that your interview with him will have no difficulties of any magnitude. I found him in a most desperately morbid frame of mind—with many cobwebs indeed obscuring his vision. One cannot but feel uneasy as to the future of a man so singularly constituted. . . .'

In his letter to Rosebery, Gladstone had placed the responsibility firmly upon him.

. . . It is my fixed assurance, founded on all I know of public life, of Great Britain, and of its people, that what I then said [at Mentmore]

[1] *Edward Hamilton's Diary.*
[2] Lewis Harcourt's Journal, quoted in Gardiner: *Harcourt*, II, 181.

was right; that you had no open choice before you; that your acceptance was predetermined by previous acts, and that the nation would not tolerate your refusal . . . the main element of the whole case, in my mind, is the solid, permanent judgement of the nation. And, as regards that judgement, and the grounds which the nation will think it has for forming it, the force of the facts is I think stubborn, and not to be denied. . . .

In his reply, Rosebery wrote that 'I will not now enter upon the points which it raises. I shall remove myself tonight to a less morbid atmosphere, and come and see you early next week.' He caught the night train to London and then went for a short solitary visit to Paris 'to clear the cobwebs out of his brain'. He returned to England on the 9th, and on the evening of the next day, after a long conversation with Spencer, returned to The Durdans. In his absence, Parliament had reassembled, and Asquith had been deputed to move the motion of no confidence in the Government on August 7th; August 11th had been fixed for the end of the great debate, and on the morning of that day Rosebery returned to London for his meeting with Gladstone.

He saw both Hamilton and West in the morning; both gained the impression that although he was dreading his meeting with Gladstone he was inclined towards accepting office. But when he called at Carlton Gardens after lunch it was to inform Gladstone that he could not change his mind. He said that his nerves were unstrung, that he could never sleep, and that in these circumstances sustained work was impossible. Gladstone was startled and upset, but in the course of an argument which lasted three-quarters of an hour he could make no impression. West told Loulou Harcourt that the interview was 'most touching and painful, and they were both nearly in tears'.[1]

The Unionist Government was defeated in the House of Commons later the same day; there were only ten Members absent (all paired) from the division, in which the Ministry was defeated by exactly forty. The large crowds in New Palace Yard took up the cheers which welcomed the Liberal Party back to office.

Gladstone was now, in his own words, 'beset left and right'; apart from the shock of Rosebery's refusal to join, other difficul-

[1] Gardiner: *Harcourt*, II, 181. The laconic nature of Rosebery's diaries on occasion may be judged from his entry for this remarkable day: '*August 11*—Durdans— lovely. To town by 10.9. Saw E. Hamilton: & Mr G at 2. To Durdans at 5.30.'

ties of a personal nature had arisen. Harcourt was being more hectoring and dictatorial than ever. Morley was gloomy and difficult over Irish arrangements, while among the voracious seekers after office Labouchere's voice was the most strident. There was now very little time left to settle these questions. The Cabinet met formally on August 12th to agree to resignation, and Salisbury repaired to Osborne in the afternoon to acquaint the Queen of the decision.

In his audience Salisbury told the Queen that he had heard from Sir Philip Currie—Under-Secretary of State—that Rosebery had told him definitely that he would not join the new Government; the Queen asked Salisbury if she should try and persuade Rosebery to change his mind, but he advised her against such action. She had, however, written to Ponsonby (who was still in London) on August 10th that 'Sir Henry will if necessary & if an opportunity offers say the Queen *insists* on Ld. Rosebery as M for FA.'[1] The opportunity does not appear to have arisen for putting the matter thus strongly, but the Queen was greatly occupied by the problem of bringing indirect royal pressure to bear upon Rosebery. The Prince of Wales had proposed on August 6th that Ponsonby should urge Rosebery in the Queen's name to take office, but the Queen—having taken the advice of Salisbury and Ponsonby—informed the Prince that 'I *must* not interfere in the formation of this iniquitous Government'. She had suggested on July 26th to Ponsonby that 'indirectly something might be done through the P. of Wales', and on August 14th the Prince did eventually appeal to Rosebery not to remain aloof from the new Government.

On August 13th Ponsonby delivered to Gladstone a singularly chilling communication from the Queen, requesting him to inform her 'if he is prepared to try and form a Ministry to carry on the Government of the country', while the *Court Circular* announced that the Queen had accepted Salisbury's resignation 'with great regret'. On the same day, Rosebery retreated from London to Mentmore, where his cousin, Henry Primrose, renewed the pressure upon him. They wrangled throughout Saturday evening, and on Sunday G. E. Buckle of *The Times* arrived for the same purpose. After Buckle had left, Rosebery and his cousin went for a two-hour walk, still arguing vehemently;

[1] Ponsonby, *op. cit.*, 217.

when they returned to Mentmore they found a sixteen-page letter from Buckle, which Rosebery described in his diary as 'powerful & affecting'. When Rosebery returned to London on the evening of the 14th his resistance was weakening.

In the flood of appeals and exhortations which descended upon Rosebery[1] there was one conspicuously absent appellant— Gladstone himself. Neither by letter nor verbal message did he contact Rosebery at this time. On August 15th he and West were to travel to Osborne, and it was with the greatest difficulty that West and Hamilton persuaded him to make a final appeal to Rosebery, saying that unless he heard to the contrary, he would put his name to the Queen as Foreign Secretary. At length, 'with rather a wry face and after some hesitation on his part and lengthened consultation with others',[2] he bowed to their advice.

I, C.G,
Aug. 15 '92.

My dear Rosebery,

I received the Queen's Communication on Saturday and I am now going off to Osborne. So late however as last Thursday the Queen made known to me her anxiety that you should take the Foreign Office. I have not yet heard from you but viewing the flight of time and all the circumstances I propose to submit your name to her today in conformity with her wish and I trust you will allow the matter to terminate in this way for the advantage and happiness of all parties as well as for the public good.

Believe me always,
Affectly yours,
W. E. Gladstone

Arnold Morley conveyed this somewhat lukewarm appeal to Rosebery, and shortly afterwards Hamilton was summoned to Berkeley Square. He arrived shortly after one o'clock, and found his friend in a state of agitation and indecision. He accused

[1] Lord Kimberley was among those who came to urge acceptance, and later stated in his unpublished memoirs—which Rosebery was loaned by Kimberley's son—that his arguments had secured Rosebery's capitulation. In a note on this passage, Rosebery wrote that 'I have always mentioned this conversation as an instance of a not uncommon hallucination. I guessed why K came and what he intended to say, but to the best of my belief he never said a word of it, but talked on different matters, and went away convinced that he had said what was in his mind. As he put on his hat in the hall he whispered something about the FO, but that was all.'

[2] *Edward Hamilton's Diary*, August 15th.

Hamilton of being an 'arch-conspirator', and added that he was exhausted by the strain of resisting the intense pressure which had been exerted. He showed Hamilton the pile of letters he had received in the past fortnight and added that he could no longer resist these entreaties. The most important factors, he said, were the letters from the Prince of Wales and Buckle and the exhortations of Henry Primrose. Hamilton said that Gladstone must be informed at once, and Rosebery, pacing round his study in great distress, wearily agreed. Hamilton almost forced him to write out a telegram, which read

So be it. Mentmore.

Hamilton seized the form in triumph and almost ran out into the Square to send it off to Osborne from the nearest post office. He then 'telegraphed enigmatically' to the Prince of Wales, Ponsonby, and Morley, rushed round to Spencer House to announce the good news 'at which Lord Spencer was overjoyed', and then went to Carlton Gardens 'to put Mrs G out of her suspense', but she was out.

West and Gladstone had proceeded to Osborne, where they received Rosebery's telegram. Their short visit was a melancholy one; the Queen, lamenting the 'dangers to the country, to Europe, to her vast Empire, which is involved in having all those great interests entrusted to the shaking hand of an old, wild and incomprehensible man of $82\frac{1}{2}$',[1] thought Gladstone 'greatly altered and changed, not only much aged, walking rather bent, with a stick, but altogether; his face shrunk, deadly pale with a weird look in his eyes, a feeble expression about the mouth, and the voice altered'. Gladstone's estimate of the Queen was almost as unfavourable—describing the interview to West as 'such as took place between Marie Antoinette and her executioner'[2]—and the audience was conducted with perfect courtesy and coldness. Both forgot the ceremony of kissing hands upon appointment, and Gladstone had to return to do so. Gladstone's room, West discovered, was excessively ugly, with pictures of Lord Sydney, Disraeli, Bishop Tait, and other 'fearful copies, daubs, and lodging-house ornaments', while a Maid of Honour was strumming on a piano next door.

When Rosebery called at Carlton Gardens on the following

[1] Newton: *Lansdowne*, 100.   [2] West: *Diaries*, 51.

afternoon he found the Prime Minister fulminating against the Queen and Harcourt. The latter had been characteristically offensive on the matter of the Peers in the Cabinet; when Gladstone had explained that he wanted to strengthen the position of the Liberal minority in the Lords, Harcourt had rejoined, 'You might as well try to strengthen the ocean by pouring into it a *petit verre* of cognac'; upon being reminded by the nettled Premier of their respective positions Harcourt had remarked, 'But it is for *us* to consider whether we shall join *you*.' '*Never*', Gladstone said to Rosebery, 'have I been so treated.'

There was general jubilation at the news of Rosebery's return to the Foreign Office, not least among the ambassadors, but Rosebery did not share this emotion. 'Rosebery will be in,' Campbell-Bannerman wrote to his cousin, James Campbell, on August 15th, 'but he is in wretched health and has refused and been over-persuaded ten times over. . . . My belief is if he gets to work it will do much to cure him.'[1] Rosebery told West rather pointedly that he resented the methods which had been employed to induce him to return to the Government; although it was not long before the interest of his work restored his good temper to some extent, it is doubtful that he ever fully forgave those who had exerted what he regarded as unfair pressure upon him. In this he rightly distinguished between friends like Hamilton who were principally thinking of himself, and political colleagues who freely talked of 'honour' and 'desertion' while solely concerned with the political dangers of his secession. Although he had behaved stupidly throughout the previous six months and had made the mistake of never making his position absolutely clear in public as well as in private, there was considerable hypocrisy in the almost tearful appeals which rained upon him; cynical and distrustful about public life, Rosebery determined that those colleagues who had almost literally begged him to join the Government should take him on his own terms. There was no written concordat on this matter, but Rosebery quickly made it plain that he was solely responsible for foreign affairs and would not tolerate interference from any quarter. There was considerable truth in the remark of Harcourt to Rosebery that 'Without you the Government would have been simply ridiculous; now it is only impossible!'

[1] Spender: *Campbell-Bannerman*, I, 124.

Hamilton, of course, was ecstatically happy on both private and public grounds, and he wrote in his diary for August 16th:

I never felt more relieved. A national calamity has been averted; the formation of a Government by Mr G has been made possible; the minds of the commercial classes will be made easy; foreign and home securities will stand steady; our interests and honour abroad will be in safe hands; a great political career has been saved from wreckage; a man of real genius born to lead others & to serve his country will be saved from a life of misery & remorse.

R has often been a puzzle to me, though probably I know him almost better than any one else; but I believe I at last understand him, & he has gone up in my estimation. My belief is—and Henry Primrose shares it—that R has a genuine dislike, or imagines he has, of public life; that he loves seclusion; that he is not really ambitious—whatever ambition he had was buried with his poor wife; that he has been totally unable to realise the importance of his own position; and that he thought his only chance of escaping finally from public life was to cut himself adrift now, or else it would (or might) be never.

Henry Primrose & I have been dining with him at the Amphitryon tonight, & he seemed quite resigned to his fate. Thus ends one of the most interesting & anxious incidents in which I ever have been or ever shall be concerned. 'All's well that ends well.'

Before he had left for The Durdans on the 15th, Rosebery had sent a brief note to Canon Rogers.

My dear old friend—
You will be glad to hear what I am sorry to tell you, that I am going back to the FO.

Y. aff.
AR.

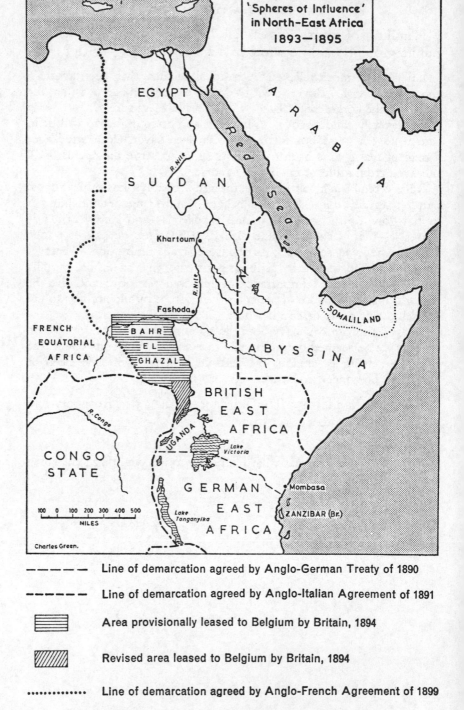

'Spheres of Influence'
in North-East Africa
1893—1895

EGYPT

ARABIA

SUDAN

R. Nile

Red Sea

Khartoum

R. Nile

Fashoda

FRENCH
EQUATORIAL
AFRICA

BAHR
EL
GHAZAL

SOMALILAND

ABYSSINIA

BRITISH
EAST
AFRICA

R. Congo

UGANDA

Lake
Victoria

CONGO
STATE

GERMAN

EAST

AFRICA

Mombasa

ZANZIBAR (Br.)

100 0 100 200 300 400 500
MILES

Lake
Tanganyika

Charles Green.

— — — — — Line of demarcation agreed by Anglo-German Treaty of 1890

– – – – – Line of demarcation agreed by Anglo-Italian Agreement of 1891

Area provisionally leased to Belgium by Britain, 1894

Revised area leased to Belgium by Britain, 1894

············· Line of demarcation agreed by Anglo-French Agreement of 1899

The 'corridor' adjoining the west side of German East Africa
provisionally leased by Belgium to Britain in 1894 under Article 111
of the Anglo-Congolese Treaty, subsequently abandoned, ran
from the north of Lake Tanganyika to the Uganda border.

CHAPTER EIGHT

FOREIGN SECRETARY

There is never a calm on the political ocean: its most serene temper is the
ground swell which follows, or the grim stillness which precedes, the storm,
often more awful than the storm itself. The unresting waves seldom permit
politicians to remain in close cordiality for any length of time. The billow
that bears one friend buoyantly on its bosom lands the other high and dry,
sometimes among strangers, sometimes among enemies. Constant changes of
atmosphere produce constantly new combinations. And so the correspondence
of statesmen who have survived their first ingenuous enthusiasm is apt, in view
of possible contingencies, to be clouded with a forbidding wariness.

ROSEBERY: *Sir Robert Peel* (1899)

ON PAPER, MR GLADSTONE's last Government was one of the
strongest and most talented of late Victorian ministries. Below
the ruling quartet of Gladstone, Rosebery, Harcourt, and Morley
were Lord Spencer (First Lord of the Admiralty), Herschell (Lord
Chancellor), Campbell-Bannerman (War), Acland (Education),
and Henry Fowler[1] (Local Government Board), while Asquith
(Home Secretary) and Sir Edward Grey (Under-Secretary of
State, Foreign Office) represented the highly talented group of
young Liberals who had entered the House of Commons since
1886. Its strength, however, was theoretical rather than actual;
paper calculations are rarely valid in political confederations, and
the government was dogged with personal animosities which
eroded its strength and led directly to the cataclysm of 1895.
With an aged and increasingly unpredictable leader, a tenuous
Parliamentary majority, a hostile Sovereign and House of Lords,
the prospects confronting Ministers were not cheerful.

[1] 1830–1911. Son of a Wesleyan Minister; Wolverhampton businessman. Mayor,
1863; MP for Wolverhampton, 1880–1908; Under-Secretary, Home Office, 1884–5;
Financial Secretary to the Treasury, 1886; President Local Government Board,
1892–4; Secretary of State for India, 1894–5; Chancellor of Duchy of Lancaster,
1905–8; Lord President of the Council, 1905–10. Created Viscount Wolverhampton, 1908.

On August 18th the retiring and incoming Ministers repaired to Osborne to surrender and receive respectively their seals of office. The Queen thought that the members of her new Government 'looked rather depressed and embarrassed', and this was exacerbated by the fact that after they had lined up in a row in front of her in the drawing-room it was discovered that both the Lord President (Kimberley) and the Clerk of the Council were missing; for a full five minutes the prospective Ministers stood uncomfortably, trying not to look at the Queen, who sat behind a table with the seals of office upon it, gazing stonily ahead. There were so many new Privy Councillors that they were sworn in in batches, and instead of rising to kiss the Queen's hand they crawled on their knees to perform the ceremony. These comic formalities were completed in an unbroken silence.

After the Council the Queen saw some of the new Ministers privately. She noted that Rosebery 'looked low and could hardly speak when I expressed my satisfaction at his accepting office, observing that he thought they would have done better to leave him where he was. I said his name would be of such importance, to which he replied: "It is but the name!" which I would not admit and told him he knew I had helped him and would do so again, which made him smile. I said work would do him good; but he replied that he had no one to look after his children.'[1] In his account of the audience Rosebery wrote that the Queen spoke 'quite maternally'. Ministers returned to Portsmouth across the Solent amid incessant lightning and peals of menacing thunder, an augury which did not escape the notice of the Unionist press.

On August 19th the new Cabinet met for the first time at 1, Carlton Gardens; the only business was Gladstone's proposal that all Ministers should resign any directorships which they held. 'I thought I was at a public meeting', Rosebery wrote to Ponsonby, 'and nearly moved Mr Gladstone into the Chair.'[2] Gladstone also announced that at future meetings of the Cabinet, Ministers would sit in chairs around the room while Gladstone himself would sit at a small table with Rosebery at his right hand. These curious arrangements did not facilitate the work of the Cabinet. It was not long before Rosebery confessed his pleasure at

---

[1] *Letters of Queen Victoria*, 3rd Series, II, 148.
[2] *Henry Ponsonby, His Life from His Letters*, 276

returning to the Foreign Office to his closest friends. Much had happened since 1886 in the foreign and domestic scene, and it was perfectly apparent to Rosebery at the outset that although he was in an infinitely stronger personal position in the Cabinet than he had been in 1886, the 'anti-Imperialist' group was also stronger and more suspicious of his policies. He was absolutely resolved to be master in his own house. Count Hatzfeldt reported to Berlin on September 1st that Rosebery had told him that 'Mr Gladstone was old, and his dominating position in the Cabinet was not what it was, whilst he, Lord Rosebery, could assure me without exaggeration that he was now almost indispensable to the inherently weak Ministry, and was therefore much stronger than formerly.' In a later report towards the end of November, Hatzfeldt wrote to Caprivi that Rosebery had told him that Salisbury's standing instructions to the Mediterranean Squadron had not been altered, and added, 'You see, my most honoured Chief, the Prime Minister, understands very little of foreign politics and knows he does not. But as he is sometimes inclined to be pro-French, I try to avoid all discussions by altering in principle nothing that I found when I took office. This is the case with those orders.'[1] Brett dined with Rosebery on September 7th and was delighted with the improvement in him. 'He is absolute at the FO,' he recorded. 'He informs his colleagues of very little, and does as he pleases. If it offends them, he retires. We shall remain in Egypt, and the continuity of Lord S's policy will not be disturbed. All this is excellent. Meanwhile his spirits have wonderfully recovered.'[2]

To Rosebery's surprise and irritation, Salisbury did not personally hand over the Foreign Office key to his successor; Rosebery felt that in view of his endeavours since 1886 to keep foreign policy out of domestic politics Salisbury might at least have communicated with him. 'I cannot say that he has acquired manners with the Windsor uniform!' he wrote to Ponsonby (on leaving office the Queen had permitted Salisbury to wear the Windsor uniform), 'which I thought never clothed any but chivalrous bosoms.'[3]

Rosebery was presented with an immediate problem. The

---

[1] *German Diplomatic Documents*, II, 169 and 202. All future references to this work will be *G.D.D.*
[2] Brett: *Journals and Letters of Viscount Esher*, I, 162.
[3] Ponsonby, *His Life from His Letters*, 276.

egregious Labouchere and his ex-actress wife had evinced a
most unwelcome ambition to represent Her Majesty in Washington. As the Queen had virtually vetoed his inclusion in the
Government, Labouchere's chances of receiving the position
were never particularly good, but the fact that *Truth* had lam-
pooned Rosebery once too often eliminated what possibility
there may have been. Furthermore, Rosebery was anxious to
improve Anglo-American relations, and was considering raising
the Washington Legation to Embassy level, which he accomplished in 1893 in the teeth of the Queen's displeasure; the
application of the Laboucheres was a joke in rather poor taste in
these circumstances, but it was quickly apparent that the matter
was more serious, since the Chief Whip, Edward Marjoribanks,
was quite prepared to purchase Labouchere's removal from the
House of Commons, and other members of the Cabinet told
Rosebery privately that the price of Labouchere's silence could
hardly be too high. Gladstone, strangely enough, took the view
that Labouchere's appointment 'would be a loss in the House
of Commons on questions of war and intervention', and 'his
claim seems not a bad one'.[1] Describing the application as 'both
tedious and impudent', Rosebery refused to consider it. Mrs
Labouchere's pleadings grew more tearful and her husband's
threats more menacing, but he was obdurate.

Mrs Labouchere called on him at the Foreign Office on November 24th with a detailed list of 'arrangements' in the diplomatic
corps while Labouchere wintered 'in Algiers or somewhere' until
matters were satisfactorily arranged. 'Your proposal', Rosebery
replied, 'comes to this. It is that Sir Clare Ford, who has been
moved to Constantinople at a considerable cost this Spring,
should be got rid of; that Sir Henry Drummond Wolff, who has
been sent to Madrid at a considerable cost, should now be transferred to Constantinople; that Sir Julian Pauncefote, who has
been doing admirable work in Washington, is to be sent away
from there to Madrid; and all this to find a post for Mr Labouchere!' He then referred to the personal attacks made on him in
Truth, and, as tactfully as possible, her bad reputation in America
which had been caused by certain incidents in a previous tour
with Lily Langtry; Mrs Labouchere did not deny this, but claimed
that it was the fault of Oscar Wilde 'whom she had endeavoured

[1] Letters to Morley of September 26th and October 5th (*Gladstone Papers*).

to keep away from Mrs Langtry' and who had spread unpleasant stories about her in revenge.

Labouchere now tried the approach minatory, the approach sentimental having failed. In his jejeune handwriting, excruciating grammar and spelling (he persisted in calling Morley 'Morly' and said that Harcourt was 'favrable' to the appointment), he wrote on November 27th to warn that 'in America, there are no heathen to convert, there is no Egypt to retain, and there is no Triple Alliance'. Marjoribanks urged Rosebery to give way, pointing out the advantages of getting Labouchere 'aloft, abroad, or below, but out of the H and C for the next Session', but Rosebery was adamant. On December 3rd he wrote to Labouchere:

. . . I should, were I to nominate you to Washington (even without a series of displacements for that purpose), be inevitably accused of having bribed into silence a formidable opponent. That is a charge to which I cannot expose myself. You on the other hand would be accused of having taken office under a chief whom you had constantly stated to be unworthy of your confidence.

There are other difficulties, but I will not detail them, for this is sufficient. . . .

Mrs Labouchere tried again on December 7th, putting forward revised proposals for the reshuffle of the ambassadors; 'I have been drinking boiling water every night, but in vain. Nothing but Washington! Washington!! Washington!!! haunts my troubled brain,' Rosebery politely replied that he had no choice in the matter, and Mrs Labouchere wrote mournfully on the 9th that 'when I *die*—if my body is opened—you will find, like "Queen Mary"—*Washington* and *Rosebery* engraved on my heart'. She had another interview with him on January 6th, in which she said that her husband would defeat the Government on its foreign policy, to which Rosebery replied that this would be 'an inestimable service' to himself. Disconcerted, Mrs Labouchere then asked him to see her husband, which he refused to do; she then burst into tears, saying that she had never been able to help her husband and that she never read *Truth*, as she thought it so dull. 'I was too polite to express my cordial concurrence,' Rosebery's memorandum of this strange conversation concludes.

All other attempts of the persistent Laboucheres—including an appeal to the embarrassed Gladstones—failed. The almost jesting nature of Labouchere's most sinister letters could not conceal the bitterness of his feelings and those of his wife. For the rest of his period at the Foreign Office Rosebery was the recipient of letters of which this is a fair example:

October 22nd, 1893.

Dear Lord Rosebery,

I see that Lord Vivian, your Ambassador at Rome, is dead. I was wondering whether this would cause a vacancy where my heart is still fixed.

Please do not trouble to answer this, for I suppose you are in correspondence with all the world just now—on things of much greater importance than

Yours very truly,

Henrietta Labouchere.

The rift with Labouchere was unfortunate. 'He evidently means to make it his "mission", as he calls it, to "crush" R,' Morley wrote to Gladstone on November 13th, 1892, adding rather primly, 'of whom he uses language that I do not care to transcribe.' Labouchere had a rare ability to coin damaging phrases, and his application to Rosebery of the most final of condemnations, that of Tacitus on Galba who, by universal consent, would have been fitted for the highest place in the State if only he had never occupied it, clung to him for many years, together with Tim Healy's aphorism that 'He is not a man to go tiger-shooting with'. The persistent jeers of *Truth*, of which Rosebery was too acutely aware, had their effect on his career, and although the attitude of some of his colleagues was cynical, it had the quality of reality. The specific proposal for Washington was lunatic, but the price which Rosebery had to pay was to prove a heavy one.[1]

These matters, although not unimportant, paled into obscurity when compared with the great issues which arose in the winter of 1892–3 and which imperilled the Ministry and warped all its subsequent activities.

Rosebery inherited from Salisbury an involved and delicate situation in Africa which was likely to be exacerbated by the

---

[1] The voluminous correspondence over the Labouchere incident and the interviews with the Laboucheres made such diverting reading that Rosebery subsequently had them privately printed; his son has recently presented a copy to the Cabinet Office at the request of the Prime Minister.

public commitments of several members of the Cabinet to the evacuation of Egypt and to the reduction of British interests in Africa. Since 1886 Salisbury had accepted Baring's assessment of the Egyptian situation, which was that evacuation had become impracticable in view of what Baring called 'the utter incapacity of the ruling classes in this country'.[1] By 1890 even Harcourt, the leading advocate of Anglo-French friendship which was constantly hindered by rival ambitions in Africa, informed the French Ambassador that 'the question is very difficult; if we retire, we leave chaos behind us; it is very difficult to take such a responsibility'.[2] Another new element in an already complicated situation was that the increasing concord between the French and the Russians had gravely affected the naval balance of power in the Mediterranean to Britain's disadvantage.

The geographical importance of Uganda was apparent to all exponents of the new Imperialism. By the 1890 agreement with Germany, Salisbury had in effect reserved for Britain the territories which eventually were known as Uganda and Kenya, and a protectorate over Zanzibar, while the Italians were offered sizeable concessions elsewhere to divert ambitions from the Nile Valley. In 1890 Captain Lugard[3] had led an expedition to Uganda under the auspices of the British East Africa Company, and had secured after active intervention a treaty from Mwanga, the tyrant of Uganda, which had given a protectorate to the Company. Having secured some assurances for peace between Christian and Moslem factions in the area, and having carried the Company's flag to the western borders of the future Uganda Protectorate, Lugard left Uganda in a reasonable state of tranquillity.

The Company, however, was in serious financial difficulties. In the December of 1890 the Chairman, Sir William Mackinnon, asked for Government assistance in the form of a guarantee on the interest of the capital required to build a railway from Mombasa into the interior. Salisbury was personally in favour of granting the request, but after violent Liberal opposition in the

---

[1] Cecil: *Salisbury*, IV, 138–9.

[2] *Documents Diplomatiques Français*, 1st Series, VIII, No. 89. (Hereafter referred to as *D.D.F.*)

[3] 1858–1945. A professional soldier before entering the service of the British East Africa Company. Later High Commissioner for Northern Nigeria, 1900–6; Governor of Hong Kong, 1907–12; Governor of Northern and Southern Nigeria: 1912–13; Governor-General of Nigeria, 1914–19. Created Lord Lugard of Abinger, 1928.

Commons, the Vote authorising the payment of £20,000 was withdrawn by the Government on July 20th, 1891. The Company reluctantly agreed to continue with the survey at its own expense at the request of the Government, and Royal Engineer officers were seconded from India to assist in the work. There appeared to be no alternative to evacuation, but the raising of over £15,000 by public subscription—principally the work of Bishop Tucker and the missionary organisations—led to a postponement of twelve months.

The situation was aggravated by wild rumours of 'atrocities' alleged to have been committed by Lugard and other agents of the Company which aroused violent reactions in France. By the April of 1892 Waddington, the French Ambassador,[1] was demanding enquiries into Lugard's conduct, and the British Ambassador in Paris, Lord Dufferin, was being warned in menacing terms of the excitement and bitterness in French political circles. The allegations found eager recipients among a certain section of the Liberal and Irish Parties, and the subject was raised no less than nine times in the House of Commons in June 1892.[2] Salisbury defended Lugard's reputation from the serious attacks made upon it by the French, but in the last few weeks of his Ministry he took two vital decisions. He formally agreed to the decision of the Company to evacuate Uganda, and appointed a Royal Engineer officer, Captain Macdonald, to report into the charges made against Lugard. This latter appointment was unfortunate; Macdonald knew nothing of Africa, having been just seconded from India to help on the railway survey, and was, moreover, bitterly antagonistic to Lugard on personal grounds.

Liberal opinion, although more than usually indeterminate, was pledged in general terms against further commitments in Africa, and Gladstone's pronouncement on the subject (March 4th, 1892) was characteristically bewildering.

> . . . I wish to state, in the most expressive terms that I can command, that I am determined for one to exempt myself, by the declaration of tonight, from every jot or tittle of responsibility connected with the undertaking [the Mombasa Railway survey]; and yet, at the same time, *I do not go so far as to deliver a final judgment.* . . .

---

[1] 1826–94. Of English descent; Ambassador to Britain, 1883–93.
[2] Margery Perham: *Lugard*, I, 329.

Harcourt and Gladstone increased the obscurity of the official
Liberal position by abstaining from the ensuing Division.

From whatever angle it was viewed, the Uganda Question
demanded urgent resolution. The personal position of Rosebery
was crucial. He had hardly entered the Foreign Office when
Waddington arrived with a long list of French grievances, accusations, and demands, and on August 24th Rosebery instructed
Sir Percy Anderson to prepare a memorandum on the situation.
This document was heavily amended by Rosebery himself at
draft stage, and amended in a strong anti-evacuationist line.

Rosebery had quickly come to the conclusion that Uganda must
be retained; since the Company could not continue,[1] the Government must take over the responsibility of administration. Although Salisbury's policy had not been clear, the decision to
support the Mombasa Railway project convinced Rosebery that
it could not be considering complete withdrawal from such a
vital area. For Rosebery there were three distinct issues on which
he was prepared to fight: the ambitions of the French must be
forestalled,[2] British influence must be preserved and confirmed,
and he alone must have the conduct of foreign policy. The last
factor was the crucial one: the Uganda crisis gave him a first-rate
opportunity for imposing his will upon his colleagues and making
it abundantly clear that he would not tolerate interference. He
laid his plans with care; the Anderson Memorandum purported
to be a disinterested official document whereas it was in fact a
Rosebery manifesto, and was circulated to the Cabinet on September 13th. On the same day, Gerald Portal, the former acting
Consul-General at Zanzibar, telegraphed to him that evacuation
'must inevitably result in a massacre of Christians such as the
history of this century cannot show', and this and other similar
warnings were distributed to the Cabinet. Foreseeing grave
difficulties, Rosebery ordered Lugard to return to Britain at once.

The Anderson Memorandum caused an immediate Cabinet
storm. 'I have read Sir P. Anderson's paper with care,' Gladstone

---

[1] By 1892 the servants of the Company were spending at the rate of £80,000 a
year, while their income was no more than £35,000. (Portal to Salisbury, February
3rd, 1892. *Salisbury Papers.* See Robinson, Gallagher, and Denny: *Africa and the
Victorians*, 309.)

[2] Rosebery's French antipathies had become apparent in 1886, and on August 12th
Waddington had complained to Salisbury of Rosebery's refusal to discuss colonial
differences. (See *D.D.F.*, 1st Series, VI, 288–90.)

wrote to Rosebery on September 17th. 'I thought it was a pleading from a Missionary society or from the Company, or should have thought so, but for the date from the FO.' Harcourt at once warned Gladstone of the political and economic perils of remaining in Uganda and prepared lengthy counter-memoranda. He wrote to Rosebery on September 18th to say that he had read Portal's telegrams 'with the greatest dismay & indignation'; the Prime Minister was excessively excited, writing to Harcourt that he was 'horrified and astonished to find how Rosebery had given way to the jingoism of the Foreign Office', while Harcourt declared that he would 'die a thousand deaths' rather than have anything to do with retention of Uganda.[1] Gladstone wrote to Rosebery on the 17th that 'I do not know who Sir G. Portal is, but his second paragraph of Sept. 15 is astonishing', but before he had received this letter (he was staying at Balmoral), Rosebery wrote to Gladstone on the 19th that the Uganda problem was 'a ticklish business and a pressing business. The company are bankrupt, they must evacuate the country, and the consequences of evacuation will, I fear, be most grave.' A Cabinet memorandum also circulated by Rosebery on the 19th stated that 'the evacuation of Uganda, according to every authority, involves not merely the restoration of the Slave Trade, but the massacre of those native Christians who do not fly and of the missionaries who will not fly'. On the same day the Prime Minister was preparing a tart reply to the Anderson Memorandum. 'I plead that I am totally in the dark as to the most important facts of the Uganda case'; getting true information was 'like gathering a history from broken Assyrian tablets'; 'In one place I am told B[isho]p Tucker and his brave band will remain till the death; in another that on the evacuation the whole of the Christians will fly. In one place the Mahommedans are to massacre the Christians; in another ... that the Christians are to massacre one another'; he ended by stating that the Unionist Government had decided upon evacuation.

This Rosebery denied on September 20th. 'It cannot be doubted that they would have held on to Uganda had they held on to office, but uncertain of their tenure, they, not unnaturally but not very fairly in view of the shortness of time, preferred to leave this embarrassing question to their successors.' In another letter on

[1] Gardiner: *Harcourt*, II, 192–3.

the same day to Gladstone, Rosebery wrote that 'there is no need and would be no question of sending a "British force" or any others to Uganda'; to Harcourt he wrote that he had little sympathy with the Company, but that the question was simply whether the Government was prepared to acquiesce to abandoning Uganda 'with its consequences'. Harcourt replied that he regarded Lugard as 'a mischievous lunatic', that the Government was arriving 'at the passing of the ways of an African policy', and that he would answer 'very decidedly "No" ' to all proposals for annexation. Gladstone instructed Rosebery to consult his colleagues, and received a whimsical but unmistakably independent rejoinder on September 22nd.

. . . I am the only Minister in London. The transient phantom of Asquith flitted through the metropolis for 15 minutes yesterday. Bryce, to whom you particularly refer me, is at Gastein three hours from a railway station, in a peculiarly inaccessible part of the Austrian Tyrol. Four Cabinet Ministers are on the Continent—I have not seen their addresses: we can send them nothing from the FO. With the others I have, on the principle you announce, felt it only loyal to rigidly abstain from communication. Kimberley has sent me a short, useful paper on my memorandum. Harcourt writes volumes. Elsewhere a vast silence. . . .

Harcourt is I fear for evacuation *sans phrase*. I know he feels deeply and earnestly on this question, and his language, though vehement is perfectly courteous and personally kind. But I do not think he sees how terribly such a course would embarrass, and, I fear—rightly or wrongly—discredit the Government. . . .

Gladstone pointed out to Rosebery in a letter on the 21st that he would more understand his concern and that of Harcourt 'had you gone through, like Harcourt and some of us, the terrible instructive experience of the Gordon Mission, in which we adopted a unanimous decision under the most seductive appearances'. On the 23rd he urged Rosebery to unite with the French to counsel moderation 'in the very strongest manner'; in another letter written on the same day—in all, Gladstone wrote three to Rosebery on the 23rd—he stated his personal position with a warning sternness.

. . . The Prime Minister, if he has been consulted on it in its various stages, is not less responsible than the Minister of the Dept. himself. And I am quite sure that any attempt of a Prime Minister to abate his

responsibility in such cases wd. be recd. with universal condemnation.
. . . This is your first case of encountering the alarming prophecies of
agents, who are either irresponsible or, naturally enough, inclined to
shift their responsibility to others. But I have had many of them; & I
see that Govts are often led into their worst errors in this way. I admit
Lugard to be a witness. I hardly attach much value to his authority.
But *if you do*, & you think you cannot, or should not, be responsible for
a decision until he comes, I am not certain that you mean things to
remain as they are in the interval? . . .

Up to this point the correspondence had been marked by
understanding, but a harsher tone began to intrude. Harcourt
prepared and circulated a memorandum on September 24th which
stated that 'Captain Lugard has probably with his Maxim gun
slain more Catholic Christians than are likely to be killed in his
absence', and that Lugard 'is so swollen with his own importance
and the value of his own reckless performances, that he has quite
lost his head, as his letters sufficiently show. Things having been
reduced to this hopeless and discreditable mess by the Company
and its Agent, we are asked what is to be done? . . . Before we
can come to any decision, we ought to have a full Report from
some impartial and capable person on the spot.' Rosebery's reply
to this document was sharp.

. . . You say you want information. So do I, so do we all. But that is
an argument that cuts both ways. If I wish to remain without sufficient
information, you wish to evacuate without sufficient information.

Gladstone wrote on the 24th that 'My views about the position
of the late Govt, formed upon the papers, is very clear & strong.
The views of some of our scattered colleagues, unsought, have
become known to me. They are all against moving to occupy.'[1]
Rosebery replied by demanding a Cabinet meeting, to which
Gladstone reluctantly consented 'with pain, though with no
hesitation'. Although he did not mention the fact to Rosebery,
Harcourt, Asquith, and Ripon had all asked for a Cabinet meeting.
His letter of September 25th continued:

[1] Asquith had written particularly strongly against annexation to the Prime
Minister, although conceding that some provision would have to be made for the
protection of those 'Englishmen & of those for whom, tho' not Englishmen, in
some way or other not at present clearly defined, we are said to be responsible'.
(*Gladstone Papers.*)

... It is the *first* time, during a Cabinet experience of 22 or 23 years, that I have known the Foreign Minister and the Prime Minister to go before a Cabinet on a present question with diverging views. It is the union of these two authorities by which foreign policy is ordinarily worked in a Cabinet; not that I have the smallest fear that this incidental miscarriage of ours will occur again. . . .

On the same day Rosebery laid down his view of Ministerial responsibility.

... I do not doubt that the First Minister shares in a special degree that of all departments. But in the popular mind a special responsibility does rest on the departmental Minister. And in strictness he shares a special responsibility with the Prime Minister.

But when the First and the departmental ministers differ, as I fear we do, the departmental cannot disengage himself of responsibility. When they agree the relative shares do not signify. But if evil comes of a policy adopted in spite of the forebodings (to use the weakest word) of the departmental minister, the burden of the last is heavy if not intolerable.

Now I am well aware of the prone-ness of interested agents to prophesy evil if their advice be not taken. But, so far as I can see at present, these prophecies take their root in the facts and common sense of the case.

I would indeed much rather suspend my judgement until Lugard returns or Macdonald reports. But, I fear, this opportunity is not open to me. It would be a great relief if we could obtain a respite till the end of the year.

I think tomorrow I will address a letter to Mackinnon pointing out how preposterous it is for him to expect a decision before Oct. 1. . . .

'I think that your view that the late Government were parties to the policy of evacuation is arguable but not correct,' Rosebery wrote in another letter to Gladstone on the 25th. 'The Mombasa railroad blocks the way. Had they accepted evacuation definitely they would never have dreamed of the railroad.'[1] Gladstone drew Rosebery's attention to the hostile attitude of the *Manchester Guardian*,[2] but Rosebery retorted that although he respected and regretted the opinion of that newspaper, 'even from the *Manchester Guardian* it would not be wise too confidently to infer the unanimity of Liberal opinion on the subject'.

[1] This was confirmed somewhat belatedly by Salisbury in a speech made on October 28th.
[2] The article had been sent to Gladstone by Morley.

Other Ministers were making their views known. Ripon circulated an unasked-for memorandum in which he stated that 'I cannot but regard with considerable suspicion the alarmist prophecies of a man so extravagant in his views and so rash in his purposes as Captain Lugard.' Asquith, Morley, Spencer, and Herschell also admitted to considerable misgivings about re- taining Uganda, while Campbell-Bannerman circulated a War Office opinion on Macdonald—who was extravagantly praised— and Lugard, who was almost contemptuously dismissed; 'The general opinion of Lugard', Campbell-Bannerman wrote to Harcourt, 'is that he is a lunatic, aiming at being a second Gordon —just what we thought.' Both Gladstone and Rosebery were by this stage very angry; Gladstone returned a telegram from Portal to Rosebery—which gave evidence of the dangers to the Christians in the event of British evacuation—with the sole comment, scrawled across the top, 'I wonder how much the transmission of this very unimportant *Jingo* paper cost.'

The Cabinet was due to meet on September 28th; Gladstone was so excited by the Uganda crisis that he could speak of nothing else, while Rosebery told West that he was suffering from a return of his insomnia and that if the disaster of Khartoum were repeated in Uganda he would never sleep again. To Herschell Rosebery wrote on the 27th that although it was clear that he would be in a minority, he would never support a policy 'of uninformed abandonment of the sphere of British influence and of leaving our missionaries & their converts to chance & the Arabs. . . . I am afraid I look to Thursday at noon with the gloom- iest forebodings.' West persuaded Rosebery to tear up another strong letter to Gladstone and urged him to compromise, but the meeting of the Cabinet was stormy and no progress was made. Rosebery and Gladstone became involved in a heated argument. Morley told West afterwards that 'Rosebery meant mischief, that Mr Gladstone had been very warm and excited with him, and that things looked black'.[1] West told Gladstone on the following morning that if matters were allowed to slide any further the Cabinet would disintegrate and that Rosebery would resign. Gladstone replied that Rosebery would do more damage to himself than to the Government if he went; West replied that this might be so, but Rosebery's defection would be a very serious

[1] West: *Diaries*, 61.

blow, and it would be worthwhile considering giving a subsidy
to the Company for a short period to give time for tempers to
cool and to work out an agreed solution. Gladstone seemed
impressed by the suggestion, and West saw Rosebery just before
the Cabinet met to warn him of this development.

After the Cabinet of the day before, Rosebery had written to the
Prime Minister what he described in his diary as 'a final summary
of my case before the Cabinet'.

. . . The pressing point before the Government is not now the
expediency of an East African Empire, nor is it the question of assisting the East African Company, nor of maintaining a sphere of influence,
nor of the Mombasa railway, nor of the intentions of the late Government.

Nor is it a question of whether it is wise to interfere in Uganda at all.

But whether . . . we are content to face the consequences of leaving
the territory, the inhabitants, and the missionaries, to a fate which we
cannot doubt.

This in face of the solemn warning of every authority conversant
with the region. . . . There is, so far as I know, not a single authority
that takes a different view.

All therefore that I ask is that I, as Foreign Secretary, and holding
a very strong view on the subject, shall not be placed in the position
of simply acquiescing, without inquiry, in an evacuation which under
circumstances of such precipitation, must in my opinion be inevitably
so disastrous. . . .

The Cabinet of the 29th was surprisingly tranquil, as Rosebery's
account in his diary records.

Cabinet in Mr G's sitting room. Much walking about of Mr G
between Harcourt & me—we did not sit down till 12.30. Bewildered
colleagues in knot all round. Mr G came up to me & said that in view
of a telegram of Portal's he saw his way to a delay of 3 months or so
in evacuation. This a compromise. The cabinet lasted little or no
time—I mute—all nearly so. No discussion—a short address only from
Mr G. Herschell, Harcourt & I appointed to draw up a *proces verbal*.
Only a round table with six places for writing. Mr G & I at the table
—a general group in front & around.

Kimberley & C-Bannerman to luncheon. This morning I did not
think I shd eat luncheon as Foreign Minister. Harcourt & Herschell
at FO at 3. Harcourt at my request dictated document to me. I sent it
to Mr G promising observations next day.

Rosebery had every reason to be satisfied with this compromise;
as he wrote to the Queen, 'The delay gives time to receive in-

formation; to elicit the real feeling of the country, which is, he is certain, against evacuation. . . . From every point of view therefore he thinks that this delay is favourable to his policy; it is not what he would wish but it is more than this morning seemed attainable.'[1] Rosebery wrote to Gladstone on the 30th to say that he interpreted the Cabinet's decision as 'giving time for information and consideration as well as for avoiding the material dangers of a hurried evacuation', but went on to warn that no expedients could obscure the fundamental difference of outlook within the Cabinet on foreign policy, and that there were bound to be future complications. This letter temporarily healed the wounds opened by the sharply personal aspect of the Uganda dispute between Gladstone and Rosebery. When Rosebery walked with Asquith to the Cabinet meeting on September 30th Gladstone took his arm ('for the first time that I remember, Rosebery remarked in his diary) and said 'with much feeling' that his conduct had been 'beyond reproach', and Rosebery replied that the differences had greatly distressed him; 'the interview signally warm & tender'.

The Uganda crisis, which was to inflame and irritate the relations between Rosebery and his colleagues for another two years, illuminated the basic division within the Cabinet. On matters of foreign policy Rosebery was virtually isolated from Gladstone, Harcourt, and Morley, but on domestic issues, and particularly over Home Rule, Harcourt and Rosebery were in considerable agreement; these alignments were distorted in a vital manner by the deep antipathy which existed between Morley and Harcourt at this time, caused by the 'Brook Street Conspiracy' and the almost daily derision which Harcourt poured on Home Rule proposals. In the correspondence between Morley and Gladstone on the Uganda crisis, Morley's comments were surprisingly mild, particularly after September 25th when Morley realised the seriousness of the situation. He was on the warmest terms with Rosebery at this time, an important factor in the situation which was due to Rosebery's offer to contribute towards Morley's election expenses at Newcastle when he had been faced with a by-election on taking office. Morley had been deeply moved by this offer, as his reply of August 25th reveals.

[1] *Letters of Queen Victoria*, 3rd Series, II, 159–60.

My dearest Rosebery,

I cannot tell you, nor even try to tell you, how your letter has moved me. It goes to my very heart, for I'm none of the stoic that I pretend to be. . . . The people here pay all expenses. I told them that they must relieve me of this burden under the circumstances. So, put the money in a box, and save it for a cruise which I will one day make in your company.

You talk of death and life, dear Rosebery. 'Tis a strange dance of shadows. I never felt it as I do today. The only thing real is the life of the affections—and your letter unseals the springs in me. I should like to keep it in my most secret archives—the letter, I mean. . . .

I believe your work will do you good.

I am interrupted by a constant succession of miseries. So no more. Always your most affectionate and grateful

John Morley.

At the best of times a Cabinet is a sensitive and uneasy body. The inevitable elements of individual incompatabilities, jarring personalities, conflicting ambitions, all render a delicate instrument subject to almost daily strains which, unless controlled by a skilful Prime Minister working in close sympathy with one or two influential colleagues, lead to eventual fragmentation. Gladstone's last Ministry lacked such a control, and its disintegration was remorseless. There was little personal sympathy between its most important members; they seldom met outside the infrequent Cabinet meetings, and it was left to men like West and Hamilton to shuttle to and fro with letters, messages, and proposals. Morley remained in Ireland for most of the time, Rosebery became a hermit in the Foreign Office, Harcourt devoted much of his formidable energy to penning harshly sarcastic memoranda to his colleagues, while Gladstone was aloof, preoccupied with Home Rule, and difficult of access. The junior Ministers, bewildered and distressed by this uncomfortable atmosphere, either lost heart or took sides. Rosebery remarked with aptness to Hamilton that this strange Cabinet was conducted 'on prize-fight principles', with the leaders sparring incessantly in the middle of a ring of puzzled Ministers.

Gladstone's position was difficult, but after making every allowance for his difficulties and the burdens which he carried, it cannot be denied that his attitude was largely responsible for the unhappy condition of his Ministry. Angered by opposition, alarmed by tendencies within the Liberal Party against which he had struggled for virtually the whole of his career, conscious of his own physical decline, confronted with bitter opposition to Home Rule, harassed by a hostile Sovereign and factious colleagues, he became increasingly averse to meeting his colleagues and retreated into the seclusion of his perhaps too devoted family circle.

The Uganda crisis was one of the most important incidents which divorced him finally from Rosebery. There was a characteristic misunderstanding over the leadership of the House of Lords, which had been offered to Rosebery on August 17th. Rosebery replied that he was 'quite indifferent' and that there were serious disadvantages in having the Foreign Secretary as leader of the Lords; Gladstone replied that he could not take this as an answer, and Rosebery definitely refused on the 19th, adding that Kimberley not only had greater abilities for the task but 'he lacks what I have—a rooted dislike for the atmosphere and habits of the House of Lords'. For some reason Gladstone still did not accept this refusal, and circulated a note to the Liberal peers to the effect that 'Lord Rosebery yields to the opinions which I have given and stated to him'. Rosebery then circulated a counter-memorandum explaining that as a misunderstanding had arisen, the matter should be postponed. Eventually, even after the most urgent appeals from his colleagues in the Lords, Rosebery definitely refused the leadership, which devolved on Kimberley. When Gladstone offered Rosebery the vacant Garter on October 4th, he replied that he had no wish for the honour but could not feel up to conducting another long correspondence on a personal matter; if the Prime Minister insisted, he would consent. The first intimation Rosebery received of the award of the Garter was when he read the news in the Press. These incidents, although trivial, further darkened the relationship between Rosebery and Gladstone, and culminated in the final harsh appraisal of Rosebery which Gladstone was to write for posterity in the document which he called his 'recorded errors'.

. . . The fatal element in this appointment was his total and gross misconception of the relative position of the two offices we respectively held, and secondly his really outrageous assumption of power apart from both the First Minister and from the Cabinet. . . .[1]

[1] *Gladstone Papers* (Brit. Mus. Add. MSS. 44,791, ff. 42–3).

This was written in 1896; in 1894 Gladstone remarked on the fact that Rosebery never confided in him politically, but added, 'He does not owe his present position in any way to me, and has had no sort of debt to pay'. In 1897 he appended a footnote: 'My bringing him to the Foreign Office was indeed an immense advancement, but was done with a belief, not sustained by subsequent experiences, in his competency and wisdom.'[1]

Rosebery himself was to say to a close friend in the last weeks of his life that his only mistake—'and a very great one'—had been to follow Gladstone. To such a melancholy condition did the spectacular promise of Midlothian degenerate.

The opening round of the Uganda crisis had convinced Rosebery that it was quite impossible for him to command support in the Cabinet for his policies, and from the beginning of September he began to gather all responsibility for the conduct of foreign affairs into his hands. It was essential that the policy of retention should be supported by public opinion and Lugard was the most convenient person to arouse it. On his return to England at the beginning of October, Lugard published an enormously long defence of his conduct and of the whole policy of annexation in *The Times* on October 6th. Although there is no direct evidence that Rosebery was behind Lugard at this time, they dined together privately more than once, and Lugard himself has written guardedly that 'Lord Rosebery was glad to utilize me in giving effect to his opposition to the views of his colleagues, and I had constant interviews with him'.[2] Lugard set out on a national lecture-tour to argue the case for annexation, and protests, petitions, and memorials urging annexation began to arrive at the Foreign Office, where they were seen and initialled by Rosebery. They numbered 174, but it was noticeable that not one Liberal organisation sent a memorial on the subject.[3] Rosebery himself came out into the open on October 20th, when he received a deputation from the Anti-Slavery Association at the Foreign Office. Declaring that 'I am only one member of a Government', he praised the work of the Association, and, speaking in a manifestly wider context, declared that 'My belief is that, having put

---

[1] *Ibid.* (Add. MSS. 44,790, f. 144).

[2] Perham: *Lugard*, I, 420.

[3] See A. Low, *British Public Opinion and the Uganda Question, October–December 1892* (*Uganda Journal*, XVIII, Sept. 1954), for a detailed analysis of this incident.

our hands to the plough in that great enterprise, we shall not be able, even if we were willing, to look back'.

It was not only Gladstone who was beginning to look askance at the independent activity of the Foreign Secretary. Ripon complained to Kimberley on November 5th about Rosebery's high-handedness, and remarked with justice that 'If he gets his way about Uganda, as I suppose he will, he will be very difficult to manage'. Kimberley, who liked and admired Rosebery, replied that he was 'in a very *ticklish* condition'.[1] 'He had a curious dread of not appearing absolute in his own house,' Marjoribanks remarked to West;[2] 'We did not send too much information from the FO to the other side of the street,' Munro Ferguson has recorded, 'and over Uganda Ld R remarked that Mr G's hair would stand on end if he knew what was going on there.'[3] It is now possible to appreciate just what was going on, and, as Miss Margery Perham has observed, had his colleagues been aware of Rosebery's stratagems 'they might well have accused their colleague of something worse than being egotistical and high-handed'.[4]

The sharp deterioration of Anglo-French relations since Rosebery's return to the Foreign Office was the subject of diplomatic comment by the beginning of October. 'The mistrust between the two Foreign Offices is, if anything, greater than even in Salisbury's time, if my observation is not deceived,' Hatzfeldt reported to Caprivi on October 12th.[5] Waddington attempted to side-step Rosebery by approaching Gladstone personally at the beginning of November to discuss Egypt. Although Rosebery had turned down a French proposal that there should be a separate French enquiry into Lugard's conduct, Gladstone told Waddington that he could see no objection to the proposal.[6] Rosebery had always disliked Waddington. 'I cannot divest myself of the idea when he enters the room that he is a churchwarden come round for a subscription,' he wrote to Gladstone on October 19th. 'The resemblance so far holds good that he brings nothing, but generally tries to take something away; and always with the unctuous air of Arthur Kinnaird reproving a customer for an overdraft.' Waddington called on Rosebery after seeing Gladstone and did not mention his interview with the Prime Minister: when

---

[1] *Ripon Papers.* [2] West: *Diaries*, 116.
[3] *Crewe Papers.* Lord Novar to Lord Crewe, March 26th, 1930.
[4] Perham: *Lugard*, I, 431. [5] *G.D.D.*, II, 179. [6] *D.D.F.*, X, 62.

he heard of it, Rosebery exploded with fury. 'He has rendered the transaction of business with him almost if not quite impossible, so far as I am concerned,' he wrote to Gladstone on November 4th. '. . . His proceedings are unprecedented I should think in the annals of diplomacy.' 'He has asked for an interview with Kimberley,' he wrote again to Gladstone on the 7th, 'so you can see he is extending his operations. He will soon begin sapping the Colonial Office and possibly besieging the Admiralty. I suggest that you send him what answer you please about Egypt with a gentle reminder that the most convenient course is to treat foreign policy through the Foreign Office.' 'Lord Rosebery, who is evidently much offended at this French action,' Hatzfeldt reported to Berlin on the 17th, 'added in strict confidence that France might now wait, before she got her way on any question whatever.'[1] Rosebery instructed Dufferin to convey to the French Government his strong complaint about Waddington's conduct, and Waddington was recalled from London in the June of 1893. On February 5th, 1893, Hatzfeldt reported that Rosebery had still not forgotten or forgiven Waddington's foray into Downing Street.[2] Gladstone, when making his judgement on Rosebery's 'outrageous assumption of power', cited this incident as evidence of his attitude.

This episode did not improve relations between Rosebery and Gladstone; according to Loulou Harcourt, Gladstone remarked to Harcourt on November 3rd after a long argument with Rosebery, 'It has come to this—either Rosebery or I must go'[3]. Rosebery's anger was probably excessive, but with a Francophile Prime Minister it was clearly vitally important to prevent a link being established between Waddington and Gladstone. 'My complaint of Waddington did not relate to his addressing himself to you and not to me', Rosebery wrote to Gladstone on November 4th, 1896, 'but to his addressing himself to you *to the exclusion of me*, for he called on me after seeing you— the very same afternoon—and never alluded to you, or the interview, or Egypt.'

Both Gladstone and Rosebery were becoming increasingly disinclined to meet each other, and when West and Hamilton remonstrated with them Gladstone replied that he did not want to

---

[1] *G.D.D.*, II, 180.   [2] *Ibid.*, 184.
[3] The unpublished Journal of Lewis Harcourt, November 3rd, 1892.

create an inner Cabinet and Rosebery said that Gladstone's deafness made it more convenient to conduct official business by letter. Rosebery complained to Hamilton on November 3rd. 'The proceedings of the Cabinet were rather painful. Mr G, he said, had lost his hold over his colleagues & showed great signs of age. He had lost his interest in almost all public affairs with an exception of foreign affairs, about which he was more active than was necessary.' On the 14th he said that he would not discuss political matters with Gladstone until the Uganda crisis was resolved, as the Prime Minister was unwilling to listen to anybody or anything, and he told West on the same day that 'Mr Gladstone is always violent and unreasonable, and snubs me at the Cabinets'.

On November 7th the Cabinet very nearly broke up over Uganda, when it was decided to send a commissioner to examine the situation;[1] Harcourt and Morley, according to Rosebery's account of the Cabinet in his diary, 'uttered sepulchral warnings and at last I solemnly advised them & W.E.G. to take their own course, wh. W.V.H. declined'. On the 11th there was another acrimonious Cabinet—described by Arnold Morley as 'very Harcourty', by John Morley as 'very rough, very rough', and by Rosebery as 'a great wrangle'—in which the Foreign Secretary again threatened to resign.

But Rosebery gained an important point by the decision to send a commissioner to Uganda, since the Cabinet agreed to send Gerald Portal. This was a very strange decision, since Portal had publicly committed himself against evacuation, but it seems certain that it was the fact that Salisbury had used Portal in a similar capacity which persuaded the Cabinet. By one of those curious processes of reasoning which distinguish the most irresolute of governments, Ministers seem to have taken the view that by appointing Portal they could not be accused of initiating a new enquiry.[2] Rosebery made it perfectly plain in a series of private letters to Portal that his job was to report against evacuation. On December 1st, for example, after telling Portal that there might be a saving clause in his instructions to cover the possibility that retention might cause insuperable difficulties,

[1] Macdonald's enquiry was solely concerned with the conduct of Lugard and other Company agents.
[2] Unfortunately the page is missing from Lewis Harcourt's Journal on which he recorded his father's understanding of the terms of Portal's mission.

he added that 'as a rather one-horse Company has been able to administer [Uganda], I suppose the Empire will be equal to it and therefore that saving clause is *mainly one of form*'.[1] On December 4th he repeated the hint. 'I may say this, as my confident though not my official opinion, that public sentiment here will expect and support the maintenance of the British sphere of influence.' Rosebery also tried to persuade the Company to stay in Uganda for another year, but the sum demanded by Mackinnon —£50,000—was impossible with Harcourt at the Exchequer, and the negotiations ended abruptly.

With Lugard speaking to enormous and enthusiastic audiences, warmly supported by a clear majority of the Press, and with Portal carefully briefed, Rosebery could contemplate the situation with some satisfaction. Having made it plain that he was to be the master of foreign policy, he took no interest in domestic matters. When the Home Rule Bill was discussed by the Cabinet on November 21st, he and Harcourt sat ostentatiously apart on a sofa, and when Spencer approached they waved him away with the remark, 'Oh no, this is the *English* bench.' Brett called on Rosebery later that day and found him in excellent spirits, just about to leave for Windsor, where the Queen invested him with the Garter. 'She said she was very glad to do it & I rose & departed in peace,' his account of the ceremony records. 'The thing did not fidget me afterwards as much as I expected. I thought it would be like a pimple on one's tongue.'

All accounts agree that Rosebery seemed to be a new man at this time. Brett went down to Mentmore early in 1893 and found Rosebery bubbling over with chaff and anecdote, doing the boxes in the long, sunny billiard room humming 'Rule Britannia', which, he genially declared, was necessary to stop him losing heart.[2] His diaries resumed some of their sardonic charm, and he was seen more in London Society. The condition of the Cabinet continued to be pitiable; 'the ship is almost as little

[1] My italics. *Portal Papers*. (*Vide* Perham: *Lugard*, I, 430–1.)

[2] A. J. P. Taylor has written that 'His main task was to deceive both his chief and his colleagues, a task which he discharged conscientiously, but only at the cost of aggravating his naturally nervous temperament to the point of insanity'. (*The Struggle for Mastery in Europe*, 341.) There is no evidence that Rosebery's health suffered in his period at the Foreign Office, and in fact his insomnia actually seems to have improved after his return to office. It was only after Rosebery assumed the Premiership in the March of 1894 that his insomnia and mental strain had serious effects.

seaworthy a craft as ever went out into a storm,' Morley gloomily wrote to him on November 14th. On November 23rd there occurred an incident which Rosebery described in his diary, and which brings the whole ramshackle machine vividly to life.

. . . A painful scene at the end. Harcourt demands prompt cabinets —falls on Fowler as a faithless accomplice,[1] on Spencer as a 'wretched peer'—Mr G resists. Rembrandt *Monte Carlo* scene wh. Asquith & I viewed from the side table. Excited men round table—pale old croupier in midst with passion seething in his face—a memorable and painful scene. . . .

On December 17th there was a final Cabinet before Gladstone departed for his Christmas holiday at Biarritz. 'Words, words, words,' Rosebery commented wearily in his diary at the end of a long 'and very unnecessary' meeting. Although the Home Rule Bill was to be the only major legislation in the forthcoming session, a Cabinet committee of Gladstone, Morley, Spencer, Herschell, Bryce, and Campbell-Bannerman was not set up to draft the measure until November 21st, barely two months before Parliament reassembled.

Rosebery spent the early part of December in Ireland as the guest of John Morley, and was promised 'solicitude without ostentation, consideration without fuss, *prévenance* without egotism, and a cup of tea with or without milk. Nobody in the world was ever so welcome as you will be to this exile of Erin.' Morley's relations with Harcourt, on the other hand, were very bad; dining with Hamilton on January 12th, Morley said that although he doubted whether Rosebery would make a successful leader of the party, his claims to the succession were growing stronger, while Harcourt was 'impossible' as a leader. When the Cabinet reassembled on January 13th acrimonious disputes arose over the financial clauses to the draft Home Rule Bill and the proposal to retain Irish Members at Westminster but to prohibit them from voting on 'exclusively British questions'; the opposition of Harcourt, Asquith, Fowler, and Acland to this part of the Bill was overruled on the 13th,[2] but Harcourt then insisted on reading

---

[1] Fowler had promised to support Harcourt in his request for more frequent Cabinet meetings, but did not do so when Harcourt raised the matter.

[2] See Gladstone's notes on this meeting (*Gladstone Papers* (Brit. Mus. Add. MSS. 44,648, f. 59)).

voluminous memoranda on the financial sections to his bored and irritated colleagues. Morley angrily told West that 'Harcourt is doing what he can to break up and destroy the Bill',[1] and Harcourt remarked to Morley on the 13th that it was 'merely a Bill *pour rire*—it is ludicrous and impossible'. A few weeks later Morley wrote to Rosebery, 'You may annex the Great Sahara, if you will, so long as you don't leave me in the wilderness without the oasis of the pleasantest friendship that is left to me, among my juniors at least. Whether we even sit in the same Cabinet again or not, is of no consequence.'

It was this acute antipathy between Harcourt and Morley which was largely responsible for Rosebery's second victory over his critics in the Cabinet; he himself was convinced that his determination over the Uganda crisis had given him his independence, and on the 14th he told Hamilton that 'he was having his own way pretty well at the FO'.

This interpretation was to be tested at once. The young Khedive of Egypt, Abbas II, suddenly dismissed the pro-British Prime Minister and replaced him with a nominee unacceptable to Baring (now Lord Cromer). Although Rosebery had received warnings that the Khedive was becoming restive, his *coup* took the Government utterly by surprise, and Cromer at once appealed for permission to take drastic action to maintain British sovereignty in a series of over-excited telegrams which at once aroused the darkest suspicions of Gladstone and Harcourt when the Cabinet met to consider the unexpected crisis on January 16th.

Rosebery's view of the Egyptian Question was exactly that set out by Baring to Salisbury on April 19th, 1892.

. . . In spite of everything that may be said to the contrary, the paramount influence of that English government over the fitful, untrained and undisciplined public opinion of this country depends mainly on the presence of a British garrison. If that influence is withdrawn or weakened, the chances are greatly in favour of the whole edifice, which has been so laboriously erected, falling about our ears. . . . We must, I think, go on as we are. . . .

This important document was subsequently amended by Baring for circulation to the new Government with the addition of a significant paragraph.

[1] West: *Diaries*, 121.

. . . It is, of course, possible that some *modus vivendi* might be found with the French by combining the settlement of the Egyptian question with that of other questions unconnected with Egypt. I do not discuss this point as it lies outside my sphere of action, but I may say that, so far as I am able to judge, any combination of the sort presents very great difficulties.[1]

Gladstone was anxious to discuss the matter with the French, and regarded an alliance on Egypt as 'a righteous cause',[2] while Rosebery considered that the main outlines of Baring's first letter to Salisbury should be adhered to. His general policy was to contrive to administer Egypt and to avert any discussion of the future of British policy. This negative attitude now became impossible, since Cromer was demanding that the Ministries of Finance, Justice, and the Interior, as well as the telegraph office, should be occupied at once. The almost hysterical nature of these first telegrams made Rosebery's task in the Cabinet extremely difficult. 'You may count on Lord Rosebery's support,' Sir Thomas Sanderson of the Foreign Office telegraphed Cromer on January 20th. 'But the attitude of French Government is very stiff and their Press is violently excited. Lord Rosebery's difficulties in the Cabinet are, as you may suppose, considerable. Pray avoid in your official telegrams expressions which can be laid hold of'.[3] 'Lord Cromer', Rosebery informed the Queen, 'has been asked to make some more practicable proposal.'

Although he did not accept Cromer's alarming reports, Rosebery considered that some gesture must be made to impress upon Egyptian and European opinion the reality of British sovereignty. Cromer, taking the hint from the Foreign Office telegrams— which he later described to Rosebery as 'rather redolent of the Gladstonian flavour'—persuaded the Khedive to dismiss his nominee and appoint a third candidate acceptable to both sides. Having made this important concession, he insisted upon at least some military reinforcement, and Rosebery agreed. To Gladstone he wrote on the 19th that 'Cromer's two telegrams of today confirm my impression of yesterday that it will be necessary to strengthen the Egyptian army of occupation as soon but as unobtrusively as possible'. His letter continued:

[1] See T. B. Miller: 'The Egyptian Question and British Foreign Policy,' 1892–4. (*Journal of Modern History*, March 1960, XXXII, No. 1.)
[2] Waddington to Ribot, January 31st, 1893 (*D.D.F.*, 1st Series, X, No. 153).
[3] Lord Zetland: *Cromer*, 198.

1 Lady Dalmeny, later the Duchess of Cleveland

2 Rosebery at Eton

3 Rosebery as an undergraduate, with Lord Lansdowne

4 Rosebery, *circa* 1870

5   Hannah Rothschild standing in front of the Rubens chimney-
piece in the Great Hall at Mentmore. This portrait by an unknown
artist hangs in Rosebery's bedroom at Barnbougle

6   Mentmore

7   The Durdans

8 Dalmeny

9 Barnbougle

10 Mr and Mrs Gladstone at Dalmeny in 1880. *Back row*: Marquess of Tweeddale; Earl of Aberdeen; Hon. Alfred Lyttleton; Marchioness of Tweeddale; Miss Mary Gladstone; Lady Rosebery; Mr Lacaita; Mr J. E. Boehm, A.R.A. *Sitting*: Lord Reay; Mr Robert Jardine; Mrs Gladstone; Mr Gladstone; Countess of Aberdeen; Lady Reay; Mr W. P. Adam; *Sitting on the ground*: Lord William Douglas; Lord Rosebery

11 Dinner at Haddo House, 1884, by A. E. Emslie. Lady Aberdeen is at the head of the table with Gladstone on her right and Rosebery on her left

12   The Earl of Rosebery, by Millais, 1885

13   The Countess of Rosebery, by G. F. Watts

14 (*Above*) Gladstone on the Front Bench, by Phil May

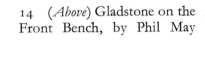

15 (*Left*) John Morley, by Harry Furniss

16 & 17 Sir William Har-
court in the House of Commons, by F. C. Gould

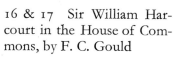

18 (*Right*) Lewis Harcourt,
by Harry Furniss

19 The end of the Home Rule Bill debate in the Lords', September 9th, 1893. The Lord Chancellor (Lord Herschell) is putting the Question and Rosebery can be seen (with his hands behind his head) on the Liberal Front Bench

20 Rosebery in 1892

21 Rosebery in the House of Lords in 1894, by F. C. Gould

The Earl of Rosebery

22 Rosebery, by Max
Beerbohm

23 Rosebery, *circa* 1905

24 Rosebery working
at 38, Berkeley Square
in 1912

25 Walking with Neil in
Hyde Park, 1915

Prevention is better than cure at all times; certainly in this instance. We have had a significant warning, and I fear if we do not take it we are at the beginning of a new and alarming phase of the Egyptian question. I propose therefore to bring the question before the Cabinet tomorrow with your permission, and to wait on you before then, should you wish to see me. . . .

Cromer may possibly take too gloomy a view of the situation. But he does not take a gloomier than I do. We have only a respite by the settlement of yesterday. And though it may be desirable to evacuate Egypt we cannot be jockeyed or intrigued out of it. . . .

The Cabinet meeting of January 20th was strongly reminiscent of the Uganda disputes. Gladstone was excited and alarmed by Rosebery's proposals,[1] telling Hamilton that 'I would as soon put a torch to Westminster Abbey as send additional troops to Egypt. It cannot be. Such proposals make me so fearful about the future. I can see nothing for it but for Rosebery to resign.' 'Morley silent, Harcourt conciliatory,'[2] Rosebery's account of the Cabinet reads. 'Mr G very hostile. . . . Kimberley & Herschell & Spencer did not go with me. Bryce the only supporter. The rest of the Cabinet absolutely mute.' Rosebery took the line that if they did not agree to Cromer's very reasonable request they faced the alternatives of leaving Egypt when ordered to go by the Khedive or sending an army at a later stage.

Rosebery had a vehement ally in the Queen, and she wrote to him on January 21st as follows:

Strictly Confidential.

The Queen thanks Lord Rosebery for his letters & telegrams wh. are all she wishes but the decision of the Cabinet is *dreadful!* How *can* they be so shortsighted & weak! How can a number of gentlemen sitting in a room together in London declare *they don't* consider the emergency to *have arisen* & that the strengthening of the garrison shall

---

[1] It is clear from several references to this fact in Gladstone's papers that Morley had told him that Rosebery's views on Egypt were similar to Gladstone's, this report, Gladstone subsequently wrote, 'appeared to guarantee them as perfectly satisfactory' (*Gladstone Papers*, Brit. Mus. Add. MSS. 44,791, f. 42). This was clearly a misrepresentation of Rosebery's views by Morley, and partly explains Gladstone's shock when the crisis broke and the Foreign Secretary's true opinions became apparent.

[2] West was talking to Loulou Harcourt when Rosebery came out of the Cabinet room and said that 'nothing could have been milder or more useful than Harcourt'; 'Loulou told his father that Rosebery's saying that he was most useful made him think he was ill' (West: *Diaries*, 123-4).

take place *when* it had done so!! Just too late. How *could* the reinforcements arrive in time? And this is the *answer* given by 'the Cabinet' to
the *repeated earnest* demands of our vy able & thoroughly experienced
Agent Ld Cromer!! It is Khartoum once more after the lapse of 8
years!

The crisis was short but intense. 'There is a Cabinet on Monday', Rosebery telegraphed to Cromer at one point, 'and if you
do not receive the powers you ask on Monday evening, the Foreign
Office will have passed into other hands.' 'I need hardly say',
Cromer replied on January 22nd, 'that if you should unfortunately
leave the Foreign Office I shall follow your example in my smaller
sphere. The result will almost certainly be that many of the high
English officials here will resign or be dismissed—in fact, the
whole machine will collapse.'[1] But in spite of the fierceness of
Gladstone's language and Rosebery's virtual isolation in the
Cabinet, he remained calm, and on the 23rd he won his point: a
battalion of troops passing through the Suez Canal was dis-
embarked at Port Said, and the crisis faded.

The Egyptian Crisis merely confirmed the lesson of the Uganda
disputes, that Rosebery held the whip-hand over his colleagues;
he did not need to brandish his resignation to make this fact
abundantly clear. In neither crisis did he get all that he wanted,
but he got far more than his critics—particularly Gladstone—
were initially prepared to give him. He had succeeded in over-
turning almost all the pre-election statements of the anti-Imperialist element in the Cabinet; whereas Gladstone had referred in
1892 to 'the burdensome and embarrassing occupation of Egypt',
Rosebery stated in a published dispatch in 1893 that 'we must
maintain the fabric of administration which has been constructed
under our guidance, and must continue the process of construc-
tion without impatience, but without interruption'. Although
irritated by what he described to the Queen as 'the tumultuous
storm of sinister telegrams that rained on the Foreign Office'
from Cromer, he had fastened on to the one important point,
which was that a demonstration of British determination to
control Egyptian administration was vital.

Rosebery was an exceptionally well-travelled and knowledge-
able Foreign Secretary, and although opinions varied about the
merits of the policies which he pursued, few critics questioned the

[1] Zetland: *Cromer* 203.

professional competence which characterised his tenure of the Foreign Office. Holding himself aloof from his Ministerial colleagues, working long lonely hours in the Foreign Office, he exercised a tight personal control over the multifarious activities of his great department. His approach to his Ambassadors was authoritarian, but he maintained close and continuous personal contact with them, and his judgement of their individual capacities was rarely proved wrong, the only conspicuous exception being Sir Clare Ford, the Ambassador at Constantinople; Rosebery refused to credit allegations circulating about Ford's private life and of his lack of attention to his work, but they were only too well-founded. In his conduct of foreign affairs Rosebery had his prejudices and blind spots, of which his ineradicable mistrust of France was the most serious, but he was a realist, and had the rare ability to separate the major from the minor factors in a complicated situation. As was demonstrated in Egypt and Central Africa, his major concessions eventually turned out to have been of little significance, whereas the apparently minor achievements were of decisive importance. His policy, as all foreign policy, was subjected to unexpected checks and strains, for the speed of diplomatic movement was increasing in the 1890's and no one could be quite sure of anything after the fall of Bismarck, with France in a dangerous temper, and the uncertainties of African ambitions constantly warping European alliances. But Rosebery, by skilfully cultivating relations with most of the European Ambassadors in London, by simulating annoyance on one occasion or flattering with his irresistible charm on another, kept Britain out of positive alignments and entanglements without ever wholly separating her from the European diplomatic struggle. He clearly appreciated the limits of British power, but was quite prepared to use that power to the maximum extent, and was not undisposed to employ bluff if occasion demanded. Foreign policy was a source of endless fascination to Rosebery, and at no other stage in his public life did he so clearly demonstrate his qualities of application to dull routine work when captivated by a subject or a problem, his intuitive shrewdness, and flexible common-sense approach to an ever-changing international situation.

Although the Egyptian crisis had been faced and overcome, it had contributed to the further deterioration of relations between

Gladstone and Rosebery. On January 22nd West again tried to persuade them to meet more often outside Cabinet meetings, but without any success. On January 29th Rosebery urged Ponsonby to propose to the Queen that she should impress upon Gladstone the necessity of making firm statements on the Egyptian Question, a suggestion which was promptly acted upon.[1] But Rosebery was obliged to amend his policy with regard to Egypt; he had written to Gladstone in the November of 1892 that negotiations about evacuation would be 'a pernicious waste of time and energy', but throughout 1893 he conducted a series of private negotiations with the Italian and Turkish Ambassadors, whose purpose was clearly to evade an ultimatum from the Powers to Britain to evacuate. 'Italy', he wrote to Gladstone on February 1st, 'is the key to the situation, and Italy is not such a fool as to join this triple conspiracy [France, Russia, and Turkey]. Nevertheless, all this gives food for thought. I feel half inclined to say: "to the Powers ye appeal, to the Powers ye shall go!" However, in any case it is a situation requiring grave consideration.' Rosebery cultivated better personal relations with the Italian Ambassador, Count Tornielli, who told Hatzfeldt with enthusiasm that 'Lord Rosebery was a statesman of determined will and a clear thinker, whose genuine sincerity inspires confidence on every occasion'.[2] Count Deym, the Austrian Ambassador, was also pleased by Rosebery's attitude towards his country and throughout the summer of 1893 Rosebery had several discussions with Deym, emphasising that the interests of the two nations in the Mediterranean were closely linked; with Rustem Pasha, the Turkish Ambassador, Rosebery had a series of confidential discussions in which little progress was made, but which had the effect— which was not fortuitous—of averting an ultimatum from the Sultan. Rustem did demand in July that Britain should give immediate and explicit recognition of Turkish sovereignty in Egypt and convene a conference of the Powers to set a date to British evacuation, but Rosebery neatly avoided committing himself.

The Parliamentary Session of 1893 was dominated by the intense struggle over the Home Rule Bill in the House of Commons, where the political world was enthralled by the amazing spectacle of the aged Premier conducting the progress of the Bill night after night against the relentless opposition of the Unionists

[1] See *Letters of Queen Victoria*, 3rd Series, II, 216–17.   [2] *G.D.D.*, 207–8.

marshalled and led by Balfour and Chamberlain (who still sat on the Government front bench). Having received its second reading on April 22nd—'Please God, in committee it will be much altered,' the Queen confided to her Journal[1]—the Bill spent the whole summer in Committee, receiving the third reading on September 2nd. In these circumstances the Foreign Secretary was left almost entirely to his own devices. Cabinet meetings became increasingly rare. 'I understand that on Monday a Bill (to "amend the provision" for the Government of Ireland), which neither you nor I have seen, is to be introduced into the House of Commons,' Asquith wrote wryly to Rosebery on February 10th. 'I send you word of this, as you may possibly like to be present, and hear what Her Majesty's Government have to propose.' 'It is wonderful how Mr Gladstone is able to put off what he does not like,' West remarked on the rarity of Cabinet meetings;[2] at the end of April Hamilton noted that the Cabinet had not met for five weeks. Friction between Morley and Harcourt increased under the stress of the arduous session. On February 13th—the day on which Gladstone was to introduce the Home Rule Bill—Harcourt sent the Prime Minister a typically harsh memorandum on the financial clauses of the Bill, on which Morley wrote with great bitterness, 'What you do is ostentatiously to hold aloof from the business, and then when others do the best they can, you descend upon them with storm and menace. That you should have on such a morning written to Mr Gladstone such a letter is the kind of thing that Brougham would have done, and nobody else that I have read of in modern public life.' On June 8th West recorded that Morley had said that Harcourt was quite impossible with his colleagues 'and it would be found out when Mr Gladstone went. He wondered if there was a precedent for sending a round-robin to the Prime Minister, asking him to dismiss a colleague!!!!'[3]

Strong criticism of the Government's African policies came from below the gangway on the Liberal side, principally from Labouchere and Dilke (who had returned to the House in 1892 as Member for the Forest of Dean). Rosebery was extremely fortunate in having Sir Edward Grey as his Under-Secretary; like Rosebery, he was idealistic, imaginative, and rich, and he shared Rosebery's radical views in domestic policies and Imperial

[1] *Letters, op. cit.,* 227.   [2] West: *Diaries,* 149.   [3] *Ibid.,* 165.

outlook on foreign affairs. Grey was one of the most promising
of the young Liberals who had entered politics since 1886, and
Rosebery had been immediately attracted to him; Grey shared
many tastes with Rosebery, not the least of which was his love of
solitude, and they worked together with rare harmony at the
Foreign Office. On March 21st he defended Rosebery's Uganda
policy vigorously in the Commons, and reported to his chief that
'the Government bench uttered murmurs, which I hope did not
reach the Reporters' Gallery; the Labbyites (the "faithful few"
as they call themselves) are indignant, and mean to fire off again
in the Appropriation Bill tomorrow. "You have put the fat in
the fire" was Harcourt's comment when I sat down.' Chamberlain
strongly supported Grey, and Rosebery remarked to Hamilton
on March 31st at Mentmore that he felt more in agreement with
Chamberlain than almost any other man in public life; he added
that he sharply resented the luke-warm support he was receiving
in the Commons from his Cabinet colleagues. He told West at
this time that he did not see why he should attend Cabinet
meetings 'as whenever he spoke, Mr Gladstone told him not to
speak'.[1] Gladstone actually refused to circulate a memorandum
Rosebery had prepared on Portal's mission at the beginning of
February, and the Foreign Secretary caused further strains in the
party by a forthright speech made on March 1st at the Royal
Colonial Institute.

. . . There is another ground on which the extension of our Empire
is greatly attacked, and the attack comes from a quarter nearer home.
It is said that our Empire is already large enough, and does not need
extension. That would be true enough if the world were elastic, but,
unfortunately, it is not elastic, and we are engaged at the present
moment, in the language of the mining camps, in 'pegging out claims
for the future'. We have to consider, not what we want, but what we
shall want in the future. . . . We should, in my opinion, grossly fail
in the task that has been laid upon us if we shrink from responsibilities
and decline to take our share in a partition of the world which we have
not forced on, but which has been forced upon us. . . .

It was probably this speech more than any other that prompted
Gladstone's grossly unfair subsequent comment that Rosebery
'was imbued with the spirit of territorial grab'.[2]
Intent upon frustrating French ambitions on the one hand and

[1] West: *Diaries*, 142.   [2] *Gladstone Papers* (Brit. Mus. Add. MSS. 44,791, f. 30).

upon retaining complete control over foreign policy in the Cabinet on the other, Rosebery was suddenly faced with an unexpected situation. Portal, far from recommending annexation of Uganda, was sending reports of a very different nature to the Foreign Office. Gladstone wrote to Rosebery on April 5th that he found these reports 'astonishing', and proposed that Portal should be recalled to Britain after he had completed his Report. Rosebery was equally astonished. On May 19th he received a characteristic-ally gloomy account from Portal (written from Kavirondo on March 3rd) to the effect that the country was arid, desolate, and unpromising, that there was universal condemnation of the Company—'on every side we come across instances of shooting, raiding, & burning villages'—and that hostility to Europeans was evident. This letter also revealed that Portal had been getting much of his information from Macdonald and from the German correspondent of the *Berliner Tageblatt*, Mr Eugene Wolf. Portal's gloom was undoubtedly intensified by the death of his brother in Uganda. It was therefore evident that he was unexpectedly receptive to stories of Lugard's alleged misdeeds, and Rosebery at once placed all possible obstacles in the way of Portal's state-ments being relayed to Ministers. On June 25th Portal told Rose-bery that he intended to report strongly against annexation, and his draft arrived at the Foreign Office towards the end of August. Rosebery told Gladstone on September 17th that he was awaiting Portal's return so that he could modify his first draft, and on November 27th he informed the Prime Minister that Portal had returned and was working to 'mature it'. 'Hitherto', Rosebery wrote, 'I have not touched it with the tongs.' After further delays, the Report was circulated on December 20th, and a week later Rosebery wrote to Gladstone that there was no urgency in the matter and that 'I considered myself bound in honour not to look at it until it was circulated to the Cabinet, and, consequently, I have only a very recent acquaintance with it'.

This last statement is clearly untrue. Portal's final Report was conspicuously less emphatic than his previous letters had sug-gested, and recommended a British 'sphere of influence' in Uganda; the question thus arises as to whether Rosebery himself had rewritten it. Miss Perham, in her admirable biography of Lugard, considers that he did; Lugard wrote to his brother on March 27th, 1894, that 'Portal did himself no good at all in Uganda

—had to write an entirely new report to order on his return'.[1] As Lugard
saw a great deal of Rosebery at this time, this evidence should
be regarded as important. Unfortunately, Rosebery's papers
throw no light on the matter, but it is clear that he delayed the
circulation of the Report, suppressed the first draft, and made it
plain to Portal that his task of 'maturing' the draft involved an
extensive change of view. Portal died on January 25th, 1894, as
a result of a disease contracted on his mission, but in spite of the
public eulogies by Ministers, his Report remained mysteriously
secret. In a memorandum dated February 25th, 1894, Rosebery
demanded a Protectorate; on April 10th—a month after he had
become Prime Minister—the Report was presented to Parliament,
and two days later it was announced that the Government had
decided upon annexation.

Rosebery's task was made immeasurably simpler by the fact
that Portal had compromised himself seriously before his Report
reached Ministers. This was due entirely to the Macdonald
Report, which arrived in June, and which even Gladstone could
not accept. 'Salisbury seems to have blundered in appointing a
personal enemy to report on Lugard's acts,' he wrote to Rosebery
on July 20th. 'Certainly a difficult situation.' The publication of
large sections of this highly confidential report in the *Berliner
Tageblatt* led to enquiries about the activities of its author, Eugene
Wolf, and on August 11th Rosebery sent a strong protest to
Portal about Macdonald's conduct; as Miss Perham observes,
'Portal's reply to this, disclaiming responsibility and playing
down the part Wolf had played, was a little less than frank'.[2]
Although a Cabinet Committee—consisting of Herschell, Harcourt, and Campbell-Bannerman—appointed to examine the
Macdonald Report was not entirely satisfied by Lugard's replies,
by the time that Macdonald himself returned to England in the
summer of 1894 his Report had been effectively discounted, and
Grey informed the House of Commons on April 17th, 1894, that
it would not even be published. There was another point which
had transpired since Macdonald had begun his work, that as he
was junior in rank to Lugard he could not properly enquire into
the activities of a senior officer. Rosebery warmly championed
Lugard, and the hapless Macdonald returned to a distinctly cold
reception.

[1] My italics (*vide* Perham: *Lugard*, I, 451).   [2] Perham: *Lugard*, I, 356.

The events of 1893 in foreign affairs had rendered the possibility of immediate British evacuation of Egypt academic. The Panama scandals at the end of 1892, which had rocked Europe and led to the dismissal of Ribot, Freycinet, and other moderate Ministers, had shaken confidence in the French nation even among the Francophile element in the Cabinet. 'My personal observation had shown me that Lord Rosebery's irritation against France has increased,' Hatzfeldt reported to Caprivi on February 5th. '... His victory in the Cabinet and the undivided support which his energetic action in Egypt won for himself throughout the country, have increased his confidence in himself, and to-day he has no doubt that if the Cabinet holds together at all, his position in it is almost unshakeable.'[1] He demonstrated this confidence by authorising Portal in August 'to protect the important interests of this country on the Upper Nile' and to 'negotiate any treaties that may be necessary for its protection'. These secret instructions were sent from Homburg, where Rosebery was on holiday,[2] and it was only a year later that his colleagues heard what had been done in their name. When the French issued menacing threats to the Siamese Government early in 1893, and followed them up by dispatching gun-boats to Bangkok and spoke of imposing a blockade, Rosebery retaliated by sending British ships to preserve the vital 'buffer state' of Siam. On July 26th the French declared a blockade, and friendly vessels were given three days to leave; matters became so critical that Rosebery sought the views of the German Government from the Kaiser who was on holiday in England.[3] The crisis passed, and a period

[1] *G.D.D.*, II, 185.

[2] He was pursued there by the lunatic Marquess of Queensberry, who, armed with a horsewhip, announced his intention of publicly assaulting the Foreign Secretary for his part in promoting his son, Drumlanrig, to the peerage. 'It is a material & unpleasant addition to the labours of Your Majesty's service to be pursued by a pugilist of unsound mind,' Rosebery wrote to the Queen. The Chief Commissioner of Police announced the removal of the nuisance in the following magnificent communication.

'Right Honourable Lord! I take the honour to advertise you that Marquis of Queensberry, in consequence of the entertainment I had with him, found it advisable to part this morning with the 7 o'clock train for Paris.

'I beg to agree the assurance of the highest consideration of your Lordship's most obedient servant.'

[3] As Mr A. J. P. Taylor has pointed out (*The Struggle for Mastery in Europe*, 343–4) this request deluded the Germans into believing that they could blackmail Britain into the Triple Alliance by making support against France conditional.

of negotiation ensued; it was not ended until the publication of a joint Declaration in the January of 1896, in which Salisbury conceded much to the French that Rosebery had refused. It is not difficult to appreciate Rosebery's indignation when Chamberlain cited the Siam question in 1900 as 'a heritage left to Lord Salisbury by his Liberal predecessors' and that 'the late Liberal Government only got peace by giving way to all the world'.

The Siam crisis was symptomatic of the profound distrust which existed between the French and British Governments while Rosebery was at the Foreign Office. 'Lord Rosebery's ... chief anxiety of all, as is evident from his apparent indifference to all other matters, is just now France,' Hatzfeldt reported to Caprivi on May 27th. 'He did not conceal it from me, and declared straight out that he was concentrating all his attention on Paris, where both the attitude of the Press and speeches by Ministers revealed extraordinary animosity against England.'[1] On June 30th Rosebery told the Queen that in view of the bitter attacks of the French Press upon Dufferin—which had been sparked off by the publication of British Embassy documents that proved to be forgeries —he had advised him to delay his return to Paris, 'for he does not think it proper that Your Majesty's Ambassador should be subjected to insult in a foreign capital'. 'The behaviour of France to Siam', he wrote to her, 'has it appears been base, cruel and treacherous. Perhaps nothing so cynically vile is on record. But that is not our affair. We cannot afford to be the Knight Errant of the World, careering about to redress grievances and help the weak. If the French cut the throats of half Siam in cold blood we should not be justified in going to war with her.'

In his conduct of foreign affairs in 1893 Rosebery had the warm support of the Queen and most of the Press, but although there was little opposition in the Cabinet Rosebery had no doubt, as he told Hamilton on July 23rd, 'that his conduct of foreign affairs was really distasteful to Mr G, & that, were it not for Home Rule, Mr G would let him know this pretty quickly'. Gladstone's suspicions erupted in the crisis which ended his Ministerial career. Although Rosebery had secured a satisfactory agreement with the Russians over the Pamirs, on the Afghanistan border, the evident *rapprochement* between France and Russia—signified

[1] *G.D.D.*, I, 191.

by the visit of the Russian fleet to Toulon in September[1]—gave a greater impetus to Rosebery's Mediterranean policy. The British naval and military intelligence had frankly admitted in a secret Minute in the March of 1892 that British naval power could not dictate policy in the eastern Mediterranean any longer. The Russian move into the Mediterranean caused something of a naval scare in Britain, and the loss of the battleship *Victoria* on manoeuvres in June gave dramatic emphasis to the alarm of the Board of Admiralty and the Press. Although not directly concerned in the dispute between Spencer and Gladstone, Rosebery made it clear that he strongly supported a vigorous naval programme to maintain the maritime balance of power.

When this crucial dispute arose in the autumn of 1893, Rosebery's standing with Gladstone had fallen even further as a result of his tepid speech in support of the Home Rule Bill in the Lords at the beginning of September. Rosebery described himself as 'a witness, but not an enthusiastic witness, in favour of Home Rule', and his speech, although witty and pointed, lacked any kind of conviction; 'I may frankly say', he remarked at one point, 'that I am by no means sure of my course. I am not certain of anything with regard to Ireland.' His speech still makes delightful reading, and sparkled with humour and erudition, but it is easy to see why Gladstone was bitterly disappointed with it. On September 9th the Bill was contemptuously rejected by the Lords by the shattering majority of 419 to 41; to the dismay of the ardent Home Rulers, 'not a dog barked'; the nation, as well as Parliament, was exhausted and bored by the controversy, and the arguments put forward by Gladstone for a dissolution were rejected by the Cabinet.

By November the controversy over the Spencer naval programme was assuming very serious proportions. The Board of Admiralty laid two programmes—a desired one and a minimum one—before Spencer in November, and by December 15th Spencer had agreed to the latter, it having been made plain to him that the alternative was the resignation of the whole Board. Even if popular opinion and the Foreign Secretary had not been insistent upon increased naval expenditure, no Victorian Government could have survived the uproar which would have followed the

[1] An Anglo-Italian naval meeting was hurriedly arranged at Taranto, but the incompetence of the Italian Navy was so notorious that no purpose was served by this rather jejeune attempt to impress the Great Powers.

resignation of the Board of Admiralty. Harcourt, in his dual role of guardian of the national purse and arch-enemy of all 'jingoistic' proposals, subjected the First Lord to a torrent of ferocious memoranda, and on December 10th Eddie Hamilton recorded that Spencer had threatened to retire 'and buy hunters', to which Harcourt retorted that 'though he has not hunting to fall back upon, he would be quite content to take himself off to Malwood and grow cabbages'. As early as November 4th Rosebery told Hamilton that he regarded a greatly increased naval programme as vitally important for the purposes of maintaining British influence and prestige, particularly in the Mediterranean. Rosebery was more depressed than ever by the unbusinesslike and undisciplined conduct of Cabinet meetings. He was extremely angry when, on November 4th, the Cabinet decided to advise the Duke of Edinburgh to renounce his annuity on his accession to the Duchy of Coburg. The language of Morley, Asquith, and Acland shocked Rosebery even more than the decision itself: 'We toss over the Queen's second son into bankruptcy or sheer dependence on his wife,' he wrote to Gladstone on November 5th, 'and without a word of care for him or for his aged mother to whom this cannot but be a cruel blow. One of the gentlest and kindliest of our colleagues [Morley] was truculent and Jacobin. It is deplorable to live under a monarchy and make a football out of it, and rejoice in starving it.' 1893 had witnessed a great improvement in Rosebery's relations with the Queen, and in a very curious audience on August 3rd she had clearly intimated to him that she wished he was Prime Minister; when he had mentioned the fact that he might take the vacant Viceroyalty of India,[1] she had replied, 'But who will you leave to me? You are the only one of the Ministry with whom I can talk freely.'

After a battle royal with Spencer,[2] Harcourt accepted the in-

[1] The problem of the Viceroyalty gave the Government considerable trouble. Lord Elgin refused the position, as did Sir Henry Norman and Lord Spencer. At one stage Rosebery spoke of taking it himself, and Kimberley wrote that 'If you go out to India, the Government will go out here'. In spite of the Queen's opposition, Elgin was induced to change his mind, and was appointed. Rosebery seems to have shared the Queen's misgivings about Elgin, as he wrote to her on September 4th that 'it seems positively sad to Lord Rosebery that more fit and aspiring men should not be found for this splendid position' (*Royal Archives*).

[2] A. J. Marder in his account of the crisis in *The Anatomy of British Sea Power* (200) suggests that Harcourt suddenly changed his mind. In fact, he carried on the struggle with Spencer until the end of December with considerable acerbity on both sides.

creased Navy Estimates, and as the year drew to a close it was painfully clear that only Gladstone was opposed to them. In his account of the crisis, written in the October of 1896, Gladstone recorded that 'When I learned Spencer's intention I at once assured Harcourt as the official dragon of the Treasury of my hearty support in resisting it. His countenance at once fell and I at once found that he had made up his mind to accept it, and accept my impending resignation as part of the arrangement. I do not suppose he was so blind as to expect the accession. But he probably had the notion of Graduated Death Duty in his head, and was so charmed with it as in some degree to excuse the expenditure on its account.'[1]

Gladstone's language became increasingly immoderate, and he noted after an interview with Spencer on December 16th that the First Lord had surrendered to the 'conspiracy' of the Admirals and had accepted most of their 'monstrous scheme'. Rosebery urged him on December 18th—the eve of a debate in the Commons on the naval crisis on an Opposition motion urging 'a considerable addition to the Navy' and a statement of the Government's naval policy, moved by Lord George Hamilton—to make a positive declaration; Gladstone did not do so, and did not even reply to Rosebery's letter; Rosebery was as hurt by this slight as much as he was annoyed by the tone of Gladstone's speech, and he refused to speak at a meeting of the National Liberal Federation at Southampton in view of his disagreements with the Prime Minister, who, for his part, was freely using the adjective 'Jingo' in private discussion of the Foreign Secretary.[2] It was decided to postpone a final decision until early in the New Year; this was Gladstone's suggestion, 'but to my astonishment Rosebery and Harcourt argued against it; but happily without effect', his record of the crisis states. 'To refuse it, even to a Prime Minister of 83, would in truth have been hardly decent.'[3]

Rosebery wrote to him on December 28th that 'a single sentence in your Navy Speech of the kind I begged for would have had an incalculable value for peace. But that word was not spoken, and the opportunity is gone.' 'The peace of Europe is less secure today than it was yesterday,' he wrote to Spencer on December 20th. Nevertheless, Rosebery was so confident of the programme passing that he told the Austrian Ambassador on December 28th

---

[1] *Gladstone Papers.*   [2] West: *Diaries*, 230–1.   [3] *Gladstone Papers*

that the increases 'will be such that there can no longer be any
doubt in any quarter that we are determined to maintain our
supremacy at sea undiminished', and that he would have resigned
if another decision had been taken.[1]

As matters proceeded ominously towards the final disintegration of the last Gladstone Cabinet, its senior members turned their
thoughts more and more towards the future. A particularly
arduous session[2] had been devoted to Home Rule and had been
wasted; already it was clear that the Lords, encouraged by public
reactions to their murder of the Home Rule Bill, would act with
greater boldness with other Government measures; there was
mounting impatience—particularly among the Radicals—at the
frustrating effect of Home Rule upon social reform. Labouchere
wrote to Dilke (October 11th, 1893) that 'we are in the hands
of an aged fetish—thinking of nothing but HR, senilely anxious
to retain power, & fancying he can do so by tricking and dodg-
ing everyone'[3]; the Fabians, acutely disappointed with the failure
to implement Newcastle, renounced their faith in the Liberals,
and G. B. Shaw published his celebrated diatribe 'To your
Tents, O Israel!' in the November issue of the *Fortnightly Review*;
the formation of the Independent Labour Party under Keir Hardie
was another manifestation of the disenchantment of English
Radicalism. The only Ministers whose reputations had risen were
Asquith and Rosebery. Harcourt was on the very worst of terms
with Morley and there was hardly a Minister who had not
writhed under the lash of the insensitive, brusque, and over-
bearing Chancellor of the Exchequer. Rosebery, although his
foreign policy was disapproved of by several of his colleagues,
had unquestionably gained considerable stature in the country. In
November he achieved a truly spectacular triumph when he acted
as mediator between the mine-owners and trade unions over the
great coal strike which had paralysed most of the industry for
several months. After six hours of discussion at the Foreign Office,
agreement was reached, and the strike called off; both sides were

---

[1] Temperley and Penson, *Foundations of British Foreign Policy*, 478.

[2] It lasted from January 1893 to March 1894; the Commons sat on 226 days,
which was 90 more than the average for the previous fifteen years. Home Rule had
occupied 82 of these days, and the work of nearly 100 days on Home Rule, Employers' Liability, and Scottish Sea Fisheries Bills was nullified by the action of the
Lords. (H. W. Lucy: *Diary of the Home Rule Parliament*, 315.)

[3] *Dilke Papers.*

warm in their praises of Rosebery's handling of the negotiations. 'Dined alone, very tired,' his Diary for November 17th records. 'But it would have been a good day to die on.'

The Liberals who looked for a leader to replace Gladstone were understandably awed and excited by this brilliant young man who had raised the Chairmanship of the London County Council almost to the level of Ministerial rank, who had received the leader's accolade as 'the man of the future', who had achieved a national reputation as Foreign Secretary, and who now appeared to possess the trust of all elements in the State. Both his past and his prospects were equally glittering, and thus, at this critical moment in the fortunes of the Liberal Party, it was the striking image of 'Citizen Rosebery' which seemed to offer positive and hopeful leadership for a party urgently seeking vital, courageous, and youthful enthusiasm. The hostility of the Prime Minister, the doubts of some Cabinet Ministers, and the shrill abuse of the handful of Radicals at Westminster, were reduced to insignificance as Rosebery was inexorably propelled towards the supreme position in the State.

ROSEBERY OR HARCOURT?

Politics are not a drama where scenes follow one another after a methodical plan, where the actors exchange forms of speech, settled beforehand. Politics are a conflict of which chance seems to be modifying the whole course.

SOREL

THE CABINET MET AT noon on January 9th, 1894. Endeavours made by Morley and other Ministers not personally committed to either side in the Naval Estimates controversy had not succeeded in abating the acute differences of opinion which existed between the Prime Minister and the majority of his colleagues. Gladstone had prepared a long statement of his case, and for fifty minutes he delivered a passionate attack against the proposals. He began with a personal reference whose content may be seen from his notes.

a Silent—and disgraced.
b A survival.
  ¾ of my life, a continuous effort for economy.
  Who could thus break himself in pieces?
c Eyes and ears.
  Warrant ample for going.
  Scanty for staying.[2]

Rosebery's detailed account of this memorable Cabinet, written immediately afterwards, should be recorded.

[1] This account of the events of January–March 1894 is based upon a detailed memorandum prepared by Rosebery which he called 'My narrative of the formation of the Government in 1894 to be used if necessary to correct false statements'; this important document (reproduced as Appendix Three, pp. 498–512) is not dated, but the fact that it is written on Foreign Office paper implies that it was written not long after the events it describes. All references to Rosebery's memorandum, which was published in the December 1951 and January 1952 issues of *History Today*, are marked thus (AR). I am much indebted to Mr Peter Stansky for having most generously permitted me to use copies he made of documents in the Harcourt Papers.

[2] *Gladstone Papers* (Brit. Mus. Add. MSS. 44,648, f. 146).

I entered late. Mr G was speaking standing up at the table (he had not yet taken his seat) speaking about the Queen's wish that Lansdowne should be made a Duke or an extra KG. When this was settled (it was agreed to offer an extra GCB or the next KG) Mr G went and took some water, resumed his seat and made a speech of 50 minutes on Spencer's naval proposals. . . .

[At the end] He then took out his watch & timed himself at 50 minutes & was gratified at having got within the hour.

Spencer followed for 5 or 6 conciliatory minutes. He said that he doubted if the Admy wd take his plan, but that they wd resign at once on seeing Mr G's adopted.[1] *Mr G* entirely disagreed as to this.

Harcourt then came with an amazing discourse. He entirely & fundamentally disapproved the estimates. As for war, nothing would induce him to remain a member of a cabinet that engaged on war. These estimates too had now gone too far. Had the Board been properly controlled at first things need not have come to this pass. But now the plan was inevitable. If we went out the Tories would pass it. And he saw the means of paying for it. He dragged into his discourse analogies & disquisitions from Mr G's budget in 1860, wh Mr G vehemently contradicted. During the latter part of Harcourt's speech Mr G wheeled round on his chair & turned his back to him.

I at length had to ask where we stood. Were we to postpone a decision for a month? This was, I believed, impossible as regarded the estimates. But as to the Govt, how should we stand? Whichever decision was taken the Govt must break up. If it broke up now it would have a few weeks in wh to endeavour to repair itself—otherwise those few weeks would be available only for leakage and the crash would take place just as Parliament met for the next session. I said we must know how we stood.

It was agreed that the estimates shd be provisionally framed on the lines of Spencer's plan.

Trevelyan differed with me. He said that we shd not sacrifice the results of the Session by breaking up now. (What he meant I do not know).

Harcourt supported my contention & drew on himself a scathing outburst from Mr G. 'I can quite understand that you wish to terminate today the little question relating to myself instead of a week or two hence. I merely wish to say that I quite understand this from your point of view, and from that point of view do not complain in

---

[1] Gladstone had proposed that Spencer's provisional Estimates should be reduced by one-half, and that the question of the other half should be postponed. It will be recalled that Spencer's programme was the smaller of the two presented to him by the Board.

the least.' Harcourt took this very calmly & merely said, not unpleasantly, 'I never said anything of the kind.'

Ultimately it was agreed that the cabinet shd discuss among themselves—Mr G saying that he should write to the Queen that the general sense of the Cabinet appeared to be in favour of some increase of the naval estimates. His last words were 'I propose to leave for Biarritz on Saturday morning.'

The Cabinet dispersed at 2.15, and Rosebery drove Morley to 38, Berkeley Square where they were shortly joined by Spencer. They agreed that as the break-up of the Government appeared to be imminent, 'now is the accepted time for our chief's resignation';[1] there is no doubt that this was the view of the majority in the Cabinet, who became, in Morley's phrase, 'this-weekers' rather than 'next-monthers'.

In the afternoon Hamilton saw Rosebery at the Foreign Office. 'He was perturbed & depressed at the outlook. Mr G had apparently carried with him not one of his colleagues, unless it should be Shaw Lefevre.' Shortly after Hamilton left, Harcourt was shown in.

He at once began speaking of Mr Gladstone's declaration and said that he supposed if Mr G carried out his threat that it meant the end of all things, and the disappearance of the Government; did I not think so? I replied that I was entirely of a different opinion. I never could dismiss from my mind the deplorable figure cut by Mr Pitt's Government on Mr Pitt's death: that our breaking up on Mr Gladstone's resignation would be so much the worse that it would be proved that the Liberal Party would have to declare itself unable even for a moment to carry on the Government after the resignation of a statesman in his eighty-fifth year; and that sooner than stomach such a humiliation I would serve in a Government headed by Sir Ughtred Kay-Shuttleworth[2] (the first name of a subordinate Minister that came into my head) or anyone else. I admitted that we could not in any case go on for long, but insisted that we should not commit political suicide.

He seemed much taken aback by this declaration, and soon afterwards retired. (AR)

Rosebery subsequently came to the conclusion that Harcourt had realised that he could not command sufficient support among

[1] Morley: *Recollections*, II, 2, states that Asquith was also present at this meeting, but there is no reference to him in Rosebery's Diary.

[2] 1844–1939. Later first Lord Shuttleworth. Secretary to the Admiralty, 1892–5; Under-Secretary to the India Office and Chancellor of the Duchy of Lancaster in the 1886 Government.

his colleagues to form a Government and had thought 'that he
would find me quite willing to fall in with his views of collapse'
(AR). This interpretation was shared by Edward Hamilton, who
saw a great deal of Harcourt, and who wrote in his Diary as early
as January 5th that 'Harcourt's being so terribly exercised in his
mind is, I expect (and no wonder), due to the difficulties which he
may foresee about himself. It is pretty well certain that his colleagues would not consent to have him even as Leader in the
House of Commons: he is probably conscious to some extent
of this, and accordingly sees that his only chance of remaining in
Downing Street, to which he is much attached, is to induce Mr G
to remain next door.' On the following morning (Wednesday,
January 10th) Harcourt remarked to Hamilton that 'it is all very
well for younger men like Rosebery and Asquith to say we shall
be able to carry on. I am an older Parliamentary hand and know
better.'

On the same day Rosebery saw Gladstone at the House of
Commons, and, as he noted in his diary, 'had a very curious
interview'. 'He spoke with much eloquence and exaltation of his
position. "The dead are with me though, it seems, not the living
—Peel, Cobden, Bright, Aberdeen, etc." On this day, however,
the acuteness of the crisis seemed to be diminished.' (AR)

The difficult and embarrassing task of telling Mrs Gladstone of
the situation had been entrusted to John Morley, and on January
9th, after dinner at Downing Street, he accomplished it, while
Gladstone and Armitstead played backgammon in front of the
fire.

It was as painful as any talk could be. However, I had no choice. I
told her that the reign was over, and that the only question was
whether the abdication should be now or in February. The poor lady
was not in the least prepared for the actual stroke. . . . What a curious
scene! Me breaking to her that the pride and glory of her life was at
last to face eclipse, that the curtain was falling on a grand drama of
fame, power, acclamation; the rattle of the dice on the backgammon
board, and the laughter and chucklings of the two long-lived players,
sounding a strange running refrain.[1]

Rosebery had made no impression upon Gladstone in his talk
with him. 'I might as well have addressed my arguments to your
hat,' he told West. 'If I had told him that we were all to be

[1] Morley: *Recollections*, II, 5–6.

stricken with leprosy, he would not have cared.'[1] But after they had recovered from the initial shock, few of the leading members of the Cabinet could bring themselves to believe that Gladstone would carry out his resolve. On January 11th Rosebery noted in his diary, 'Long walk with Asquith. The crisis apparently over.' Gladstone entered upon business as if nothing had happened, and in the morning he saw Edward Marjoribanks, who repaired to the Treasury, where he found Harcourt with Hamilton, who recorded the following conversation.

He (E. M.) had been commissioned to put two questions to Mr G. Might the Navy Estimates be prepared on the Spencer line, which Mr G's colleagues had accepted? Might they, during his absence, meet in Cabinet? He said 'Yes' to the first query; but 'No' to the second, unless they first obtained his leave. Harcourt took the 'No' to imply some wavering on the part of Mr G; for if Mr G really intends going why should not the rest of the Cabinet meet to discuss the programme of next Session? On the strength of this ray of light, and the report of a talk which Algy West had with Mr G this morning, together with the fact that Mr G had been asking for further information about the Admiralty proposals, Harcourt took a more cheerful view of the position of affairs.

Rosebery—to whom Hamilton immediately reported—agreed with Harcourt's estimate of the situation. 'There was something decidedly comic and ludicrous about the explosion of this tremendous bomb unnecessarily,' Hamilton records Rosebery as saying to him. 'His sense of humour, he said, was too strong to prevent his laughing. Mr G, he believed, would stay on after all, & it was undoubtedly best from a party point of view.' On the same evening Hamilton dined with the Marjoribanks, and found Morley and Spencer optimistic about Gladstone's intentions, although Morley confided to Hamilton that he was slightly shocked by Gladstone's inconsistency. 'You were right from the first,' he added; 'Mr G ought never to have taken office at all.'

This optimism was not shared by West or Hamilton, but at this stage they could not convince any Ministers of the reality of Gladstone's resolution. Gladstone—'very glum & (for him) very silent'—sat next to Hamilton at another dinner at the Marjoribanks on Friday evening (January 12th), and gave no hint of yielding an inch. West found Morley 'miserable at the shattering

[1] West: *Diaries*, 237.

of his idol, being convinced (wrongly) that Mr Gladstone's attitude was all acting, and that his anguish was for nothing'.[1] Even at this early stage Morley was playing a careful game. He gave Gladstone the impression that he was numbered among his supporters while being the most outspoken of the 'this-weekers' in conversation with his colleagues. Thus, on January 25th he wrote to Gladstone, 'So far as I can observe, the tide is setting as strongly as ever, or even more strongly than before, in the *wrong* direction. I cannot discover in the process a single good indication the other way. There is not likely therefore to be much prospect of anything like a swing round among our friends.' From his daughter Mary, Gladstone discovered that Morley had deceived him. 'My daughter tells me you told her my decision was wrong,' he wrote curtly to Morley on January 29th. 'I told her you had not told me.' Morley, in a somewhat uncomfortable letter on February 2nd, tried to explain that he agreed entirely with Gladstone about the disastrous long-term dangers of the naval programme but that he was even more alarmed by 'the dire, certain and immediate mischief' which would ensue if Gladstone resigned on the issue of the Estimates and publicly stated the cause of his departure.

On Saturday, January 13th, the Gladstones departed for Biarritz, the Prime Minister delivering a Parthian shot by informing Marjoribanks that there was no purpose in him coming, as he would not be talked round. When the additional complication of Easter being early that year was brought to the Prime Minister's attention (the Estimates having to be decided before that time), he merely cited the precedent of 1874, when Parliament met in the second week in March and got through essential financial business by the end of the month.

On the morrow of the inopportune flight to Biarritz, Ministers pondered the situation with some seriousness. The possibility of Gladstone's retirement had been a feature of the Liberal Party for so long that it seemed incredible that it should occur and in such a manner, but it was obvious that there must be a decision within a few weeks. Rosebery's cynical amusement at the spectacle was merited. With under a month to go before the return of Parliament, the Queen's Government was bereft of its principal measure, its naval estimates, and its leader; it could not hold

[1] West: *Diaries*, 242.

meetings until Gladstone returned to England at some unspecified date; in brief, it had no notion whether it was to be permitted to continue in existence at all, and, if it were, who was to
lead it.

If Gladstone resigned—and at this stage it was a very big 'If'
in the minds of his colleagues—who was to succeed? Rosebery
and Harcourt were the only two serious contenders, and Harcourt
had succeeded in making himself so objectionable that even those
Ministers who did not wholly trust Rosebery—such as Morley—
supported him because they disliked Harcourt even more. But the
barrier of the Peerage was not one which could be lightly dismissed.

Any possibility there may have been of a peaceful development
of the argument over the succession was bedevilled by the
intrigues of Harcourt's charming, popular, but unscrupulous son,
Loulou. Having set his heart upon his father becoming Prime
Minister, Loulou began the task of undermining Rosebery's
position with a cold ruthlessness which was to poison the Liberal
Party for the next decade. 'Few men have appealed less to the
gallery than Mr Harcourt,' A. G. Gardiner wrote of Loulou in
later years. 'He does not scan far horizons. He does not declare
any vision of a promised land. He has no passionate fervour for
humanity, and is too honest to pretend to any. He is a practical
politician, with no dithyrambs. He loves the intricacies of the
campaign more than the visionary gleam, the actual more than the
potential, present facts more than future fancies. He is the man
without a dream.'[1] Loulou's only dreams concerned his father,
whom he adored, but he was fully aware of the acute difficulties
facing Sir William. Morley was alienated; Asquith and most of the
younger Ministers were Rosebery men; Marjoribanks at this
stage regarded Harcourt as an impossible leader of the party,[2]
while it was obvious that the Queen would place every conceivable obstruction in Harcourt's path. Loulou told Brett frankly
on January 14th that he had 'worked for ten years at wire-
pulling, and now he must reap the fruit'.[3]

Another difficulty which Loulou had to surmount was the lack

[1] *Prophets, Priests, and Kings.*

[2] *Edward Hamilton's Diary,* January 14th. Marjoribanks subsequently told Rosebery that he believed that the party and the Cabinet would have followed Harcourt
if he had succeeded Gladstone.

[3] Brett: *Journals and Letters,* I, 181.

of resolution shown by his father. 'He has hardly any ambition,' Loulou wrote in his Journal at the beginning of January. 'I have a double dose for him'; on January 4th he wrote, 'I wrote to W. V. H. today . . . that if Gladstone goes the Queen will send for Rosebery, who must refuse to form a Government, but that if he attempts it W. V. H. must refuse to serve *under* him.'[1] His father's early attitude lacked this Corinthian resolution. 'In any case, he said, the Government would not last long, and it might as well go to pieces under Lord Rosebery as under himself.'[2]

It is important to realise that, during the complicated man-oeuvres of the next few weeks, it was Loulou and not Sir William who made all the running. This was a fact which Rosebery himself later acknowledged by saying again and again that he would be very happy to restore friendly relations with Harcourt 'were it not for Loulou'.

Loulou correctly judged that the most important single member of the Cabinet apart from the two contestants was John Morley, and on January 10th—the day after Gladstone's announcement to the Cabinet—he called on Morley, who remarked in conversation that 'Rosebery keeps as mum as possible, as *the* (and then correcting himself) or one of the possible successors'. 'I did not like this indication of a change in J. Morley's opinions and pledge given to me at Malwood four years ago, that he would support W. V. H. to the last as against Rosebery as Mr G's successor,' Loulou recorded in his Journal.[3] On the next day they met again at the House of Commons.

. . . J. Morley added: 'The future is very dark and, my dear Loulou, it is a great pity that the Malwood compact has been broken up, and broken not by my act or desire.' All this was said with great emphasis, and I knew what he meant, but did not desire to pursue it then.[4]

On January 12th Loulou again reproached Morley for changing his mind, and Morley retorted that the events of the past eighteen months, starting with the 'Brook Street Conferences', had forced him to the conclusion that he could not work under Harcourt, and added, 'possibly not even with him.' 'I said he might at least have informed me sooner that his "compact" with

[1] Lewis Harcourt's unpublished Journal, January 4th and 10th.
[2] *Ibid.*   [3] *Ibid.* (Quoted in Gardiner: *Harcourt*, II, 263.)
[4] Lewis Harcourt's unpublished Journal, January 11th.

me at Malwood was broken,' Loulou recorded, 'but that I accepted the fact. . . . I told J. M. that I had given up the ten best years of my life and other things beside in the hope of making W. V. H. Prime Minister, and I should not give in without a fight, and that I meant W. V. H. to be first or out of it altogether.'[1]

Morley was playing a very much more complicated game than Loulou—or anyone else at the time—realised. Although it is not possible to state definitely what his purpose was in deliberately misleading both sides in the crisis, it is reasonable to deduce that he was intent upon using his important independent position to its maximum advantage. Morley was ambitious, and already some of those most closely concerned in the crisis were entertaining suspicions about these ambitions; 'There is an idea that the "other office" to which J. Morley aspires is the Foreign Office', Hamilton noted on January 14th; '—an idea scarcely credible.' The events of the following week were to reveal how justified these suspicions were. But by the middle of January Morley had misled Gladstone over his views on the Naval Estimates crisis, had told Loulou that he could not serve under Harcourt, and told Asquith that he would serve under neither Harcourt nor Rosebery.[2]

What was Rosebery's attitude to the to-ing and fro-ings that now gripped the Liberal hierarchy? He himself has described his position in his account of the crisis.

Some of the Ministers were in constant communication with me— notably Asquith, John Morley, Acland and Spencer. . . . But I myself was passive, for I was engrossed by the business of my great depart- ment. I had indeed during this Government become purely a depart- mental Minister—content to hold aloof provided I were left alone in my special work. And, provided this condition were observed, I did not trouble myself greatly about the future. In the first place I did not believe that Mr Gladstone would resign at this time, and on this question; and, secondly, if he did, I was convinced that Harcourt would try and make any Government of which he was the chief pleasant to his colleagues and successful. My invariable language was 'Harcourt will try and make his own Government a success, but he will take care that no one else's is.' And I was prepared to serve under him, or indeed under anybody who would prevent the Government from falling to pieces on Mr Gladstone's retirement.

[1] L. Harcourt's unpublished Journal, January 12th.
[2] West: *Diaries*, 242.

But I can say this of no other Minister. I now think it quite possible that had my colleagues been placed between the devil and the deep blue sea, that is, had they been placed in the position of choosing between Harcourt and their extinction, they would have submitted to Harcourt. But I did not think so then, for their language was violent in a contrary sense, as used or reported to me. John Morley indeed, who was the most vehement, declared that nothing would induce him to serve under Harcourt as Leader of the House of Commons—much less Prime Minister. It was not till Feb 13 that I noted a tendency in him to yield this point. But Asquith, Acland and Spencer were equally firm to me as to the impossibility of Harcourt being Prime Minister. For some reason or another he had offended all, and made all shrink from the idea of his being placed in authority over them. (AR)

The possibility of a third member of the Cabinet being chosen as leader was, surprisingly enough, not seriously considered.[1] Loulou saw Brett on January 14th, who, according to Loulou, reported that Rosebery 'was much more determined to be Prime Minister after Gladstone than he had ever seemed to be before', and they agreed that 'the creation of a second Lord Liverpool in the person of Spencer or Kimberley would be absurd, and that if it came to W. V. H. serving under anyone it would be better a man of Rosebery's parts'.[2] Loulou saw Rosebery—who makes no reference to the fact in his account—on the 15th, and urged him to make concessions on the Estimates, but, according to Loulou, Rosebery was evasive. Loulou met Hamilton after leaving Rosebery, and told him that he was just going to Althorp to sound Spencer, and implied that his father would either be Prime Minister or out of the Government by Budget Day. Hamilton, when he saw Rosebery, found him 'still very sceptical about Mr G's present intentions', and quite prepared to serve under Harcourt if he was allowed complete freedom at the Foreign Office.

Loulou's visit to Spencer was a very bold stroke, since he told Spencer that he was authorised by Rosebery to say that he would agree to reductions in the Estimates 'to make Gladstone's course easier. . . . I told him bluntly that it was impossible for W. V. H. to serve under Rosebery; that I should do all I could to prevent it, even if W. V. H. wavered on the subject. . . . I also told him

[1] Hamilton considered that a Kimberley leadership would be the only way of keeping the Cabinet together, and urged this course—without effect—on Ponsonby on February 25th. (Sir F. Ponsonby: *Side-Lights on Queen Victoria*, 387–9.)

[2] L. Harcourt's unpublished Journal, January 14th.

John Morley was contemplating not being in the next Government, which was a shock to him.'[1] Loulou's attempt to stampede Spencer into accepting Gladstone's bisection of his Estimates and thereby to avert the succession crisis reveals the extent of the blow he had received by Morley's abrogation of the Malwood Compact. But Rosebery, who must have had a shrewd idea of what Loulou was up to, wrote to Spencer on the same day to say that the best way of averting a crisis was to remain 'absolutely quiescent until the return from Biarritz—proceeding with the estimates as framed by you'. This effectively killed Loulou's ingenious plan, and, as Mr Peter Stansky comments, 'On the surface Rosebery might affect a lordly calm, pacify Loulou by claiming not to believe in the crisis, and tell others that he did not wish to move from the Foreign Office, but by urging Spencer to stick to his plan he was in fact creating, whether deliberately or not, a most favourable position for his own appointment as Prime Minister.'[2]

It seems unlikely that it was a deliberate step towards the leadership, but it was clearly vitally important to the Foreign Secretary that the naval programme should not be emasculated even further for the convenience of the Prime Minister. But his own account of the crisis is disingenuous. 'As I have stated', he writes, 'I was immersed in my department. I took occasional "constitutionals" with Asquith or John Morley, and other Ministers dropped into luncheon, and thus I was kept informed. Otherwise I should have known little or nothing.' (AR) In fact he kept a close watch on events, and used Hamilton in particular as an informant. 'Should you learn anything that is important I should know, or should you be able to give me any interesting history,' he wrote to Hamilton (January 8th), 'pray communicate it.' But although he knew that he was in a very strong position if Gladstone did retire, all the evidence confirms that he remained sceptical of this possibility until a late stage. There was no need to make plans or rally adherents, so none were made and no offers of future preferment were whispered.

'The news that reached us from Biarritz was conflicting,' Rosebery recorded. 'Armitstead wrote that Mr Gladstone was un-

---

[1] L. Harcourt's unpublished Journal, January 15th.
[2] *The Leadership of the Liberal Party, 1894–9* (unpublished Harvard University thesis, 1961), 96.

moved. Mrs Drew wrote that there was more hope and some chance of a reprieve.' (AR) West arrived at Biarritz on January 19th, and found Gladstone 'very silent', while Acton, who had been staying for a few days, reported that Gladstone had come to 'the absolute conclusion' that he must resign. 'He was loud, unreasoning, inurbane, in proclaiming his old fixity, and he spoke to me at first as if his colleagues were divided,' Acton sadly wrote to Bryce. 'He had a list 1. of those against him, 2. of those with him, and 3. of those who were not committed.'[1] An examination of these lists reveals how far the old man deluded himself about the situation; he thought that Arnold Morley, John Morley, Shaw-Lefevre, Trevelyan, Fowler, Bryce, and Mundella supported him, and he even indicated that Harcourt, Ripon, and Campbell-Bannerman might help.[2] 'Generally', Acton reported to Bryce, 'he was wild, violent, inaccurate, sophistical, evidently governed by resentment. Now and then, for a moment, he collected himself, and was full of force—but never full of light or able to see any argument but his own.' When West told him that he had brought 'many prayers and entreaties' from his colleagues, Gladstone exploded, 'What is the good of prayers! I have had hours of conversation with J. Morley and Acton, and they have not produced a single point or reason to alter my decision.' He was taking his stand against militarism, and Ripon, Asquith, and Acland were undecided on the matter; 'He fancied that John Morley was with him, but at this interview he was so occupied and angry that I hardly knew what he thought.'[3] Gladstone also told West that he was immovable on the Estimates—'You might as well try to blow up the rock of Gibraltar'—and West decided that he should return to London to inform the Cabinet of this obduracy. Gladstone, having seized upon what he regarded as a mighty issue of principle, had become almost incoherent in his animosity towards the Spencer programme; in one of his personal memoranda written after his resignation he took the view that his attitude bore signs of 'Providential ordination'.

West's report—made on the 23rd—merely irritated the Cabinet, and Rosebery—who was laid up with a strained ligament—told Hamilton on the 25th that the situation was evidently very

---

[1] *Bryce Papers.*
[2] *Gladstone Papers* (Brit. Mus. Add. MSS. 44,776, f. 39).
[3] West: *Diaries*, 251.

serious and that Palmerston's prophecy that Gladstone would destroy the Liberal Party and die in a lunatic asylum looked as though it might be fulfilled.

Loulou was still obstinately advocating a 'neck or nothing' policy on his father, but with little success; in a long conversation on the evening of January 26th Harcourt—'to my disgust'—told his son that he would serve under Rosebery 'for the sake of the Party'.

I tried to convince him that it would be an impossible position; that he would lose rather than gain respect in the House of Commons by doing it. He only said in reply that the next Government is sure to go to pieces quickly, that he would just as soon it did so in Rosebery's hands as his own; and that he would not have it said of him by the Party that he had prevented or made difficult the formation of a new Government by standing aside on a personal question. He also said 'It is always better that people should ask why you are *not* in a particular place than ask why you are in it.'[1]

West returned to Biarritz, but Acton was now in London and the reports of Gladstone's wild language spread among the members of the Cabinet. Rosebery told Hamilton on the 29th that he still could not believe that Gladstone would retire; he also expressed distaste at the idea of having to give up the Foreign Office for the Premiership, since 'it would be like taking a good ploughman and promoting him to the place of head gardener'.

On the next day the great secret, which had been wonderfully kept, was out, broadcast in the midday editions of the *Pall Mall Gazette*. Although the announcement caused a considerable sensation, the paragraph in the paper merely mentioned that Gladstone would retire at the end of the Session on grounds of health and family reasons; there was no reference to the crisis over the Naval Estimates, which allayed fears that there had been a Cabinet leak.[2] But appeals to Biarritz for an official disclaimer of the story only evoked what Hamilton called 'a thoroughly *Gladstonese*

[1] L. Harcourt's unpublished Journal, January 26th.
[2] Hamilton wrote in his diary on January 21st that 'Mr G's Cabinets have been able to keep their own counsel ever since Chamberlain & Dilke ceased to be colleagues'. Hamilton also stated (March 9th) that the information, which was nothing more than an inspired guess, had been offered to The Times and the Daily Telegraph, who had refused to credit it. There is no evidence to corroborate the opinion of A. J. Marder (*Anatomy of British Sea Power*, 203) that the story was deliberately circulated by unspecified members of the Cabinet to assess reactions.

denial' which increased the public speculation. His colleagues, whose impatience with their leader was becoming very pronounced, thought the old man was deliberately tantalising them, 'vacillating and playing a game,' as Rosebery sadly described it to Hamilton on February 1st, and were probably not much wrong. 'What isolation!' West (again at Biarritz) remarked in his Diary. 'Not a word from any colleague!!!'[1]

On Monday, February 5th, there came a new development. Gladstone asked Welby for information about dissolutions, particularly about the earliest date on which the Committee of Supply could be set up in a new Parliament. This request was regarded as having sinister overtones, and on the same evening West left Biarritz for London with a letter from Gladstone to Marjoribanks urging an immediate dissolution on the issue of the House of Lords, who had spent a profitable fortnight mutilating the Employers' Liability Bill and the Parish Councils Bill. Rosebery had told Hamilton a few days earlier that he suspected 'that a *volte face* is imminent, and we think that the ground on which it will be put is the action of the House of Lords'.

The Cabinet rejected the proposal out of hand, Harcourt describing it as 'absolutely insane' and Marjoribanks as 'preposterous'. 'Colleagues in town, namely all the Peers, Asquith, Fowler, and A. Morley strongly against proposal to dissolve,' Kimberley telegraphed to Biarritz. 'The break-up of 1874 and 1886 will pale before the smash now,' Rosebery told West, while Harcourt told the ubiquitous Hamilton—at Malwood to discuss Budget matters—that Gladstone's proposal 'is the act of a selfish lunatic'. Subsequent events have made the idea appear rather less absurd than it seemed to his colleagues, and Gladstone frequently lamented the failure to take what he always regarded as a priceless opportunity. But the suddenness of the proposal irritated the Cabinet, many Liberals did not relish the prospect of fighting another election on the issue of the Lords' rejection of Home Rule, and the party managers were decisively opposed to a 'snap' election on an unprepared party. But the fundamental reason for the curt rejection of the proposal was the fact that Gladstone had forfeited the confidence and even the respect of the majority of his colleagues; this disillusionment is the dominant feature of the private correspondence of Ministers at this time, and it was

---

[1] West: *Diaries*, 267.

decisive. West, furthermore, can hardly have been an enthusiastic emissary, since he wrote mournfully to Bryce on February 8th that 'Things have got blacker & blacker every day, & I am broken hearted; a sudden idea came into Mr G's head that the difficulties might be got over by a sudden dissolution & he charged me to find out the views of his colleagues on the point.'[1]

On February 11th Loulou Harcourt, clearly seeing that his father's hopes of the succession were rapidly dwindling, made un-authorised but tempting offers to John Morley. Rosebery—whose informant was almost certainly Morley—records the event as follows:

He offered him, in fact, all the Kingdoms of the World if——. If his father became Prime Minister he would give J. Morley the Ex-chequer and the emissary sketched two alternative Budgets either of which J. Morley could master in a few days. The next proposal was more insidious. If, on the other hand, Sir W. H. did not become Prime Minister, he would preserve a benevolent neutrality (out of office, presumably), *provided J. Morley became Prime Minister*. Sir William, of course, knew that I could never give the Foreign Office to J. Morley for more reasons than one, and so by the suggestion he hoped to create a soreness, and in fact did so. He thus, too, probably gave the first idea of the Foreign Office to J. Morley, an idea which germinated. (AR)

Rosebery's account, although correct in its main features, makes the natural mistake of assuming that Loulou was his father's representative, whereas he was working entirely inde-pendently of Sir William. His account needs amplification, for there were two meetings between Loulou and Morley on Febru-ary 11th. It was after the first one—in the morning—that Loulou met Marjoribanks and asked him if he thought Morley coveted the Foreign Office; this suspicion had been germinating in Loulou's mind for several days, and was confirmed by Marjoribanks. At the afternoon meeting, Loulou said that it had always been his father's intention that Morley should go to the Foreign Office, and, before he left, casually mentioned the alternative of the Exchequer.

I told J. M. he would do the Exchequer very well and that if W. V. H. were Prime Minister he could have the offer of it. . . . J. M. was rather pleased at the idea and would like to be Chancellor of the Exchequer.

When Morley expressed doubts at being able to work with Harcourt, Loulou assured him that there would be no difficulties

[1] *Bryce Papers.*

on that score.[1] Thus Morley, by nature slightly more vain than most politicians, had both the Foreign Office and the Exchequer dangled before him by Loulou, and naturally assumed that the offer stemmed from the father. As he had received no offers of any kind from Rosebery, it is not to be wondered that he began to waver.

Loulou returned to Brook Street well content with his day's work, only to discover to his consternation that his father was still opposed to the 'neck or nothing' policy. Loulou had clearly underrated his father's enjoyment of office, and, in particular, his enthusiasm for his draft Budget, already in an advanced stage of preparation, which included a drastic and revolutionary scheme of death duties. Loulou was obliged to accept the disagreeable fact that in the event of Rosebery being summoned by the Queen on Gladstone's retirement his father would continue at the Exchequer. The evening was spent by the Harcourts in drawing up a list of assurances to be demanded from Rosebery in this eventuality, which could be made public if Rosebery rejected them. These 'conditions' were extremely drastic. Harcourt was to be 'free to act and speak on all questions as they arise with perfect independence and without the necessity of any previous consultation with the PM', he should be consulted on all questions of Foreign Policy before any decisions were taken, he should approve all Government appointments, and should possess an equal right with the Prime Minister as to the recommendations for and distribution of Honours.[2] These terms were not prepared as the basis for a working arrangement between the Leader of the Commons and a Peer Premier, but to give the Harcourts the reality of victory out of their defeat. It is often said that these conditions were not unreasonable, but to present them in the form of an ultimatum and to have them formally agreed by both parties was unusual and unfair.[3] This is a strange interpretation, for Harcourt was in effect demanding that whereas he, as the second Minister, should have complete freedom of action and expression on all questions as they arose without even consulting the Prime Minister, the Prime Minister would have to receive the benediction of the Leader of the House of Commons before

[1] L. Harcourt's unpublished Journal, February 11th.
[2] *Ibid.*
[3] See, for example, W. S. Churchill, *Great Contemporaries*, 24.

announcing any policy or even recommending Ministers to the Queen. If accepted, the conditions would have made Harcourt Prime Minister in all but name; if rejected, they were to be published to the House of Commons to reveal Harcourt's solicitude for the rights of that assembly to have a dominant voice in the affairs of the nation.

Meanwhile, Mr Gladstone, still inwardly fuming against his colleagues, had returned to Downing Street, and the Cabinet met on February 12th in a somewhat strained atmosphere. For an hour they solemnly discussed the Lords' amendments to the Parish Councils and Employers' Liability Bills (the latter being abandoned on February 20th), and Gladstone announced that there would be a Cabinet dinner on Saturday, February 17th. About the future of his Government and his own intentions the Prime Minister said not a word. The situation was intolerable, and the temper of Ministers deteriorated with every day that passed. On February 13th Rosebery walked with John Morley, and had a disagreeable surprise.

Whether from the emollient efforts of the son or perhaps from a feeling of difficulty as to making his position intelligible to the public, he this day began to waver as to vetoing Harcourt's leadership of the House of Commons. (AR)

Morley was also extremely upset by an incident which had occurred on the previous day, but which he had merited. 'All my vexations at the frantic embarrassments in which we are plunged', he wrote to Rosebery, 'seemed to melt away tonight when I helped the old man into his greatcoat, and saw him painfully trudge off alone, refusing my escort.' In later years Rosebery dictated a private memoir of John Morley; much of it consists of incidents referred to elsewhere, but one comment on his ambition to become Foreign Secretary is worth inserting at this point.

John Morley was a very lovable man, but very difficult to understand. . . . He wanted, I believe, to succeed me as Foreign Secretary—an impossible appointment, partly because his wife could not have received the Ambassadors' wives, she having a slight cloud on her, John having anticipated the ceremony of marriage. . . . But I truly loved him, and we got on very well together.

Morley is a tragic figure. It would be easy to mock his painfully obvious and invariably unsuccessful gyrations in the succession crisis, and it is true that he cut a pathetic figure, earning neither the fear nor respect of either side. Like so many extremely intelligent men, he was incapable of self-analysis, and undoubtedly seriously overrated himself. 'To see where he fell short as a judge of men you have only to turn to the two volumes of his *Recollections*,' Haldane has written on Morley. 'There you find how he wished to rule and how he had not it in him to rule, at least to the extent he desired.'[1] He was undoubtedly jealous of Rosebery's effortless advance to the highest offices and of his advantages of wealth and position to which Morley had not been born. As has already been noted, he was particularly jealous of Rosebery's success as an author; as he remarked to Loulou at this time, 'Rosebery is a peer, with great wealth, an air of mystery, an affectation of literature, and is probably going to win the Derby.'[2] His relationship with Rosebery was a strange combination of great personal affection, warm admiration, jealousy, and suspicion, and his bewildering inconstancy made him a difficult political colleague upon whose loyalty and constancy it was impossible to rely.

After the Cabinet of February 12th matters continued to remain in suspense for several days. On February 17th the Cabinet dinner was held at 10, Downing Street. West asked Gladstone if he intended to announce his resignation to his colleagues, but Gladstone replied that he was not, as they knew of it already. When West suggested that Ponsonby should be warned, Gladstone said that the following week would be soon enough. ' "For, before that", he said, "we shall know what the Lords will do, and they may alter things, for in the case of a dissolution I should go to the country with them." '[3] If West recorded this remark correctly, Gladstone was still clinging to his hope of forcing a dissolution and appealing to the country on the cry of 'the Peers against the People'. Certainly he made no hint of retirement at the dinner, whose first surprise was that oysters and cold entrées—both of which Gladstone was known to detest—were served. When Rosebery, who was sitting at the Prime Minister's left hand, remarked lightly that it was obvious that he had not chosen the dinner, Gladstone merely replied that the oysters had been sent by an admirer. 'We ate our dinners expectantly,' Morley has written;

[1] Haldane: *Autobiography*, 99.   [2] Gardiner: *Harcourt*, II, 269.
[3] West: *Diaries*, 278

the coffee found the oracle dumb; and in good time a crestfallen flock departed.'[1]

After dinner, [*Rosebery's account records*] as it was a Cabinet dinner and as the world was all agog with curiosity, I said to my host that if any secret matters were going to be discussed we ought to look to the doors. 'Certainly,' said Mr Gladstone with great composure, 'if any-one has any topic to raise it should be done now.' This was all that passed and made a deservedly popular story. But though the position had its humorous, it also had its tragic side, as the Cabinet were left in absolute ignorance of what was going to happen—whether they were to live or whether their thin-spun life was to be slit by the resignation of the Prime Minister. Never since Lord Chatham's premiership was a Government so absurdly or unpleasantly situated in relation to its head. Mr Gladstone was, I imagine, angry with us for not 'rallying' (to use his own expression) to his views on the Navy, and so kept us at arm's length. I am sure he did not intend to embarrass us by keeping his intentions a secret; he was only in a condition of righteous wrath; but the result was the same. (AR)

Ministers, as they donned their great-coats and made their farewells to their host, were extremely angry. 'Gladstone made fools of us,' Kimberley remarked with uncharacteristic acerbity to West;[2] 'J. Morley asked W. V. H. what he thought of the affair,' Loulou noted. 'W. V. H. replied, "I feel as I did at the Home Office when a high sheriff told me he had three times tried to hang a man and failed, and I had to go down to the H of C and say that the man deserved to be hanged, but I had reprieved him".'[3]

On February 20th Kimberley told Rosebery that if he were summoned by the Queen he would advise her to send for Rose-bery, and on the same evening Harcourt told Morley of the 'conditions' which he and Loulou had prepared on the 11th, but omitting the one about patronage. Loulou came round himself to Morley's house early the next morning to add this condition and to dangle the Exchequer once again; 'Morley made various *façons* about not being up to the work of the Exchequer, but I could see that he was really pleased and relieved at what I said,' Loulou recorded.[4] Loulou had been surprised when he had heard of his father's conversation with Morley, since it implied an

---

[1] Morley: *Recollections*, II, 9.   [2] West: *Diaries*, 279.
[3] Gardiner: *Harcourt*, II, 262.
[4] L. Harcourt's unpublished Journal, February 21st.

acceptance of Rosebery's succession, and his early visit to Morley was to try and remove this impression. Harcourt himself was extremely cheerful on the 21st, telling Hamilton that he and Morley were 'fast friends again' and that everyone in the Cabinet, particularly himself, was prepared to waive all personal claims and feelings for the common good.

Morley hastened to inform Asquith, Rosebery, and Spencer of Harcourt's conditions. Although Rosebery makes no reference to his reactions in his account, Spencer told Loulou that Rosebery had said that if he accepted the terms he would merely be 'a dummy Prime Minister',[1] and Asquith records 'Rosebery strongly averse to serving "over" Harcourt'.[2]

The implication of Harcourt's terms were clear enough. 'If Rosebery can, and does, accept these conditions', Loulou wrote in his Journal on February 22nd, 'he will have put himself in a humiliating position and struck the greatest blow at the House of Lords which it has ever received. On the other hand, if the re-construction of the Government were to fail or were to proceed with W. V. H. remaining outside, and he was to read this paper in the H of C as the explanation of what had happened, there is not a man in our party in the H of C, and I suspect very few in the country, who would not support him in it.'[3] Rosebery was so indignant and contemptuous that he told Hamilton on the 21st that he 'would decline point-blank to accept the Premiership on such terms, however much he might be pressed by his colleagues to form a Government'. On the afternoon of the next day there was a strange development: Hamilton was in his room at the Treasury when Harcourt stalked in and said 'I wish you to under-stand that what I have said to you does not apply to Rosebery. Nothing would induce me ever to serve under him.' In his account Rosebery states that this message was delivered imme-diately, but Hamilton's diary reveals that it was not wrung out of Hamilton until the following Sunday (February 25th).

On February 23rd Mr Gladstone summoned another Cabinet meeting. It discussed the Queen's Speech which would close the Session, and as the meeting was breaking up Gladstone at last broke his silence on the subject of his imminent retirement, which, to his colleagues' relief, would be on grounds of his health. The

[1] *Ibid.*   [2] Spencer and Asquith: *Asquith*, I, 89.
[3] L. Harcourt's unpublished Journal, February 22nd.

accounts of this episode vary considerably. Rosebery wrote that 'Mr Gladstone said a few vague words as to the time when his co-operation with the Cabinet would cease, but they were so vague that they produced no impression, and no one said anything in reference to them'. (AR) Morley, on the other hand, has written that 'the words fell like ice on men's hearts, there was an instant's hush, and we broke up in funereal groups'.[1]

After the meeting Loulou Harcourt saw Spencer, and sought a statement of his action should he be summoned by the Queen; Spencer said that in that event he would advise her to send for Rosebery. Loulou said that Morley was now in favour of Harcourt, and that the animosity against his father among his Cabinet colleagues seemed to be abating. 'Spencer said rather slowly, and, I thought, regretfully, that he believed this to be the case.' Spencer did not appear to be greatly disturbed by Loulou's observations, and the shrewd intriguer realised that the game was all but lost.[2]

'The next day' (Saturday, February 24th), Rosebery's memorandum continues, 'was a day of small calamities to me.' He had been invited to Sandringham by the Prince of Wales, and planned a few hours at Newmarket. His account of the vicissitudes of his journey in his Diary is even better than that in the memorandum.

Arrived at Liverpool St 11.1. Train gone, boxes with it. Messenger wringing his hands. Started in special in pursuit. Arrived Newmarket. *Ladas*[3] slightly amiss; could not gallop. On the heath when only squall of day, & pressing personal telegram from Queen to ask me to Windsor tonight. Telegraphed to Sandringham for luggage to return, to FO to stop messenger & retreated to London. Arrived 6.30. Every stitch gone to Sandringham. Telegraphed to Windsor that I was coming naked but not ashamed by 7.15. Ultimately rigged myself out. Arrived Windsor. Telegram from P of W to beg me to come tomorrow for the night. This the last straw. Refused point blank. After all this, the Queen had nothing to say!

Rosebery, of course, had assumed that Gladstone had informed the Queen of his decision to retire and wanted to see him, but in fact the Prime Minister had rather mysteriously asked the Queen (through Ponsonby) if she could keep a secret on a highly

---

[1] Morley: *Recollections*, II, 9.
[2] L. Harcourt's unpublished Journal, February 23rd.
[3] *Ladas II* was Rosebery's Derby favourite.

confidential piece of political information; she had replied that she must be free to consult whom she wished. 'The very mystery of Mr Gladstone's communication made me rather surmise that it was not resignation,' Rosebery wrote. (AR)

Rosebery had already written a valedictory letter to Gladstone on February 24th which must have helped to remove some of the soreness of the past eighteen months.

My dear Mr Gladstone,

I cannot forbear writing you a few words, and the bitter thought is that they may be the last that I shall address to you as a colleague. For, though you never told the Cabinet expressly or in terms, I can scarcely doubt after what you said yesterday that it is your intention to retire from office in the forthcoming week.

Since I entered Parliament I have always been your follower. Since 1879 I have been more closely and personally attached to you. And though there have been differences, and are, there are many fewer than might have been anticipated in view of the difference in age and conditions. We have seen, if I may say so, glorious days together—the recollection of which still stirs my blood—you as chief and I as esquire. And now all is passing or past, and it is a moment of anguish—to all your colleagues I believe—most particularly to me.

I fear that the present, but I hope temporary, condition of your eyesight gives you only too good a reason for resignation. But it would be affectation to deny that there is also a difference of opinion—opinion is perhaps too weak a word, for with me it is a matter of faith. In this one point at any rate we are agreed—that it involves the peace of the world. Unfortunately we are at the poles asunder as regards the means.

On this point I could say much. I have held aloof of late—partly because I could not bring myself to believe in your intention—much more it is painful to be in a relation of acute difference on so vital a point. Nor do I believe for a moment that anything I could say would change your views, for I am no more your equal in argument than in anything else. But I could at least convince you that from my point of view my policy is not less than yours founded on peace and not on oppression.

It is hard to be thus parted; and once more I deeply regret that you do not leave me, as I so ardently wished, in my retirement. But whatever happens you cannot change my present feeling to yourself. Goodbye is a hard saying:—hard at all times, but scarcely tolerable when I think of what you are and have always been to me, of the old Midlothian days, of the times of storm and sunshine in which I have stood by your side, and, above all, of the time to come, when that may not be.

y. affectionately,

AR

'We have still the recollections of battles fought, possibly even victories won, side by side in a good cause,' Gladstone replied; '& we also have still the hope, and as far as depends upon our poor human wills, the determination that personal relations shall remain absolutely unchanged.'

Harcourt's conditions were now generally known to the leading members of the Cabinet, and they had been enclosed in a lengthy paper which emphasised that only one peer—Lord Russell—had been a Liberal Prime Minister since Melbourne and that that precedent was not encouraging. There was also a move afoot—which Loulou was suspected of being behind[1]—for a number of Radical MPs headed by Labouchere to petition Marjoribanks against a peer being Prime Minister. Rosebery heard of Harcourt's declaration to Hamilton from Hamilton himself on February 25th, and remarked 'I see now it is war to the knife'. Marjoribanks was alarmed by Labouchere's 'round-robin', and told Rosebery that 'there was a growing feeling in the House of Commons against a Peer being Prime Minister. On this I said that I was delighted to hear it—might it grow!' (AR)

Marjoribanks' position throughout the succession crisis was equivocal—perhaps understandably as a Whip—but his wife, the beautiful and charming Lady Fanny, took it upon herself to tell Loulou that his father's conditions were intolerable and that Spencer might act as a stop-gap leader; but Loulou, who had once toyed with this idea, had long since abandoned it.[2] On the 26th there was a short Cabinet. 'Harcourt oleaginous', Rosebery drily noted in his diary; and on the next day Rosebery drew up a personal memorandum on the situation. Harcourt was impossible; he himself would far prefer to remain at the Foreign Office: 'Of the work of the Prime Minister, nay, of current domestic politics, I am as ignorant as a man can well be'; 'A Liberal Peer as Prime Minister heading a score of dubious peers

[1] Unfairly, as it happened. But Rosebery's supporters, with good cause, tended to see Loulou behind every anti-Rosebery move.

[2] L. Harcourt's unpublished Journal, February 25th.

would be a ridiculous spectacle'; Harcourt's terms 'would not be entertained by any man of self-respect'.

. . . The matter then resolves itself into a choice of evils: either the irksome yoke of Harcourt, or a ministry headed by a reluctant peer in face of strenuous opposition in the House of Commons, headed by Harcourt.

The choice, though one of evils, seems simple enough. Indeed, the Government might under the second supposition meet with an early and ignominious defeat.

I have always urged a Harcourt Ministry in this event, on the simple common-sense ground that he would try and make his own government a success, and any other a failure.

The question then arises if anything has caused me to change my view. I can truly say that I know of nothing. . . .

He went on to describe the change of atmosphere caused by Loulou's intrigues, Harcourt's 'deliberate declaration against me' to Hamilton, and the nature of his conditions of taking subordinate office 'make it impossible for me to serve under him without loss of self-respect and even of character'. He foresaw his complete subordination as Foreign Secretary, which he could not tolerate.

. . . As I work it out then, the case is clear. Harcourt may not be personally palatable to all of us. But he deserves the Premiership by inheritance, he will do his best to make his ministry agreeable and successful, and his ability to do so is unquestionable. Moreover, if he does not obtain it he will place himself at the head of the extreme party and will exercise his undoubted powers as a belligerent.

For me it is also clear that I could not hold the Foreign Office under him, and my retirement from the Foreign Office is (though I tried another solution) equivalent to my retirement from the Government.

It is fruitless to speculate what would have happened if the question of the succession had been formally put to the leading members of the Cabinet or even referred to the Parliamentary Party. In the former case the result would undoubtedly have been a virtually unanimous Rosebery victory, but in the latter, Harcourt might have won. But the choice of the successor lay in the Queen's hands, and, as has been already noted, if she had sent for either Spencer or Kimberley, they would have advised her to entrust the formation of a new Government to Rosebery. There was the possibility that Rosebery himself might advise her to summon Harcourt, but this was effectively destroyed by two important factors: the intense antipathy towards Harcourt shown by almost every leading member of the Cabinet, and Loulou's unscrupulous intrigues of the previous weeks, about which Rosebery was well informed by Morley, Spencer, and Asquith. The Liberal Press, when the issue became a matter for public debate, almost entirely deserted Harcourt and strongly backed Rosebery. The pressure put upon him to accept the Premiership by his colleagues now became very great indeed. In later years he regretted that he had not compelled Harcourt to take the place, if only to emphasise that he did not command the confidence of his colleagues, but it is very difficult to see how he could have done this in the absence of any clear opinion by the party. To complete Harcourt's public humiliation, the Radical 'round-robin' was a dismal fiasco, which even Morley did not take seriously. Thus, to an extent which many historians have failed to comprehend, Harcourt was astonishingly isolated at this time, in public and in the private discussions among the party leaders. Birrell—then Liberal Member for West Fife—was possibly right when he later wrote that 'We back-benchers all knew, how could it be concealed from us? that Harcourt thought the place belonged to him; and had we been consulted, his it would have been,'[1] but if this was the case, the Liberal rank and file was conspicuously silent. At the time, Rosebery advanced to the Premiership with hardly a voice raised in opposition, and the farcical Labouchere 'round-robin' only served to emphasise this fact.

Rosebery dined at Buckingham Palace with the Queen on February 27th, but nothing was said about the one burning question of the hour. 'Q. very rheumatic', Rosebery noted in his diary '. . . She now knows through Ponsonby the truth, but said nothing.'

Two days later, on March 1st, Mr Gladstone presided over his last Cabinet meeting. After the business was ended Kimberley tried to make a few appropriate remarks but broke down almost at once. Rosebery's account continues:

Mr G was about to reply when a cry of 'Stop!' was heard. It was the Chancellor of the Exchequer. As soon as he had arrested Mr G's

[1] *Things Past Redress*, 137.

attention he pulled from his pocket a handkerchief and a manuscript and at once commenced weeping loudly. Then he said, 'I think I can best express my feelings by reading the letter I have addressed to you, Sir, on this occasion'—on which he declaimed to us a somewhat pompous valedictory address of which I only remember vaguely a long-drawn metaphor taken from the solar system. Mr Gladstone was obviously disgusted. He said a few cold words, and always referred to this Cabinet as 'the blubbering Cabinet'. (AR)

'Of those who were present there are now few survivors,' Asquith subsequently wrote, 'but which of them can forget the expression on Mr Gladstone's face, as he looked on with hooded eyes and tightened lips at this maladroit performance?'[1] Morley's account, characteristically, was somewhat more dramatic.

Mr Gladstone, who had sat composed and still as marble, closed the scene in a little speech of four or five minutes—the sentences of most moving cadence, the voice unbroken and serene, the words and tones low, grave, and steady. . . . Then he said in a tone hardly above a breath but every accent heard, 'God bless you all!'[2]

Whether Gladstone was disgusted or moved—'A really moving scene,' he noted in his diary—the moment of separation had definitely arrived. On the afternoon of the same day he made his last speech in the House of Commons, vigorously and even passionately attacking the House of Lords.

After the Cabinet had broken up, Morley, Asquith, Acland, and Spencer lunched with Rosebery at 38, Berkeley Square. Upon being asked to make a definite declaration to them, he replied by reading to them a short memorandum which he had prepared.

My position seems to be this: I share all the views held against a Peer being head of a Liberal Ministry.

My wish is to remain at the Foreign Office. I know nothing of the other post, and should be in every way unsuited to it.

But if it be absolutely necessary for party purposes that I should exchange the one place for the other, it is clear—to make the arrangement barely possible:—

   1. That it must be in obedience to a clear and decisive call.

[1] *Fifty Years of Parliament*, 216.
[2] Morley: *Recollections*, II, 10. Rosebery told Mary Drew in 1919 that he vividly remembered Morley walking out of the Cabinet with him and saying 'Wasn't Harcourt nauseous?' (Lucy Masterman: *Mary Gladstone*, 487.) In his diary Rosebery merely noted on the Cabinet, 'A horrid scene.'

2. that there must be complete harmony and confidence between me and the leader of the House of Commons.

3. that as I cannot remain in the Foreign Office I must be unfettered in my selection of the Foreign Minister.

Summed up it comes to this—that there must be cordiality and confidence between the Prime Minister on the one hand, and the Party, the leader of the Commons and the Foreign Minister on the other.

Without these conditions it is clear that an experiment, sufficiently difficult in itself, must break down, and another combination must be sought.

R.   March 1, 1894

'A general agreement to these terms, as being fair and moderate, was expressed.' (AR) Morley's account is more definite, and clearly inaccurate.

Rosebery at last definitely accepted the obligation, and agreed that he would *under any circumstances* undertake to go on with the task, if the Queen sent for him.[1]

Although far too late to affect the immediate issue, Loulou's strategy was having its effects on Morley, as Rosebery's account demonstrates.

His manner had quite changed, and he was now grave and pre-occupied. He went on murmuring as if to himself, 'Yes, I suppose you have a right to demand the nomination to the Foreign Office, but . . .'; and 'would not a man in the House of Commons, say, like Campbell-Bannerman, be a much wiser choice?' I do not think I replied as I was determined to maintain that point.

At six o'clock this cloud of preoccupation had obscured the entire firmament. John Morley sate on the sofa in my room at the FO and declared his determination not to remain in his 'back kitchen' as he called the Irish Office. I cannot remember if I had declared at luncheon that I should appoint Kimberley, but I think I had. Anyhow, it was known and it was suggested that J. Morley should go to the India Office if he would not remain at the Irish Office. But since the an-

---

[1] My italics. Morley: *Recollections*, II, 16. Morley had written to Kimberley on February 25th to advise him not to recommend Rosebery to the Queen if he was summoned 'unless it is clearly and definitely understood beforehand that R. would go on with the business. It is obviously of the very first importance that plans should be ready and not half a day lost—both on account of the pressing demands of parliamentary business, and in order to put an extinguisher at the earliest possible moment on the excitement, gossip, and general distraction and clamour which is sure to arise, and to go on swelling until definite solution is known. . . . I only write now to press that R. should make up his mind *now*.' (*Kimberley Papers*.)

nouncement about the FO he had become quite intractable. Acland walked away with him in despair, but wrote me a reassuring note afterwards. (AR)

Mr Gladstone travelled to Windsor on March 2nd. He had decided that if his advice were sought as to his successor he would suggest Spencer,[1] but Rosebery had already been informed by the Prince of Wales on the evening of March 1st and in a short interview at Marlborough House on the following morning that the Queen intended to summon him upon receiving Mr Gladstone's resignation. His accession was so assured that Loulou, hearing from Marjoribanks that Hamilton had reported to Rosebery the declaration of his father, hastened to assure him that he had misinterpreted Sir William's remarks, and 'that W. V. H. *wished* for a Rosebery Government and thought it the best solution of the situation'; Loulou added that he hoped it was appreciated that neither he nor his father had ever indulged in 'anything that savoured of intrigue'! Hamilton replied that he admired Loulou for the gallant fight he had put up on behalf of his father, and promised to deliver the message.[2]

Morley came to see the Harcourts on the afternoon of the 2nd to urge Sir William to accept Rosebery's accession. According to Loulou's Journal—which is, generally speaking, a remarkably accurate document—Morley said that he had convinced Rosebery that a peer Foreign Secretary was unacceptable and that Rosebery had consented to Campbell-Bannerman. Harcourt said that he would prefer to have Morley himself at the Foreign Office, 'but J. M. said this was impossible on account of the Queen and also because he had no great house, etc.'[3] It is probable that Morley's intention in conveying this serious misrepresentation of Rosebery's statement was simply to make Harcourt more receptive to the idea of a Rosebery leadership, but the workings of his mind were so tortuous at this stage that it is impossible to deduce what he hoped to achieve. Harcourt read out his list of conditions again, and his account of the interview concludes:

[1] *Recollections*, II, 11. In a memorandum dated July 25th, 1894, Gladstone wrote: 'My choice on the whole would have fallen on Spencer; less brilliant than either [Rosebery or Harcourt], he has far more experience, having entered the Queen's service over thirty years ago. He has decidedly more of the very important quality—weight.' (*Gladstone Papers*, Brit. Mus. Add. MSS. 44,470, ff. 145–6.)

[2] *Hamilton's Diary*, March 2nd, and L. Harcourt's unpublished Journal.

[3] L. Harcourt's unpublished Journal, March 2nd.

I told him as I had done before, that I intended to allow no personal considerations to stand in the way of any arrangement which was thought advantageous or necessary to keep the Party together, but that if I was to undertake the lead of the H of Commons I must satisfy myself that I was to act under conditions which should make such a position tenable. . . .

He suggested that I should personally see Rosebery and come to some understanding before the question assumed a definite shape. I expressed my willingness to do this and begged him to communicate this to Rosebery.[1]

Rosebery had spent the morning at Willesden, tending his wife's grave, and had lunched with Hamilton at 38, Berkeley Square. He said that his remark about serving under Harcourt but not over him had not been meant seriously, but that only those who had endured Harcourt as a colleague could appreciate the extent of his deficiencies. Pressure from the Prince of Wales, his colleagues, and even Dr Reid, the Queen's physician, had made him convinced that he would be summoned. He had no illusions about his position. 'It was wide insight and no pusillanimity that made him slow to yield to our pressure,' Morley has written.[2] To Ponsonby Rosebery wrote on March 2nd:

I have received the Queen's gracious message through the Prince of Wales. It would not be proper, I conceive, that I should address her on the subject of it, so I write to you with the intention that you should read this letter to her.

It would be affectation to deny that I have often seen it suggested that I might succeed Mr Gladstone when he should retire. In view of that I have kept myself sedulously in the background; I have not made a speech or written a line for publication. I have done this deliberately to avoid this *damnosa hereditas*. And I delivered the only speech that I did make (that on the Irish Government Bill) in the full hope and expectation that it would put an end to any question of my heading a Liberal Government. My reasons were these:—

(1) I am altogether unfitted for the post, as regards capacity and knowledge.

(2) I am in an office where I believe I can do good work and where a change might do harm. Why, then, should I be taken out of a round hole and put into a square one?

[1] *Harcourt Papers.* Memorandum by Sir William Harcourt, March 2nd.
[2] *Recollections*, II, 15.

(3) The House of Commons is justly jealous of the headship of a Liberal peer.

The Liberal Prime Minister, if a Peer, will be dependent entirely on the leader of the House of Commons. While the House of Commons is settling the affairs of the Country under its leader, the Prime Minister will be shut up in an enemy's prison with an intrepid band of twenty followers.

The Radical case announced last night, though not, I believe, formidable in itself, is right in this—that a Liberal Peer, as Prime Minister, is in a wholly false position. He cannot control the House of Commons or his representative there; he can only watch them from the Strangers' Gallery.

(4) I am very sceptical as to the apparent movement in my favour. It is I believe negative, and arises much more from dislike and distrust of one of my colleagues than from anything personal to me. In their anxiety to avoid him they can see no issue or chance of safety but through me.

These are the objections that I see and which I express without reserve, for I think it my duty to make the Queen aware of them.

Believe me,
Yours sincerely,
AR

'I went out of all this turmoil by the 5.30 train [to Epsom],' Rosebery's account continues. 'John Morley called as I left the Foreign Office and drove with me to the station. He had been spending two hours with Sir W. Harcourt, who had read him his memorandum of conditions, "with every word of which", said Morley, "I agreed". ' (AR) The purpose of Morley's visit was, of course, to arrange a meeting with Harcourt, but when the Harcourts had heard nothing by eight o'clock Sir William wrote to Morley that he assumed that Rosebery did not wish to see him. Morley replied at 8.45 that 'Rosebery was just starting for Epsom when I saw him, and I had only a few minutes with him. He did not receive my proposition with much favour and thought that as the time for official or quasi-official communication was so near, it might be as well to wait. I am sorry that my intervention has come to little. . . . I don't intend to meddle more, if I can possibly help it. The angers of celestial minds are too much for me.'[1]

Harcourt replied at 9.45:

[1] *Harcourt Papers.*

Your report is what I expected. But I do not regret that I should have proposed, though Rosebery has refused, that we should have a friendly discussion of difficulties beforehand.

It clears the situation.[1]

Mr Gladstone, who had been Queen Victoria's First Minister for a total of nearly fourteen years, was not asked for his advice about his successor. Ponsonby sounded him informally on the morning of March 3rd before and after the aged statesman attended morning chapel at St George's, but Gladstone declined to speak on the subject before it was raised by the Queen. He did, however, describe the Labouchere deputation as having no significance, and said that 'presuming that the Queen would send for one of the present Ministers, he said he could not agree that a peer was impossible. . . . But he did not advocate anyone specifically.'[2] But at the final audience the vital topic was not even alluded to.

Rosebery travelled up to London on an early train from The Durdans on the morning of March 3rd and sent a brief note to Harcourt as soon as he reached the Foreign Office.

My dear Harcourt,

I received as I was starting for Durdans yesterday, a message through John Morley that you would welcome a friendly conference on the situation. I should welcome it too.

I see you are going to the Council. I would be at your disposal at your return.

Yrs sincerely,
AR

The Council was being held at Windsor to approve the Speech proroguing Parliament, and was attended by Gladstone, Kimberley, Ripon, Spencer, and Harcourt. At some stage of the proceedings—accounts differ, although it was probably before the Council—Harcourt was ushered into the Royal presence by mistake and had to be ushered out again. Some doubt has been thrown upon this excellent story through the fact that there is no reference to it in the Queen's Journal, but in the May of 1899 Rosebery

[1] *Harcourt Papers.* The proposal for the meeting, of course, did not originate with Harcourt but with Morley. Marjoribanks told Loulou on the next day that Morley had misinterpreted Rosebery's remarks (Journal for March 3rd).

[2] *Letters*, 3rd Series, II, 369.

asked her if it was true, and she replied that it was. 'She laughed heartily at the recollection. "Yes, that was terrible. No one knows to this day how it happened—no one can explain it. You were not there that day—it was Mr Gladstone that I sent for." '[1]

Ponsonby called on Rosebery at the Foreign Office at 3.30 with a letter from the Queen inviting him to form a Government; Rosebery told him that he would accept, but would insist upon choosing his own Foreign Secretary.[2] He wrote a formal reply to the Queen to the effect that he could not resist her appeal and 'will endeavour to carry out Your Majesty's wishes'. To his colleagues he communicated the following message:

I desire to inform my colleagues that the Queen has asked me to form a Government.

I have undertaken, under great pressure and under a strong sense of my various disabilities, to attempt the task.

Under these arduous circumstances, I would ask my colleagues for their cordial co-operation.

So far as the Queen was concerned, the matter was agreeably settled, and she instructed Ponsonby to tell Rosebery that she was 'immensely delighted'.[3]

John Morley, however, was even more discontented than ever. He told Loulou on the afternoon of March 3rd that Rosebery was planning to make the Foreign Office a 'secret bureau controlled by himself', and gave Loulou to understand that if Harcourt refused to accept Kimberley as Foreign Secretary he would support him. Loulou took the opportunity of remarking yet again that Morley would make an admirable Foreign Secretary!

Harcourt—who returned from Windsor after Morley had left and told Loulou that he did not know what had happened except that Spencer had not been invited to take the Premiership—assumed that the Cabinet circular had cancelled Rosebery's previous invitation, but Marjoribanks called at 5.30 to say that

[1] Rosebery's 'Betting Book', May 1899.

[2] The Queen suggested that Rosebery should hold both positions—as Salisbury had—but he considered that such a combination would be unacceptable to the Liberal Party.

[3] She did, however, write to Lord Rowton a letter to be communicated to Salisbury stating that 'her wish to see him again at the head of affairs is as great as ever; but she feels she could not act differently than she has done at the present time. It must be remembered that the present Government have still a majority in the House of Commons.' (*Letters*, 3rd Series, II, 368–9.)

Rosebery was waiting for a reply. Shortly afterwards Morley re-appeared at Brook Street, fulminating against '*any* Peer being put at the FO. He said he did not think he *could* join the Government under the circumstances and would go off at once to Berkeley Square to present an ultimatum. W. V. H. said "Shall you stick to it?" and J. M. replied, "Yes, I think I shall".'[1]

Rosebery and Harcourt met at 11, Downing Street at 6.30—not 5.30 as Rosebery states in his memorandum—and the meeting seems to have been cordial. Harcourt did not read out his list of 'conditions' because, as he himself recorded, 'I knew he was aware of its contents, and did not desire to have the appearance of formally imposing conditions.'[2] The one major subject on which they could not agree was the nomination to the Foreign Office; Rosebery said that he intended to appoint Kimberley, at which Harcourt 'declared himself greatly perturbed. He was convinced that the House of Commons would never acquiesce in the Premiership & the Foreign Office both being held in the House of Lords &c, &c. I declared however that on this point I could not yield, so he took it *ad avizandum.*' (AR) Harcourt believed that Rosebery had accepted all his conditions except that over the Foreign Office dispatches and the appointment of the Foreign Secretary.[3] This can hardly have been the case, as Rosebery's account states 'Of this interview I have preserved no written record'—a very rare event with him—'but briefly the whole matter turned on the Foreign Secretaryship'. (AR) This was, of course, the one really vital 'condition' which Harcourt was trying to impose and which Rosebery was determined to resist, but there is no evidence that Harcourt referred to his terms—on the grounds that Rosebery knew of them already—or that they were discussed. It can only be assumed that Harcourt thought that Rosebery's willingness to discuss matters with him contained the implied acceptance of his terms.

[1] L. Harcourt's unpublished Journal, March 3rd.
[2] Memorandum by Sir William Harcourt, quoted in Gardiner: *Harcourt*, II, 271.
[3] *Vide* L. Harcourt's Journal for March 3rd: 'The question of consultations in respect of appointments was also mentioned, and no difficulty raised on that subject. I asked Morley if he understood that W. V. H.'s conditions were generally accepted by Rosebery, and he replied: "Yes, fully, with the exception of the disputed point about the FO communications."' Rosebery, however, wrote to Ponsonby on March 4th that 'I have refused to submit to any conditions not ordinarily imposed on a Prime Minister'. Lord Crewe's account makes no reference to the Harcourt conditions.

The principal participants in this strange drama spent the evening in the company of friends, Rosebery dining alone with Eddie Hamilton at 38, Berkeley Square, and Morley and the Harcourts being among the guests at Kimberley's Pricking Sheriffs dinner. 'No discredit to the host,' Morley has written, 'his kitchen or his cellar, the meal was not convivial.'[1] According to Rosebery's account, Morley told Acland that neither he nor Harcourt would tolerate Kimberley's appointment (AR), but in fact Harcourt and Loulou spent an enjoyable hour taunting Morley with such effect that, according to Loulou, he left 'swearing he would not join the Government and would send another ultimatum in the morning, etc. The situation is delightful to me, for J. M. is *the* man who has deprived W. V. H. of the first place and now he finds himself discarded and of no importance.'[2] Campbell-Bannerman had also expressed disquiet about Rosebery's proposal, but Loulou realised that 'the thing must go on on Rosebery's terms and we must make the best of it'.[3] But March 3rd was a very bitter day in the life of Mr Lewis Harcourt, for which he was to extract a full recompense in the course of time.

Rosebery, meanwhile, was dining quietly with Eddie Hamilton. The events of that extraordinary day had brought pleasure to at least one person. Lady Leconfield wrote to him:

I see your name wherever I turn, & though it could not make me think of you oftener, I must send you one line with my best, & very deepest, love. I thank God that I have lived to see this day. . . . If only our darling Hannah could have shared it with you; it seems more than ever bitter that she should have been taken away before the full fruition of all her hopes, but the name that you gave her is for ever hers, & whether in life or death, all the glory you gain here must be reflected in her. God bless you ever.

Edward Hamilton described his dinner with Rosebery in his Diary.

. . . While at dinner, a box came from Windsor saying that the Queen was highly pleased that R had accepted her commission and was ready to see him at any time. All she hoped was that she should not be

---

[1] *Recollections*, II, 10.
[2] L. Harcourt's Journal. His contempt for Morley may be judged from the fact that he allowed A. G. Gardiner to quote this passage in his biography of Harcourt (II, 269).
[3] L. Harcourt's unpublished Journal, March 3rd.

obliged to see much of Harcourt. We sat till about 10.45, when he ordered his carriage round to drive down to the City to see his old friend Canon Rogers. 'As I can't', he said, 'offer him a Bishopric, I will pay him the greatest compliment I can by announcing myself as Prime Minister first to him.'

Before we parted, he asked me what I thought would have been said had he declined the task? I said, it would be considered that he showed the white feather. I held that he had no choice but to accept what the Queen, the Party, & the Country expected him to do. 'Perhaps so,' he replied, 'but I call you to witness that I undertake the duty of forming an administration with the greatest reluctance. The Foreign Office was an ambition of mine, I admit. I consider it by far the finest post to occupy. In doing what I have done today, I consider that it is the most daring act of my life, unless I except what I did just 32 years ago, which was steering the *Defiance* at Eton without ever having been on the river.'

The Prime Minister then stepped into his carriage, which clattered away across the peaceful Square in the direction of the City.

CHAPTER TEN

PRIME MINISTER

A First Minister has only the influence with the Cabinet which is given him by his personal argument, his personal qualities, and his personal weight. All his colleagues he must convince, some he may have to humour, some even to cajole; a harassing, laborious, and ungracious task. Nor is it only his colleagues that he has to deal with; he has to masticate their pledges, given before they joined him, he has to blend their public utterances, to fuse as well as may be all this into the policy of the Government: for these various records must be reconciled, or glossed, or obliterated. A machinery liable to so many grains of sand requires obviously all the skill and vigilance of the best conceivable engineer. And yet without the external support of his Cabinet he is disarmed.

ROSEBERY: *Sir Robert Peel* (1899)

ROSEBERY ASSUMED THE HIGHEST OFFICE in the State under circumstances which could hardly have been less inspiring. As Sir Winston Churchill has related, 'The Liberal Government, holding office by the Irish vote, assailed vehemently by the far more solid Unionist array, was struggling along under the freshly-used veto of the House of Lords, by majorities which sometimes fell below twenty, towards an ugly election. It was a bleak, precarious, wasting inheritance.'[1] The internal schisms within the Cabinet were of even greater significance. The Harcourts were bitterly disappointed, did not conceal their mortification, and determined (particularly Loulou) to make the Government unworkable;[2] Morley was similarly embittered by the events of the past six weeks, while below the gangway on the Government benches in the House of Commons there lurked an out-

[1] *Great Contemporaries*, 23.
[2] 'W. V. H. told Marjoribanks that he was still willing to do anything necessary for the Party advantage, but that he would have nothing but *official* relations with Rosebery after this. He also said that he does not see that any personal communications would be necessary between a Prime Minister in the Lords and the Leader of the House of Commons, as the Leader would act on all occasions on his own initiative and responsibility.' (L. Harcourt's unpublished Journal, February 28th.)

spoken element in the party which would use every opportunity for deriding and attacking the new Prime Minister. A bleak inheritance indeed!

The immediate problem was whether Harcourt and Morley were going to insist upon the Foreign Secretary being in the Commons. Harcourt wrote to Morley at 8 a.m. on the morning of March 4th urging him not to go too far in threatening Rosebery, 'as it was not any use taking up a position which he could not maintain'. 'I hope you will see me before you deliver any *ultimatum*,' Harcourt wrote. 'What we can and ought to obtain is an arrangement which shall secure a *sufficient communication* between the FO and the H of C. This may be made a condition. I doubt if we shall succeed on the question of *personnel*, which is more difficult. It would be a mistake to make a demand on which we cannot insist.' Morley replied at 9 o'clock that he was considering his course of action. 'The Sabbath calm is favourable for such business,' he wrote mysteriously; 'I will come to see you when my purpose is shaped.'[1]

Harcourt then wrote to Rosebery,

> March 4th, 1894. 9 a.m.
> Treasury Chambers,
> Whitehall, S.W.

My dear Rosebery,

I shall be glad to have some further conversation with you in the course of the day with a view to coming to some understanding as to the relation and communication between the FO and the H of C. I hope we shall be able to arrive at a good *modus vivendi* on this important subject.

> Yours, etc.,
> W. V. Harcourt

Rosebery replied at once:

My dear Harcourt,

By all means. But one thing must be made clear. I cannot have any conditions imposed on me which have not been accepted by previous Ministers. I must either be a real Prime Minister or I will not be Prime Minister at all.

I am more sensible of my own deficiencies than anyone else can possibly be, and of my unfitness for the post I hold and still more for that I am asked to hold. But for that very reason I cannot be a party to either office suffering limitation or detriment while in my hands.

[1] *Harcourt Papers.*

Of course I do not know what it is that you propose in regard to the relations of the House of Commons with the Foreign Office. But I desire to clear the ground beforehand. It is, however, necessary to remember that we must lose no time in settling the point, as the time is short enough for what has to be done and it will be still more inadequate if a new arrangement has to be made.

Yours sincerely,

R

Morley's account of the ensuing events states,

It would be better, I said [to Harcourt], that we should take independent action. Harcourt at once drove to Berkeley Square, surrendered the point, and generally fell in with a Rosebery premiership.[1]

Rosebery's version—based obviously upon a report from Morley—is similar; he states that Sir William, deserted by his fickle ally, came to his house at 10 a.m. to say that 'out of a sincere wish to facilitate arrangements he would not press his objections to Kimberley'.[2] (AR) What actually happened was that Loulou wrote to Morley again at 11.10 a.m. to ask him to come to a rapid decision 'as my father has to see R on the subject'. Morley replied at 11.40, 'I have not had any communication from R, nor with him. I think that we had better act independently—your father and I. My course is shaped by different general considerations, and by the special consideration of Ireland. Meanwhile, I go at least as far as your father's note of this morning, and shall probably go further, whatever others do. But I must once more feel the Irish ground. I have pretty well decided not to remain in Ireland.'[3]

It was upon receiving this letter that Harcourt went to Berkeley Square. Harcourt's account of the interview was more detailed than Rosebery's.

I told him that apart from his condition as a peer I admitted Lord Kimberley to be the fittest person for the purpose, and that I could not designate any special person in the House of Commons to occupy the post. . . . I said that I was of the opinion that the Foreign Secretary should communicate as fully and freely with the Leader of the House of Commons as he did with the Prime Minister. To this Lord Rosebery

[1] Morley : *Recollections*, II, 17.
[2] In his Diary Rosebery noted that the interview was 'before noon'; in his memorandum Harcourt gives the time as 1 p.m. (Gardiner : *Harcourt*, II, 272).
[3] *Harcourt Papers.*

agreed, and it was understood that I should communicate with Lord
Kimberley for the purpose of giving effect to this object, so that the
Leader of the House of Commons should have notice not only when
foreign affairs reached a crisis but *ab initio* when affairs were beginning
at all to 'creak'.[1]

This was a remarkably weak ending to the crisis over the
famous 'conditions', and the one concession that Harcourt extracted from Rosebery, although not unimportant, was a distilled
version of the original demands. It has so often been assumed
that Rosebery did accept Harcourt's terms that it is necessary to
emphasise the point that there is no evidence, either in Harcourt's papers or Rosebery's, to confirm this deduction. It is
sometimes held that as Rosebery knew of them, and that they
were the price of Harcourt's adhesion to the new Cabinet, he
accepted them by implication. Sir Winston Churchill has given
some currency to this view by stating that 'a formal contract was
novel. . . . However, in the end Harcourt exacted his conditions.'[2] This was not Rosebery's understanding, for at the vital
interview on March 4th when he invited Harcourt to remain at
the Exchequer Harcourt only raised the matter of the Foreign
Office. Rosebery told Hamilton on March 29th that he had told
Harcourt 'that having much against his will accepted the ungrate-
ful task of forming a Government he intended to be a real Prime
Minister and not a merely nominal one. *Thereupon Harcourt gave
up his game and fell into line.*'[3] Thus the notion of a formal contract
between Rosebery and Harcourt existed solely in the imagination
of the Harcourts. It is probable, however, that the other members
of the Cabinet who knew of the conditions assumed that Rosebery
had accepted them. And thus a political legend was born.

All the other members of the late Cabinet called on Rosebery
throughout the day and agreed to remain in office. Marjoribanks
had a long walk with Rosebery and agreed to remain on as Chief
Whip, but returned ten minutes later to announce that his father,
Lord Tweedmouth, had died, and that he had succeeded to the
title. 'This was a terrible loss,' Rosebery noted, 'for he was a
consummate Whip.' (AR)[4] The event removed from a position of

[1] Gardiner: *Harcourt*, II, 272.   [2] *Great Contemporaries*, 24.
[3] *Edward Hamilton's Diary*, March 29th (my italics).
[4] According to his gushing biographer, Lady Aberdeen, 'The brilliant parties at
Brook House, the successful founding of the Liberal Social Council by Lady
Tweedmouth, and the pains taken by both Lord and Lady Tweedmouth to bring

great influence in the House of Commons a close friend of Rosebery's, and Marjoribanks' successor, Tom Ellis, never really
achieved a close relationship with the Prime Minister.

Morley had had a terrible day. After Harcourt had gone to see
Rosebery he anxiously wrote to Loulou that when he had spoken
of 'acting independently' he had been referring solely to the
Foreign Office issue. Mrs Morley was urging him to leave the
Irish Office, and 'pursued me even to my dressing-room and
plied me with friendly appeals'.[1] He saw Rosebery in the afternoon, and, according only to Rosebery's account (AR), was
offered the Lord Presidency of the Council. Morley says[2] that he
agreed to join the Government to prevent a Harcourt premiership,
but this is clearly moonshine. He agreed to dine with Rosebery,
and before he left for Berkeley Square saw Loulou. 'J. M. asked
me anxiously if I thought there had been "trickery" on Rosebery's
part. I replied "Plenty, but what did you expect?" If it was not
pitiable it would be amusing to see the poor ladder lying kicked
in the gutter after it had ceased to be useful.'[3] Rosebery urged
him to remain at the Irish Office, and eventually Morley—
'head plunged between his hands'[4]—agreed. But on the following
morning—after an unhappy domestic scene—Morley's discontent exploded again. The occasion was a small conference of
Ministers at 38, Berkeley Square, called to decide upon Kimberley's successor at the India Office. 'We sat as usual round a table,'
Rosebery has recorded, 'but Harcourt sat apart, behind me, near
the window, his chin and nose in the air. I informed the conclave
that Morley declined it [the India Office], and we all came to the
conclusion that Fowler was the proper man to be nominated.
When this was settled Morley asked with vehemence if he was to
understand that Fowler's appointment was agreed upon. I replied that I so understood it, but, observing his tone, asked him
if he could think of anybody else. He replied "No", and flounced

Liberal politicians of all shades together, would form a chapter in themselves. And
it must be remembered that all this political work was carried on side by side with a
very full participation in general society, where Lord and Lady Tweedmouth were
so popular, and with time of leisure and country life spent in fishing, shooting,
deer-stalking, hunting, pursuits in which both excelled.' (I. Aberdeen, *Edward
Marjoribanks*, 23.) Nonetheless, Marjoribanks had been a good Whip.

[1] *Recollections*, II, 19.
[2] *Ibid.*, II, 18.
[3] L. Harcourt's unpublished Journal, March 5th.
[4] Morley: *Recollections*, II, 20.

out of the room, when we continued our business without him.' (AR)

Shortly after this incident Morley wrote to Rosebery,

I hope that I shall not be asked or expected to take part in such councils as those of this morning. I propose to confine myself strictly and absolutely to the business of my department, *plus* attendance at Cabinet councils, *plus* steady obedience to the call of the whips for my vote. Perhaps I should have set this out more clearly in my letter of this morning. I thought you understood. It is as much as I can do, to pull thro' the business of the office, and other burdens must be borne by younger men. This is the position which I announced at the FO the other afternoon.

I think you ought to tell Harcourt the understanding on which I retain office.

This letter followed one which expressed Morley's willingness to remain at the Irish Office on the understanding that 'I am not to be either asked or expected to take part in debates on non-Irish subjects, nor to address meetings outside of Parliament'. This was absurd, and Loulou was as disgusted—for a different reason—as Rosebery. 'I told him I thought he was behaving extremely badly to W. V. H.,' Loulou recorded, 'who depended on him as deputy leader in the H of C. I said "It is *you* who are responsible for my Father's present position and it is *you* who desert him when he wants your help in the House of Commons". Morley was surprised—tried explanation—that his action was directed against R not W. V. H., but I stumped out of the room with simulated anger and concealed amusement.'[1]

On March 6th Morley again wrote to Rosebery, asking for a reply to his letter, 'accepting the terms laid down in my letter about the Irish Office. That will complete the contract.' Rosebery, deeply hurt, sent a cold reply.

Foreign Office,
March 6th, 1894

My dear J. M.

I have no choice but to accept your 'conditions'.

I won't disguise from you that I am deeply pained by them.

You would not have imposed them on Mr Gladstone, or, I believe, on anybody else. It is because your perhaps most intimate political friend undertakes the Government, largely because of your action, that

---

[1] L. Harcourt's unpublished Journal, March 5th.

you insist on a pound of flesh bond which sets forth an absolute want of confidence and a cold denial of all assistance or co-operation. Had I known that this was to be your definite attitude I certainly would not have undertaken the Government, and if I could honourably now, I would give it up.

Yours ever,
R

By this time Rosebery was Prime Minister. On the afternoon of March 5th he had travelled to Windsor and had kissed hands in the Prince Consort's room which, the Queen told him, had been unchanged since his death. On his return to London he called on George Murray to ask him to be his private secretary—a characteristic gesture which helps to explain why men like Murray and Hamilton were devoted to him—and dined with Ferdinand Rothschild and Hamilton, who recorded that he seemed in good spirits.

He had little reason to be. The Harcourts—particularly Loulou and Lady Harcourt—were profoundly embittered by their reversal,[1] and unfairly attributed to Rosebery intrigues and machinations comparable to their own. Morley was holding himself aloof. Asquith mentioned to Rosebery at this time that although Morley was difficult to manage he was at least a perfect gentleman; 'Yes,' Rosebery replied drily, 'but I am not sure whether a perfect lady would not best describe him.' The arrangement with Harcourt over foreign affairs was loose, and Rosebery did not intend it to be anything else. Having controlled foreign policy for eighteen months he did not intend to relinquish his hold. The possibility that the 'Malwood Compact' would be renewed did not dispose him to weaken his authority on this aspect of government at least.

His relations with the Queen were complex and embarrassing from the outset. He knew that she was hostile to his Ministry, although personally sympathetic, and she made this abundantly clear when she wrote that 'She does not object to Liberal measures which are not revolutionary & she does not think it possible that Ld Rosebery will destroy well tried, valued, & necessary institutions for the sole purpose of flattering useless Radicals or pandering to the pride of those whose only desire is their own

---

[1] Hamilton recorded in his diary for March 6th that although Harcourt seemed as genial as ever, his wife broke down, and said that Rosebery had not treated her husband fairly.

self gratification.' On March 8th she took violent exception to references to disestablishment bills for the Scottish and Welsh Churches in the Queen's Speech. Rosebery rightly considered that the measures, to which the party was committed, could not be dropped, and after anxious consultations with Ponsonby—in the course of which Rosebery intimated that he would resign if the Queen persisted—the obnoxious phrase was altered to 'Measures dealing with the ecclesiastical establishments'. Harcourt gave him robust support in this controversy, declaring 'I highly approve of the position you have taken up, and will stand by you to the last. It is impossible on such a matter to give way an inch.' But the tone of Rosebery's relations with the Queen had been established. She used her experience and authority, and the knowledge that Rosebery was anxious to have her sympathy and assistance, to dictate to the Prime Minister on virtually every aspect of his policy. At the same time, she carefully maintained her contacts with the Unionist leaders to an extent which Rosebery never suspected. The tone of her letters to him was maternal but authoritative, and the relationship caused Rosebery considerable difficulty. On March 11th, the day before he was due to make his first speech as Leader of the party to the Liberals in the morning and his maiden speech as Prime Minister in the Lords in the afternoon, she urged him not to commit himself 'but [to] be as *general* & to a certain extent as vague as he can be. He need not say anything agst what he feels himself pledged to. But he can do this & say nothing to discourage his Party & yet not commit himself too strongly. What the Queen says here, she does in the *Name* of *one* who can no longer be a comfort & support to him & who also felt very anxious on this subject.' The reference to Hannah was perhaps questionable, and Rosebery replied that 'His position is of course an almost overwhelmingly difficult one, but he will try not to lose heart'.

March 12th was indeed, as Rosebery noted in his diary, 'a terrible day'. In the morning he addressed a party meeting at the Foreign Office, and even Hamilton—who committed 'the grave impropriety' for a civil servant of attending—noted that the applause for Harcourt was considerably greater than that for Rosebery. Nonetheless, the fear of the Whips that Labouchere would mar the harmony of the proceedings by objecting to a Peer leader did not materialise. The absolute unanimity of the

Liberal Press in its hailing of Rosebery was probably not without effect in this matter. In his speech Rosebery declared that 'We stand where we did. There is no change in measures—there is only a most disastrous change in men.' He said that he sympathised with the view of the deputation which had waited upon Marjoribanks, 'But,' referring to the inconvenience of having a Premier in the Lords, 'I am not one of those who think he is under a stigma or bar. I have not so learned the Liberalism in which we were brought up. It is not at this stage of our development that I am prepared to make a new genus of exclusion, to create a fresh disability, so that in future there is to be written over the doors in Downing Street, "No Peer need apply." ' His remarks on Home Rule were more warmly received. 'It will be pressed to the forefront, and, as far as in me lies, pressed to a definite and successful conclusion.' 'The meeting today was very near freezing point, except when one name was mentioned,' Acton reported to Gladstone, 'but there was no hitch.'

After attending the first meeting of the new Board of Treasury, Rosebery lunched with Hamilton, a large crowd cheering the Prime Minister when he emerged from his house to drive to Westminster. Disaster struck in the House of Lords that afternoon. After welcoming Rosebery to his new position, Salisbury said that Home Rule now stood in suspense, and that the issue hung on the acceptance or rejection of the principle by England. Rosebery opened his first speech as Prime Minister with a noble tribute to Gladstone. 'He heard the guns saluting the battle of Waterloo, he heard some of Mr Canning's greatest speeches, he heard the Reform debate in 1831 in this House, and Lord Brougham's memorable speech. He was, over half a century ago, the right-hand man of Sir Robert Peel's famous Government; and when, to this coating of history which he acquired so long ago, is added his own transcendent personality, one cannot help being reminded of some noble river that has gathered its colours from the various soils through which it has passed, but has preserved its identity unimpaired and gathered itself in one splendid volume before it rushes into the sea.'

He then replied to Salisbury's speech, and fell headlong into the somewhat obvious—and probably unintended—trap.

The Noble Marquess made one remark on Irish Home Rule with which I confess myself in entire accord. He said that before Irish Home

Rule is concluded by the Imperial Parliament, England as the predominant member of the Three Kingdoms will have to be convinced of its justice and equity. That may seem to be a considerable admission to make, because your Lordships well know that the majority of Members of Parliament elected from England proper are hostile to Home Rule. . . .

The Commons members of the Cabinet grouped on the steps of the Throne, and the phalanx of Liberal MP's at the Bar, heard these injudicious words with stupefaction. Their new leader was in effect saying that the tremendous efforts of the past eighteen months had been worthless, and that Home Rule would have to be held in abeyance until there was an English majority to support it.[1] Morley has related his subsequent interview with Rosebery, who was 'not particularly agitated, though he knew pretty well that he had been indiscreet'.

'I blurted it out,' he said. 'For Heaven's sake,' said I, 'blurt out what you please about any country in the whole world, civilised or barbarous, except Ireland. Irish affairs are the very last field for that practice.' R: 'You know that you and I have agreed a hundred times that until England agrees, H R will never pass.' J M: 'That may be true. The substance of your declaration may be as sound as you please, but not to be said at this delicate moment.'[2]

At the Cabinet meeting on the following morning there were no recriminations, Spencer reporting to Gladstone that Rosebery 'was exceedingly good about the incident, humble without false humility & very considerate for Harcourt & the members of the House of Commons'.[3] But in the Commons that afternoon the storm broke, Redmond denouncing Rosebery with harshness and describing his contention as 'preposterous and insulting to the Irish people', and an amendment to the Address moved by Labouchere—which practically abolished the powers of the House of Lords—was carried by two votes.

Although the division was taken in a small House at dinner-time—when many Liberals were paired—as a start to a Premiership this could hardly have been more catastrophic. The fact that

[1] Strangely, Acton did not appreciate the importance of the passage, and reported to Mary Drew that Rosebery's speech was 'so serious, so strong, so convinced, and so victorious and confident, as to alter his position and raise him to a higher level in the country and in Ireland. Everybody I saw was deeply impressed.' (*Mary Gladstone Papers.*)

[2] Morley: *Recollections*, II, 21.   [3] *Gladstone Papers.*

many Irish Members voted in the majority emphasised the seriousness of the rebuke to the Prime Minister. *The Times* eagerly declared that Rosebery had shattered the fabric of Liberal policy at one blow, while the Queen, appalled by the passing of the Labouchere amendment, delivered an angry rebuke to the Prime Minister for the negligence of the Whips.[1] Rosebery, although angered by the violence of Redmond's invective, admitted that the notorious sentence was unfortunate; he had, as Sir Robert Ensor has remarked, 'betrayed the amateur'.[2] The House of Commons had to be asked to negative the whole Address and substitute a new one. Fortunately, Rosebery was due to make a speech at Edinburgh on March 17th, and Morley and Tom Ellis both implored him to repair the damage done by the 'predominant partner' speech. Ellis wrote that although the party was 'sobered and steadied' by the defeat on the Address,

... There is, however, especially among the more keenly friendly of our own people and of the Irish, a most ardent expectation for further light on the memorable sentence of Monday. The sentence is being read as if great questions affecting Ireland, Scotland and Wales could not be legislatively settled in accordance with the wishes of the electorate of the respective nationalities without the assent of a majority from England. Your reference to this conception of Monday's sentence will be microscopically examined on Sunday and Monday. ...

At Edinburgh[3] Rosebery argued that his reference to 'the predominant partner' was a platitude in the sense in which he made it, since it was obvious that more English votes were required in support of Home Rule. The criticisms of his speech, he added tartly, 'were not animated by that benevolence which alone makes criticism at all tolerable'. Although Dillon—who was present at

---

[1] 'Here is a nice wigging for both of us,' Rosebery wrote to Harcourt, enclosing the Queen's letter. 'The spirit of George III survives in his descendent,' Harcourt replied.

[2] *England, 1870–1914*, 216.

[3] Randolph Churchill moved a motion n the Commons on March 19th to the effect that as there was a by-election pending at Leith, Rosebery had infringed the laws and liberties of the Commons. Balfour did not support him, and H. W. Lucy has recorded that 'Lord Randolph stood at the table, sad wreck of a man, attempting to read a carefully-prepared manuscript in a voice so strangely jangled that few could catch the meaning of consecutive sentences. As soon as he rose members began to move towards the door. When he sat down he had talked the place half-empty—he at whose rising eight years ago the House filled to its utmost capacity.' (*Diary of the Home Rule Parliament*, 327–8.)

the meeting—said that he was satisfied, Ellis reported that
'Edinburgh has cleared the air. Irish and British members, instead of being nervous and suspicious, are hopeful and buoyant',
and Morley reported favourable Irish reactions, the *Annual
Register* remarked with justice that 'independent Irish criticism
which found vent in Ireland and elsewhere was sceptical and
contemptuous.' Colonel Bigge wrote to the Queen—holidaying
in Florence—that he would be 'very surprised if public opinion
is convinced by the explanation offered by Lord Rosebery of what
he said in the House of Lords'.

Having cast, by his inopportune frankness, the gravest doubts
among his Liberal supporters as to his reliability on the basic
tenets of the Liberal programme, Rosebery soon found himself
beset on three fronts. The Queen, particularly on the subjects of
the House of Lords or Church Disestablishment, subjected Rosebery to a stream of indignant and even minatory epistles to which
he laboriously tried to reply. In Foreign Affairs the unresolved
crisis in Central and Northern Africa threatened to become a constant source of friction within the Cabinet, while Harcourt's
Budget proposals very nearly led to a serious rupture. The relationship between Rosebery and Harcourt, which had been
surprisingly cordial in the first weeks of the Ministry, never
recovered from this episode.

Harcourt's proposed scheme—in fact the creation of Alfred
Milner, then Chairman of the Board of Inland Revenue—included
the introduction of a graduated death duty. Harcourt at one stage
also envisaged a graduated income-tax, and Loulou had actually
prepared such a scheme before it met strong opposition from
Milner, and was eventually abandoned. Harcourt made a move
in this direction, however, by increasing income-tax from 7*d.* to
8*d.* in the £, and relieving incomes below £500 of taxation. The
kernel of the death duty proposals was to extend to every type of
property the existing probate duty, under the new name of
estate duty. In a letter to Rosebery on March 23rd Harcourt
anticipated that the new duty would yield only about £1 million
in the current year, but would bring in 'between £4,000,000 and
£5,000,000' in future years.

These proposals perturbed many Gladstonians, and, most
notably, Gladstone himself, who recorded that it was 'by far the
most Radical measure of my lifetime', and that it was too violent,

since 'it involves a great departure from the methods of political caution established in this country where reforms, particularly financial reforms, have always been considerate, and even tender'. Rosebery was concerned by the social implications of Harcourt's proposals, as was natural for a great land-owner, and also by the possible political effects. The drift away from Liberalism of the great families—indeed, by now almost a stampede—which had supported it and led it for generations was an event which alarmed Rosebery. The 'horizontal' division of parties was a prospect which depressed him, and, on a more practical level, the removal of great wealth was having serious effects upon the party funds. He saw the dangers inherent in making the Liberals a party of shop-keepers and dependent upon big business for its funds and recruits. He believed, as did Gladstone, that the Liberal Party should be the one national party, embracing all elements and all classes in the nation. No doubt his view of the contribution of the great families to Liberalism was tinged with romanticism, but there was much to be said in its favour. Lord Crewe, sometimes regarded as 'the last of the Whigs', although considerably more radical than ever Rosebery was, has written with justice about Campbell-Bannerman that he 'shared in a degree the limitations seen in some of the nineteenth-century Liberals who were great commercial figures, especially those whose devotion inclined them to measure affairs all over the world with a British foot-rule'.

The brief honeymoon between Rosebery and Harcourt had shown signs of strain before Harcourt read out most of his Budget speech to his bored colleagues on April 2nd, 'and with a little encouragement, which was not given, they would have been treated to the whole of it', as Rosebery remarked to Hamilton. Harcourt had already announced on the subject of Uganda that it would probably destroy the Government 'and the sooner the better', and on April 7th Rosebery wrote to the Queen that 'The Cabinet is perfectly harmonious, indeed unanimous, with one exception, but the voice of that exception never ceases during the sitting of the Cabinet'.

After carefully considering Harcourt's draft Budget, Rosebery wrote a private memorandum for the Chancellor of the Exchequer, couched in a mild enough tone, but setting out his 'apprehensions' about the Death Duties scheme as at first prepared. As this document has never been published[1] it is necessary to summarise the arguments which Rosebery put forward for Harcourt's consideration. He was concerned first by the alienation of property.

. . . Property in this country is an enormous and insidious force; it influences innumerable employees and dependants; it subscribes the election funds; its mere panic is a power. I think it difficult to over-estimate the resources of property as a political engine. . . . [The proposals] will raise a most formidable enemy against us, perhaps the most formidable. Will it give us any compensating friends?

We should secure the friendship, indeed, of the persons who possess less than £500 a year. Are these likely to be grateful, or numerous enough to help if they are? I am doubtful on both points.

If we wish to counterbalance property, it must be by the help of the masses. The masses do not appear to support the Liberal Party as much as we have a right to expect. It is not necessary now to investigate why this is so: the fact is sufficient. But will this scheme bring them back? It gives them nothing, if they be tee-totallers: if they drink spirits, those spirits are further taxed. So we can hardly hope for much enthusiasm or active support from the masses. . . .

He went on to express his concern about the possibility of 'a horizontal division of parties, in which the Liberal Party would rest on nothing but a working-class support, without the variety and richness and intellectual forces which used to make up that party'. He drew Harcourt's attention to the American experience, which was that taxation of capital resulted in calculated professional evasion, and expressed his concern at the possibility of the breaking-up of estates and art collections; he suggested that special provision should be made for the latter category of property as it brought no income and if it had to be sold would result in a disastrous expatriation of the nation's treasures to America. His memorandum concluded,

. . . We bring about these far-reaching results, not less ultimately operative perhaps than the Code Napoleon in France, for what? To raise a million, which is in effect to be handed back to the incomes of £500 a year. And the result is that, while all other classes are heavily taxed for a common interest, the maintenance of an adequate efficient navy, this fortunate section will not merely contribute nothing, but will be actually in pocket by the transaction. . . .

[1] Rosebery refused permission for it to be published in Gardiner's *Harcourt*. The copy in Rosebery's papers has only recently been found.

I hope therefore that the graduation may be mitigated as far as possible. Proposals of this kind should be introduced with gentleness, and high graduation appears to me in any case to be essentially a war tax. . . .

As a Peer I have no vote on, or contact with, finance, and as an individual I may be credited with a personal interest in the matter, though that may be easily exaggerated. My opinions may therefore not be of great value; I only give them for what they are worth.

This was a very mild memorandum, typical of the sort of document which freely passes between Ministers, and particularly from a Prime Minister to a leading colleague. Rosebery made one slip, when he failed to make it clear that when he spoke of 'the persons who possess less than £500 a year' he was referring to the income-tax payers below this limit, who were exempt from paying tax on the first £120 (Harcourt raised it to £160), which was considerably more than the average working-class income. But the phraseology in the memorandum was ambiguous, and it gave Harcourt an opportunity which he did not miss. The Harcourts were leaving the House of Commons on the evening of April 4th when the memorandum was handed to the Chancellor in a dispatch box. 'W. V. H. much amused at the high Tory line taken by R', Loulou noted, 'and said "I wonder what the *Daily Chronicle* would think if they could see this?".'[1] When Loulou returned to Downing Street after dining at the Savoy he found that his father had written 'an admirable memo. in reply to R's', which was promptly dispatched to 38, Berkeley Square, where Rosebery resided until the beginning of 1895 when repairs drove him reluctantly to 10, Downing Street.

Rosebery had had little experience of Harcourt's extraordinary ferocity in departmental disputes, but neither Spencer nor Campbell-Bannerman would have been greatly surprised by the nature of Harcourt's startling reply to the Prime Minister's memorandum. Harcourt wrote to Spencer that 'R's disquisition would have been thought extreme in its Toryism by Lord Eldon. There is nothing to do with rubbish of this sort except to treat it with the contempt it deserves'.[2] Spencer, although he did not entirely share Rosebery's views, disapproved strongly of Harcourt's outrageous reply, which can be read with amazement even today, together with Rosebery's sardonic comments.

[1] Gardiner: *Harcourt*, II, 283.   [2] *Ibid.*, 287.

Harcourt: . . . You are not, as I am, old enough to remember the great battle fought by Mr Gladstone in 1853 on the Succession Duties. That contest secured for him the lasting hatred of the landed proprietors and the enthusiastic support of the Liberal Party. The fears which your Memorandum express are a faint echo of the panic and terrorism of that time. The Tories, openly, and the Whig Magnates, covertly, feared and hated his policy. He had however the advantage of the courageous and strenuous support of Aberdeen and Granville. I have no doubt that we shall have a 'formidable enemy' in those who find themselves deprived of monopolies which they ought never to have possessed and privileges which enrich them at the expense of their poorer fellows.

Rosebery: The Budgets may resemble each other. But there is a difference in the men.

Harcourt: That this class may be alienated from the Liberal Party I am not disposed to dispute. If it be so, the Liberal Party will share the fate of another Party which was founded 1894 years ago, of which it was written that it was 'hard for a rich man to enter into its Kingdom.'

Rosebery: Cant.

Harcourt: I think it is highly probable that there are 'many young men who will go away sorrowful, because they have great possessions.'

Rosebery: No. It is the young men who are to inherit great possessions who will suffer. So this refined innuendo is beside the mark.

Harcourt: You say that the only compensation which we shall receive is in the friendship of the men under £500 per annum. You ask two questions: first, whether they are 'numerous enough to help'. Secondly, whether they are likely to be 'grateful'.

As to the first question, the answer is easy—they form ninety-nine hundreds of the population and certainly nine-tenths of the constituencies. As to the second question, gratitude is a very uncertain quantity. The only method I know of securing it is to deserve it.

Rosebery: What! The *income tax payers under 500£ a year!* for that is the class to be benefited, not the *incomes* under 500£. If Sir W. H. is right there is no need of old age pensions.

Harcourt: . . . You say 'that the masses do not appear to support the Liberal Party as much as we have a right to expect'. If that is true, so much the worse for the Liberal Party.

It is probably more the fault of the Party and of its leaders than of the masses.

It does not appear to me that we are likely to secure 'their enthusiasm or active support' by appearing as the defenders of fiscal privileges and exemptions of the wealthy which are universally condemned.

You desire to avert the 'cleavages of classes'. The hope on your part is natural, but you are too late. 'The horizontal division of parties' was certain to come as a consequence of Household Suffrage. The thin end of the wedge was inserted and the cleavage is expanding more and more every day.

Rosebery: Nonsense. The Tories are prepared to give nearly as much as we are, or quite; but they have a fair representation of all classes.

Harcourt: I do not wonder at your casting a longing lingering look on the 'variety and richness and intellectual forces' which have passed away, but these are not the appanage of democracy.

Rosebery: What then was the 'appanage' of Athens?

Harcourt loftily dismissed Rosebery's fears about the effects of the taxation of capital and declared that large estates prudently administered would not suffer. His memorandum continues,

... Your argument seems to involve that it is necessary to maintain an unequal incidence of taxation in order to avert the breaking up of large properties irrespective of the character of their possessors.

Rosebery: My argument involves nothing of the kind.

Harcourt: This is a very fine old Tory doctrine—it is one which the Liberal Party are not likely to accept.

Rosebery: Insolence is not argument.

Harcourt concluded with a prolonged peroration about the mighty principles at stake. 'The fate of the present Government and the issue of the next Election are temporary incidents which I view with philosophic indifference (*Rosebery:* !!Coriolanus.) ... What I care for as long as I have any personal responsibility for the public finance is to establish principles of fiscal equality which are worthy of the Liberal Party and which if defeated today will have a resurrection hereafter. I am sorry that my views of the political bearings of my financial proposals should be so completely in antagonism to yours. Like you I admit I may be wrong, but like you I desire to place them on record and I should be glad that your Memorandum and mine should be laid before the Cabinet on Friday. It seems hardly fair to me in our respective positions that your elaborate protest against the Budget should be buried in our respective bosoms.' On this, Rosebery remarked, 'Mine has never entered my bosom; your views not merely pervade London in a red box but are recited to the loungers in the lobbies.' At the end of what he described as 'this farrago' Rosebery wearily wrote, 'Mr Pitt said "Patience".'

It might be considered that on the merits of the argument Harcourt was in the right on the main issue; but this is to miss the point of the dispute. Rosebery had not attacked the Budget, he had merely expressed some apprehensions, which he was more than entitled to do; Harcourt, having delivered with undisguised glee his lengthy diatribe, agreed to Rosebery's proposal that the maximum be reduced from 10 to 8 per cent. In a note written in 1898 Rosebery said that he took 'little notice' of Harcourt's offensive harangue, but Hamilton's diaries—and the fact that Rosebery returned to the subject four years later to prepare a memorandum on the episode—reveal that he was deeply angered by it. He told Hamilton on April 10th that Harcourt had not even behaved like a gentleman, and on the 16th he said despairingly that the Budget would be the ruin of the country, by breaking up large properties and driving away capital, and that he would have to be a party to it. 'He is too timid,' his friend commented.

Rosebery never considered that he had opposed Harcourt's proposals, nor really had he. He declined to have the two memoranda placed before the Cabinet, which enchanted Loulou—'I thought that coon would come down, but I did not expect him to do it so quickly and so completely'[1]—and the principles of the Budget were approved by the Cabinet. By a strange irony, Harcourt was among the first victims of his Budget, and he spent his last months in rather sad circumstances at Nuneham attempting to salvage as much as he could from his family's fortunes when heavy duties were payable on his nephew's estates.

Apart from Spencer and Morley—who, according to Rosebery, took his side when he read Harcourt's philippic—the rest of the Cabinet were unaware of the cause of the acute personal division between the Prime Minister and the Chancellor, although they could note its effects. 'Harcourt was in a very bad humour this morning,' Hamilton noted on April 7th. 'One must never attach much importance to his blurtings out, but increased bitterness against Rosebery was very marked. He alluded to their having interchanged views on the Budget proposals. He sneered at R's memdm. and prided himself at having in his reply torn R's arguments to pieces.' Morley told Hamilton on April 16th that 'Rosebery must try and get Harcourt off his nerves . . . at the present moment his wisdom is dimmed by the Harcourt spectre'. This was a counsel of unreal perfection; Harcourt was, after all, the second man in the Cabinet and the Leader of the House of

[1] Gardiner: *Harcourt*, II, 287.

Commons; if he was going to react so offensively to the mildest of criticisms Cabinet work was clearly going to be impossible.

Rosebery misjudged the Harcourts in one respect, for neither the father nor the son revealed that Rosebery had criticised the Budget until the December of 1896, when Loulou—with his father's approval—sent the documents to Labouchere, who published an article based on them in the *Pall Mall Gazette*. Labouchere's article went too far in suggesting that Rosebery had flatly opposed the Budget, but there was enough truth in the story to justify Rosebery's anger at this breach of Cabinet secrecy. Kimberley asked him at Mentmore if it was true that he had opposed the Budget, and Rosebery denied that he had. Kimberley's report to Ripon is interesting, since it shows that the rest of the Cabinet were completely unaware of the rift.

I asked him whether there was any foundation for the *Pall Mall* statement that he had opposed Harcourt's budget. I never heard anything of the kind, but I thought it just possible that something might have taken place behind the scenes which I did not know. As I expected, R said there was never any opposition on his part to the Budget. The only suggestion he made was that the maximum death duty should be 8 instead of 10 pr. ct., & you will remember it was settled at 8 pr. ct. after a slight discussion in the Cabinet.[1]

Foreign Affairs provided numerous harsh exchanges in the Cabinet. The Anglo-German Agreement of 1890 and the Anglo-Italian Agreement of 1891 recognised the Sudan as a British sphere of influence, and Britain claimed that the failure of any other Power to protest established her claim. Rosebery had long been anxious to divert the Belgians away from the area, and on March 5th negotiations were opened with King Leopold in Brussels. Kimberley and Rosebery envisaged a kind of package deal, whereby Leopold would recognise the British sphere of influence on the Upper Nile, in return for which the British would lease to him the regions which corresponded to the former Egyptian provinces of Equatoria and Bahr-el-Ghazal on the understanding that he claimed no rights of sovereignty. The results of such an arrangement would have been to stifle possible threats from the West to the Nile, while the secret clauses of the Anglo-Italian Agreement of May 5th, 1894, gave the Italians the region of Harrar and encouraged them to dispute the claims of

[1] *Ripon Papers.*

Menelek, Emperor of Ethiopia, who claimed all the territory up to the right (eastern) banks of the Nile, and had ambitions to push his empire as far as Khartoum and Victoria Nyanza. If—as appeared probable—the French backed Menelek and the Italians took fright, the situation would have become extremely serious.[1]

The Cabinet were not informed that these important negotiations with Leopold were to be opened, but on March 27th Kimberley, after consulting Rosebery, told Harcourt, who replied, 'Many thanks for your note. I will take an opportunity of speaking to you on the matter.' It is clear that he had completely failed to note the significance of the negotiations, and the fact that he was immersed in preparations for his Budget was probably the principal reason. On April 12th the Treaty was secretly signed in London, and a copy was sent to Harcourt on April 21st. Upon its receipt the Chancellor erupted.

. . . You know [he wrote to Kimberley on April 22nd] that when I undertook the lead of the H of C I stipulated for and received a distinct assurance that I was to be kept in full and constant knowledge of all important transactions in the FO from their initiation, and that nothing of importance was to be done without my privity.

I regard this Belgian Agreement as a distinct breach of that promise.

When you hinted to me that something of the kind was going on, I indicated my doubts as to the policy. I fully expected—and permit me to say I had the right to expect—that I should have been fully informed before it went on to completion. As you know I have never been allowed to see the document before it was signed. If I had, I should strongly have protested against it, and required that it should be brought before the Cabinet. This has been rendered impossible. The Cabinet and I[2] myself are informed of it as a concluded affair in a circulation box ten days after the signature of the agreement.

You professed to inform the Cabinet at its last meeting of what was going on in the FO, and were absolutely silent on this Agreement which was then signed.

The mutilation of the Portal[3] Report (which I accidentally dis-

---

[1] Article III of the Treaty, whereby Leopold leased to the British a corridor running along the eastern border of the Congo State and adjoining the western frontier of German East Africa, was a Foreign Office addition for which Sir Percy Anderson was responsible. It was this part of the Treaty which aroused the German opposition to the Treaty. (See map on page 252.)

[2] The copy of this letter, published in Gardiner, *Harcourt*, II, 313, is littered with mistakes. The words 'This has been rendered impossible. The Cabinet' are omitted.

[3] Misquoted as 'the Postal Report' in Gardiner, *op. cit.*

covered[1]), and this secret[2] Agreement kept back from me and from the Cabinet till it is too late to discuss it have left on my mind the most painful impression. . . . I must request that this Treaty shall be published at once, and that I shall be at liberty to take such course as I think fit with regard to it.

The House of Commons has a right to expect that I shall answer to them for the Foreign Policy of the Government. The only answer that I can now return is that the Foreign Policy of the Government is transacted by the First Lord of the Treasury and the Foreign Secretary in the House of Lords, and that they take particular care that I shall know nothing of these Foreign Affairs. . . .

Harcourt's wrath, for once, was wholly justified, and Kimberley's weak reply that the onus of asking to see the Agreement lay upon him was ruthlessly destroyed.

. . . To say that something is about to be done, and then to do it without further consultation or communication is merely delusive.

I consider I have been very badly treated, not in this matter only, but in the whole of the undertaking that I should be kept informed as to what is going on. It is impossible for me to say that I want this or I want that, when I have no means of knowing what this or that is. . . .

I feel that there has been no real desire to deal fairly or frankly with me in this matter, on which a solemn assurance was given. . . .

Morley (April 25th) added his censure to that of Harcourt.

I agree with the Chancellor of the Exchequer in thinking that this Agreement ought not to have been concluded without express reference to the Cabinet. . . . I wish to put on record my distrust of the proceeding, and my regret that nothing was said about it before it was arranged.

The Cabinet met on April 23rd, and agreed to send Sir Percy Anderson to Brussels to discover if Leopold would agree to abandon the Treaty. This decision was not carried out, but Harcourt did not check up on the matter, and the views of the Cabinet were thus deliberately flouted by Rosebery and Kimberley. One suspects that neither was particularly worried about Harcourt's bluster at this stage, and relied upon his preoccupation with his Budget. But on May 3rd further correspondence with Leopold was laid before the Cabinet, and Harcourt in his anger and astonishment described the actions of the Foreign Secretary as

---

[1] Misquoted as 'discussed' in Gardiner, *op. cit.*

[2] Misquoted as 'second' in Gardiner, *op. cit.*

'dangerous and dishonourable'. Kimberley, although a mild man, was stung by this onslaught, and replied that 'I confess I do not understand the cause of your wrath. Nothing has been done except to induce the King to agree that the secrecy which you and others objected to should be put an end to.' Harcourt retaliated that 'whilst I have received all sorts of despatches from the FO on very immaterial subjects, these communications which have been going on upon a matter in which I was known to take a very deep interest, have been studiously withheld from me for a whole fortnight'. 'I can assure you I had no intention to keep back the despatches', Kimberley replied on May 4th. 'I sent you some time ago the first despatch about the King's negotiations with France. You sent it back to me yesterday.' Harcourt had circulated a characteristic memorandum to the Cabinet on May 3rd.

. . . The whole thing is a wanton provocation of France, made all the more mischievous by the underhand manner in which it has been conducted. The exasperation produced by this *shady* proceeding will of course embitter all the questions which we have at issue with France in Egypt, Siam and Uganda. I am of opinion that there is only one safe and respectable course, and that is to cancel an Agreement which would never have been made if the Cabinet had been allowed to discuss it. . . .

Morley and Asquith expressed strong agreement with Harcourt, and on May 4th the Cabinet returned to the question. Both the Harcourts assumed that the Cabinet decided to support Sir William, that the Treaty was to be cancelled, and that Anderson was to be sent to Brussels for this purpose. Again, Anderson was not sent, but although Harcourt discovered this, the fact does not seem to have unduly troubled him. Rosebery, in his account to the Queen, reported that the Treaty would be cancelled 'on condition that the King signed a more general agreement, recognizing that he only occupies a position in the British sphere under the authority of your Majesty's Government, and that he must evacuate it on due notice from your Majesty's Government. This would secure our rights and put the King right with the French.'

Leopold was under strong pressure from the French—who had a delegation actually in Brussels from April 16th to 23rd—to grant them access to the Nile, and he wanted to abandon the British Treaty. This the Foreign Office refused to permit, and fater a modified version was signed on May 12th—to hoodwink the French into believing that it had been negotiated after their delegation had returned from Brussels—it was published on May 21st.

At this delicate moment Harcourt discovered Rosebery's 'Homburg Instructions' to Portal of the previous August, and descended with fury upon both Kimberley and Rosebery with the resounding declaration that Rosebery had deliberately ignored the views of his colleagues and had conducted Foreign Affairs by himself, a practice not attempted since Palmerston's dismissal in 1851. But having put Rosebery in a thoroughly uncomfortable position, Harcourt then let the matter drop. His tactics were playing more and more into Rosebery's hands, since it was clear that Harcourt was more interested in attacking Rosebery than in keeping a close supervision over Foreign Policy, about which he knew very little. His outbursts in the Cabinet, his childish huffiness, his abusive language, and the jeering harshness of his memoranda had created considerable sympathy for Rosebery among the members of the Cabinet. Ripon—by no means a supporter of the tactics of the Foreign Office—characterised this emotion when he wrote to Kimberley on May 5th, 'I hope you will not trouble yourself about the rude expressions in Harcourt's minute. They are unpardonable, but they are not worth notice, coming from one so uncontrolled in his habitual speech.'[1] As Asquith has written, Harcourt's 'lack of any sense of proportion, his incapacity for self-restraint, and his perverse delight in inflaming and embittering every controversy, made co-operation with him always difficult and often impossible. Cabinet life under such conditions was a weariness both to the flesh and the spirit.'[2]

But although Harcourt muffed the opportunity of bringing home to his colleagues the fact that they were not expected to play any part in the foreign policy of the Government, he did succeed in seriously damaging the Anglo-Belgian Treaty. The Germans had reacted to its publication with an anger almost as great as that of the French, and Article III (concerning the corridor adjoining German East Africa) was abandoned by the British Government, again without consultation with the Cabinet. Harcourt sent his usual protest to Kimberley on July 16th, adding that 'of course I agree with the cancelling of one-half of this agreement, but the tearing up of it in small pieces instead of dealing with it as a whole is in my opinion an impolitic course

---

[1] *Ripon Papers* (copy).   [2] Asquith: *Fifty Years of Parliament*, I, 252.

which only exposes us to fresh humiliations'. The abandonment
of Article III—which had been inserted by the Foreign Office at
a late stage, without any warning to either Kimberley or Rosebery that the Germans had already given warnings about British
interference with the corridor adjoining German East Africa—
could not repair the damage. Leopold asked the British Government for permission to renounce his gains under the Treaty.
Rosebery wished to refuse, but he and Kimberley were overruled by a clear majority of the Cabinet on August 13th, and the
hapless Treaty dissolved ignominiously to the joy of Berlin, Paris,
and Sir William Harcourt. 'Fancy our foreign affairs being in the
hands of two men unfit to manage a public-house,' he remarked
contentfully to Ripon.[1]

This serious defeat for the Prime Minister was followed by
another humiliation. Informal discussions between Hanotaux
and Phipps—the British Minister in Paris—about the possibility
of a limited agreement on Egypt were held in August and
September, and by mid-September had reached a promising
stage. At this point Harcourt arrived in Paris in the course of a
holiday, learned of what had been going on, and fired off angry
letters to Kimberley and Morley. 'The instructions to Phipps',
he wrote to Morley on September 15th, '. . . should be *settled by
the Cabinet*. These men are quite incapable by themselves of
handling any matter of serious importance and I think we have
already had as much snubbing and eaten as much dirt as we can
swallow.'[2] Rosebery's subsequent abandonment of the discussions was one of the few occasions on which his conduct of
Foreign Affairs was approved of by the Chancellor.

These bitter disputations left an ineradicable impression on the
Prime Minister. For a while he clung to the hope that Harcourt
would resign after his Budget was passed, but by July he had to
abandon this hope. Harcourt's Budget had been ecstatically
received by the Liberals, and his conduct of the lengthy Committee Stage had won warm tributes in the Commons from both
sides. His proud boast that he never had to use the closure irritated his colleagues profoundly, and all other Government
business was seriously held up while the Finance Bill crawled
through Committee. This triumph made Harcourt more unbearable than ever, and he once told Lady Tweedmouth that

[1] West: *Diaries*, 207.   [2] *Harcourt Papers* (copy).

her husband was 'nothing better than a fetcher and carrier for Rosebery'. On August 1st he was dined by his Commons supporters in honour of his handling of the Budget. 'Sir William was in a combative mood', the *Annual Register* for 1894 recorded, 'and had little that was amiable to say about anybody but his hosts. He made no reference to Lord Rosebery, and more than once spoke of himself as "the commander-in-chief".' Rosebery told Hamilton on July 12th that he was considering holding a rival dinner for *his* supporters on the same evening!

Within a few months of Rosebery's accession to the Premiership some of his colleagues were privately expressing alarm at his conduct of business. An early Cabinet circular (April 25th) had emphasised the fact that Mr Gladstone was no longer at the head of affairs.

A rumour has reached me (to which of course I attach no credence) that four of the confidential Ministers of the Crown have arranged to spend this evening in the contemplation of a courtesan at a minor theatre.

It is however difficult to put a stop to a report which has obtained circulation; and I would implore all members of the Cabinet to so spend this evening as to be able to establish a satisfactory alibi.

A public visit to inspect their own effigies at Madame Tussaud's would be both pleasing and popular: while for those to whom this might be too great a strain it might be useful to bear in mind that Mr Haldane QC, MP, lectures on 'Schopenhauer and the Ideal London' at the George Odger Coffee Tavern, 3 Cowslip Terrace, Clerkenwell Green, at 8 precisely (there will be a collection).

AR

His distribution of patronage—which he detested—contained some appointments so bizarre as to arouse merited suspicions of frivolity on the part of the Prime Minister. The Queen advised him (June 4th) to take 'a more serious tone' in his speeches, '& be, if she may say so, less *jocular* which is hardly befitting a Prime Minister'. This criticism could be applied with even greater force to his public appointments. That of Frederick York Powell— who had been a law tutor at Christ Church when Rosebery was an undergraduate—to the Regius Professorship of History at Oxford in succession to the great Froude was a case in point. Rosebery had in fact favoured S. R. Gardiner, who had refused, and Rosebery's letter of invitation to Powell lay unopened for several days as the eccentric recipient suspected that it was a tax demand. Powell's inaugural lecture to a huge audience was almost a scandal. 'He came in very late', Sir Charles Oman recalls, 'and looking rather bored, with two or three scraps of paper in his hand. He made a few disjointed remarks for about twenty minutes, intimated that he had never known his predecessor Froude, so could not speak about him, and complained that Oxford was destitute of the proper apparatus for original research. When we were expecting him to warm up to some eloquent thesis, he suddenly slapped down the last of his scraps, observed that he had no more to say, and departed.'[1]

The circumstances surrounding the appointment of Bishop Kennion (1845–1922) to the See of Bath and Wells in 1894 were no less comical but had considerably happier results. Kennion, who had been at Eton with Rosebery, had met him on his Australian tour in 1883–4, and Rosebery had noted 'I believe he is both a saint and a man of business. I have rarely been so fascinated.' Kennion had then been Bishop of Adelaide, and when he returned to England in the summer of 1894 some friends at the Athenaeum solemnly told him that it was his duty as a retiring Colonial Bishop to call on the Prime Minister. The fact that it was Derby Day added greater piquancy to their jest, and the innocent Bishop called first at Downing Street, whence he was sent to 38, Berkeley Square, where he was received somewhat coldly by a butler. He left his card with the butler, and when Rosebery returned, considerably exhilarated and cheered by a large crowd in the Square, he was presented with Kennion's card. Rosebery was at the time wrestling with the problem of the Bath and Wells bishopric, and was delighted to be reminded of his old friend, who was subsequently appointed.

Another appointment—that of Reginald Brett to the Commissionership of Works—excited the indignation of Tom Ellis, who wrote to Murray:

. . . Brett's appointment is simply *execrable*. I have already received a very strong hot letter about giving such an appointment to a man with about £6,000 a year with five houses in town and country who has 'always left his party in the lurch.' It will do Lord R and the party immense injury. See how the whole thing looks! A Primrose is promoted and a rich personal friend—who has never done the party a

[1] Sir Charles Oman: *Memories of Victorian Oxford*, 205.

good turn—is placed in his stead. It will be looked upon as Whiggery with a vengeance. Ugh! . . .

On June 6th there occurred one event in this unhappy year which afforded Rosebery real delight, but which did not endear him any further to many of his supporters. *Ladas II* had enjoyed a marvellous season, and started in the Derby at 9 to 2 on. Rosebery was up at six o'clock with several of his Durdans guests to see *Ladas* canter on the Downs, and when the horses went to the start he anxiously drank a glass of champagne. 'The Lad' told him that *Ladas* was bound to win as Rosebery had seen a hedgehog running in the garden in the morning, but only when his horse passed the post an easy winner did Rosebery relax and say triumphantly, 'At last!' Scenes of ecstatic enthusiasm followed, and Chauncey Depew genially telegraphed from America 'Only Heaven left'.

Three weeks later the members of Loder's who had fared so disastrously in 1869 gave a dinner in Rosebery's honour, who responded by reciting a postscript to *Pretender's Derby*.

So sung your Bard in '69, with cheerful lamentation,
His hopes were past, his horse was last, and all was desolation;
The name of Ladas *clung to him, a hissing and a scorn,*
And he began to sorrow that he ever had been born.

But life is long and youth is young and it is weak to brood,
So his potsherd was discarded and his ashes were shampooed.
And he set himself in earnest a courser to acquire,
That should write the name of Ladas *in characters of fire.*

The search was long and painful, though his horses did abound,
Few, few were swift, and few could stay, and fewer still were sound.
One here and there discredited his colours in a race,
Some vanished into sausages, some vanished into space.

But after patient waiting his drooping hopes were cheered,
For at last the steed of destiny and victory appeared,
As handsome as Apollo and swifter than a bird;
So the flouted name of Ladas *for him was disinterred.*

I trust the hopes of Oxford and the Loders' cash he bore,
And the wounds of '69 were healed in '94:
For Ladas *won the Derby amid consoling cheers—*
After a painful interval of five and twenty years.

R.—24

A quarter of a century—O vanished years and gold!
Count not the withered thousands, nor the faded years unfold.
Count not the price indeed, for then would victory seem dear;
Let the recording Angel be ready with a tear.

Your Bard was Senior Censor then—or something of the kind—
But there were other censors to his errors far from blind;
Some cursed him as a sportsman, and others still more keen
Damned his followers as faddists—whatever that may mean.

So all he reaped was buffets, applied on either cheek,
Which he bore—all things considered—with resignation meek.
While his winnings were requested for churches and for cnapels,
So that Derbies—in fruition—resemble desert apples.

One certain gain alone accrues—experience beyond price—
So let the battered veteran administer advice.
(Of course ye will not take it, ye Loders bold and free),
'Let others own the horses that ye go out to see.'

Another moral yet there is, if moral can be found
In what is so immoral and obviously unsound;
To bet may be unlawful, to race may be a sin,
Still in racing, as in everything, it's always best to win.[1]

This was emphatically not the opinion of a large and highly articulate section of the Liberal Party which claimed to represent 'the Nonconformist Conscience'. Rosebery vainly protested that it was absurd to tolerate the ownership of unsuccessful racehorses and then to recoil in horror when one of them won the Derby. His flippant riposte to one critic that Cromwell had also owned racehorses did not assuage the nonconformist wrath. Speaking at the Gimcrack Dinner of 1897 to a more congenial and sympathetic audience he remarked that 'I made the discovery, which came to me late in life, that what was venial and innocent in a Secretary of State or a President of the Council was criminal in the First Lord of the Treasury. I do not even know if I ought not to have learned another lesson—that although without guilt or offence I might perpetually run seconds or thirds, or even run last, it

[1] When the Prince of Wales won the 1896 Derby, Rosebery remarked to his servant that he supposed everyone would say that the other horses had been stopped, and he received the reply 'No doubt, but I am bound to tell your Lordship that many people thought the same thing when *Ladas* won, and you were Prime Minister!'

became a matter of torture to many consciences if I won.' The racing world and London Society were delighted by Rosebery's Derby triumph, but the sterner element in the Liberal Party, which had always relished Gladstone's somewhat ascetic example, found it more than ever difficult to accept as his successor a man who wore the mantle so negligently. The Derby victory confirmed doubts which had been rising as the months passed. 'Rosebery's speeches have not been up to the mark,' Hamilton remarked in his diary on June 21st. 'They have been a little too flippant and made people think that, for a Prime Minister, he is not serious enough or sufficiently in earnest.'

Rosebery's shyness was a serious deficiency in the First Minister. Morley, Asquith, and Acland invited him on three separate occasions to dine with them in the House of Commons to meet Liberal Members but he refused. Acland later told the Webbs that Rosebery 'had been intolerable as head of the Cabinet, shy, huffy, and giving himself the airs of a little German king. . . . He complained that his colleagues never came to see him, but when we did go he had hurried off to The Durdans or to Dalmeny. Then after a Cabinet he might ask one of us to come to lunch, but of course we had, as busy Ministers, already mapped out our day with deputations and parliamentary work. If we pleaded a previous engagement, he would seem offended.'[1] This account is certainly tinged with malice, but it is in part confirmed by the remarks of other Ministers. Complaints of Rosebery's aloofness and inaccessibility occur even in Hamilton's diary, and although the cause was shyness and indecision the effect was wholly unfortunate.

Some attempts were made to arrange a *modus vivendi* between Rosebery and Harcourt, but without any success. Rosebery was so embittered by Harcourt's actions and language over Uganda, the Belgian Agreement, and the Budget that he resisted all entreaties. On one memorandum of Harcourt's he tartly wrote 'Can *la bêtise humaine* further go?' and when Harcourt asked for a CB for a Treasury official Rosebery coldly replied that there was none available. Even the devoted Hamilton, who fully appreciated the delicate situation, thought that Rosebery was being ungenerous and narrow-minded. 'He might have made more allowances for Harcourt—his weaknesses, his temper, & his disappointment,' he

[1] Beatrice Webb: *Our Partnership*, 276-7.

wrote in his diary on July 20th; 'shown himself willing to be very civil to Harcourt; consulted Harcourt on honours & appointments, & occasionally flattered him. No one is more open to a little bit of flattery than Harcourt.'

Spencer and Morley approached Harcourt on July 19th, and were told that Rosebery must make the first move. Loulou's account of the conversation between Morley and Harcourt should be recorded:

At 6.30 J. M. came to see W. V. H. . . . [and] begged him to 'make it up' with R. as it was so unpleasant for the other colleagues to feel there was a 'gulf of ice' between the two sides of the table (they sit opposite one another at the Cabinet). J. M. says R. sees nothing of his colleagues except perhaps Asquith and knows nothing of what is going on or of his duties as Prime Minister.

W. V. H. replied 'That is your fault; he is your choice; you can't expect me to educate him in the duties of his position and if you want me to go in every morning to talk as I used to with Mr G—well, I won't. I endeavour to preserve relations of perfect civility with him when we meet at the Cabinet and as long as we are outwardly on good terms that is all that can be asked.' . . .

J. M. appealed to W. V. H. to make some advance to R. . . . [but] W. V. H. replied that he knew R. too well to make advances to him at such a moment and that if the positions were reversed he should consider such an approach an insult. He told J. M. he quite realised that he (W. V. H.) should lead the Party in Opposition and that this would not make him regret the death of the Government, but warned J. M. that when the dissolution comes he will fight it only as the member for Derby. . . . J. M. knew that Spencer had been on a similar mission without success, and W. V. H. thinks they both came as emissaries from the rest of the Cabinet—though they do not say so.'[1]

Spencer and Morley tried again in September, but with no success, Harcourt writing to Spencer with some bitterness that 'You and your friends have informed me sufficiently frankly you do not regard me as fit to lead. Why then should I pretend to take the initiative only in order that you may repudiate me? As you know, I am not a supporter of the present Govt. I have a great personal regard for all of you and contemplate your proceedings with an impartial curiosity and a benevolent neutrality. I quite agree that your position is a difficult one and I wish you well out of it. And I see that your leader is announced for a good many

[1] L. Harcourt's unpublished Journal, July 19th.

speeches in which he will no doubt develop his policy with his accustomed clearness—and then you will know what to think and do. It will be quite time enough when your plans are declared for me to consider how far I can support them. . . .'[1] This was an insane attitude to adopt, but these episodes revealed how bitterly Harcourt nursed his defeat of March. Asquith wrote at this time that 'Arnold Morley has urged that R has no producible case against H, nor perhaps has he. The full case can only be known to colleagues, by all of whom it is felt to be irresistibly strong: the public only suspect.'[2]

Haldane echoed the dismay of most Liberals when he remarked to West at this time that Rosebery wanted to be a Pitt but was ending in being a Goderich.[3] The Cabinet appeared to have no positive ideas about contemporary problems, and this impression was fully justified. A good example of the indecision and timidity which characterised its work was its attitude to payment of Members of Parliament. The Trades Union Congress, meeting at Norwich early in September, passed a motion in favour of this innovation, and Rosebery asked for his colleagues' views. All were enthusiastic, only Bryce expressing the view that payment of election expenses was more urgent. Harcourt, Arnold Morley, John Morley, and Asquith wanted the reform introduced in the next Session. But in spite of this rare unanimity, nothing was done, and the members of the Cabinet who approved the proposal so warmly do not seem to have even mentioned it again except in the vaguest terms.[4] Rosebery himself was acutely aware of this widespread disappointment, but he was working under very great difficulties. His relationship with the Queen caused him almost as much vexation as that with Harcourt. On April 7th he sent her a long and lucid memorandum on the subject of the House of Lords, which contained the pithy and accurate summary

[1] Gardiner: *Harcourt*, II, 307–8.   [2] Spender and Asquith: *Asquith*, I, 93.
[3] West: *Diaries*, 303.
[4] Asquith's position may be explained by the intense opposition of his second wife —he married Margot Tennant in the May of 1894—to the proposal. In the November of 1897, when the subject was raised again, she wrote to Rosebery that 'I told Henry I wd. rather he walked over my body than advocated such a mad change in our constitution. I want you in talking to him or any other of our colleagues to put yr. foot firmly down. A greater folly for one party to go in for cannot be imagined. Henry has promised me he *won't* vote or speak for it.' Nevertheless, it was a Government headed by Asquith which eventually introduced payment of Members of Parliament in 1911.

of the situation that 'When the Conservative Party is in power, there is practically no House of Lords: it takes whatever the Conservative Government brings it from the House of Commons without question or dispute; but the moment a Liberal Government is formed, this harmless body assumes an active life, and its activity is entirely exercised in opposition to the Government. . . . It is, in fact, a permanent barrier against the Liberal party.' The Queen entirely rejected this practical assessment of the manifestly scandalous nature of the House of Lords, argued that the Lords were of far greater significance than the Commons, and described any agitation against the Lords as 'a most revolutionary Proceeding'. The Prime Minister's rejoinder was not without a sting; he had never denounced the House of Lords, although Russell, Hartington, and Chamberlain had, and it was dangerous to ignore a potentially dangerous situation. On April 14th he politely remarked that the Lords might occasionally represent the true feelings of the country better than the Commons, 'that can scarcely be the case at present when the country has chosen a Liberal House of Commons to represent it, while nine-tenths of the House of Lords are opposed to that party'. On May 14th he set out the difficulties of his position at great length. He had inherited a policy, a cabinet, and a Parliament for which he had not been responsible; the Leader of the House of Commons was bitterly opposed to him, while 'Lord Rosebery in the meantime is shut up in a House almost unanimously opposed to his ministry, and, for all political purposes, might as well be in the Tower of London'; he was thus obliged to make speeches out of Parliament—a proceeding which the Queen always hated—and could not withdraw measures agreed to by the party before he re-joined the Cabinet in 1892. 'What then does Your Majesty expect of him?' he enquired, letting a hint of irritation enter an otherwise courtly epistle; he was determined to quit politics for ever after the Government fell.

In the autumn of 1894 his relations with the Queen entered a more uncomfortable phase. The National Liberal Federation had held a special one-day meeting at Leeds in June in order to pass two vehement resolutions against the Lords, and throughout the latter part of the summer Rosebery was meditating upon the possibilities of an all-out attack on the Lords; Morley visited

Dalmeny in September and reported to Harcourt (September 21st) that his host 'is full of the H of L and what line ought to be taken'.[1] He delayed warning the Queen until October 24th that he intended to proceed by Resolution of the House of Commons directed against the Lords. In a speech at Bradford on the 27th he posed the question, 'When the dissolution comes, what will the election be fought upon? Will it be fought upon Disestablishment or Home Rule or the liquor question? . . . The next election will be fought on none of these, but upon one which includes and represents them all—I mean the House of Lords.' He went on to describe the Lords as 'a great national danger,' announced that the Commons would move a challenging Resolution to end an intolerable situation whereby the Liberal Party had to go 'hat in hand to the House of Lords to ask it to pass your measures, in however mutilated a shape they may wish', and concluded, 'We fling down the gauntlet; it is for you to back us up.'

The Queen was scandalised; she appealed to Salisbury for advice and enquired 'is the Unionist party fit for a dissolution *now*?' She wrote to Rosebery that he had committed a grave impropriety by not consulting her—'not to speak of not obtaining her sanction'—before advocating such changes in the British Constitution. This Rosebery politely denied, and he pointed out that his speech was made to a partisan audience of over five thousand people, 'and it is impossible to argue points under such circumstances in the style appropriate to a drawing room or a library'. On November 3rd Ponsonby was ordered to inform Rosebery that the Queen would not consent to the Resolution being tabled without an appeal to the country.

Rosebery's agitation against the Lords never got off the ground, for he was promptly disavowed by his colleagues. He had consulted none of them before delivering his Bradford speech, and they were highly indignant. A Cabinet meeting broke up on November 9th without agreement being reached, and after Harcourt, Morley, Asquith, and Acland, had all protested at the independent action of their leader. On the 26th he was completely overruled. According to Loulou's account, the meeting ended when Harcourt declared, 'I hope it is clearly understood that nothing is settled'.

[1] *Harcourt Papers.*

Everyone replied 'Oh, yes, nothing is settled'. W. V. H. said, 'It does not matter to me, as I am not going to speak in the country, but those who are had better understand that nothing is settled.'

There was a chorus of questions *why* he was not going to speak—to which he replied 'Because I don't know what to say'.[1]

Rosebery saw the Queen on December 7th at Osborne and deliberately steered the conversation on to the subject of the House of Lords, but he could only intimate to her that if the Resolution was tabled it would only be in a very mild form. The Queen, although relieved, was extremely annoyed with Rosebery. Two years later she commented to Sir Henry James that

He never seemed really to know his own mind. I scolded him for taking up so strong a position against the House of Lords. I telegraphed to him and wrote to him. I did not like his talking about revolutions. He came and saw me, and all he said was I need not trouble, as his views had fallen flat in the country. I did not think that this was a right position for my Prime Minister to take up, and I was not sorry when he was turned out.[2]

On December 11th Rosebery returned to the subject in a speech at Devonport, but the fire and fury of Bradford had almost entirely disappeared, and the speeches of other Ministers emphasised the isolation of the Prime Minister. Balfour, in a wickedly brilliant speech at Haddington on December 21st, dwelt on 'the comedy of the situation'.

There are sixteen members in this Cabinet. I believe and suppose that each of these sixteen gentlemen has a private plan for dealing with the House of Lords, and these sixteen private plans are fighting it out among themselves, with no very assured prospect, so far as I can see, that the fittest is likely to survive.

Thus 1894 closed in embittered recriminations between the separate sections of the Liberal Party and the derisive contempt of the Unionists. By-elections, which had been reasonable from the Liberal point of view up to the autumn, began to show new trends. Rosebery had been forced to abandon a treaty which was the centre-piece of his African policy; he had been humiliated by Harcourt over the Budget; he had been disavowed over his proposed attack on the House of Lords. Of the Liberal Press, only

---

[1] L. Harcourt's unpublished Journal, November 26th.
[2] Askwith: *Lord James of Hereford*, 250.

the *Daily News* remained faithful to him, and in the Cabinet he seemed to have not a single ally. His memoranda and comments on his Premiership in later years made dispiriting reading, and their predominant note is querulousness; he was never given a fair chance, his colleagues were weak, Harcourt's manners were frightful, Loulou took every opportunity of undermining his position, and so on. There was justification in these complaints; he had been treated badly by his colleagues; he was in an extremely difficult position as a Liberal Peer-Premier; he was often criticised unfairly; but the first eight months of his Premiership had illuminated his principal political defects of impatience, lack of proportion, sensitiveness to criticism, and deep resentment of opposition which had been apparent since he had first held junior office.

Yet out of this disastrous period something else had emerged. He had tried to conduct his Cabinet as a reasonable man, and had bowed to the majority decision on two occasions, even though in the case of the Anglo-Belgian Treaty he had struggled to avert the consequences of that decision by failing to dispatch Anderson. But at the close of 1894 it is possible to see a new defiance in Rosebery's attitude towards his colleagues and even the Queen. 'The party of a small England, of a shrunk England, of a degraded England, of a neutral England, of a submissive England, has died out,' he truculently declared to an enthusiastic Sheffield audience on October 25th, but aiming at a wider and more hostile body of Liberal opinion. But fortune, which had treated him so cruelly, was not to permit him the opportunity of re-establishing the authority which he had lost since he had accepted the Queen's Commission.

CHAPTER ELEVEN

'THE VEILED PROPHET'

It does not signify which of the two [Fox and Shelburne] was to blame for this mutual mistrust; that it existed is sufficient. It would be too much to maintain that all the members of a Cabinet should feel an implicit confidence in each other; humanity—least of all political humanity—could not stand so severe a test. But between a Prime Minister in the House of Lords and the Leader of the House of Commons such a confidence is indispensable. Responsibility rests so largely with the one, and articulation so greatly with the other, that unity of sentiment is the one necessary link that makes a relation, in any case difficult, in any way possible. The voice of Jacob and the hands of Esau may effect a successful imposture, but can hardly constitute a durable administration.

ROSEBERY: *Pitt* (1891)

BY THE BEGINNING OF 1895 it was evident that the Government's temporary popularity evoked by the Death Duties Budget was ebbing rapidly. By-elections testified to the apathy of the Liberal supporters and the mounting confidence of their opponents. Forfarshire renounced its allegiance in November, Brigg followed suit in December, and in January the Conservative candidate at Evesham more than doubled his majority. Rosebery's proposed onslaught on the Lords as envisaged at Bradford had been flagrantly ignored by Harcourt, who raised the tattered banner of Local Option. In a major speech at Cardiff on January 19th—a location selected to emphasise the party's commitment to Welsh Disestablishment—Rosebery made the ingenious but unconvincing explanation that the issue of the Lords meant dissolution, and that before that happened 'I want to get something more done for the people'. 'Filling the cup or, in Asquith's phrase, 'ploughing the sands', was the policy he enunciated. Rosebery promised Welsh Disestablishment, curtailment of the liquor trade, and 'one man, one vote', a programme which may have excited the Cardiff Liberals, but which aroused very little enthusiasm elsewhere. John Morley tried to restore Home Rule

to its old predominant position in the party's programme—
having given a pledge to the Irish that it would be 'the first
and principal policy' in the Address—but Rosebery and Harcourt,
in one of their rare meetings (on January 24th), agreed that
this was impossible. There was a violent Cabinet on the following day, in which, according to Loulou's Journal, Morley 'resigned at least six times' but was overruled. The eventual Address
was not inaptly described by Rosebery as 'a *reductio ad absurdum*
of the circulation box'.

The almost incessant quarrels in the Cabinet, the contemptuous
abuse directed against him by the extreme section of the Liberal
Press, and the wearying difficulties with the Queen, had all contributed towards a serious breakdown in the health of the Prime
Minister. Sleep almost entirely deserted him, he brooded too
much, and allowed trivial incidents to assume disproportionate
importance in his mind. 'Shut up with four hundred Tories in the
Lords', he wrote to E. T. Cook, then editor of the *Westminster
Gazette*, 'a Prime Minister deserves extra consideration, but never
a colleague ever defended me, though one and all, except Harcourt, begged me to form a Government. I was sent for by the
Queen and urged on by them, but never chosen by the party. If
they like, therefore, I will clear out and let the party be united
under Harcourt and Morley, with Dilke and Labby and Phil
Stanhope, who are their only followers.'[1] For some weeks he had
been searching for an opportunity to present his colleagues with
an ultimatum, and this came on February 18th, when, in the
Debate on the Address in the Commons, Courtney, Dilke, and
Labouchere delivered venomous attacks against the Prime
Minister to which Harcourt in his reply to the debate made no
reference.

Rosebery summoned a Cabinet meeting on February 19th and
read a prepared statement expressing his disgust at this lack of
support.

. . . I cannot call to mind a single instance in which any individual
in the party or the Ministry has spoken even casually in my defence
within the walls of Parliament. I limit myself to the walls of Parliament, though, so far as my knowledge goes, that limitation is almost
superfluous. . . . I have waited patiently and I hope uncomplainingly

[1] Saxon Mills: *Sir Edward Cook*, 164. The letter is not dated, and no copy has been
discovered.

for a year in order to see whether there would be any change. There has been none. On the contrary, the last two nights have been taken up with a debate on a vote of want of confidence directed obviously and especially against the head of the Government. The discussion has been marked with more than the usual violence against the Prime Minister, and there has been no defence and only one word of association with him.[1] There was not even an indication that the government and the Liberal party did not share the hostility expressed towards the Prime Minister. It seems strange that on the lowest grounds neither the Party nor my colleagues view the position of the head of the government as one of the smallest importance or relevance to themselves. . . .

The difficulties to which I allude have been hard to bear; indeed, I could not undertake to face another session like the last. But I have borne them because I have felt that the arduous task of the Liberal Party should not be complicated by personal incompatibilities. What I complain of and what has rendered my position untenable is not that circumstance. Nor is it the attacks upon me; it is the total—or almost total—absence of ordinary support.

God knows I never sought my present office and would have done anything consistently with honour to avoid it (or even joining the Government in 1892) and I renounce it to say the least without regret. I am aware that technically my resignation puts an end to the administration. But that is only technical. There need be only one Minister the less, and that Minister wishes all success to the Government which he leaves. . . . I beg no one of my colleagues to blame himself, for I blame nobody but myself.

Rosebery's account of this strange Cabinet continues as follows:

The paper was followed by a long rambling amiable discourse from Harcourt, who said that we were all friends, that he had deliberately thought it best not to answer Dilke (which was not the question), that people had tried to make mischief between us but that they had failed & that my departure would break up the Govt & possibly the party. Many warm & almost angry protestations followed from the Cabinet, who unanimously declared that the Cabinet could not go on without me. Campbell-Bannerman took occasion to remark that Labouchere & others thought they had grounds for believing they had supporters in the Cabinet. This brought up Harcourt, who denied that he had any relations with Labouchere.

Thereupon I said that I did not doubt this, but that he was unguarded in conversation with regard to the Govt & his colleagues

[1] By Campbell-Bannerman.

& that people were only too ready to fetch & carry such dangerous gossip.

Then he declared that he had never talked against my colleagues—especially against me. In the end, my colleagues asked me to adjourn a final decision until the Cabinet on Thursday, to which I agreed.

The Cabinet broke up in some consternation. Rosebery's dramatic sense—which was seldom misplaced—had certainly effected a shock upon his colleagues, Kimberley subsequently describing his announcement as 'a thunderbolt'. Within a few hours, letters of loyal support and sympathy began to pour from the pens of Rosebery's colleagues. The announcement of an utterly unexpected Liberal victory at Colchester on the same day[1] undoubtedly strengthened Rosebery's position since it seemed to show that the electorate was returning to the Liberal fold. 'This conversation will put things on a *far* better basis,' Harcourt wrote. 'I have an unhappy sort of feeling that you have rather hardened your heart against me', John Morley wrote in supplicating terms, 'for reasons to me unknown. But if you care to see me in this day of stress, you will send for me.' Most members of the Cabinet thought that Rosebery meant what he said, and there were anxious confabulations. Asquith saw Harcourt and urged him to take the lead if Rosebery really did go, and he and Morley told Harcourt that Rosebery had given them previous warning of his Bradford speech; Harcourt had doubts about what the Queen's attitude would be, but Loulou was convinced that Rosebery was not in earnest, and Harcourt's plans for Cabinet reconstruction—which included Fowler as Chancellor of the Exchequer—were short-lived. On the next day Rosebery saw all his major colleagues and received warm promises of loyal support, but Harcourt had to listen to some hard sayings.

Harcourt (according to Rosebery's account of their interview) began by saying that 'if there is anything I can say or do to help you I will do it for your sake and for my sake and the sake of the Party. That is what I came up to say and I beg you to bear it in mind.'

I told him I would weigh what he said & thanked him.

I took the opportunity in conversation of telling him that if he thought I had sought or wished to be PM he was thoroughly mistaken.

He replied that he did not wish to discuss that point.

[1] See page 379.

I replied nor did I but that I wished him once and for all to understand that.

I also called his attention to the absolute absence of all personal relations between the leaders of the two Houses, that I had never received a single communication from him on the business of the H of C since I had been PM, that this was the first time he had been in my room during that year, and that I was resolved to put an end to a state of things which under the peculiar circs of the Budget it had been possible to endure but which would be intolerable for another session.

I instanced as a specimen of his proceedings his announcement to everyone last year that he was going to resign without a word to me. He denied that he had ever said that he thought of resigning; he had said that he thought he might die, but that was another thing. I was sorry that I could not accept that denial, for, as I told him, he had e.g. openly declared his intention of resignation at F. Rothschild's table, & to multitudes of other people.

These are only some salient features of the interview, which was cold & stiff. The intention of V. H. evidently was that the declaration I have just noted should stand on the record, & that was his object in coming.

Harcourt's account, as related to Loulou, was that he had allowed Rosebery 'to run on for some time, and described it as being like playing a big salmon; you had to let him have plenty of line when he made his rushes and then reel up slowly afterwards'.[1]

At a Cabinet on the 21st, Rosebery, speaking very quietly, told his colleagues that as he had received satisfactory assurances for the future he was prepared to withdraw his resignation. In later years, in a note on these important papers, Rosebery wrote: 'It would of course not have been possible for me to resign; but it was the only way in which I could restore any discipline, or deal with the open and insulting disloyalty of one member of the Cabinet at least. . . . I called a Cabinet to play the last card left to me, and on the whole it succeeded.'

The cause of Cabinet unity was immeasurably strengthened on the same evening in the House of Commons when Fowler, in one of the most brilliant debating speeches ever made by a Minister under attack, routed the Opposition to such a paralysing extent that the Motion of Censure on Indian Cotton Duties utterly

[1] Gardiner: *Harcourt*, II, 350–1.

collapsed, and, amid scenes of wild excitement, the Government which had been hanging on by its eyelids for the past week with majorities of ten to twenty, recorded a majority of nearly two hundred in a full House. A few days later, while the political world was still humming with excitement at Fowler's triumph, Harcourt crushed a potentially serious motion on bimetallism. It seemed that the Government had turned the corner, and back-bench morale rose to a higher point than at any moment since the summer of 1893.

This was clearly the moment for Rosebery to re-establish his personal authority on the same lines as in 1892–4; he had taken office on the express desire of the majority of his colleagues; either he had his own way or he went. Relations between Morley and Harcourt were still strained. Morley complained to Ellis in January that 'having been broken in health by his own labours for Ireland, he was not going to be broken in reputation by remaining in a Cabinet which was so violently anti-Irish'. Ellis replied that Harcourt at least had recently spoken on the Irish Question. 'Yes,' said Morley, wagging his head, 'I was not unfavourably impressed by the speech on first reading it, but I am going to scrutinise it *very carefully* this evening.' 'What an occupation for a man's leisure hour!' George Murray, who reported the incident, wrote to Rosebery.

Any plans which the Prime Minister may have had to impose his will upon his colleagues were irretrievably destroyed by an illness whose seriousness has not been sufficiently appreciated by historians.

For several months he had been sleeping very badly, and for long periods suffered from almost complete insomnia which had eroded his health in a manner that startled and distressed his closest friends. He managed to give a public appearance of confidence and well-being but in private he was near despair. Randolph Churchill's death in January had distressed him deeply, although it had been long anticipated. He had taken to going on long night drives as he could not sleep, and in these solitary journeyings he brooded deeply upon the misery of his existence. 'Toughness when nothing particular was happening was not the form of fortitude in which he excelled,' Churchill has written,[1] and this temperamental disability for a Prime Minister was

---

[1] *Great Contemporaries*, 22.

exacerbated tenfold by the terrible sleeplessness which plagued him at all moments of crisis when he could not see his course. His colleagues, from whom he increasingly divorced himself, had no idea of the mental and physical strain under which Rosebery was suffering at this time. Campbell-Bannerman described him at this period as 'most patient and good-natured',[1] but this was purchased at a heavy price.

Within a week of the delivery of the ultimatum to the Cabinet on which he pinned so many hopes, Rosebery suffered what was nearly a complete breakdown in health, a serious attack of influenza being the final factor. Sir William Broadbent hastened to The Durdans on February 25th and was horrified to find that Rosebery's pulse was barely perceptible and the lips were 'quite ghastly'. The influenza was cured reasonably quickly, but the physical collapse which it had directly accelerated was slow to respond. On March 8th Broadbent reported to Reid, the Queen's physician, that there was little improvement, and he told Brett on the 13th that he had never come across such a serious case of chronic insomnia and if there was not some speedy improvement 'there must be a fatal termination'. Brett visited The Durdans and had a long drive with Rosebery in his carriage. 'He was not cheerful,' Brett wrote to a friend, 'and we talked over every imaginable thing. He complains of loneliness. Marriage frightens him—he cannot believe in a fresh disinterested affection. As if that mattered to anyone who understands love!' Rosebery remained acutely depressed, frequently complaining of loneliness. Eddie Hamilton came to The Durdans on March 17th and was alarmed by his friend's appearance and gloomy conversation. He counted himself fortunate if he had two hours' sleep a night, and could not see how he could carry on the Premiership in these circumstances. Brett came again on the 21st.

Rosebery telegraphed for me. I went down. He was worse than last week, after three sleepless nights.

He began 'This is my wedding day!' That was depressing enough.

. . . He got very irritable and angry with the servants, and said to me 'I am unfit for human society'. In reality he is broken down with illness and worry. He lies awake thinking all night. Whether it is temporary or permanent God knows, but it is terribly painful to witness.[2]

[1] Spender: *Campbell-Bannerman*, I, 166.
[2] Brett: *Journals and Letters of Viscount Esher*, I, 188.

Rosebery was extremely exercised by what he regarded as the unforgivably inept negotiations conducted by Harcourt over the Speakership which became vacant upon the unexpected resignation of Speaker Peel. Campbell-Bannerman wrote Rosebery a very long letter asking for the position, since he could not on health grounds—and did not on personal grounds—desire a position in the Liberal hierarchy. 'It is the first time, I think, that I ever pushed myself, and if it were not a serious matter with me I shd shrink from doing it now.' Rosebery was distressed and surprised, and gently told Campbell-Bannerman in a kind letter on March 11th and in the course of an unhappy interview at The Durdans on the 17th that the proposal was out of the question.

The Cabinet met on March 12th—neither Rosebery nor Campbell-Bannerman (who had a cold) attended—and agreed that no Minister should be appointed. Harcourt in the meantime had formally approached Courtney, but on the 15th it was evident that he could not command Liberal-Unionist support, and declined. The Unionists announced their intention of putting forward their own candidate—Sir Mathew White Ridley—and Rosebery believed strongly that the Speaker must be found in the Liberal ranks. Harcourt took a high-and-mighty House of Commons attitude, and virtually told Rosebery to mind his own business. 'Speakers are not Shakespeares,' Rosebery tartly replied on the 16th; 'they are usually under-secretaries or whips. We should have a score of possible Speakers among our party.' He suggested Haldane—whom he privately approached—Frank Lockwood, or Mr Gully, an obscure back-bencher 'of whom I hear good things'. Harcourt replied that these names 'are absurd and out of the question. I really could not be responsible for recommending to the Chair persons whom I regard as quite incompetent for that position'. He proposed—to Rosebery's intense anger—to approach Courtney again. Donald Crawford reported to Rosebery (March 15th) that 'Courtney sits in the Library . . . gazing on all with a meek and genial smile. C. Bannerman's wife, distrusting his interior, put him to bed for a week. Ridley at the Speaker's last night, after taking a furtive inventory of the furniture and pictures, was playful over his chairmanship of the Scottish Grand Committee. Of the very outsiders, Gully has taken to dining in the House, Hanbury has grown much larger and more generally dignified, Justinian [Haldane] patronises from a more distant and elevated point, but much more kindly than before. Well, it makes the House a much more pleasant place. Half are in the running, and they are very kind to the other half.' 'It is impossible to allow the points of the various candidates to be canvassed like those of a slave auction,' Rosebery angrily wrote to Harcourt on the 17th. 'I propose therefore to call a Cabinet . . . to discuss & if possible solve this question.' Harcourt replied that it was a House of Commons matter, and told Murray that if Rosebery interfered he would resign. Rosebery, forbidden by Broadbent to travel to London, nursed his indignation with difficulty. 'I cannot endure the party humiliation of again seeking a Speaker among my opponents,' he wrote to Gladstone on March 18th.

The Cabinet, baffled by the turn of events, made another approach to Courtney through Morley. Courtney told Morley that a three-quarters majority of the Liberal-Unionists would be sufficient and that the Government should inform the Opposition that Ridley's candidature would be unacceptable. This was on March 20th, and Rosebery, when informed, protested strongly at this 'humiliating' procedure, which put the Government in the position of suppliants to the Liberal-Unionists. He said that if his Commons colleagues were 'really unanimous' he would accept their decision with reluctance. On the 25th the Liberal-Unionists held a short, poorly attended meeting in which they agreed to support Ridley, and the rather unattractive personality of Courtney was removed from the field. 'It is scarcely possible', Rosebery wrote bitterly, 'to exaggerate the humiliating position in wh the Govt has been placed by this hunting of Courtney & hanging on the smiles of the LU party.' Harcourt replied to the protestations from The Durdans with the bland statement that 'I do not myself take any profound interest in the question, which seems to me of secondary importance' (March 26th), and he told Murray on the following day that he had washed his hands of the whole business and that Ridley would certainly defeat any Liberal nominee. Murray protested strongly at Harcourt's conduct in placing the responsibility back upon Rosebery, who had consistently drawn his attention to the folly of his conduct. Rosebery refused to accept the poisoned chalice; it was, he tartly remarked, a 'House of Commons matter' as someone had said. Harcourt replied that the nominee would have to be Gully 'who knows nothing and whom nobody knows', and that 'if it is thought better to arrive at Ridley through a defeat of the Govt I personally have no objection'. Rosebery—fortified by Liberal backbench opinion—insisted upon a party candidate, and the obscure Mr Gully—who was, however, a close friend of Herschell—was propelled towards a position to which he was elected on April 10th by eleven votes and which he occupied with little distinction. Nonetheless, the party challenge laid down by Balfour had been met and resisted, and Harcourt was obliged to commend to the House of Commons the man whom a few weeks before he had dismissed so contemptuously.

Rosebery's illness had temporarily improved relations between himself and Harcourt before the Speakership crisis flared up, and on March 31st he told Hamilton that 'if it were not for Loulou' matters would be improved further. Brett records that he met Loulou at the beginning of March and found him 'most vindictive' towards Rosebery, 'whereas Sir William has recovered his equanimity'. Harcourt was a man of such strange moods that it is possible that his desire to work cordially with Rosebery—expressed through Hamilton—was genuine enough, but at the first opportunity he hurled himself with elephantine delicacy into bitter controversy.

Rosebery's physical condition at the beginning of April was still deplorable. He was haggard with insomnia and strain, and the depressing after-effects of the influenza were evident. 'Conducting an inherited Govt. with 5 per cent of one House & a majority of ten in the other does not exactly represent the exuberance of power, & certainly not its intoxication,' he wrote to Haldane on April 26th, 'but it reminds one of the darker portions of Frederick the Great's campaigns.'[1] On April 12th he told Hamilton that for the first time in his life he understood why people committed suicide. The recollection of these months haunted him for the rest of his life. 'I cannot forget 1895,' he wrote in 1903. 'To lie night after night, staring wide awake, hopeless of sleep, tormented in nerves, and to realise all that was going on, at which I was present, so to speak, like a disembodied spirit, to watch one's own corpse as it were, day after day, is an experience which no sane man with a conscience would repeat.'

[1] *Haldane Papers.*

It was in this unhappy physical and mental condition that he had to grapple with Harcourt over what he rightly regarded as the last vestiges of his control over national affairs. His African policy was in shreds; the Anglo-Congolese Treaty had failed ignominiously, the Anglo-French discussions had been abandoned, and ominous reports of French infiltration were coming in. The only alternative to negotiation was intimidation, and in reply to a Commons debate on the alleged French encroachments on the Niger and in the direction of the head-waters of the Nile on March 28th, Edward Grey categorically placed the entire Nile valley within the British sphere of influence, and stated that a French advance into this area would be regarded as 'an unfriendly act'. This important statement was made without Rosebery's prior knowledge, but Grey knew his mind completely, and Rosebery at once endorsed his remarks. As Murray wrote to Bigge on April 2nd, 'all the circumstances of Grey's declaration on Thursday night were very fortunate. If it had been premeditated, it could scarcely have been made without the express sanction of the Cabinet; and I shudder to think of what the feelings of that august body would have been, if they had been asked to take such a step in cold blood. As it was, neither they—nor indeed anybody else—knew anything about it beforehand. . . . It has enabled Lord Rosebery to commit the Cabinet to a policy of which, I should think, none of them cordially approve, and to which not a few are violently opposed. I am afraid you will think my sentiments very unconstitutional but they are (otherwise) sound.'[1] There was much sound and fury, but Harcourt and Morley were confronted with the choice of demanding a disavowal of the declaration and losing Grey, or endorsing his statement. Grey clearly had a majority of the House of Commons, the Press, the Queen, and the Prime Minister behind him, and the issue was never seriously in doubt. Nevertheless, Harcourt and Morley lodged vehement protests. Harcourt wrote to Kimberley (March 29th) that Grey's declaration was made contrary to the views of the Cabinet, and that Grey had deliberately departed from the prepared statement which had been agreed to by him. 'The whole of the mischief which has arisen and which I fear is irremediable', Harcourt wrote again to Kimberley on the 30th, 'comes of your determination against which I have so often remonstrated, not to let me know

[1] *Royal Archives.*

what the FO was intending to do or say in matters on which you knew there was a strong difference of opinion.' 'I only hope', came the daily broadside of March 31st to the hapless Foreign Secretary, 'for the sake of peace that the French Govt may under this very unnecessary provocation show that good temper and good sense in which they have hitherto set us an example very deserving of our imitation.' On April 1st there came a formal demand that Harcourt should see and approve all Parliamentary answers to questions on Foreign Affairs and that he himself should make all statements of importance on the subject. Rosebery strongly resisted this proposal. 'Nothing shd be done to diminish, impair, or reflect upon the present position of E. Grey,' he wrote to Kimberley on April 2nd. 'He is one of the most important members of the Govt; for his being outside the Cabinet is the direct cause not of his failure, but of his great success as reptve. of the FO. Moreover he is *persona gratissima* to the H of C, popular, admired, and respected. Any attempt therefore to take out of his hands what he has been doing with such consummate skill wd be resented by many besides himself, and by none more than—yrs AR.'

There is no direct evidence to support the general view—echoed by the new French ambassador, Courcel[1]—that Rosebery (who saw Kimberley at The Durdans on March 27th) had prepared the statement. Grey's account is very mysterious, since he claimed in his memoirs that he had transferred the firmness which Kimberley had impressed upon him from answers to questions on the Niger to those on the Nile. This disclaimer has convinced no student of the period except his biographer, G. M. Trevelyan, who for once attributes a degree of stupidity to his hero which it is difficult to credit. As one observer has pointed out,[2] Grey had already used the prepared Niger answers. It seems clear that in making his famous 'Declaration' Grey was repeating—either consciously or otherwise—the views expressed to him on numerous occasions by the one Minister he admired—Rosebery. To this extent, therefore, Rosebery must be held to be personally responsible for the statement.

[1] See his report to Hanotaux of March 28th (*D.D.F.*, XI, 630–1).
[2] W. L. Langer, *The Diplomacy of Imperialism*, I, 264–5. Temperley and Penson (*Foundations of British Foreign Policy*, 501) also refuse to accept Grey's account (*Twenty-five Years*, I, 18) and that of Trevelyan (*Grey of Fallodon*, 69).

'Though there was some grumbling in the usual quarters,' as Rosebery reported to the Queen, the Cabinet approved Grey's declaration on March 30th, and Rosebery was determined that Harcourt's ultimatum on Foreign Affairs statements should be resisted. At the Cabinet it was not Harcourt but Morley who made the greatest fuss; he stated that unless the Declaration was overturned he would resign, and when Rosebery said that he entirely approved of Grey's statement, Morley angrily replied that he must go. Harcourt, on the ground that his resignation would damage Anglo-French relations even further, persuaded him to relent.[1] Nevertheless, some concession to Cabinet feeling was necessary, and on April 1st Grey published a letter in *The Times* which stated that they had omitted the words 'and Egyptian' in their report; although this qualification made little practical difference to the impact of the Declaration, there was at least a hint that the interests of the two countries might be separated at a future date, and Morley (according to Loulou Harcourt's Journal for April 1st) was satisfied. Rosebery, in a note on Morley written many years later, remarked that 'John never further alluded to the subject of his resignation'.

Having been subjected to two more characteristically offensive Harcourtian letters in which the Chancellor threatened resignation,[2] even the mild Kimberley could tolerate this stream of wounding missives no longer. 'The position is really almost impossible,' he wrote to Rosebery on April 6th. '. . . How is the business of the country to be carried on successfully under such conditions? . . . Harcourt practically insists upon playing the role of joint Prime Minister. How can I serve two masters, with one of whom happily I have no differences . . . but with the other of whom I have, to put the matter mildly, little in common?' 'It is impossible to conceal from ourselves, or at any rate it is impossible for me to conceal from myself', Rosebery replied, 'that there is a deep seated & radical difference between Harcourt & myself on questions of foreign policy. His view is broadly that in questions between G. Britain & foreign countries, foreign countries are always in the right & G. Britain always in the wrong.' 'I cannot compromise on these vital matters,' he wrote again on April 7th,

---

[1] Langer, *op. cit.*, I, 266, wrongly assumes that Rosebery's reference in his report to the Queen (*Letters*, II, 491–2) to 'one resignation threatened' was to Harcourt.
[2] Quoted in full in Gardiner: *Harcourt*, II, 337.

'& I confess I view the approach of the critical moment with a certain sense of relief. So I suspect do you.'

Criticism of the handling of Foreign Affairs was not confined to the Cabinet, and indeed from the collapse of the Anglo-Congolese Agreement a hopeless muddle seemed to overtake the Foreign Office. The massacre of thousands of Armenians in the autumn of 1894 aroused Mr Gladstone from his retirement, and Bryce and Harcourt in the Cabinet echoed his demands for more vigorous action by the Government. 'I reckon myself as a man of peace in foreign affairs,' Harcourt wrote to Kimberley on December 2nd. 'In fact I am one of those mean-spirited "Little Englanders who have ceased to exist", but there is a point of humiliation at which even my gorge rises, and we have swallowed our full peck of dirt in this business, and it is time we should have some regard to our own dignity and self-respect, and not allow our nose to be tweaked by the Grand Turk, unless we mean to allow ourselves to be the laughing-stock of Constantinople and of Europe.' But by the summer of 1895 Harcourt had become far less bellicose, and he and Morley strenuously opposed any suggestion that the British Fleet should force the Dardanelles, for once in complete agreement with the Prime Minister. But the impatience of many Liberal supporters was echoed by the contempt of Europe. Another public sign of weakness was the refusal of the Government to co-operate with Russia, France, and Germany over the Sino-Japanese war which ended in the April of 1895 with a complete victory for Japan. Rosebery, although overruled by his colleagues, let it be known in diplomatic circles that he regretted the decision.

Rosebery's determination to keep the Foreign Office independent of Harcourt was given an immediate opportunity for test. The Nicaraguan Government had expelled a British Vice-Consul, and the British Government demanded £15,500 compensation; arbitration was requested by the Nicaraguans and refused, and three British warships seized Corinto and inflicted a humiliating defeat upon a minor state. Harcourt—for once clearly in the right—was outraged, but his prestige in the Cabinet had fallen so low that Rosebery and Kimberley—who, however, was extremely unhappy about the incident—were able to pursue their policy. Morley's 1894 prognostication that the Foreign Office would become a secret bureau controlled by Rosebery had been fulfilled. Rosebery refused to have anything to do with Harcourt, and never met him outside Cabinet meetings, which were kept to the irreducible minimum. Tempers were getting short; Murray constantly urged Rosebery to give at least the impression of being open to argument, but to no avail. At the end of a characteristically acrid Cabinet meeting on May 27th, in which Morley and Harcourt had urged postponing a decision on the Uganda railroad, Rosebery said to Morley that he hoped they would be friends again when they were no longer colleagues. 'Perhaps,' said Morley, and flounced out of the room.[1]

The Welsh Disestablishment Bill, the major measure of the Session, dawdled through Committee in May, to the mounting exasperation of a group of independently-minded Welsh Liberals already dominated by Lloyd George. When Asquith, whose lack of interest in the measure was ill-concealed, refused an important amendment moved by Lloyd George on May 20th, the disgust of the Welsh minority was manifest. Ellis, of whom much was expected by the party leaders in controlling the Welsh, had bungled his work. 'Tom Ellis, a charming and gifted man, and one of my greatest personal friends,' Asquith has written, 'was more at home among the children of light than with the children of this world, with whom a Chief Whip is in daily and even hourly converse.'[2] Gladstone began to take an unwelcome interest in the measure, and for a time there was a possibility that he would actually appear in the Commons to attack it, an impression strengthened by the somewhat dramatic cancellation of his 'pair'. Ellis, although aware of this impending step, did not inform the leader of this ominous event until it was publicly announced on June 19th.

The effects of his illness were now clearly apparent upon Rosebery. He was irritable, even petulant, and becoming absurdly petty over trivial matters. In May 'Blackie' Hope expressed the desire to become Secretary of the Office of Works, but Rosebery brusquely refused to make the appointment because, he alleged, Hope had been a Conservative faggot voter in the 1880 Midlothian election. Hamilton protested strongly at this ridiculous pettiness, but without effect. But Hamilton realised, which other

[1] At a Cabinet on the following day Rosebery gained his point, and Government support for the undertaking was announced.
[2] Asquith: *Memories and Reflections*, I, 190.

people could not, that a man who is getting barely any sleep for night after night cannot be expected to adopt a reasonable attitude on every question. On May 8th, while making a short speech at the National Liberal Club, Rosebery broke down, lost the thread of his remarks, and recovered himself with difficulty in an embarrassed silence. A brief yachting holiday and the tonic of the unexpected victory of *Sir Visto* in the Derby did little to improve his health or his general depression.

The Government was clearly disintegrating in public as well as in its Cabinet conclaves. By-elections, disappointing at the end of 1894, became disastrous in 1895. Since the beginning of April four safe Liberal seats had been lost, and the one victory which the Government recorded in February evoked accusations of a nature which did it far more harm than any number of defeats. The sitting Unionist Member for Colchester, Captain Naylor-Leyland, unexpectedly resigned at the beginning of February, and it was quickly apparent that although the Unionist organisers were taken completely by surprise, the Liberals were not, and won the by-election on February 19th, in spite of statements by the Liberal candidate, the wealthy contractor Sir Weetman Pearson (later Lord Cowdray), to the effect that pressure of business would preclude frequent attendance to his Parliamentary duties. Naylor-Leyland then announced that he had joined the Liberal Party, and subsequently received a baronetcy in June. The uproar which this cynical announcement created was tremendous,[1] and it was widely stated by disgruntled Unionists that there had been some very suspicious transactions between Naylor-Leyland and the Liberal Whips before he had announced his strange resignation from the Commons. It was not easy to see what other services Captain Naylor-Leyland—who was only thirty-one years of age—had rendered to the State. The details of these *sordida* seem to have disappeared; the only direct reference in Rosebery's papers to payment being made for an honour was one of £5,000 by Lipton, the tea magnate, for his knighthood, and this application was made before Rosebery became Prime Minister. But it is evident that Arnold Morley—and probably Ellis as well—was engaged

[1] Oddly enough, the *Manchester Guardian* was the only newspaper of any importance which did not condemn the nomination. Even *The Speaker*, edited by Rosebery's great friend, Wemyss Reid, violently attacked it, for once supported by *Truth*, which delivered a tremendous philippic.

upon the selling of honours at this time, and it seems probable that the Naylor-Leyland business was characteristic of his tactics.[1]

The Liberal finances were in an unhappy position in the 1890's. The widening of the franchise and the Corrupt Practices Act of 1883 had virtually compelled the parties to increase their national expenditure; the general election fund in 1880 had been just over £30,000, but by 1895 it was nearly £80,000, while the annual expenditure of the central party organisation had grown proportionately. The events of 1886 had removed almost all the men of wealth from the Liberal Party, and by 1891 it was agreed by Arnold Morley and Schnadhorst that rich industrialists could be persuaded to make large contributions to party funds in return for promises of peerages or other favours when the party returned to power. Rhodes paid £5,000 on condition that the Conservatives' Egyptian policy would not be reversed, and Schnadhorst regarded himself as responsible for supervising Rhodes' interests, although he does not seem to have put any pressure upon Rosebery (who was ignorant of the arrangement). In 1891 Arnold Morley and Schnadhorst found two rich Liberals, James Williamson and Sydney Stern, who were prepared to pay for peerages, and when Morley and Tweedmouth informed Rosebery in 1895 that Gladstone had agreed to this ignoble transaction he was extremely angry, and refused to believe the story. Morley persuaded Gladstone to inform Rosebery that it was true, and Rosebery reluctantly agreed that the matter must go forward. He felt very strongly that he was put in an impossible position—having already pledged himself against creating any new peerages—and in his letters to Williamson and Stern he made it plain that he offered the honours under protest. In a speech on March 28th, 1896, he publicly declared that he had been compelled to create these two highly controversial peerages as a result of pledges made without his knowledge by his predecessor. Rosebery's elder son recalls the intense anger and even disgust with which his father spoke of this wretched business, and the incident is probably characteristic of his general ignorance of this aspect of party arrangement. Like Gladstone, he preferred not to know what was going on in the murky regions of the party organisation and did not care very

[1] See H. J. Hanham, *Victorian Studies*, March 1960, 'The Sale of Honours in Late Victorian England'.

much. He approved the Naylor-Leyland baronetcy when he was deeply involved in other matters, and probably did not give the matter a second thought. To this limited extent, he must be held to blame for the merited obloquy which was hurled upon the Ministry.[1]

The final crisis of Rosebery's miserable Premiership arose, of all things, over a proposal to erect a statue to Oliver Cromwell in the precincts of the Palace of Westminster. The Cabinet approved the project, and after a typically acrimonious argument over the possible sites, asked the House of Commons to approve the vote of £500. The Irish Nationalists promptly erupted; 'Drogheda, and all the other deeds of two centuries and a half before blazed into memory as if they had happened yesterday,' John Morley has ruefully recorded.[2] On June 17th Rosebery was surprised to be told casually by Ellis that in view of the unexpectedly fierce opposition from the Irish, the vote might have to be withdrawn. Rosebery caustically remarked that 'This Government is not strong enough to do so weak a thing', but at 10.15 p.m. on the same evening, having heard other rumours to the same effect, he telephoned Ellis to ask what was going on; Ellis replied that the Commons members of the Cabinet had met and had decided to withdraw the vote. This was done by Morley amid 'wild cries of aboriginal joy from our Irish friends'. Rosebery told Ellis that this was outrageous, that no one had consulted him, that a Cabinet must be summoned forthwith, and that he would not endorse the supine attitude of his colleagues. He then wrote a memorandum which reveals the extent to which his temper and sense of proportion had been affected by the events of the past months.

. . . This is an admirable object lesson of the way in which the affairs of the government have been carried on. . . . It is obviously impossible for me to remain responsible for the conduct of business under such circumstances. I do not blame anyone. It is possibly a necessity of the situation. But at any rate one thing is clear, that no one with the commonest self-respect can remain the head of the Govt under such circumstances, and it is for me now to consider whether

---

[1] Hamilton considered that Arnold Morley was 'the principal culprit: but R. ought to have put his foot down and declined point blank to fulfil any pledge of so disgusting a kind.' (Diary, July 7th.)

[2] *Recollections*, II, 48.

it is possible for me consistently with honour to continue to hold my present position. . . .[1]

His colleagues were spared this final absurdity, with the Prime Minister's perennial chant 'I do not blame anyone', when it was clear that that was exactly what he was doing. On June 21st the end came.

It had been a bad week, with the Cromwell Statue fiasco on Monday, a Government defeat in a Standing Committee on an amendment to the Factory Bill on Tuesday, and a majority of only seven in the House on a major amendment to the Welsh Disestablishment Bill on Wednesday. On Thursday Campbell-Bannerman announced the end of the prolonged and embarrassing negotiations which had led to the supersession of the aged Duke of Cambridge as Commander-in-Chief of the Army, and on the same evening a snap vote to reduce his salary on the grounds that he had failed to secure enough cordite for the army found Ministers in a minority. It was significant that the Welsh Liberals were almost entirely absent from the division lists, and both Harcourt and Asquith were apprehensive of a defeat on the remaining clauses of the Bill on the following Monday. The situation had become intolerable, for the Government was living on sufferance, dependent upon every use of their supporters in straight clashes with the Opposition, and through this fact having to lean upon Unionist support against their extreme supporters. Even if measures passed the Commons, the Lords could do what they liked with them. Ministers had to ask 'What will the Irish say?' 'What will the Welsh say?' 'What will Labby and his friends say?' and then 'What will the Lords do?' The party, and particularly the Cabinet, was in a condition of physical and mental exhaustion when the chance blow came, and although under normal circumstances the cordite defeat would have been regarded as a mere nuisance, Ministers eagerly snatched at this opportunity of deliverance from an utterly impossible and humiliating position. There was, in fact, an overwhelming sense of relief that the end had come.

There was an informal meeting of Ministers at the House of Commons after the cordite division—not attended by Rosebery,

[1] Rosebery subsequently commissioned the statue—by Thornycroft—and contributed £3,000; it was sited outside Westminster Hall facing Westminster Abbey, and was unveiled by Rosebery himself in 1899.

who was enjoying the shortest night of the year on the verandah at The Durdans—and it was decided that Ellis should replace the Welsh Bill with Supply for Monday to give an opportunity for rescinding the vote if necessary. A red-lined Whip, the most imperative of summonses, was issued to all Liberal Members for the Monday.

The Cabinet met on the following morning; they had to decide whether to resign, to dissolve, or to carry on and prepare for a dissolution at the earliest possible moment. Harcourt, Ripon and Tweedmouth supported Rosebery's argument that immediate resignation was their best course, and this powerful if unusual combination eventually overcame the arguments of Morley, Asquith, Fowler, and Kimberley who favoured dissolution. Ellis was called in, and—according to Loulou Harcourt's Journal for June 22nd—urged delay, since he was not ready for an election, and Robert Hudson (who had replaced Schnadhorst as Secretary of the Liberal Central Office) had told him that a sudden resignation with no comprehensible electoral cry and with half the work of the Session uncompleted would be 'suicidal'.

This extremely sensible advice made no impression upon the Cabinet; they were, to a man, sick of office, and, in any event, Campbell-Bannerman obstinately refused to withdraw his resignation and ask for the rescindment of the cordite vote. The Cabinet had not agreed by lunch-time, but in an afternoon meeting of nearly two hours (4 to 5.45 p.m.) agreed to resign, and Rosebery travelled to Windsor to inform the Queen of the decision. As Asquith has observed, 'The Cabinet was so impressed by the unusual—the almost unprecedented—spectacle of their [Rosebery and Harcourt] cordial agreement with one another, that it deferred to their combined authority.'[1] By 9 p.m. the Queen had dispatched a message to Salisbury to invite him to form an administration.

Rosebery intended to inform his colleagues at a last meeting on the 27th that he could never again work with Harcourt and that he would retire from public life, but, as he told Hamilton, 'everybody was so amicable and so friendly to me that my heart failed me, and I had to allow matters to slide for the moment'. Harcourt had called on him—'the first time since I have been PM', Rosebery noted in his diary—on June 23rd and again on the

[1] Asquith: *Fifty Years of Parliament*, I, 262.

next day, and the conversations appear to have been reasonably cordial. Nonetheless, he determined to announce definite separation from Harcourt after the general election. 'It is not possible', he wrote to Campbell-Bannerman on July 27th, 'that the sham of partnership can be carried on any longer.'[1]

On June 24th he dined for the last time in Downing Street, the Gladstones also being present. 'Illuminated by Lord Rosebery's irresistible charm', Mary Gladstone has written, 'we had a most delightful evening, the late and the present Prime Ministers being merry as boys out of school.'[2] On June 28th Rosebery had his final audience with the Queen, at which she invested him with the Thistle, and 'To London—free', he wrote thankfully in his diary. 'There are two supreme pleasures in life,' he wrote in 1899. 'One is ideal, the other real. The ideal is when a man receives the seals of office from his Sovereign. The real pleasure comes when he hands them back.'[3]

The Liberal Party confronted the electorate in the July of 1895 with a series of laughably conflicting policies which bewildered its supporters and invited the ridicule of its opponents. Harcourt and Morley in particular seem to have approached the elections dominated by a kind of political death-wish. On February 13th Loulou Harcourt had recorded a conversation between his father and Morley in which Morley remarked, 'we shall all have our own manifestoes; you at Derby and I at Newcastle'. 'W. V. H. said, "I shall have no manifesto; I shall say to my constituents 'I have been your member for 15 years and I hope to be so again'. " '[4] Tweedmouth put his finger on the fatal weakness of the party when he wrote to Gladstone (July 12th) that 'our weak spot is the want of one leader and one policy to conjure by'. Rosebery still urged an all-out attack on the Lords, but was ignored; Morley spoke solely on Home Rule, while Harcourt perplexed and irritated the electors of Derby with expositions on the merits of Local Option. 'The Liberals', as Mr Peter Stansky justly remarks, 'were becoming known as the party of faddists, a collection of cranks, each with his own cure for the ills of the nation.'[5]

---

[1] *Campbell-Bannerman Papers.*   [2] Mary Drew: *Catherine Gladstone*, 259.
[3] *Sir Robert Peel* (1899).
[4] L. Harcourt's unpublished Journal for February 13th, 1895.
[5] Stansky, *op. cit.*, 306.

The consequence of these divergencies was electoral catastrophe, which swept away both Harcourt and John Morley—both of whom returned to the House of Commons within a few months— Shaw-Lefevre and Arnold Morley, while other senior Ministers had their majorities seriously reduced. Whereas 124 Unionists were unchallenged, only 10 Liberals were allowed an uncontested election, a contrast which illuminated the efficiency and enthusiasm of the two parties. The Liberal majority of 43 was converted into a Unionist majority of 152—the worst defeat suffered by either political party since 1832, although in terms of total votes cast the Unionists only had a national majority of just over 40,000—and the accession of Devonshire and Chamberlain to the new Government formalised the relationship of the Liberal-Unionists with the Conservatives.

Rosebery surveyed this holocaust with a certain sardonic satisfaction. 'I expected this overthrow,' he wrote to Ripon, 'and think it a great blessing to the Liberal party . . . we have offended every interest by the Newcastle Programme (to which I have never adhered): three leaders proclaimed three different policies. . . . But there was a more general & deeply rooted cause—Mr G's general policy since 1880.'[1] On October 18th he made three speeches in one day at Scarborough in which he blamed the defeat of the Government upon its concentration on local issues which did not interest the majority of the people. He was clearly right, but both the timing and the content of the speeches were not happy; as the *Annual Register* remarked with truth, the Scarborough speeches 'were a general disappointment'.

They did not meet the wishes of those who wanted a definite lead, for they gave no lead at all. They abolished the old programme and substituted no other for it. The Irish and Welsh parties resented the disparagement of Home Rule and Church Disestablishment; the Radicals, who were clamourers for a strong policy, were aggrieved at getting none; and even timid Liberals, who hesitated about many things, were disappointed to find Lord Rosebery in the same case. Whatever the purpose they might have been intended to serve, the speeches did not strengthen Lord Rosebery's claim to the confidence of his party.

'My Scarborough speeches will make the Radicals—rather the faddists—furious,' he wrote to Hamilton after the dust had

[1] *Ripon Papers.*

settled, 'but I counted on that beforehand, and do not care, as the Duke of Wellington used to say, a twopenny damn.' This attitude, however justified, was not the most desirable in the leader of a party which had just suffered a humiliating defeat, and boded ill for the future. To Canon Scott Holland he wrote on August 21st:

I do not need consolation with regard to this general election. It was inevitable, and can scarcely fail to do good. The Liberal Party had become all legs and wings, a daddy-long-legs fluttering among a thousand flames: it had to be consumed in order that something more sane, more consistent, and more coherent could take its place. . . . It sees in its purgatory that it must concentrate itself, and that it cannot gain victories as a mad mob of dervishes, each waving his own flag and howling curses on everyone else's. . . .

The people will come back to us. Liberalism has always been founded among the masses not on aspiration but on discontent. The masses are, comparatively speaking, contented just now. May they remain so, even if Liberalism should suffer thereby.

I count too as clear gain the defeat of Socialism of the rabid kind and the separation of Socialism from Liberalism. But it is always possible that that may happen which has happened in Belgium—the elimination of Liberalism, leaving the two forces of Socialism and Reaction face to face. Whether that shall happen here depends on the Liberal Party. . . .

In Rosebery's opinion the first essential step was to formalise the divorce from Harcourt. 'No earthly power will induce me to take part in the dishonest hypocrisy of the last year or two,' he told Wemyss Reid. 'Nothing will lead me again to consent to anything like a dual leadership between myself and a man whom I cannot trust.' 'The firm of Rosebery and Harcourt', he wrote to Gladstone (August 26th) 'was a fraud upon the public.'

The opportunity for making his decision known soon arose. On August 10th Spencer wrote to him to suggest Spencer House as a suitable meeting-place for the ex-cabinet, and Rosebery replied that his connection with Harcourt had been purely official, that it had ended with the defeat of the Government, and that he declined to have any relations with him. A copy of this letter was sent to Harcourt, who seems to have been genuinely hurt by its tone, and wrote, on August 14th in the last letter which passed between the two men, that he was pained by Rosebery's attitude and could not comprehend it. 'I have never known anything ever approaching his [Harcourt's] power of self-deception,' Gladstone wrote to Rosebery on the 25th. Harcourt told Spencer that he regarded Rosebery's letter as 'a damned piece of impertinence', and that he had no intention of retiring from the Liberal leadership in the Commons, and, in Spencer's words, 'assumed the air of absolute ignorance that any serious difference had existed between him and R'.[1] 'What will be the issue I neither know nor foresee,' Rosebery wrote to Gladstone. 'I only feel an immeasurable relief.'

Only the members of the ex-cabinet were told of the situation[2] and the arrangement whereby Harcourt led the party in the Commons and Kimberley in the Lords, with Rosebery as titular leader, creaked on for another year. It was a wholly unfortunate arrangement, since the discrepancies between the speeches of the two leaders was painfully obvious. Thus, on March 3rd, 1896, Rosebery recommended a policy of 'concentration' of ideas within the Liberal Party in a speech to the Eighty Club; on the 11th Harcourt, in the words of the *Annual Register*, 'seemed to go out of his way to depreciate Lord Rosebery's policy of "concentration"'. On January 15th, 1896, Haldane went to Mentmore 'full of Harcourt's wish for a reconciliation, etc. I told him that I stood absolutely by my letter of Aug. 12,' Rosebery recorded, 'that had I not written it already I wd write it today: but that (1) of course any one cd act as intermediary with a view to independent common action: or (2) what I shd much prefer, that I shd retire, & leave the opposition without what is practically an element of division—myself.'

There were several other attempts to bring the two leaders together, even Gladstone offering his services. Asquith was particularly active, but after successive weekends at Mentmore and Malwood, wrote to Ripon on January 10th, 1896, that 'Mentmore is unyielding, except perhaps to the extent of informal & indirect communications through some intermediary. Malwood, on the

[1] See Gardiner: *Harcourt*, II, 375–6, for Spencer's account.

[2] Loulou Harcourt sent the correspondence between his father, Spencer, and Rosebery to Labouchere in the November of 1896, together with information about Rosebery's alleged opposition to the 1894 Budget (see above, page 347), and an article based on this information was published in the December 7th issue of the *Pall Mall Gazette*. Rosebery somehow discovered who the informant had been but wrote to Hamilton (November 20th), 'I shall notice nothing unless the illustrious sire takes the field in person!' Ripon regarded this incident as 'a most gross breach of confidence'.

other hand, is bland with conscious innocence, willing to forgive and forget the past, and ready to meet the other at any time & place. . . . My own opinion is that the only hope of a real *modus vivendi* is by some kind of advance *from* the New Forest.'[1] Ripon, however, was not convinced, and declined to approach Harcourt as Asquith proposed.

In mid-January there was a Liberal conclave at Mentmore attended by all the Liberal leaders with the conspicuous exceptions of Harcourt and Morley. On the following Monday Lady Fanny Tweedmouth gave a reception to which both Rosebery and Harcourt were invited, and, according to Hamilton, they 'conversed together very amicably'. Morley reported to Spencer, however, that Rosebery had gone up to Harcourt and had insisted on shaking his hand in a characteristically dramatic manner, and that Harcourt had not been particularly impressed with the sincerity of the episode.[2]

Rosebery absolutely refused to entertain any suggestion that he might settle his differences with Harcourt, and in this twilight period of their joint leadership they only met occasionally, and then by accident. Rosebery's elder son remembers driving with him in his carriage to the dentist; as it drew up, Harcourt emerged from the dentist's door, putting on his hat; 'My God!' said Rosebery, slumping back into the cushions and the darkness, 'drive on!' Eddie Hamilton tried to persuade Rosebery in the February of 1898 to invite the Harcourts to a ball he was giving for his daughters; Rosebery eventually invited Sir William and Lady Harcourt to a reception but not Loulou, and the Harcourts refused; when Loulou's engagement was announced in December 1898, Rosebery sent his congratulations to Harcourt but not to Loulou. Hamilton was distressed by this rancour. 'I doubt if R. will ever forgive Loulou,' he wrote in his diary for December 1st, 1898.

Throughout 1896 Rosebery gave no hint that he was awaiting his opportunity to retire from the leadership. In fact he seemed to have shaken off his malaise of the past two years and to be more gay and confident than since the death of his wife. He began to be seen more in London Society, and was regarded by many of the younger Liberals as the only leading member of the party who realised that the Newcastle Programme and Home Rule were out-

---

[1] *Ripon Papers.*   [2] *Spencer Papers.*

dated as electoral cries. They did not comprehend his bitter disillusionment with party politics, and the strength of his resolution to sever what he called his 'Gladstonian chains' once and for all. Either he would lead and hold power, or he would go his own way, and he was convinced that until the Liberal Party changed its outlook and philosophies there was no place for him in it. Already it is possible to see the germination of his intention to hold a lofty and independent position above the party maelstrom. Sitting in the garden of the Alhambra in the May of 1896 he confided these thoughts and intentions in his 'betting book' in a memorable and revealing note.

The only sure base of success in politics, as in other enterprises, is faith; not of course religious faith only. That is the highest, but politics have passed outside its realm.

It was faith that animated the triumph of Ferdinand & Isabella, & drove the Moors out of Spain, that made Spain one, Christian & powerful; just as it was the want of faith, the distrust in the powers of faith, that degraded religion to persecution & ruined Spain.

It was faith that inspired the Crusaders, the Saracens & the Puritans: faith of another kind made Cobden a conqueror & so Howard & Wilberforce & Garibaldi—an inspired fool, but still inspired.

But Faith alas! has gone out of English politics. It has ceased to be a contest of creeds—it is a game, in which, as in other games, a good deal of cheating takes place, & in which as in other such games it is best for an honest man to look on.

The best part of British politics is that it opens high spheres of administration & diplomacy . . . in which every faculty may be freely employed without any consideration but patriotism & public duty.

Faith, if it lurks at all in our politics will be found, I suspect, in a few Socialists.

1896 was dominated by two political events. The fiasco of the Jameson Raid in the last days of 1895 brought up the crucial problem of the direction of British policy in Africa. The revelation that Rhodes was directly implicated in the Raid which was ostensibly designed to 'liberate' the repressed 'Uitlanders' in Johannesburg did not shock British opinion as greatly as might have been expected, principally as a result of an ill-timed telegram of congratulation and support sent to President Kruger by the Kaiser. Jameson and his men returned to England for trial, but were virtually hailed as heroes. Rosebery's public statements on these matters were few, but consisted of severe condemnation of the Raid and of the conduct of the Government which, reacting to the popular interpretation, refused to condemn Rhodes. In the Debate on the Address in January—which, as the *Annual Register* remarked, 'put an end to rumours which had been of frequent occurrence during the recess with reference to his withdrawal from the leadership of the Opposition'—Rosebery was scathingly contemptuous about the eulogies heaped on Chamberlain's conduct in repudiating the Raid, for, although willing to lay 'a meagre and a tardy chaplet on the opulent shrine of the Colonial Secretary', he did so with reluctance as he had only been doing his duty. He described the Raid as an Elizabethan venture, and derided the deplorable verses on the subject written by the new Laureate Alfred Austin which had appeared in *The Times* and which had extolled Jameson and his men. It was conspicuous that Harcourt, in the Commons, paid glowing tributes to Chamberlain. In private, Rosebery entertained strong suspicions that Chamberlain had been privy to Rhodes's plans, and at a speech at Newton Abbot on May 15th he demanded a 'searching and impartial inquiry', and opposed the proposal—supported by Harcourt—that the matter should be referred to a Select Committee of the House of Commons.[1]

The other major event of 1896 was the massacre of the Armenians in Turkey, which appalled the British, and particularly the Liberal, conscience. Rosebery, although stingingly critical of the craven attitude of the Government, refused to advise independent action, although in a speech to the Eighty Club on March 3rd he spoke contemptuously of the inanition of the European powers in the face of 'the cruel mercies of the barbarous Kurds'. He was savaged by Massingham in the *Daily Chronicle*—which had reversed its previous pro-Rosebery line—for this attitude, and dubbed 'the veiled prophet' by that organ. Mr Gladstone, incensed by the reports from Constantinople, emerged from his retirement to castigate his ancient foe and to advocate a European crusade against 'the great assassin' and, failing that, unilateral British action. Rosebery replied in an open letter to Dr Guiness Rogers[2] in *The Times* of September 14th that although he fully shared Gladstone's horror at the atrocities, he

[1] See Appendix Two for the examination of the allegation that Rosebery had foreknowledge of the Raid (pages 494 to 497).
[2] A notable Liberal cleric who had led the anti-Turk agitation.

could not support an 'impulse' by the Liberal Party of this nature. On September 14th Gladstone made a vehement appeal for positive action by the British Government at Liverpool, although he was extremely vague about what form this should take. Of the Liberal leaders only Asquith—rather surprisingly—supported Gladstone, but the rank and file and the majority of the Liberal Press were in favour of more strenuous methods than Rosebery was prepared to support. 'There was nothing very definite in the position taken up by Lord Rosebery,' the *Annual Register* commented on his speeches in the summer of 1896, '. . . but what attracted more attention was the marked way in which he abstained from any reference to his colleagues. Rumours of his resentment at the scant courtesy he received from those in the House of Commons began to circulate once more, especially when it became evident that a course of action was frequently decided upon by them without any reference to him.' This was particularly irritating to members of the party, since the Liberals suddenly started to win by-elections, and recaptured no less than three seats in the late summer.

Having pondered Gladstone's speech at Liverpool and the reactions of the Liberal Press, Rosebery retired to Dalmeny—or, more literally, Barnbougle—to consider his course of action. Harcourt—who had been urged by Loulou to take a strong Gladstonian line—spoke to his constituents on October 5th, and came down by implication on Rosebery's side. The *Daily Chronicle*, however, hailed his speech as being anti-Turkish, and Massingham, in a sulphurous leading article, attacked Rosebery fiercely and accused him of trying to 'drag' the Liberal Party 'into a sham Palmerstonian revival'. It is almost certain that this gross and deliberate misrepresentation of Harcourt's speech was the decisive factor which propelled Rosebery towards resignation, since he had been watching Harcourt's speeches closely during the year for one sign of blatant disloyalty.[1] It is doubtful that he contemplated a complete severance from public life, which, as he had already learned, was difficult to accomplish. In his subsequent conversations with his closest friends—particularly Hamilton—

[1] This view is strengthened by Munro Ferguson's interpretation of the resignation contained in a letter to Campbell-Bannerman of October 12th (*Campbell-Bannerman Papers*) in which he specifically referred to Rosebery's indignation at the attitude of the *Daily Chronicle*. (See also Lady Betty Balfour's account on page 393.)

we come across a new phrase which was destined to become famous, 'the clean slate'.

He said that he had been tied to Gladstonian chains ever since he had taken a prominent part in politics. It commenced with the Midlothian Campaign: he had been bound to Mr G for the next 16 years; and then was left with the thankless task of acting as Mr G's political executor and of winding up his political estate. He could stand it no longer; he wanted to start with a *tabula rasa*; and to put him in the position of doing this, he was bound to take a very drastic step.[1]

It was the old conflict between politics and power; Rosebery revelled in the latter and detested the former with a genuine hatred, which found expression in his final and memorable description of 'this evil-smelling bog'. But he hesitated for several weeks, sitting alone in Barnbougle, consulting no one, wanting no one. Subsequently explaining this silence to Hamilton, he said that the one thing he had learned from the events of 1892 and 1894 was that his judgement was almost invariably correct when he was left to work things out for himself. Haldane came to Dalmeny at the beginning of October, 'but though he was sensible of vague mutterings and gloom, and something going wrong he did not know how serious it was, though he walked up and down to Barnbougle in the wet gravel in his evening pumps for ages'.[2]

The political world was therefore wholly unprepared for the shock of the publication in the newspapers on October 8th of a letter from Rosebery to Tom Ellis informing the latter that, so far as Rosebery was concerned, the Liberal leadership was vacant. It was a perfectly executed manoeuvre. Rosebery did not even tell his private secretary of the letter to Ellis, and wrote out the copies for the Press himself. These were dispatched on the evening of October 7th too late to make any evening edition, so that the mine was sprung on the morning of the 8th. 'I wish you to know from myself that I have resigned the leadership of the Liberal party—that is, if I ever held it, of which I am not quite sure,' he wrote to Gladstone. 'I will not disguise that you have, by again coming forward and advocating a policy which I cannot support, innocently and unconsciously dealt the *coup de grace*, by enabling discontented Liberals to pelt me with your authority. But, as you

[1] *Edward Hamilton's Diary*, October 16th, 1896.   [2] West: *Diaries*, 330.

well know, the situation has long been almost impossible and almost intolerable, and I for one am glad that it should cease.'

'Your letter is an acknowledgement of receipt for a stab under the fifth rib,' Gladstone replied, 'and regarded in that view it is not only kind, but kindness itself. I can desire nothing more than to follow it. Our political relations have been tragical enough, but you have prevented their carrying any infection into the personal sphere. Will it surprise you when I tell you that my first knowledge of a difference between us was when I read the letter stating that sole action meant European war?'

Some of the members of the ex-cabinet were aghast at what they regarded as this betrayal. 'In taking the step he has, R has acted selfishly,' Asquith remarked to Hamilton on November 3rd. 'He has no doubt improved his personal position for the moment, but in doing so he has sacrificed the interests of his colleagues and friends.' 'You have handed us over to Harcourt without escape,' Ripon wrote bitterly, 'and you are not ignorant of all which that means.' Asquith was staying with the Balfours at Whittingehame when the bombshell from Dalmeny was exploded, and his immediate reactions may be glimpsed from a letter from Lady Betty Balfour to Mrs Barbara Webb.[1]

... Asquith heard on Wednesday night from his chief of his intended resignation & tried by wiring him & the Lib Whips to stop it but without success, as the papers had the news. Margot was bursting with it on Wed. night but managed to hold it in till Thurs. morning. Then her great desire was to be the first to tell Arthur [Balfour], who never reads the papers for himself. . . . [But] Frances[2] as soon as she returned from her drive walked into his study & told him the news, thus ousting Margot! . . .

Arthur thought it finally proved that Rosebery had no stuff in him, was a mere sack to tumble to right or left, & that it was a monstrous behaviour to his colleagues. Asquith felt it as a great blow; he minded not having been consulted, & he is determined to leave politics rather than serve under Harcourt. Margot was convinced that the party would unite to persuade him to retake the leadership. All agree that he resigned on the feeblest pretext, for with the exception of Glasgow (whose opinion now is nothing worth) the *Methodist Times* & the *Daily Chronicle*, the whole party have supported Rosebery in his

[1] This unpublished letter, together with others of great interest, were placed at my disposal by Mr David Holland of the House of Commons Library.
[2] Lady Frances Balfour, Arthur Balfour's Sister-in-Law.

Armenian views, even Harcourt. Margot owns, however, that both Harcourt & Morley had this year behaved most disloyally to Rosebery, & that he did feel being their leader was *hell*. . . .

Asquith returned [from Dalmeny] at 7 in the evening & with him Mr Evan Charteris & Francis Horner. Asquith had found Haldane & Fowler at Dalmeny, but they all three failed to shake the resolution of their chief. The only thing apparently which did shake his confidence in having done the right thing were two telegrams, one from Ld Wemyss saying 'Bravo, Archie', & one from Sir Charles Tennant saying 'Heartfelt congratulations'. These two did almost persuade him to withdraw his resignation. Apparently resentment of Harcourt's behaviour, & the attitude of the *Daily Chronicle* were the two things which decided Lord R. to seize this opportunity of freeing himself from what had become an intolerable position. Armenia was only a pretext. . . . His colleagues are so afraid of his going because of what may happen next. . . .

The dynamic thirty-one-year-old Alfred Harmsworth—the future Lord Northcliffe—arrived at Dalmeny to interview Rosebery for his new *Daily Mail*, not yet six months of age. Rosebery was surprised and intrigued; 'I thought the *Daily Mail* came from the other camp,' he remarked, to which Harmsworth replied, 'The *Daily Mail* is independent and Imperial'. They lunched together, Asquith also being present, and Harmsworth later reported in the *Daily Mail* that 'the man who had this morning startled the world appeared as merry and sunburned as though he had just returned from the moors or the links'. When the name of Gladstone was mentioned 'there was, I thought, a tone of sadness in the cheery voice'. Asquith, the other luncheon guest, was not as impressed as Harmsworth by the dramatic element in the situation.

Rosebery was due to speak at the Empire Hotel in Edinburgh on the next evening (October 9th). West—who was staying at Dalmeny—spoke to Asquith just before the meeting and 'we had a gloomy, melancholy, and useless talk'. Rosebery had left Dalmeny after his guests, scribbling down the heads of arguments, and arrived on the stroke of seven o'clock at the meeting, 'ashy pale, and with that unseeing look I know so well', West recorded.

Never had Rosebery spoken to a more excited and expectant audience than when he rose that evening. He started very quietly, but his exquisite voice was so clear and the impact of his personality so extraordinary that the enormous audience settled into a kind of trance which surprised and awed those members of the

platform party who had never heard Rosebery speak to an Edinburgh audience. He was listened to in a deep and almost reveren-
tial, silence, which was broken with tremendous applause whenever he paused. John Buchan has described the speech as 'one of
the most dignified and moving of valedictory speeches ever
spoken by a British statesman'.

. . . Perhaps Mr Gladstone has been the indirect cause—or the latest
indirect cause—of the action which I have thought right to take. . . .
But let none think that for that reason I have regretted his intervention in the Armenian question. It is now seventeen years since Mr
Gladstone came to Midlothian. I remember then making a speech in
which I said that we welcomed the sight of a great statesman, full of
years and full of honours, coming down at his advanced period of life
to fight one supreme battle on behalf of liberty in Europe. Little did I
think then that seventeen years later I should see a still nobler sight, a
statesman—the same statesman—fuller still of years, and, if possible,
fuller still of honours, coming out and leaving a well earned retirement, which the whole world watches with tenderness and solicitude,
to fight another battle, but I hope not the last, on behalf of
the principles in which his life has been spent. Whatever our differences on public policy may be, what has passed between Mr Gladstone
and myself goes too deep, is too rooted, too entwined in all that I
value or hold holy in public and private life for me to forget, even for
a moment, what I owe to him. . . .

He defended his action on the Armenian Question on the in-
controvertible argument that unilateral action either meant war
or inevitable humiliation if the nation shrank from such an
extreme step. 'If there is one rule of diplomacy which I regard as
sacred, it is this—you should never put your foot farther than you
can keep it down.' He politely dismissed Gladstone's remarks
about 'the phantom of a European war'.

. . . I believe it is no phantom at all. I do believe that there was a
fixed and resolute agreement on the part of the Great Powers to resist
by force any single-handed intervention by England in the affairs of
the East. . . . You know what a European war means. It means the
massacre, the slaughter of hundreds of thousands of people; it means
the ruin and devastation of the regions it invests; it means danger to
many countries, and perhaps worse to this country, almost our national
existence. . . . I can conceive nothing more futile, more disastrous,
more dangerous, than such a policy as this.
It is, then, against a solitary and feverish interest in the East that I

enter my protest. Some persons, some guides of public opinion, are trying to work up in this country the sort of ecstasy which precedes war, even if it does not intend war. Against that I protest, and against that I will fight. . . .

He said that he resigned the leadership to promote unity in the Liberal Party, and, with a side-thrust at Harcourt, pointed out that a Liberal leader in the Lords required 'very exceptional support', 'which you never got,' responded the audience, emerging briefly from its trance. After paying a magnificent tribute to Asquith which was enthusiastically received, he ended on a characteristically dramatic note, by saying quietly that, as a Peer, he had no constituents; he had turned slightly away from the breathless audience, and, suddenly facing them, said, 'But you, the people of Edinburgh, are my constituents', and sat down amid scenes of frenetic enthusiasm. There were loud cries for Asquith, who rose, and said:

I do not think that I am seriously risking whatever reputation I may have or aspire to as a political prophet if in my forecast publicly stated to you to-night, I say that the more maturely and deliberately the Liberal party throughout the kingdom reflect upon the circumstances of the case, the more strongly will they come to the conclusion that the decision arrived at three years ago, that Lord Rosebery was the only fit successor to Mr Gladstone, is a decision which has been ratified by events, and that, at any rate in so far as it lies within their power, they are not willing to recede from it.

In the crowded streets of the city the familiar cry of 'Rozbury! Rozbury!' greeted the audience of the Empire Theatre as they streamed out of the building, where they also waited, an enormous crowd in the gas-lit November gloom, for the hero of the evening, who returned to Dalmeny through the wildly enthusiastic throng with some difficulty.

Rosebery, his ordeal over, was in wonderful form at dinner at Dalmeny, where the large company included West, Bryce, Haldane, Tennant, and Lady Leconfield. It seemed incredible that this brilliant being, holding the table enraptured with searching criticisms of Macaulay, Carlyle, and Gibbon amid the splendours of the superb Dalmeny dining-room, could be permitted to leave public life. Haldane, Fowler, and Bryce were so excited by the Edinburgh speech that they told West after dinner that they were convinced that Rosebery would shortly resume the leadership at the insistence of the rank and file of Liberals. Haldane wrote to his mother from Dalmeny that 'it is only the beginning of the battle but a battle which we hope to win. Asquith, Henry Fowler & I are in his party & the whole time is spent in consultation & talks—nothing but politics—Rosebery in grand spirits.'[1]

Champagne, although a wonderfully rare quality in polemical disputations, has no lasting qualities. Rosebery's followers, although probably influential and numerous, were left without a leader. Acland wrote to Tom Ellis, 'It is rather sad for us and men like us with the hopes we brought into public life from Oxford and our homes and have found that those we earnestly desired to uphold and follow have, through the grave defects you mention, given us such a bad time. . . . I am more than ever convinced that "isolation" which R might have lessened so much if he had been less sensitive about the intrigue and more ready to initiate meetings instead of complaining at home, has been our great bane.'[2] Acland was very bitter about a cold letter Rosebery had written to him in reply to one of sympathetic support. 'The letter is marked *confidential*,' Acland wrote to Ellis, 'but a future editor of his life could publish it as though [it was] to an almost complete stranger. . . . I would have given anything to have rounded off this little bit of my life and correspondence without this sting (quite unconsciously given by our self-centred friend) left behind.'[2] These emotions were widespread among Rosebery's supporters; Morley took the earliest opportunity of attacking him; the party as a whole did not know where to turn; there was even a lunatic suggestion (which died a rapid death) that Gladstone should return to hold the leadership until things calmed down. Eventually, the question of the leadership was shelved, and Harcourt and Kimberley continued to rule in their respective spheres. 'K & H may work together as R & H never did,' Ripon wrote to Spencer on October 15th, 'but it is a miserable state of things.'[3] Rosebery himself had no plans, no ambitions. He had severed himself from his 'Gladstonian chains', and, if recalled, would only return as the real and not the titular leader. For the moment he was determined to remain aloof and silent, but the shoals of ecstatic letters of sup-

[1] *Haldane Papers.* Haldane to Mrs Haldane, October 11th, 1896.
[2] *Ellis Papers* (National Library of Wales). I am grateful to Mr Nevile Masterman for sending me copies of this and other letters in Ellis' papers.
[3] *Ripon Papers.*

port which poured into Dalmeny—over five hundred in the first
week—showed that this determination might prove difficult to
maintain. But, for the moment, he had his beloved books to turn
to, and it was with immense pleasure that he dismissed from his
mind the internecine struggles of the Liberal Party and immersed
himself in the lonely fastness of St Helena and the last phase of the
life of Napoleon. He attended a luncheon in his honour at the
City Liberal Club on December 17th. 'A genial gathering,' he
wrote in his diary. 'My last public engagement in the world!'

The period of approximately three years which elapsed between
Rosebery's resignation of the party leadership in the October of
1896 and his reluctant return to politics on the outbreak of the
South African War is a curious interlude in Rosebery's life. His
pattern of life underwent a significant change in 1897 when he
bought the Villa Delahante at Posilipo near Naples for £16,000;
the purchase of the villa had long been an ambition of himself
and his wife—'we spent an hour of rapture at the Villa Delahante', he wrote to Lacaita on September 27th, 1882; 'Hannah
was amazed and stupefied by the beauty of the place'—but since
her death he had lost interest and his bid was considerably lower
than the minimum price asked (approximately £25,000) and
he did not expect it to be accepted; his elder son was with him
when Rosebery opened a letter, stared at it in amazement, and
said, 'My God, I've bought a villa in Naples!' For the next ten
years he was absent from England for several months in each
year, and this physical separation added considerably to the difficulties of those Liberals who passionately desired his return to the
leadership. For many years, as E. T. Raymond has written,[1]
'Dalmeny became a St Germain, and it was long before the dream
of a Rosebery restoration was quite banished'. His public activities in these years were mainly confined to addresses on largely
non-controversial subjects, and contained some of his most
memorable images. He seemed to be drawn more and more into
the company of his books and in the past. His appreciation of
Burns at Dumfries on July 21st, 1896, remains perhaps the most
perfect of these spoken essays. In the afternoon he spoke at the
Drill Hall, and dwelt upon the wretched circumstances of Burns'
death.

[1] *The Man of Promise*, 188.

In this place and on this day it all seems present to us—the house of anguish, the thronged churchyard, the weeping neighbours. We feel ourselves part of the mourning crowd. We hear those dropping volleys and that muffled drum: we bow our heads as the coffin passes, and acknowledge with tears the inevitable doom. Pass, heavy hearse, with thy weary freight of shattered hopes and exhausted frame; pass, with thy simple pomp of fatherless bairns and sad moralising friends; pass, with the sting of death to the victory of the grave; pass, with the perishable, and leave us the eternal.

On the same evening he spoke on the same subject at St Andrew's Hall in Glasgow, and did not flinch from discussing Burns' private life and its implications.

Mankind is helped in its progress almost as much by the study of imperfection as by the contemplation of perfection. Had we nothing before us in our futile and halting lives but saints and the ideal we might well fail altogether. We grope blindly along the catacombs of the world, we climb the dark ladder of life, we feel our way to futurity, but we can scarcely see an inch around or before us. We stumble and falter and fall, our hands and knees are bruised and sore, and we look up for light and guidance. Could we see nothing but distant unapproachable impeccability, we might well sink prostrate in the hopelessness of emulation and the weariness of despair.

Is it not then, when all seems blank and lightless and lifeless, when strength and courage flag, and when perfection seems as remote as a star, is it not then that imperfection helps us? When we see that the greatest and choicest images of God have had their weaknesses like ours, their temptations, their hours of darkness, their bloody sweat, are we not encouraged by their lapses and catastrophes to find energy for one more effort, one more struggle? Where they failed we feel is less dishonour to fail; their errors and sorrows make, as it were, an easier ascent from infinite imperfection to infinite perfection.

Man, after all, is not ripened by virtue alone. Were it so this world were a paradise of angels. No! Like the growth of the earth, he is the fruit of all the seasons; the accident of a thousand accidents, a living mystery, moving through the seen to the unseen. He is sown in dishonour; he is nurtured under all the varieties of heat and cold; in mist and wrath, in snow and vapours, in the melancholy of autumn in the torpor of winter, as well as in the rapture and fragrance of summer, or the balmy affluence of the spring—its breath, its sunshine, its dew. And at the end he is reaped, the produce, not of one climate, but of all; not of good alone, but of evil; not of joy alone, but of sorrow—perhaps mellowed and ripened, perhaps stricken and withered and sour. How, then, shall we judge any one? How, at any rate, shall we judge a giant, great in gifts and great in temptation; great in strength and great in weakness? Let us glory in his strength and be comforted in his weakness. And when we thank heaven for the inestimable gift of Burns, we do not need to remember wherein he was imperfect, we cannot bring ourselves to regret that he was made of the same clay as ourselves.

Rosebery's addresses and appreciations in these years are among the most delightful he ever delivered. Over sixty years later it is possible to be charmed by them, and to reflect upon his astonishing breadth of interests. Whether the subject was Burns, Burke, Wallace, the old parts of London—when he first suggested that the LCC should put plaques on houses where eminent men and women had lived—love of books, the duty of public service (his Presidential Address on October 25th, 1898, to the Associated Societies of the University of Edinburgh), the civil service, oratory, Scottish history or racing (the Gimcrack Dinner of 1897), his touch was infallibly sure. He could make people laugh, his knowledge sat lightly upon his shoulders, and when he quoted it was as if he were reaching into a vast library of information and anecdotage and casually lighting upon the most apposite quotation. A small volume of his speeches was published in 1899 to his surprise, and quickly ran through several editions.

His main literary task in these years was *Napoleon: The Last Phase*, first published in 1900,[1] which was a detailed and vivid study of the conflicting accounts of Napoleon's incarceration on St Helena. It was a subject which had fascinated Rosebery for many years, and he had gathered a remarkable collection of Napoleonic relics, including Napoleon's superb travelling library, and the cushion on which his head rested after his death. Brett was staying at The Durdans in 1899 when the actual shutters from Napoleon's bedroom were delivered. Although Rosebery enjoyed writing and the company of his books, the polished charm of his essays was acquired by immense care and prodigious re-writing. As he grew older, this passion for amendment grew upon him, and in both the cases of *Lord Randolph Churchill* (1906) and *Chatham: His Early Life and Connections* (1910) there was an

---

[1] Lord Crewe states inaccurately (*Rosebery*, II, 601) that it was first published in 1908.

immense amount of re-writing, to the despair of those who had to undertake the typing.

The picture of Rosebery's activities in this period is therefore somewhat tesselated. His diaries deal with his lengthy travellings abroad, his addresses and speeches to learned societies and the like, prodigious slaughter of the Dalmeny, Rosebery, and Mentmore game, and the occasional record of important events. In 1898 his lifelong association with Gladstone ended, after months of distressing agony. At the great funeral in Westminster Abbey he was one of the pallbearers.

A noble sight and ceremony. Mrs Gladstone a figure of indescribable pathos. Supported by her two sons she knelt at the head of the coffin, and when it was lowered seemed to wish to kiss the ground, saying 'once more, only once more' (I was close) with a dim idea, I think, that she was to kiss him, but the two sons gently raised her.

One by one, his small circle of intimate friends was becoming smaller. Ferdinand de Rothschild, Frank Lockwood, Canon Rogers,[1] Harry Tyrwhitt, and Randolph Churchill all died between 1894 and 1900, and to a man so reluctant to make new friends their loss was irreparable. The marriage of his younger daughter to Lord Crewe in 1899 was the start of the disruption of the devoted family circle; the children still visited him constantly, but their interests in their careers and marriages naturally meant that Rosebery saw far less of them, and his letters and diaries reveal how sadly he contemplated this inevitable state of affairs.

Rosebery's position after 1896 was a source of perplexity to the political world. 'I hear from miscellaneous quarters a good deal of grumbling about Rosebery, who took himself off abroad a week ago,' Hamilton wrote on January 22nd, 1897. '. . . His own immediate late colleagues seem to be more than ever sore; and a good many of the rank and file to be complaining of being handed over *nolentes volentes* to the tender mercies of Harcourt. The idea, I am afraid, is gaining ground that he has done for himself politically for some time to come.' It seemed impossible that such a man, in his early fifties, with a glittering record, and still commanding considerable public interest and enthusiasm, should

[1] He died on January 19th, 1896. Rosebery saw him on the 15th, and recorded in his diary that his old friend was 'calm and cheerful, but realised "that he had not above ten years to live" '.

divorce himself from public life. After a visit to Dalmeny in the November of 1896, Ripon wrote to Spencer that 'I found Rosebery full of life, & evidently beginning already to work for a future leadership free from the Harcourt connection'. Harcourt might affect indifference, but both he and Loulou were acutely conscious of the brooding shadow from Dalmeny which darkened the leadership, and it was small comfort to reflect that Morley, the fickle ally of 1892–4, was Harcourt's only declared supporter on the Liberal front bench. But, as Asquith wrote to Milner in the January of 1898 about Rosebery, 'there are many who cannot forget or forgive his timely escape, in a life-boat constructed to hold one person, from the water-logged ship. And for the moment there is no one else whose name is even generally acceptable, let alone a rallying-cry for a broken army. The fact is that people have been so accustomed for more than a generation upon both sides to leaders who are obviously marked out for the post (Palmerston, Gladstone, Disraeli, Salisbury) that they are bewildered by the problem of choice. In the end it will no doubt solve itself by the action of natural forces, but in the meantime the effectiveness of the party as a political instrument is crippled.'[1] Rosebery himself, in countless letters (many of which were never sent) and personal memoranda, set out his position in these years. In the February of 1897, at Naples, he wrote that

I resigned the leadership of the Liberal party not to destroy that party but to promote its union. With the same object I have ever since remained persistently silent and refused all engagements. . . .

This view does not necessarily imply my permanent silence or retirement.[2] It is of course difficult to fix an arbitrary limit of time for this and I shall not attempt to do so. But six months under the circumstances would appear a decent minimum.

Beyond this I am bound to say that I have had a revolting experience of the higher positions in British government, and that it will take some time to wash out of my mouth the taste of the last administration. . . .

This was rather ambiguous, and his actions increased the bewilderment. He refused even to subscribe to Liberal Party funds, writing to Munro Ferguson (January 10th, 1898) that 'I have formally retired from public life. That is the case as it stands. I may re-enter it, but that is beside the question. I have cut myself off from all connection with the Liberal party, and have left it

---

[1] *Milner Papers.*   [2] My italics.

under the *apparent* guidance of the politician I most profoundly distrust. . . . Contribution implies agreement & even approval. Now I cannot agree with, or approve blindly, what has been done or may be done by the Liberal party.' 'Neither duty, business nor pleasure summon me,' he wrote contentfully to Munro Ferguson from Naples on February 20th, 1897. 'Here I have summer and solitude and repose, all of which I enjoy intensely. . . . Nor do I honestly know of any one in either House of Parliament (except yourself) who wishes me back. And as I do not wish myself back we are almost unanimous! . . . I have no engagements and no plans. I am very well and very happy. In England I should be worried by all sorts of people, and saying "No" all day long.' Edward Hamilton, who was now more intimate with Rosebery than anyone else, wrote in his Diary in the October of 1897 after a dinner with him and Haldane at Brooks' that 'Rosebery certainly seems to take a keener interest in politics than he has done; though he probably would not admit this'.

Through Rosebery's personal notes and letters we can see the rapid growth of a philosophy which he later described as the doctrine of Efficiency. In the August of 1898, while staying at Gastein, he wrote that he believed that the party system had become irrelevant in English politics since the great issues of the past which had created the parties had either been resolved or had disappeared. 'The people', he wrote in this revealing memorandum, 'are more concerned with men than with measures—men whom they trust rather than measures they espouse. . . . Problems are either becoming too large for parties to deal with, or parties, owing to the above or other causes, are becoming too weak to deal with them.'

The demands for Rosebery to return to the leadership became more insistent as the months passed and it was painfully evident that the leadership of Harcourt and Morley was flaccid. With the exception of Massingham's *Daily Chronicle*, the Liberal Press was hostile, Wemyss Reid's *Speaker* being particularly caustic. Harcourt and Campbell-Bannerman had been prominent members of the Select Committee[1] which investigated the events leading up to

[1] According to Margot Asquith (*Autobiography*, II, 28) Chamberlain tried to get Asquith to serve on the Committee; when she asked him why he had refused, Asquith replied, 'Do you take me for a fool?' Campbell-Bannerman was also reluctant to be a member, but was over-persuaded by Harcourt. (The correspondence is in the *Harcourt Papers*.)

the Jameson Raid in 1897 and which exonerated Chamberlain
while condemning Rhodes. The Report was published on July
20th, 1897, and Liberal back-bench opinion, inflamed by what
they regarded as their leader's dereliction of duty, was not
assuaged by the disinclination of Harcourt to debate the Report,
and when Philip Stanhope did initiate a debate in defiance of his
leader, 38 Liberals supported the Government, 69 supported
Stanhope's motion of censure, and 15 ostentatiously abstained.
In a further division the whole Liberal front bench again supported the Government, and Liberal suspicions that Harcourt and
Campbell-Bannerman had been 'squared' by Chamberlain—or at
the very least, as Herbert Paul later wrote, that they had been
'out-manoeuvred and over-reached'—gained ground. Morley
defended Harcourt in public, but in private described the enquiry
as 'a scandalous mess',[1] while Sir Robert Reid, whose political
star was rising fast, delivered a savage attack on his leaders in a
speech to the Eighty Club, echoed by Ronald Munro Ferguson
in a speech at Leith in the January of 1898 which some believed
had its inspiration at Dalmeny. But although Rosebery described
the South African Committee in private as 'perhaps the greatest
political blunder, if not crime, of my time', he refused to declare
himself publicly. 'I have never read a document at once so shame-
ful and so absurd,' he wrote to Wemyss Reid; 'one would laugh,
did one not cry.' But to Edward Cheney he wrote in the July of
1898,

   . . . Why should I leave this life of happiness with my friends and
children in my home? There is no vacancy, no summons, no call of
duty. Even were it otherwise, my latest experience of politics & politicians has given me a scorn of politics & politicians, a *saeva indignatio*
as Swift says in his epitaph, which keeps me aloof from the profession
& the professors. I feel like Walpole that my trees cannot lie, and I
have what Walpole lacked, the inestimable love of books. Leave me
then in my tranquillity, & let the good & great men in active political
life still bandy their sonorous charges of inconsistency & folly, and
divide the seals & wands & keys when there are seals & wands &
keys to divide. Even at that sublime though invidious moment they
will not be so happy as is
                              Yrs sincly
                                   AR

---

[1] *Spencer Papers.*

It is evident that Rosebery had definitely decided by this stage that he would return to public life only on his own terms and only in response to a positive request by a large section of his colleagues. Up to the middle of 1898, no such request had arrived. Rosebery was perfectly sincere when he spoke of his love of solitude, which had grown upon him sharply since 1896. 'My party dispersed,' he wrote in his diary at Dalmeny in the November of 1897; 'Alone at last!', and his diary frequently makes the reference to 'delightful solitude'. 'Should a definite concrete demand or proposition come to me from the party,' he noted significantly on July 30th, 1898, 'I would judge it & deal with it on its merits. . . . But it would need a very clear conviction of duty to make me abandon my present happiness in private life.' 'The leadership', he wrote to an imploring correspondent at this time, 'cannot be doffed or donned like a great-coat! As to the people, who, as you say, wish for my return & express confidence in me, they may be numerous, but they are certainly dumb. Glad am I that they are so, for I have never of late years been so happy as since my "abdication".'

Rosebery told Hamilton on March 7th, 1898, that if he started to make political speeches it would be said that he was undermining Harcourt's position. 'Poor Liberal party!' he said, 'what a plight it is in! No policy, and nobody to expound it. But it was itself greatly to blame. For the last thirty years it has leaned absolutely on Mr G. It has been like a man who has become accustomed to get about with a crutch only, and when that crutch is withdrawn, helplessness and hopelessness ensued.'

This position of Olympian aloofness was perceptibly changed in the autumn of 1898. It would be unwise to assume that the movement for Rosebery's return to the leadership was confined to the remnants of his personal political *entourage*. Harcourt's authority had received a heavy blow over the South Africa Committee, and there were ominous reports of the intense enthusiasm at Rosebery's speech in support of the Progressives in the LCC elections at St James's Hall on March 2nd. The Executive Committee of the Home Counties Liberal Federation demanded 'an early settlement of the question of the leadership of the Liberal Party', which did not suggest any measure of enthusiasm for Harcourt's leadership and demonstrated the fact that most Liberals did not regard the matter as settled. The Nottingham Liberal Federation tried to initiate a debate on the matter at the annual meeting of the General Committee of the National Liberal Federation, while the *Daily Mail* publicly mocked Harcourt by running a competition for suggestions for a new Liberal programme and leader. Harcourt, who disliked Harmsworth and knew he was a fervent admirer of Rosebery, naturally assumed that this was part of a deliberate campaign, and even Loulou was worried. The Oxford University Eighty Club and Palmerston Club elected Rosebery as their chairman by enormous majorities over Harcourt. These were pin-pricks, but they still hurt. The Fashoda Crisis, however, was the decisive blow.

On September 2nd, after a lengthy and arduous march, Kitchener won an overwhelming victory over the Khalifa at Omdurman; by September 10th, having heard of the arrival of Major Marchand and a small French party at Fashoda on the 5th, Kitchener moved south to meet him. The two men met at Fashoda on September 19th, treated each other with great courtesy and common sense, and in effect returned the problem to the politicians. British and French public opinion were equally aflame, and a period of acute tension between the two countries followed before France had to give way.

Rosebery, in a speech to the Surrey Agricultural Association at Epsom, intervened to declare that he was 'ministerially and personally' responsible for the famous Grey Declaration of March 1895, and delivered a threatening speech in which he said that 'if the nations of the world are under the impression that the ancient spirit of Great Britain is dead, or that her resources are weakened, or her population less determined than ever it was to maintain the rights and the honour of its flag, they make a mistake which can only end in a disastrous conflagration'. Ten days later, at Perth, on October 22nd, he spoke in the same vein of the necessity to 'wipe out' the 'humiliation' of Gordon's death, while Asquith and Grey hastened to add their unqualified support. This dealt the final blow to Harcourt's tottering leadership, even the *Daily Chronicle* joining the chorus of criticism; at a Mansion House dinner held on November 4th it was conspicuous that Rosebery and Kitchener were the heroes of the occasion and Harcourt's speech was listened to 'with something like impatience', as his biographer remarks.[1] 'R told me he had several

[1] Gardiner: *Harcourt*, II, 471.

public engagements ahead,' Hamilton wrote on September 14th. 'As long as he keeps himself *en évidence* there is no need for him to commit himself immediately to a return to politics.' In the middle of December Harcourt and Morley—who had just undertaken the enormous task of writing Gladstone's *Life*—exchanged lengthy epistles of mutual commiseration in which they informed one another and a puzzled public that they declined to be subjected to further disloyalties and misrepresentations and withdrew their services from the disposal of the Liberal Party.

There was considerable bitterness in the Liberal ranks about the manner of this announcement. 'What a pity it is when big causes and interests get into the hands of grown up children who will not play in the same nursery!' Asquith wrote to Campbell-Bannerman, who described the event as 'a gratuitous bungle'; Fowler called it 'a foolish fiasco', while Spencer told Asquith that Rosebery, Harcourt, and Morley had treated the party 'abominably'.

The choice of successor really lay between Asquith and Campbell-Bannerman. There was a strong Asquith faction led by Spencer, Ripon, and Tweedmouth and supported by Tom Ellis and Haldane, but Asquith was not prepared to accept the offer, principally upon financial grounds. Of all the party nabobs, only Morley's advice was not solicited, a snub which he felt deeply and which he never forgot. Campbell-Bannerman, however, intimated that he was prepared to consider any offer favourably, and duly accepted. 'He is evidently quite keen about it', Haldane reported to Rosebery (January 4th, 1899), '& does not mean to have his allotted cubic inches encroached upon by the ponderous figure of the Resigned One—or to be disturbed by the sharp elbow of the Unresigned One [Morley]. I see no reason why the new arrangement should not work. Asquith will support it in a very friendly way.' The appointment was not enthusiastically welcomed by the party at large, and there was a very real danger that a 'bring Harcourt back' movement led by Labouchere might mar the contrived unanimity of the party meeting summoned to the Reform Club to elect the new leader.

Although Rosebery liked 'C-B', he was determined that the position of the Liberal-Imperialists should not be weakened, and in May 1899 he addressed the City Liberal Club, and 'speaking in a disembodied way', urged the virtual abandonment of Home

Rule and a combination of 'the old Liberal spirit with the new
Imperial spirit', an exhortation which revived ancient and fundamental cleavages. Harcourt retorted angrily in a speech on the
next day that Rosebery apparently envisaged the scrapping of the
Liberal programme. Although Rosebery's public appearances had
been few since the summer of 1898, they had been notably provocative without giving any hint of a return to active politics.
Hamilton remonstrated with him, but he retorted that he had
said nothing which would preclude his return 'if the call were
really emphatic'. Hamilton's account of his conversation continues:

. . . He could not and would not make a bid for the leadership himself. It was all very well to say that his quondam colleagues wanted
him back and were working to bring this about eventually; but he
failed to see that there was any such eagerness on their part. They did
not tell him so, and indeed rarely came near him. He was moreover not
conscious of his being under great obligations to them. They had not
stood by him, as they might, *vis à vis* Harcourt, who he knew was
intriguing again with Labouchere.

Was Rosebery in the arena or above it? His friends asked for a
definite answer, but he disappeared into a haze of vague gener-
alities about having quitted public life, that only 'some unsuspected crisis' would bring him back, and that he reserved full
freedom of action. To Hamilton he privately confided that he had
been both gratified and disturbed by the amazing scenes of
enthusiasm when his younger daughter had been married to
Lord Crewe in London on April 20th. With respect to the bride
and groom, it had been obvious that the real attraction of the
occasion for the crowds had been the ex-Premier. To a man so
sensitive to atmosphere, such manifestations of popularity and
admiration were extremely important, and almost certainly led him
to speak out with such partisan gusto to the City Liberals in May.
But having advanced, he promptly retreated again, and his attitude merited Asquith's intense annoyance—expressed by Margot
Asquith to Hamilton on May 9th—at Rosebery's lack of co-operation with his friends and physical remoteness, which made him
'almost impossible to get hold of'. Morley, in one of his happier
phrases, compared Rosebery to 'a dark horse in a loose box', and,
when Rosebery pressed for further explanation, replied (May 27th)
that

. . . I see from Murray's dicty (a work that I hope you possess and read) that a dark horse is one about whose racing powers little is known. That would never do in this case. I thought it meant a horse of whose powers and chances its owner was well aware, only he kept to himself his purpose of being a starter. As for loose boxes, the last I saw was Ladas's, which you showed me. I pictured myself entering it with analytic instruments, and confronting the noble animal, with ears back, heels skittish, and a slight ugliness in the eye. Anyhow, I laughed when I thought of it, and I knew that you would too—as you do.

Even Hamilton could make nothing of Rosebery's attitude. 'He fairly puzzles me,' he wrote on April 20th. 'Does he intend to return to active politics? If so, he might at any rate be frank about it with his intimate friends. If he does not intend to come back, why should he continue to take such an interest in party developments and party concerns? and is he not by maintaining his public character rather posing as a possible leader under false pretences?' It was also becoming clearer to Hamilton—virtually the only person who regularly saw Rosebery at this time—that he had not forgotten 1894–5, and in a conversation at The Durdans on June 11th Rosebery broke out bitterly against his former colleagues; their behaviour had been 'outrageous'; he had been subjected to 'greater ignominy' than any other modern Prime Minister and they had not supported him. 'What he likes—(at least this is my belief)', Hamilton shrewdly remarked in his diary after this outburst, 'is to figure largely in the mind of the public and at the same time to be independent and thus not over-weighted with responsibility. And this is just what he has got though he declines to admit it. . . . He refuses to budge one inch in the direction of emerging from his shell. He declares he is a fatalist, and it is only by fate that he could possibly find himself so situated as to be forced into taking the helm again. He sincerely hoped that such a fate did not await him.'

The 'unsuspected crisis' was at hand in the summer of 1899. By June the deteriorating relationship between the British Government and the Boers was arousing alarm in the Opposition ranks. Campbell-Bannerman expressed the concern of the party at Chamberlain's conduct of negotiations at Ilford on June 17th, and, after private conversations with Chamberlain on the 20th and 22nd, warned the Government that the Liberals could not support 'any open military demonstration such as the dispatch of a force to the Cape'. On July 28th he went further, and pronounced that a war with the Boers—for such an eventuality now appeared likely—'would be one of the direst calamities that could occur'. Morley, with considerable courage in view of the popular temper, strongly opposed the proposition that the mightiest nation in the world should go to war with 'this weak little Republic'. 'It will bring you no glory,' he declared on September 15th at Manchester. 'It will bring you no profit, but mischief, and it will be wrong. You may make thousands of women widows and thousands of children fatherless. It will be wrong. You may add a new province to your Empire. It will still be wrong.'

The Liberal Party was acutely divided. Campbell-Bannerman had robustly declared upon taking the leadership in letters to Asquith, Haldane, and Bryce that 'This Jingo and anti-Jingo division is purely fictitious. . . . We have no vital differences among us.' Campbell-Bannerman was disgusted by a letter by Harcourt to *The Times* in January, describing it to James Campbell as being full of 'bad English, bad taste, bad feeling, bad tactics. . . . The whole thing is sickening.'[1] An attempt by Labouchere to recall Harcourt to the leadership did not further improve the relations between Campbell-Bannerman and the 'Little England' wing. But as the months passed his sympathy with Harcourt and Morley became manifest. The two anti-Imperialists were surprised and jubilant at their capture. 'The boasted unity of the party has been conspicuously refuted,' Harcourt wrote warmly to Morley on March 1st. It was true, and the events of the summer of 1899 only served to make the division glaringly apparent. As Robert Reid —later Lord Loreburn—wrote angrily to Bryce in 1900, 'Harcourt means to spend the rest of his days with Loulou's help in combating "Imperialism". I know what that means; it means pursuing his miserable personal quarrel.'[2]

Asquith, Grey, and Haldane were in general support of the Government, being friends of Alfred Milner, and suspicious of Kruger. Rosebery, while sharing their distrust of the Boer intentions, was not under the Milner spell to the extent that his younger supporters were, possibly because of his part in the formulation of the Death Duties Budget; there are few direct references to Milner in Rosebery's papers, but in private con-

---

[1] *Campbell-Bannerman Papers.*   [2] *Bryce Papers.*

versation he did not conceal his dislike of him. As Lord Crewe—
who saw much of him at this time—has written, Rosebery
'thought that negotiations with the Transvaal Government had
been sadly mismanaged, and that in a sense Milner was greatly
responsible for the war'.[1] He believed that Chamberlain had been
privy to the Jameson Raid, and distrusted his 'rasping diplomacy'.
He considered that a more dexterous diplomacy by negotiators
whom the Boers trusted would have averted a war, but, as he
wrote to Grey on October 21st, 'if Kruger & his like had remained in power, the problem would probably have had to be
solved by the sword'. On July 23rd, at The Durdans, Rosebery
told Hamilton and Nathaniel de Rothschild that 'nothing would
induce me to come back into political life, short of the most distinct and emphatic public call'. The Boer ultimatum at the beginning of October, and the almost immediate opening of hostilities,
swept all his doubts and misgivings aside; although he considered,
as he told Grey, that 'the whole affair has been greatly bungled',
he at once declared in a public letter (October 11th) that the
nation must close its ranks and 'relegate Party controversy to a
more convenient season. Without attempting to judge the policy
which concluded peace after the reverse of Majuba Hill, I am
bound to state my profound conviction that there is no conceivable Government in this country which could repeat it.'
These were ominous words for the Liberal Party; 'Rosebery's
letter is a masterpiece of cunning and meanness,' Harcourt wrote
bitterly to Morley. 'The kick administered in the last sentence to
the dead lion is thoroughly characteristic, and that from the bear-
leader of the Midlothian Campaign.'[2]

Rosebery appeared to be determined to provoke Liberal
schism. On October 26th he received the freedom of Bath, and
unveiled tablets commemorating the Pitts, declaring that Chatham
was 'the first Liberal Imperialist. . . . I believe that the party of
Liberal Imperialism is destined to control the destinies of this
country.' He then turned to the emotionally dangerous topic of
'Majuba', which he described as 'a sublime experiment'.

. . . It was an attempt to carry into international policy the spirit of
the Gospel itself, and, had it been successful, we should have been
entitled to believe that mankind had taken a great stride forward. . . .
Now we know how that magnanimity was rewarded. We may feel

[1] Crewe: *Rosebery*, II.   [2] Gardiner: *Harcourt*, II, 510.

perfectly confident, we who followed Mr Gladstone, that were he now alive, and had control of the destinies of this country, it would not be possible for him, nor would it enter his contemplation, to make terms after this war such as were made after the skirmish of Majuba Hill. . . . It was with a deliberate and constant encroachment on the terms of the settlement that the Boers rewarded the sublime magnanimity of Mr Gladstone.

This, make no mistake, is no little war; and we cannot, at this critical juncture, afford to waste time in polemical discussions. When I think of this little island of ours, so lonely in these northern seas, viewed with such jealousy, and with such hostility, with such jarred ambition by the great empires of the world, so friendless among nations which count their armies by embattled millions; when I think of this little island, of the work which it has undertaken, of the Empire which it has founded and which it is determined to maintain; when I think of the high pressure under which we live, of the responsibility which we have undertaken, I say with Chatham, 'Be of one people; forget everything for the public'.

Parliament had reassembled on October 17th, and the Liberal Party presented a condition of vexatious disarray. Asquith, Fowler, Grey, and Haldane—vehemently supported by the *Daily News*—had declared their approval of the Government's determination to revert to war; the extreme anti-war section, small in numbers but highly articulate, was represented by Lloyd George and Labouchere; Campbell-Bannerman, trying to hold a central position in which he condemned the Government but reluctantly agreed that Kruger's ultimatum had left them with no choice, was under intense pressure from Harcourt and Morley to move further in the direction of the section quickly dubbed 'the pro-Boers'. Rosebery's Bath speech opened old wounds at a delicate moment. 'Fancy the statue of Pitt held up for the Liberal Party of the future to fall down and worship,' Harcourt indignantly wrote to Loulou, 'shades of Fox and Grey!' 'His hold on our people is limited,' Harcourt wrote again to his son shortly afterwards. 'I doubt whether even in ten years he will be capable of leading a party. He is too selfish, too trivial, too much a *poseur*, and I fancy what he admires in Chatham was his isolation, which ended in his choosing to act with no one, till no one would act with him. . . . He will never take the rough and tumble of party warfare, but keep himself for the *réclame* of safe displays at intervals.'[1] Writing to Grey

[1] Gardiner: *Harcourt*, II, 512.

on October 21st Rosebery said that he thought that the Liberal Party 'is nearing its final cataclysm. The Rump will break with the Imperialist section and ally itself with the Irishry. All this in the long run must tend to do good.'

In the first division on an amendment to the Loyal Address the Parliamentary Liberal Party disintegrated into angry fragments, and Rosebery received a vivid account of the circumstances behind this public collapse from Edward Grey.

46, Cadogan Square,
October 22nd, 1899.

My dear Rosebery,

. . . The front bench councils which preceded the division on Thursday were very stormy. I have been to Fallodon for Sat & Sunday, but after this interval of peaceful reflection I am still of opinion that the difference in the party is cut deeper than ever. After the Fashoda division[1] I minimized it, but this time I shall do nothing of the kind. I have several speeches before me, at least three, and by the time they are over the difference in the party will be unmistakeable—unless the Harcourt-Morley party fail to follow up their line.

It is disagreeable to have to say that the Government's mistakes were not the cause of the war, but if one did say they were, one could not with credit cease to denounce them & urge that the only way for the country to redeem its moral character would be to turn out the Government for having caused an unnecessary & cruel war. This is a line which I think public opinion would condemn, but I have an active & (I hope) intelligent conviction that it is not true. The Government deserves to be turned out, but for other reasons.

I didn't think the division on Thursday represented the feeling in the party; people did not realise how much the division that evening must govern the line & tone of subsequent speeches; and there was of course no guidance, except Harcourt's and Morley's from the front bench. The *final* reason for this was want of time—it was ridiculous after Chamberlain's speech to leave only half an evening for debate—but the previous discussions about speaking or voting were long & at the last angry, & the course of the debate has destroyed all compromise amongst us as to speaking, if any other occasion arises in the House.

You cannot feel more independent than I do at this moment, but I

---

[1] In the February of 1899 the Liberals had split over the question of Sudan policy. Grey spoke vigorously in support of the Government, but although Campbell-Bannerman appeared to agree with Grey in the course of his speech, voted with Morley against the Government.

shall endeavour not to commit you, even by implication, to anything at Glasgow; however, people will talk whatever one says.

Yours sincerely,

E. Grey.

Rosebery had agreed to stand as a candidate in the Rectorial Election of Glasgow University, and this pending contest aroused keen political interest in the autumn of 1899. Haldane wrote to Rosebery on October 23rd that 'our minority is depressed tonight. Fowler talks of retiring, Asquith is silent. But it is not so with E. G. or myself. We are going to Glasgow to shew a little sport. No reference of course to H or M but to support the "independent" candidate. We do not feel dismayed by the numbers on Thursday. Half of the 92 were of our mind, & nearly all the abstentions were so. If, as it must, the demonstration from the end of the front Oppn Bench means war, we think we have the best position. E. G. talks of leaving the front bench, but I am pressing him to remain.'

The catastrophic news of military disaster in South Africa added immeasurably to the strains within the Liberal Party.[1] The jeering delight of the Irish at the news of every British defeat inflamed equally the Conservatives and the Liberal Imperialists, while the mocking invective of the 'pro-Boers' and the supine leadership of Campbell-Bannerman created an intense personal bitterness between the separate Liberal sections. The Liberal Imperialists were in a particularly vulnerable position; a by-election at Bromley and Bow was the portent, since although the Liberal candidate supported the war he was branded as a 'pro-Boer' by the Unionists and was crushingly defeated. As one Liberal Imperialist remarked to J. A. Spender—editor of the *Westminster Gazette*—'it is one thing to go to the stake for principles you believe in, and quite another to be roasted alive for causes you abhor'.[2] This situation, which put the career of every Liberal Imperialist MP in jeopardy, had two major consequences; pressure upon Campbell-Bannerman to give a positive lead to the party rather than occupying a nebulous position vaguely 'left of centre' was in-

[1] The *Annual Register* for 1900 estimated the Liberal supporters of the Government in Parliament at 62; opponents of the war at 68; approximately 27 who were uncertain in their allegiance, and a small element—represented by Campbell-Bannerman and Herbert Gladstone—who tried to follow a middle line.

[2] Spender: *Life, Journalism and Politics*, I, 101.

creased, and the Liberal Imperialists turned almost desperately to Rosebery for protection.

The Bath speech, followed by his triumphant election as Rector of Glasgow University, appreciably raised Rosebery in the estimation of his followers. Haldane was one of many who wrote enthusiastically in this bleak period to say that Rosebery's support 'comes as refreshment to those who have felt themselves out of it just now for want of a creed & a leader'. Although he declined to involve himself in these internal struggles within the party, Rosebery continued to urge national unity in a series of elegantly phrased and wildly applauded speeches. His restored popularity gave him an immense attraction to the Imperialist minority in the Parliamentary party, and their exhortations propelled him reluctantly back into the political arc-light. He had always been an interesting personality; at the beginning of 1900, as the tide began to turn in the war, interest in his intentions increased considerably. 'You are the hope—at this moment the only hope—of the men who stand for all that is best in the Liberal party,' Wemyss Reid wrote to him. '. . . There was a time when we who believed in you & clung to you were comparatively few in number. Now we are a great army ready to march to victory if you will but put yourself at our head.'

'Lord Rosebery has severed the last tie that bound him to any political organisation,' Sir Almeric Fitzroy noted on February 24th, 1900, 'but reserves to himself the right, as the Chatham of the day, to influence politics by the sheer force of his personality.'[1] By the early summer of 1900, even the most uncompromising enemies of the war in the Liberal Party were casting uneasy glances at this perplexing political phenomenon. Rosebery was but fifty-two years of age; his general popularity in the country had never stood higher; it seemed that he had recovered his health and his nerve; he stood out above the party strife as the one Liberal with a national reputation and a national following. To his entranced supporters and his anxious opponents it appeared that he held the leadership of the party in his grasp once again.

[1] Fitzroy: *Memoirs*, 35.

CHAPTER TWELVE

THE LIBERAL LEAGUE

*Independence is at once the choicest and the least serviceable of all qualities
in political life. Independence in a public man is a quality as splendid as it is
rare, but it is apt to produce and develop acute angles. Now a colleague with
acute angles is a superfluous discomfort. And independence in a great orator
on the Treasury Bench is a rocket of which one cannot predict the course.*

ROSEBERY: *Introduction to the Windham Papers* (1913)

A SERIES OF BRITISH VICTORIES in South Africa in the summer of 1900 misled the British people and their Government into
believing that the Boer War was virtually ended, and the disputations within the ranks of the Opposition increased in bitterness as
their electoral prospects grew steadily more sombre. The Liberal
Party had reached that dangerous point in an internecine dispute
when the victory of either section had become far more important
to the participants than the future of the party as a whole. Each
side clutched at portents, whether from by-elections or any dis-
cernible shifts in the personal fortunes of their leaders, and threw
all notions of caution aside. The Liberal Party, although it had not
lost its hold upon a large and devoted section of the electorate,
seemed to gain a masochistic pleasure out of its frequent schisms
in the House of Commons. On July 25th, for example, the party
split violently over a motion proposed by a notorious 'pro-Boer',
Sir Wilfred Lawson, to reduce the Colonial Office Vote; Campbell-
Bannerman advised a general abstention, but Grey led 37 Liberals
into the Government lobby, while over 30 'pro-Boers' voted with
Lawson. After a meeting with Grey and Asquith—who had
abstained from the division, but privately told Grey that he supported him—Haldane wrote from the House of Commons to
Rosebery urging him to take the lead. 'I do not know whether
you will consider that what has happened makes a difference to
you. But if you choose to emerge & lead those Liberals who may
be called "Lord R's friends" with Asquith & Grey as lieutenants

in the House, I think things will work out. . . . *We* have the machinery & the Whips & the future, & this means that we grow & become the party.'

Rosebery was now being pushed towards a decision from which he shrank. 'Politics may possibly come to me, but I shall not go to them,' he wrote to Wemyss Reid from Gastein on July 1st. 'It is not the whispers of half a dozen friends which will induce me to exchange a life which I love for a life which I hate. . . . It might strike a cynic that there is something strange in this reported anxiety to see me in the field before the General Election. The party has done very well without me for four years. During that time it has committed considerable blunders, and has, to put it mildly, not gained upon the country. It now sees itself on the brink of a catastrophe, and desires—or is said to desire—to see a new leader before the election, i.e. a new scapegoat.' 'While there is, so far as I can judge, this universal desire for your return to the leadership,' Reid replied warningly on July 11th, 'there is at the same time among many, including some who have been your warmest political adherents, a strong feeling that patriotism itself demands your return to the helm in the great crisis (national rather than party) through which we are passing; & that if you do not come back now you will have missed your chance. . . . When a man means to cross a stream it will not do for him to sit on the bank until all the water has run past. Sooner or later he must wet his feet.'

Parliament was dissolved in September, and was followed by the 'Khaki Election', in which all Liberal candidates were tarred with the pro-Boer brush, and the cry 'A vote for the Liberals is a vote for the Boers' rang from every Unionist platform. Rosebery told Hamilton on August 8th that he was determined to keep aloof from the elections, but on the eve of the voting he issued a private manifesto in the form of an open letter to Lambton, the hero of Ladysmith, who was a Liberal candidate; he strongly attacked the Government but declared that he could never support any settlement of the war which would nullify the sacrifices made by the nation. His silence had bewildered and angered his friends, and his intervention did not improve matters. Although several seats changed hands, the 1900 election hardly altered the party representation at Westminster, the pre-election Unionist majority of 130 being increased to 134. More significantly, however, this majority was 18 smaller than that of 1895. A new friend of Rosebery, Winston Churchill,[1] although elected as a Unionist for Oldham, was not deceived. 'I think this election,' he wrote to Rosebery on October 4th, 'fought by the Liberals as a soldiers' battle, without plan or leaders or enthusiasm, has shown so far the strength, not the weakness, of Liberalism in the country.'

After the elections, Rosebery disappeared once again into his cloud of mysterious reserve. 'Rosebery has not improved his position,' Asquith wrote to Herbert Gladstone. 'He was afraid to plunge, yet not resolute enough to hold to his determination to keep aloof.'[2] 'He is at present too dark a horse for any wise man to put his money on,' Lord Ripon remarked. The Liberal Imperial Council, under the erratic leadership of Lord Brassey, formally disassociated itself from Campbell-Bannerman, and on November 15th the exasperated leader of the party delivered a highly provocative attack upon the Council at Dundee and raised the question of Rosebery's position. 'I shall hold the door wide open,' he had told the anxious Herbert Gladstone, 'but I shan't ring the dinner-bell or hang out a flag of distress.' The appeal consequently lacked warmth. 'The door has always been open for Lord Rosebery's return,' Campbell-Bannerman declared. 'We should welcome him and rejoice to see him standing among his old comrades and taking his share in carrying on, as he so well can, the work which they have been endeavouring to prosecute in the most unfavourable circumstances during his absence. Of one thing you may be quite sure—that Lord Rosebery will never come back to put himself at the head of a section.' 'Most of the MP's & other people whom I have heard discussing the matter agree that C-B acted in perfect good faith,' Reid wrote to Rosebery on November 22nd, 'but that he bungled the business atrociously.'

It is unlikely that this was a correct interpretation of the

[1] Rosebery's first impressions of Lord Randolph's son were not favourable. He met him at Guisachan—the Scottish seat of Lord Tweedmouth—just after Churchill returned from South Africa, with his name ringing through the land as a result of his escape from a prisoner-of-war camp. Churchill, voluble and enthusiastic, regaled his fellow-guests with his reminiscences until a late hour one evening before Rosebery arrived, and when, on the following evening, Rosebery rose to go to bed, the rest of the company, terrified at having to endure a further lecture from this talkative youth, leaped up, and, in Rosebery's own words, 'I was almost jammed in the door'. This unfavourable impression, however, was quickly removed.

[2] Mallet: *Herbert Gladstone*, 177.

Dundee speech. Campbell-Bannerman, like Haldane, Grey, Asquith, and Reid, wanted to bring Rosebery into the open. 'As long as he is merely looking over the wall', he wrote to Sydney Buxton on November 21st, 'there will be peace for us.' He lunched with Rosebery at Dalmeny in the February of 1901, and found him 'perfectly friendly, deeply interested, but immovably aloof. . . . Of course I had no overtures to make and our conversation was quite general.' To Ripon he wrote that Rosebery had appeared 'not steadfast and unmoveable, but unmoveable without being steadfast'.

The pressure being exerted upon Rosebery by his supporters— particularly Reid, Grey, and Haldane—was assuming formidable proportions by the end of 1900. 'If you choose to draw the sword & lead those who need you at this low ebb in their fortunes,' Haldane wrote (October 16th), 'you will not lack devoted followers.' Rosebery simply replied that he could see no sign that his return to partisan politics was generally desired, and that even if it was, there was more value in independence. Fowler spoke of his 'commanding influence'; Rosebery retorted by pointing out that the Liberal Imperialist candidate whom he had publicly supported in the election (Lambton) had been beaten by over four thousand votes and was bottom of the poll. 'Talk about commanding influence! Few letters have accomplished more!'

In November, Rosebery delivered his eagerly awaited Rectorial Address at Glasgow, which was dominated by a magnificently eloquent defence of the concept of Empire.

How marvellous it all is! Built not by saints and angels, but the work of men's hands; cemented with men's honest blood and with a world of tears, welded by the best brains of centuries past; not without the taint and reproach incidental to all human work, but constructed on the whole with pure and splendid purpose. Human, and yet not wholly human, for the most heedless and the most cynical must see the finger of the divine. Growing as trees while others slept; fed by the faults of others as well as by the character of our fathers; reaching with the ripple of a restless tide over tracts and islands and continents, until our little Britain woke up to find herself the foster-mother of nations and the source of united empires. . . .

. . . And mark this. In all that I have said there is no word of war, not even the beat of a drum or the distant singing of a bullet. To some, the Empire is little else, and that makes many hate the word. That is

not my view. Our Empire is not founded on the precedents associated
with that name, it is not the realm of conquest which that term has
been wont to imply. It has often used the sword, it could not exist
by the sword, but it does not live by the sword. . . .

Grey and Haldane were ecstatic in their praises. 'Your address
made me feel that a rift was made in clouds', Grey wrote enthusiastically, 'through which I saw a fine & inspiriting prospect with
a glowing light upon it.' 'It gives us what we needed to work
upon', Haldane wrote, '—the foundations of a constructive peace
policy. The suggestions in it are limitless, & the oratory of it,
if I may say so, simply admirable.'

The winter of 1900–1 witnessed a perceptible decline in the
reputation and authority of Campbell-Bannerman. Grey demanded
assurances that he would not support a move to recall Milner, and
Haldane described his leader as 'a weak and foolish man'. An
attempt by Haldane on January 24th to arrange a *modus vivendi*
between Campbell-Bannerman and Rosebery failed, but their
private relationship remained friendly. Munro Ferguson was
probably the most vehement of the opponents of the leader, but
Rosebery refused to accept his violent criticisms. 'Remember that
he is thoroughly straight,' he had written in the March of 1899,
'a gentleman, a friend of yours, a Scot, and do not be hasty to
despair of him or even criticise him.' This pleasant relationship
created in the dark days of 1894–5 was irretrievably destroyed by
the events of the summer of 1901.

Even at this stage it is easy to detect in the letters of even
Rosebery's most devoted followers a germinating feeling of
dismay at his inaction and inaccessibility. The second complaint
was well justified, and partly explains his increasing remoteness
from the political scene. He was out of Britain for five weeks in
1900, twelve weeks in 1901, eight in 1902, twelve in 1903, nine
in 1904, and seven in 1905; furthermore, his habit of moving from
one of his great houses to another without any warning was often
disconcerting to his supporters. Time and again, at important
moments, they simply did not know where Rosebery was, and
his restlessness became more noticeable every year. One afternoon he would be working quietly at 38, Berkeley Square, and
then on an impulse would order his carriage and set off for King's
Cross, arriving at Dalmeny early the next morning; an emissary
to The Durdans would learn that the great man had just departed

for Mentmore; visitors to Dalmeny would discover that he was shooting at Rosebery, over twenty miles away.

Keeping a track on their leader was not the least of the irritations confronting Rosebery's supporters. 'I have nothing new to say with regard to the position as it affects yourself,' Reid wrote to him in April. 'You know already how impatient many of those who regard themselves as your friends are; they speak quite angrily when your name is mentioned.' 'If he doesn't come into the open in the next two years his chance will be gone anyhow,' Grey wrote to Munro Ferguson on October 18th, 1900, 'and he may at any time get an ultimatum from some of us that we are not going on any more without him.'[1] Reid and J. A. Spender tried constantly to 'draw' Rosebery, but without effect. As Spender has written,

He was the most uninfluenceable of men. Time after time I have left him, thinking that possibly I had made some impression on him, only to discover a few days later that he had done the one thing that I had urged him most strongly not to do. Then I would lose my patience and fling out at him in the *Westminster*, but it made no difference. He would ask me to come again, smile at my disappointment and displeasure, and be his old charming self, talking of Napoleon and Pitt and Horace Walpole, and telling stories of Dizzy and Mr Gladstone.[2]

Rosebery spent the spring of 1901 travelling around Europe, marvelling with an engagingly childlike awe at the beauty of the Coliseum in moonlight, Vesuvius in a sunset, and Gastein on a summer's evening. 'After dinner to the Coliseum,' he noted on March 27th. 'A band playing, then a rocket or two, the Bengal Lights, the last vulgar. But before they began I was profoundly impressed with the scene—the great gaunt skeleton of time in which there once throbbed so full & tumultuous a life, where the dusty Pagan crowd thronged as to a bullfight to see the torn Christian furnish sport, this imperishable monument which defies time and watches impassively the vicissitudes of Rome, now containing a small crowd of tourists, listening to an Italian military band, & waiting for the paltry fireworks, with the cold moon looking cynically down.' Most of April was spent in Naples at the beloved Villa Rosebery, and after a brief return to England, May and June found him in Gastein. It is not surprising that his

---

[1] Trevelyan: *Grey*, 78.   [2] *Life, Journalism and Politics*, I, 65.

supporters were impatient and indignant. 'Although Asquith and Grey and I stuck by him tightly we did so at the peril of our political lives,' Haldane subsequently wrote,[1] 'because we never knew when he would retire altogether and leave us in the lurch. He would make no sacrifice of himself.'

While Rosebery was thus progressing around Europe in the spring and early summer of 1901, events were moving rapidly in England. The capture of the *Daily News* by an anti-Imperialist syndicate and the dismissal of E. T. Cook—'Cook of Berkeley Square', as Harcourt was wont to call him—was a severe blow to the opponents of Campbell-Bannerman. By a strange irony, the proprietor of the *Daily Chronicle* dismissed Massingham at almost the same time and reversed that paper's pro-Boer policy, so that the politics of both papers were forcibly changed. But the loss of Cook's influence upon the *Daily News* was a far more serious reverse to the Imperialists than the fortuitous reversal of the outlook of its rival. Harcourt reported at this time that he found C-B—to use his famous sobriquet—'full of fight and with a much stiffened back', declaring that he was tired of 'trying to accommodate everybody by paring down a phrase here and a proposal there until nothing was left' and that he would take his own line, regardless of the 'Lib-Imps'.[2] It was not long before this new mood in the leader found occasion for expression.

Failure to negotiate with the Boers had driven them to a policy of guerrilla warfare which had proved disconcertingly successful. The British retaliated by wholesale burning of farms and by massing thousands of women and children in concentration camps. These tactics, although possibly justified on military grounds, aroused profound indignation in the Liberal ranks even before ugly stories of gross mismanagement and even cruelty began to circulate. Miss Emily Hobhouse—who returned from South Africa in the same boat that bore Milner to his peerage and the laudations of the City of London—laid before Campbell-Bannerman evidence of the appalling condition of some of these camps. At a banquet given by the National Reform Union at the Holborn Restaurant on June 14th, which was attended by Harcourt and Morley, Campbell-Bannerman delivered his judgement.

[1] Maurice: *Haldane* I, 159. It should be noted that Haldane's chronology is inaccurate in the memorandum from which this extract is taken.
[2] Gardiner: *Harcourt*, II, 527.

A phrase often used is that 'war is war', but when one comes to ask about it one is told that no war is going on, that it is not war. When is a war not a war? When it is carried on *by methods of barbarism* in South Africa.

The impact of this sentence was traumatic, and the vilification which was hurled at Campbell-Bannerman's head from all sides was reminiscent of the hatred against Gladstone after the death of Gordon. The phrase was injudicious in the sense that Campbell-Bannerman had not intended to slander British troops, but after he had disclaimed any such intention in the House of Commons on June 18th, he proceeded to support the motion for the adjournment moved by Lloyd George, who had unleashed a vitriolic attack on Milner; Haldane, Grey, and Asquith were among the fifty Liberals who abstained in the division.

On June 20th came the first signs of violent reaction to this inept performance, Asquith attacking his leader with surprising fierceness in a speech to the South Essex Liberals at the Liverpool Street Station Hotel. The Liberal Imperialists arranged for a dinner in his honour on July 19th, and the process of dining and counter-dining—'war to the knife and fork', as Henry Lucy wittily remarked—had begun. The *Westminster Gazette* commented acidly upon the situation.

There was a dinner on June 14th at which speeches were made which gave great offence to the Imperialist section of the Liberal party. There was a dinner on June 20th at which Mr Asquith answered the speeches which gave offence. There is now to be a dinner in recognition of the speech which answered the speeches which gave the offence to the Liberal Imperialists. There will next be a dinner in recognition of the speech which gave the offence which was answered by the speech which led to the dinner in recognition. The Liberal Party will thus dine and counter-dine itself out of existence or else be dissolved in the laughter of that observant man in the street or balancing elector whose suffrage it so greatly desires to obtain.

Campbell-Bannerman decided that a crisis of confidence had definitely arisen, and a party meeting was hurriedly arranged for July 9th at the Reform Club. He took a very tough line at this meeting, inviting the party to expel those who opposed his leadership. 'I say to you deliberately and emphatically that we shall never restore healthy efficiency to the Liberal Party in the House of Commons unless these rebels are put down, and I

appeal to solid, earnest, loyal men—and I am sure I see no others
here—to lend their aid in extinguishing them.' The Liberal Party,
the party of freedom of discussion, of individual liberty, had never
thus been exhorted. Asquith, clearly uncomfortable, said that he
was pained and surprised to realise that it was believed that there
was anything personal in his criticism of the leadership, but that
it was either affectation or political dishonesty to pretend that
no differences on fundamental policy existed in the party. Grey
was more combative, pointing out that the leader himself was
not innocent of creating severe difficulties for loyal party members
and that others apart from Campbell-Bannerman were suffering
from the schisms within the party.

Although the leader received his vote of confidence, the
political atmosphere remained sulphurous. 'We have had an awful
fortnight,' Campbell-Bannerman wrote to his old friend William
Robertson on July 13th, 'but it has all ended well for the moment.
I have the whole party except perhaps six men with me: and even
on the SA question (whatever they may have the courage to say
publicly—that is another question) they with very few exceptions
take my attitude. But the intriguers will go on as opportunity
offers.

'The Asquith dinner is a stupid blunder. They cannot make it
innocent, do as they like; it has the taint of its origin about it;
and, honestly, every single man I have spoken to condemns it,
and wishes it given up. *This includes A himself*, but he is so thirled
to Grey and Haldane that he seems unable to offend them by
openly renouncing. . . . It is a striking picture of the obstinacy of
the two I have named, and also of the weakness of A. I suspect
Milnerism is at the bottom of it! But those gentry have made A
their tool in a great plot against me.'[1]

At this delicate moment Rosebery intervened. He had been
greatly shocked by the Holborn Restaurant dinner, which he
described to Spender as 'a sinister event'. 'There was nothing un-
foreseen or unexpected about it. C-B knew exactly who he would
meet, and met them. Moreover, he made them a speech such as
they might have made themselves. I do not see therefore how a
schism can be avoided. Indeed I think it must have been in the
minds of the organisers to bring one about.'[2] He regarded
Campbell-Bannerman's crime as twofold; through his complicity

[1] *Campbell-Bannerman Papers.*   [2] Harris: *Spender*, 107.

in 'the conspiracy of silence' in the South Africa Committee 'which had deliberately and firmly shut its eyes to the central matter of the complicity of the Government'[1] he had contributed to the war situation; now he was publicly expressing himself on the side of Harcourt, Morley, and the anti-Imperialists, and had, by one injudicious phrase, given the Unionists a cry which could be disastrous for all Liberals.

Rosebery hastened home from Gastein, and on July 8th was summoned by the King. 'He wished to consult me as to seeing C-B and impressing upon him the encouragement that his utterances about the war gave to the Boers and appealing to him as a patriot to desist,' Rosebery's record of the conversation states. 'I urged him to do nothing of the kind, and he agreed to give up the idea.' Without warning anyone,[2] Rosebery declared in a letter to *The Times* on July 17th that he would not return to party politics but felt bound to point out the fundamental nature of the controversies in the Liberal ranks.

. . . There is a great Liberal force in the country, but it must make up its mind about the war. Neutrality and an open mind make up an impossible attitude. The war is either just or unjust, the methods either uncivilised or legitimate. But this is not a transient difference of opinion. It is based on a sincere fundamental and incurable antagonism of principle with regard to the Empire at large and our consequent policy. One school or the other must prevail if the Liberal party is once more to become a force. A party cannot be conducted on the principles of Issachar. . . .

To add to the consternation of Asquith, Grey, and Haldane, it was then announced that Rosebery would address the City Liberal Club luncheon on the 19th, thereby giving the strong impression that he and Asquith were working in concert and incidentally seriously affecting the publicity which the Asquith dinner had expected to receive on the morrow. 'Had it not been for *The Times*, which, with great insight, reported both Rosebery and Asquith verbatim,' Haldane has written,[3] 'we should have been in a great difficulty because he [Rosebery] had not backed us up in what he said.' Grey was the first of the Imperialist group to

[1] A private note written by Rosebery on June 15th.

[2] Not even Hamilton, who wrote in his diary on July 17th, 'Although I am supposed to enjoy Rosebery's full confidence, he never gave me a hint of his bombshell which he exploded this morning.'

[3] Maurice: *Haldane*, I, 159.

express strong public disappointment at Rosebery's attitude. 'The position of standing aside from party politics cannot last,' he declared to an audience at Peterborough on the same day that Rosebery's letter appeared. 'It is true that lookers-on see most of the game. Yes, but they do not influence the result.' 'To be an ally of a man of genius', Grey wrote to his wife on August 16th, 'you have either to pay the price which he askes (sometimes an impossible one) or serve him for nothing. I sometimes think that the reason why Rosebery attracts so much attention is that the genius in him lifts him up so that he is conspicuous in the crowd, a head taller than it; people keep looking and admiring, no one else can stand so tall, but those who are quite close see that his feet aren't upon the ground. It's as if God dangled him amongst us by an invisible thread.'[1]

On July 19th Rosebery made his eagerly awaited speech to the City Liberals, which served to perplex and dismay his supporters even further.

. . . For the present at any rate, I must proceed alone. I must plough my furrow alone. That is my fate, agreeable or the reverse; but before I get to the end of that furrow it is possible that I may find myself not alone. But that is another matter. If it be so, I shall remain very contented in the society of my books and my home. If it be so, I shall wait for those circumstances to arise before I pronounce with any definiteness about them. . . .

Asquith handled his speech on the same evening with great skill, and from this moment definitely emerged as the leader of the Imperialist wing. 'You are going to plough your furrow,' Grey wrote to Rosebery on July 20th. 'Some of us too are setting to work to plough a furrow, which goes in the same direction. We ought not therefore to come into conflict, but the situation needs delicate handling and for the present there is some soreness. In the first place, Asquith has come through a very trying time and has in my opinion saved the situation, as far as the "centre" of the Liberal party is concerned. Without him, and if he had not stood by us, there would have been a secession of myself and a few, but *very few*, others from the Liberal party before you had come back. Now, if there is a split, it will be a much less one-sided affair. Asquith has been very staunch to us & we are very chivalrously disposed towards him.' Haldane had a long conversation

[1] Trevelyan: *Grey*, 79–80.

with Asquith on the 21st and reported to Rosebery that he minded 'the loss of prestige which arose from the *appearance* of the great sacrifice & effort of his life being jumped upon. But he is quite aware that this was an appearance only, & that the reasons for it lay far beyond the moment. He sees that it is wisest that the furrow should be ploughed separately. But *his* furrow he has been ploughing at great pain to himself, & I think he needs every consideration that can be given for the effort & sacrifice he has made.'

Rosebery strongly believed that the Imperialist movement 'should be Asquithian', as he told Grey on June 29th, but it would at least have been helpful if he had given his friends some warning of his actions. 'Whatever comes or goes,' Asquith wrote to him on July 22nd in terms which read strangely in view of the fact that the two men were popularly supposed to be working in concert, 'our old & tried friendship, rooted in such deep soil, can (I hope & believe) never suffer any change. But I hope also that your "furrow" will prove not to be divergent, or even parallel, but sooner or later (& the sooner the better) to be one in which E. Grey & I & all your real friends & associates can lend a hand.'

The pressure upon Rosebery to give a decisive lead to the Imperialist wing of the party was given greater emphasis by an important event which occurred towards the end of July. Alarmed by the deteriorating condition of the war, and convinced that a negotiated peace was not only necessary but possible, he privately approached Salisbury and Balfour with a proposal that a private emissary from each side should meet secretly to discuss the outstanding points of difference between the two sides. Such a meeting, he urged, would not publicly compromise either Government but would be a starting-point for more formal armistice negotiations.

Through Mr Arthur Markham he received intelligence on July 9th that M. Edouard Lippert,[1] then travelling on the Continent, considered that the time was opportune for ending hostilities, and told Markham that Kruger was anxious for peace 'on the basis of a federal states of South Africa', but refused to negotiate with Chamberlain. Lippert had asked Markham to approach Rosebery to see if he would be prepared to act as intermediary between Kruger and Salisbury. Rosebery asked Lippert and Markham to

[1] One of the original dynamite concessionaires, and close to Kruger.

call on him at Berkeley Square, which they did on July 18th.
Lippert made the point that all previous negotiations between the
two sides had failed not so much on the point of amnesty to the
Boers, but because of Boer mistrust of Chamberlain and Milner.
Rosebery's memorandum of this conversation ends, 'I called on
Lord Salisbury the same day at the House of Lords and communicated the proposals to him, as well as my answers.' On July
25th Salisbury wrote to him that 'it is wisest to adhere to the
beaten roads of negotiation', to which Rosebery replied on the
same day.

Dear Lord Salisbury,

Many thanks for your note.

I regard it as a negation to all idea of negotiation, and do not doubt
that you have ample grounds for that determination. But I wish, in one
line, to make the position clear.

Of course the Boers would like to see Milner and Chamberlain (&
Rhodes) blown sky high! But they know that is not possible. Nor is
any removal of Milner possible, even were it desirable on other
grounds, which it is not.

The question then resolves itself into this—is it worth while to
appoint a private agent to meet a private agent with credentials from
the other side with a view to finding out if there is a possibility of
peace on reasonable terms. In my judgment—or rather according to
my information—it is worth while & there is such a possibility. But
that is for you to judge.

It occurred to me that you might appoint one of your late colleagues (such as Goschen) who has no official character, but in whom
you would have complete confidence, & who would not commit you.
My impression is that that was the course adopted at the end of the
war with the American colonies. Chamberlain & you would, of course,
direct negotiations, but would not equally of course be brought into
actual contact with the other negotiator.

Forgive my troubling you, but in view of the terrible drain of the
war I do not like to neglect a chance of ending it. I went to the House
of Lords this afternoon to try and see you but you were not there, so
I am obliged to inflict this letter on you.

Yrs sincly,

AR.

'I most entirely & earnestly share your desire that this terrible
drain of life and money should cease,' Salisbury replied on July
31st, 'but we have to take care lest in trying to arrest it we could

only succeed in prolonging it. . . . If such a negotiation was known to be on foot, it would be widely read on the Boer side as a proof that we are exhausted and disposed to give in. I do not see how it is possible to guard against this danger.'

Salisbury had shown Rosebery's letter to some of his colleagues —presumably including Chamberlain—but on August 3rd Chamberlain made a belligerent speech in the Commons which, according to Lippert and Markham, ended what hopes there might have been for the Boers to approach the British to open peace negotiations. And on this unsatisfactory note, the incident ended.

It was this episode which was the decisive factor in persuading Rosebery to accept an invitation to address a meeting at Chesterfield on December 15th. The announcement created a sensation which took contemporary politicians completely by surprise and which at this length of time it is difficult to fully understand. E. T. Raymond has amusingly but accurately described the excitement.

The expectancy that reigned reminded old politicians of the Midlothian days. Quiet people in far-away corners of the earth were perplexed by Reuter telegrams giving daily bulletins of what was supposed to be in Lord Rosebery's mind. The public at home were whipped up into a frenzy of curiosity. For a moment De Wet and Delarey were forgotten. Generals disappeared momentarily from the illustrated papers, and the space was filled with photographs of Lord Rosebery in all ages and all attitudes. . . . In short, the Chesterfield meeting was advertised with a completeness still unsurpassed. By an ironic destiny the consistent scorner of the arts of the publicity agent was himself the beneficiary of a master-piece of political puffery.[1]

With his few supporters beginning to lose heart, Chesterfield could not have come at a more opportune moment. Even Haldane and Grey were depressed by their leader's erratic performances, his mysterious silences, and his even more mysterious utterances. Haldane told Hamilton on November 1st that Rosebery's reputation had suffered a decline on both sides of the House of Commons, and on November 11th—to take only one example of several—he felt impelled to complain that although he and Grey were fighting for their political lives Rosebery would not confide in them. 'We shall not lose the faith that was instilled into

[1] Raymond: *The Man of Promise*, 201.

us,' Haldane's letter concluded, 'but shall continue to follow out the lines which you laid down for us—to be ours, with or without yourself.'

Chesterfield swept away these doubts—for the moment. The occasion could not have been more daunting for the orator when he rose on December 15th flanked by Fowler, Grey, and Asquith in a hall crammed with serried ranks of Liberal notables. He began by dealing with the tragic South African question, and, although he defended the concentration camp system on grounds of military necessity, he strongly attacked the Government for its inept handling of negotiations with the Boers, and singled out Milner for particular censure. Reminding the audience of the grim examples of the Netherland's resistance against Spain and the history of Lord North's administration, he urged either a meeting 'at a wayside inn' between two representatives from each side— the course he had unsuccessfully urged upon Salisbury—or the opening of official negotiations by Kitchener. 'We are bound to the Boer people, for better or worse, in a permanent, inevitable, and fateful marriage. . . . I want to bind, to heal, not to keep open, the mortal wound which is being caused by this war.'

He then turned to the more explosive topic of the condition of the Liberal Party. In a note written in 1898 he had expressed his conviction that the country would never trust the Liberals until they were free from the Irish Nationalists, and at Chesterfield he developed this point. The party must become independent of the Irish; it must achieve unity; it must 'clean the slate' and re-state its principles.

. . . It is six years since the Liberals were in office. It is sixteen since they were in power. Meanwhile, the world has not stood still; but there is Toryism as great in Liberal circles, as great and as deep, though it may be less conscious, as in the Carlton Club. There are men who sit still with the fly-blown phylacteries of obsolete policies bound round their foreheads, who do not remember that while they have been mumbling their incantations to themselves, the world has been marching and revolving, and that if they have any hope of leading it or guiding it they must march and move with it too. I hope, therefore, that when you have to write on your clean slate, you will write on it a policy adapted to 1901 or 1902, and not a policy adapted to 1892 or 1885. . . .

My advice is not to move much faster than the great mass of the

people are prepared to go. If the Liberal Party has not learnt that
lesson in its many years of affliction, then it has learned nothing. My
last piece of advice to the Party is that it should not disassociate itself, even indirectly, from the new sentiment of Empire which occupies
the nation.

He developed the curious philosophy of 'Efficiency', particularly attacking Parliament and implying strongly that it was not
efficient or representative. 'I am quite sure that my policy does
not run on Party lines, but it is not to Party that I appeal. I appeal
to Caesar—from Parliament with its half-hearted but overwhelmingly majority for the Government and its distracted and dis-
united Opposition—I appeal to the silent but supreme tribunal
which shapes and controls in the long run the destinies of our
people, the tribunal of public opinion and common sense. If that
fails us, we are lost indeed, and I know of nothing else that remains to avail us.'

In one respect Chesterfield was a spectacular success. The
idea of the meeting 'at a wayside inn' was arresting to a nation
sickened by war, and unquestionably altered the climate of opinion both in Britain and Africa, while the insistence upon magnanimity to the Boers appealed to the highest instincts of the most
generous nation in the world. The principles of the peace of
Vereeniging which was concluded between Kitchener and Botha
in the summer of 1902 were almost identical to those urged by
Rosebery at Chesterfield.

On the domestic parts of the speech opinion was more sharply
divided. Rosebery received an enormous number of enthusiastic
congratulations, and Grey was so excited that he sent Campbell-
Bannerman—with what the latter thought 'd——d egotism and
impertinence'—an ultimatum that he had felt obliged to choose
between himself and Rosebery, and had chosen Rosebery. Haldane told Hamilton on December 24th at Chatsworth that
Chesterfield 'has made all of us ready to work our fingers off for
Rosebery, if, as I think, he means to lead'. John Morley, however,
struck a different note. 'I only want to be left alone in my shell,
but people come flaming to my door with a Chesterfield broadside
in their hands—I mean broadsheet, don't I?—clamouring for a
riposte, and I vainly plead dilapidated vocal chords. However, I
bid you good night, all the same, and wish you well, only reminding you and myself of Pascal's saying that three parts of the mis-

chief in the world would be avoided if men would only sit still in their parlours.'

It would have been unnatural had Campbell-Bannerman surveyed the extraordinary enthusiasm which Rosebery could still arouse without a certain degree of jealousy and impatience. Campbell-Bannerman had never entertained serious personal ambitions until he found himself, after a series of accidents, in the Liberal leadership. But having arrived at this position, he clung to it with a wholly unexpected tenacity. He had the failing—not uncommon in public life—of regarding all criticism in a personal light and he did not forget, nor did he forgive. But although his Parliamentary performances were usually lamentable, his basic common sense and political shrewdness were very important factors; he was a very limited man, but he led a party which was bewildered by the gyrations of his unquestionably more able but less reliable predecessors. The Liberal rank and file may have admired Rosebery but they instinctively trusted 'C-B'.

Campbell-Bannerman at once put his finger upon the central weakness of Chesterfield. A political party long in opposition requires, above all things, tender handling, and a rekindling of the Faith. A period of political misfortune and consequent depression is the last occasion on which a party's leaders should raise disquieting fundamental questions which can only lead to further schismatic bitterness. Campbell-Bannerman perceived this, but Rosebery never seems to be aware of this basic political fact, thereby demonstrating his chronic insensitiveness to the rank and file membership of a national political party. Notions which were stimulating and even exciting at Dalmeny, Cloan, or Fallodon merely aroused bewilderment or anger in less glittering abodes. Until his disastrous conversion to Home Rule, Gladstone had never stepped as a party leader too far ahead of his supporters, and he had the extraordinary facility of raising all fundamental issues to a plane which was so exalted that his followers marvelled rather than cursed. Chesterfield was not so much a challenge as a slap in the face; Rosebery's greatest oratorical triumph was, politically, his most disastrous utterance. He had not rekindled the Faith, but had derided it, and had proposed in its place a new policy which bore little relation to Liberalism and which was based upon a vague doctrine of 'Efficiency'. For once Harcourt expressed the amazement and anger of the party at Chesterfield when he wrote to Loulou, 'All the traditions, the pledges, and the faiths of the Liberal Party are to be wiped out. . . . The whole language is an insult to the whole past of the Liberal Party and a betrayal of its growth in the future.'[1]

Herbert Gladstone had been anxious to arrange a meeting between Campbell-Bannerman and Rosebery since the elections to discuss differences. 'The clear wish of the vast majority of Liberals is that you should have the active co-operation of Rosebery for general party purposes,' he had written to the leader after the 1900 elections,[2] and after Chesterfield he wrote enthusiastically to Campbell-Bannerman about the prospects for reunion.

. . . It seems to me that there is so much that is broad, generous, & wise in what he says, so much tending to a definite plan of peace under an alternative Govt, that we ought to sink differences for the sake of getting rid of the present hopeless regime & of getting substantially nearer a peaceful settlement. . . . I expect we shall find that the bulk of our men will say that R's speech gives both sections the opportunity of sinking their differences & that it should at once be laid hold of. . . .[3]

Campbell-Bannerman, who was more concerned with the domestic aspects of Chesterfield, was noticeably less impressed.

I have your meditations upon Chesterfield [he replied to Gladstone on December 18th]. I agree that the views on peace and war go very far and are not unreasonable, though it is unfortunate that they run counter to the very two things our people in the country care most about—Milner and Camps. I also agree that Aaron, KC, and Sir E. Hur,[4] who were there to hold up the prophet's hands, must have held up their own at some of the things they were expected to swallow. . . .

All that he said about the clean slate and efficiency was an affront to Liberalism and was pure claptrap. Efficiency as a watchword! Who is against it? This is all mere *rechauffé* of Mr Sidney Webb, who is evidently the chief instructor of the whole faction.

It is not unfavourable to the chance of unity, in the war and peace issue: but ominous of every horror in general politics, if it is meant seriously. However, we can talk this over.

What is a 'fly-blown phylactery'?

Fly-blow is the result of a fly laying the egg from which maggots come in meat; no fly out of Bedlam would choose a phylactery (if he found one) for such a purpose. . . .[5]

[1] Gardiner: *Harcourt*, II, 536–7.   [2] Mallet: *Herbert Gladstone*, 180.
[3] *Campbell-Bannerman Papers*.   [4] Asquith and Grey.
[5] Spender: *Campbell-Bannerman*, II, 14.

Campbell-Bannerman decided that it would be opportune for him to meet Rosebery, and lunched at Berkeley Square on December 23rd. It is difficult to regard this decision as anything more than a tactical exercise. Rosebery recorded his impressions of their conversation immediately after Campbell-Bannerman left— as was his invariable habit with important conversations— whereas the leader's account was for external consumption, a fact which may account for their conspicuous dissimilarities.

Rosebery recorded that he thought Campbell-Bannerman 'much changed (I had not seen him for many months). He had lost his tranquil and portly ease, seemed aged and shrunk and irritable (for him). He began talking about substantial agreement &c and I somehow fell at once into Irish Home Rule and stated definitely that I could have nothing to do with Mr Gladstone's policy, and that much had happened since 1902. . . . This rather disconcerted C-B, as he had just declared himself at Dunfermline in favour of Irish Home Rule. He tried to soften down my declaration, but I was emphatic.'

They then moved to the delicate topic of 'methods of barbarism'. C-B said that the effect of the phrase had been greatly exaggerated, but Rosebery retorted that the impact upon himself at Gastein had been very strong. When Rosebery taxed him further, 'he said nothing and offered no explanation. He gave me the impression of not being very proud of it. He spoke however with complacency of his recent tour in Devonshire and Lancashire, and with great bitterness (quite unlike him) of the "rebellion" attempted in Scotland which had been "put down and squashed by our fellows". He named Haldane and Munro Ferguson with peculiar asperity. I inferred that union between his section and Asquith's was more remote than ever. (More especially as the same evening Haldane proposed himself at Mentmore and spoke with an acrimony which could be scarcely exceeded of C-B.)

'C-B ended by acknowledging, in reply to my remark in justification of Asquith, that he (C-B) had definitely thrown himself into the arms of the Pro-Boer section, that his private opinions had always been with that section. (This I had never doubted.) . . . In the midst of the conversation he said that he must catch his train and hurried off.'[1]

[1] *Vide* Crewe, *Rosebery*, II, 573–4, for the full text of Rosebery's account.

Campbell-Bannerman's account of the meeting—speedily conveyed to his colleagues—was very different. 'I thought that the straightest thing was to see him and ask him what he was up to,' he wrote to Bryce on December 25th. 'I told him that it was intolerable and mischievous that I and my friends should be held up to condemnation because we were unwilling to work with him. I told him firmly that there was no impediment on our side. . . . Will he then co-operate and consult? Impossible: left the Liberal party five years ago; is not "in communion with you", in ecclesiastical phrase. Ireland is in itself enough to keep him away. . . . Used all the old Unionist arguments. When said if appealed to, he would do all he could to help, what did he mean? It is from the country not from the Party that the appeal must come. Has no more to do or say: his cards are on the table. . . . No more speeches: far more importance attached to this one than he ever intended; will take an active part in H of L. . . . I tackled him about clean slate, shibboleths, etc. Explains that he only meant to be done with N[ewcastle] programme. Would apply Liberal principles as occasion demanded or allowed. . . . For good or evil, there it is. The country does not know all this: thinks we are selfishly excluding a broad-minded statesman. It may be clever but it is diabolically unfair and mischievous.'[1] 'The interview was in the friendliest spirit,' he wrote to William Robertson on the 29th, 'but I ascertained that he *will not* rejoin: will not even co-operate on the war. . . . I pointed out to him that the public were being led to believe that he was a patriot anxious for reunion, while I and others were jealous curmudgeons refusing it. He did not dissent much, but disclaimed any such intention.'[1] He wrote to Ripon, Gladstone, and Harcourt in almost identical terms, and Herbert Gladstone—who ten days before had been extolling Chesterfield—wrote bitterly in reply, 'Ye Gods, what a man! Well, let us see what "the country" says. So far as I know, every useful & capable political being in the country is broadly either Conservative or Liberal. The rest are mostly opinionated drones . . . His position is lamentable & it seems to me the height of selfishness. That you kept up a friendly talk fills me with envy, for I should have lost my temper at once. But what a prospect! And is England to be saved by such a man?'[1]

It was not long before the Press—and particularly that section

[1] *Campbell-Bannerman Papers.*

R.—29

known to be close to Campbell-Bannerman and Gladstone—begin to state that the leader had approached Lord Rosebery in the most friendly manner to seek Liberal unity and had been rebuffed. Reid reported to Rosebery on January 5th, 1902, that 'a deliberate attempt is being made . . . to make it appear that you have repulsed C-B when he would fain have said "ditto" to you. This is the latest phase of the ugly tricks that the Anti-R clique have played so long.' Shortly afterwards Rosebery learned from Herbert Gladstone that Campbell-Bannerman had told his colleagues of their conversation, and Rosebery wrote to Gladstone on January 10th that 'this sort of thing destroys all confidence in communication, & renders it indeed impossible'. On the 13th he protested to Campbell-Bannerman himself. 'I confess it never occurred to me that our private, confidential (& interrupted) chat, as between old friends and colleagues, was in any sense formal or intended for communication to others.' 'If it had been my intention to make any public or formal use of what passed between us, you may be sure I should have first conferred with you,' Campbell-Bannerman replied. 'But though we talked as friends I cannot leave out of sight my responsibility as leader of the Party in the Commons, & I was *bound* to repeat the gist of our talk, of course in the strictest confidence, to my Cabinet colleagues. In reply to a letter from Grey I also told him. That is all I have done. For what has happened in the Press I am in no way responsible. I need not say that if the answer you gave me was rather more peremptory than you really wished to make it, no one wd be better pleased than I.'

'I have just found your letter on my return from Cowes,' Rosebery curtly replied. 'I gather from it that I completely misunderstood the character of our conversation.' And so, with the exception of one formal letter of 1907, the correspondence between Rosebery and Campbell-Bannerman, which had lasted for over twenty years, comes to an abrupt and melancholy conclusion.

On that same evening (January 23rd), speaking at St James's Hall, Campbell-Bannerman challenged Rosebery publicly to declare his position. 'I do not know how it may be elsewhere,' he declared, 'but it is hard to see in this country how a public man can take an effective part in public life in detachment from all political parties'; he went on to question whether any man had the right to adopt such an attitude. Asquith retaliated swiftly on the following evening at Hanley, disassociating himself from his leader's strictures on Rosebery, and urging all Liberals to support the policy of Chesterfield. When Parliament reassembled, Campbell-Bannerman made provocative speeches in favour of Home Rule on January 20th and 21st, and the Liberals again presented a dismal spectacle in debate and the division lobbies. Relations between the two sections of the party were now extremely bitter, with Haldane and Munro Ferguson working to establish a Scottish National Liberal Association to declare support for Chesterfield and attack Home Rule. But Asquith, Grey, and Haldane were still plagued by the silence from Dalmeny. 'I think you should make a sign to Grey & Asquith,' Haldane wrote to Rosebery on January 3rd. 'We are all anxious to help, but we all feel we have been a little sat on.'

The public rupture, however, could not be long delayed. Rosebery had been particularly impressed by the bitterness of Campbell-Bannerman's language against the Lib-Imps in their conversation, and on February 14th he spoke at Liverpool in strong defence of his friends, repeating the demand for independence from the Irish and 'the clean slate'. Campbell-Bannerman replied at Leicester five days later that so long as he was leader of the Liberal Party, Home Rule was not to be wiped off the slate.

I do not know down to this moment of speaking whether Lord Rosebery speaks to me from the interior of our tabernacle or from some vantage point outside. I put that question publicly to him a month ago, but he does not answer it, and I frankly say that I do not think it is quite fair to me not to do so. . . . I am not prepared to erase from the tablets of my creed any principle or measure or proposal or ideal or aspiration of Liberalism. . . . Who is to write on 'the clean slate'? Who is to choose what is to be written?

To the surprise and delight of his supporters, Rosebery's reply was immediate and, for once, clear. In a letter to *The Times* on the next morning (February 20th) he wrote:

Speaking pontifically within his tabernacle last night, my friend Sir Henry Campbell-Bannerman anathematised my declarations on the 'clean slate' and Home Rule. It is obvious that our views on the war and its methods are not less discordant. I remain, therefore, outside his tabernacle, but not, I think, in solitude. Let me add one word more at this moment of definite separation. No one appreciates more heartily than I do the honest and well-intentioned devotion of Sir Henry to the Liberal Party and what he conceives to be its interests. I only wish I could have shared his labour and supported his policy.

Asquith was the first prominent Liberal to declare his allegiance to Rosebery, asserting that the Irish problem was neither settled nor shelved, but that English opinion must be won over by 'step by step' methods: 'To recognise facts is not apostasy. It is common sense.' The National Liberal Federation, however, while welcoming 'the powerful stimulus' given by Rosebery to settlement of the South African War, rejoiced in 'the practical unanimity of the Party', and besought all Liberal MPs to support Campbell-Bannerman.

The immediate effect of these public dissensions was the formation of the Liberal League, which was formally announced after a series of conclaves at 38, Berkeley Square. Rosebery became President, with Asquith, Grey, and Fowler as Vice-Presidents, while a Mr Robert Perks—a staunch admirer of Rosebery and a Liberal MP since 1892—and Mr William Allard were responsible for the organisational work. Haldane, Grey, and Munro Ferguson were, however, the most active members of the League from its earliest days. Fowler was generally regarded as 'unsound', although a powerful acquisition, while Asquith's relationship with the League was ambivalent. His biographers state that he regarded it as 'a useful piece of machinery to keep within the party the considerable number of moderate men who at that moment had been alienated by Campbell-Bannerman and were attracted to Lord Rosebery . . . he by no means wished to push the quarrel to extreme lengths'.[1] Haldane's interpretation was less flattering. 'London Society came, however, to have a great attraction for him, and he grew by degrees diverted from the sterner outlook on life which he and I for long shared. . . . From the beginning he meant to be Prime Minister, sooner or later.'[2] That Asquith was

---

[1] Spender and Asquith: *Asquith*, I, 143.

[2] Haldane: *Autobiography*, 103. It was commonly said at the time that Margot Asquith was 'ruining' her brilliant husband by whirling him round London Society, and that he was beginning to drink too much. Rosebery's papers are absolutely silent on this subject; he liked and admired Asquith, but in private conversation in his family he deplored the bad influence which Margot had upon her husband. There was a ludicrous story—possibly spread by Margot herself—that Rosebery had wanted to marry her himself; when Lady Leconfield was asked about this story by an eminent lady, she replied simply, 'If Archie had wanted to marry Margot, he would have.'

concerned about his position is evident from some of his conversations with Rosebery at this time. 'Walk & *serious talk* with
Asquith as to his present inactivity & future prospects,' Rosebery's diary for March 19th, 1903, records. Rosebery regarded the
League as 'my only formal connection with public life. It is a
protective and defensive body.' 'He is willing, he says, to assist,
and give a leading hand to, men like Asquith & Co.,' Hamilton,
recorded after a conversation at Mentmore in September 1902,
'but more he will not do, at any rate unless he has some more
positive proof that the Liberal party want him.'

What, then, did the Liberal League really 'stand for'? Its principal purpose was to give unity, and through unity, protection to
those Liberals who disliked and distrusted Campbell-Bannerman's leadership and his predilection for obsolete policies. It
could claim that the young men of the party were supporting it,
and certainly the young men of talent. Rosebery, Asquith, Fowler,
Grey, Haldane, Rufus Isaacs, Edwin Montagu, Josiah Wedg-
wood, Cecil Harmsworth, Sir Edward Tennant, A. E. W. Mason,
and Munro Ferguson were the most conspicuous members of the
League, and when this glittering company was compared with
Campbell-Bannerman's aged and ineffective troupe it was naturally assumed that the hours of his leadership were numbered.
This was not the view of the leader himself. 'My own idea', he
wrote to Herbert Gladstone on the formation of the League, 'is
that R is already being found rather "thin", and as he goes on
creating he will be less and less accredited. The truth is they have
nothing to found a new league upon, and they have been goaded
into it by *The Times* and other similar advisers. My intention is to
leave them alone for the most part.'[1]

The truth was that the Liberal League contained such a diver-
sity of personalities and so many individual interpretations of its
functions that it did not present a serious challenge to the leadership. In spite of its talk of setting up independent League candidates and of forming its own local associations, its leaders
lacked the resolution—and the desire in most cases—to create a
party within the party. It was unfortunate in that its most active
adherents, particularly Haldane, Perks, and Munro Ferguson, were
unpopular among Liberal MPs for personal reasons. Beatrice
Webb was exaggerating when she described Perks as 'a repulsive

[1] *Campbell-Bannerman Papers.*

being—hard, pushing, commonplace . . . a blank materialist who recognizes no principle beyond self-interest',[1] but he was clearly not an attractive or persuasive lieutenant, and it is significant that Wemyss Reid told Rosebery in the January of 1902 that he regarded Perks, Haldane, and Munro Ferguson as serious liabilities in the House of Commons. They were all possessed of monumental tactlessness. In 1913 Rosebery asked Munro Ferguson to walk with him in Hyde Park, and he replied that he would not do so 'as it might harm my political career'. Rosebery at once broke off all personal contacts with him, replaced him as one of his executors, and returned his letters. The rift was healed later, but it is not a bad example of Munro Ferguson's tactlessness.

Nonetheless, the League was by no means a derisory body. *The Times* of November 6th, 1900, had estimated the number of Liberal-Imperialist MPs at 81. Alfred Harmsworth swung his already considerable newspaper empire behind the League, Asquith and Fowler ostentatiously sat at a distance from Campbell-Bannerman on the Opposition front bench, and for a time at least every word that Rosebery said was reported and widely studied, whereas the utterances of the official leader were almost completely ignored. The League gave refuge and encouragement to many Liberals who would have left politics or joined the Unionists rather than subscribe to the Little-Englandism of Campbell-Bannerman, Harcourt, and Morley, and it gave them hope for the future. Even the Lloyd George extreme left wing of the party expressed its willingness to serve under a Rosebery leadership, so great was the respect which he still obtained in the country. Although his critics worked incessantly to undermine confidence in him, they could not delude themselves that he was —with the exception of Chamberlain—potentially the greatest elemental force in British politics, and for a time they were genuinely alarmed. At the Leeds by-election in the July of 1902, a Liberal League candidate electrified the political world by converting a Unionist majority of over 2,500 into a Liberal majority of nearly 800, and there were heated arguments as to whether this was a symptom of Ministerial unpopularity or support for the Imperialist wing of the Liberal Party. It was not surprising, in

[1] *Our Apprenticeship*, 231-2. Mrs Webb's reliability as a judge of character may be gauged from her description of Eddie Hamilton—then Permanent Financial Secretary to the Treasury—as a 'flashy fast Treasury Clerk'.

these circumstances, that far too many Liberals sat ostentatiously on the fence for the comfort of the indefatigable Herbert Gladstone.

The fundamental weakness of the League lay in its vagueness of purpose and in the exasperation of its Vice-Presidents with Rosebery. 'I hear nothing from R,' we find Grey writing to his wife on January 28th, 1902, just before the announcement of the formation of the League, 'and what I hear of him is rather tiresome and petty. He has a habit of hiding his light, and making it seem as if the light that was in him was darkness. I am all for letting him go his own way, but I don't think I can help him much to play his game at present. It is an *underground* game, which is all right for him; but for us, who are in the House here, it is difficult to take part in it without playing the *underhand* game. We are in contact with much from which he is free.'[1] Alfred Harmsworth's enthusiasm for the League soon faded, in spite of his great admiration and affection for Rosebery. Harmsworth lived at 36, Berkeley Square, and the two men walked together in Hyde Park two or three times a week when they were both in London; in spite of this close friendship—or, possibly because of it—Harmsworth soon entertained serious doubts about Rosebery's firmness of purpose. By 1903 he was sadly describing Rosebery as 'hopeless'.[2] After making a brilliant attack on the Government and delivering a formidable defence of the League at Glasgow on March 10th which, as Haldane wrote, 'made me feel happy politically for the first time for years,' Rosebery then withdrew again. It was not long before the recriminations broke out again, and Haldane wrote on July 19th to him that

. . . No one can foresee the future—& it is not possible for Asquith, for example, to pledge himself to a definite line in circumstances which we can none of us forecast. You will not mind my adding that the uncertainty as to what can & cannot be avoided in the future is trebled by your withdrawal from any sort of candidature for the nation's leadership. I am not, as you know, challenging your decision or complaining. I am only saying that it makes the future very uncertain. . . . It is this really that brings a certain element of depression into our councils. . . .

It was at about this time that A. G. Gardiner dined with two of Rosebery's most devoted supporters, one a Member of Parliament

[1] Trevelyan: *Grey*, 80.   [2] Pound and Harmsworth: *Northcliffe*, 221, 289.

and the other a Peer. The commoner said that 'Rosebery is a man
whom you never know how you will catch. He may be all smiles
to-day and to-morrow you will find him cold and remote as an
iceberg.' 'Yes,' said the Peer, 'he came down to the House this
afternoon to support my motion, and delivered an excellent
speech. I met him in the lobby afterwards, stopped him, and
thanked him for his support. He turned on his heel without a
word and walked away.'[1] But in spite of these rebuffs and disappointments, Rosebery's name still had an extraordinary stature
in the country. As Lord Newton has written in reminiscence,
'The belief in certain quarters still remained that Rosebery was a
mystery man who could put everything right if he were given the
chance, and that vague belief continued to exist for a considerable
time.'[2]

Hamilton stayed at Dalmeny in October 1902 and while driving
in the park after dinner on the 12th, told Rosebery that his
attitude bewildered and disappointed his friends. 'It is all very
well for you to talk of my many friends,' Rosebery replied, 'but
as far as I can see they don't come tumbling over one another.
There is no proof of their longing to support me. If they do, why
don't they join the Liberal League?'

A most revealing letter from Rosebery to Wemyss Reid on
November 14th shows to what an extent the irritation was not
confined to one side.

 . . . In this business I am working for others—not for myself. It
has never occurred to me that I could ever be in office again: I renounced all such ideas years ago. I have held office for a short time,
but never power. I would never hold office again without power, and
it is humanly speaking impossible that I should ever hold office with
power. If power did come to me it would come too late. No, I am
working entirely for Asquith & Grey & the younger members of the
party. For them I am endeavouring to rally a party which shall save
Liberalism, by placing it on a practical basis. . . .

I remember we had a gardener many years ago, whose defect it was
not to be a good manager of his men. He used to be seen with his coat
off digging energetically while his subordinates stood around and
sympathetically watched him. That is the position which Liberal
Imperialists have generously marked out for me, until I find that it
is my grave that I am digging. When they realise that—or when I
am in it—they will probably begin their spade work.

<hr>

[1] *Prophets, Priests and Kings.*   [2] Newton: *Retrospection,* 113.

But gloomy as is my course, I cannot terminate it by my own act. It may probably end in a complete breakdown of health, for no one but myself knows the strain and sleeplessness produced by these long speeches to great meetings which the League and the public so cheerfully urge. In the meantime, I am bound to those who have stood by me, and I believe that some day—not perhaps in my time—the cause will be triumphant. But the blunders of the last few years will take long to undo, and it is uphill work to counteract the daily lies of the little-England press with so little of defence, much less counter-attack. . . .

The conclusion of the South African War at the beginning of the summer of 1902 had removed one of the *raisons d'être* of the League, but the disposal of this running sore in the internal relations of the Liberal Party could not efface the acute schisms which the Boer War had precipitated. At the end of November Spencer made an unsuccessful attempt to arrange a meeting between the two wings of the party, to be represented by himself and Campbell-Bannerman on the one side and Rosebery and Asquith on the other. 'I cannot help thinking', Spencer wrote to Rosebery on November 30th, 'that since the S. African war has ended, there ought to be no difficulty in the whole Liberal Party, & its leaders, uniting for combined action, and in putting an end to the schism which except on one or two special questions appears to exist amongst us.' To this well-meaning proposal Rosebery replied that he was not available for the next ten days, 'but Asquith would answer all the purposes you mention much better than I should'. 'I am very sorry to find that your engagements for the present will prevent your joining the small meeting to which I referred in my letter of yesterday,' Spencer replied with justifiable coldness. 'I certainly shall not go on with the proposal until you can come. Pray let me know when that will be.'

Relations between Rosebery and Campbell-Bannerman had been noticeably worsened by an episode at the end of May, when Gladstone was present at a rally in Leeds at which Rosebery was the principal speaker. Campbell-Bannerman was surprised at Gladstone's presence, and remonstrated with him. 'If I refuse to go to Leeds,' Gladstone replied, 'what would be said of me after preaching unity?'[1] 'Our loyal people throughout the country will be completely bamboozled when they see the leading officials of

---

[1] *Campbell-Bannerman Papers.*

the Party joining, *not on some particular subject*, but in general politics, with one who has publicly cried off from us,' Campbell-
Bannerman wrote in reply. 'The whole meeting in fact has its
genesis in the purpose *ad majorem* R *gloriam*.'[1] Gladstone ignored
his leader's advice, and the story got around to Rosebery, possibly through Gladstone himself.

To the Liberals, still locked in their bitter internecine squabbles,
incredible deliverance came in the May of 1903. In the course of a
single speech to the Unionists of West Birmingham on May 15th,
Chamberlain hurled the Unionist Party into a controversy of
mortal ferocity. He himself called his speech 'A Demand for
Inquiry', but it consisted of a trenchant and provocative exposition of the case for Imperial Preference and Tariff Reform,
coupled with a critical analysis of the deficiencies of Free Trade.
Few speeches in modern political history have achieved a more
shattering effect. Free Trade was not so much an economic
doctrine as an article of faith, the sacred cow of British domestic
politics since God knew when. For any politician to challenge it
was startling enough; for the most formidable Minister in the
Government to do so was staggering; and the spectacular potentialities of the situation were given greater emphasis by that fact
that Balfour—who had succeeded Salisbury as Prime Minister
twelve months before—explicitly relegated Imperial Preference
to 'a hypothetical future' on the same day that Chamberlain exploded his bombshell at Birmingham. 'This reckless criminal
escapade of Joe's is the great event of our time,' Campbell-
Bannerman gleefully recorded. 'It is playing Old Harry with all
party relations. . . . All the old war-horses about me are snorting
with excitement. We are in for a great time.'

Party politics at once leapt into intense life. Campbell-Bannerman appealed for unity 'to resist this mad and dangerous
excitement', and Asquith began a tour of speeches in which he
hammered remorselessly at Chamberlain's proposals. Rosebery's
first reactions were cautious, to the dismay of his followers, and
he rejected an approach by Harmsworth (September 1903) to
join an anti-Chamberlain crusade. 'I am not a person who believes
that Free Trade is part of the Sermon on the Mount', he informed
the Barnsley Chamber of Commerce on May 19th, 'and that we
ought to receive it in all its rigidity as a divinely appointed dis-

[1] *Campbell-Bannerman Papers.*

pensation,' but shortly afterwards he came out vehemently against Chamberlain's concept of an Imperial Zollverein at Burnley as tending to dislocate, and in time dissolve, the unity of the Empire. 'How strange it all seems', he wrote to Robert Murray Smith on February 8th, 1904, 'to look back to the days of the Imperial Federation League and to find an "imperial statesman" copying our perorations but not imitating our abstinence from commercial federation schemes. My fear about the whole matter is this. The colonies have always regarded our fiscal as sacred. "We know you can't alter your free trade system" has always been their burden. But now Mr C has upset all this. He will, I think, fail. But the colonies will always be hankering for his scheme which is a bounty to them without any return from them. No wonder they shout "Vivat Josephus". But will they ever settle down again to the old position "No interference with the fiscal policy of either mother or children"? You have always justly said "Hands off" as regards your fiscal system. The day may come when we shall have to say the same to you. If J C succeeds—which Heaven forbid—his epitaph may yet be "Having wrecked both parties in the State he set to work to wreck the Empire".'[1]

The autumn of 1903 saw the resignation of Chamberlain from the Government and the withdrawal of the most important Free Trade Unionists; the country awaited the decision of the Duke of Devonshire with breathless attention; when he went, after days of agonising indecision, the fate of the Ministry was virtually settled. A section of the younger Free Trade Conservatives—notably Winston Churchill and Lord Hugh Cecil—entered into secret negotiations with the Liberal whips to co-ordinate action against the Government.[2]

The Liberal League refused to disband itself in spite of the

[1] Smith (1831–1921) was Agent-General for Victoria, 1882–6, and had met Rosebery on the latter's Australasian tour of 1883–4. I am indebted to Smith's great-granddaughter, Mrs Maclean of Dochgarroch, for placing his papers at my disposal.

[2] Consuelo, Duchess of Manchester, held a courageous dinner-party on November 6th, to which Balfour, Devonshire, Austen Chamberlain, Rosebery, and Churchill were invited. Balfour and Devonshire sat on either side of the Duchess during the meal, but when the ladies retired there was an awkward silence, as men who had spent the preceding weeks in acrimonious public disputation sought for safe topics of conversation. 'We gallantly talked about sleeping compartments, & all passed off well,' Rosebery recorded.

virtual unanimity of the party, and naturally gave more and more the impression of a disgruntled minority pursuing a vendetta against Campbell-Bannerman. Rosebery continued to champion 'Efficiency'—which embraced the proposal that Kitchener should take over the War Office—to the embarrassment of his supporters and the puzzlement of his audiences. There was no desire on the part of Campbell-Bannerman to share his leadership with Rosebery. 'We must not rush too precipitately into the opposite extreme to estrangement,' he wrote to Robertson in reply to a suggestion that Rosebery might be invited to take the chair at one of the leader's meetings, 'and my feeling is that the best way to obliterate the evil effects of the past is to say as little about it as possible. . . . We must also remember that although you and I have no *arrière pensée* in the matter whatsoever, My Lord is unco' kittle cattle to drive and is as easily scared as a hare!'[1] To Herbert Gladstone he wrote on November 9th that if Rosebery returned 'and bears his share of the work and responsibility I shall be delighted. But if the idea is that he should mount and ride the horse and should dictate what we are to do and say, we cannot, of course, have him on such terms; at least, it would not last long; and I greatly fear from his isolation and his being surrounded by adulating toadies, that may be his view of the proper relationship!' Gladstone was disappointed. 'What our people want now is to wipe out the past altogether & to drop everything wh may tend to keep up friction,' he replied, urging Campbell-Bannerman to extend the hand of friendship publicly to Rosebery.[1]

Rosebery's position remained a complete mystery. Would he be prepared to accept the leadership of the party if offered? His public statements were conflicting. Would he take office in a Campbell-Bannerman Ministry? No one knew. He had reserved full freedom of action for himself, but what did that mean in terms of practical politics? His frequent disappearances to the Continent made personal access extremely difficult, and when he was run to earth he expressed himself so vaguely that anxious adherents and would-be adherents left Berkeley Square bewildered and often angry. 'Rosebery lent himself to cross-examination with unfailing good humour,' Spender has written, 'but always in the end I retired baffled and had to report that no one would know till the last minute of the twelfth hour. And no

[1] *Campbell-Bannerman Papers.*

one did.'[1] In the June of 1903 Hamilton made a last appeal to his friend to give a positive lead to the party, but Rosebery sent in reply 'a chilling, heart-breaking note'. 'It is hopeless, evidently,' this best of friends wrote in his diary, 'and one must reluctantly give up the idea of his ever being of any real use to his country. So all these splendid talents are to be thrown away: & all one's cherished hopes dashed to the ground.' Harmsworth sent a courier to Mentmore in the August of 1903, offering to place the whole of his newspaper organisation at Rosebery's disposal, on the condition that he could arrange the timing of Rosebery's speeches to ensure the maximum publicity. Rosebery was sitting on the lawn under the shade of a garden tent with Spender when the courier arrived. Spender laughed, but 'Rosebery, too, laughed, but he was also visibly angry',[2] and the offer was peremptorily refused. Almeric Fitzroy's comment on Rosebery's speech in the Lords on the second reading of the Education Bill on December 6th, 1902, had a wider application. 'Lord Rosebery's illuminants were of the nature of *feux d'artifice*, brilliant, yet leaving the darkness all the greater when they had burnt themselves out.'[3]

Rosebery himself thought and wrote a great deal about his personal position at this time. 'The Liberal Party', he wrote to Hamilton on June 11th, 1903, 'need not be in the least afraid of my offering myself to them as leader. I was in that position once and am not likely to solicit it again.' On September 30th he drew up for his own interest a memorandum giving seven unanswerable objections to his return; he was anathema to the 'pro-Boer, pro-Armenian, pro-Macedonian and generally hysterical section of the party'; the Irish distrusted him; Harcourt and Campbell-Bannerman were markedly unfriendly; his health—a factor which seemed to weigh heavily with him at this time—was poor, and he found it quite impossible to retain names and faces; he loved his solitude and his books; he dreaded the recurrence of his insomnia, which still plagued him before and after a public meeting; 'I cannot forget 1895.' His contempt for the party system was gradually increasing. 'I have never seen a more pitiable exhibition than they [the Government] have presented in endeavouring to escape discussion and so maintain a united front,' he wrote to Hamilton on August 15th, 'unless it be the failure of the Opposi-

---

[1] Spender, *Life, Journalism and Politics*, I, 107.   [2] *Ibid.* II, 172.
[3] Fitzroy: *Memoirs*, 113.

tion to bring them to book. One more disastrous evasion of opportunity to be reckoned by the Recording Angel against the present Opposition management. . . . I am inclined to think that the disgust of the country with both front benches will aid the extremists—Socialists, Labour, Independent Labour, or what not —and I don't blame the voters for this.'

Rosebery also felt very acutely the destruction of old friendships which his return to politics had caused. 'You are lucky to be allowed to "love J M",' he wrote sadly to Spender. 'No one loved him more sincerely than I, and I have no idea why the pleasure is no longer permitted to me.'[1] His solitariness was becoming more conspicuous every year, as friends died or were alienated, and as his family grew up. 'I see less of him now than I ever did,' Eddie Hamilton wrote sadly on March 1st, 1904. 'He does not volunteer my company as he used to do: & when I propose myself he is apt to make excuses. It may be merely that his love of isolation is growing upon him.'

As the cause of Liberal unity strengthened throughout 1903 and 1904, his political position sensibly declined. The position of an independent statesman aloof from partisan politics has some point when there is a national emergency and partisan politics are either unreal or dull: when that emergency has passed, and party politics are exciting and interesting, the independent statesman is left stranded; he must either descend into the arena or disappear politically. Statesmen who await a national summons frequently wait for ever. Rosebery's position has a certain similarity to that of Mr Adlai Stevenson in 1960; his supporters, although limited in number, admired him intensely—perhaps too intensely—and he retained great respect and genuine affection: but at moments of crisis, when implored to give a positive lead, he was either silent or ambiguous, and the army which his great talents had drawn to his side began to silently steal away in the direction of less attractive but more positive leaders. And so Rosebery moved sepulchrally from one great house to another, from one country to another, reading much, writing much, pondering the affairs of his country incessantly, keeping his own counsel. And when at last he raised the banner, he found that his army had noiselessly disappeared, leaving only a handful of excessively devoted courtiers to accompany him into the wilderness.

[1] Harris: *Spender*, 108.

Spencer, still anxious for a *détente*, asked him to give the dinner to Liberal Peers on the eve of the opening of Parliament in the January of 1904. Rosebery refused, saying that 'it would give rise to all sorts of baseless inferences; and as one must suffer fools gladly—or otherwise—it is best to avoid giving them the opportunities'. Spencer expressed his regret, and then asked him to return to the Opposition front bench in the Lords, as 'an effective symbol of united action which I trust is now to be'. Rosebery again declined, and also refused to attend a meeting of the Liberal leaders at Spencer House, in spite of frantic appeals from Tweedmouth not to dismiss this opportunity of at least demonstrating a willingness for unity. King Edward VII intervened in the autumn of 1904 through Brett—now Lord Esher—but the appeal from Balmoral was curtly rejected by Dalmeny. Spender was deputed to approach Rosebery, but found him 'quite uncompromising' and 'absolved by the action of the Liberal leaders themselves. He had made his overtures at the time of the Chesterfield speech and later, and they had been rejected.'[1] He read another personal memorandum to Spender, in which he wrote that 'I have in fact at this juncture the confidence of neither the Crown, the House of Commons, either party, or the public at large. Those are strange foundations on which to rear political ambitions, had I any desire that way.'

In 1904 Lord Lansdowne concluded the Anglo-French Agreement to the applause of both political parties. Rosebery's voice was raised in solitary opposition. 'My mournful and supreme conviction in the matter is that this Agreement is much more likely to lead to complication than to peace.' In private, he was even more despondent: 'It will lead you straight to war.' 'You are leaning on an aspen,' he said to Grey in the summer of 1905 in tragic tones, 'and the German Emperor has four millions of soldiers and the second best navy in the world.'[2] His mistrust of France was of course deep-rooted, and with justification. He was generally accused of Germanophilism by all parties, and his dwindling band of allies wrung their hands in despair at his erratic judgement. History has taken a somewhat different view of Rosebery's alarm, but it is little solace to be applauded by posterity; politics is a matter of the hour. Nonetheless, although universally criticised by his countrymen, Rosebery was still

[1] Harris: *Spender*, 109.   [2] Trevelyan: *Grey*, 84.

enormously respected by the European Powers. On June 7th, 1905, he dined at Lansdowne House to meet the King of Spain, and it was particularly noted that the ambassadors were very anxious to shake his hand and enquire after his health. 'There is no barometer so sensitive as the corps diplomatique', Rosebery noted in his diary, '—too sensitive in the present instance, & so misled!'

As the doomed Ministry tottered from one by-election catastrophe to another, the Liberals began to formulate Cabinet plans —that most satisfying of all political pursuits—in earnest. Harcourt had died in 1904, but it was evident that Campbell-Bannerman remained his disciple; the problem was what was going to happen to the senior members of the League. Campbell-Bannerman's popularity in the constituency parties was not reflected at Westminster, where he continued to lead the Opposition with extraordinary inefficiency. There are few contrasts so startling in modern British politics as the incompetence of Campbell-Bannerman as Leader of the Opposition and his ease, authority, and ability as Prime Minister. This was a factor which —quite reasonably—the younger men of the party never anticipated, and which subsequently made their opposition to him appear less sensible than in fact it was. The men who mattered were Asquith, Grey, and Fowler, since their exclusion from any Liberal Government was almost unthinkable; to a lesser extent, Haldane was an important factor, since it was generally believed that he dominated Grey. It is quite clear that by the summer of 1905—and possibly earlier—they had abandoned Rosebery as the leader of the Liberal Imperialist wing, and were looking to Asquith, whose position was both delicate and perilous, as their leader. Hamilton's Diary, now in its last volume,[1] contains several reports of the disenchantment of Rosebery's former friends and allies. 'I have had a letter from Reay,' he writes in a tremulous hand on September 8th. '. . . He complains of Rosebery: never sees him now. Indeed, he (R) sees nothing of his friends.' On October 10th Hamilton paid a last sad visit to Dalmeny. 'Rosebery does not "open out" to me as he used to do; but I could detect no

---

[1] Hamilton's physical decline had been inexorable since 1902. 'My downward course is slow, very slow, but sure,' he wrote on May 31st, 1905. On July 3rd he decided to stop writing in his Diary, but he resumed it in September for a few months.

greater willingness to come forward & make himself useful. What he still liked is his independence & freedom. He never seems to give a thought of [*sic*] others or of his country.'

In the August of 1905, however, Campbell-Bannerman made a last half-hearted approach to Rosebery through Spencer, who was shortly to suffer a mortal stroke, and whose debility had been painfully apparent for several months. Their conversation at The Durdans was recorded by Rosebery in his 'betting book'.

I bathed & dressed early [for dinner] after a long walk with Asquith, so that Spencer found me dressed in the billiard room at 7.30. He came & sat by me & began almost at once, 'I hope, Rosebery, you will join us when we form the next Govt', or words to that effect. I turned it off onto the fertile topic of J. Morley, with whom S had had many difficulties, e.g. J M had cut him for weeks if not months after the Harcourt resignation, because apparently J M had not been chosen as his successor. As the clock chimed 8 I said it was time for him to dress, but S was not to be ruffled. As I moved to the door he said 'But Rosebery, I hope you will let me say this, that I hope you will be with us when we come in,' or some such words. So I murmured something about all that having passed by for me, that I had resigned in 1896 & that that was a definite act. Then he said something—I know not what exactly—about my powers of speaking, but I did not & do not understand what that had to do with the question. So I replied 'Oh, you will have plenty of speakers without me', and by that time had got into the hall, where the conversation had to drop wh I had been eluding all day.

I respected him for sticking to his point & for the kindly intention of his, but it was I thought irksome & unnecessary.

This was the last overture, and Rosebery was told by Spender in 1913 that Campbell-Bannerman 'was not very anxious that it should succeed'. Asquith and Haldane stayed at Dalmeny in October, but never mentioned the formation of the 'Relugas Compact' with Grey of a few weeks before at Grey's fishing-lodge at Relugas, whereby the trio would refuse office unless Campbell-Bannerman went to the Lords. In fact, Haldane was in communication with the King through Francis Knollys, warning him of the difficulties which were likely to arise if Campbell-Bannerman was invited to form a Government. 'If Rosebery had been coming to his right place at the head of affairs we could have gone anywhere with the confidence that the tone could be set,' Haldane wrote to Knollys. 'But it seems now as if this were not to be, and we have to do the only thing we can do, which is to think out and follow a plan of concerted action.'[1]

Rosebery had as usual spent much of the year abroad, returning to win the Derby for the third time with *Cicero*: the King proposed his health at the Jockey Club dinner. 'I said I was ashamed to win the Derby thrice, when so many of my colleagues had never won it once,' Rosebery wrote in his diary. 'This was greeted with a loud hoarse cheer—from Hartington—the only cheer I tell him he ever gave me!' There was an enormous celebratory party at The Durdans to which much of the population of Epsom was invited, consumed vast quantities of food and drink, and were soothed by no less than three bands playing in the gardens. Apart from these enjoyable diversions, Rosebery was engaged upon his memoir of Randolph Churchill and in discussing the official biography which Winston was just completing. The summer of 1905 was spent by Rosebery in various social and official functions, none of them political. There was the comic opening of the Bathgate Reservoir near Edinburgh; 'I standing on a peninsula in a bleak lake and addressing people on a distant bank'; a strange cricket match at Windsor where a team of Eton boys played one captained by Prince David,[2] in which, after some prior arrangements, he scored 17—'the fielding was immensely loyal'—and Prince Albert[3] achieved 'one or two runs with the assistance of the field, & then was bowled, returning to the pavilion with the Eton boys cheering, he proud & flustered. It gave me a lump in my throat—the whole scene so redolent and pathetic'; and a bizarre dinner with the Asquiths, where Rosebery met Belloc—'a foreign looking gentleman'—and Chesterton—'a big burly Bohemian-looking man, reminding me a little of Birrell'; G. W. E. Russell, of whom a little went a long way with Rosebery, transfixed the company as he sat down at the table by saying 'in a loud but tender whisper to Lloyd George, grasping his hand, "*My* leader!!". . . I escaped at 10.45.'

His shyness had always made relations with Asquith rather difficult, as Rosebery himself later admitted. 'Intercourse between us has been too rare both for my own pleasure as a friend, and also for the political objects in which we were publicly united,'

---

[1] Haldane: *Autobiography*, 160.
[2] Later King Edward VIII (now the Duke of Windsor).
[3] Later King George VI.

he subsequently wrote to Asquith on December 28th. 'I knew you were overwhelmingly busy and did not like to trouble you. Moreover, there was a certain shyness on my part, and reluctance to appear to interfere too much in a political future in which I had renounced my official share. You, I think, have much the same shyness, and even in conversation we waited for the other to begin.' This fact partly explains the events of the autumn of 1905, but it is curious that neither Haldane nor Asquith even hinted at the Relugas Compact or the fact that Asquith and Campbell-Bannerman were preparing a declaration on Irish policy which would embrace Asquith's 'step by step' policy and the leader's determination to retain Home Rule as a major part of his programme. While these crucial negotiations were in train, Rosebery continued to preach the doctrine of 'Efficiency'. In a preface to a book called *Great Japan* by Alfred Stead which was published at this time he strongly attacked the concept of party government.

. . . It is considered as inevitable as the fog, yet its operation blights efficiency. It keeps out of employment a great many men of precious ability. It puts into place not the fittest, but the most eligible from the Party point of view. . . . That is, very often, the worst. Efficiency implies the rule of the fittest. Party means the rule of something else, not of the unfittest, but of the few fit, the accidentally not unfit, and the glaringly unfit.

'Is this great man with us or against us?' Campbell-Bannerman wrote to Herbert Gladstone on October 21st. '. . . Is he going to the country on the ticket of "Efficiency, and no party government", or what is the game?'[1] No one had the faintest idea.

On October 25th, at Stourbridge, Rosebery demanded a positive statement of official Liberal policy on Home Rule. 'Any middle policy—that of placing Home Rule in the position of a reliquary, and only exhibiting it at great moments of public stress, as Roman Catholics are accustomed to exhibit relics of a saint— is not one which will earn sympathy or success in this country.' Home Rule, he insisted, must either be made a major measure for the first session of a new Parliament, or be abandoned for the time being. Having secured the prior agreement of Asquith—who did not communicate the fact to Rosebery[2]—Campbell-Banner-

---

[1] *Campbell-Bannerman Papers.*

[2] Rosebery neither saw nor communicated with Asquith between October 22nd— when Asquith left Dalmeny—and December 11th.

man replied on November 23rd at Stirling that 'the opportunity of making a great advance on this question of Irish Government will not be long delayed'. The *Freeman's Journal*, the organ of Irish Nationalism, assumed that the Stirling speech meant that although Home Rule would come 'step by step', the first part of the legislation would be presented to Parliament immediately a Liberal Government was formed.

Meanwhile, Rosebery was engaged in a Liberal League political tour in Cornwall.[1] On November 22nd he spoke to what he described in his diary as a 'dour, granitic & silent' audience of, several thousands at Penzance, and on the 24th, at Truro, to a crowd of nearly nine thousand—'It was like preaching in a cathedral', he noted—he revealed that he was entertaining misgivings about the implications of Stirling. He had decided that it meant a return to 1892, and on November 25th, at Bodmin, in what he privately described as 'probably my last platform speech', he came out decisively against the unfurling of the Home Rule banner. The vital sentences, punctuated with wild applause, were as follows:

> ... I object to it mainly for this reason: that it impairs the unity of the Free Trade party, and that it indefinitely postpones legislation on social and educational reform [*cheers*] on which the country has set its heart [*renewed cheers*]. I will, then, add no more on this subject, except to say emphatically and explicitly and once and for all that I cannot serve under that banner [*cheers*].

These startling observations convulsed the political world. The Unionists—and most political commentators—naturally assumed that Rosebery was speaking for the Liberal League, and therefore for Asquith, Grey, Fowler, and Haldane. The Ministry was in a desperate situation; Chamberlain derided Balfour's parliamentary tactics as 'humiliating' on November 3rd, declared that he would 'rather be part of a powerful minority than a member of an impotent majority', and demanded a dissolution; on the 14th he captured the National Union of Conservative Associations, succeeding where Randolph Churchill had so narrowly failed in 1884; a week later at Bristol he formally disassociated himself

---

[1] Allard had actually proposed in October that Campbell-Bannerman should arrange another date for the Stirling speech, as it would conflict with Rosebery's Cornish tour. 'Did you ever know such a piece of impertinence?' Campbell-Bannerman exploded to Gladstone. (*Campbell-Bannerman Papers.*)

from Balfour's last attempt at a compromise between the embattled Tariff Reformers and Free Traders. Bodmin, apparently demonstrating acute Liberal differences, provided a gleam of hope to the stricken Unionists.[1]

Rosebery was quickly apprised of the true situation. Grey wrote to him with uncharacteristic sharpness on the 27th that 'your speech has put me in the most disagreeable fix I have ever been in. C-B's Stirling speech wasn't intended to be as you take it. Asquith discussed Ireland with him in London; got an assurance that C-B agreed with his (A's) Irish declaration; and Asquith now telegraphs to me that he regards the sense of C-B's speech, which you denounced, as quite innocuous. There is a pleasant situation for me! If it wasn't for feelings of porsonal friendship I shouldn't mind; but as it is I feel full of strange eaths. I can't desert Asquith & I want to defend you. I feel dead beat at last.'[2] Rosebery subsequently described this letter as 'the greatest blow I ever had in my political life', but there were more surprises.

Harry Paulton, a young MP and an enthusiastic Liberal Leaguer, sent Rosebery disconcerting news of Asquith's reactions to the Bodmin speech on November 27th.

. . . I called at Asquith's chambers in the Temple on my [way] through this aftn—saw him and was never more taken aback in my life. I found him, so far from being pleased as I expected, very much put out and, indeed, angry. He has interpreted C-B's speech in an entirely opposite sense & says that everyone has done so, including Haldane from whom he had received a letter which I saw. They regard your utterance as a positive *disaster*!

To me this came as a shock indescribable. I don't know any more how to put a meaning upon words when I find these men looking on C-B's speech as explicitly repudiating all intention of dealing with Home Rule in the next Parlt!

'But,' I said, 'in that case where is the difficulty? You & Grey have only to say that Ld R's interpretation is mistaken & that on behalf of

---

[1] It has often been stated that Balfour was encouraged by the Bodmin speech to resign at the beginning of December; in fact, he had circulated a Memorandum to the Cabinet on November 25th putting forward the arguments in favour of resignation as opposed to dissolution, and stating that 'My own leanings towards a December resignation took shape' before Chamberlain's belligerent speech at Bristol on the 21st. (See Chilston: *Chief Whip*, 331.)

[2] Asquith's telegram to Grey was as follows: 'Hope you will repudiate R's interpretation of Stirling speech which is perfectly innocuous sense. Asquith.' (Trevelyan: *Grey*, 94 (footnote).)

yourselves, of C-B & of the Party you repudiate such meaning & intention'. His reply was that you had damned the whole lot with the charge of officially raising the Home Rule flag.

I argued it from your point of view, quoting the *Freeman's Journal* interpretation, but no—he held that such attacks were natural both from the Irish & the Tories but wrong & unjustifiable from one in your position.

All that was amazing & disconcerting enough. . . . I was much more staggered & concerned when he went on to say that it might involve grave consideration of the League's position, which wd require to be thought more at leisure. He was quite convinced that Edward shared his views & wd say so tonight. . . .

Rosebery subsequently accepted Asquith's explanation that he had been about to send him a telegram on Stirling and his conversations with Campbell-Bannerman, but had thought that he had finished his Cornish tour at Truro, and their friendly relationship was not permanently impaired. But his immediate reactions were bitter. Spender dined with him at The Durdans on the 28th, and reported his host's mood to Herbert Gladstone, who wrote to Campbell-Bannerman that 'R is in a savage and despairing temper. He denounced A & G in unmeasured terms, accusing them of having abandoned him, saying that he had done with public life, having no party and no friends. He had consulted those with him in Cornwall, and they all agreed that your Stirling speech meant Home Rule. His brain was not good enough to interpret the language of a speech, and he was not fit therefore to take a leading part in politics. Of course now he is "sorry he spoke", but he sees no way of unsaying it.'[1]

'How could I guess at that conference?' Rosebery wrote to Grey on the 28th. 'How could I divine it? Is it not a pity that I should be kept entirely in the dark with regard to a matter of such supreme importance, particularly when I was on a speaking tour? All I can say is that I was in a house full of people who all took the same view as I did. What is more important is that the Irish press did the same.'[2] Of the 'Relugas trio', Grey was the only one who seems to have felt any remorse over their treatment of Rosebery. 'Of course,' he wrote to Munro Ferguson on December 1st, 'Asquith & I ought to have bethought ourselves to warn R not to take C-B's speech as he did; but to speak frankly I don't think

[1] Mallet: *Herbert Gladstone*, 200.   [2] Trevelyan: *Grey*, 94.

C-B's speech should have given the Cornwall party quite the impression it did.'[1]

The damage was done, and as the days passed Rosebery's isolation was painfully apparent. Spender (November 29th) implored him to state publicly that explanations since Bodmin had cleared the air and that he was now satisfied that Free Trade and not Home Rule was the vital issue before the electorate and would support the Liberals in the elections. Every hoarding, Spender warned, would be plastered with Unionist slogans, 'Lord Rosebery's advice to electors, "Don't fight under the Bannerman's Banner", "What isn't good enough for Lord Rosebery to fight for isn't good enough for you to vote for." ' Rosebery refused; it was up to the leader to make the position clear. 'The speech means another Parliament devoted to Ireland. . . . The only person who can say my interpretation is wrong is the orator himself.' 'Twice has C-B raised voice and said nothing,' he wrote to Grey on December 1st. 'This is significant. He could put an end to the present situation in a sentence by saying that you and Asquith rightly interpreted his utterance and that I interpreted it wrongly. The responsibility rests with him and his silence.'[2]

Campbell-Bannerman had no wish to end the situation. Spender—probably incorrectly—had gained the impression at The Durdans on the 28th that Rosebery had not finally decided to refuse office and was still prepared to help in the elections.

Warned that Balfour was about to resign, Campbell-Bannerman had returned to London, and was awaiting the summons to the Palace when Spender called on December 4th. Spender's account of what must have been Campbell-Bannerman's most satisfying hour may properly conclude the history of the ill-fated Liberal League, which, although it struggled on for four more years with dwindling support, was effectively killed by Bodmin.

The scene is still vividly in my memory. He was wearing a long frock coat with black trousers, and his hat was—rather oddly—on the table beside him with black gloves hanging out of it. The blinds were half drawn, and one might have thought the scene to be for a funeral. But he was in the highest spirits and overflowing with little quips which never failed him in good times or bad. He said he was expecting a summons from 'Jupiter' (he nearly always spoke of King Edward as 'Jupiter') and it might cause him to get up and leave me abruptly at

[1] Trevelyan: *Grey*, 95.   [2] *Ibid.*, 95.

any moment, but in the meantime he was very glad to have news of 'the Lord' ('Barnbougle' or 'the Lord' were his usual designations for Rosebery). Did he come this time with sword or olive branch? I made my unauthorised communication and left him to judge, saying what I could for the expediency of letting the Bodmin quarrel rest, even if he could not see his way to say anything soothing. Then he twinkled all over, as only C-B could twinkle, and after some moments of apparent reflection delivered his ultimatum:

'Will you please tell Lord Rosebery that within two hours from now I expect to have accepted the King's Commission to form a Government, and that being so, I can obviously say no more about the Irish question until I have had an opportunity of consulting my colleagues.'[1]

[1] *Life, Journalism and Politics*, I, 126–7.

CHAPTER THIRTEEN

THE LONG EVENING

Does not history tell us that there is nothing so melancholy as the aspect of great men in retirement—from Nebuchadnezzar in his meadow to Napoleon on his rock?

ROSEBERY: *Napoleon: The Last Phase* (1900)

FORTIFIED BY THE RESOLUTE attitude of his wife, Sir Henry Campbell-Bannerman resisted the ultimatum of the three confederates of the 'Relugas Compact', and after several days of anxious confabulation they agreed to join the Government, Asquith going to the Treasury, Grey to the Foreign Office, and Haldane to the War Office. Rosebery was not consulted by the trio, and only Edward Grey—in a series of brief scribbled messages—kept him informed of the confused negotiations which preceded the capitulation. Although he went out of his way to explain to them that he had not expected to be consulted, Rosebery was undoubtedly hurt by their silence. Campbell-Bannerman, having completed his ministerial arrangements, advised the King to dissolve Parliament, and the Unionist Party which had ruled for almost twenty years virtually disappeared in the election, Arthur Balfour himself being among the ranks of the defeated.

Campbell-Bannerman, having thus dramatically removed the stigma of leading a Government with a House of Commons minority, could afford to be generous. Rosebery's elder son, Lord Dalmeny, had reluctantly consented to become Liberal candidate for Midlothian at the request of his father, and had resigned his commission in the Army for this purpose. He won the seat convincingly, and was invited to second the motion for the Address in the Commons. Surprised and delighted, he told his father of this honour, but Rosebery stiffened and coldly remarked, 'If you accept C-B's invitation you are no son of mine'. Although this well-meant approach was thus bleakly ignored, there was a move in the Government ranks to make use of Rosebery's abilities. The

King proposed that he should become Ambassador at Washington, and Edward Grey was enthusiastic; Eddie Hamilton dictated a last stricken aʃ peal—'I am not likely to trouble you with many more requests. I do beg that you won't dismiss the idea'—but Rosebery refused what he described in his diary as 'this fantastic idea', and Bryce it was who went to Washington.

Although he could not admit it, Rosebery's relevance as a public figure had disappeared after the Liberal triumph. In a long personal memorandum written at Naples in the summer of 1905 he had pondered the implications of a Liberal victory. 'I have done my best for the cause [Liberal Imperialism], but have been baffled by the party machine,' he wrote. 'I acknowledge that I did not realise the strength of the party machine—the *ingens Machina*. But the machine is a permanent force; it will retain its jealousy of and enmity to whatever is extraneous to it. And I should be infinitely weaker than now in opposition. I am indeed beginning to doubt if the fierce play of party admits of an independent political position. It is little to say this, for everybody has long been convinced of it. I am not quite but nearly convinced.' He doubted if the League could survive, since 'Politicians do not care to preach and parade in a wilderness. The fruitful oasis of bounty and patronage will be elsewhere.' The analysis was correct, for after 1905 the League rapidly declined into a poor joke, only a handful of devoted nonentities refusing to face this unpalatable fact. Over eighty Liberal MPs belonged to the League, and three of its four Vice-Presidents were in the Cabinet, but its influence was so negligible that even the Vice-Presidents tended to forget that it existed.

But nothing that had occurred—or was to occur in the next five years—could dim Rosebery's reputation in Scotland, and in the November of 1906, in pouring rain, he unveiled the Memorial to the Scots Greys in Edinburgh with a perfect little speech.

Honour to the brave who will return no more. We shall not see their faces again. In the service of their Sovereign and their country they have undergone the sharpness of death, and sleep their eternal sleep, thousands of miles away in the green solitudes of Africa. Their places, their comrades, their saddles, will know them no more, for they will never return to us as we knew them. But in a nobler and a higher sense, have they not returned to us to-day? They return to us with a memory of high duty faithfully performed; they return to us with the inspiration of their example. Peace, then, to their dust; honour to their memory. Scotland for ever!

His links with the Government were entirely personal. John Morley, Edward Grey, and Winston Churchill—who, upon being asked by Rosebery if he was satisfied with the under-secretaryship at the Colonial Office, replied, 'They bought me cheap'—saw him often and had good political talk. Grey had suffered a terrible calamity when his wife was killed in an accident in the December of 1905, and this disaster brought him even closer to Rosebery. Among Rosebery's accounts of conversations with Grey, one is memorably pathetic.

June 11th, 1906

Dined alone with E. Grey.

He lives entirely in the past, describes himself as 'waiting'. Waiting for the door that has closed behind her to open for him, hoping it may be soon. His only ease is to immerse himself in the past. His present life is purely mechanical. In reply to my question he said he would take the premiership as he would take anything else that came to his hand. He spoke sublimely about life. . . . He felt that if he was destined to meet her again he should feel a better man to be with her from the experience of grief.

Rosebery's independence from the Government was publicly demonstrated by ostentatiously sitting on the cross-benches in the Lords, 'his head leaning back on his linked hands, his heavy-lidded light blue eyes fixed in a curious, impassive stare—a sphinx whose riddle no man can read,' as a contemporary commentator wrote.[1] He declared in the March of 1907 that he owed the Government neither allegiance nor confidence, 'perhaps not even the common courtesies of life', and it was not long before he was to be found among the Ministry's most persistent and articulate opponents. In the August of 1907 he descended upon the House of Lords and turned his still formidable powers of sarcastic invective upon the unfortunate Secretary of State for Scotland, John Sinclair, whose Scottish land policy had excited Rosebery's wrath. Sir Almeric Fitzroy was present on this occasion.

The contemptuous tone of his references to the Secretary for Scotland indicated the measure of his esteem for that amiable henchman

[1] A. G. Gardiner: *Prophets, Priests and Kings.*

of the Prime Minister, for whom I could not withhold a meed of sympathy, as he sat a few yards off on the steps of the throne, trying to look as if he was enjoying the castigation of somebody else.[1]

Rosebery even opposed the introduction of Old Age Pensions as being 'objectionable because non-contributory, financially inopportune, and threatening to the reserve resources on which the country should rely for war'. His real reason for opposition to this hesitant measure of social reform was, however, rather more sensible, for he dreaded a competition between the two parties for lavish distribution of public money to particular sections for electioneering purposes. But his public statements seemed to be pure Toryism to his amazed supporters, and it was not surprising that the Duke of Devonshire should visit The Durdans in the April of 1907 to discuss concerted opposition to the Government. Both were out of sympathy with their parties, Devonshire being contemptuous about the Unionists—'up to the neck in Tariff Reform'—and Rosebery proposed that they should sit on the cross-benches. 'I said that I loathed politics & office, but that I thought that the present majority was dangerous & uncontrolled, & would have been still more so had the LCC elections returned a large progressive majority. . . . That I thought however disagreeable it might be, history would censure us and rightly if we remained apathetic at this juncture.' The Duke joined Rosebery on the cross-benches, but died in the following year.

The Liberal League limped along with dwindling support and attracting little interest. Rosebery addressed what he thought would be its last meeting on March 12th, 1908, and noted that 'My speech even worse than usual—partly from trying to pack too much into it, partly from using notes, partly from a clammy afternoon audience, partly from my being out of touch with politics.' Lord Eustace Percy attended the meeting incognito and reported to Almeric Fitzroy that it was 'quite the most dismal gathering he had ever attended. Lord Rosebery was obviously ill at ease; what little cheering was elicited came from Percy and his friends'.[2] This was not surprising, since the annual meetings of the League were simply occasions for Rosebery to attack the Government. 'I venture to predict', he stated at the 1907 meeting, 'that at no distant time the Liberal Party will find itself squeezed out between Socialism and Conservatism. Socialism can

[1] Almeric Fitzroy: *Memoirs*, 329   [2] *Ibid.*, 342–3.

promise much more to the predatory elements in politics; Conservatism can afford much more confidence to those who wish to keep things as they are.'

These criticisms afforded little concern to the Government, for Rosebery's personal following in the Liberal Party was virtually non-existent; he was, as he admitted in his last speech to the moribund League in 1909, 'the retired raven on the withered bough'. A. G. Gardiner expressed a general opinion when he wrote of Rosebery at this time that he was 'a lonely man, full of strange exits and entrances, incoherent, inexplicable, flashing out in passionate, melodramatic utterances, disappearing into some remote fastness of his solitary self'.

The light has vanished from the morning hills, the vision has faded in grey disenchantment. He is the Flying Dutchman of politics—a phantom vessel floating about on the wide seas, without an anchor and without a port. It is significant that his latest work should deal with 'The Last Phase' of Napoleon, for it is that solitary figure standing on the rock of St Helena and gazing over sea at the setting sun of whom he most reminds us. Behind, the far-off murmur of the great world where he was once the hero, now lost to him for ever; before, the waste of lonely waters and the engulfing night.[1]

His health, which—apart from the serious insomnia of 1895— had been remarkably good throughout his life, began to deteriorate, and in the January and February of 1907 he was seriously ill with a high fever which started as influenza in Naples. 'At this period', he later remarked, 'I was a perfectly cheerful, healthy and well-preserved corpse. But as time went on I became an impatient and uncomfortable corpse. Once, I was reduced to a point below being even a corpse.'

Although it was not unexpected, his overwhelming defeat for the Chancellorship of Oxford in the same year—Curzon being elected by 1,101 votes to Rosebery's 440—was another manifestation of his personal decline. The King came to The Durdans in the June of 1907 to urge him—with an unintentionally felicitous mixture of metaphors—'to rise like a sphinx from your ashes', but with no success. The King often confided in him, and when it was evident that Campbell-Bannerman's health was declining rapidly, asked him whether he ought to summon Asquith or Grey. Rosebery's advice is not recorded in his account of this

[1] *Prophets, Priests and Kings.*

audience, but it is almost certain that he recommended Asquith, for whom he had always had an immense respect, and whom the party evidently favoured. He was distressed by the fact that after Asquith had assumed the Premiership the King took a deep-rooted dislike to him, describing him on one occasion to Rosebery as 'having no manners at all—very common. Also very weak.'

Rosebery's own relations with the King were strained on occasion, and there was a hapless dinner at Naples on board the *Victoria and Albert* in 1906 when he turned up in a Yacht Squadron mess jacket, to the horror of the King, and then proceeded to joke about it, which was more than the King could bear, and, according to Fritz Ponsonby, 'he eyed Rosebery angrily all through dinner'. The King asked Rosebery to stay after dinner, but then disappeared to play bridge for several hours, at the end of which he returned and merely bade Rosebery good-night, and the distinguished guest departed in a very angry frame of mind.[1] On another occasion, also witnessed by Ponsonby, Rosebery and the King fell out during an Ascot house-party at Windsor, and Rosebery sulked all week. 'If anyone tried to draw him into conversation he turned an eye like a fish on them and withered them with biting sarcasm. So everybody avoided him.' After several days of this Rosebery himself got bored, and on a warm night on the terrace held court first to Ponsonby then to almost all the house-party who were attracted by Ponsonby's shouts of laughter; eventually the King was guided by the gaiety from the terrace, but when Rosebery saw him he stopped talking at once, there was a dead and uncomfortable silence, and the King remarked that he must return to his bridge.[2] These stories are not untypical of this period of Rosebery's life, and the impatience with fools or bores which had always been characteristic of him became more pronounced. He could be cruel when irritated, and Bonar Law was genuinely shocked by the contemptuous ease with which Rosebery made King George V look a fool in a private luncheon at Buckingham Palace; once a young lady to whom Rosebery had taken a strong dislike remarked at a glittering dinner that she had just read a certain book; 'It is, indeed, interesting information to us to know that you are capable of so intellectual a pursuit,' Rosebery coldly remarked, turning

[1] Lord Sysonby (Sir Frederick Ponsonby): *Recollections of Three Reigns*, 224
[2] Sysonby, *op. cit.*, 272–3.

away from her with an almost perceptible sniff of disdain.

His alienation from the Liberal Government had been conspicuous before Lloyd George's 'people's Budget' of 1909 brought matters to a head. The Budget proposed increases in death duties, the introduction of super-tax, children's allowances, and revised land taxes. The land taxes—20 per cent on the unearned increment in land values, to be paid either when the land was sold or passed at death; a capital tax of $\frac{1}{2}d$. in the £ on the value of undeveloped land and minerals; a 10 per cent reversion duty on any benefit accruing to a lessor at the end of a lease —provided the issue on which the real battle was fought. Defending the Dukes as 'a poor but honest class', Rosebery categorised the Budget as 'a social and political revolution of the first magnitude' and in a hard-hitting speech at Glasgow on September 10th, 1909, he declared that the Budget was not Liberalism but pure Socialism, 'the end of all, the negation of faith, of family, of property, of monarchy, of Empire'. This onslaught upon 'this inquisitorial, tyrannical and Socialistic Budget' was the culmination of a series of attacks on the principle of State 'paternalism', of which the most eloquent was his address as Chancellor of Glasgow University in the June of 1908. Paternalism, he argued, was merely a form of despotism, and 'I distrust a despotism even when exercised in the name of liberty and adorned by the word Benevolent, for I know the benevolence to be accidental and the hypocrisy permanent'. He continued:

The State invites us every day to lean upon it. I seem to hear the wheedling and alluring whisper: 'Sound you may be; we bid you to be a cripple. Do you see? Be blind. Do you hear? Be deaf. Do you walk? Be not so venturesome. Here is a crutch for one arm; when you get accustomed to it you will soon want another—the sooner the better.' The strongest man if encouraged may soon accustom himself to the methods of an invalid; he may train himself to totter or to be fed with a spoon. . . . The lesson of our Scottish teaching was 'level up'; the cry of modern teaching is 'level down'; 'let the Government have a finger in every pie,' probing, propping, disturbing. Every day the area for initiative is being narrowed, every day the standing ground for self-reliance is being undermined; every day the public infringes—with the best intentions no doubt—on the individual: the nation is being taken into custody by the State.

Asquith reacted sharply to the Glasgow speech by resigning

from the Liberal League, and Grey and Haldane followed suit; not to be outdone, Rosebery resigned from the Presidency, and what was left of the League collapsed completely. To John Morley he wrote immediately after Glasgow that

> . . . there is no question of a 'change' of party for me. I am only, as I have been for years, a crossbench man. If like you I dip into theology for my metaphor I should say that the analogy is not between an Anglican becoming a Roman, but rather of a Roman declaring himself, like Dollinger, an Old Catholic.

> I am where I have been any time the last thirteen years. But no doubt the Liberal Party has marched on with seven league boots, and I with my painful pumps am left in the mud. The Liberal Party is young, and I approach the Grand Climacteric: I like to think that that is the real reason of our difference. . . .

But after 'flinging down the gauntlet' at Glasgow, Rosebery himself picked it up in the Lords barely a month later (November 24th), when he declared that although he loathed the Budget he would not vote against it. The Unionists, who had expected much from him, were dismayed and angered, and Curzon accused him of treachery in the course of an acrimonious and highly-charged debate. Rosebery had forfeited the respect of both sides. G. P. Gooch, then a young Liberal MP for Bath, stood at the Bar of the House of Lords while Rosebery was speaking. 'He was deeply moved, raising both arms above his head and letting them fall dramatically to his side. As we stood and listened at the bar we found it difficult to believe that he had been for a brief space our Commander-in-Chief.'[1] The House of Lords, ignoring all counsels of moderation, rejected the Finance Bill by the enormous majority of 350 to 75 on November 30th, and on December 2nd the Commons passed an angry resolution before the Government appealed to the people.

As Rosebery had foreseen, the Unionists—who had been doing excellently in by-elections before the Lloyd George Budget—were heavily defeated at the General Election, but the Liberals had little cause for exultation since they had lost their independence from the Irish and Labour.[2] Dalmeny—whose captaincy of

[1] G. P. Gooch: *Under Six Reigns*, 152.
[2] The figures were Liberals 275, Conservatives 273, Labour 40, Irish Nationalists 82, giving the Government a majority of 124 over the Conservatives with Irish and Labour support.

Surrey had made him a more familiar figure at Kennington than Westminster—did not stand again for Midlothian, but Neil Primrose was elected for Wisbech. On all sides the question was raised, 'What is to be done about the Lords?'

The situation tempted Rosebery to return to his hobby-horse of Lords Reform. He had sat as Chairman of a Select Committee set up in 1907 as a result of a House of Lords Reform Bill introduced by Lord Newton, but his conduct of the chair had not been happy. 'It must be admitted', Lord Newton himself has written guardedly, 'that Lord Rosebery was less successful as a Chairman than might have been anticipated, for he allowed the members to stray from the point under discussion, frequently made discursive if entertaining speeches himself, and conveyed the impression that he was physically unequal to the moderate strain of work involved. He was also liable to fits of discouragement; I remember receiving from him one day a telegram announcing that in consequence of some minor difference of opinion he intended to resign from the Committee and it was only with difficulty that he was induced to continue.'[1] Curzon, another member of the Committee, told Esher that Rosebery 'made a very bad chairman, and he now understood R's failure to deal with affairs or with men. His two great faults are his tendency to treat grave matters frivolously and his feminine sensitiveness to criticism. He is always saying, "The Committee, I observe, will not accept favourably any suggestion of *mine*," and such like phrases.'[2] Rosebery, in fact, was becoming something of a bore. His penchant for writing to the newspapers had developed to such a point that he was ready to write to *The Times* or *The Scotsman* on the most trivial of subjects, such as the proposal to build a lunatic asylum near Epsom or the movements of Scottish regiments.

His Committee's recommendations, if they had been accepted, would have reduced the size of the House of Lords to less than 400, and would have considerably curtailed the hereditary element. But they were not even debated. When Parliament reassembled in 1910 he lost little time in producing Resolutions for Reform, and a packed House listened to his speech on March 14th; but, as Fitzroy noted, 'he had an immense audience, but somehow failed, with all his earnestness and rhetorical skill, to produce an effect commensurate with the pitch to which expecta-

[1] Lord Newton: *Lansdowne*, 363.   [2] Brett: *Journals and Letters*, II, 329.

tion had been carried'.[1] Rosebery also felt that he had failed. 'I confess I thought that it fell very flat', he wrote to Lady Stanhope, 'and that the audience was very chilly. One felt all the time as if one was climbing an Alp. I kept my eye on Jem[2] to see that he did not fall asleep.' He urged the Lords to accept at least the principle of Reform.

'The alternative is to cling with enfeebled grasp to privileges which have become unpopular, to powers which are verging on the obsolete, shrinking and shrinking until at last, under the unsparing hands of the advocates of single-chamber government, there may arise a demand for your own extinction, and the second chamber, the ancient House of Lords, may be found waiting in decrepitude for its doom.' His three resolutions—that there should be a strong and effective second chamber, that this could best be achieved by the reform of the existing House of Lords, and that the possession of a peerage should not give of itself the right to sit and vote—were duly passed, but the sudden death of King Edward on May 6th and the convening of an all-party conference to try to reach agreement left the matter in abeyance for some months. When the conference failed, Rosebery brought forward two detailed resolutions[3] on November 17th, but on the next day the Government announced that Parliament was to be dissolved in ten days' time Before the dissolution, the Parliament Bill—designed to remove any powers concerning Money Bills from the Lords and to permit them only the power of delay (two years) in other legislation—came before the Lords, and a series of hostile Unionist resolutions were passed without a division.

In the political manoeuvrings which took place, Roesbery had little part, but J. S. Sandars, Balfour's confidential secretary, was startled when on a raw November afternoon in London 'a small mackintoshed figure hailed me out of the gloom—"How are you getting on, & what are our prospects?" It was Rosebery. He pro-

[1] Fitzroy: *Memoirs* 399.
[2] The present Lord Stanhope.
[3] '(1) That in future the House of Lords shall consist of Lords of Parliament: (*a*) chosen by the whole body of hereditary peers from amongst themselves, and by nomination of the Crown; (*b*) sitting by virtue of offices and of qualifications held by them; (*c*) chosen from outside. (2) That the term of tenure for all Lords of Parliament shall be the same, except in the case of those who sit *ex officio*, who would sit so long as they held the office for which they sit.'

posed a walk—rain notwithstanding & I cd. but consent. We soon came upon T[ariff] R[eform] and Ref[erendum]. I said what if A. J. B. promulgated the policy on Tuesday—dramatically he stopped, took me by the sleeve, & said "We should win the Election".[1] But although the Referendum Pledge was given, the second General Election of 1910 was as inconclusive as the first in the sense that the party balance remained virtually the same; but it effectively settled the fate of the Lords.

Party politics had not been marked by such bitterness and even hatred within living memory; the announcement that the King had agreed to permit a sufficient creation of Peers to swamp the opposition to the Parliament Bill if it were rejected again plunged the two parties into savage mutual denunciation. Asquith was deliberately howled down in the House of Commons with roars of 'Traitor' and 'Who killed the King?', while F. E. Smith, bringing to British public life something of the panache and daredevil imagery of Randolph Churchill, represented the unreasoning personal ferocity of the Unionist invective. The fact that the Liberals were now reliant upon the Irish for their Parliamentary majority, and were consequently shackled to the millstone of Home Rule once again, further inflamed party passions, Churchill, Redmond, and Lloyd George answering the Unionist onslaught with equal vigour.

The Parliament Bill passed the Commons after the 'Kangaroo' closure—by which device whole sections of a Bill can be voted upon without debate—had been invoked to counter the Unionist obstruction at Committeee Stage. The Lords amended the Bill heavily, and the Commons rejected the amendments; throughout the torrid summer of 1911 political passions reached a crescendo of bitterness in the debate in the Lords on August 9th and 10th. There was naturally great interest in what Rosebery's attitude was to be. He had already protested against the Bill as 'ill-judged, revolutionary, and partisan', that while one House of Parliament was in process of effacement the other was being reduced to the level of a salaried board (a reference to the introduction of payment of Members), and that the Government, ignoring the appeal of the Archbishop of Canterbury for conciliation, 'had wrung the

---

[1] A. M. Gollin: *The Observer and J. L. Garvin*, 261. The Referendum Pledge was made by the Unionists to the effect that they would put the question of Tariff Reform to a national referendum if elected.

dove's neck and served it up on the olive branch'. But, having thus delighted the 'die-hard' Unionist peers led by the ancient but lively Lord Halsbury which had determined to reject the Bill and hang the consequences, Rosebery almost immediately disappointed them by implying—in a brief and vague speech—on the second day of the debate that he would abstain. This speech was melodramatic and unimpressive, even Kilbracken sadly noting that it was 'something in the style of a mid-Victorian tragic actor', but later in the evening, after a stream of speeches, and amid mounting excitement and tension, Rosebery suddenly darted forward from the cross-benches and announced that he would vote for the Government. The Bill passed by a mere seventeen votes, and Rosebery never entered the House of Lords again.

This inept and theatrical performance effectively destroyed what influence Rosebery still possessed, but his own account, in a private letter to the King, reveals that 'When I returned to the House after dinner I was informed that there were 20 peers who would vote for the Government if I said that I would. I should never have forgiven myself if I had abstained and if in consequence the large creation of peers had taken place.'[1]

Rosebery's last official task was to announce the new reign at Vienna, and he later declined an invitation to accompany the King and Queen on their State Visit to India. When pressed by Stamfordham he quoted in reply the passage from *Pickwick* when Mr Tupman wanted to go to a party dressed as a brigand.

'Tupman: "Why not Sir?"
"Because Sir," said Mr Pickwick, "Because you are too old, Sir."
"Too old!" exclaimed Mr Tupman. "And if any further ground of objection be wanting," continued Mr Pickwick, "you are too fat, Sir." '

In the Coronation Honours, determined that none of Asquith's would-be Peers should usurp any title remotely connected with himself, Rosebery became Earl of Midlothian and added to his other titles the Viscountcies of Mentmore and Epsom.

E. T. Raymond, always a waspish commentator, but for once correct, has written of Rosebery at this period that

His interventions were perfectly timed, but were anachronistic. His comments had always a point, but were seldom to the point. His

[1] *Royal Archives.*

speeches, as speeches, were interesting, perhaps even better in form than at any other time; but as practical contributions to political thought they were nothing, or rather less than nothing, since one speech often contradicted another. It seemed as though the last control had snapped, and the infinite contradictions of Lord Rosebery's temper and intellect and circumstances, of his instincts and his acquired mental habits were allowed unrestricted play. . . .

The sombre figure in the House of Lords, with the sphinx-like eyes and the brow on which 'deliberation sat and public care', was for years marked as a portent of some momentous intervention. Its anticipated appearance on a public platform was long sufficient to induce speculations as to new and important political combinations. But in due course it was found that the croak was only a croak, an unusually musical one; the gramophones of the Press ceased to reproduce it in full; and Lord Rosebery, while still far from old as politicians go, seemed to belong to a past as remote as his master Gladstone's.[1]

His oratorical power was still remarkable, although the theatrical element had become rather too predominant. The European scene filled him with despair, which he communicated to Churchill, who has written that 'He felt in his bones, with his finger-tips, all that subterranean, subconscious movement whereby the vast antagonisms of the Great War were slowly, remorselessly, inexorably assembling. He had laboriously inspected the foundations of European Peace; he saw where the cracks were, and where a subsidence would produce a crash. His heart responded instinctively to any readjustment or disturbance of the balance of power. In Rosebery's time Foreign Affairs and war dangers were invested with a false glamour and shrouded in opaque ignorance. But when some school-teacher was dismissed in Upper Silesia Rosebery said to me, "All Prussia has been shaken." '[2]

In the June of 1909 he was persuaded—with considerable difficulty—to deliver the speech of welcome to the first Imperial Press Conference at the White City. At one stage he excused himself on the ground that he had to attend the King's Ascot house-party, but Lord Burnham was deputed by the organiser of the conference, Harry Brittain, to approach King Edward, who gutturally pronounced 'I excuse Rosebery Ascot', and, in spite of more wrigglings, the bird was snared. It was one of Rosebery's

[1] Raymond: *The Man of Promise*, 223 and 226.
[2] Churchill: *Great Contemporaries*, 26.

most brilliant performances, the diners almost unconsciously moving from their places at the tables to group themselves under the platform, enthralled by Rosebery's voice and authority. His message was one of gloom; Europe was heading for catastrophe, 'this calm before the storm is terrifying', 'there never was in history so threatening and overpowering preparation for war'. 'Deeper and deeper grew the silence,' A. G. Gardiner has recorded, 'and the gloom as he pictured the menace that encompassed us. And when in a thrilling whisper he spoke of the peace that hung over Europe being charged with such a significant silence that "we might almost hear a leaf fall" we felt as though the enemy were already off Tilbury docks. And at that moment there was a roar like the roar of a hundred guns outside. For an instant we thought that Lord Rosebery had uttered his warning too late and that our doom was sealed. But then the truth flashed on us. It was ten o'clock—the hour at which the fireworks display began in the Exhibition grounds outside.'[1] Spender, commenting on the extraordinary skill with which Rosebery held the attention of his audience to the end of his speech, although almost drowned by the thunder of the fireworks, has described it as the most remarkable performance he had attended in his life.[2]

Rosebery seemed to have relapsed into a kind of seigneurial pessimism, lamenting the passing of Britain's greatness and surveying the contemporary scene with a moody melancholy. One exception was his Rectorial Address to the University of St Andrews in the September of 1911, which ended

Be of good cheer. I have seen life and death and glory chasing each other like shadows on a summer sea, and all has seemed to be vanity. But I remain in the conviction that, though individuals may suffer, when we take stock of a century at its end, we shall find that the world is better and happier than it was at the beginning. *Sursum corda.* Lift up your hearts, for the world is moving onward. It is guided from above, and guided we may be sure with wisdom and goodness which will not abandon us. That is the comfort which even in blackest darkness must afford light.

In 1910 Rosebery published his last book, *Chatham: His Early Life and Connections*, which was based upon the unpublished Dropmore Papers at Boconnoc. It was not particularly well reviewed, and many commentators took the opportunity of

[1] *Prophets, Priests and Kings.*   [2] *Life, Journalism and Politics*, I, 227.

drawing comparisons between the later Chatham and Rosebery, and John Morley was one who considered that Rosebery had consciously moulded himself upon Chatham as the great aloof arbiter of party squabbles.[1] But, just as his *Pitt* was rather over-rated, his study of the young Chatham has never received the attention which it deserves.

He had severed himself finally from public life, and became even more of a solitary figure. He had given the Villa Rosebery to the British Government in 1909, and, with his children now grown up and living their own very full lives, wandered rather aimlessly from one of his lovely houses to the other. The restoration of friendly relations with John Morley gave him great happiness, and their correspondence resumed the charm and warmth of earlier years. One extract from a letter from Morley shows why, in spite of all that had happened in the past, Rosebery still loved him.

. . . Your glorious chair will be the undoing of me. When you dropped me the other day, I strolled home, and sat in it for an hour or more, recalling my happy visit to Dalmeny, the constant kindness of the giver over long trying years, his singular considerateness in my sore domestic tribulation, and finally, as always happens after a meal with you, of the score of things I had meant to speak about, and didn't. . . .

His comments on politics and politicians grew more harsh as the years passed. 'Politics, always dirty and debasing, are now dirtier and more debasing than ever,' he wrote in 1914. 'A gentleman will blithely do in politics what he would kick a man downstairs for doing in ordinary life.' There was some attempt to make him play the part of the Elder Statesman, but he had had enough. Fritz Ponsonby came to Mentmore in 1914 when the Irish crisis was threatening to plunge the country into civil war to sound Rosebery on a proposal of the King that he should convene an all-party conference. After a dinner when they were attended by 'a butler and three ponderous footmen', Ponsonby was driven round and round the park and given little positive advice. 'He gave me the impression that he had lost touch with the political world and that he was unwilling to rouse himself to take any serious view of the problem,' Ponsonby wrote. 'We returned to the house about eleven o'clock and at once Lord Rosebery went

[1] Fitzroy: *Memoirs*, 425-6.

to bed, as he said if he began talking he would lose that sleepy feeling one gets from driving.'[1]

After his final retirement from politics he became increasingly obsessed with the failure of his life. Shortly before his death he commented that his main fault had been Pride, or, more precisely, *hubris*. This is a judgement which even his most severe critic might hesitate to accept as the sole cause, and equally questionable are his other notes in this period of introspection.

The secret of my life, which seems to me sufficiently obvious, is that I always detested politics. I had been landed in them accidentally by the Midlothian Election, which was nothing but a chivalrous adventure. When I found myself in this evil-smelling bog I was always trying to extricate myself. That is the secret of what people used to call my lost opportunities, and so forth. If you will look over my life you will see that is quite obvious. But nothing is so obvious as the thing which one does not wish to see.

I saw in some book the other day that I was described as a failure, and this led me into a train of thought which whirled me from myself. But let me say at once that according to the usual apprehension of the word the description is sufficiently accurate. What! a man who has been more or less in public life for a quarter of a century, who has never enjoyed an instant in power, and has now been long in seclusion without a follower and almost forgotten, what can be a greater failure?

In this second note Rosebery went on to examine examples of failure, and concluded that 'the ambitions of the wise' were not the material prizes of life but 'a well-ordered life of work, friend-ship, family affection and, if possible, religious faith; congenial work, a healthy existence, pleasant relations of family and friend-ship, and reverent loyalty to God'.

It would be unwise to be misled by these jottings. No man who has devoted three-quarters of his active life to politics relishes facing the fact that his life has been a failure, and Rosebery was a proud and sensitive man. It was characteristic that he should have undertaken this personal audit, but the conclusions were evi-dently intended as solace for a bruised and chastened spirit; it is unlikely that they succeeded in their purpose.

When the Great War broke out in the August of 1914 Rosebery was an anxious but detached observer of the catastrophe which he

[1] Lord Sysonby: *Recollections of Three Reigns*, 287-9.

had dreaded for over thirty years. 'When a European war breaks out', he had remarked to Hamilton two decades earlier, 'it will be interminable.' He found comfort and hope only in the solidarity, loyalty, and energy of the Empire. 'Our enemy fondly hugged himself that the Empire was a loosely compacted structure which would fall to pieces at the first touch of the antagonist. Lies! Lies! Lies! A nation which has been fed on lies for the last twenty years cannot hope to thrive in any enterprise' (Edinburgh, September 18th, 1914).

Rosebery's national work in the war was characteristic of that undertaken by many elderly men in public life, consisting mainly of speeches at bazaars and ex-servicemen's organisations, visits to hospitals, appeals for money and recruits, and patriotic addresses to already enthusiastic gatherings. Dalmeny was loaned as a hospital, and Rosebery spent most of the war in the south. Through his friendships with the King, the Asquiths, Churchill, Kitchener, and Fisher he was kept well informed of the series of military and political crises which destroyed Asquith's leadership.

His relationship with the Asquiths was a source of some embarrassment, since Margot pestered him with a series of frantic rambling appeals to support her husband, and kept telling him of Henry's poor health, the incompetence or disloyalty (and sometimes both) of his colleagues, and their poverty, which compelled her in 1915 to sign a contract for her memoirs. To these strange epistles Rosebery replied as politely as possible, but when Asquith invited him to become High Commissioner of the Church of Scotland in 1915 he was surprised and irritated, and ignored the request. He had never been impressed by the necessity of preserving this anachronistic and expensive functionary, but Asquith persisted, and Rosebery was compelled to reply. 'If I was astonished at your first invitation I was stunned by your second,' he wrote to the Prime Minister on March 10th. 'I think I can trace the first to a poor joke of mine . . . but I cannot understand the repetition. I suppose that if at this time of stress I was required to sweep a crossing, and could do it efficiently, I ought to accept it. But there is no call of patriotism to go and entertain the General Assembly at Holyrood, and, being single, I am ill fitted to meet it if there were. No one indeed would be the worse if the office were suspended during the war or altogether abolished afterwards.' Rosebery subsequently called on Asquith to clear up this silly misunderstanding, and they went on to discuss the vacant Provostship of Eton. Rosebery favoured Walter Durnford—in whose house his two sons had been—or Dr Montague Rhodes James, Provost of King's College, Cambridge, but then Asquith 'to my speechless astonishment', said 'You are the right man'. Rosebery demurred, but Asquith followed him to the door urging him to consider the proposal. He was definitely tempted. 'It was a delightful dream to toy with,' he wrote sadly in his 'betting book', 'but only a dream.'

He followed the progress of the war with increasing despondency. Kitchener told him that the Cabinet deserved the Victoria Cross for the courage in declaring war without any adequate supplies of arms, ammunition, and general military equipment; Fisher sent him long accounts of Churchill's conduct of the Admiralty, which were not notably complimentary. Fisher's distrust of Churchill germinated early, and was based mainly upon his dislike of Churchill's personal *entourage* and his interference in military enterprises in France and Antwerp when he should have been attending to his duties at the Admiralty. Rosebery followed the tragic course of this amazing love-hate relationship with a perplexed fascination, and was not surprised when it dissolved in the May of 1915, the Dardanelles Expedition being the final factor. The present Lord Rosebery recalls an occasion when Fisher met his father and himself on a walk in Berkeley Square shortly after Fisher's resignation, and, oblivious of the startled glances of the passers-by, the embittered old man upbraided the Government loudly and fiercely.

The King's dislike and distrust of politicians in general and his Ministers in particular had not abated with the outbreak of war, and Rosebery, not an unsympathetic listener, heard many denunciations of his Ministers from the King. When Lloyd George assumed the Premiership in 1916 he and the King were anxious that Rosebery should join it in a senior position without any departmental duties, but the offer was declined.

Had he joined the War Cabinet he would hardly have been an inspiriting element, as the sickening loss of life filled him with a depression which found its outlet in a series of passionate speeches devoted to the subject of the hideous folly of war. The Zeppelin raids stung him to write to *The Times* calling for reprisals, and he was haughtily rebuked by Sir Evelyn Wood, who quoted Marmont's saying, '*les représailles sont toujours inutiles*,' a philosophy more suited to the kind of war in which the gallant Field-Marshal had distinguished himself than the brutal squalor of 1916. Rosebery's depression was very marked. 'How kind of you to remember my centenary,' he wrote to Grace, Lady Wemyss, on May 10th, 1917, 'for though I am only 70 I feel more like the other thing. The last few years have come with the weight of decades. Anyhow, in the present state of the world, I would rather be 70 than 7. It is a better thing to be going out of the world than coming into it, at any rate for those accustomed to the atmosphere of the last half of the nineteenth century.' ' "Lighten our darkness" is the prayer always in my mind, for it is difficult to see much light,' he wrote to Northcliffe (February 21st, 1918). 'Russia, on whom we depended so much, collapsed in treachery and anarchy, Greece a phantom, Rumania overwhelmed, the cursed havoc of the submarines and the damnable imbroglio of our party politics. Nevertheless, though all crumble round us, we shall be staunch. *Impavidum ferient ruinae.*' 'Our "allies" crumble,' he wrote to Lady Stanhope. 'But an anti-socialist may view with complacency the result of Socialism in Russia, were it not so damaging to our campaign. Every competent general dismissed, and the army commanded by a rhetorical young civilian! The worst monarchy could not do worse!' Mary Drew lunched with him in the March of 1916 and shared 'a scrap of chick and some lettuce', and found her old friend 'terribly down over the war and the apparent bleeding to death of these mighty Kingdoms'. He said that he had no wish to live, and wanted to fall asleep and pass, but dreaded pain. He was also pondering whether to destroy all his papers, as he intended to put any possibility of a biography 'out of court'. He said that he was sure Chamberlain left the Government in 1886 with great reluctance and would have stayed had Gladstone managed him more intelligently; he described the 'unauthorised programme' as 'one of the worst actions in politics'.[1]

The careers of his two sons were prospering. Dalmeny had rejoined the Army and rose rapidly, becoming Military Secretary to Allenby after winning the MC and DSO in France. Neil had married Victoria Stanley, daughter of the 17th Lord Derby in 1915, and, after he had been recalled from military service in France, became Under-Secretary for Foreign Affairs and later Joint Parliamentary Secretary to the Treasury. Neil possessed

[1] Lucy Masterman: *Mary Gladstone*, 484.

much of the charm and fascination of his father and had also inherited his superb rich voice. Rosebery's relations with Neil were, as Lord Birkenhead later remarked, 'among the most touching in a life full of idealised love. The two men were indeed more like brothers in their easy and affectionate intimacy than like father and son.'[1] In the May of 1917 his political career suffered an unexpected set-back when he was not given higher office in the Government. Neil appears to have considered that Lloyd George had violated a private agreement whereby, after a period in the Whips' Office, he would be given a ministerial appointment. Whatever the cause, he rejoined the Bucks Yeomanry, was posted to Palestine, and was killed on November 17th near Gaza by a stray bullet which hit him in the head after the Turks had surrendered their position. It was the last shot of the engagement, and with it went his father's most cherished ambitions. It may be that he overrated Neil, but the blow of his death was almost mortal.

Henry Skelton, vicar at Mentmore, was instrumental in arranging Rosebery's last speech, which was delivered to the congregation of the tiny Mentmore church in the August of 1918. Skelton, young and enthusiastic, even prepared a few notes for Rosebery—'for which I have often blushed with shame at the thought of'—but he refused to commit himself, being frightened of breaking down. On the afternoon of August 4th Skelton received a short note, 'I have been trying all day to muster up courage to give an address this evening, but I cannot. Rosebery.' But he came to the service, and at the door agreed with Skelton that if he felt that he could do it he would make a signal; otherwise Skelton would deliver the sermon as usual. When the moment came, Skelton began to move to the pulpit, but Rosebery suddenly put his hand up, rose from his place in the front pew, and walked to the pulpit, where he delivered his last speech. His text was 'Lift up your hearts', but forty years later Skelton could only recollect Rosebery's 'really terrible' denunciation of the Kaiser. When Lady Battersea heard rumours of this sermon and referred to them in a letter, Rosebery replied that he had been 'bullied into the pulpit', and that it had caused him great anguish, and 'It is my last speech, & in no sense a sermon'. When she asked, 'Why should it be the last?' he replied simply, 'Because I cannot make posthumous speeches.'

[1] Lord Birkenhead: *Points of View*, II, 126.

In fact, one last undelivered speech survives. Invited by Skelton to address evensong exactly a year later, he sent a message to be read to the congregation.

My dear Mentmore Friends and Neighbours.

I had hoped to speak to you on August 3rd this year, as I did on August 4th last year: and I had prepared something to say. But when the time came I was not strong enough, and so the Vicar has permitted me to send you this message through him.

The clouds are dark, and there are storms lowering around; there are wars and rumours of wars all over the world; it is not difficult to see sore times ahead. How are these to be faced? Not, I am sure, by ignoring God and following every wayward vision of social revolution.

It is a dark problem. My hope is that you will remain a united little community of honest and industrious Christians: then you may be an oasis in the midst of a disturbed nation. If you continue in that spirit there will be nothing to fear. I do not expect to be with you then and so I write this.

If I do not return to you let these be my last words, which I send you from the bottom of my heart: God bless you all.

By the time this message was delivered, Rosebery had been prostrated by a stroke while shooting at Rosebery early in the November of 1918. He was taken to Randolph Crescent—where he had rented a house for the duration of the war—and lay either unconscious or delirious for several days. On November 11th the excited crowds celebrating the Armistice marched joyfully to the Crescent to demand a speech from their champion of past battles. It was a moving scene, with the crowd of many thousands calling the ancient chant 'Rozbury! Rozbury!' in the evening gloom. But the orator did not appear, and the crowds slowly dispersed.

Dalmeny had set out at once from Palestine for Edinburgh when he heard of his father's grave condition, but communications were bad, and it was over six weeks before he reached Randolph Crescent. He found his father slipping away from life, and ordered that he should be moved at once to Dalmeny, which had now been evacuated as a hospital. Rosebery began to recover almost as soon as he re-entered his home, and within a remarkably short time had improved so much that he occasionally came down to the library in the evening, delighting in Lady Leconfield's conversation and his son's two children. The recovery was maintained throughout 1919, although it was apparent that he was permanently paralysed, and was incapable of writing, all his letters being dictated to his private secretary. 'I am a poor worm still in bed,' he wrote to Skelton, 'and not likely to get up.' 'The doctors are buoyed by hope, but I am not,' he informed Stamfordham. Mary Gladstone visited him at The Durdans and wrote that 'It is rather pitiful, the helplessness of his physical condition and the undimmed brilliancy of his mind'. Edmund Gosse was walking down Farm Street in the May of 1919, pushing Lord Reay (who had broken a leg) in a wheel-chair, when they saw a closed motor car.

Ld Reay said, 'R must be coming out; I want to say something to him.' Next moment there emerged a little withered figure in a railway-cap of cloth, who stood blinking in the sun. Snow-white hair, closely-shaven drawn parchment cheeks, dull eyes that gazed out blankly. I should, positively, not have known who it was. Lord Reay spoke cheerfully to him, and he shook hands with us both, but said not a word; stood there, without a smile, then turned, still not speaking, and was pushed by two servants into the motor, which had the blinds drawn down. Lord Reay, ten years his senior, very much animated by excitement and distress, looked quite young, and turning to me said "We have seen a dying man! What a rapid and fatal change! We ought not to have stopped, nor have spoken! Who could guess that he had suddenly become like that?' It really was terrible. . . .

Oh! That sad yellow phantom of a shrunken Rosebery—I can't tell you what it was![1]

Rosebery's recovery of his full mental powers was entirely the result of the last public controversy in which he was engaged. His son used to read the main items from the newspapers to him every morning, and towards the end of the November of 1919 he remarked, 'I see that Turnhouse Aerodrome is up for sale.' 'But that's my property,' Rosebery exclaimed in amazement, seizing the newspaper. The Ministry of Munitions was offering the aerodrome and $178\frac{1}{4}$ acres of land 'for disposal as a whole, or the buildings and the land on which they stand'. The land had been taken over in the war under the Defence of the Realm Act for use as an aerodrome, which had subsequently been closed, and Rosebery—the arch-enemy of State interference—opened the engage-

---

[1] Evan Charteris: *Life and Letters of Sir Edmund Gosse*, 447–8.

ment with a sarcastic letter to *The Scotsman* in which he pointed out that the land was his and that the Ministry had no conceivable right to offer it for sale. The Permanent Secretary, Sir Howard Frank, retorted on December 1st that the Government was within its rights to purchase the land and 'to secure to the taxpayer as large a return as possible for expenditure necessitated by the war, and to avoid the waste involved in the destruction of expensive buildings which may be of permanent utility for industrial or other purposes'.

Frank was very quickly out of his intellectual depth, and the readers of *The Scotsman* followed the subsequent correspondence with rare pleasure. Rosebery called the action of the Ministry 'a lawless proceeding', and declared, 'I cannot share your indifference to the distinction between meum and tuum, and even to the Eighth Commandment'. On December 12th he really let fly.

... I had hoped that our controversy was ended, as we approach the question from such different points of view as regards honesty and morality that it seemed useless to continue firing from such long range. We are indeed as far apart as the poles, or as honesty from dishonesty. No one moreover can be better aware of my position than yourself. I did not answer your last letter in detail for it seemed (forgive me for saying so) to consist only of a tedious recapitulation of exploded contentions. . . .

To me I confess it is a matter of indifference, if I am to be robbed, whether it is by a pickpocket or a burglar. You have, as you well know, no equitable claim or title to Turnhouse. And to sell my best farm to recoup your Department's wasteful expenditure is an unscrupulous depredation unworthy of any honest Minister. I have been a Minister myself, and should have blushed to countenance such malpractices. You seem to glory in them. Times are changed. . . .

Frank's rejoinder to this onslaught did not lack spirit.

I received your letter of the 12th after I had read it in the evening papers. To accuse us of being robbers and pickpockets and lacking in honesty and morality does not appear to me to be very convincing.

It would seem that the charge that you really bring against us is that of carrying out the intentions of an Act of which you say you have never heard, but which after full discussion passed through the House of Lords. If you regard our conduct as unscrupulous I can only regret it. . . .

We do not claim the right to sell your farm without paying you the full value together with compensation for such loss, if any, as you may sustain by reason of being deprived of it.

I am sending a copy of this letter direct to the Press, as in forwarding your letters to the newspapers you omitted to send those I had written to you.

Howard had now shifted his ground, which was the result of an admission by the Ministry in reply to a formal protest by Rosebery's solicitors that they were not empowered to convey the property to a purchaser. Enormously encouraged and exhilarated by the sudden talk of compensation and by the fervour aroused by the controversy in the country—comparable to that excited by the Crichel Down affair in 1954—Rosebery hit back strongly at Frank on December 16th.

As a matter of fact I did send your last letter to the Press with mine, but it does not seem to have attracted the Editor.

You resent being compared to a burglar or a pickpocket, but when anyone attempts to rob me of my land I regard him as a thief.

What is the case? You built a few huts at an insane cost, on the edge of a fine farm, and now you claim to confiscate the farm to conceal the shameless waste of public money perpetrated by your Department.

You claim without a blush to protect the taxpayer. It is from you, however, that he needs protection, you who have spent £68,000 on those squalid huts. No wonder you wish to hide this extravagance. What I complain of is that you wish to hide it at my expense.

That is the whole story. I cannot go on repeating it, or continuing a futile discussion. Your position, if sinister, is manifest; so is mine. You propose to sell a rich farm of mine against my will. It is unnecessary to repeat what honest men think of such conduct. The public must decide, and I think it has.

As to the House of Lords, I have not set foot in it since 1911.

At this point Sir Howard wisely withdrew from the diverting but unequal contest. 'I still do not understand your grievance,' he wrote in a final pained letter on December 17th. '. . . I have no intention of replying to the personal attacks you have made on me. . . . This correspondence is therefore closed so far as I am concerned.' The incident was closed as well, as certain senior Ministers, alarmed by the storm which the correspondence had aroused, ordered complete capitulation. There was one final incident which occurred before the controversy ended. The Ministry's Parliamentary Secretary, F. G. Kellaway, MP, delivered an extraordinary public and intemperate attack on Rosebery at Crewe, accusing him of lack of patriotism, selfishness, and making some adverse observations on 'his record'. The resultant explosion—published in *The Times* of December 18th—was no less than he deserved.

> . . . The Department have let loose one of their understrappers to deliver an invective against me. He says that he knows my record. I cannot reciprocate. He comes from the Ministry of Munitions, but I do not know whether he is a Minister or a Munition.
>
> I rejoice in the violence of his language, because that is always a sign of a weak case, which it is intended to obscure. His invective lacks point, but that will improve with age and experience, and Mr Kellaway may yet live to annoy somebody. I rejoice that he calls my letter waspish, because a wasp implies a sting, and I certainly meant to plant a sting to fill the void which ought to have been occupied by a conscience. Before the department sent out this dove from the ark they ought to have taken more pains about the paper fastened under its wings. . . .
>
> Mr Kellaway mouths a good deal about patriotism. Patriotism is a sacred word, and should not be prostituted to perorations. I am not afraid of my record of patriotism, though no doubt it does not equal Mr Kellaway's. . . .

Many years later, a Minister who had been indirectly involved in the dispute sought out Rosebery's son—who had by then succeeded to his father's titles—and apologised for Frank's conduct. 'There is no need,' Lord Rosebery replied. 'Had it not been for Turnhouse my father would not have lived for another ten years.'[1]

It cannot be pretended that they were very happy years. His mind retained all its old vigour, but physically he was sorely afflicted. But some of his best letters belong to this rather sad period. 'My lower jaw is as firm as the rock of Gibraltar, but my upper jaw is as loose as Rahab,' he wrote to his dentist. Mary Drew urged him to read Haldane's Autobiography, but he replied, 'No. I have read his *Secret Memorandum*, which was enough.' When approached by Mrs Drew to help in financing G. W. E. Russell he replied that 'I cannot conceive anything more undesirable in literature than a reproduction of any more of his writings; whereas you think they would be inspiring. What they would inspire I will forbear to ask, but anyhow I will have no hand in it.' The publication of the Diaries of Algernon West annoyed him

[1] Rosebery had a hundred copies of the complete correspondence privately printed under the title *Turnhouse: An Object Lesson.*

considerably. 'I think that it was a terrible breach of confidence for a man in his position to keep that diary and to leave it for publication,' he wrote to Mrs Drew. 'It would have been more courageous if he had done it himself in his lifetime. Certainly it caused me no little annoyance, though I liked him well enough.' When Baldwin became Prime Minister he remarked to his son, 'It is a strange experience to realise that the Prime Minister of Great Britain is a man of whom one has never heard.' On his oldest enemy he wrote to Stamfordham in the February of 1925 that 'I regard the House of Lords as emasculate and degraded, and I know of no operation which would put it in a better position'.

The enthusiastic and devoted John Buchan considered that a collection of Rosebery's speeches and addresses would make an excellent book, and was so persistent that Rosebery reluctantly gave his permission. The two volumes of 'Miscellanies' were published in 1921, and were well received. Rosebery's attitude was characteristic. 'I have nothing whatever to do with them,' he wrote to Mrs Drew. 'I do not even know what they consist of. They are being published by John Buchan. . . . I dislike the whole thing more than I can say.' 'They are only a *rechauffée*, a collection made by John Buchan, in which I have no share,' he told Lady Battersea. 'The fact is John Buchan was strong and I was weak.' When Mrs Drew urged him to send a copy to St Deiniol's, he replied that he possessed only one copy, 'and I do not propose to waste money in purchasing any more'.

His interest in Church affairs did not diminish, and Skelton received a gloomy account of the condition of Christ Church, Epsom.

I must now tell you that we have now a Mr Hooke from Southampton (as all the Bishop's nominees are) who has come with the reputation of having emptied two churches, and is now on the way to emptying Christ Church. However, he seems a very good and amiable man, a great contrast to his predecessor, who filled the evening Church with a rather mixed congregation, and employed such buffoonery that a girl coming from his evening service was heard to say to another girl 'It's as good as a music-hall, I call it.' However, that poor man died, and had to be replaced at once from Southampton, in the way I have described.

John Morley, Randall Davidson, Frederic Harrison, Winston Churchill, and George Murray were among the few visitors who penetrated Dalmeny or The Durdans. Once, lunching at The Durdans, Churchill said that he could not undertake the biography of Marlborough, which Rosebery was urging upon him, since he could not surmount the obstacle of Marlborough's betrayal of the Brest Expedition, for which he had been excoriated by Macaulay. 'The aged and crippled statesman arose from the luncheon table', Churchill has related, 'and, with great difficulty but sure knowledge, made his way along the passages of The Durdans to the exact nook in his capacious library where "Paget's Examen" reposed. "There", he said, taking down this unknown, out-of-print masterpiece, "is the answer to Macaulay."' [1]

The infirmities of age were descending rapidly upon him. 'I suppose in one's old age one tumbles about like a tee-to-tum,' he wrote to Lady Battersea after a particularly bad fall at The Durdans, 'and hunting men rather enjoy these accidents, which add to the zest of the chase. But then I never was a hunting man.' In 1925 a doctor mistakenly diagnosed diabetes, and prescribed a course of insulin injections which nearly proved fatal. Rosebery sank into a coma, and his children were urgently summoned. Lady Crewe arrived from Paris to find to her surprise and delight that her father had recovered. 'If this is death', he said to her, 'it is absolutely nothing.' To Skelton he wrote, 'Pain is what I dread most.'

By the beginning of 1929 it was evident that the end could not be much further delayed. His eyesight had deteriorated so badly that he was virtually blind, and the outside world saw him only when he drove out for his nightly ride in his carriage to listen to the nightingales. They saw a hunched, wizened, almost sepulchral figure, slumped in the cushions. John Buchan was occasionally his companion on these rides. 'It was a melancholy experience for me', he has written, 'to see this former Prime Minister of Britain crushed by bodily weakness, sorrowing over the departing world and contemptuous of the new. It was sadly reminiscent of the old age of Chateaubriand. I went for a drive with him, I remember, at The Durdans on an April day in 1929. . . . I had never seen Surrey more green and flowery, but he was unconscious of the spring glories and was sunk in sad and silent meditations.' [2]

There is one last picture of him. In the January of 1929 Lord

[1] Preface to Volume I of *Marlborough, His Life and Times*.
[2] Buchan: *Memory-Hold-The-Door*, 157.

and Lady Stanhope lunched with him at The Durdans, and
although they were saddened by his physical disabilities, which
made even eating a hazardous and embarrassing undertaking,
they were struck by the fact that his real charm in congenial
company and the vivacity of his conversation were as remarkable
as ever. Lord Stanhope's account of part of their conversation—
written immediately upon his return to Chevening—records:

At lunch—we three were alone together—the conversation turned
to the personality of great men, & I asked if Disraeli had a great
presence or was more peculiar. Lord Rosebery at once replied that
Disraeli was more peculiar, adding 'But he was always very kind to
me.' I asked if Dizzy was not rather alarming & Rosebery said 'I was
never frightened of him.' Then he said 'Munro Ferguson & I agree
that we should have done better to have followed him.' I said, 'I suppose it was your one mistake,' to which Rosebery replied, 'Yes, but a
very big one.' I then remarked that Novar[1] had since changed over—
he is now a Conservative—and Rosebery retorted '*He* definitely calls
it ratting.' I then said 'If you had followed Dizzy, what a difference it
would have made in history,' to which Rosebery replied, 'I don't
agree with you,' but was obviously pleased when I said, 'Then we must
agree to differ.'[2]

On the evening of May 20th, 1929, Rosebery sank into a coma,
and in the early hours of the morning of May 21st, with his son
and Lady Leconfield by his bed, he died. He had given instructions that a record of the Eton Boating Song was to be played as
he died, and this wish was actually carried out, although it is
doubtful if he heard the haunting music, redolent of hot summer
afternoons, the quiet laughter of friends, and the golden days of
his young manhood.

He was buried at Dalmeny, in the family vault in the exquisite
Kirk where he had worshipped for over fifty years. The cortège
passed through Berkeley Square on its passage through London,
and an account by a witness of this event is my last quotation.

Many people waited one night in Berkeley Square to see the dead
Lord Rosebery borne past his house in the Square on his way to his
grave in Scotland. It was a place very near the spirit of that strange
statesman; and over it, too, hung the shadow of dissolution, for
Lansdowne House was soon to be dust and ashes, and the old grandee

---

[1] Munro Ferguson had been created Lord Novar in 1920.
[2] *Stanhope Papers.*

Square, which had housed so many Prime Ministers in the past, was to be changed out of recognition.

Many years before, in a paper he read on disappearing London, Rosebery spoke of those little unchanged parts of old London that you sometimes come on hidden behind regions of new buildings, giving you the same surprise that you had when you came on patches of snow long after the frost. Berkeley Square seemed to be one of those survivals, and the man who had himself appeared to be a survival of another era, seemed to be lingering there as his coach came slowly by the red-brick mansion with the carved primroses on its façade.

The crowd that waited there included many tall men like footmen and some little men like jockeys. The great doors of the mansion stood open as though a caller was in sight. When the procession of funeral cars came slowly round the bend of the Square, their lights gilding the sashes of the windows, the household staff appeared on the steps, the crowd uncovered, the policemen stood at the salute. Lord Rosebery in his oaken coffin crowned with flowers went very slowly past his doorstep with never a stop.

Then the funeral coach moved on more quickly through the familiar sallow Mayfair streets and on to King's Cross, where the familiar train was to bear him for the last time to the home of his ancestors.[1]

What is one to make of this strange, sad life, and this perplexing career? As Mr John Raymond has remarked, 'Rosebery has been the subject of many varying judgments, each of them more subjective than is usually the case when politicians are assessed.'[2] Rosebery's character has a Hamlet-like quality which renders it open to every kind of interpretation. As E. T. Raymond has observed, 'By omitting certain sets of facts, and placing others in a strong light, he can be proved almost anything we like—a man before his age, a man behind it; a strong, far-seeing statesman, a sentimentalist bemused by his own incantations and catchwords; a patriot too pure for the vulgar commerce of politics, a politician too slippery to be trusted by men themselves not over-particular. . . . His admirers will have him all godhead. His detractors make him all clay feet.' In Spender's view his unhappy premiership was 'too swiftly attained and too gravely embarrassed', and Mr Algernon Cecil considered that this episode kept him 'like a burnt child dreading the fire'. Guedalla, representing a common

[1] James Bone: *London Echoing*, 172–3.   [2] *The Doge of Dover*, 42.

view of Rosebery, described him as 'political caviare, a morsel of public life which it is distinguished to enjoy . . . it is his tragedy that there is no place in politics for Peter Pan'. Bernard Shaw's jibe that Rosebery was a man who never missed a chance of missing an opportunity expresses another point of view, that of the political extrovert who turns aside with contempt from hesitation, pusillanimity, and doubt.

Another school of thought represents Rosebery as a kind of throw-back to the grandee Whigs, magnificent but anachronistic. Mr Algernon Cecil belongs to this school, and has written of Rosebery that 'British diplomatic history will always salute him, yet as one about to die. He was the last pure-blooded survivor of his race—of the old Whig breed that served us in a period of transition so well. He carried his honours with excellent grace. He seemed as if born to figure in such regal congresses as the world once knew, and to return the tennis balls of diplomacy in the grand manner of former times. Occasion failed him for this. Yet not Clarendon nor Granville bore the old luggage of the Whigs into the lumber-room with a finer air, or left among the archives of latter-day diplomacy a more delicate perfume.'

Many of those who fell under the magic of Rosebery's charm and erudition lament that he never had the opportunity to show his great qualities. Buchan has written that the tragedy of Rosebery's life was that 'his work was with second-rate problems, the ordinary party scramble among half-truths, and both the task and the rewards came to seem to him too trivial to be worth his care', and Churchill has echoed this comment: 'Rosebery flourished in an age of great men and small events.' Others proffer the excuse of 'the spoiled child'. 'No one ever had the same advantages,' Randall Davidson, who loved him greatly, once remarked. 'A most definite and inimitable personality, everything both to allure and compel. And yet here he is, the most tragic example in our time of a wasted and ineffectual life. It is largely, yes almost entirely, his own fault, but it is the fault of former years rather than of now.'

Arguments can easily be marshalled to support or contradict any of these judgements. Undoubtedly his character was not tempered in his formative years by competition and probably suffered from excessive adulation; his resentment at criticism— however mildly expressed—and his moodiness were clearly the result of the circumstances of his earlier years. But sufficient allowance has rarely been made for his shyness, which too often gave an impression of aloofness which was not intended, and for the insomnia which plagued him for over half his life. There is something inexpressibly pathetic in the picture of him walking through London in the early hours or prowling around Mentmore or The Durdans, his long, solitary night drives, his hours of loneliness at Barnbougle as the black mass of the Kirk-caldy hills lightened imperceptibly and the cold glittering waters of the Forth materialised stealthily from the gloom. By nature pessimistic and introspective, these dragging hours gave him time to ponder too deeply, to nurse wounds, and, if only on occasion, to indulge in self-pity. His most conspicuous failing was a complete inability to stand back, as it were, from himself, and try to judge his actions from the point of view of others. Most of mankind—and particularly political mankind—is selfish, or self-absorbed; Rosebery was rather more self-enfolded, preoccupied with himself, and the effect upon himself of his course of action. He ran through his political friendships with a reckless profligacy, only that with John Morley really surviving. Esher once wrote of him that 'He is too lacking in frankness for perfect intimacy', and this was the result of his shyness, his timidity in facing un-pleasant problems, and his sensitive self-absorption. He did not have the gift of laughing and forgetting; few men have, when it comes to the test, but Rosebery carried a natural aversion to opposition and criticism to excessive limits. His accounts of the major episodes in his career are characterised by a note of self-justification; they are often querulous, frequently petulant, and dominated by a mood of pained incomprehension. Gladstone, Granville, Harcourt, Morley, and Campbell-Bannerman cannot have been so wrong or so unfair as Rosebery believed; he searched for some failing in manner or approach in others, never in himself. Even when he does criticise himself, it is a half-hearted self-analysis which does not convince either the author or the reader.

The question must needs be asked, What was he doing in politics at all? This is the most difficult question of all, and one which cannot easily be answered. He inherited a family tradition on both his father's and mother's side of public life; he was brought up in political surroundings, educated in the most politically-conscious of schools, and from an early age was fascinated by the interplay of personality and circumstance in political history; a great landowner, with no need to seek an income or make a career, politics was a natural outlet for an ambitious and idealistic young man. But these facts do not fully explain why he set himself at an early age to acquire knowledge, to devote himself to political life, to make the acquaintance of political leaders. Although compassion is one of the most rare and admirable of impelling powers in a public man, it is difficult to believe that Rosebery's radicalism went very deep, and his concept of social improvement involved very little participation on the part of the prospective beneficiaries. He had the most common weakness of social reformers, a strong taste for dictation; his chairmanship of the London County Council demonstrated not only his enlightenment and competence, but also this basic defect. So long as he was responsible, could 'do something for the people', and, moreover, could say what that 'something' was to be, all went well. But he was not ready to fight over details, and he was sufficiently intelligent to realise that every 'panacea' has its defects; he was, indeed, strongly nostile to doctrinaire treatment of any subject, and had a deep-rooted aversion to 'isms'. But what should have been his greatest strength was in fact a serious weakness in the politician. He would have preferred to have conducted all the business of the State with quiet reasonableness, with himself in command; when faced with opposition he either retired in a huff or conceded the point. Nothing in his official career is more illuminating than his second tenure of the Foreign Office in 1892–4. After early rebuffs he worked in secret, adopting the attitude, 'Here is my policy; here I stand. Take it or leave it, it is of no consequence to me.' In 1893 his colleagues had no choice, but when the tactic was constantly repeated in later years, different circumstances prevailed. This is really the 'secret' of Rosebery's failure as a politician. He went into politics partly because of personal ambition—although this should not be exaggerated—and partly because he felt that he could handle power. Probably he could have, but in a modern Britain power cannot be achieved by such methods as Rosebery adopted.

As he himself has remarked, 'No one reads old speeches,' but Rosebery's speeches still make remarkably attractive reading. The humour, the learning, the common sense, the prescience, even, which he brought into public life gave his speeches a quality which rarely failed to delight and enlighten his listeners. His Imperialism was neither an ignoble nor a bigoted concept, for he had a real feeling for *la mission civilatrice* of the British Empire, allied with a realistic appreciation that charity is best administered by a strong central agency. So much that he prophesied has come to pass that there is a temptation to regard him as a great political sage, but sages who move in a vacuum do not greatly influence events. Politics is a struggle for power; Rosebery wanted the power, but shrank from the struggle.

It is difficult to calculate the precise effects of his wife's death. To a man so sensitive, so anxious for sympathy and understanding, the loss of the one person who really understood his complex and febrile personality was a terrible blow. It may be argued that there is something fundamentally unsound about a character which suffers so severely from such a loss, but that is hardly the point. Rosebery deliberately gave the impression of being reticent and almost cold, but in fact he was very warm-blooded, with a mercurial temperament which veered from the heights to the depths of emotion, sensitive to atmosphere, quick to resent intrusion, too easily attracted by the dramatic and by the pleasure of making a fine gesture. Such a nature requires sympathy and patience, which his wife supplied. It is not fanciful to trace in Rosebery's relations with Gladstone and the Queen a desire for a similar sympathy and comprehension.

But, although 1890 may fairly be regarded as the turning-point, it is evident that Hannah Rosebery's death only illuminated the basic weaknesses of Rosebery's personality for political life. The story of his disastrous leadership of the Liberal Party is not entirely one of Harcourt's gross disloyalty, jealousy, and meanness of mind; Rosebery's feminine sensitivity and sulking moodiness, his disinclination to take other colleagues into his confidence, and his constant endeavour to avoid unpleasantness by trying to divert difficult problems away from Harcourt, all played their part. *Capax imperii nisi imperasset.*

His failure to lead was of decisive importance in the history of the decline of the Liberal Party, for the internecine controversies that rent the party from 1894 to 1905 gave the Labour Party its opportunity for emerging from its derisory insignificance in 1895 (when Keir Hardie lost his seat in the House of Commons) to its triumph in the General Election of 1905. The abdication of

leadership by the Liberal Party in this period—for which Rosebery must bear a considerable part of the blame—sealed its doom
as the party of the Left. As time passes, it is becoming clearer that
their victory in 1905 was a 'freak' result so far as the Liberals
were concerned; within five years they were reduced to virtual
parity with the Conservatives, and their dismally remorseless
extinction since then is a matter of history. Professor D. W.
Brogan has recently commented that

To the Labour intellectual . . . it is in my experience an axiom that
the Labour Party (whether you date it from 1900 or 1906 or 1918) was
bound to replace the Liberal Party as the party of the Left. It had
received the Mandate of Heaven, as the Chinese used to put it. Now
this doctrine (which should be distinguished from the similar but not
identical Marxist doctrine) ignores the role played by *luck* in the
replacement of the Liberal Party by the Labour Party.[1]

In the final analysis, as Mr Cecil has written, 'It is the enigma
of a striking personality and not the portrait of a great Prime
Minister that rivets the eye.' Even if the effects of his strange
career were principally negative, although there may be no place
for a Peer in modern British politics, nor room for doubts and
independence, and although Rosebery may have been too far
removed from the existence of ordinary people to be their champion, the tragedy of his life cannot be obliterated by the subsequent wisdom of detached critics. Even his most severe detractors
cannot wholly ignore the intense admiration he aroused, the
great hopes which he inspired, the sound sense and shrewdness of
his judgement when it was unclouded by personal prejudices, and
the extent of the difficulties with which he had to contend.

*Here lies one who meant well, tried a little, failed much. Surely that
may be his epitaph, of which he need not be ashamed.*

---

[1] 'The Future is Behind Us?' (article in *Encounter*, January 1960).

APPENDIX ONE

Genealogical Table

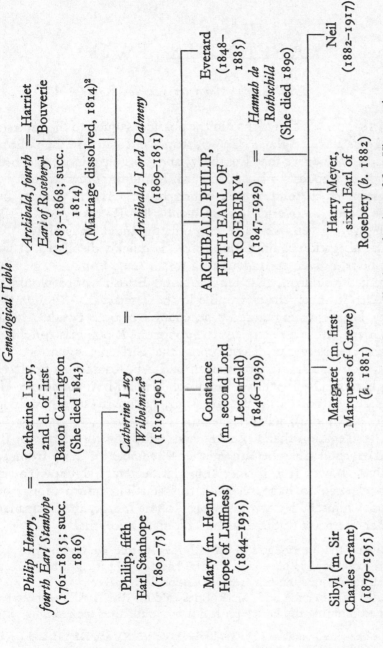

Philip Henry,
fourth Earl Stanhope
(1761–1855; succ.
1816)

=

Catherine Lucy,
2nd d. of first
Baron Carrington
(She died 1843)

Archibald, fourth
Earl of Rosebery[1]
(1783–1868; succ.
1814)

=

Harriet
Bouverie

(Marriage dissolved, 1814)[2]

Philip, fifth
Earl Stanhope
(1805–75)

Catherine Lucy
Wilhelmina[3]
(1819–1901)

=

Archibald, Lord Dalmeny
(1809–1851)

Mary (m. Henry
Hope of Luffness)
(1844–1935)

Constance
(m. second Lord
Leconfield)
(1846–1939)

ARCHIBALD PHILIP,
FIFTH EARL OF
ROSEBERY[4]
(1847–1929)

=

Hannah de
Rothschild
(She died 1890)

Everard
(1848–
1885)

Sibyl (m. Sir
Charles Grant)
(1879–1955)

Margaret (m. first
Marquess of Crewe)
(b. 1881)

Harry Meyer,
sixth Earl of
Rosebery (b. 1882)

Neil
(1882–1917)

[1] Received an English barony, 1828.   [2] He married, secondly, Anne, daughter of first Viscount Anson.

[3] She married, secondly (1854), Lord Harry Vane, later fourth and last Duke of Cleveland.

[4] Created Earl of Midlothian, Viscount Mentmore, Viscount Mentmore, Baron Epsom of Epsom, 1911. K.G., 1892; K.T., 1895.

APPENDIX TWO

Lord Rosebery and the Jameson Raid

WHEN PUBLIC INTEREST in the possible sequels to the Jameson Raid was at its height in 1896–7, stories circulated in the political world to the effect that Rosebery, and possibly Ripon, had been privy to Rhodes's plans. Edward Hamilton drew Rosebery's attention to these rumours, which he vehemently denied, but some recent discoveries in the Chamberlain Papers by Miss Ethel Drus[1] have given them a certain circumstantial plausibility.

The allegation against Ripon may be quickly dismissed. It was that he had given an undertaking to the Cape Commissioner, Sir Hercules Robinson, that ten thousand British troops would be supplied in the event of trouble in the Transvaal. Although this story has been unguardedly accepted by some South African historians, it has no evidence to support it; Ripon was convinced of the necessity for discouraging the Uitlander agitation, and turned down a similar application by Loch, Robinson's predecessor, in 1894. Neither Miss Drus nor Mr C. M. Woodhouse, MP (the joint author—with the late J. G. Lockhart—of a new biography of Rhodes), believes the story.

The allegation that Rosebery had had prior knowledge of the Raid reached Chamberlain in the November of 1896 from Sir Graham Bower (the former Imperial Secretary at Cape Town), who claimed to have received this startling information from Rhodes himself. He wrote to Sir Robert Meade, the Permanent Under-Secretary of State at the Colonial Office, that

> During the interview with Mr Rhodes he told me that he had told Lord Rosebery his plans and that he had thought it right to do so as the latter was making him a Privy Councillor.
>
> Later on, after the raid, Mr Rhodes told me that Lord Rosebery had warned him that the Police must not move till after the rising. . . .

[1] *Bulletin of the Institute of Historical Research*, Vols. XXV and XXVII, and *English Historical Review*, Vol. LXVIII.

I desire to add that Lord Rosebery's name was given to me in the strictest confidence and that in communicating the conversation to you in so far as it affects Lord Rosebery it is on the honourable understanding that it will only be used confidentially.

Meade took this letter to Chamberlain, who wrote to Lionel Phillips—a Uitlander leader who had seen the correspondence between Rhodes and Rutherford Harris, his agent in London—to enquire if there was any truth in the story. Phillips's reply, however, is not in the discovered Chamberlain Papers.[1]

Bower subsequently regretted writing this letter and wanted it to be destroyed, and as late as 1902 he tried to retrieve it, telling Bryce that Robinson had dictated it.[2] Rosebery, when approached by Ripon on the suggestion of Meade, denied that he had any prior knowledge of Rhodes's plans or that he gave the warning about moving the police as alleged by Bower.

The evidence for a story which has been stated as a fact by some historians[3] is therefore extremely flimsy. The Rosebery Papers give no clue, except in a negative sense, in that the correspondence between Rhodes and Rosebery, and the latter's accounts of conversations with Rhodes, contain no hint of any foreknowledge on Rosebery's part about Rhodes's intentions. One particular correspondence is an important element in Rosebery's defence. Rhodes wrote to him in the August of 1895 to ask him to assist him in his request to Chamberlain that the Bechuanaland Protectorate—which he ostensibly wanted as a railroad, but in fact as a jumping-off point for Jameson—should be handed over to the British South Africa Company. Rosebery sought Ripon's advice. Ripon had never been enthusiastic about this proposal, but in the June of 1895, immediately before the fall of the Government, he had circulated a Cabinet Memorandum supporting the project. But by August he had changed his mind, and he advised Rosebery not to write to Chamberlain—'there is no saying what use an unscrupulous fellow like Joe might make of your intervention'—and that the time for handing over the area had not yet arrived. In his original letter to Ripon, Rosebery had said 'I am not very

[1] *Bulletin*, XXV.
[2] *Bryce Papers*.
[3] See J. Van der Poel, *The Jameson Raid*, 23; E. A. Walker, *A History of Southern Africa*, 445; Bell, *Flora Shaw*, 177; and H. Sauer, *Ex Africa*, 258. Lady Pakenham, however (*Jameson's Raid*, 321), wisely reserves judgement, and gives Rosebery the benefit of the doubt.

anxious to write to Chamberlain, but I like to help Rhodes when I can', but he took Ripon's advice and told Rhodes that he could not intercede.[1]

This incident is of course extremely significant, for, unless he was playing an extraordinarily Machiavellian game, it clearly shows that Rosebery had no idea of the importance of Bechuanaland to Rhodes's plans, and was therefore unaware of the plans themselves.

In any event, the story is *prima facie* highly improbable, if not positively absurd. Rosebery was the only Liberal leader who declined to praise Chamberlain for his prompt disavowal of the Raid; his public reason was that Chamberlain was only doing his duty, but in private he explained to Edward Hamilton that 'he had the best reasons for believing that there was truth in the rumours that in the Transvaal business, culminating in the Raid, Chamberlain's hands were not clean'.[2] As Rosebery had seen Rhodes on several occasions in the late summer of 1896, it is reasonable to deduce that the informant was Rhodes himself. Rosebery believed that Chamberlain, whom he had never liked, had been behind the Raid, which was why he demanded a complete enquiry, opposed the nomination of a Parliamentary Committee on the grounds that it could not work quickly enough, and was bitterly contemptuous of the Report of the Committee when it was published. He was in his period of silence after his resignation of the leadership of the Liberal Party, but his private notes leave no doubt of his feelings. In one memorandum written in the June of 1901—his ire aroused by Campbell-Bannerman's notorious 'methods of barbarism' speech—Rosebery wrote that the Committee 'had deliberately and firmly shut its eyes to the central matter of the complicity of the Govt. Yet both the guests of the National Reform Union were parties to this conspiracy of silence.' It is, to put the matter mildly, unlikely that Rosebery would have pressed for a complete and impartial enquiry into the background to the Raid if he himself was likely to be implicated. Mr Woodhouse, who has also examined the complete Rhodes-Rosebery correspondence, has written to me that 'There is nothing on the record to incriminate Rosebery at all'.

[1] *Ripon Papers* and *Rhodes Papers* (C27/58).
[2] *Edward Hamilton's Diary*, October 26th, 1896 (Brit. Mus. Add. MSS. 48,670, f. 30).

Rosebery's account of a subsequent conversation with Rhodes is of some interest in the tangled history of the Jameson Raid and in the formulation of the scheme of Rhodes Scholarships, of which Rosebery was one of the original Trustees.

May 9, 1898

Long walk with C. Rhodes.

The Raid cost him & Beit[1] close on 400,000£ each—near 800,000£ in all.

Has brought Beit into the [scholarship] scheme. Beit childless. C.R. has pointed out that his remote heirs will probably dissipate his fortune in follies.

He thinks the income may be 500,000£ a year. Scheme of offering to colleges of each colony & of U.S.—this more doubtful—to pass 3 men through Oxford or Cambridge. . . .

The complete telegrams a perfect picture. The one of Miss Shaw's that escaped merely a specimen—& that or others (I am not sure which) severely edited by Jackson.[2]

They were about to refuse the name Rhodesia; but suddenly announced they gave way. Otherwise he might have acted differently.

J.C. fought the paragraph (wh. C.R. regards justly as an imputation on his personal and political honour) for 20 min. Hicks-Beach bowed his head & assented.[3]

The suppressed telegrams wh. it was impossible to elicit were actually in the bag of Pember QC[4] while the discussion was going on!

[1] Alfred Beit, Rhodes's colleague.

[2] W. L. Jackson was the Unionist Chairman of the Committee, and was a former Chief Secretary for Ireland. The telegrams referred to were almost certainly those from Miss Flora Shaw (who subsequently married Lugard) to Rhodes, which were demanded by the Committee on June 1st. They were sent to Jackson as Chairman, and he handed them into the Committee on June 29th. They contained some suspicious passages relating to Chamberlain and Rhodes, but Miss Shaw, by a brilliant *tour de force*, was able to explain them away in the face of some mild questioning. The implication of Rhodes's remark to Rosebery is that Jackson was in league with Chamberlain and 'edited' these vital telegrams before they were submitted to the Committee.

[3] This was the paragraph criticising Rhodes which Chamberlain subsequently went out of his way to repudiate in the House of Commons. It was alleged that Rhodes threatened to release the 'missing telegrams' unless Chamberlain made his defence.

[4] Rhodes's counsel at the Committee of Enquiry. The interesting implications of this statement require no elaboration.

APPENDIX THREE

Rosebery's account of the events leading to his accession to the Premiership, January to March, 1894

This document is undated, and is entitled 'My narrative of the formation of the Government in 1894 to be used if necessary to correct false statements. It is unfinished in form, but in substance contains, I think, all the necessary facts.' It has been published in the December 1951 and January 1952 issues of *History Today*.

ON TUESDAY, JANUARY 9, 1894, in a speech of fifty minutes, Mr Gladstone announced to the Cabinet his intention to resign if the Admiralty estimates for the coming year were maintained at their proposed figure, stating that he could truthfully attribute his resignation to physical infirmity. He argued against the proposals in passionate language, but said that he did not wish to be wholly unaccommodating, and as he could not and would not attempt to frame a departmental estimate, he would simply propose to bisect the new charge and postpone one half till a future occasion. This did not seem a tenable or logical suggestion and it was quite clear that the Cabinet was almost unanimously in favour of the original estimate. Harcourt indeed as Chancellor of the Exchequer supported Mr Gladstone's views. He entirely and fundamentally disapproved of these estimates. But if they were not agreed to the Government would break up and the Tories who would succeed would agree to them. Moreover, he saw his way to finding the money. He was consequently prepared to acquiesce in the Admiralty demands. It was observed that during the latter part of this discourse Mr Gladstone, who had several times indignantly interrupted him, turned his back on his Chancellor of the Exchequer.

It is unnecessary to describe the regret with which Mr Gladstone's announcement was received. It may safely be said that it created a feeling of consternation in the mind of every person present. There had for a few days been vague rumours that Mr

Gladstone objected to the naval estimates and threatened extreme courses. But there are always rumours of this kind floating about Cabinets, and there was implicit confidence that Mr G's ingenuity and great, though unconscious, tenacity of office would overcome the difficulty. Now that Ministers found themselves immediately in face of the approximate loss of this noble and puissant figure they were appalled. Little was said in this sense, but the aspect of the Council was unmistakable.

It was, however, pointed out as delicately as might be that whatever the result might be the decision must not too long be postponed. Whichever decision was taken the Government must break up. The sooner, then, that it broke up the better. Otherwise the next few weeks would be passed in leakage and gossip and drift, ending in a wreck just before the new Session, when there would be no time to re-compose the Government or make any preparations for Parliament. That would be a disaster.

This view was generally held, but the course deprecated was the one adopted, and the disaster so long foreseen was what actually occurred. The discussion branched off into a rather painful scene between Mr Gladstone and Sir W. Harcourt, and it was finally suggested that Ministers should discuss among themselves what could be done: one of those flabby proposals which are hurriedly adopted in order to put an end to an intolerable position. Mr Gladstone closed the Cabinet by saying 'I propose to leave for Biarritz on Saturday morning'.

In the afternoon Sir W. Harcourt expressed a wish to see me and came to the Foreign Office. He at once began speaking of Mr Gladstone's declaration and said that he supposed if Mr G carried out his threat that it meant the end of all things, and the disappearance of the Government; did I not think so? I replied that I was entirely of a different opinion. I never could dismiss from my mind the deplorable figure cut by Mr Pitt's Government on Mr Pitt's death: that our breaking up on Mr Gladstone's resignation would be so much the worse that it would be proved that the Liberal Party would have to declare itself unable even for a moment to carry on the Government after the resignation of a statesman in his eighty-fifth year; and that sooner than stomach such a humiliation I would serve in a Government headed by Sir Ughtred Kay-Shuttleworth (the first name of a subordinate Minister that came into my head) or anyone else. I admitted that we could not in any case go on for long, but insisted that we should not commit suicide in despair.

He seemed much taken aback by this declaration, and soon afterwards retired.

I was at the time a good deal perplexed by the object of this visit and by Sir W's demeanour. But I have no doubt that it had begun to dawn upon him that he could not form a Government and that the best way of concealing his impotence was that the Government should come to an end; that he regarded me as the only person who could continue the Government and made no doubt from my reluctance to return to Office in 1892 that he would find me quite willing to fall in with his views of collapse.

Mr Gladstone left for Biarritz on the Saturday (Jan. 13) as he announced. I saw him on the previous Wednesday (the day after the Cabinet) at the House of Commons when he spoke with much eloquence and exaltation of his position. 'The dead are with me though, it seems, not the living—Peel, Cobden, Bright, Aberdeen, etc.' On this day, however, the acuteness of the crisis seemed to be diminished, and on the Thursday (Jan. 11) it seemed to be past. Mr Gladstone entered upon business as usual, and those most in his intimacy believed that he had made up his mind to remain. On the Friday again it seems he took an official farewell of one at least of his private secretaries.[1] On the Saturday he disappeared as it were from our ken, and the Cabinet heard nothing more from him directly until his return. It was understood, however, that he expressly refused leave for any Cabinets to be held in his absence.

It is very difficult to give a clear or consecutive view of what happened in London during the next few weeks. Naturally the Cabinet had to preserve its burning secret (which was wonderfully kept) and to prepare for the possible eventuality (for it was not regarded as more) of being left without a chief within ten days or a week of the reassembling of Parliament.

Some of the Ministers were in constant communication with me—notably Asquith, John Morley, Acland and Spencer. Some I think remained passively awaiting the stroke of fate whatever it might be. Among these I should reckon Trevelyan, Lefevre, Fowler, and perhaps Bryce. Shaw-Lefevre went to Mr Gladstone shortly after the Cabinet of Jan. 9 to say that he was in

[1] Spencer Lyttleton.

agreement with him—whether generally or particularly, I do not know, nor does it matter. Mr G afterwards said that he had greatly underrated Shaw-Lefevre who he now thought would make a good Colonial Governor. Of Kimberley, Ripon and Herschell I saw I think little. But I myself was passive, for I was engrossed by the business of my great department. I had indeed during this Government become purely a departmental Minister —content to hold aloof provided I were left alone in my special work. And, provided this condition were observed, I did not trouble myself greatly about the future. In the first place I did not believe that Mr Gladstone would resign at this time, and on this question; and secondly, if he did, I was convinced that Harcourt would try and make any Government of which he was the chief, pleasant to his colleagues and successful. My invariable language was 'Harcourt will try and make his own Government a success, but he will take care that no one else's is'. And so I was prepared to serve under him, or indeed under anybody who would prevent the Government from falling to pieces on Mr Gladstone's retirement.

But I can say this of no other Minister. I now think it quite possible that had my colleagues been placed between the devil and the deep blue sea, that is, had they been placed in the position of choosing between Harcourt as Prime Minister and their extinction they would have submitted to Harcourt. But I did not think so then, for their language was violent in a contrary sense, as used or reported to me. John Morley indeed, who was the most vehement, declared that nothing would induce him to serve under Harcourt as Leader of the House of Commons—much less Prime Minister. It was not till Feb. 13 that I noted a tendency in him to yield this point. But Asquith, Acland and Spencer were equally firm to me as to the impossibility of Harcourt being Prime Minister. For some reason or another he had offended all, and made all shrink from the idea of his being placed in authority over them. Arnold Morley, indeed, afterwards told me that he took a Whip's view and would have served under any person selected to lead the Party; and Edward Marjoribanks, taking also a Whip's view, expressed his conviction that the great mass of the Cabinet would have done the same.

To return to what passed after Mr Gladstone's departure for Biarritz on Jan. 13—I can tell little of personal knowledge, because, as I have stated, I was immersed in my department. I took occasional 'constitutionals' with Asquith or John Morley, and other Ministers dropped into luncheon, and thus I was kept informed. Otherwise I should have known little or nothing.

Undoubtedly the most active person at this juncture was Mr Louis Vernon Harcourt, the Chancellor of the Exchequer's eldest son. He was, naturally enough, determined to leave no stone unturned to procure the succession for his father. Very shortly after Mr Gladstone's departure he called on John Morley and asked him if the compact between him and his father still held good.[1] Morley in a fury replied that it did not, and that if he wished to know the reason why he should know it at once. Morley then proceeded to deliver a philippic against Sir William, recapitulating with exactness and sincerity all the causes of complaint which he (Morley) and the Government had against the Chancellor of the Exchequer. Mr Harcourt listened with admirable patience and composure, and at the end appeared to admit the justice of these censures, but referred them to his father's idiosyncracies which Morley should know and condone. This, however, Morley declined to do and the interview ended most unsatisfactorily for the Ambassador.

Of this conversation I only knew from Morley himself, who told it us immediately. What chiefly impressed us in it was the revelation of a secret understanding between Sir W. Harcourt and Morley of which all the Cabinet was unaware. It then transpired that in 1891, I think (at any rate before the General Election of 1892), Morley had been staying with Harcourt at Malwood, and had then agreed with him that they would never agree to a peer being Prime Minister. That was all that we heard at the time. In 1896, however, J. Ellis, staying at Malwood, learned from Mr L. Harcourt more precise details. But this authority is not in any sense reliable, and I have stated all that is pertinent to this narrative.

Mr Harcourt was, however, indefatigable in his efforts, though he did not come to me. Nor did I see anything of his father after the interview of Jan. 9.

On the 23rd of January Sir A. West, who had accompanied Mr Gladstone to Biarritz, paid a flying visit to London. He brought with him the record of a conversation with Mr Gladstone in which he expressed himself as unmoved in his purpose of resignation. 'You might as well try and blow up the Rock

[1] See pages 241 *n* and 301 on the 'Malwood Compact'.

of Gibraltar with your own hands as try and move me.'

At this time I was confined to bed with a strained ligament in my leg and saw scarcely anybody.

On the 31st of January (I think) the *Pall Mall Gazette* announced Mr Gladstone's resignation, which was contradicted in a strange communication from Sir A. West evidently composed by Mr Gladstone.

The news that reached us from Biarritz was conflicting. Armitstead wrote that Mr Gladstone was unmoved. Mrs Drew wrote that there was more hope and some chance of a reprieve. Those who knew best were, I think, of opinion that the resignation would not come on this occasion, mainly perhaps for the reason that resignation on the return from Biarritz would be so hard a measure and create such cruel difficulties for the Government.

On Feb. 6 there was a new phase. Sir A. West again came over from Biarritz with a letter to Marjoribanks, the Chief Whip, suggesting a dissolution because of the misdeeds of the House of Lords. All the available Ministers were unanimously against this proposal—they scarcely even considered it serious. Of the measures mentioned in Mr Gladstone's letter Home Rule had been rejected five months before without a ripple of national emotion; Betterment was as yet an immature proposal; the Employers' Liability Bill had been amended in a sense which a large section of the population supported and in a spirit more apparently popular than the enactment proposed; the Parish Councils Bill remained a great measure in spite of the Lords; and the Scottish Fisheries Bill was perhaps the most preposterous measure ever presented to Parliament. There was not the remotest chance of arousing any feeling against the Lords on these issues, and just resentment would be felt by Liberals at being put to the trouble and expense of another General Election so soon after the last and without the opportunity of proposing further measures of British domestic reform.

So Kimberley telegraphed to Biarritz that we were strongly and unanimously against the proposal. A few days afterwards Mr Gladstone returned to London.

On Feb. 11 Mr L. V. Harcourt made a further attempt on Mr John Morley. He offered him, in fact, all the Kingdoms of the World if——. If his father became Prime Minister he would give J. Morley the Exchequer and the emissary sketched two alternative Budgets either of which J. Morley could master in a few days. The next proposal was more insidious. If, on the other hand, Sir W.H. did not become Prime Minister, he would preserve a benevolent neutrality (out of office, presumably), *provided J. Morley became Foreign Minister*. Sir William, of course, knew that I could never give the Foreign Office to J. Morley for more reasons than one, and so by the suggestion he hoped to create a soreness, and in fact did so. He thus, too, probably gave the first idea of the Foreign Office to J. Morley, an idea which germinated.

On Monday, Feb. 12, we had a Cabinet. There was not a word, however, as to the subject of the last Cabinet; only a summons to a Cabinet dinner on the ensuing Saturday, Feb. 17.

The next day I went to see John Morley in Elm Park Gardens and walked back with him. Whether from the emollient efforts of the son or perhaps from a feeling of difficulty as to making his position intelligible to the public, he this day began to waver as to vetoing Harcourt's leadership of the House of Commons.

On Saturday the 17th was the Cabinet dinner at Mr Gladstone's in Downing Street. Herschell was on his right and I was on his left. He talked to me, I think, almost entirely of trees. But he also told me, which was interesting, that just before his examination in Greats he gave himself a week's repose, which he spent in hearing the Reform Bill debate in the House of Lords. I laughingly told him that I could see that he had not ordered the dinner as it included oysters and cold entrées—both of which he detests.

We all thought that the banquet was to be the opportunity for Mr Gladstone to declare his intentions, but I was soon undeceived. After dinner, as it was a Cabinet dinner and as the world was all agog with curiosity, I said to my host that if any secret matters were going to be discussed we ought to look to the doors. 'Certainly,' said Mr Gladstone with great composure, 'if anyone has any topic to raise it should be done now.' This was all that passed and made a deservedly popular story. But though the position had its humorous, it had also its tragic side, as the Cabinet were left in absolute ignorance of what was going to happen—whether they were to live or whether their thin-spun life was to be slit by the resignation of the Prime Minister. Never since Lord Chatham's premiership was a Government so absurdly or unpleasantly situated in relation to its head. Mr Gladstone was, I imagine, angry with us for not 'rallying' (to use his own expression) to his views on the Navy, and so kept us at arm's length. I am sure he did not intend to embarrass us by keeping his intentions a secret; he was only in a condition of righteous wrath; but the result was the same.

John Morley was the only exception to this general ban. As I understood he had explained to Mr Gladstone that he was in general agreement about the Navy, but that his duty compelled him to remain in Office. Any other course would be a desertion of Ireland. But even Morley shared to a limited extent in our disgrace. He wrote to me on Feb. 13 a note from which I extract a sentence as showing this and Morley's sense of our deplorable condition. 'All my vexations at the frantic embarrassments in which we are plunged seemed to melt away tonight when I helped the old man into his great-coat, and saw him painfully trudge off alone, refusing my escort.' I remember Morley's expatiating on this refusal.

On Tuesday, Feb. 20, Mr Gladstone addressed an enigmatical letter to Kimberley which I subjoin as I cannot interpret it. . . . Kimberley brought it to me in order to take the opportunity of saying that if he were sent for by the Queen, as leader in the House of Lords, he could only advise her to send for me.

During the evening of the same day Sir W. Harcourt came to John Morley's room at the House of Commons. They had a very long interview in which Sir William had, as Morley reported, to listen to many hard sayings. But the object of his visit was to announce his willingness to make any sacrifice, even to the extent of undertaking the lead of the House of Commons under someone else as Prime Minister; on two conditions: (i) He must see all Foreign Office dispatches. (ii) He must be free to take any decision in the course of debate without previous consultation. Next morning at 9 a.m. he sent his son to Morley to explain that he had given himself away in the freedom of conversation, but that in any case he must add a further condition—which related to patronage I think. But I did not take a note of it and indeed Sir William wiped out the whole transaction so far as I could be considered as being concerned within forty-eight hours.

Next day (Feb. 21) Morley summoned Spencer, Asquith and myself to hear his report of this conversation, but I have no note or recollection of what occurred.

On Thursday, Feb. 22, Sir W. Harcourt took the marked

step to which I referred above as wiping out as far as I was concerned his previous declaration.

Edward Hamilton, one of my most intimate friends, a clerk in the Treasury, was seated in his room when the Chancellor of the Exchequer stalked in, and said, 'I wish you to understand that what I have said to you (in former conversations) does not apply to Rosebery. Nothing would induce me ever to serve under him.' Having said this he at once or almost at once stalked out again.

This, of course, was intended as a message to me, and was at once delivered.[1] I heard afterwards that Harcourt had been annoyed, I do not quite understand why, by my saying, quite truthfully, that 'I had served under him and with him but could not undertake to serve over him'. However, I took his announcement as being definite.

The next day (Friday, Feb. 23) we had a Cabinet to discuss the Queen's speech closing the session. Harcourt declared that our policy must be one entirely of 'resistance to the House of Lords'. This seemed negative, but is not pertinent to this narrative.

After the Cabinet Mr Gladstone said a few vague words as to the time when his co-operation with the Cabinet would cease, but they were so vague that they produced no impression, and no one said anything in reference to them.

The next day was a day of small calamities to me. I was to go to Sandringham, taking Newmarket on my way. I missed my train and my compartment with all my red boxes had gone with it. I pursued it in a special train. At Newmarket I received a pressing personal telegram from the Queen asking me to dine with her as she particularly wished to speak to me. So I hurried back to London (finding there that all my clothes had gone to Sandringham) and thence to Windsor. I was, of course, under the impression that the Queen had heard that Mr Gladstone intended to resign and wished to see me. But she had nothing whatever to say to me. Something, however, had happened. Mr Gladstone had on that day sent for Sir H. Ponsonby, and had asked him if the Queen could keep a secret if he told her one. So Ponsonby asked the Queen. 'From everybody?' she enquired in reply. Ponsonby said 'Yes', on which she flatly declined, and said she

[1] It was not. See page 313.

must be free to consult friends. She believed the secret to refer to dissolution. I told Ponsonby that I regretted her answer.

I did not know of this until night, after I had seen the Queen, when Ponsonby told me. I suppose she telegraphed for me thinking that I could throw some light on the secret, but, of course, under no circumstances could I have said anything. Nor indeed, though I could guess the secret, could I tell positively what it was. The very mystery of Mr Gladstone's communication made me rather surmise that it was not resignation; and I never felt sure of his resignation until he announced it to the Queen four days afterwards.

The next day I returned to London, where I saw Asquith and Campbell-Bannerman who had come from Marjoribanks. Marjoribanks had been summoned yesterday to Harcourt who had read a long memorandum to him. It set forth that the First Minister should be in the House of Commons. But that if that could not be, he would, if it were the general wish, lead the House of Commons under certain conditions: (1) that he should take independent decision in the House of Commons if the course of debate should render it necessary; (2) that he should see all Foreign Office dispatches; and (3) that he should have some control of patronage, and another which I forget.[1] (After his message by Hamilton I did not pay much attention to all this.) On this I again made the remark that it might be difficult to serve under H but that it would be still more difficult to serve over him.

Marjoribanks had also said that there was a growing feeling in the House of Commons against a peer being Prime Minister. On this I said that I was delighted to hear it—might it grow!

I could see that both Asquith and Campbell-Bannerman were much disquieted by Marjoribanks' tidings. On Feb. 27 I drew up for my own satisfaction a full Minute of my views on the general and personal aspects of the situation. . . .[2]

When I wrote this it will be seen that I was not sure if Mr Gladstone would resign or not. But next day (Feb. 28) he saw the Queen at Buckingham Palace for half an hour and intimated his intention of resigning. . . . That afternoon Sir H. Ponsonby came to see me from the Queen to ask my advice as to the

[1] That Harcourt could summon meetings of the Cabinet.
[2] This long document is summarised on pages 316–7.

course she should pursue in the event of Mr Gladstone's resignation. I have no memorandum of the conversation. . . .

On March 1 Mr Gladstone held his last Cabinet. After the business was concluded Kimberley said that he could not allow our meeting to terminate without saying in a word how painful it was to us to part with our chief, and in a moment the honest old fellow was sobbing, unable to proceed. Mr G was about to reply when a cry of 'Stop!' was heard. It was the Chancellor of the Exchequer. As soon as he had arrested Mr G's attention he pulled from his pocket a handkerchief and a manuscript and at once commenced weeping loudly. Then he said, 'I think I can best express my feelings by reading the letter I have addressed to you, Sir, on this occasion'—on which he declaimed to us a somewhat pompous valedictory address of which I only remember vaguely a long-drawn metaphor taken from the solar system. Mr Gladstone was obviously disgusted. He said a few cold words, and always afterwards referred to this Cabinet as 'the blubbering Cabinet'.

After this scene had ended, Spencer, Acland, Asquith, and J. Morley came to luncheon with me. We were at first employed in discussing what had just occurred, but presently they began to press me as to whether I would definitely state my position with regard to the premiership. In reply I read them the short paper which follows.

Foreign Office

This is the paper which I read to J. Morley, Asquith and Acland at luncheon in Berkeley Square on March 1, 1894.

———

My position seems to be this: I share all the views held against a Peer being head of a Liberal Ministry.

My wish is to remain at the Foreign Office. I know nothing of the other post, and should be in every way unsuited for it.

But if it is absolutely necessary for party purposes that I should exchange the one place for the other, it is clear—to make the arrangement barely possible:

1. that it must be in obedience to a clear and decisive call.

2. that there must be mutual harmony and confidence between me and the leader of the House of Commons.

3. that as I cannot remain at the Foreign Office I must be unfettered in my selection of the Foreign Minister.

Summed up, it comes to this—that there must be cordiality and confidence between the Prime Minister on the one hand, and the Party, the leader of the Commons and the Foreign Minister on the other.

Without these conditions it is clear that an experiment, sufficiently difficult in itself, must break down, and another combination must be sought.

R.

March 1. 1894

A general agreement to these terms as being fair and moderate was expressed. But I had to go to the Foreign Office, and so we broke up agreeing to meet for further discussion there at 6 o'clock.

I gave John Morley a lift in my brougham as he was going to the Irish Office. His manner had quite changed, and he was now grave and preoccupied. He went on murmuring as if to himself, 'Yes, I suppose you have a right to demand the nomination to the Foreign Office, but . . .'; and 'would not a man in the House of Commons, say, like Campbell-Bannerman, be a much wiser choice?' I do not think I replied as I was determined to maintain that point.

At six o'clock this cloud of preoccupation had obscured the entire firmament. John Morley sate on the sofa in my room at the FO and declared his determination not to remain in his 'back kitchen' as he called the Irish Office. I cannot remember if I had declared at luncheon that I should appoint Kimberley [to the Foreign Office], but I think I had. Anyhow, it was known and it was suggested that J. Morley should go to the India Office if he would not remain at the Irish Office. But since the announcement about the FO he had become quite intractable. Acland walked away with him in despair, but wrote me a reassuring note afterwards.

To-day I received a note from the Prince of Wales conveying to me 'a message from the Queen that should she offer me the premiership she hoped that I would accept it, and stand by her'. (He repeated this at an audience I had with him next day.)

This same day, March 1, a procession of Liberal Members insignificant in number and headed by Labouchere waited on Marjoribanks, the Chief Whip, to protest against a peer being made prime minister. Dilke went some way with it but seeing the exiguity of the numbers stole off.

The next day I wrote to Ponsonby a letter to be read to the Queen in answer to her message.[1] . . .

At the same time I had an urgent letter from Dr Reid written by command of the Queen to urge me to form a Government on grounds connected with her own health.

I went out of all this turmoil by the 5.30 train. John Morley called as I left the Foreign Office, and drove with me to the station. He had been spending two hours with Sir W. Harcourt, who had read him his memorandum of conditions 'with every word of which', said Morley, 'I agreed'.

The next day Mr Gladstone resigned. He named the privy councillors who were to attend from the colleagues who had served longest with him. Among these was Harcourt in connection with whom there occurred an inexplicable incident. After the Council the Queen had sent for Mr Gladstone for an audience. Suddenly the door opened and Sir W. Harcourt stood before her. She asked him what was the matter. He replied that he understood she wished to see him. The Queen said, 'No,' and he retired.

At 3.30 Ponsonby arrived with a letter from the Queen appealing to me on behalf of herself and the Government to form a Government. I at once replied.[2] . . . Later on I sent her a further telegram, begging her to write a kind letter to Mr Gladstone, and telling her that, as I had heard, he should not consider his resignation as accepted until he received some communication from her.

Ponsonby wrote to say that the Queen was 'immensely delighted' with my acceptance, as she had feared a letter such as I had written the day before.

I now circulated to my colleagues the following notice.[3] . . . I then (at the instance of J. Morley, I think) had an interview with Harcourt after his return from Windsor about 5.30.[4]

Of this interview I have preserved no written record. But briefly the whole matter turned on the Foreign Secretaryship. He made no reference to his message through Hamilton, and professed no unwillingness to serve in the new Government. But when he heard that Kimberley was to be my successor at the

[1] See pages 322–3.
[2] Rosebery's letter is printed in *Letters of Queen Victoria*, 3rd Series, II, 373.
[3] See page 325.   [4] See page 326.

Foreign Office he declared himself greatly perturbed. He was convinced that the House of Commons would never acquiesce in the Premiership and the Foreign Office both being held in the House of Lords, etc., etc. I declared, however, that on this point I could not yield, so he took it *ad avizandum*.

That night Kimberley gave his Pricking Sheriffs dinner. Both Harcourt and Morley were present. Before dinner Morley came up to a Minister (Acland) and said with great excitement that the new arrangement was already dead, that I had formally announced that Kimberley was to be Foreign Secretary, that Harcourt would not stand it and that he would not stand it. At dinner they sat next each other and declared an alliance hostile to the new arrangement.

It was not of long duration. Very early next morning Louis [*sic*] Harcourt appeared at Morley's bedside to say that his father had sent him to concert action with Morley as agreed the previous evening. But the fit had already passed or the moment was unseasonable. Morley declared that they had better proceed separately, and that he was averse to joint action. Consequently, finding himself deserted by his ally, Harcourt appeared at my house at about 10 o'clock to say that out of a sincere wish to facilitate arrangements he would not press his objections to Kimberley.[1] He had prefaced this by a note which I subjoin with my reply.[2] . . .

Later in the day I called on J. Morley with Asquith when J.M. suggested that he should become President of the Council. I sent an invitation to my colleagues to call on me, which they all did. I took a long walk with Marjoribanks, the Chief Whip, making arrangements. Ten minutes after we had parted he returned to say that he had just received a telegram announcing his father's death, and his accession to the House of Lords. This was a terrible loss, for he was a consummate Whip.

John Morley dined alone with me. I pressed naturally upon him that his relinquishment of the Irish Office at this juncture would arouse great suspicion, but I told him that so far as I was concerned the India Office was at his disposal. Eventually he agreed to remain at the Irish Office, but next day accompanied it with a

[1] Although this account is broadly correct, it is inaccurate in details, and what is believed to be the authoritative account is on pages 330–2.

[2] Quoted in full on pages 330–1.

letter of conditions. I thought it best to allow this document to remain unanswered in the hope that the squall might pass over, but next day I received a demand for a written reply, which I sent and subjoin.[1] . . .

On the next day (Monday) I called a meeting of a few colleagues to consider new appointments, especially that to the India Office vacated by Kimberley's appointment to the Foreign Office. We sat as usual round a table, but Harcourt sat apart, behind me, near the window, his chin and nose in the air. I informed the conclave that Morley declined it, and we all came to the conclusion that Fowler was the proper man to be nominated. When this was settled Morley asked with vehemence if he was to understand that Fowler's appointment was agreed upon. I replied that I so understood it, but, observing his tone, asked him if he could think of anybody else. He replied 'No', and flounced out of the room, when we continued our business without him.

[1] This correspondence is summarised on pages 334–5.

NOTES ON SOURCES

Unpublished Documents

THE PRINCIPAL SOURCE OF MATERIAL has been the *Rosebery Papers* at Barnbougle Castle, on the Dalmeny Estate, near Edinburgh. This extremely large collection consists of the private and official papers of the fifth Earl of Rosebery, most of the private papers of his mother, the Duchess of Cleveland, including her Diaries and manuscript autobiography for the years 1819–51, and some of the papers of the last Duke of Cleveland and Everard Primrose. The Rosebery Papers are uncatalogued and largely unclassified, and it is possible that the collection is not yet complete. As has been mentioned in the Preface, more documents were discovered as late as the February of 1962. So far as is known, Rosebery kept every letter he received, and he had the admirable habit of keeping copies of many of his letters, and of almost all official correspondence. His letters to Lord Novar, Canon Rogers, and Ouseley Higgins were returned to the Rosebery family and are in the collection. A great quantity of official correspondence of the 1894–5 Administration—particularly Foreign Office correspondence—has been preserved. It is thought that Rosebery only destroyed his correspondence with his wife and his letters to Miss Mary Fox (although her letters to him were not). Much of Lady Rosebery's correspondence with friends has been preserved.

The *Papers of Sir Edward Hamilton* at the British Museum contain much important information relating to the politics of the years 1880–1905 and in particular to Rosebery. The Diaries (Additional Manuscripts 48,630–83) take more the form of a Journal, and appear to be based upon other diaries which Hamilton kept, as it is evident that he wrote up several days at a time, and there are occasional inaccuracies in dates which require some care to be used when the Diaries are being quoted from. Fortunately, in the case of Rosebery, it is easy to confirm these.

Letters from Rosebery and his wife are listed Additional Manuscripts 48,610–11.

The *Papers of W. E. Gladstone* at the British Museum contain an enormous quantity of papers relating to Rosebery, but of particular importance are Gladstone's notes of Cabinet meetings from 1892–4 (Add. MSS. 44,648), his correspondence with Rosebery (44,288–90), W. P. Adam (44,095, ff. 1–126), E. W. Hamilton (44,189–91), Morley (44,255–7), and Sir Algernon West (44,341–2), and Gladstone's autobiographical memoranda (44,790–1). Miss Agatha Ramm has rendered a notable service by editing the complete Gladstone–Lord Granville correspondence in four volumes covering the years 1868–86. Unfortunately the last volumes (1878–86) were not published until this work was virtually completed. In spite of numerous works on Gladstone, it is remarkable how fruitful the Gladstone Papers remain for students of nineteenth-century politics. Although the cataloguing of the papers is normally beyond praise, several letters from Gladstone to Rosebery on the subject of Uganda were incorrectly placed in the 1893 volume—which probably explains why they have escaped the attention of historians—but this error has now been rectified.

The *Papers of Mary Gladstone* (Mrs Drew) at the British Museum contain letters from Rosebery, listed Add. MSS. 46,226.

The *Papers of Herbert (later Lord) Gladstone* at the British Museum are still heavily 'restricted'; letters from Rosebery (45,986), Campbell-Bannerman (45,987–8), and Harcourt (45,997–46,002) are not at present available. This irritating restriction does not greatly signify in the case of Rosebery, since copies of many of his letters to Gladstone are at Dalmeny, and other copies are in the Campbell-Bannerman Papers; the latter collection also includes copies of most of Campbell-Bannerman's letters to Gladstone. This correspondence is listed in the *Campbell-Bannerman Papers* as Add MSS. 41,216–7, and Rosebery's letters as 41,226; Morley's letters are to be found in 41,223.

The *Papers of Sir Charles Wentworth Dilke* at the British Museum (Add. MSS. 43,874–967) should be handled with great caution in view of their heavy and careful editing undertaken by the Dilkes and Miss Gertrude Tuckwell. Of interest are the correspondence with the Roseberys (43,876), Dilke's edited Diaries (43,924–8), autobiographical notes for his memoirs

(43,929), and the memoirs themselves (43,930–41). The documents relating to the alleged implication of the Roseberys in the Crawford Case are found in Add. MSS. 49,454 (ff. 20–2).

The *Papers of Lady Battersea* (British Museum Add. MSS. 47,909–64) include several papers relating to her father, Anthony de Rothschild, and husband, Cyril Flower, Lord Battersea. Of particular use in this work were Lady Battersea's Diaries (47,929–63), and Rosebery's letters to her husband and herself (47,910).

The *Stanhope Papers* at Chevening, Sevenoaks, Kent, contain much interesting information about Rosebery and his parents, and a long correspondence between himself and Evelyn, Countess Stanhope.

The *Papers of Lord Randolph Henry Spencer-Churchill* are at present divided between Chartwell, Westerham, Kent—where the bulk of the papers reside—and Blenheim Palace. The manuscript and notes of Sir Winston's biography of his father are at Blenheim.

The *Harcourt Papers* are at Stanton Harcourt, Oxfordshire. The most interesting single document is the unpublished Journal of the late Lord Harcourt (Lewis Harcourt). The present Lord Harcourt gave me permission to examine his father's papers, but I have relied with complete confidence upon the detailed notes taken by Mr Peter Stansky of Harvard University, Massachusetts.

I have to acknowledge the gracious kindness of Her Majesty the Queen for her permission to examine and quote from the *Royal Archives* at Windsor Castle. Lord Crewe had obtained copies of almost all Rosebery's correspondence with the Queen in 1930, which greatly reduced my work on the archives. But although most of the papers relating to Rosebery have been published either in Lord Crewe's biography or in the *Letters of Queen Victoria*, there are some important exceptions.

Miscellaneous

Among other collections of unpublished papers which I have examined, Rosebery's correspondence with Lord Ripon (British Museum Add. MSS. 43,516) and some letters from Lady Betty Balfour to Mrs Barbara Webb (loaned to me by Mr David Holland) have been of interest. Rosebery's letters to the eighth Duke of Devonshire and T. Ellis were copied in 1930 for Lord

Crewe. Mr Nevile Masterman, who is engaged upon a new study of Ellis, has drawn my attention to some interesting documents in the *Ellis Papers* (National Library of Wales) and has made copies for me. Mr Stansky has performed the same kindness in relation to the *Bryce Papers* and *Asquith Papers* (at the Bodleian Library, Oxford), as well as the *Spencer Papers* (at Althorp) and the *Haldane Papers* (National Library of Scotland, Edinburgh). Mrs Maclean of Dochgarroch sent me Rosebery's letters to her great-grandfather, Robert Murray Smith, and Bishop Skelton sent me a memoir of his period as Vicar of Mentmore and letters from Rosebery, shortly before his sudden death. Lord Beaverbrook undertook an examination of those papers of Bonar Law and Lord Curzon which are in his possession, but few letters of any importance were found.

On publication of a request for documents in the *Daily Telegraph* and *The Times Literary Supplement* I received a great quantity of letters and recollections of Rosebery for which I am very grateful. I am particularly indebted to Mr F. S. Brown, Rosebery's secretary for twenty-five years, for his personal recollections and much other assistance in the compilation of material.

SELECT BIBLIOGRAPHY

I am most grateful to the trustees, publishers, or authors who hold the copyright of those books marked with an asterisk for their permission to quote from them.

Rosebery

A. Wallace: *The Earl of Rosebery, His Words and his Work* (1894)

Speeches of Lord Rosebery, 1874 to 1896 (1896)

C. Geake (Ed.): *Appreciations and Addresses delivered by Lord Rosebery* (1899)

Jane T. Stoddart: *The Earl of Rosebery, K.G.* (1900)

T. G. F. Coates: *Lord Rosebery, His Life and Speeches* (1900)

E. Rodgers and E. J. Moyle: *Lord Rosebery* ('Men of the Moment' Series, No. 2, 1902)

J. Renwick: *Life and Work of Lord Rosebery* (1909)

John Buchan (Ed.): *Miscellanies Literary and Historical of the Earl of Rosebery* (Hodder & Stoughton, 1921)

*E. T. Raymond: *The Man of Promise, Lord Rosebery* (Fisher Unwin, 1923)

E. H. Thruston: *Lord Rosebery, Statesman and Sportsman* (1928)

*Marquess of Crewe: *Lord Rosebery* (Murray, 1930)

Essays on Rosebery appear in the following works:

*(Sir) James Barrie: *An Edinburgh Eleven* (1889)

*T. H. S. Escott: *Personal Forces of the Period* (Hurst & Blackett, 1898)

S. H. Jeyes: *Prime Ministers of Queen Victoria* (1906)

*A. G. Gardiner: *Prophets, Priests and Kings* (Dent, 1909)

* (Sir) Winston S. Churchill: *Great Contemporaries* (Butterworth, 1937)

*Algernon Cecil: *Queen Victoria and Her Prime Ministers* (Eyre & Spottiswoode, 1953)

*John Raymond: *The Doge of Dover* (MacGibbon & Kee, 1960)

*Sir Keith Feiling: *In Christ Church Hall* (Macmillans, 1960)

Among Rosebery's writings the following may be particularly noted:

Pitt (Macmillans, 1891)

Sir Robert Peel (Cassells, 1899. Reprinted from *The Anglo-Saxon Review*)
Napoleon: The Last Phase (A. L. Humphreys, 1900 and 1904; Hodder & Stoughton, 1922)
Lord Randolph Churchill (A. L. Humphreys, 1906)
 Chatham: His Early Life and Connections (A. L. Humphreys, 1910)

 Introductions to:

 The Love Episode of William Pitt (privately printed, 1900)
*G. Home: *Epsom, Its history and surroundings* (1901)
 G. Tomline: *Pitt* (1903)
*Alfred Stead: *Great Japan* (1905)
 A. Vandal: *L'Avènement de Bonaparte* (1912)
The Windham Papers (1913)

Contemporary Pamphlets

The great majority of these ephemeral publications are of no more than passing interest to the biographer of Rosebery. *The Merrypebble Gems* (1882) is an excellent example of a type of scurrilous pamphlet freely circulated at the time of, or immediately after, the Midlothian campaigns of 1879–80. A satirical account of the 1894–5 Ministry, *The Earl and the Knight* (1897), is interesting because, although inaccurate in details, the antagonism between Harcourt and Rosebery is described with sufficient accuracy to arouse suspicions that it is the work of someone with inside knowledge. Edward Hamilton at one time suspected that Reginald Brett may have been the author, but this seems improbable.

Many of Rosebery's speeches were published singly or in small collections shortly after they were delivered in pamphlet form. I have not noted these individually in this bibliography, but I have made use of a complete set at Dalmeny.

Biographies and Autobiographies

*H. H. Asquith: *Fifty Years of Parliament* (Cassells, 1926)
*Margot Asquith: *Autobiography* (Butterworth, 1920)
*J. A. Spender and Cyril Asquith: *Life of Lord Oxford and Asquith* (Hutchinsons, 1932)
*A. G. Gardiner: *John Benn and the Progressive Movement* (Benn, 1925)
*Augustine Birrell: *Things Past Redress* (Faber, 1937)
*John Buchan: *Memory-Hold-The-Door* (Hodder & Stoughton, 1940)
*J. A. Spender: *Life of Sir Henry Campbell-Bannerman* (Hodder & Stoughton, 1923)
 J. L. Garvin: *Joseph Chamberlain* (Macmillans, 1932–3)

(Sir) Winston S. Churchill: *Lord Randolph Churchill* (Macmillans, 1906, and Odhams, 1951)

*R. Rhodes James: *Lord Randolph Churchill* (Weidenfeld & Nicolson, 1959)

 J. Saxon Mills: *Life of Sir E. T. Cook* (1921)

*Faith Compton Mackenzie: *William Cory* (Constable, 1950)

*F. Warre-Cornish (Ed.): *Letters and Journals of William Cory* (Oxford, 1897)

*James Pope-Hennessy: *Lord Crewe, The Likeness of a Liberal* (Constable, 1955)

*Lord Zetland: *Cromer* (Hodder & Stoughton, 1932)

 Bernard Holland: *The Eighth Duke of Devonshire* (1911)

*Roy Jenkins: *Sir Charles Dilke, A Victorian Tragedy* (Collins, 1958)

*W. F. Monypenny and G. E. Buckle: *Life of Disraeli* (two-volume edition, Murray, 1929)

*Lord Zetland (Ed.): *Letters from Disraeli to Lady Bradford and Lady Chesterfield* (Benn, 1929)

*M. V. Brett (Ed.): *Journals and Letters of Viscount Esher* (Nicholson & Watson, 1934)

*Lord Esher: *Cloud-Capp'd Towers* (Murray, 1927)

*Sir Almeric Fitzroy: *Memoirs* (Hutchinsons, 1925)

*Mary Drew: *Catherine Gladstone* (Nisbet, 1919)

*Lord (Herbert) Gladstone: *After Thirty Years* (Macmillans, 1928)

*Sir Charles Mallet: *Herbert Gladstone, A Memoir* (Hutchinsons, 1932)

*Lucy Masterman: *Mary Gladstone, Her Diaries and Letters* (Methuen, 1930)

 John Morley: *Life of W. E. Gladstone* (Macmillans, 1903)

 Philip Magnus: *Gladstone* (Murray, 1954)

*G. P. Gooch: *Under Six Reigns* (Longmans Green, 1958)

 Lord Fitzmaurice: *The Second Earl Granville* (Longmans, 1901)

 Viscount Grey of Fallodon: *Twenty-Five Years* (Hodder & Stoughton, 1925)

*G. M. Trevelyan: *Grey of Fallodon* (Longmans Green, 1937)

*Lord Haldane: *Autobiography* (Hodder & Stoughton, 1929)

*Sir F. Maurice: *Haldane* (Faber, 1937)

 D. Sommer: *Haldane of Cloan* (Allen & Unwin, 1960)

*A. G. Gardiner: *Life of Sir William Harcourt* (Constable, 1923)

*Lady St Helier: *Memories of Fifty Years* (Arnold, 1909)

*Lord Kilbracken: *Reminiscences* (Macmillans, 1931)

*Lord Newton: *Lord Lansdowne* (Macmillans, 1929)

*Sir Henry Lucy: *Sixty Years in the Wilderness* (Smith, Elder, 1912)

*Margery Perham: *Lugard, The Years of Adventure* (Collins, 1956)

 Cecil Headlam (Ed.): *The Milner Papers* (Cassells, 1931–3)

*John Morley: *Recollections* (Macmillans, 1917)

*Lord Newton: *Retrospection* (Murray, 1941)

*Lord Ponsonby of Shulbrede: *Henry Ponsonby, His Life from his Letters* (Macmillans, 1942)

*Lord Sysonby (Sir Frederick Ponsonby): *Recollections of Six Reigns* (Eyre & Spottiswoode, 1951)

F. E. Hamer (Ed.): *The Personal Papers of Lord Rendel* (Benn, 1931)

*Lucien Wolf: *Life of Lord Ripon* (Murray, 1921)

Lady Gwendolen Cecil: *Life of Robert, Marquis of Salisbury* (Hodder & Stoughton, 1921–32)

*Wilson Harris: *J. A. Spender* (Cassells, 1946)

* J. A. Spender: *Life, Journalism and Politics* (Cassells, 1927)

*B. Webb: *Our Partnership* (Longmans Green, 1948)

*H. G. Hutchinson (Ed.): *The Private Diaries of Sir Algernon West* (Murray, 1922)

Edith H. Fowler: *Life of Henry Fowler, First Viscount Wolverhampton* (1912)

Miscellaneous

*James Brinsley-Richards: *Seven Years at Eton* (Bentley, 1883)

*John Bateman: *Great Landowners of Great Britain and Ireland* (4th ed., 1883)

*G. W. E. Russell: *Portraits of the 'Seventies* (Fisher Unwin, 1916)

*G. E. Buckle (Ed.): *Letters and Journals of Queen Victoria*, Second and Third Series (Murray, 1928–30)

*E. T. S. Dugdale (Ed.): *German Diplomatic Documents, 1871–1914* (Methuen, 1928)

*R. C. K. Ensor: *England, 1870–1914* (Oxford, 1936)

H. Temperley and L. Penson: *Foundations of British Foreign Policy* (Cambridge U.P., 1938)

*Sir Charles Oman: *Memories of Victorian Oxford* (Methuen, 1941)

W. Langer: *The Diplomacy of Imperialism* (Knopf, New York, 1951)

Ethel Drus: 'A Report on the Papers of Joseph Chamberlain relating to the Jameson Raid and the Inquiry' (*Bulletin of Institute of Historical Research*, XXV, 1952)

Ethel Drus: 'The Question of Imperial Complicity in the Jameson Raid' (*English Historical Review*, October 1953)

Ethel Drus: 'Select Documents from the Chamberlain Papers concerning Anglo-Transvaal Relations, 1896–9' (*Bulletin of Institute of Historical Research*, XXVII, 1954)

S. Maccoby: *English Radicalism, 1886–1914* (Allen & Unwin, 1953)

*A. J. P. Taylor: *The Struggle for Mastery in Europe* (Oxford, 1954)

*A. Low: 'British Public Opinion and The Uganda Question, October–December 1892 (*Uganda Journal*, XVIII, September, 1954)

*H. J. Hanham: 'British Party Finance, 1868–1880' (*Bulletin of Institute of Historical Research*, XXVII, 1954)

Roy Jenkins: *Mr Balfour's Poodle* (Heinemann, 1954)

H. J. Hanham: *Elections and Party Management: Politics in the Time of Disraeli and Gladstone* (Longmans Green, 1959)

Elizabeth Pakenham: *Jameson's Raid* (Weidenfeld & Nicolson, 1960)

T. B. Miller: 'The Egyptian Question and British Foreign Policy, 1892–4' (*Journal of Modern History*, March 1960)

*A. M. Gollin: *The Observer and J. L. Garvin, 1908–14* (Oxford, 1960)

*P. Stansky: *The Leadership of the Liberal Party, 1894–9* (unpublished Harvard University thesis, 1960)

*R. Robinson, J. Gallagher, and Alice Denny: *Africa and the Victorians* (Macmillans, 1961)

*Agatha Ramm: *The Political Correspondence of Mr Gladstone and Lord Granville* (1868–76, Royal Historical Society, 1952; 1876–86, Oxford, 1962)

INDEX